Free Trade in the Twenty-First Century

Max Rangeley · Daniel Hannan
Editors

Free Trade in the Twenty-First Century

Economic Theory and Political Reality

Editors
Max Rangeley
The Cobden Centre
Buckingham, UK

Daniel Hannan
House of Lords
Parliament of United Kingdom
London, UK

ISBN 978-3-031-67655-0   ISBN 978-3-031-67656-7 (eBook)
https://doi.org/10.1007/978-3-031-67656-7

© The Editor(s) (if applicable) and The Author(s), under exclusive license to Springer Nature Switzerland AG 2025

This work is subject to copyright. All rights are solely and exclusively licensed by the Publisher, whether the whole or part of the material is concerned, specifically the rights of translation, reprinting, reuse of illustrations, recitation, broadcasting, reproduction on microfilms or in any other physical way, and transmission or information storage and retrieval, electronic adaptation, computer software, or by similar or dissimilar methodology now known or hereafter developed.
The use of general descriptive names, registered names, trademarks, service marks, etc. in this publication does not imply, even in the absence of a specific statement, that such names are exempt from the relevant protective laws and regulations and therefore free for general use.
The publisher, the authors and the editors are safe to assume that the advice and information in this book are believed to be true and accurate at the date of publication. Neither the publisher nor the authors or the editors give a warranty, expressed or implied, with respect to the material contained herein or for any errors or omissions that may have been made. The publisher remains neutral with regard to jurisdictional claims in published maps and institutional affiliations.

This Springer imprint is published by the registered company Springer Nature Switzerland AG
The registered company address is: Gewerbestrasse 11, 6330 Cham, Switzerland

If disposing of this product, please recycle the paper.

Preface

"Free trade, the greatest blessing a government can bestow on a people, is in almost every country unpopular", wrote Lord Macaulay in 1824. In the 200 years since, average global incomes have risen, at a conservative estimate, by 3000%—having previously barely sloped upwards at all. Globalisation and open markets have been miraculous poverty-busters. Take any measure you like: literacy, longevity, infant mortality, female education, calorie intake, height. We have never had it so good.

Yet Macaulay's observation is, if anything, even truer today. We enjoy a standard of living that previous generations would have attributed to wizards or gods; yet we remain deeply suspicious of the economic system on which it rests.

To economists, the benefits of specialisation and comparative advantage are so obvious as to be uncontroversial. Free trade is one of the very few precepts that can be said to command general acceptance within their profession. But, even more than in Macaulay's day, there is a chasm between what economists take for granted and how most non-economists see things.

Surveys of economists and non-economists show that the latter are more hostile towards imports, likelier to think that economic growth exists to support jobs rather than the other way around, and readier to believe that a nation should produce its own food and other resources.

Hence this book. We have brought together the best writers in the field, economists and non-economists alike. Some are academic specialists. Some are former trade negotiators. Some are politicians—including two former prime ministers—who have had direct experience of negotiating trade deals and then needing to sell them to their electorates.

Our ambition is for the essays that follow to become a standard text for students. Our authors, by and large, do not defend free trade with graphs, equations, or formulae. As the American economist Kenneth E. Boulding wryly put it, "mathematics brought rigor to economics; unfortunately it also brought mortis". Instead, they explain, in human terms, why the removal of economic barriers is a mighty force for poverty alleviation, conflict resolution and social justice.

One of the curiosities of the present debate is that almost all the moral fervour lies with the protectionists, whether of the Trumpian or Corbynite variety. The people who protested against TTIP and the CPTPP, who picketed G20 meetings and railed against the "neo-liberal order" were genuinely convinced that they were standing up for the masses against corporate interests. Yet, as we show in the pages that follow, the opposite was true. Free trade benefits the vast majority of people, but its biggest beneficiaries are those on low incomes, the highest proportion of whose budgets generally go on the most protected goods, above all food. Conversely, its biggest losers are those politically connected lobbies that have distorted the rules in their favour.

We hope, in the essays that follow, not only to set out the definitive case for free trade in the twenty-first century but also to recapture some of the moral fervour of its original advocates, the sense that they were engaged in a great and just cause.

Both editors of this book are trustees of the Cobden Centre, a British educational think-tank named after the great Victorian radical who, more than anyone else, can be said to have ushered in the unprecedented period of peace and prosperity in the late nineteenth century.

On 15 January 1846, in Manchester, on the eve of the victory of the Anti-Corn Law League, Cobden gave a speech which is worth quoting at length.

> I have been accused of looking too much to material interests. Nevertheless I can say that I have taken as large and great a view of the effects of this mighty principle as ever did any man who dreamt over it in his own study. I believe that the physical gain will be the smallest gain to humanity from the success of this principle.
> I look farther; I see in the free-trade principle that which shall act on the moral world as the principle of gravitation in the universe,—drawing men together, thrusting aside the antagonism of race, and creed, and language, and uniting us in the bonds of eternal peace. I have looked even farther. I have speculated, and probably dreamt, in the dim future—ay, a thousand years hence—I have speculated on what the effect of the triumph of this principle may be. I believe

that the effect will be to change the face of the world, so as to introduce a system of government entirely distinct from that which now prevails.

I believe that the desire and the motive for large and mighty empires; for gigantic armies and great navies—for those materials which are used for the destruction of life and the desolation of the rewards of labour—will die away; I believe that such things will cease to be necessary, or to be used, when man becomes one family, and freely exchanges the fruits of his labour with his brother man.

We know what happens when the world moves away from Cobdenite principles. It happened at the beginning of the twentieth century, with cataclysmic consequences. Indeed, it was precisely as a reaction to the horrors of the two wars, the Holocaust and the Holodomor that delegates from the free nations met in Bretton Woods in 1944 and agreed to a progressive reduction in trade barriers—a policy which led to the creation of what is now the World Trade Organisation and to seven decades of unprecedented democracy as well as unprecedented prosperity.

That process is now going into reverse. Trade is falling as a proportion of global GDP, and we are seeing a revival of the doom-loop between political instability and autarkic tendencies. The owl of Minerva, wrote Hegel, spreads its wings only with the gathering of the dusk. If ever there was a time to remind ourselves of how fortunate we have been in the economic order we have enjoyed, that time is upon us.

Buckingham, UK Max Rangeley
London, UK Daniel Hannan

Contents

The Philosophy, Politics and Ethics of Free Trade

Adam Smith's Moral Sentiments, Society, and Free Trade   3
Verno L. Smith

Reflections from the Inside Out: What Libertopia Tells Us
About the Nature of Markets in Trade   13
Tim Evans

The Foundations of Free Trade   31
Patrick Barron

The Psychology of Protectionism   43
Eamonn Butler

Free Trade for Peace, Prosperity, and Progress   65
Thorsten Polleit

The Cultural Politics of Free Trade in Britain   77
Stephen Davies

Free Trade and Austro-libertarianism   95
Walter E. Block

Ludwig von Mises on Trade, Human Development,
and Human Progress   117
Mark Thornton

The Viewpoints of Senior Policy-Makers

The International Trading System: A Practitioner's Perspective — 135
Tim Groser

Why Free Trade Is Difficult to Achieve in Practice — 159
Syed Kamall

Free Trade: A Ministerial Perspective — 187
Lord Peter Lilley

My Experiences of Global Trade Negotiations — 201
Liz Truss

Revising Globalising — 215
Tony Abbott

Free Trade Under Siege: Analyzing Contemporary Trade Policies — 225
Barbara Kolm and Miguel Del Valle

Mrs. Thatcher's Prescient Bruges Speech — 257
Daniele Capezzone

The Case for Free Trade—Why We Need to Keep Making It — 275
Douglas Carswell

Let Free Trade Work Its Magic in the UK: Lord Moynihan of Chelsea, OBE — 287
Jon Moynihan

Monetary Economics and Global Trade

The Monetary System of Free Trade — 321
Keith Weiner

Twin Deficits—How Are They Related? — 351
Alasdair MacLeod

Big Players and the Volatility of Exchange Rates — 365
Roger Koppl and Marta Podemska-Mikluch

Fix Money Fix the World — 379
Dominic Frisby

Economic Policy and Trade: The Good, The Bad and The Ugly

Free Trade in the Nordic Countries — 405
Hannes H. Gissurarson

Old Lessons for the New Protectionists — 429
Phillip W. Magness

Free Trade Is Not Free: Why Deglobalization Is (Unfortunately) Here to Stay — 445
Keith Jakee and Stephen Turner

Export Subsidies — 469
Veronique de Rugy

Germany's Costly Hidden Export Subsidies — 487
Gunther Schnabl

Trading Away Freedom: How Non-trade Elements Came to Dominate Trade Agreements — 505
Iain Murray

Trade Adjustment Textbook Chapter — 533
Scott S. Lincicome

Challenges in Export Growth and Financial Compliance for Latin America — 553
Jorge Jraissati

Free Trade and Free Markets

How Free Trade Helps Businesses Thrive — 567
Daniel Lacalle

Colombia's Uber Wars: Anarchy, Legalism, and the Politics of Regulatory Capture — 579
Daniel Raisbeck

Globalization, Long May It Reign — 601
Deirdre Nansen McCloskey

Social Market Economy, Ordoliberalism and Neoliberalism. An Introduction — 617
Annette Godart-van der Kroon

Revealing the Benefits of Trade to University Students   631
Anthony J. Evans and Wioletta Nawrot

Free Trade Myths and Realities   643
Wayne Winegarden and Rowena Itchon

Free Trade Versus Interventionism   659
Jörg Guido Hülsmann and Karl-Friedrich Israel

Globalization: Free Trade Versus Managed Trade   675
Richard M. Ebeling

The Philosophy, Politics and Ethics of Free Trade

Adam Smith's Moral Sentiments, Society, and Free Trade

Verno L. Smith

Adam Smith's fundamental case for free trade was first expressed not in his celebrated second published book (Smith 1776; hereafter *WN*), *The Wealth of Nations*, but in his first published book (Smith 1759; hereafter *TMS*), *The Theory of Moral Sentiments*. *WN* had offered a theory of economy that explained the political economy of his day and how the rising commercial as well as traditional agricultural activity of Europe and the world accounted for their growing prosperity and well-being. But before he could write coherently on economy and its foundation in free trade, which addressed the citizens and statespersons of his time, it was appropriate that he write on the origins and consequences of the emergence of the order that constituted society. That development was the grand achievement of *TMS*.

Let me explain why.

V. L. Smith (✉)
Economic Science Institute, Chapman University, One University Drive, Orange, CA 92866, USA
e-mail: vlomaxsmith@gmail.com

The Rules We Learn to Fashion and Follow Are Motivated by Our Desire to Get Along with Each Other

From his study of human action in history, literature, and art, Smith believed that the stuff of which society was made emerges and lives dynamically in the rules we learn to create and follow that enable us to get along with each other. That learning begins in earnest about the time that we first have playmates. This is when we first encounter others who are strangers in the sense that they are not part of the family we were born into. Consequently, they are not as partial or protective as our parents in interacting with us. The child "…thus enters into the great school of self-command; it studies to be more and more master of itself; and begins to exercise over its own feelings a discipline which the practice of the longest life is very seldom sufficient to bring to complete perfection" (*TMS*, p 204).

Society is thus created by the rule-following actions of ordinary people in their ordinary daily interactions, not elites, although well-stationed people may recognize its importance and contribute to the practice, or even to the philosophy of civility.

In *TMS*, all such rules of order are comprehendible under either beneficence or justice.

The Rules of Beneficence Originate in Our Feelings of Gratitude for Properly Motivated Beneficial Actions

Beneficence concerns the great variety of good things we do for each other in our neighborhoods and friendly gatherings, which are of central importance in creating community, and that naturally may scale up to form an orderly society compounded of neighborly communities. But the rules of beneficent engagement have not this intentional purpose and achieve any larger ends by simply supplying the ground-level elements that are aggregate-able into a larger compatible whole.

Smith's first proposition on beneficence (BP 1) states: "Actions of a beneficent tendency, which proceed from proper motives, seem alone to require a reward; because such alone are the approved objects of gratitude, or excite the sympathetic gratitude of the spectator." (*TMS*, p 112).

Thus do English speakers refer colloquially to having incurred a "debt of gratitude" when, out of the goodness of someone's heart, a beneficial service is performed for them: "But of all the duties of beneficence, those which gratitude recommends to us approach nearest to what is called a perfect and complete obligation. What friendship, what generosity, what charity, would prompt us to do with universal approbation, is still more free, and can still less be extorted by force than the duties of gratitude. We talk of the debt of gratitude, not of charity, or generosity, nor even of friendship, when friendship is mere esteem and has not been enhanced and complicated with gratitude for good offices." (*TMS*, p 113).

Observe that it is the emotions of gratitude that drive our responses when another chooses a beneficial action toward us. The beneficiary of a neighbor's service of kindness feels a compulsion to reward the action in some way appropriate for that person. Your neighbor brings in your empty trash barrel from curbside when you forget to do it. She may have saved you a police citation. Out of your gratitude, you subsequently fill a bag with avocados you picked off your tree and take them to her. She is not at home, so you leave them on her doorstep. She will know from whom they came and why. Nor is the order of moves important. You might have given her a bag of avocados and she subsequently brought in your trash barrel. Neighborhoods are filled with locally shared public and private decentralized information that supports a mutual help-exchange system, much as in any market for pricing goods and services. According to Smith, the required reward out of gratitude in BP1 must come from the design or intention of the person benefited. You do not and cannot feel absolved of your duty merely because she was enriched from a lottery win or was generously favored by some other independent event. You are happy for her in her unanticipated prosperity but only you can discharge your own debt of gratitude.

Smith's second proposition on beneficence (BP2) states: "Beneficence is always free, it cannot be extorted by force, the mere want of it exposes to no punishment; because the mere want of beneficence tends to do no real positive evil. It may disappoint of the good which might reasonably have been expected, and upon that account, it may justly excite dislike and disapprobation: it cannot, however, provoke any resentment which mankind will go along with." (*TMS*, p 112).

Thus, does Smith recognize that a person has the unmolested right to not be beneficent toward anyone. BP2 is an essential corollary of BP1 because beneficence is meaningless if not freely and voluntarily chosen. Hence, choosing not to act beneficially is not a cause for punishment that the community will sanction.

Progressive political candidates and their policies constantly call for an increased redistribution of income from richer to poorer citizens by means of the federal income tax since its authorization by the 16th Amendment to the constitution passed in 1913. Government has thus implemented progressive tax rates through majority rule processes that allow lower-income citizens to benefit by paying a smaller share of their income in taxes than those with higher incomes.

But does this violate BP2? I think not because no one—certainly not Adam Smith—defends government as a non-coercive institution. Majority rule democracy is by construction coercive toward minorities. The private sector certainly provides numerous clubs and associations which might charge lower fees for lower-income members such as students. But these tend to be predominantly voluntary associations, with exceptions such as coercive union labor and business cartels. The Organization of the Petroleum Exporting Countries (OPEC) is a cartel that imposes production quotas on its members, which they routinely violate. "In every single quarter from 1993 to 2005, total OPEC production exceeded the sum of its members' quotas. In this period, an OPEC member over-produced its quota by an average of 6.7%." (Ghoddusi et al. 2017, p 2).

The Rules of Justice Originate in Our Feelings of Resentment for Improperly Motivated Actions that Are Hurtful

Justice concerns the control and limitation of the hurtful things we do to each other. As Smith emphasizes, justice is more important than beneficence: "Society may subsist, though not in the most comfortable state, without beneficence; but the prevalence of injustice must utterly destroy it." (*TMS*, 125).

The first proposition on justice (JP1) states: "Actions of a hurtful tendency, which proceed from improper motives, seem alone to deserve punishment; because such alone are the approved objects of resentment, or excite the sympathetic resentment of the spectator." (*TMS*, p 112).

A corollary extension of JP1 is that the greater and more irreparable the evil in hurtful actions, the greater the resentment of the sufferer and the greater the appropriate punishment: "Death is the greatest evil which one man can inflict upon another and excites the highest degree of resentment in those who are immediately connected with the slain. Murder, therefore, is the most atrocious of all crimes which affect individuals only, in the sight both of mankind and of the person who has committed it. To be deprived of that which we are possessed of, is a greater evil than to be disappointed of what we have only the expectation. Breach of property, therefore, theft and robbery, which take from us what we are possessed of, are greater crimes than breach of contract, which only disappoints us of what we expected. The most sacred laws of justice, therefore, those whose violation seems to call loudest for vengeance and punishment, are the laws which guard the life and person of our neighbor; the next are those which guard his property and possessions; and last of all come those which guard what are called his personal rights, or what is due to him from the promises of others." (*TMS*, p 121).

Neither of the Two Pillars of Society—Beneficence and Justice--Are Derived from Utilitarian Consequentialiest Motives

Adam Smith's methodology of analytical thought is implicitly founded on two important distinctions not made by modern utilitarian theorists:

I. A distinction between *being self-interested* and *acting self-interestedly.*
II. A distinction between the *origins of action* and the *consequences of action.*

Thus, in respect to I, Smith says:

"Every man is, no doubt, by nature, first and principally recommended to his own care; and as he is fitter to take care of himself, than of any other person, it is fit and right that it should be so…Though it may be true, therefore, that every individual,
in his own breast, naturally prefers himself to all
mankind, yet he dares not look mankind in the face, and
avow that he. acts according to this principle. He feels
that in this preference they can never go along with him,
and that how natural soever it may be to him, it must
always appear excessive and extravagant to them. When
be views himself in the light in which he is conscious that
others will view him1 he sees that to them be is but one of
the multitude, in no respect better than any other in it. If
be would act so as that the impartial spectator may enter
into the principles of bis conduct, which is what of all things
he has the greatest desire to do, he must upon this, as upon
all other occasions, bumble the arrogance of his self-love,
and bring it down to something which other men can go
along with. They will indulge it so far as to allow him to
be more anxious about, and to pursue with more earnest

assiduity, his own happiness than that of any other person. Thus far, whenever they place themselves in bis situation, they will readily go along with him. In the race for wealth, and honours, and preferments, be may run as hard ·as he can; and strain every nerve and every muscle, in order to outstrip all his· competitors. But if he should justle, or throw down any of them, the indulgence of the spectators is entirely at an end. It is a violation of fair play, which they cannot admit of. This man is to them, in every respect, as good as be : they do not enter into that self-love, by which he prefers himself so much to this other, and cannot go along with the motive from which he hurt him. They readily, therefore, sympathize with the natural resentment of the injured, and the offender becomes the object of their hatred and indignation." (*TMS*, pp 119–20)

In respect to II, we need only note that the origin of action in beneficence resides in the emotions of gratitude, while in justice the origins arise from the emotions of resentment.

The Rules of Justice Define Property

Notice carefully that these protections define property[1]:

Protection from murder yields property in our bodies.

Protection from theft and robbery conveys property in the products of body and of mind in the body.

Protection from the violation of contractual promises provides us with property in each other's promises. This protection includes compensatory judgments for the victims rather than only the punishment of violators which is expected to deter future crime. Criminal punishment does nothing in compensation for the loss suffered by the aggrieved family and friends of the person murdered.

The Theory of Economy

Observe that when Adam Smith came to write *WN* the essential groundwork had already been laid in *TMS*, which explains why he thought *TMS* was his most important contribution.

---

[1] These are implicit in our interpretation and are not made explicit in *TMS*.

Consider in the above light, from *TMS*, Smith's central theorem in WN: "This division of labor, from which so many advantages are derived, is not originally the effect of any human wisdom, which foresees and intends that general opulence to which it gives occasion: It is the necessary, though very slow and gradual, consequence of a certain propensity in human nature which has in view no such extensive utility; the propensity to truck, barter, and exchange one thing for another." (*WN*, p 15).

Why this propensity in people everywhere to engage voluntarily, enthusiastically, and freely, in trade? Smith immediately speculates: "Whether this propensity be one of those original principles in human nature, of which no further account can be given; or whether, as seems more probable, it be the necessary consequence of the faculties of reason and speech, it belongs not to our present subject to enquire. It is common to all men, and to be found in no other race of animals, which seem to know neither this nor any other species of contracts." (*WN*, p 15).

Smith here immediately punts in answer to his own question. More significantly, however, he neglects to relate the answer to his rhetorical question to what he has already carefully developed and articulated in *TMS*. Moreover, the answer in *TMS* is not primarily about reason but rather finds the origins of social exchange in feelings of gratitude and is seen as an on-the-ground product of the Author of Nature.

For a more satisfactory foundation for the human propensity to trade, *TMS* has already developed and articulated beneficence prepositions BP1 and BP2. Someone—it might be you—has offered to benefit another with units of a good or service and this other is (non-coercively) prepared voluntarily to reward that action with a different good or service that is believed by this other that you will like. In *TMS*, people are long practiced from antiquity in such exchanges, separated in time, if they live in orderly communities. So, what is to be expected if a neighbor, or even a friendly stranger, offers to give something good now in exchange for something good now from you? Such people are already well-practiced in acting beneficially toward others, while others, in discharge of their debt of gratitude, regularly reward that action with an appropriate recompense. They act in accordance with the principle that giving leads to receiving. Indeed, in *TMS*, reciprocity follows from Smith's BP1 and BP2: "Of all the persons, however, whom nature points out for our peculiar beneficence, there are none to whom it seems more properly directed than to those whose beneficence we have ourselves already experienced…Kindness is the parent of kindness." (*TMS*, p 331).

Thus kindness, which is not coercible, begets kindness in return and reciprocity follows from BP1 and BP2. Economic trades merely make social exchanges coincident and simultaneous in time. Who, that is well-practiced in such exchanges over time, is not going to be drawn to trade?

Trade combines self-love with beneficence and through markets, creates wealth via enabling the division of labor or specialization in the development of skills and products.

Can Smith's Principles of Free Exchange and Free Trade Be Extended to Electorate Decision Making? An Experimental Investigation

Adam Smith articulated a theory of the emergence of orderly society based on voluntary individual exchange in creating and following the rules of justice and beneficence and the extension of these rules to a market exchange economy. These classical liberal principles also have led to the formation of liberal constitutional government regimes that rely on majority rule in public decision making. Yet, as indicated above, majority rule is coercive in forcing minorities to bear the full burden of their dis-preferred outcome. The winner-take-all nature of majority rule directly incentivizes wasteful spending as each side attempts to form a majority constituency.

I want to close by reviewing a mechanism for electorate public decision that is non-coercive in the sense that non-dominant losers are compensated based on their expressed preference. Versions of the mechanism have been tested in laboratory experiments, so I can summarize some of the findings (Oprea et al. 2007).

Suppose the citizen constituents of an electoral district must each decide whether they favor or oppose a proposition to change local zoning law to prohibit locating a retail business in certain residential neighborhoods. Those living in households near vacant lots are likely to suffer substantial declines in property value; others less so, and a few may even see a benefit in being not too distant from convenient shopping. Observe, that this is fundamentally an economic choice problem.

If the decision is based on the accustomed one-person-one-vote majority rule, there are certain to be winners and losers depending on the majority outcome. Hence, majority rule necessarily constitutes a mechanism for confiscating the "property" of losers by denying them their preferred choice.

Suppose instead that each voter submits a bid for, or against, the proposition specifying how much they are willing to pay to have their option prevail. Let M be the sum of bids for either option while m is that for the alternative, where $M > m$ is the winning choice. The option with the largest sum of bids is the winner and, by definition, is sufficient to reimburse each loser in the amount of their bid. Hence, each winner pays the amount of their bid; each loser pays nothing and receives a compensatory cash payment equal to the amount of their bid.

The resulting settlement holds the promise that it betters the welfare of the electorate compared with majority rule voting.

Laboratory experiments have been reported for 36 compensation elections for groups of size 6 and 18 the details and controls for which can be obtained from the reference.

The subjects in the experiments were assigned values for each of two options and were free to bid as little or as much of their value as they chose and were under no requirement to bid more for their preferred option, as such would be infeasible in any real application. Hence, subjects were free to misrepresent their preferences if they hoped to gain via the compensation process.

Here are some general findings or results from the experiments based on prior questions that were posed: Subjects tended strongly to bid higher the greater their value for an option. The bids did not reflect important attempts to profit from bidding on dis-preferred options. Subjects tend to bid a larger proportion of their value in large cohorts compared with small cohorts.

Summary

In TMS, Smith develops a theory of society founded on the rules ordinary people fashion and follow out of their day-to-day living motivated by their desire to get along with each other. These rules fall under the two categories of beneficence and justice. The former concerns the good things we do for each other, while the latter is about limiting the bad things we do to each other in our neighborhoods and communities. These in turn may scale up to entire societies and nations. Beneficence is about our compulsion to reward out of the debt of gratitude we feel toward the good-hearted actions of others which is the source of reciprocity. Justice is about the natural tendency to feel resentment and to punish actors who engage in murder, theft, robbery, and the violation of contractual promises. Society thus emerges from bottom-up voluntary liberal and liberating processes tending to increase happiness and reduce unhappiness.

We learn from *WN* that a free-market economy accounts for the division of labor and wealth creation as an unintended consequence of free voluntary trade. But people in societies that are well-practiced in voluntary social exchanges across time are sure to find attractive the simultaneous giving and receiving that characterizes every voluntary trade.

Overlooked by Adam Smith in *WN*, the propensity to truck barter and trade is a natural outgrowth of the emergent rules of beneficence. The rules of justice support property, an essential condition of market-based economies that are wealth creating.

Vernon L. Smith
Chapman University
2002 Nobel Laureate in Economics.

References

Ghoddusi H, Ghoddusi M, Masoud N, Rastad M (2017) On quota violations of OPEC members. Energy Econ 68. https://www.researchgate.net/publication/320515582_On_quota_violations_of_OPEC_members

Oprea RD, Smith VL, Winn AM (2007) A compensation election for binary social choice. Proc Natl Acad Sci 104(3):1093–1096. https://doi.org/10.1073/pnas.0609866104

Smith A (1759) The theory of moral sentiments; or, An Essay towards an Analysis of the Principles by which Men naturally judge concerning the Conduct and Character, first of their Neighbours, and afterwards of themselves. To which is added, A Dissertation on the Origins of Languages. New Edition. With a biographical and critical Memoir of the Author, by Dugald Stewart (London: Henry G. Bohn, 1853). In the public domain. Available at: https://oll.libertyfund.org/titles/smith-the-theory-of-moral-sentiments-and-on-the-origins-of-languages-stewart-ed

Smith A (1776) An inquiry into the nature and causes of the wealth of nations. Edited, with an introduction, notes, marginal summary and an enlarged index by Cannan E. Volumes I and II. Muethen, London, 1904. In the public domain. Available at: https://oll.libertyfund.org/titles/smith-an-inquiry-into-the-nature-and-causes-of-the-wealth-of-nations-cannan-ed-in-2-vols

Reflections from the Inside Out: What Libertopia Tells Us About the Nature of Markets in Trade

Tim Evans

To Be Human Is to Trade

Trade is an inevitable activity of human existence. In all periods, people have engaged in transactions that involve the exchange of goods, services, and ideas. Not only has trade helped societies adapt their responses to risk and uncertainty but it has also played a central role in intergroup relations be they cordial or predatory. Long before the invention of money for private exchange (Ingham 2004), elements of trade formed part of the earliest human interactions. Among prehistoric peoples, goods, services, and ideas were exchanged as gifts, tributes, or as part of a barter economy (Watson 2005: Introduction). Beyond early hunter gatherer communities which strove to maintain self-sufficiency, long-distance trade could be found. Indeed, since its beginnings in the Palaeolithic and Neolithic periods, the impulse to trade has developed, eventually spurring immense civilisations and empires. It was the development of maritime trade connecting the Mediterranean, Indian Ocean, and South China Sea, along with the creation of the Silk Road (Beckwith 2011), that established what we recognise today as the foundations of the world's modern commercial and trading systems.

In more recent times, exploration, cartography, and technology have all played their part in the creation of an increasingly interconnected world. Whether by choice or design, trade remains a core function of the human

T. Evans (✉)
Business and Political Economy, Middlesex University, London, UK
e-mail: T.Evans@mdx.ac.uk

© The Author(s), under exclusive license to Springer Nature Switzerland AG 2025
M. Rangeley and D. Hannan (eds.), *Free Trade in the Twenty-First Century*, https://doi.org/10.1007/978-3-031-67656-7_2

condition. Across all periods of boom and bust, war and peace, to be human is to be involved in the vicissitudes of its all-encompassing activities. However, what we mean by trade and what we mean by a market are not always easy to discern. In an attempt to overcome confusing ideas and terminology, this chapter touches on the ethical, epistemological, and economic nature both of markets and trade. In so doing, it not only examines what we mean by the 'market', but it also presents an 'ideal type' construct concerning the underlying institutional architecture of trade.

Rise of Modern Free Trade

Up until the middle of the seventeenth century, English overseas trade was marginal in comparison to that of the Dutch and Spanish who dominated trade across the Atlantic, Europe, and parts of the Middle East. It was in response to their successes that from the 1650s onwards England's Parliament introduced regulations called the Navigation Ordinances, which were designed to primarily prevent the Dutch from having a role in the country's importation markets (Israel 1997: 305–318). As had occurred in other places and times, the English used state intervention to dictate that only its vessels would be allowed to import goods into or via its ports. Ushering in a new era of protectionism (Harper 1939), the Navigation Ordinances entrenched a mercantilist outlook which following the Act of Union in 1707 was extended to cover Scotland too. Together, these interventions entrenched a protectionism that dominated British trade for more than a century (Loschky 1973: 689–691).

However, with the rise of modern industry and manufacturing from the late eighteenth century onwards, merchants and manufacturers began to look beyond a protectionism that echoed the fixed quantity of wealth fallacy. By the first half of the nineteenth century, British industry was not merely innovative, but its pioneers recognised the growing risks of imposing import duties. Understandably, they feared such policies would encourage others to respond in kind against them. It is against this backdrop that from the 1820s onwards, British merchants and entrepreneurs, particularly in economic powerhouses such as Glasgow, London, and Manchester, started to argue for what they called 'free trade' and the abolition of all manner of duties. Starting with the 1823 Reciprocity of Duties Act, which enabled the bilateral signing of mutual trading agreements with other countries, more liberal approaches to trade started to incentivise the production and export of more competitive goods.

By the 1840s and 1850s, a virtuous cycle of cheaper production, international competitiveness, higher exports, and prosperity, came to capture the high ground of debate. Despite protestations from several merchants, land owners, and shipowners (who persisted with the view that their country's interests would be better served by protection), John Bright worked in partnership with Richard Cobden to establish what became known as the Anti-Corn Law League (Briggs 1957: 496–503). The League highlighted the ways such measures artificially raised food prices and protected landowners' interests by levying taxes on imported wheat. In 1846, Parliament repealed the Corn Laws and during the early 1850s, Britain further repealed or reduced duties on more than 250 items. By the close of 1860, the country had virtually abandoned nearly all its remaining protectionist measures.

Despite temporary deviations to reintroduce import duties during the economic headwinds of the late 1920s and 1930s, Britain has broadly remained a champion of liberal trade throughout the twentieth and early twenty-first centuries. Although in the early twentieth century it gifted preferential treatment to traders within its Empire (Glickman 1947: 439–470), the country has generally continued to disport a market-oriented outlook.

Unilateral Free Trade

In recognising free trade to be a mutually beneficial process, there are of course those economists who also advocate its unilateral application. Ever since Adam Smith in the late eighteenth century, numerous economists have supported a policy of one-sided, or non-reciprocal trade as a means of encouraging the world's poor to accelerate their development for the benefit of all. As the US economist Paul Krugman wrote in 1997: "The economist's case for free trade is essentially a unilateral case: a country serves its own interests by pursuing free trade regardless of what other countries may do" (Krugman 1997: 113).

While advocates of unilateralism welcome the post-war liberalisations of the General Agreement on Tariffs and Trade (GATT) and its successor the World Trade Organisation (WTO), many economists rightly consider such ways of working to be overly cumbersome. Recognising unilateral free trade to be of benefit, they want a more efficient approach.

Notwithstanding this, in the early twenty-first century, a tension is also recognised between those economists who believe in unilateral free trade and those who accept it faces practical challenges. Generally, the latter group support a policy of unilateral free trade but recognise that (a) a foreign government's protectionism can inflict damage in the home country and (b) retaliatory tariffs can cause foreign governments to reduce or terminate tariffs so as to derive gains in the home country over the longer-term. To mitigate such matters, one has to consider an economically derived comparison between the scale of the damage that foreign-government protectionism imposes on the domestic market, against the damage done at home by the domestic government's protectionism.

Casting doubt on the wisdom of retaliation, the logic of unilateralism is strengthened further when one considers the interest-group pressures that invariably lie at the causal root of most protectionist measures. As public choice theorists point out, in the political marketplace there are always incentives for vote motivated politicians and self-interested officials to address the most vociferous interest groups and offer visible short term benefits (Butler 2012). Just as in life the squeakiest wheel gets the grease, so in politics, the loudest and boldest often win legislative favour against the dispersed interests of consumers.

Complexity, Epistemology, and Ethics

In considering the socio-economic benefits of the industrial revolution, it becomes clear that over the past 200 years market-based societies have enabled people to live healthier, wealthier, and happier lives than ever before. Since the early nineteenth century, market-based societies have facilitated an unprecedented unleashing of growth and potential. Mindful of the developments, in 1922, Friedrich Von Hayek encountered the 'Austrian School of Economics' under Professor Ludwig Von Mises. Profoundly affected by its teachings, Hayek spent much of the rest of his life exploring its truths. The Austrian School is important because it sees modern society as a web of complex and subjective human interactions in which prices act as signals for human behaviour. For the Austrian economist:

> …the free market and the language of price are the very sources and mechanisms of wealth, the diversity of goods produced by many individuals is richer and more useful, ensuring greater and more widespread wealth than any system which attempts to control from the centre. A diversity of different attempts to predict future needs is what guarantees innovation. The role of market pricing is partly that of allocating resources to the preferred use. Its more important role however, is that of transmitting information about preference and relative scarcities. Only markets can effectively utilise information dispersed throughout millions of economic agents. Profit is a signal which demonstrates

that the entrepreneur is doing the right thing for people he cannot know. Price is therefore the language of the complex or extended order of modern societies. The knowledge utilised in this extended order is greater than that which any single agent such as a government department can possibly acquire (Graham and Clarke 1986: 7).

For Hayek and other Austrian School Economists, the market has been historically beneficial because it is economically efficient while also protecting individual liberty: "[It is] a procedure which has greatly improved the chances of all to have their wants satisfied. It is the only procedure yet discovered to which information widely dispersed among millions of men can be effectively utilised for the benefit of all – and used by assuring to all an individual liberty desirable on ethical grounds." (Hayek 1976a: 70–71).

Whereas exponents of economics from Adam Smith to Friedrich Hayek have defended free markets and free trade on the basis of wealth creation and a moral society, the Russian-born American philosopher Ayn Rand rooted her argumentation in an individualist ethics and epistemology. For her, the "…moral justification of capitalism does not lie in the altruist claim that it represents the best way to achieve 'the common good'…the moral justification of capitalism lies in the fact that it is the only system consonant with man's rational nature, that it protects man's survival qua man, and that its ruling principle is Justice" (Rand 1967: 20).

To Douglas J. Den Uyl and Douglas B. Rasmussen (Den Uyl and Rasmussen 1986), the unique feature of Rand's defence of markets is that it neither considers capitalism to be a necessary evil or that it is justified by its outputs. Instead, the essence of capitalism is centred on its protection of individual rights. If individual rights are being respected, then that society is to some degree capitalist. Based on an essentially Aristotelian model of human action, Rand's stresses the creative power of the mind. The degree to which one's knowledge increases is argued to be a function of one's ability to effectively solve problems. The creative mind is identified as the dynamic, inspirational force behind human progress: "Men of genius in both the sciences and the arts are those who do not allow themselves to be held down by received wisdom" (Den Uyl and Rasmussen 1986: 166).

Under Rand's philosophy, which she called 'Objectivism', the fundamental choice facing living things is productive or destructive action. Because we have no automatic means for the furtherance of our lives, we are forced to make choices concerning which courses of action to take. Free market capitalism is not merely a "social system based on the recognition of individual rights"; more importantly: "it is the basic, metaphysical fact of man's nature – the connection between his survival and his use of reason – that capitalism recognises and protects" (Rand 1967: 19).

In '*For the New Intellectual*', Rand uses two philosophical ideal types to depict the enemies of capitalism, the Witch Doctor and Atilla: "The essential Characteristic of these remain the same in all ages: Attila, the man who rules by brute force, acts on the rage of the moment, is concerned with nothing but the physical reality immediately before him, respects nothing but man's muscles, and regards a fist, a club or a gun as the only answer to any problem…" (Rand 1961: 14). The Witch Doctor wishes to avoid empirical evidence and the world of demonstrable reality: "[He is] the man who dreads physical reality, dreads the necessity of practical action, and escapes into his emotions, into visions of some practical realm where he wishes to enjoy a supernatural power unlimited by the absolute of nature" (Rand 1961: 14). For Rand, both the Witch Doctor and Attila exist with a "consciousness held down to the perceptual method of functioning, an awareness that does not choose to extend beyond the automatic, the immediate, the given, the involuntary, which means an animal's epistemology, or as near to it has a human consciousness can come" (Rand 61: 14). She continues: "It is against the faculty of reason that Attila and the Witch Doctor rebel….Both dread the fact that 'nature, to be commanded, must be obeyed.' Both seek to exist, not by conquering nature, but by adjusting to the given, the immediate, the known" (Rand 1961: 15).

Rand's theory of rights links to her conception of human nature. For her, "the source of rights is man's nature". Rights are a necessary condition of man's particular mode of survival: "Thus, for every individual, a right is the moral sanction of a positive of his freedom to act on his own judgement, for his own goals, by his own voluntary, uncoerced choice. As to his neighbours, his rights impose no obligations on them except of a negative kind; to abstain from violating his rights" (Rand 1967, 322).

Life is not guaranteed. In recognition of this metaphysical fact, Rand holds that rights are freedoms of action and not guarantees of anything. Property rights are not conceived to be rights to things, but only the freedom to pursue courses of action with respect to material goods. If certain goods and services are to be guaranteed to individuals—as protectionists and welfare theorists demand—some people, by implication, must be coerced to provide for others. Apart from the fact that what is guaranteed is conditional upon the productivity of some, and hence no guarantee at all, there is in principle no limit to what one could claim must be guaranteed. Here, the state becomes not merely inefficient and ineffective, Hayek's grounds for opposition, but it is also rendered fraudulent. Rand argues that the rhetoric of state protectionism and welfarism actually assumes people do not possess rights. Instead, their advocates rely on the notion that somehow rights are the gifts of the state, and that therefore like all benefactors, the state possesses the power to remove its generosity when it so desires. Because the state is ultimately its own arbiter, it has no obligation to respond efficiently to demands.

For Rand, the best we can do is to establish conditions which will allow for choices that are essential for the pursuit of life. To establish these social conditions without reference to anyone's particular circumstances is to treat each individual equally. It is against this backdrop that property rights denote the right to certain courses of action as opposed to specific objects: "The right to life is the source of all rights – and the right to property is their only implementation. Without property rights, no other rights are possible. Since man has to sustain his life by his own effort, the man who has no right to the product of his effort has no means to sustain his life. The man who produces while others dispose of his product is a slave" (Rand 1967: 20). For Rand, the fact that capitalism involves the pursuit of self-interest is not only good but morally virtuous. Objectivists argue that capitalism induces, through the process of rational self-interest, material advancement:

> Whatever one's line of work, a competitive and free market tends to push one toward the achievement of the best one is able to produce within a given context. Because there are no guarantees that past achievements will not be bettered, there are strong incentives to continue to produce at the maximum levels. Moreover, those who are innovative and hard-working are not held to the level of the mediocre and the slothful since there is the full expectation of reaping the rewards of one's efforts. In short, capitalism is a system directed towards achievement. (Rand 1967: 20)

Countering the Marxist claim that progress under capitalism is the result of exploiting the surplus labour of workers, Rand contends that capitalism removes sacrifice from social relations. The popular belief that capitalism exploits workers is contested. Collectivism, in whatever variety, is a system wherein some are sacrificed for the sake of others. At the root of collectivism's sacrificial nature is the willingness to operationalise the holistic 'needs of society' view and thereby override individual interests. For Rand, surplus or profit is the product of individuals, not a class phenomenon. In a market society, no one is coerced to associate with other individuals if one finds it detrimental to personal interests. This is not to deny that difficult choices or disagreeable situations cannot be avoided. Instead, it is to suggest that capitalism holds the promise that the products of one's own efforts will not be expropriated without one's agreement.

Similar to Rand, the German sociologist Franz Oppenheimer made a distinction between politics (the state) and the market (Oppenheimer 1926: 24–27). As Murray Rothbard explains, Oppenheimer argued that there are two mutually exclusive ways of acquiring wealth:

> …one he called the 'economic means'. The other way is simpler in that it does not require productivity; it is the way of seizure of another's goods or services by the use of force and violence. This is the method of one sided confiscation, of theft of the property of others. This is the method which Oppenheimer termed 'the political means' to wealth. It should be clear that the peaceful use of one's reason and energy in production is the 'natural path for man: the means for his survival and prosperity on earth. It should be equally clear that the coercive, exploitative means is contrary to natural law; it is parasitic, for instead of adding to production, it subtracts from it. The 'political means' siphons production off to a parasitic and destructive individual or group; and this siphoning not only subtracts from the number producing, it also lowers the producer's incentive to produce beyond his own subsistence. In the long run, the robber destroys his own subsistence by dwindling or eliminating the source of his own supply. But not only that; even in the short run, the predator is acting contrary to his own true nature as a man.' (Rothbard 2009: 14–15)

For believers in genuine markets and free trade, political systems and states have been created less by benign processes of 'social contract' and more by conquest and force. Believing in the private supply of public goods, many free marketeers argue it is important to envision ways in which free markets can be applied to areas from which they are excluded.

Water Privatisation as an 'Ideal Type' Market Construct

One such example is presented by Walter E. Block and Peter L. Nelson in their book, *The Case for Privatising Oceans, Rivers, Lakes, and Aquafers* (Block and Nelson 2016). Arguing that privatisation of the earth's waters would usher in a new age of global growth, they point out that water covers approximately 75% of the earth's surface while land merely represents around 25%. However, while the former accounts for less than 1% of global GDP, land represents more than 99% of global GDP. Accepting that part of the reason for this disparity is that more people live on land than water, they go on to detail the ways in which property rights can redefine the boundaries of economic debate.

For Block and Nelson, the fact that most water remains unowned represents a global tragedy of the commons. In reminding us of problems associated with 'government failure', the authors point out that in the Soviet Union, 97% of land was state owned, accounting for 75% of crops, whereas 3% of the land was privately owned, accounting for a disproportionately high 25%. Arguing that when something is unowned, economic agents lack the incentives to protect, care, or look after it, they argue that it is because of a lack of property rights that the world's oceans suffer from oil spills, overfishing, pollution, piracy, and other problems. In arguing for the full privatisation of the world's water, the authors not only see private ownership as more efficient and effective but, like Rand, they believe those who argue 'property is theft' are morally wrong.

For Block and Nelson, water ownership is not simply about delivering growth. It will also lead to new and innovative forms of dispute resolution. In examining problems involving existing laws that govern the seas (Law of the Sea, Admiralty Law, and Law of Salvage), they envision a world in which law would be privately produced and enforced. Discussing law through the prism of contract and discovery, they outline the sorts of rules they believe would emerge to deal with issues of homesteading, dereliction, or abandonment. Theoretically, they argue that water privatisation would best be established by a homesteader who melds labour with natural resources and who claims the right of ownership accordingly. Hostile to centralised control, they argue property rights are best earned by sweat and toil.

At a practical level, it is not for entrepreneurs to know in advance what will and will not work. What matters is the incentivisation of discovery and solutions. For example, the market may invent new forms of underwater electric fence to keep fish within specific areas. Or it may facilitate GPS-enabled buoys designed to track high-value protean. From an entrepreneurial perspective, what matters is experimentation.

In a series of provocative thought experiments, Block and Nelson discuss a number of challenges. For example, concerning the water cycle and issues relating to evaporation and precipitation, they acknowledge the challenges of trying to tag and trace drops of 'owned water'. Concerning rivers and the case of someone lacking legal access to a plot they own 'midstream', they suggest the sorts of ways players would game solutions. Concerning flooding, fishing, erosion, piracy, and endangered species, they explain why they remain optimistic that private property rights would provide better solutions than any coercive authority.

While it is possible to argue that the authors might not take sufficient account of the fact that humans are land creatures, and that working with water imposes significant additional costs, their work is nevertheless important because it challenges the ways in which we think about concepts such as a 'free market' or 'global free trade'. In a world of 'water socialism' is it appropriate to even use such terminology?

Social Power and Terminology

Economists often describe the world's first major period of globalisation as that which emerged between 1870 and 1914. However, it was Adam Smith in *The Wealth of Nations* more than a century before who noted that in each period of history: "People of the same trade and profession seldom meet together, even for merriment and diversion, but the conversation ends in a conspiracy against the public, or in some contrivance to raise prices…" (Smith 1904, Book I, Chapter X). For Smith, professions and trades popularise their preferred versions of the 'public good' so as to successfully lobby politicians to gain legislative favour. Two centuries later, in the 1970s, Barry Hindess and Paul Hirst (Hindess and Hirst 1977) went further by arguing that in the drive for such corporatism genuine free markets and free trade never exist. Instead, they are always socially, legally, and politically bounded. For example, even the basic unit of modern capitalism, the firm, is built on the statutes of limited liability as introduced by the government in the middle of the nineteenth century.

In exploring the language and thought processes used to describe markets, the US economist David Friedman argues that while it is one thing to show there is something government could do to improve an outcome, it is quite another to show what politics would do in reality. On this, he says:

> That would require a theory of governmental behaviour comparable in power and precision to the theory of market behaviour from which the original efficiency theorem and the inefficiencies due to failures of its assumptions were derived. No widely accepted theory of that sort exists, and much of the large and growing literature that attempts to produce such a theory seems to suggest that government intervention is more likely to worsen than to improve market outcomes. (Friedman 1999: 7)

For Friedman, the question is not whether political markets work under conditions of zero transaction costs and perfect information, for under those conditions the private market is also efficient. The significant question is how badly each system breaks down when the assumptions are relaxed. On this, he states:

> Economic efficiency is a strong requirement for the outcome of any real world system of institutions, since an outcome is efficient only if it could not be improved by a bureaucrat god – a benevolent despot with perfect information and unlimited power over individual actions. While it may be seen as an upper bound on how well an economic system can work, one might think that using that bound to judge real systems is as appropriate as judging race cars by their ability to achieve their upper bound – the speed of light" (Friedman 1999: 7)

Countering the claim that there are areas of human activity too important to be left to the market, Friedman retorts:

> My response would be that the market is, generally speaking, the best set of institutions we know of for producing and distributing things. The more important the good is, the stronger the argument for having it produced by the market. Both barbers and physicians are licensed; both professions have for decades used licensing to keep their numbers down and their salaries up. Government regulation of barbers makes haircuts more expensive; one result, presumably, is that we have fewer haircuts and longer hair. Government regulation of physicians makes medical care more expensive; one result, presumably, is that we have less medical care and shorter lives. Given the choice of deregulating one profession or the other, I would choose the physicians. (Friedman 1999: 7)

Friedman's insights underscore the need for economists to be more precise with their terminology. In economics, as in other disciplines, muddled language leads to inadequate diagnoses. For example, while many economists argue that public goods are in some way consonant with tax-funded provision, they are often beguiled by normative judgements far removed from the realities of economic history.

Private Supply of Public Goods

While today it is widely believed that there are many goods and services essential to a society's functioning that can only be produced by the state, Stephen Davies points out that: "The historical evidence does not support arguments for the necessity of the state as a provider and regulator. Instead, it lends support to the thesis that the market is capable of producing private solutions to the problem of 'public goods'" (Davies 1987: 2).

For example, in Britain between the mid-eighteenth and mid-nineteenth century, a plethora of private law-enforcement agencies developed on the market. While some used newspaper advertisements and rewards to catch criminals, others were professional detectives or thief-catchers. The most significant players in this market were the voluntary associations for the prosecution of felons. Initially set up by citizens to defray the growing cost of criminal prosecutions, they developed new services such as crime prevention and the provision of insurance. Between 1744 and 1856, more than 450 such associations existed (Shubert 1981). By the 1830s, the largest was the Barnet Association which started to resemble a private police force. Providing a service to members that was inexpensive and effective the sector served an increasingly broad socio-economic customer base.

In education, E. G. West (West 1965) and Philip Gardner (Gardner 1984) have demonstrated that before the introduction of compulsory state education in Britain in 1870 and 1880 an overwhelming majority of youngsters were accessing high-quality private schooling from an increasingly diverse and entrepreneurial range of providers many of whom served the poor.

Similarly, in the early decades of the nineteenth century, the supply of water and sanitation services was increasingly provided by chartered private water companies. While in areas such as Ashton-under-Lyne, providers were effective in providing a stable and high-pressure water supply (Holland 1846), elsewhere, there were problems. As many observers commented at the time, the main challenge was the parlous state of local government and a lack of competition. For example, while London had more than 300 providers, they were forced to operate under a complex web of approximately 250 local Acts.

Despite these challenges, late Georgian and early Victorian Britain witnessed the development of an astonishing array of market-based organisations. In the area of justice, private arbitration services abounded. To mitigate risks of fire, the country saw the arrival of private insurance companies, such as Sun Alliance. And when it came to saving lives at sea, it welcomed the establishment of the Royal National Lifeboat Institution (RNLI). Founded in 1824 (Meek 1999: 2) and staffed mainly by unpaid volunteers, the RNLI remains to this day a successful charity which receives no money from the public purse.

By the middle of the nineteenth century, the solutions being offered through the private supply of public goods were increasingly blocked by powerful interests aligned to the state. Whereas interventionists had a unifying ideology in Benthamism, mid-Victorian elites were also spurred on by a mounting fear of a moral decay. Believing economic development was undermining social cohesion they believed the market was encouraging an amoral 'state of nature'. The main objection to independent education was its perceived lack of moral instruction. Against the associations for the prosecution of felons was the belief that in focusing on property and person, 'moral' offences such as prostitution and inebriation were being ignored. Even the debate concerning sanitation came to be viewed as much about morals as about sewerage. From the 1840s onwards, state interventionism at national and local levels was not only being spurred by collectivist notions of morality; they were being encouraged by conservative elites.

Weberian State

By the early twentieth century, the German sociologist Max Weber reflected that the modern state is that political organisation whose: "Administrative staff successfully uphold the claim to the monopoly on the legitimate use of physical force in the enforcement of its orders" (Weber 1922: 29, translation). While previously, the private supply of public goods had been commonplace, he argued it was only with the ending of the Thirty Years War (1618–1648) and the signing of the Peace Treaty of Westphalia that the centralising authority of the modern state started to emerge.

For Weber, the emerging nation states of the eighteenth, nineteenth, and early twentieth centuries were distinguished from previous periods of governance by two key features. The first is the state's monopoly on force and violence within a given territory. The second is the idea of absolute sovereignty denoting territorial integrity and the right to non-intervention. It is through its protection from what he characterised as 'local racketeers and outside marauders' that the state consolidates and performs its purpose. Any re-emergence of a system that tolerates the private production or enforcement of law represents a failure in statecraft that is tantamount to undermining the state's own "quintessential function and signifier of being" (Small 2006: 12).

Today, a century on, the statecraft Weber described is itself giving way to new forms of governance. While the Weberian state relied on a binary division between official and unofficial structures, in many parts of the world, such demarcation lines are starting to blur. As the US defence and security expert Sean McFate has pointed out, in many countries people have already entered an increasingly fluid age in which states are being disintermediated and hollowed out by an ever broader array of private alternatives. Detailing the inexorable rise of non-state actors, he says that: "The privatisation of war changes warfare in profound ways, and this could fundamentally alter the distribution of power within the world system. Should this trend continue, states will no longer enjoy a monopoly of force to uphold rule of law, and new kinds of actors will rise to challenge them, sometimes existentially" (McFate 2020: 1).

Towards a Vision for Markets in Trade

It is with all of this in mind that it is not only important to learn from the past but to recognise where we are today. In gaining altitude, such insights not only encourage reflection but they help us to imagine scenarios for the future.

In an attempt to avoid muddled terminology and thinking, this chapter has sought to locate the idea of markets and trade as core features of the human condition. In highlighting the ethical, epistemological, and economic foundations of capitalism and unilateral free trade, it has also argued that it is only those societies that respect varying degrees of 'property in and of the person' that have managed to turn human prosperity into a sustainable reality for millions of people around the world. Since the start of the industrial revolution, it is the market-oriented societies that have unleashed people's economic potential so that they can enjoy healthier, wealthier, and happier lives. However, in questioning what is meant by the term 'free trade' on a planet where private property rights are precluded from 75% of its surface makes for an interesting thought experiment. As does the history of privately produced public goods in areas such as law enforcement, education, emergency services, and water and sanitation provision.

Such reflections are important because in failing to articulate coherent definitions of what is and is not meant by such terms as 'free market' and 'free trade', too many scholars make assertions that misdiagnose issues of causality. Unlike classical liberals and libertarians, Marxist, National Socialist, Fascist, Keynesian, neo-Keynesian, and neo-liberal thinkers invariably apportion blame to markets where no property rights exist in the first place (Tyler and Crampton 2002). Similarly, mainstream commentators often fall into the scientistic trap of making overly mathematicised and normative statements that fail the test of time. Not only do they deny the complexity and unpredictability of human action, but they often end up promoting mathematical models which are incapable of accurate predictions in the real world.

It is against this backdrop that not only should state failure be more readily criticised, but we should start to envision what genuine markets in trade might actually entail. Away from the heady top-down world of supranational 'blockification' as exemplified by the European Union, Central American Integration System, and the Gulf Cooperation Council—or indeed, the international corporatism of the WTO—genuine markets would be led by consumers. Putting to the side actually existing polities, borders, and controls, a free market world would include features such as the private production of law, enforcement and money, as well as private property rights on land and water.

Private Law, Enforcement, and Money

Just as the failings of public law-enforcement agencies are giving rise to an ever more sophisticated and international private security sector, so excessive delays and backlogs in public courts are incentivising private-sector alternatives. Today, it is almost impossible to find a contract between firms and consumers that does not contain provision for arbitration. In Western countries such as the UK and the USA, private courts now compete with public courts across broad range of civil disputes. Private security and dispute-resolution services not only herald more efficient and effective provision, but they also incentivise higher levels of transparency and satisfaction.

History presents many examples concerning the private production and enforcement of law. For example, across mediaeval Europe, the Law Merchant (lex mercatoria) governed almost all aspects of commerce and trade. Based on reciprocity and reputation, it evolved overtime. Even today, most international trade is largely governed by merchants, as they produce, arbitrate, and enforce key elements of their own law.

The US academic, Bruce L. Benson, argues that free markets in law would encourage the development of more individual and cooperative arrangements (Benson 1990). On the market, he argues these would include insurance and treaty-style agreements between competing protection organisations. Lawbreakers would be punished through the payment of full restitution to injured parties including the coverage of costs associated with bringing an offender to justice. Threats of ostracism and boycotts would incentivise convicted criminals to pay debts. And private courts would reward those judges who developed the best reputations for impartiality and clear judgements.

Again, in a world of propertarian markets, money and finance would no longer be subjected to state regulation and top-down control. Instead, central banks, fiat currencies, and the world of finance would all come under the purview of private property rights and open competition (Hayek 1976b). On the market, state failure with inflation, deflation, and bank runs would be dealt with by entrepreneurs building more sustainable and stable business models.

Reflections Beyond Libertopia

The reason all this matters to trade is because without an underlying institutional architecture founded on property rights, not only are market processes diluted, but the claim that they are in anyway 'laissez-faire' is exposed. Undermined by coercion, politics, and sectional interest, economics merely becomes a branch of public policy.

For markets to be meaningful, trade would have to be governed by privately produced and enforced law. Through property rights and contracts, security arrangements would replace defence. Consumer standards would replace regulation. And victimless crimes would be rendered moot as the law focused on contractual disputes and tort damages arising from actual aggression in the form of burglary, assault, or pollution. Although markets would logically establish their own private supreme court (Birch 1998), its jurisdiction would denote a new type of governance built on the principle of non-coercion. In such a utopia, externalities would be internalised through private property rights (Cheung 1978). Information asymmetries would be minimised through brands and commercial free speech (Micklethwait 1993). And the demand for monopolies would be met through private supply.

Alongside growth would come new and better forms of private health, education, and welfare, not least for the poor (Tooley and Dixon 2005). Without a politically derived uniformity of rules determining what constitutes a doctor, teacher, or electrician, training and quality standards would be driven by choice, innovation, and reputation.

As a theoretical exercise, the point here is not to actually build such a world. Instead, it is to recognise that all the scary things that most mainstream trade experts and economists believe would happen without the state are the very things that usually happen with it. Beyond a world of tariffs, quotas, and duties, there may not be a viable or practicable libertarian utopia. But what there certainly are are several useful market concepts and ideas worth considering, especially if one is trying to think in economic terms.

As we consider the nature of markets in trade, it is these reflections that will more powerfully hone and improve our thinking. After all, the way polities think and operate internally often reflects their boundaries of discourse concerning external behaviour and the wider world of trade relations. That is why thinking about what we mean by 'free markets' and 'free trade' are, in and of themselves, so important.

Bibliography

Beckwith C (2011) Empires of the Silk Road: a history of central Eurasia from the Bronze Age to the present. University Press, Princeton

Benson BL (1990) The enterprise of law: justice without the state. Pacific Research Institute for Public Policy, San Francisco

Birch P (1998) Anarcho-capitalism dissolves into city states. Legal Notes Number 28. Libertarian Alliance, London

Block WE, Nelson PL (2016) The case for privatizing the oceans, rivers, lakes, and aquifers. Lexington Books, Maryland, USA

Briggs A (1957) Cobden and bright. Hist Today 7(8)

Butler E (2012) Public choice: a primer. Institute of Economic Affairs, London

Cheung SNS (1978) The myth of social cost: a critique of welfare economics and the implications for public policy. Hobart Paper 82. Institute of Economic Affairs, London

Davies S (1987) The private supply of 'public goods' in nineteenth century Britain. Historical Notes Number 3. Libertarian Alliance, London

Den Uyl D, Rasmussen DB (eds) (1986) The philosophic thought of Ayn Rand. Illinois University Press, Illinois

Friedman D (1999) Should medicine be a commodity? [online]. http://www.daviddfriedman.com/Academic/Medicine_Commodity/Medicine_Commodity.html. Accessed 18 Jan 2024

Gardner P (1984) The lost elementary schools of Victorian England. Croom Helm, London

Glickman DL (1947) The British imperial preference system. Q J Econ 61(3)

Graham D, Clarke P (1986) The new enlightenment. Macmillan in association with Channel 4, London

Harper LA (1939) The English navigation laws: a seventeenth-century experiment in social engineering. Columbia University Press, New York

Hayek FA (1976a) Law, legislation and liberty. The mirage of the social justice, vol 2. Routledge and Kegan Paul, London

Hayek FA (1976b) Denationalisation of money: the argument refined. Hobart Papers Number 70. Institute of Economic Affairs, London

Hindess B, Hirst P (1977) Mode of production and social formation. Palgrave Macmillan, London

Holland PH (1846) Report on the Ashton under Lyne Water Works. Towns Improvement Company, London

Ingham G (2004) The nature of money. Polity, London

Israel JI (1997) England's mercantilist response to Dutch world trade primacy, 1647–74. In: Conflicts of empires: Spain, the low countries and the struggle for world supremacy 1585–1713. Hambledon Continuum, London

Krugman P (1997) What should trade negotiators negotiate about? J Econ Lit 35(1)

Loschky DJ (1973) Studies in the navigation acts: new economic non-history? Econ Hist Rev 26(4)

McFate S (2020) Mercenaries and privatized warfare: current trends and developments. Paper prepared for the United Nations Working Group on the Use of Mercenaries Office of the United Nations High Commissioner for Human Rights, Geneva, Switzerland

Meek N (1999) The plausibility of large-scale, hi-tech, voluntarily-funded emergency organisations: the example of the Royal National Lifeboat Institution. Libertarian Alliance, London

Micklethwait B (1993) How and how not to achieve good taste in advertising: free market regulation is better than government regulation. Political Notes 74. Libertarian Alliance, London

Oppenheimer F (1926) The state. Vanguard Press, New York

Rand A (1961) For the new intellectual. Signet Books, New York

Rand A (1967) What is capitalism. In: Capitalism the unknown ideal. New American Library, New York

Rothbard MN (2009) Anatomy of the state. Mises Institute, Auburn, Alabama

Shubert A (1981) Private initiative in law enforcement: associations for the prosecution of Felons, 1774–1856. In: Bailey V (ed) Policing and punishment in nineteenth century Britain. Croom Helm, London

Small M (2006) Privatisation of security and military functions and demise of the modern nation-state in Africa. Occasional paper series, vol 1, Number 2. African Centre for the Constructive Resolution of Disputes, Durban, South Africa

Smith A (1904 [1776]) An inquiry into the nature and causes of the wealth of nations. Methuen and Company, London

Tooley J, Dixon P (2005) Education is good for the poor: a study of private schools serving the poor in low-income countries. CATO Institute, Washington, DC

Tyler C, Crampton E (2002) Market failure or success: the new debate. Edward Elgar Publishing, Cheltenham

Watson P (2005) Ideas: a history of thought and invention from fire to Freud. Harper Collins Publishers, New York

Weber M (1922/1968) In: Roth G, Wittich C (eds) (trans) Economy and society. Bedminster Press, New York

West EG (1965) Education and the state. Institute of Economic Affairs, London

The Foundations of Free Trade

Patrick Barron

There are two irrefutable foundations to free trade: That free trade is part and parcel of, one, human action, an a priori science, and, two, that man owns himself. We shall examine these concepts below.

The A Priori Foundation of Free Trade

Economic science is a social science and not a natural science. The two "sciences" differ markedly in several important respects, the most important of which is that economics is based upon a priori knowledge and the natural sciences are based on a posteriori knowledge. A priori knowledge is derived by following logical deductions from irrefutable maxims. A posteriori knowledge is based upon induction from observation, usually conducted in controlled environments. Inductive knowledge can only validate or invalidate theories. No theory can ever be validated for all time, since it is always possible for some new observation, hitherto unobserved, to contradict the theory. In contrast, and to the exasperation of many natural scientists, deductive knowledge cannot be disproven by observation; it can be disproven only by the exposure of faulty logic.

P. Barron (✉)
West Chester, PA, USA
e-mail: patrickbarron@msn.com

Man Acts

The irrefutable maxim that is the foundation of economic science is "***Man Acts***". This statement cannot be refuted, for to attempt to do so validates the maxim; i.e., one acts when one states that man does not act. All of economic science, including the a priori foundation of free trade, follows logically and irrefutably. Let us expand our explanation of irrefutable logical maxims by stating that "***Man Acts Rationally***". Again, one sees that to argue that man does not act rationally does not follow logically from the proposition that Man Acts. If man does not act rationally, then one cannot argue the point without proving it. This is not the same as stating that man may act in error. One may act in error and still act rationally. I once bought a set of very nice women's golf clubs and all the accessories for my wife, believing that owning new clubs, shoes, etc. would entice her to take up the game that I loved. I was quickly shown to have acted in error. I did act rationally, despite the fact that my wife thought that I was out of my mind. Not the same thing, you see.

Natural scientists might have told me that all previous evidence, gathered by the induction process of observation over the years, should have proven to me that my wife just did not want to play golf. Ah, but here I could have argued that no amount of evidence could possibly prove such an assertion. I could have argued that I had detected subtle changes to her outlook on the great game. In other words, I undoubtedly believed that I had seen evidence to the contrary, mistaken though it may have been. Such is the difference between deduction and induction. One can never assert that my wife will never take up the game of golf; i.e., such an assertion can never be proven. My wife just has not taken up the noble game ***yet***. Despite her protestations to the contrary, she might change her mind in the future.

Self-ownership

The intellectual support of free trade is further provided by the concept of self-ownership. Man owns himself. No one else owns him. Thus, man is free to act as long as he harms no one. For millennia man was held to be subservient to a pharaoh, king, emperor, or warlord. Its most recent expression can be found in the concept of the Divine Right of Kings. But the rise of Christianity ultimately destroyed the foundations of this concept. For, if man is formed in God's image, how can one man claim to be formed as a natural master and others as natural servants?

Immanuel Kant and the Humanity Principle (Atwell 1986a)

The most thorough explanation of man's primacy was developed by Immanuel Kant. The recognition of the self-ownership of man meant that man was an end and could not be used as a means to an end. Kant's **Humanity Principle** could be discovered by reason alone. But what is the origin of reason? Enter religion. Kant claimed that the existence of reason itself is an intimation of the existence of God. All of ethics and, as it happens, all of economic progress flows from this one maxim. Christianity teaches that man is formed in the image of God and the implications of this have proven to be tremendous for economic progress. It has taken a long time, and the process can be reversed, which it may be doing right now, as Christianity has been abandoned by huge numbers in the West. Nevertheless, here is the argument: if man is formed in the image of God, then all individual men are equal to one another in their rights, which derive from God and cannot be derived from other men. In the eyes of God, the lowest person on the social scale is equal in his God-given rights to the highest and most exalted anywhere in the world, whether a captain of industry, king, or president.

The concept of the rule of law emerged in the West to protect the individual's natural rights by giving him equal protection under the law; i.e., equal with all other men, no matter how exalted. Other protections of the individual followed, such as the right to government by representatives elected by the people themselves and trial by a jury of one's peers. Magna Carta is the best-known example of this statement, for the king was forced to admit that all men had rights that could not be taken away, regardless of social rank.

The political liberation of man that stems from accepting that he is made in the image of God has gradually been extended to include economic liberation. In the West, it gradually came to be accepted that economic rights were protected under the banner of political rights. This makes sense since taking away a man's economic rights cannot be justified without taking away his political rights. In communist Cuba, all legal jobs are owned and controlled by the state. One of the ways the Cuban tyrants keep people in line is to place them on an economic blacklist, prohibiting their employment anywhere in the country. Since the state owns all businesses, such a penalty can be a death sentence. There is no way such an ostracized person can earn a living; he must become either a beggar who lives off the handouts of others, a criminal, or he starves.

It is no wonder that most communist regimes forbid organized religion. They must deny that man has any God-given rights, only state-given rights, which, of course, may be taken away at any time and for any reason, even for no reason at all but just to terrorize the populace into fearful submission. Some totalitarian regimes recognize state-controlled or state-authorized religion, which elevates the tyrant to God-like status. The state uses such pseudo-religions for purposes of internal control and as outlets for their propaganda. The pharaoh was a God and the people were treated as beasts of burden. The "official" religions of the Middle Ages come to mind, too, proclaiming that the king was placed on his throne by "divine right" and to oppose him was to oppose God. In modern times Shinto Japan elevated the emperor to God-like status, which the allies forced the Japanese to abandon at the end of World War II. Today communist North Korea requires its population to worship the Kim family, and Red China forces Roman Catholics to take orders from its own Chinese Patriotic Catholic Association. These state religions do not elevate man to enjoying equal political and economic rights; they are used as a tool of the state to set up a privileged, parasitic class, whether one calls them aristocracy or vanguards of the proletariat.

The Logic of Unilateral Free Trade

Free trade is both a human right and the one trade policy that will deliver the greatest economic benefit to those who practice it. It follows logically from the irrefutable maxim that Man Acts that the goal of all economic life is to improve the quality of life of the individual. Since only individuals act, economic science is based upon "methodological individualism". It functions not to serve certain groups, and it especially does not function just to serve producers. Furthermore, unlike macroeconomics, government statistics are of limited value, since it is impossible to quantify an individual's satisfaction gained from economic activity. How much a person's welfare increases from work, consumption, or leisure cannot be measured with mathematical tools.

In addition to formulating the Humanity Principle, Immanuel Kant gave us the **Categorical Imperative** (Atwell 1986b); that for something to be ethically valid it must be binding always and everywhere regardless of one's inclination. An example of a violation of the categorical imperative is the government's claim that it has to right to use the police power of the state to prevent us from buying a good or service from foreigners. These measures are justified as good for "the economy." If that were so, then you and I should be allowed to force our neighbors to buy goods that we produce instead of goods that people in other towns or states produce! But extortion is a crime, unless committed by the government. But there are many such violations of the categorical imperative all around us. For example, tariffs on foreign steel benefit only *some* people—US steel companies, their stockholders, and their employees—at the expense of everyone else.

The Law of Comparative Advantage

Methodological individualism exposes other macroeconomic fallacies. I will discuss just a few. David Ricardo explained that trade is founded on the Law of Comparative Advantage (Montevirgen 2024); i.e., that trade expands the specialization of labor to minimize one's opportunity costs. For example, it makes no economic sense for basketball star Michael Jordan to skip a few games in order to paint his living room. His opportunity cost would be very high; i.e., he would forgo the opportunity to earn vastly more money by playing basketball than by saving the cost of paying someone to paint his living room. The Law of Comparative Advantage extends infinitely, from the individual to the family to the neighborhood, etc. to cover the entire world. Political boundaries are irrelevant.

Say's Law

Macroeconomics' invention of "lack of aggregate demand" attempts to deny the validity of Say's Law or the Law of Markets (Investopedia Team 2024). Jean Baptiste Say most clearly explained that supply must precede consumption. In other words, inherent in supply is the wherewithal for consumption. Think of an Iowa farmer who gazes over his vast corn crop. The farmer sees the wherewithal for satisfying all his many needs. He will exchange his corn crop for a widely accepted medium of indirect exchange, money, in order to purchase all the necessities of life. If his crop failed, he would face dire straits. Printing money and giving it to him, as advocated by macroeconomists, merely debases the medium of exchange and causes higher prices for the rest of society, a violation of Kant's Humanity Principle.

Bastiat's "the Unseen"

Frédéric Bastiat pointed out what should be obvious to all; i.e., that state directing of resources may indeed cause certain "seen" statistics to go in the desired direction, but these same resources could have been directed to any number of more highly desired ends. Furthermore, there may be ends that never were realized at all. In other words, if we are forced to pay more for something simply because it is "made in America," we will have less money for satisfying other desires. Bastiat's famous essay "That Which Is Seen, and That Which Is Not Seen (Bastiat 2022)" was a devastating attack upon mercantilist direction of the French economy. We can "see" that the glazier benefits from the broken window, but we do not "see" all the benefits that had to be forgone.

Tariffs can certainly be justified using the tools of the macroeconomists, who view individuals are mere cogs in a machine known as "the economy." But once we start to consider individuals as acting human beings with their own values, desires, and rights, we cannot justify taxing, manipulating, and coercing those people for the sake of a politician's goals for the artificial construct known as "the economy."

Two Common Objections to Free Trade

In spite of centuries of sound economic theory describing the benefits of free trade, we continue to hear two objections to free trade. We even sometimes hear these from friends who consider themselves generally to be in favor of free trade, even unilateral free trade.

The first objection I will call the Donald Trump objection—the claim that imports have cost Americans good-paying jobs, from which the nation has never recovered and cannot recover as long as we allow imports to replace American-made products. The second I will call the essential industries objection—the claim that there are some products that America must produce itself, no matter what the cost or inefficiency, in sufficient quantities to ensure access to these products in time of war.

Objection Number One: Free Trade Causes Unemployment

The first objection is easiest to dismiss, for it attempts to refute Ricardo's the "Law of Comparative Advantage". Peaceful cooperation among peoples of the earth has no limit. Just as Pennsylvanians find it advantageous to import pineapples from Hawaii rather than attempt to grow them, Americans find it advantageous to import many goods from people who just happen to live in foreign countries. Absent government intervention to restrict one's own citizens from entering into peaceful cooperation to produce any legal product or service, all will find employment and all will be wealthier. The corollary is that even those who are less skilled in *all* things can find useful employment in an unhampered market. This is the "Law of Absolute Advantage" (Investopedia Team 2023), a corollary to the "Law of Comparative Advantage."

The Law of Comparative Advantage is also revealed once producers create a surplus. Savings produce capital, which produces more wealth when individuals are allowed to engage in the productivity-enhancing division of labor via trade. The resulting products and services cost less than previously, yet employment is not destroyed. It is transferred to better uses, which enrich all. Both sides expect that trade is beneficial and must be allowed to freely trade their surplus product. The political location of individuals engaged in such trade is completely irrelevant to the wealth-enhancing benefits of trade.

The logical conclusion of restricting international trade for just one or two so-called threatened industries is the demand that *all* products be protected. Advocating an autarkic society is to argue in favor of the Fallacy of Composition (Nikolopoulou 2023); i.e., that what might be good for one industry—for example, allowing domestic steel producers to extort higher prices from customers—cannot be extended to all industries. This is akin to standing in a giant circle with everyone picking the pocket of the person to the right while having his pocket picked by the person on the left.

The source of our societal problems, even those correctly identified, such as persistent unemployment, must be found elsewhere. As Ludwig von Mises would advise, one must find the proper means to arrive at the ends desired. If the US really does suffer from collapsing industries, restricting trade is not the solution but will exacerbate the problem. In other words, trade restrictions to cure unemployment are the wrong cure and will cause even more harm to society.

Unfortunately, in modern-day America, there are many suspects to which one can assign economic decline. American industry is hampered by a panoply of regulatory red tape and outright restrictions at federal, state, and local levels. One needs only to consider the effects of the Environmental Protection Agency, the Occupational Health and Safety Administration, the Federal Food and Drug Administration, and not to mention similar agencies at the state level. Plus, the disaster that is public education (regulated mostly by the states) and ever-increasing regulations on economic life at the local level. (My tiny township government in southeast Pennsylvania recently informed us homeowners that we needed to obtain a township-issued permit in order to resurface our driveways. So, now I need government permission to maintain my property in good repair!).

Objection Number Two: Essential Industries Must Be Protected

This is the national security objection; i.e., that the US must maintain a minimum production level of essential war-related products. This is not an argument in favor of economic efficiency. Quite the opposite. Furthermore, little or no evidence is offered that nations have lost wars due to running out of essential products, although it undoubtedly is true that denying the enemy all kinds of goods and services does reduce a nation's war-making capability. Nevertheless, one can make a good case that this concern is unlikely to be a factor by taking a closer look below the surface of this argument.

Stating the "Essential Industries" Case

Let us assume that China wants to drive US steel manufacturers out of business. It succeeds by offering US steel users—manufacturers of buildings, bridges, autos, etc.—high-quality products at low prices for an extended period of time. After US steel production has been reduced to zero, China suddenly refuses to sell steel to us and, as a consequence, we cannot build essential war material that requires steel components. We surrender to China, withdraw our military protection to allies, and/or accede to China's demands, whatever those may be.

The Response

Note that for a long period of time, perhaps years or even decades, China must subsidize steel production, which drains its public coffers and actually reduces its own war-making capacity. (China cannot build its own battleships, for example, if it is subsidizing construction of ours.) In the meantime, the US enjoys an increase in its standard of living. We build up our country in many ways, from new and improved bridges to a revitalized domestic auto industry (remember, cheap, high-quality Chinese steel is subsidizing US car makers). Now China embargoes steel shipments to the US and makes threats of some kind. Our modern battle fleet, the product of cheap Chinese steel, is at our immediate disposal.

Meanwhile, our modern infrastructure, built with cheap Chinese steel, allows us to rush stockpiled war material, also built with subsidized Chinese steel, to our fleet and onward to our overseas bases and the battle area. We then gear up for the possibility of a protracted war by placing orders for steel with the other thirty-odd nations of the world who are eager to sell us high-quality steel but who have been shut out of the American market by subsidized Chinese steel.

Now, I ask you ... is this not the more likely scenario?

Importing subsidized products—perhaps *especially* products essential for war—increase a nation's war-making capacity rather than diminish it. We build up all aspects of our nation's economy, including the defense sector, by using products with the best combination of quality and price, whether ***imported or not***. Doing so allows us either to spend less for the same level of defense or increase our defense by spending the same amount of money but getting more war material in return. Our theoretical potential enemy has actually helped us defend ourselves and our vital interests abroad.

Trade Agreements Are Not Necessary

The common assumption behind any discussion of these debates and crises is that a country cannot stand alone in the world and needs to negotiate trade and monetary terms with its trading partners, who may require the country to adopt measures that are antithetical to its interests. Is this really the case? Is it possible for a nation to free itself from all international agreements, manage its own currency as it sees fit, and trade robustly with the rest of the world?

No Country Can Harm Another Economically Without that Country's Consent

In order to accept the wisdom of international noninterventionism in economic affairs, one must understand that no country (or bloc of countries, such as the EU) can harm another economically without that country's consent, meaning its tacit compliance. In other words, a country can adopt its own trading and currency policies and need not be influenced or harmed by the actions of any other country. But first of all, we need to understand the definition of "harm."

No Harm

In his book *No Harm: Ethical Principles for a Free Market*, Dr. T. Patrick Burke explains that harm consists only in physical harm or the threat of physical harm. It is not characterized by discrimination or a demand for special trading terms. The most common example of real, physical harm is war. War destroys the assets of others. Likewise, blockades cause real harm, because the blockaded nation is threatened by the destruction of its outgoing or incoming goods. Just because it does not choose to fight to break the blockade or is powerless to do so does not mean that it is not harmed. However, a refusal of one country to allow its citizens to trade with another—for example, the EU's recent restriction on its members that prevents them from importing Iranian oil–does not harm Iran. Iran has not been harmed in the T. Patrick Burke sense. It cannot demand that the EU allow its citizens the right to import Iranian oil. However, EU citizens *are* harmed, because they are physically prevented by the police power of the state from exercising their preferences.

An internal example would be for a person to refrain from trading with a local merchant, due to some personal disagreement that his wife has with the merchant's wife. That merchant is not harmed by the trade that he does not enjoy. However, in our example, the husband is harmed, because his wife prevents him from enjoying a preference that would improve his satisfaction. Most likely, the husband must travel farther and pay more for goods or purchase inferior goods. At the nation-state level, the European Union harms its own citizens, for they must pay more for oil, buy inferior oil, or suffer some kind of inconvenience. Otherwise, why would they have purchased Iranian oil in the first place? One could even go so far as to say that the EU wages war against its own citizens and not against Iran, for, undoubtedly, there are police sanctions that the EU would employ against its members for violating the Iranian trade prohibition.

Regulatory and Monetary Trade Interventions Harm Only Those Who Impose Them

I will continue to use the EU case as illustrative of my thesis that a nation adopting unilateral free trade cannot be harmed except by its own consent. The EU has adopted many onerous regulations on trade in goods and services with which its members must comply as a condition of EU membership. The EU has erected trade barriers for many goods and services against non-EU members. For example, the EU prohibits the importation of most agricultural products from Africa. Either there is an outright prohibition against importing African foodstuffs or the African nations cannot comply with complex and onerous regulations such as the prohibition against genetically engineered food. A country that wishes to trade with the EU either complies with EU demands or must find buyers elsewhere.

This practice does not fall into the Burkean definition of harm as regards Africa. It does, though, constitute harm to citizens of the EU. African countries are left in the same position as before: remember, no one and no nation has an entitlement to the trade of others. But we must assume that the EU prohibits African foodstuffs because its citizens would have purchased them in the absence of the prohibition; otherwise, the prohibition would not be necessary. Therefore, the EU regulations or prohibitions against the importation of African foodstuffs harm only EU citizens themselves. The African nations are perfectly free to pursue sales elsewhere in the world, although it is true that their standard of living would have been higher without the EU regulations and prohibitions.

The same is true of currency interventions. The United States has complained for some time that China intervenes in its own currency markets to hold down the value of the Yuan in order to increase export sales. The US position wrongly claims that it is harmed because domestic companies lose sales to cheaper Chinese goods. But this is wrong. Viewed from the standpoint of Burkean justice, domestic companies do not have an entitlement to domestic sales. And viewed from a practical standpoint, America enjoys an outright subsidy from China. China sells the United States goods below cost and causes its own citizens to suffer higher prices; that is, higher Chinese domestic prices are caused by its currency intervention that gives American importers more Yuan than the free-market rate, which is based on purchasing power parity. Currency interventions to spur exports are paid by the exporting country's own citizens in the form of higher domestic prices. Should America foolishly prohibit the importation of Chinese goods, either by quotas or tariffs, it would cause harm only to its own citizens, who would be forced to pay higher prices, in addition to other economic dislocations.

Conclusion

A free trade policy does not rest on evidence that nations who adopt it enjoy superior economic performance. Free trade rests on a priori, irrefutable maxims: Man Acts, Self-Ownership, Kant's Humanity Principle, and Burke's No Harm Principle. Data gathering and analysis to prove or disprove the advantages of free trade are irrelevant and unnecessary. Nations may deny their citizens the right to trade freely with foreign nations, but only their own citizens are harmed. Thus, negotiating free trade agreements is unnecessary. Unilateral free trade is the default policy that will generate the most satisfaction for those who adopt it.

Bibliography

Atwell JE (ed) (1986a) Nijoff International Philosophy Series (NIPS, vol 22) ends and principles in Kant's moral thought. The principles of humanity, pp 105–137. https://doi.org/10.1007/978-94-009-4345-2_6#citeas

Atwell JE (ed) (1986b) Nijoff International Philosophy Series (NIJS, vol 22) ends and principles in Kant's moral thought. Ends and the good will, pp 13–32. https://doi.org/10.1007/978-94-009-4345-2_4

Bastiat CF (2022) That which is seen and that which is not seen. Mises Institute, 25 Nov 2022. https://mises.org/library/which-seen-and-which-not-seen

Burke TP (1998) No harm: ethical principles for a free market. Paragon House, St. Paul, MN, USA

Investopedia Team. Absolute advantage: definition, benefits, and example. Investopedia, 20 Sept 2023. https://www.investopedia.com/terms/a/absoluteadvantage.asp#toc-understanding-absolute-advantage

Investopedia Team. Say's law of markets theory and implications explained. Investopedia, updated 26 Apr 2024. https://www.investopedia.com/terms/s/says-law.asp

Kant E (2006) Groundwork of the metaphysics of morals. The University Press, Cambridge

Montevirgen K (2024) Comparative advantage economic theory. Britannica Money, 14 Mar 2024. https://www.britannica.com/money/comparative-advantage

Nikolopoulou K (2023) Fallacy of composition: definition & examples. Scribbr. Rev 30 Oct 2023. https://www.scribbr.com/fallacies/fallacy-of-composition/

The Psychology of Protectionism

Eamonn Butler

The Rationality of Free Trade

Nearly all economists agree that the most rational and wealth-creating trade policy is to maintain free and open trade; yet our irrational human psychology usually persuades us to do exactly the opposite.

Throughout recorded economic history, people have generally believed that wealth comes from selling things, while buying things represents a loss. Countries therefore created the huge legal and regulatory structures of *mercantilism*, intended to make themselves wealthy by selling as much as possible abroad, while buying as little as possible from other countries and promoting domestic production.

In *The Wealth of Nations*, the pioneering economist Adam Smith ridiculed the absurdity of this policy (Smith 1776). Why, he asked, should anyone try to make wine, very expensively, in chilly Scotland, when it could be bought, much more cheaply, from balmy France? And he pointed out that both sides benefit from such trade. They each give up something they value less for something they value more. The French might get the money, but the Scots get the wine. Both count themselves as better off. Indeed, neither would bother to trade unless they did. In this way, free exchange creates value all around. The best policy, therefore, is not to cripple trade with tariffs and

E. Butler (✉)
Cambridge, UK
e-mail: eamonn@adamsmith.org

controls but to facilitate it: to let the people of the world trade freely, boosting human value and prosperity with each of their multitude of transactions.

Despite this fairly obvious lesson, the old mercantilist attitudes still persist today. Governments almost everywhere still resist open trade and favour their country's own producers. So why are we so irrational?

The Psychology of Protectionism

The answer lies in the depths of human psychology. The human brain, like that of other animals, evolved principally for survival in a world full of dangers and conflicts. Our uniquely advanced skills of reasoning came much later. No wonder that this upstart portion of the mind has a hard time restraining the deep visceral doubt, fear, prejudice, aggression, and ignorance that affect everything we do.

This weakness of reason against our much deeper psychology exists in trade policy as well. And it shows itself in many ways.

Loss aversion. Human beings weigh potential losses more heavily than potential gains. That is probably a useful evolutionary trait, keeping us out of harm's way. But it shapes our attitude to trade too—fearing the potential costs of competition more than the comforts of protectionism.

Selective memory. For the same reason, our memory of bad things is much sharper than that of good ones. Regarding trade, if friends have lost jobs because of foreign competition, that affects us far more than any recollection of competition delivering better products from abroad.

National identity. People have strong attachment to their national identity and a bias against outsiders. This leads them to favour their own country's interests—and products—over those of others.

Political conflicts. Human beings are aggressive. This trait might have helped our evolution as we competed for scarce resources and expanded into new places. But political tensions often lead to trade being used as a weapon to cause damage to an enemy, rather than as a rational, beneficial policy.

Perceived loss of agency. One of the most alarming of human emotions is a sense of powerlessness. In the economic sphere, this may lead to calls for the government to 'take control' of trade through protectionist measures that reduce the country's dependence on others.

Perceived fairness. Humans have evolved with strong feelings for fairness and equality, traits that perhaps served us well over our long history of living in small groups (Hayek 1976). That prejudices them against competition that might adversely affect poorer citizens or poorer countries.

Conspiracy theories. Humans seem naturally disposed to believe that life is controlled by some greater power. They commonly believe that economic life is controlled by global elites. That may induce them to call for trade barriers to prevent their economy from being corrupted by such forces.

Ignorance. Humans naturally avoid unnecessary effort. Most people do not bother to learn about economic theory, for example, because they cannot see the relevance to their specific situation. This may cause them to overlook the potential benefits of trade and the potential damage of trade restrictions.

Overconfidence bias. Humans in general, and politicians in particular, tend to believe they have the ability and knowledge to intervene positively in economic life. But economic processes such as trade are complex: attempts to control them always give rise to unforeseen and often undesirable consequences.

Herd instinct. As social beings, we are disposed to act in ways that gain the approval of others (Smith 1759) and we prefer to be in groups of similar people. When people see that most other countries raise trade barriers, therefore, they are disposed to join in and be part of that protectionist community.

Confirmation bias. Humans tend to seek out and interpret information in ways that confirm their pre-existing beliefs or biases. Those who support protectionism will tend to blame free trade for every job lost or business that moves abroad, and this soon becomes the prevailing popular view.

Emotional appeals and framing. It is easy to illustrate the specific downsides of free trade, such as jobs lost to competition, in emotional ways. The benefits of trade, being more general, arouse less human emotion. This bias can again increase the support for protectionism against that for open markets.

Countering psychological biases. Many of these psychological biases reinforce each other. Countering them needs not just reliable facts, but psychology such as appeals to shared values, sympathetic treatment of concerns, and storytelling narratives about the positive benefits of free trade.

How Trade Barriers Reveal Our Psychology

Before looking at these psychological biases in more detail, it is interesting to reflect on how the nature of real-world protectionist measures reveals just how much they are driven by loss aversion, nationalism, fear, paranoia, ignorance, the herd instinct, and all the rest.

If a country aims to reduce or exclude goods coming in from abroad, the simplest measures are probably tariffs on imports, or subsidies and currency manipulation to make its goods cheaper abroad, or quotas on how much others can import into the country, or outright bans on a product being imported at all. These tariffs, currency manipulations, quotas, and controls are common. But they reveal something of the psychology behind them.

Tariffs. For example, in 2018 the United States government applied a 25% tariff on steel imports from various countries, with the intent of giving American steel producers a price advantage. This measure raised steel prices for American manufacturers and their customers, even though the rational policy may have been to buy steel from cheaper (and higher quality) producers in Asia and elsewhere. But those dispersed costs of steel tariffs have a much smaller emotional impact than the decline of steelmaking towns in the Midwest 'rust belt' and the plight of laid-off steelworkers and their families.

Subsidies. Many countries subsidise their exports to make them cheaper. These subsidies can take various forms, such as direct cash payments, tax incentives, or low-interest loans. Though such export subsidies are a cost to the taxpayers of those countries, the cost is hard to see. But the mercantilist idea that wealth comes from exporting and poverty from importing is easy to understand and is thus a driver for protectionism.

Currency manipulation. China today, like others in the past, is accused of intervening in currency markets to manage down the value of their currency, and with it the price of their exports to other countries. This again is a cost on local taxpayers, But it is even harder to see than subsidies to export industries. So again, the mercantilist idea triumphs.

Quotas. Many countries impose quotas on imports, particularly agricultural goods. They include the European Union (e.g. sugar, meat and dairy products), India (e.g. edible oils, pulses), Japan (e.g. rice, beef) and many more. Though advanced farming technologies mean that decreasing numbers of people are employed in the sector, a country's fields and plantations remain a very visible part of the environment, eliciting more emotional concern for farmers than for less visible workers. Agricultural protectionism is also driven by the fear that reliance on food imports could be a strategic threat in times of conflict. When the Russian-Ukraine war started in 2022, for example, the price of soybeans, vegetable oils and grains all rose sharply.

Import bans. Some imports have been banned outright by various countries, including the United States (e.g. Cuban cigars, Iranian carpets and virtually all North Korean products) the United Kingdom (e.g. certain Chinese communications technologies) and Saudi Arabia (e.g. pork and alcohol).

Such bans perhaps reflect cultural identity and in-group bias. The US restrictions may be motivated more by the political divisions with these countries rather than any significant military threat to the United States. The UK bans speak of the fear of security threats (though provides a convenient excuse to favour domestic manufacturers). The Saudi restrictions are motivated by the desire to preserve the country's religious identity.

Local content and production. In-group bias is nowhere clearer than in the 'buy local' and domestic content requirements practised by many countries.

'Buy local' policies, like the US Buy American Act, require or encourage government agencies, public institutions, or companies to give procurement preference to domestically produced goods and services. The rational policy might be to follow Adam Smith's advice and buy from the best-value world supplier, but the cost of 'buy local' policies is obscure and the thought of benefiting domestic workers is psychologically appealing.

Through domestic content requirements, some countries mandate that a certain percentage of a product's value must be sourced domestically. This measure aims to protect domestic industries and jobs by ensuring that a portion of the production process remains within the country. For example, Indonesia requires a minimum local content in mobile phone assembly, while France and Canada have domestic content requirements in films and television productions.

Loss Aversion

Looking now in more detail at the psychological biases that are manifested in protectionism, a good place to start is loss aversion—the fact that humans regard potential losses as more urgent and more important than potential gains.

When we encounter something unexpected and potentially threatening to us—suddenly seeing a spider on the pillow, perhaps, or being in an airliner buffeted by stormy weather—we are gripped by a cold, instant, adrenaline shock and apprehension. Such a response is no doubt a valuable evolutionary reaction to imminent danger, preparing us for flight or fight. If, by contrast, something potentially good happens to us—we come across a long-lost friend or win a basket of fruit in a raffle—we enjoy a feeling of warmth, but nothing so heightened or immediate.

The same loss aversion conditions how we regard economic gains and losses too, including those resulting from trade policy. People have a genuine fear of job losses, wage cuts, and the general insecurity caused by economic disruption. This fear might be fuelled by trade-related concerns about the impact of outsourcing abroad, or cheaper products undercutting domestic producers. And the fear is much sharper, especially in the minds of those who feel their own jobs are most at risk, than the blurry abstract notion that trade liberalisation might improve consumer choice. It makes people more likely to favour the certainties of protectionist policy over the uncertain possibilities of open trade.

It is also very common. For example, the prospect of Brexit—Britain's departure from the European Union—raised concerns from automotive and bank workers that the EU would raise trade barriers against an independent Britain, while agricultural workers worried about the loss of EU subsidies and the potential competition from producers abroad once the protection of high EU food tariffs ended.

Similarly, the 1994 North American Free Trade Agreement (NAFTA), which aimed to create a free trade zone between the United States, Canada and Mexico, was widely resisted by US manufacturing workers who feared (often correctly) that their jobs would be outsourced to much cheaper workers in Mexico—concerns which, among others, led US President Donald Trump in 2017 to demand a renegotiation, and weakening, of the agreement.

Selective Memory

Negative experiences with international trade can create a perception that trade is universally harmful. Probably for the same self-preservation reasons that human beings rate bad experiences more significantly than good ones, we recall bad things more easily and more vividly than we do good things. And (in a trait which psychologists call the *availability heuristic*, we tend to make judgements based on our most vivid and most easily recalled memories.

In trade, this phenomenon may be seen where industries have suffered decline due to foreign competition or outsourcing to cheaper countries. Such selective memory may lead people to overestimate the negative impacts of trade and underestimate the positive ones, leading in turn to calls for protectionism. The very strongest memories, of course, will be those in which individuals themselves, or their friends and communities, have been displaced by foreign competition. Their perception of the positive benefits of free trade (such as having a greater choice of cheaper, imported goods) will be much less acute.

Economic Nationalism

A great deal of trade protectionism can be linked to the near-universal human sense of national belonging, and people's desire to preserve their unique national and cultural identity. Adherence to national identity may show itself as pride in the country and its culture and institutions. Equally, this *in-group bias*, as psychologists call it, may come out in less positive ways—as distrust, contempt or hostility to foreigners, for example, or in protests against immigration, or in racial, religious or political tensions. But there is no denying that such feelings are strong.

Emotional nationalism spreads easily into the economic sphere, and into trade policy. The opposition to immigration, for example, is often intensified by the idea that immigrants are taking local jobs. This may well be true, particularly in the lower-paid manual occupations, because immigrants are generally willing to work more cheaply, thus depressing local wages. And the opposition to foreign immigrants can turn into opposition against open borders more generally.

Migration and Jobs

In the debate over immigration and border security between the United States and Mexico, for example, US producers have expressed fears that immigrants, both legal and illegal, could displace American workers, particularly in sectors like agriculture and construction. Such concerns have made discussions on trade agreements between the two countries difficult.

Where nationalism is rife, the interests of the nation-state will be regarded as much more important than any benefits of global economic integration, which are of course less immediately obvious and arousing. International trade and commerce may be seen as a threat, not only to domestic industry, but also to the nation's identity, cultural heritage, values, traditions, language, religion, social cohesion, institutions, and way of life. The desire to preserve these things may lead people to support protectionist measures to secure existing economic structures against erosion by foreign competition.

Cultural Imperialism

Much of the nationalist opposition to global trade is based on the argument that the culture of a nation could be swamped by others that are economically more powerful, particularly the United States. This supposed homogenising spread of Western ways and values has been objected to as 'McDonaldisation' or 'cultural imperialism'.

The concern is greatest with respect to poorer countries, where campaigners (both in those countries and in richer ones) have expressed concerns that globalisation will see traditional crafts being replaced by cheaper mass-produced goods, undermining local craft industries and culture. There are also concerns about heritage sites being overwhelmed by mass tourism and commercialisation.

But rich countries also strive for cultural exceptions in international trade. France, for example, seeks to protect its cultural industries (e.g. film, television, and publishing) with subsidies and regulations to promote domestic over foreign content. India too, with its thriving 'Bollywood' film industry, has imposed protectionist restrictions on foreign films. Canada, likewise, has maintained cultural exceptions in trade agreements, allowing it to provide subsidies and support to domestic cultural producers.

Such policies have sparked many trade disputes. But internationalists argue that they are ill-founded. Countries have always taken what they see as the best things from others, while still preserving their own unique culture. And if poorer countries in particular can become wealthier as a result of trade, they are then in a better position to preserve and protect those features of their culture that they regard as most unique and important.

Manufacturing Independence

Mercantilist and nationalist ideas are mutually reinforcing. In the 1960s and 1970s, for example, poorer countries used the *import substitution* argument to boost their national and economic independence from richer ones. Governments created new manufacturing industries, making steel, cars, domestic appliances, even electronics and aircraft, all protected by trade barriers and foreign exchange controls.

These 'infant industries' soon came to be regarded as national champions, feeding local nationalism. But this made it harder to square up to their problems. And without the pressure to compete, the protected industries were often costly and inefficient, and so reliant on subsidies from crony governments that corruption spread and the 'infants' never 'grew up' (Butler 2021). This experience was quite different from that of the Asian 'tiger' economies, which opened up to trade and exploited their comparative advantages such as low labour costs.

Security

The key duty of any national government is to protect the security of citizens from criminals at home and enemies abroad. Once again, nationalism and mercantilism can be mutually reinforcing as people argue that domestic industries must be protected to safeguard national security.

It may well be unwise for a country to outsource its defence technologies, leaving its defence at risk to supply chain problems or even to suppliers who might turn. In the digital era, cybersecurity has become an issue too, with governments restricting foreign access to critical infrastructure to counter the possibility of cyber warfare, espionage or data theft. For example, in 2020 the US and UK banned imports of the Chinese company Huawei's telecommunications equipment.

There may be legitimate concerns about security threats of these kinds. But it is not obvious that economic protectionism is the best response. Security threats require both targeted and far-reaching responses, such as investment in cybersecurity, intelligence sharing, and diplomatic, cultural and other non-economic initiatives.

Energy industries, such as oil, gas and renewable energy, are also seen as so essential to a nation that dependence on foreign supply could be a threat. Hence there are calls for protectionist controls to ensure the stability and availability of energy resources, particularly during times of geopolitical volatility or disruptions in global energy markets. Again, these concerns may sometimes be legitimate. For example, when the Russian-Ukrainian war broke out in February 2022, Germany and other European countries had become highly dependent on Russian oil and gas, opening them up to energy supply blackmail that restricted their willingness to intervene. But it is hard to know how far calls for controls on energy supply are about genuine security concerns and how far they are motivated by nationalism and protectionism.

Nationalism and protectionism also coincide in intellectual property disputes, where countries accuse each other of stealing trade secrets, or trademark violations, or patent and copyright infringement. They may argue that others have inadequate regulatory standards, leaving their rights violated and creating barriers against market access. Such concerns can lead to the imposition of trade restrictions, economic sanctions and controls over the activities of foreign nationals in the country. For example, the United States has accused China, India and South Korea of intellectual property theft, and the European Union has made the same claims against China and Russia.

Agriculture is more protectionist than probably any other sector. Often, it is argued that controls are necessary for a steady supply of home-grown food in case of hostilities with foreign suppliers or disruptions in supply chains. But the nationalist desire to protect the rural way of life might be a stronger motive. That might certainly help explain the ingenuity that is devoted to protecting agriculture, with arguments about farm subsidies, pesticide use, animal welfare, labelling, genetically modified products, chlorine-washed meat, fishing quotas, and much else.

Political Conflicts

Human beings' natural aggression and in-group nationalist bias can of course lead beyond animosity between nations and to open hostilities. That may prompt protectionist restrictions on trade for the purposes of replacing imports, supporting domestic industries and boosting war industries.

But trade restrictions themselves can also be used as a hostile weapon against others. Countries may use *sanctions* to weaken enemies (and rogue states) by banning their imports. Examples include the US embargo on goods from Cuba aimed at weakening Castro's communist government, or the 2006 sanctions on Iran designed to pressure it into halting uranium enrichment, or the 2014 sanctions on Russia in response to its invasion of Crimea. Such measures, however, do not necessarily hit the target. Countries may find other willing buyers for their products; and while sanctions may leave ordinary citizens facing shortages and higher prices, the government elites who make the decisions may be largely unaffected.

Moreover, the imposition of protectionist controls in peacetime can also increase the possibility of war. Protectionist measures may be seen as unfriendly or even hostile, straining trade relationships and causing animosity, potentially leading to 'tit-for-tat' response measures, reduced cooperation, deterioration of diplomatic relations, military tensions, and open conflict.

Trading nations, being dependent on others for the supply of many of the goods they want and need, face obvious pressure to preserve good relations with their trading partners. The more that their citizens benefit from trade, the greater this pressure will be. Trading nations have much to lose from conflicts that disrupt supply chains or dislocate production. As a remark attributed (probably wrongly) to the nineteenth-century French political economist Frédéric Bastiat puts it: "If goods do not cross borders, armies will."

Fear of Loss of Agency

Equally, high levels of trade dependence on other countries can evoke feelings of vulnerability. Competition and the use of economic power from abroad can be seen as potentially disruptive. People may worry that an excessive reliance on foreign goods is a risk to national security and economic stability. And (in what psychologists call *psychological reactance*) if individuals see free trade as a threat to their freedom or autonomy, and feel powerless against it, they are likely to call for protectionist measures in the hope of reducing this perceived dependency.

Critics of globalisation, too, object to open trade on the grounds that poorer countries would lose their powers of economic self-determination in the face of the greater economic power of richer nations.

Perceived Fairness

Humans have strong feelings for fairness and equality. This may have evolved during our long evolution in small groups, where it is easy to see and sympathise with the losses and misfortunes of others. It is possible that our ancestors living in these small groups would all benefit from an equitable sharing of resources. A different culture may be needed for our much larger societies to work (Hayek 1976), with self-interest being the basis of economic life and progress (Smith 1776). Whatever its origin, this perception of fairness and unfairness is a powerful driver of protectionism.

Distributional effects. For example, trade liberalisation can have distributional effects within a country, impacting different groups unequally. The arrival of cheap food and manufactures from low-cost countries, for example, may see farm and industry workers in specific areas facing job cuts or wage stagnation. Because human beings have a strong psychological sense of fairness, there may in consequence be calls for protectionist controls in the hope of avoiding these distributional effects. These calls will be strongest, of course, among the groups directly affected. Thus, workers and trade unions may demand import restrictions, such as tariffs, quotas, or stronger labour and product standards on goods from low-wage countries.

Free trade may have distributional effects between countries too, and the perceived unfairness of this can again bolster protectionism. Critics in both richer and poorer nations argue that liberalisation disproportionately benefits developed countries, reinforcing global economic inequalities. They also argue that trade can result in the exploitation of poorer countries, particularly in terms of environmental degradation such as deforestation, pollution, or mining.

While the countries most affected are likely to have most psychological reactance against such threats, the better-financed campaigners in richer countries may have more leverage in the international debate. That leverage can be seen in the attention captured by anti-globalisation protests at major international events, such as World Trade Organisation (WTO) meetings and G20 summits.

Whatever the source, there are widespread demands for special and differential treatment for developing countries, such as longer transition periods before trade is fully opened, exemptions for environmental sectors such as lumber, agriculture or mining, and suspension of some of the normal obligations implied in free trade.

Market access. Countries often argue that their products face unfair trading practices from others, such as domestic content rules, 'dumping' goods at artificially low prices, manipulating their currency, subsidising their industries or violating intellectual property rights. These accusations may be true or may simply reflect the accusers' own psychological biases. Either way, they can fuel disputes, and not always between richer and poorer nations. The United States, for example, frequently complains of unfair trading practices by the EU, South Korea, Japan and Canada.

If nations feel that their trading partners are engaging in unfair practices, they are more likely to support protectionist measures as a way to 'level the playing field' and restore trade fairness. Thus the US and EU have complained about China's state support of its solar panel and electric vehicle industries, the EU and the US complain about each other's promotion of their aviation industries (notably Boeing and Airbus), and Japan and South Korea dispute microchip production.

Other examples abound, partly because it is sometimes difficult to identify when a country is covertly supporting an industry, and if so, by how much. The resulting investigations into dumping, subsidies and other protectionist measures can load both sides with large costs that are ultimately borne by consumers.

Conspiracy theories. Human beings are deeply willing to believe that their world is being controlled by forces beyond them. Thus the belief in some almighty deity is as old as humankind. Less positively, conspiracy theories abound, such as claims that the 1969 moon landing was faked, that Princess Diana was murdered by the British establishment, or that COVID-19 vaccines contained microchips that allowed people to be tracked.

One does not have to believe that the global economy is controlled by some secret group (e.g. the Illuminati) in order to acknowledge that potent forces, such as the power of self-serving governments and big businesses, might have a strong influence in shaping it. Such forces may be seen as a threat to a nation's economic independence, fuelling calls for protectionism to keep them out. Furthermore, the thought that strong governments or financially significant international businesses welcome globalisation for their own purposes, rather than for the general human benefit, can undermine trust in free trade. These perceptions make a country's desire to protect its domestic industries against such forces more likely.

The belief that powerful economic forces are at work naturally manifests itself in demonstrations and protests at G7 and OECD summits of world leaders. They are even common at G20 meetings, which include some developing countries, and at those of the World Trade Organisation, which aims to promote open world trade even more widely between its 164 member nations.

There may be legitimate weight in the argument that larger and richer countries are in a better position to take advantage of trade than poorer ones, and even that such power can be exploitative. At the same time, however, the argument also provides a convenient excuse to keep trade barriers high.

Ignorance of Economic Realities

The *rational choice* hypothesis underpins much economic theory. Individuals, it supposes, weigh up the costs and benefits of their options—say, whether to buy a particular product or not—to determine what works best for them.

However, the American economist Anthony Downs gave this hypothesis a new twist. Looking at the economics of how people make political choices, he pointed out the *rational ignorance* of voters (Downs 1957). It takes people time and effort to educate themselves on the details and merits of different policies and candidates. But the chance of their vote making a difference in an election is minute. So (to the frustration of politicians and advocates of democracy) they generally spare themselves the effort of self-education and vote according to their prejudices.

There is a good measure of ignorance (rational or otherwise) in economic choices, including trade decisions, too. While economists agree that free trade benefits everyone in the long run, most people know little of the theory behind that, and of how economic processes work more broadly. Instead, their choices about trade are made on the basis of more naïve perceptions and personal prejudices.

Zero-Sum Thinking

The old mercantilist idea that trade is a strictly adversarial relationship, with winners and losers, remains strong. Many people, including political decision-makers, believe that one country's gain must come at another's expense. This perception, a prominent example of economic ignorance, can fuel support for protectionist measures as a means to secure income and resources for domestic industries and workers.

Trade imbalances. Zero-sum thinking is nowhere more common than in disputes about bilateral trade imbalances. A positive balance with another country is seen as a measure of success; a negative balance is seen as a failure. Even the language used—'trade surplus' and 'trade deficit'—reflects this belief. Such cases fuel demands to 'bring trade back into balance'. Thus, Brazil, the United States, and India have complained about their trade deficits with China; and Germany is criticised by its neighbours for running persistent trade surpluses with them. Often, the mere existence of a deficit is taken as evidence that the other side must be cheating—manipulating its currency or subsidising its exports, say—and that protectionist measures are therefore justified.

However, this thinking arises out of economic ignorance. Trade is international and trading patterns and supply chains are complex. While a country may run deficits with some, it may run surpluses with others—just as individuals may run a 'deficit' with their hairdressers, but a 'surplus' with their employer. A narrow focus on bilateral trade imbalances produces misguided policies that disrupt trade relationships and their mutual benefits.

Rigid negotiation stances: Zero-sum thinking can also be observed in rigid trade negotiation stances, where countries approach trade talks believing that any concession made by one party must be offset by an equal concession from the other party or parties. The adoption of these stances is reinforced by the natural human desire to be in control of things: thus, countries may deliberately keep their tariffs high and controls tight in order to have 'bargaining chips' to spare in negotiations. But this makes it difficult to reach mutually beneficial agreements that would promote overall economic welfare over the long term.

Other priorities. Free trade is also resisted because countries come to regard other priorities, such as environmental or security concerns, as more important. There may be some merit in such commitments, though often they reflect the large emotional pull of such issues, in contrast to the less obvious benefits of free trade. But in many cases, the prioritisation of these issues over trade arises out of economic ignorance.

Anti-globalisation groups' focus on 'food miles', for example, allows campaigners to argue that food should be sourced locally in order to prevent the environmental damage done by transporting it over long distances, sometimes halfway around the world. The same argument can be extended to almost any other product too. But the reality is that goods are transported in huge bulk in massive container ships, or in the otherwise empty cargo spaces of passenger aircraft. This makes their transportation cheap and of little environmental impact in terms of the large volumes involved. Most 'food miles' are the last mile in the consumer's car from the supermarket to the home. Also, producing food and other goods at home—think of all the heating needed to grow Adam Smith's fabled grapes in chilly Scotland—would very often be even more financially and environmentally costly than importing them.

Overconfidence Bias

Why do people gamble, since in the long run they can only lose? Mostly, it is because human beings greatly overestimate their ability, knowledge and chance of success in almost everything they do.

This overconfidence bias is greatest in people with low ability or knowledge in particular areas, who lack the expertise to appreciate their own limitations—a circumstance called the Dunning-Kruger effect, named after the Nobel psychologists who first studied it (Kruger and Dunning 1999). Thus, novice investors overestimate their ability to outsmart the stock market and make high returns because they do not fully understand the companies they invest in and do not take adequate advice. Likewise, most new businesses fail because entrepreneurs underestimate the full costs and risks of trading and the possibility that customers may not much like what they provide. And many do-it-yourself enthusiasts take on tasks that really require professionals, leading to disappointing, over-costly, or even unsafe results.

The problem is particularly common in politicians, whose success, self-confidence and charisma may cause them to make misguided policy decisions and unrealistic promises because they overestimate their ability to predict and control complex phenomena such as the social and economic life of entire countries, which of course includes trade. But precisely because trade is so complex, involving networks of economic relationships, global supply chains, and diverse national interests, the information that policymakers have about it can be patchy, or oversimplified, or unable to capture its many intricacies. This limited understanding can again lead to overconfidence in the effectiveness or outcomes of trade policy decisions.

Protectionist measures. This overconfidence bias can lead policymakers to enact protectionist measures, greatly overestimating the ability of such interventions to protect domestic industries and promote economic growth.

The same overconfidence may lead them to ignore the complex economic factors, supply chains, geopolitics and global dynamics that shape international trade. They may therefore underestimate the potential damage done by protectionism, such as the unintended consequences of reduced competitiveness in the country's businesses and its dependence on inefficient industries that face little pressure to improve, leading to higher consumer prices.

In addition, trade barriers can disrupt the flow of intermediate goods, components, and raw materials, affecting the productivity of industries that rely on global value chains. This falling productivity can harm not only domestic industries but also those in other countries, prompting retaliatory tit-for-tat protectionist measures that strain countries' trading and diplomatic relations and make conflicts more likely.

Trade agreements. Policymakers may also overestimate their bargaining power or the potential benefits they can achieve through negotiations. They may believe they can secure terms more favourable than what is realistically achievable, leading to an unwillingness to compromise that leads to prolonged or unsuccessful negotiations, thwarting mutually beneficial outcomes.

Unwillingness to learn. Human beings are notoriously reluctant to admit their mistakes. Overconfidence bias can reinforce this reluctance, hindering policymakers' willingness or ability to learn from past trade policy mistakes. When policymakers are overly confident in their decisions, they may be less likely to acknowledge and rectify previous errors. This can lead to a repetition of ineffective or detrimental trade policies, hindering economic growth and global cooperation.

Herd Instinct

As social beings, humans desire social acceptance. They therefore try to be part of the wider group, conforming to the ways, thoughts, beliefs and emotions of the wider group. Hence the allure of fashion trends, viral social media phenomena, and crowd behaviour. There is undoubtedly some evolutionary merit in this social cohesion, though it can have its downsides. In the economic sphere, for example, herd behaviour can lead to panic buying or bank runs and stock market panics. There is also the problem of groupthink—that when people are surrounded by others who share similar views and beliefs, they may become overconfident in their opinions and less open to critical assessment of the options.

In trade, herd behaviour can induce countries to adopt protectionist measures. When countries see others adopting restrictive trade policies such as import tariffs and export subsidies, they may be more inclined to think that such practices are entirely normal, and they may therefore be more willing to copy them and less willing to critique them or consider alternatives. And as protectionist ideas spread through the world's voting populations, it raises the pressure on policymakers to adopt such measures.

Trade blocs. The establishment of a trading bloc, whereby the countries of a particular region agree to trade relatively openly between each other but raise tariffs and other barriers against others, can also produce a herd mentality in which country after country rushes to join the bloc and be one of the 'insiders'. The remarkable expansion of the EU and other customs unions are examples. However, by having often very high barriers against non-members, such trading blocs do not always enhance the idea of free trade more generally.

Reaction to crises. Major global economic events, such as financial crises, recessions or military conflicts, can also set off herd behaviour in trade policy. In times of economic uncertainty, countries may resort to protectionist measures in order to safeguard their domestic industries against the economic contagion from abroad. It might start with those who are most affected, but then herd thinking can kick in, reinforced by the fear of loss, such that many other countries (even those relatively unaffected) raise barriers too. The 2007–08 financial crisis, which affected mainly Western economies but induced protectionism elsewhere too, might be an example.

Confirmation Bias

Confirmation bias is the tendency to interpret evidence as confirmation of one's existing beliefs or theories. It influences what information we search for (such as who and what we choose to read on social media) and even what information we recall and what we forget. We tend to believe what we want to believe rather than judging things on their real merits.

In terms of trade, confirmation bias means that those who are already disposed towards protectionism (probably a majority of the population) will tend to blame free trade for every job lost or business that moves abroad; and (economists apart) this becomes the prevailing view.

Similarly, the evidence on job losses may be chosen and presented selectively. It may be easy to see when a particular industry loses out to foreign competition, but hard to see all the new jobs, lower prices and greater choices that might be created by more open trade. Hence, job losses are seen as confirmation of the need to raise trade barriers and the other evidence is ignored.

Another example is the selective attitude to trade imbalances. Overconfidence bias plays its part in this too. Countries, full of confidence in their own trading abilities, may regard a trade surplus with others as entirely normal. A trade deficit, on the other hand, will be seen as an indication that the country's trading partners must be engaging in some kind of unfair cheating. So the political focus is entirely on deficits rather than surpluses. This in turn then reinforces the notion that deficits are unfair and raises the pressure for protectionist options against them.

Confirmation bias also reinforces the herd mentality. Trade decision-makers may seek validation for their policies by looking for support in the actions of other countries. And if many of those countries maintain a number of protectionist barriers, as is usually the case, this will be taken as supporting proof of the normality and wisdom of protectionism; while the few who promote generally open trade will be seen as foolishly errant exceptions.

Framing Issues

These various human biases mean that the way trade issues are presented can make a big difference in terms of the political pressure and intellectual drift towards protectionism. Different framing, such as a focus on the potential losses from trade—a focus that results from several of the biases already mentioned—may resonate more strongly with individuals and sway their attitudes towards trade restrictions.

Emotional appeals can also affect public opinion. Messages that evoke fear, anger, or resentment towards foreign competition play into people's natural biases and make protectionist arguments more persuasive, as can the framing of trade issues in terms of national security threats, job losses, cultural erosion or economic decline.

Selective reporting in media coverage is another factor. As a result of our fear of losses, bad news sells better than good news, so the media will be more inclined to focus on the problems caused by trade rather than the benefits. This further amplifies concerns about potential losses and reinforces the protectionist narrative.

Human beings are also more persuaded by real stories than by abstract principles. Calls for action from media outlets or campaigners and politicians, therefore focus on hard cases (such as families who have lost their livelihood due to foreign competition) or on specific examples (e.g. dumping, national security, labour standards, product safety testing, data and privacy breaches, environmental degradation, or animal welfare issues). A few serious, heart-wrenching problems caused by trade and competition can sway public and political opinion far more effectively towards protectionism than countless hours of debate and discussion on the benefits of free trade can sway them against.

Conclusion: Countering Psychological Factors

When faced with all these human fears and biases, how can proponents of free trade ever expect to prevail? Their task is difficult, but there are a number of communication strategies that might help.

The first is to provide factual information. Emotional appeals can be strong, but emotions are often driven by perceptions that may not always align with reality. Making people aware of the realities may help them to overcome their emotional biases. Highlighting the benefits of open trade with statistics on job creation, economic growth, and increased consumer benefits are a part of this. But free trade advocates also need practical examples and case studies to illustrate the beneficial outcomes of free trade.

Second, proponents of trade should stress the shared values that open trade promotes, including the benefits of economic prosperity, cooperation, cultural exchange, and global stability. Trade can be framed as a means to lift people out of poverty, foster innovation, and enhance living standards for individuals and communities; and advocates can show how open trade can lead to greater opportunities for all, including job creation, access to a wider range of goods and services, and improved standards of living.

Third, it is essential to understand and address the specific concerns that pull people towards protectionism. These might include job losses, economic displacement, safety or cultural anxieties; but it is important to acknowledge these concerns and provide evidence-based arguments that show how trade can mitigate these challenges. Trade advocates must also provide real-world examples of individuals and industries that have successfully adapted to global competition, and must demonstrate the potential for reskilling, retraining, and support for affected workers.

Fourth, a free trade strategy must foster engagement and dialogue with concerned individuals and groups. This includes workers, industries, communities, and advocacy groups. It must listen to their perspectives, understand their experiences, and address their concerns. It must strive, through constructive discussion, to find common ground and explore potential solutions that balance the benefits of open trade with the need for support and protection for affected individuals or industries.

Such a strategy will also use real stories to highlight the negative consequences of protectionism. It will explain how protectionist measures can lead to higher prices, reduced competition, limited choices, and reduced economic growth, focusing not just on the facts but on real cases with emotional appeal. For example, it might show the damage done to people in poorer countries facing high EU and US tariffs that prevent them from selling their produce in these protectionist places.

At all points, it is important to humanise the impacts of open trade through personal narratives and stories that highlight the positive effects trade can have on individuals, communities, and businesses. This human-centred approach will take account of the many fears and biases that lure people toward protectionism and instead will highlight success stories from individuals who have thrived due to global trade, emphasising the widespread opportunities and benefits it has provided. Such stories can resonate deeply and help counter people's natural biases towards protectionism.

References

Butler E (2021) An introduction to trade and globalisation. Institute of Economic Affairs, London

Downs A (1957) An economic theory of political action in a democracy. J Polit Econ 65(2):135–150

Hayek F (1976) The mirage of social justice. Routledge, London

Kruger J, Dunning D (1999) Unskilled and unaware of it: how difficulties in recognizing one's own incompetence lead to inflated self-assessments. J Pers Soc Psychol 77(6):1121–1134

Smith A (1759) The theory of moral sentiments. Andrew Millar, Alexander Kinkaid, J. Bell, London and Edinburgh

Smith A (1776) An inquiry into the nature and causes of the wealth of nations. W. Strahan, T. Cadell, London

Free Trade for Peace, Prosperity, and Progress

Thorsten Polleit

Introduction

Classical economic thinking of the eighteenth century, including Adam Smith, was in favor of free trade, based on the idea of the law of "absolute advantage": Countries should specialize in what they are most efficient at, then exchange these products, and so people of both countries would be better off when compared with a situation of no specialization and no-free trade.[1] In his *Principles of Political Economy and Taxation* (1817), David Ricardo (1772–1823) expounds that if each country should produce what it is *most* best at, or even least worst at, what it has a *comparative*, not an absolute, *advantage* in producing.[2] For instance, even if country *1* is more efficient than country *2* at producing *both* commodities *A* and *B*, it pays country *1* to specialize in producing *A*, which (we assume) it is *most* best at producing, to buy commodity *B* from country *2*, even though it is better at

---

[1] See Rothbard (1995), Classical Economics, p. 94. Note that the idea of "absolute cost advantage" is relevant if and when factors of production (labor and capital) are *mobile* across countries. In Ricardo's theoretical framework the factors of production are *immobile* across countries.

[2] See Ricardo (1817), Priniciples of Economics and Taxatioin, Chaps. 22 and 25. Rothbard points out, however, that the origin of the 'law of comparative cost advantage' is falsely ascribed to David Ricardo. Already in 1814, James Mill (1773–1836) had expounded the rudimentaries of the law. See Rothbard (1995), Classical Economics, pp. 96–8.

T. Polleit (✉)
Königstein Im Taunus, Germany
e-mail: polleit@firm-investor.com

producing *B* but does not have as great a comparative advantage as in making commodity *A*.

If, then, the government of country *1* imposes a protective tariff on imports of commodity *B*, and it decrees an industry producing commodity *B*, this special privilege then will injure the consumers in country *1* as well as those in country *2*. Country *1* loses the advantage of specializing in the production of what it is most best at since many of its scarce resources are inefficiently tied up in the production of commodity *B*. In effect, the protective tariff in country *1* disrupts the efficient structure of the division of labor around the world—for in a free market system, all lines of production are effectively interrelated. The law of comparative cost advantage also suggests that no country of the earth should be left out of the international division of labor under free trade. For *even if* a country has no absolute advantage in producing *anything*, it still pays for its trading partners to allow it to produce what it is *least worst* at.

Law of Association 1.0

However, there is much more to the law of comparative cost advantage than meets the eye. It was Ludwig von Mises (1881–1973) who realized that Ricardo's theory does not only make a convincing case for free trade on a global scale but that it actually explains the process of civilization of mankind, in which the division of labor—which, of course, implies, among other things, the inequality of man in terms of preferences, interests talents and endowments—is essentially the driving force. As a result, Mises called Ricardo's law the universal "law of association", and he put it succinctly:

> The law of association makes us comprehend the tendencies which resulted in the progressive intensification of human cooperation. We conceive what incentive induced people not to consider themselves simply as rivals in a struggle for the appropriation of the limited supply of means of subsistence made available by nature. We realize what has impelled them and permanently impels them to consort with one another for the sake of cooperation. Every step forward on the way to a more developed mode of the division of labor serves the interests of all participants. In order to comprehend why man did not remain solitary, searching like the animals for food and shelter for himself only and at most also for his consort and his helpless infants, we do not need to have recourse to a miraculous interference of the Deity or to the empty hypostasis of an innate urge toward association. Neither are we forced to assume that the isolated individuals or primitive hordes one day pledged themselves by

a contract to establish social bonds. The factor that brought about primitive society and daily works toward its progressive intensification is human action that is animated by the insight into the higher productivity of labor achieved under the division of labor.[3]

In this context, it should be mentioned that Mises considers economics to be an *a-priori science*. The term a-priori refers to a logically irrefutably true statement, a statement that is self-evidently true, and that cannot be denied without causing a logical contradiction.[4] Mises argues that economics is but a part of the (much) larger discipline of the *science of the logic of human action* (which he called "praxeology").[5] In view of the science of economics, Mises noted:

> Its statements and propositions are not derived from experience. They are, like those of logic and mathematics, a priori. They are not subject to verification and falsification on the ground of experience and facts. They are both logically and temporally antecedent to any comprehension of historical facts. They are a necessary requirement of any intellectual grasp of historical events.[6]

Mises also realizes that Ricardo's *law of association* is praxeologically valid, implied in the a-priori logic of human action and that it effectively provides an important element in the aprioristic explanation of mankind's civilizational progress:

> Neither history nor ethnology nor any other branch of knowledge can provide a description of the evolution which has led from the packs and flocks of mankind's nonhuman ancestors to the primitive, yet already highly differentiated, societal groups about which information is provided in excavations, in the most ancient documents of history, and in the reports of explorers and travelers who have met savage tribes. The task with which science is faced in respect of the origins of society can only consist in the demonstration of those factors which can and must result in association and its progressive intensification. Praxeology solves the problem. If and as far as labor under the division of labor is more productive than isolated labor, and if and as far as man is able to realize this fact, human action itself tends toward cooperation and association; man becomes a social being not sacrificing his own concerns for the sake of a

---

[3] Mises (1998), Human Action, pp. 160–1.
[4] See Tetens (2006), Kants "Kritik der reinen Vernunft", pp. 36–7; Höffe (2007), Immanuel Kant, pp. 57–63.
[5] See, for instance, Hoppe (1995), Economic Science And The Austran Method; also Rothbard (2011), Economic Controversies, Section One, Chaps. 3–5.
[6] Mises (1998), Human Action, p. 32.

mythical Moloch, society, but in aiming at an improvement in his own welfare. Experience teaches that this condition-higher productivity achieved under the division of labor is present because its cause-the inborn inequality of men and the inequality in the geographical distribution of the natural factors of production is real. Thus we are in a position to comprehend the course of social evolution.[7]

Law of Association 2.0

In the Ricardian theory world, the production factors labor and capital are assumed to be *immobile* across countries. How would the international division of labor be affected once we assume that labor and capital are *mobile*?[8] In such a case production would take advantage of the most suitable regions. Raw materials would be produced in those parts of the world where (other things being equal) the highest yield on investment could be achieved. Likewise, manufactured goods would take place in regions that yield the highest return on capital (and transport costs for moving goods to consumers would be the lowest). Also, labor would move towards those regions where real wages (for a given kind of employment) are the highest.

Of course, natural conditions tend to change over time. For instance, hitherto fertile regions become barren; or changes in coastlines offer new opportunities for fishing. In addition, technological progress makes hitherto economically unattractive regions attractive, as, say, transport and logistic costs decline. That said, ongoing changes in the conditions under which production takes place continually lead to a movement of labor and capital to places which are most favorable for production—to places where the yield for a given employment of labor and capital is the highest.

As a rule, people will move away from regions in which there is a relative abundance of labor and thus relatively low real wages towards regions where there is a relative shortage of labor and thus relatively high real wages. The same holds true for the allocation of capital: Firms will employ their capital in regions where there is relative scarce supply of capital and thus relatively high returns on capital, withdrawing it from regions where there is relative abundance of capital and thus relatively low returns on capital. There will be a tendency towards the same wage rate across the regions of the world. The outcome will be that some regions are more densely populated and other

---

[7] Mises (1998), Human Action, p. 161.
[8] See, for instance, Mises (1951), Socialism, p. 227.

regions less densely populated. Likewise, the yield on capital employed will tend towards a unified rate, with different regions having different levels of capital-intensive production. An economic equilibrium is attained when the marginal productivity of all capital and labor is the same in all regions of the world.

Of course, the free movement of capital and, labor in particular, might become a source of conflict (actually it often does in reality). For instance, the inflow of labor reduces the real wages in regions of immigration (compared with a situation of no immigration). People in regions of immigration would therefore be in favor of protectionism (restricted labor immigration). However, as has been pointed out earlier, a system that protects the interests of groups damages productivity in general and, in the end, injures everybody—including even those favoring protectionism. The economically convincing key solution to all potential problems related to (im-)migration is the unconditional respect and enforcement of private property rights.[9] The explanation is as follows.

Any owner of property (land, house, apartment) must, of course, be free to invite people from around the world, provided he pays the costs of his invitation of guests causes (for, say, food, transport, housing, insurance, health care, etc.). Likewise, firms must be free to hire people from abroad, provided they pay the costs the employment entails—that is wages plus pensions, unemployment, and health care costs. In other words, in a free market, the costs of inviting (employing) migrants would have to be "internalized", predictably leading towards "restricted immigration". If, however, a government would "open the borders" to migration, allowing "unrestricted migration" against the interests and wishes of the property owners, conflicts will inevitably result as immigration costs are "externalized".

The more countries engage in unrestricted free trade, and the higher the mobility of labor and capital are, the lower will be the international migration pressure—that is number of people moving from low-real-wage-regions to high-real-wage-regions. In contrast, if high real-wage countries engage in protectionist policies against low-wage areas, immigration pressure would be kept high or even raised. That said, the unconditional respect for private property and, in addition, the need for internalizing all (current and future) costs related to migration is a key factor for coming to terms with the migration problem. Any government action, however, compromising or even undermining private property would not solve but perpetuate, even intensify, the migration problem.

---

[9] See, for instance, Hoppe (1998), The Case for Free Trade and Restricted Immigration.

Government Interference

To take full advantage of the division of labor, nationally and internationally, free trade is required—which means that everyone should be free to buy and sell the goods and services as he wishes. What is more, division of labor and free trade not only improve the material standard of living of all participants involved, they also work towards a lasting and peaceful cooperation among men. This is easy to understand: People engaging in a division of labor develop a mutual interest in their well-being: If producer A decides to rely on producer B in economic terms and vice-versa, both will suffer losses if their respective trading partner goes out of business (for whatever reason). As a result, and out of self-interest, both producers develop a mutually beneficial "harmony of interests".

Government-imposed protectionism restricting free trade or even abolishing it altogether (through, say, protective tariffs, trading contingencies, sanctions, import probibitions, etc.) does not only economically harm all consumers worldwide in terms of lowering their material living standard. What is more, anti-free-trade policies also affect the division of labor negatively, thereby loosening or even destroying existing links between producers and ultimately consumers and thus destroying the "harmony of interests" among people, even raising the risk of war among nations. It is this (praxeological) insight that makes liberal and libertarian thinkers (especially those conceptualizing economics as an a-priori science) rejecting any government market interventions outright, especially in the form of free trade restrictions.

However, it certainly cannot be argued that free trade would, or could, be a guarantor that peace can be maintained among or within states.[10] While free trade undoubtedly brings people literally closer together, provides them with an economic incentive to cooperate peacefully on a permanent basis, it can be overwritten by other factors—first and foremost by peoples' "war-minded attitude", which typically comes with the spreading of anti-liberal ideas: ideas hostile to the free market system such as, for instance, interventionist, imperialist, socialist and communist ideas. It is in this context that Mises, in view of the causes of WW I (and WW II), wrote the following words:

> Only one thing can conquer war—the liberal attitude of mind which can see nothing in war but destruction and annihilation, and which can never wish to bring about a war, because it regards war as injurious even to the victors. Where Liberalism prevails, there will never be war. But where there are other opinions

---

[10] See, for instance, Eberling (2002), Can Free Trade Really Prevent War?.

concerning the profitability and injuriousness of war, no rules or regulations, however cunningly devised, can make war impossible.[11]

From the viewpoint of sound economics, it can be argued that prosperity and peace for the people of the world will only be achieved and maintained if we divorce from false economic ideas and policies which, in turn, can be traced back to the acceptance of false economic theories. That said, free trade will not, and can not, prevent war among nations when people no longer believe in peace. Free trade is therefore ultimately premised on the idea that human affairs should be based on the principle of voluntary action and mutual consent. To this end, the necessary condition is the renunciation and outright rejection of all imperialist, militarist, protectionist, statist, and socialist ideas. Free trade in itself is conducive to peace and prosperity and, no doubt about that, indispensable for mankind's civilizational progress.

State and War

At this point, a critical view of the state (as we know it today) is required. In 1919, Mises published a book entitled "Nation, State, and Economy", presenting an explanation as to why the catastrophic WW I could come about.[12] The war occurred, so Mises, because of the departure from the idea of free markets, free trade, individual freedom, and equality before the law; it was the abandonment of liberalism and the rise of the state as we know it today that led to WW I. However, this may not come as a surprise if an a priori analysis is applied. The latter reveals that the modern state is aggressive both internally and externally, and it also has an incentive to wage wars against other states in order to assert its interests. State and war go hand in hand, so to speak. To explain this in more detail, a few economic considerations need to be put forward.

It is a logical, undeniable truth that man has goals that he seeks to reach by employing means. Also, man prefers more means over fewer means and prefers an earlier satisfaction of wants to later satisfaction. As a rational being, he realizes sooner or later that the division of labor is advantageous for him, as it increases the output of his work (as was explained earlier). Division of labor, nationally and internationally, means that everyone carries out the work they can do at the comparatively lowest cost. The division of labor

---

[11] Mises (1953), The Theory of Money and Credit, p. 395.
[12] See Mises (1919, 1983), Nation, State, and Economy.

requires exchange. After all, if they organize themselves based on the division of labor, most people no longer produce for their own direct needs, but almost everyone produces for the needs of their fellow human beings. It is the division of labor that makes people recognize each other as mutually useful in dealing with their life challenges.

A system of free markets, if practiced consistently, would sooner or later allow people around the world to grow into a very tightly-knit division of labor. The result would be permanently peaceful and productive cooperation among the people. Because war is entirely alien to the system of free markets, people who know and experience the productive effect of the division of labor on a worldwide scale have no incentive to engage in something like war, as it would be against their personal interests. But, unfortunately, there is no system of markets in this world that is, or would ever have been, truly free. For many centuries, especially since the beginning of modern times, there has been the state.[13]

Initially, there was a state in the form of the feudal lord and the king. Then, there was the emperor. In the more recent past, there has been the republic, the dictatorship, and the modern democratic state. We may ask: What exactly is the state? You might respond: "The state, that's all of us" or "We cannot do without the state, because nobody would build roads and schools, support the needy, ensure justice and security". However, the logic of human action brings to light a rather different kind of answer. From that point of view, the state (as we know it today) is a coercive monopoly of power. Rothbard defines today's states as the territorial, coercive monopolists with the ultimate decision-making power over all conflicts in their territories and as taking also the "right" to levy taxes.

This kind of state is, of course, not a natural institution, has not been created voluntarily by people, nor could it have arisen in a system of free markets, because in free markets, there is only voluntary exchange; there is no forced action brought about by coercion and violence. The German sociologist, physician, and economist Franz Oppenheimer (1864–1943, who, incidentally, was the doctoral supervisor of Ludwig Erhard (1897–1977), the father of the German social market economy and the second chancellor of the Federal Republic of Germany) determined unequivocally that the state is in fact based on coercion and violence. In his book "The State" (1915), Oppenheimer writes that the state:

> … essentially and almost completely during the first stages of its existence, is a social institution, forced by a victorious group of men on a defeated group,

---

[13] See, for instance, Polleit (2022), Markets Are Peaceful but the State Is Not.

with the sole purpose of regulating the dominion of the victorious group over the vanquished, and securing itself against revolt from within and attacks from abroad. Teleologically, this dominion had no other purpose than the economic exploitation of the vanquished by the victors.[14]

Rothbard and Oppenheimer inform us that the state is an aggressive institution and especially aggressive inward. The ruling class, through use of state power, strives not only to maintain its power over the ruled class but also to expand it through prohibitions and bans, regulations and laws, higher taxes, and much more. The reason for this is obvious: If the state has the territorial monopoly of power to ultimately decide all conflicts in its territory, and if it also has the power to levy taxes (including the inflation tax), then the state (the people who exercise its power) will, of course, make greater and more use of it. The ruling class prefers more means over fewer means, and it prefers an earlier satisfaction of wants over a later satisfaction.

Put simply, the state (as we know it today) becomes larger and more powerful over time, and the citizens and entrepreneurs under its command are increasingly pushed around, their freedoms curtailed. However, the state will not only become larger and more powerful "internally" but also externally as soon as it gets a suitable opportunity to do so. States that feel ideologically linked to each other have an incentive to form a cartel, to eliminate competition between them. An example of such a state-cartel, which increasingly centralizes its power, is the European Union. But if states pursue different interests and follow different ideologies, they have an incentive to aggressively and belligerently build up and expand their power. World history is full of wars between states motivated in this way.

Large states are, of course, particularly aggressive toward the outside world because they can relatively easily obtain the means necessary to pursue an aggressive foreign policy, such as money, weapons, and soldiers. When large states follow different ideologies, the danger of war between them is very great. An example of this is the many military conflicts, especially in the form of proxy wars, between the United States and the former Soviet Union. One can see that the modern state is aggressive in an economic sense, so armed conflicts between states are not a tragic coincidence but a logical consequence. Incidentally, this is a fundamental insight that the Prussian general Carl von Clausewitz formulated in 1832, declaring: "War is a mere continuation of politics by other means."

So if we want to prevent war effectively, as Mises said, we must limit the state and thus place firm limits upon politics and politicians. Wrote

---

[14] Oppenheimer (1922), The State, p. 15.

Mises: "Whoever wants peace among nations must seek to limit the state and its influence most strictly." And we must also unconditionally embrace the concept of the free market, because it, and not the state, supports peace and prosperity for the people on this planet. There are only two ways human cooperation occurs: through voluntary means or through coercion. The free market with its division of labor stands for voluntary cooperation; coercion and violence are the means of the state. There is an important point that we need to make: law and security are indispensable if people in a community want to get along peacefully and productively. But the goods of justice and security can, of course, also be provided under the system of free markets. A state monopolist is not needed.

The Case 'Enlightenment'

Economics can do much to make the world more peaceful and thus ethically and morally better. Anyone who learns how a system of free markets works, and what benefits it brings to all participants involved, will have no reason to call for a state (as we know it today). This insight also helps us to understand why small states and small political entities are more peaceful and prosperous than large states and large political entities. It is no coincidence that the people who rely on the system of free markets and organize themselves in small units are peaceful while also earning the highest per capita income. Switzerland, Lichtenstein, Monaco, Singapore, and Hong Kong come to mind.

Anyone who thinks that the solution to the Russia–Ukraine conflict lies in the further rearmament of states, in sanctions, and in the end of the cross-border division of labor and trade is making a serious mistake. The problem of war is not solved when the aggressor is defeated, but only when the ideologies that lead to war are completely discredited and no longer appeal to the people. The Königsberg philosopher of the Enlightenment Immanuel Kant (1724–1804) noted that peace must be established; it does not come by itself.[15] I would add that peace requires, as a necessary condition, people voluntarily cooperating with each other in free markets, engaging in the division of labor and free trade. It is not established by the state. Rather, the opposite is true.

---

[15] See Kant (1795), Zum ewigen Frieden.

Literatures

Eberling RM (2002) Can free trade really prevent war? Mises daily article, 18 March, Ludwig von Mises Institute, Auburn, US Alabama

Höffe O (2007) Immanuel Kant. C. H. Beck, München

Hoppe HH (1998) The case for free trade and restricted immigration. J Libertarian Stud 13(2):221–233

Hoppe HH (1995) Economic science and the austran method. Ludwig von Mises Institute, Auburn, US Alabama

Kant I (1795) Zum ewigen Frieden. Ein philosophischer Entwurf, Philipp Reclam jun., Stuttgart

Mises LV (1919, 1983) Nation, state, and economy. Contribution to the politics and history of our time, library of congress

Mises LV (1951) Socialism. An economic and socialical analysis. Yale University Press, New Haven

Mises LV (1953) The theory of money and credit. Yale University Press, New Haven, Conn

Mises LV (1998) Human action. An economic treatise, Scholar's edn. Ludwig von Mises Institute, Auburn, US Alabama

Oppenheimer F (1922) The state: its history and development viewed sociologically. B.W. Huebsch

Polleit T (2022) Markets are peaceful but the state is not. Mises Wire, Ludwig von Mises Institute, Auburn, US, Alabama, 25 Mar

Ricardo D (1817, 1929) Priniciples of economics and taxation. G. Bell and Sons, Ltd., London

Rothbard MN (1995) Classical economics. An Austrian perspective on the history of economic thought, vol II. Ludwig von Mises Institute, Auburn, US Alabama, pp 81–99

Rothbard MN (2011) Economic Controversies. Ludwig von Mises Institute, Auburn, US Alabama

Tetens H (2006) Kants "Kritik der reinen Vernunft". Ein systematischer Kommentar, Philipp Reclam jun., Stuttgart

The Cultural Politics of Free Trade in Britain

Stephen Davies

Today, arguments for and against free trade are conducted almost entirely in the language of economics. The arguments on both sides appeal to economic analysis and theory to justify their positions and the main justifications advanced for either position are economic ones, to do with the economic consequences of free trade or protection for things such as growth, development, the well-being of consumers and producers, or the distribution of income within society. It would seem that this is an economic argument, made initially by economists, and concerned with economic policy narrowly understood.

On one side, advocates of free trade put forward the case first set out over two hundred years ago by David Ricardo, founded on the principle of comparative advantage. This is a much more radical analysis than Ricardo himself or many subsequent advocates of free trade have realised, with extensive implications. Those implications have not generally been set out in contemporary discourse, which focuses instead on the benefits of free trade, even unilateral, for consumer well-being, economic efficiency (and consequently wealth and growth), and deeper economic integration. The other side often put forward technical critiques of Ricardo's original thesis, with the implication that it is not a general principle but a special case but these have not withstood research (Irwin 1996). The more common and politically

S. Davies (✉)
Institute of Economic Affairs, London, England
e-mail: SDavies@iea.org.uk

© The Author(s), under exclusive license to Springer Nature Switzerland AG 2025
M. Rangeley and D. Hannan (eds.), *Free Trade in the Twenty-First Century*, https://doi.org/10.1007/978-3-031-67656-7_6

effective argument has been the neo-mercantilist one, first set out systematically by Henry Carey and Friedrich List and subsequently by a series of economic historians. In this the argument is made that while free trade is beneficial to the dominant power or core of the world economy it is not for the less developed (or underdeveloping) periphery which needs protection to develop to the point where it can trade on equal terms with the core. In this vision, as put forward by contemporary figures like Ha Joon Chang, free trade is undesirable for all except the few core countries until all of the world has reached an equal stage of development (Chang 2002). Since this is very unlikely to ever happen the argument resembles the well-known prayer of the young Saint Augustine to be given chastity 'but not just yet'.

Both of these kinds of arguments are economic. It is economic goals such as development and growth that are at the heart of them and one policy or its reverse (free trade or protection) is justified and the other damned, on the basis of its economic consequences. However, if we look to the past, of many parts of the world but of Britain in particular, a very different picture emerges. Historically, economic arguments initially played a small part in the cases for and against free trade and economists were not initially the most prominent figures, particularly on the Free Trade side. Instead, a whole range of non-economic arguments were made and it was these that gained purchase. Consequently, these arguments became incorporated into political discourse both elite and popular. Even more, they became a central part of an entire popular culture and set of attitudes and beliefs. Expressed at the level of 'metapolitics' through images, narratives, popular history, and poetry, the arguments for free trade became an important part of British national identity for many, not least the working class. A rival kind of Protectionist popular culture with its own images emerged at the end of the nineteenth century and was ultimately victorious in the 1930s—although this proved to be a Pyrrhic victory. In the United States, it was Protectionism that became embedded in popular culture and national identity, in the same way that Free Trade did for a long time in Britain.

This should lead us all to think about and question the centrality of technical economic arguments to the debate over trade and trade policy. It should also lead us to revisit Ricardo's original argument and to recover the radical implications of his insight, which go far beyond what is commonly defined as economics. The history of the popular culture of Free Trade in the United Kingdom, and of Protectionism in the United States, should also remind us of the persistence of these kinds of narratives and sensibilities at an almost subterranean level, from which they can re-emerge to influence politics once more—as we are currently seeing in the US.

Protectionism was the predominant economic policy followed by British governments in the eighteenth century. High tariffs and duties on imported goods were combined with special grants and support for domestic manufacturing the two being known as the 'mercantile system'. This was the policy of the dominant Whig party—the Tories were at that point a free trading party, but as they were a perpetual opposition force that had no practical effect. In the years after the Seven Years War, the old Tory party faded away and Britain entered an era of purely factional politics. This however made no difference to economic policy and the 'mercantile system' persisted, despite strong criticism from people such as Adam Smith. In the 1780s a party division re-emerged with the Whigs now in opposition and a revived Tory party in government led by Pitt the Younger. This remained the case right up until 1832. Initially, both of the parties supported protectionism and the associated system of taxes, duties, subsidies and monopolies. One reason for its wide support in the political class was that the trade policy was a central part of a general system that worked to cement the power and privileged economic position of a highly self-aware ruling class, composed of great landowners and privileged merchants (the two were actually hard to distinguish). This political and economic system, often known by the label attached to it by its critics, 'Old Corruption', came under increasing intellectual and political assault during the 1820s, from the emergent radical Whig and liberal movements (the term 'liberal' was first used as a political label in Britain in 1826).

During the 1820s, there was a gradual movement on the part of the Tory government away from protectionism and high tariffs, particularly while William Huskisson was Chancellor. However, the central elements of the system remained in place. Above all, there were the Corn Laws, a complicated system of controls on the importation of grain linked to the price level of domestic grain that had been introduced in 1815. Effectively grain could only be imported free of duty if the price of domestic produce went above a certain (high) level. The lower the domestic price, the higher the duty. The aim of course was to protect domestic agricultural interests, particularly large landowners, against cheaper Continental grain. The effect was to keep the price of food of all kinds but above all bread, truly the staple food of the time, at a high level—certainly higher than it would have been under a regime of free trade in grain. This clearly bore down most heavily on the poor and on people of average or low incomes in general.

This was the context for a campaign against the Corn Laws that began with Parliamentary protests in the 1820s and gained force during the 1830s. In 1838 a truly national campaigning body was set up, the Anti-Corn Law

League. What followed was eight years of mass campaigning and propaganda which culminated in the repeal of the Corn Laws in 1846. Although there were still a vast array of tariffs and duties in place, the keystone of the system had been ripped out. At the time Britain was actually a more protectionist country than France and remained so for some time, but the years after 1846 saw a steady abolition or reduction of the remains of protectionism until by the 1870s Britain had become a truly free trading nation. The repeal and subsequent shifts had a dramatic domestic effect—a recent study estimates that the immediate result of repeal was to raise the living standards of 90% of the population and reduce those of 10%—the latter being almost entirely those on higher incomes through landownership (Irwin and Chapeliev 2021). These effects accelerated markedly after about 1850, when grain from North America became available in large quantities for the first time, and played a central part in the dramatic improvement in living standards that took place between 1850 and 1900.

The story of the Anti-Corn Law League and the campaigning efforts of Richard Cobden and John Bright has been told many times—in fact, the way that story has been told is something we will examine but the contemporary economists' take on what happened is seriously wide of the mark. Their picture is one in which as economic understanding developed, and in particular after Ricardo's landmark work in 1821, so the critique of protectionism gained force and generated the understanding and arguments that drove the successful campaign for repeal. In fact, this is not true. Had the campaign for Free Trade followed that pattern, of being inspired by economic analysis and employing arguments from that discipline, then it would almost certainly not have had the kind of political success it ultimately had. Its victory would have been far more partial and limited. Most importantly, even if there had been a move towards free trade as policy because of economic arguments, this would not have had the major and very long-lasting cultural impact that actual repeal campaign did.

If we look at the actual records of the movement, including the private correspondence of its leading figures and their public speeches and pronouncements, as well as the mass of ephemeral material produced by less well-known figures, several things become apparent. The first is that economists as such, people like Nassau Senior and Robert Torrens, played almost no part in the campaign. (This was in marked contrast to their prominent role in another reform campaign of the time, the one to reform the Poor Law). The other very striking feature of these sources is that appeals to economic theory and the like played a comparatively minor part in most speeches, advocacy and propaganda. Other kinds of arguments and motives were much more prominent.

One set of arguments and motives made by the repealers was that they did not see the campaign against protectionism and were in favour of Free Trade in isolation. It was not a single and simple question of economic policy. Rather, it was an assault on an entire social and political system at one of its vulnerable points, that of trade policy. It was chosen as much from reasons of political expediency as from intellectual economic analysis. Richard Cobden had initially considered launching a campaign for reform of the House of Lords and the institution of the peerage before deciding to concentrate on a campaign to repeal the Corn Laws because he judged, it would have a greater chance of success. He also concluded that the consequential impact of victory would be greater—trade policy was not only a vulnerable point in the system of (as he saw it) aristocratic rule but also one where victory for the cause of reform would have extensive consequences, because of the way it interacted with other issues such as the nature of the fiscal system and the economic power of landlords (Hinde 1987; Edsall 1987).

The campaign for Free Trade was thus not a matter of technical economics, which people who disagreed about other things could unite behind. It was, and was seen to be, one of a range of issues that together formed the emerging radical liberal attack on the Establishment. It was connected to opposition to: a political system dominated by and run in the interest of a landed aristocracy and a small merchant oligarchy; a critique of British foreign policy (including colonialism) and the system of government debt that supported it; and a structure of public finance that relied primarily on taxes that fell more proportionately heavily on the great majority of the population than on the wealthy.

This was reflected in the way that many of its leading figures and supporters were also involved in or supportive of other campaigns, such as 'religious liberty' (church disestablishment), reform of the land and game laws, administrative reform, the reconstruction of local government, the extension of the franchise, 'aboriginal protection' and anti-slavery, and (for many) free education. It was therefore something that arose from the wider ecology of liberal and reform politics in early and mid-Victorian Britain. That is why the arguments made in favour of repealing the Corn Laws gave more emphasis to things like the need for reduction in the political power of the aristocracy and reform of the public institutions of the state than to technical economic arguments. However, unlike some of the other demands or campaigns, it was able to attract support from many who were sceptical of some of the other radical proposals such as church disestablishment. This was because of the form the campaign and its aftermath took.

The second point that becomes apparent from the study of the sources such as the speeches of Cobden and Bright is that in addition to radical politics, the Free Trade campaign had intellectual inspirations that were only tangentially related to economics. One was what was known as the 'condition of England question'. This was the term used to describe a range of related social issues to do with the living conditions of the new industrial working class in the rapidly expanding towns and cities of Britain and also the conditions of the rural poor. The latter was in fact the more pressing issue because there were larger numbers of impoverished people both absolutely and proportionally in the rural districts and the social problems of those areas were more acute and pressing than even those of new cities such as Manchester. People like Cobden and other radicals were well aware of this. One of the reasons for advocating a move to Free Trade was that it was seen as an absolutely essential measure if the challenge of improving the 'condition of the people' was to be met without a revolution. It was seen as something that would reduce the cost of food but also lead to an improvement in agriculture so as to elevate living standards in the countryside. So a powerful motive for the campaign for free trade was not simply an argument about economic efficiency but a more general agenda of social improvement and melioration. In this, as in other cases, the economic analyses, to the extent they were used, were employed as a backup to something that had a different motive.

Another important inspiration was the way that at the popular level economic arguments had become combined with religion, above all with Dissent and Evangelical Anglicanism. This is the phenomenon that has been ably set out by Boyd Hilton, in his *'Age of Atonement'* (Hilton 1988). He identifies the way in which popular evangelical Christianity from the 1790s onwards came to draw economic arguments and conclusions from its theology and ethics. Anglican, Dissenting, and Church of Scotland figures like Sydney Smith, Hannah More, Thomas Chalmers, and W J Fox argued for a range of economic policies such as Free Trade as being the consequences or derivatives of Christian doctrines such as divine providence. They would sometimes employ the vocabulary of people such as Smith or Ricardo (and even more often Malthus) but this was again a case of using the writings of economists in an instrumental fashion, rather than being motivated by them. For religious writers who were also political activists, such as Fox, their politics, including their support for Free Trade, was a consequence of their religious faith and its application to the questions of the day. The same was clearly true for the main leaders of the Free Trade campaign, with Coben as an Anglican and Bright as a Quaker both strongly motivated by their religious convictions. The campaign was thus about moral reform and the application of moral principles to public policy as well as being about radical reform of the political and social order.

The two were combined in the final motive, which had a prominent place in all of the arguments, which was the connection between Free Trade and peace (Mongredien 1871). It is clear from his speeches and writings that for Cobden this was the main reason for advocating Free Trade. The belief was that not only would it undermine the fiscal system that supported a war making state while being driven by the financial demands of war, but it would also connect and integrate the peoples of the different parts of the world that self-interest and greater mutual understanding would remove the impetus for war. For him wars and the military establishments that fought them were not in the interests of the mass of the population but only of a small ruling class (Hinde 1987). They were able to gain popular support for their bellicosity, he thought, because fear, and ignorance of other peoples and parts of the world, led the mass of the population to identify their interests with those of their rulers. If economic integration was allowed to proceed through unrestricted trade, the result would be an economic order that no longer aligned with the political one, it was thought. The result, for Cobden, would be what he called the 'municipalisation of the world' in which large states and empires would dissolve into a constellation of small communities and city states. This pacifism was thus a major motive for the campaign and as such it also figured prominently in the arguments made by its advocates.

No sooner had the Corn Laws been repealed than the history of the movement and its results began to be told. Some of the early accounts, such as that of Archibald Prentice, came from participants in the campaign (Prentice 1853). Later on, there were journalistic and academic ones and as the decades passed more serious historical narratives were written and published. Examples of these were works such as *Free Trade and Protection* by Henry Fawcett, and *History of the Free Trade Movement in England* by Augustus Mongredien (Fawcett 1879; Mongredien 1881). Finally, at the end of the century and in the first decade of the twentieth, there were works produced as part of the controversy over the revival of protectionist sentiment, and the organisation by Joseph Chamberlain of the Tariff Reform campaign in 1903. These works combined defences of Free Trade with retrospective historical accounts of the original success of the free traders in the 1840s and the impact of their victory over the following decades. There were many of these, with leading examples being *The Free Trade Movement and its Results*, by Armitage Smith, *The Fall of Protection*, by Bernard Holland, *Free Trade* by Lord Avebury, and *The Triumph of Free Trade*, by Russell Rea (Smith 1969; Holland 1913; Avebury 1904; Rea 1920). The very first of these 'third generation' accounts, published in 1881, was Morley's *Life of Cobden* (Morley 1903). Despite its title and biographical structure, this was not so much a life of its subject as a detailed account and defence of his views and philosophy, illustrated by the narrative of his life and campaigns.

These historical and controversial accounts add to the analysis just given. If we read them, we will notice that the story of the victory of Free Trade and the fall of protection is told in a particular way and given a certain kind of framing. In the early works, the repeal of the Corn Laws was presented as a milestone or key victory in a longer story. That was the story of progress, economic, social, political, and moral. The campaign and its victory were described as coming from a social awakening and a transformation of consciousness and culture as much as intellect and belief. The kinds of origins and reasons for the campaign set out above were all given great prominence. Free trade was explicitly made a part of the wider concept of 'Reform'—a category that included such varied causes as extension of the franchise, reform of the penal code, anti-slavery, disestablishment and religious liberty, the fight against 'taxes on knowledge', and temperance. This was Whig history but of a popular and radical kind. This framing can be seen clearly in the title of one of these early works, Alexander Somerville's "*Free Trade and the League: A Biographic History of the Pioneers of Freedom of Opinion, Commercial Enterprise, and Civilisation in Britain from the Times of Serfdom to The Age of Free Trade in Food, Manufactures, and Navigation*" (Somerville 1853). (Interestingly, Somerville later fell out with Cobden over the latter's pacifism, which he rejected). As this title shows, Free Trade was cast not so much as an economic doctrine but as a moral and political one, and associated with other liberal and radical ideals.

In the 1870s, the works of authors like Fawcett and Mongredien retained that framing but made it less prominent. More technical economic arguments now made their appearance and these works were more concerned with explaining what for the authors was a puzzle. This was the failure of other countries, particularly the United States, to adopt the British policy of unilateral free trade, and the movement towards renewed protectionism of emerging powers such as Germany and Italy. As this gained ground and began to evoke a response in the United Kingdom, so the third wave of historical accounts were written, as part of what was by then a major public debate. These works retreated from technical economic argument. Instead, empirical statistical evidence was used to show the benefits that free trade had brought in terms of higher wages, cheaper food and essentials and lower prices in general. This was combined with a reiteration of the kinds of narrative set out by the first generation of authors such as Somerville and Prentice, so that the cause of Free Trade was seen as being the centrepiece of the general liberal movement of progress and improvement. This was combined with an account in which commitment to Free Trade and the array of associated values was made a central part of British national identity. The British nation was cast as being a liberal and free trading one, with campaigns such as anti-slavery and the work of the Anti-Corn Law League key episodes in the formation of that identity and its victory over its rivals.

In fact, after the 1880s, Free Trade was the central feature of a liberal cultural politics. This is brilliantly captured and analysed by Frank Trentmann in his book, *Free Trade Nation* (Trentmann 2008). He captures the essence of this politics in a speech made by the Liberal leader (and future Prime Minister) Sir Henry Campbell-Bannerman to a mass Free Trade rally held at Alexandra Palace in 1904, held to commemorate Cobden's centenary. In his speech, Campbell-Bannerman said:

> We stand today at a parting of the ways. One road – a broad and easy one – leads to protection, to conscription, to the reducing of free institutions to a mere name ….And the other road leads to the consolidation of liberty and the development of equity at home, and to treaties of arbitration and amity, with their natural sequences in the arrest and ultimate reduction of armaments, and the lightening of taxation, which presses upon our trade and grinds the faces of the poor. (Trentmann, p. 1)

In that passage, with its biblical allusions, Campbell-Bannerman captured the central features of the way Free Trade was defended at that time. First, its nature as a moral value, something good beyond any purely economic benefits it would bring. Second, its association with a kind of class politics that emphasised equity and the elevation of the condition of the poorest. Third, its central connection to peace and a particular theory of international relations and their desired evolution. Fourth and linked to that, the connection of opposition to free trade with militarism, authoritarianism and (as other passages in the speech made clear) imperialism and military aggression. Fifth, the explicit connection to smaller and cheaper government—the classic Gladstonian principle of 'retrenchment'. Finally, and tying all of these together, the idea of free trade as the principal value and practical method of liberalism in the widest sense and of the liberal idea of progress.

This kind of cultural politics of Free Trade was the main feature of a kind of resurgence of classical liberalism in Britain in the Edwardian era, beginning with Campbell-Bannerman's critique of the imperial policy of the Unionist government in South Africa and culminating in the massive electoral triumph of 1906. It took the form however of more than speeches or writings, however eloquent. What Trentmann identifies is a whole array of forms of popular culture that embodied the argument and message that Campbell-Bannerman (and other such as Morley) were setting out.

Free Trade and the campaign for it, were important elements of popular history and figured in literary accounts, with the 'Hungry Forties' a recurring background or episode and the victory of the Anti-Corn Law League portrayed as a new dawn. Biographies, which were widely read then as now, were an important element of this. There were many lives of Cobden and Bright besides the canonical work of Morley as well as accounts of other figures in the movement for Free Trade. The lives of Cobden and Bright belonged to the popular genre of the 'exemplary life' and all of them clearly and firmly connected Free Trade to all of the other liberal values and campaigns. One classic example was J A Hobson's *Richard Cobden: The International Man,* which highlighted the connections between Cobden's support for Free Trade and his pacifism and anti-imperialism (Hobson 1919). Hobson's firm belief in this shows how this affinity or connection, between Free Trade and liberal or radical principles such as democracy and popular rule and self-rule was one of the main things uniting older Gladstonian liberals and the New Liberals (of whom Hobson was a leading light).

As Trentmann describes in detail, there was also a whole range of depictions of the case for Free Trade in visual media. These included posters and political advertising, as well as postcards and whole range of objects including things as varied as ornamented mugs and tea ware, furnishings and decorations. Certain images were recurrent as visual representations of the values of Free Trade—the best known being the contrast between the shrivelled, costly and meagre loaf of Protection and the plump, large, and cheap one of Free Trade (Trentmann 2008).

A crucial part of all this was the centrality and significance given to consumption as both an activity and a value. Citizenship was defined in terms of consumption rather than production and the economic life of the national community was defined by and oriented around consumption as the primary end of economic activity. This had a direct connection to the associated political values. Consumption was both universal and individual. It was universal because it was something everyone did, whereas production as an activity was not, particularly if it was understood narrowly. It was individual because each consumer had their own specific preferences and identity. In contrast, production divided the population into distinct categories. However, despite its individualised quality, there was also a common interest shared by all consumers, that the widest variety of goods be available in the highest quality and cheapest price possible.

It was this that made Free Trade the central feature of politics and economics built around consumption. There was a connection between consumption and both democracy and equality in its liberal version (equal status and esteem) because each consumer's purchasing had equal standing to any others in terms of status and it was the demand of consumers that ultimately directed economic activity. Consumption also brought cooperation between people in different social classes and parts of the world, because of shared tastes and the way that satisfying the needs of consumers required friendly trade and relations between consumers in one part of the world and producers in another. By contrast, a focus on production, organised as it was on a national level, tended towards an emphasis on competition between nations and people in different parts of the world.

In popular liberal cultural politics Free Trade thus united citizenship and popular empowerment, peaceful international relations, social equality, and improvement—all connected to individuals and their families being given free unfettered access to commodities and services. The politics of Free Trade and consumption also connected that with other values such as personal thrift, industriousness, temperance both with and without a capital T, low taxes and government frugality.

What though provoked the flowering and crystallisation of this liberal thought in which Free Trade had such a central place? It was a response to a rival and emergent kind of political vision and popular culture. This had started to appear in the 1880s and then appeared full grown in the 1900s, most notably in the campaign for Tariff Reform launched by Joseph Chamberlain in 1903. One early sign of the emergence of this new kind of politics and popular culture was campaigns by business interests for Fair Trade, meaning reciprocal tariffs, rather than unilateral free trade. Another was the work of economic historians such as William Ashley and William Cunningham, which was critical of free trade as an economic policy and explained Britain's economic success and development as due to mercantilism (Cunningham 1881, 1904). The full-blown variant of this kind of politics was, like the Free Trade one, a complete and interlinked constellation of values and images, inspired not by economic arguments but by a set of values.

One was the idea of international relations as being completion between rival nations. Linked to this was a frank imperialism, with Empire seen as both inevitable and the just reward of the successful. Another element was a producer's vision of the national economy, which saw economic life as having the primary purpose not of enriching consumers and making their lives more pleasant and spacious but of building up national productive capacity and thereby increasing national power. This was connected to a specific political programme, of protectionism both for generating revenue and developing domestic industry while the government provided more direct assistance. This was combined with a policy of 'Imperial free trade' or preference in which the British Empire became a customs union with internal free trade with a common external tariff against other parts of the world such as Germany and the United States. The intention was to turn the Empire into a coherent and cohesive political unit that could rival emergent great powers, again most notably Germany and the US but also Russia. Another aspect was a major expansion of the functions and spending of government, not least various kinds of welfare spending. This was not linked to egalitarianism but to a very frank defence of social differentiation and was justified not on social justice grounds but as an aid to 'national efficiency'. Finally, there was an explicit connection to nativism and hostility to so-called 'alien immigration' (referring mainly to Jews in the British case).

As with Free Trade, there were also connections that seem strange because they are not obvious. One was advocacy of conscription and popular militarism. The latter was an important aspect of the social life of Britain after roughly 1890, with organised volunteer reserve organisations springing up all around the country. Another connection was with the idea of physical fitness and exercise, seen as being a patriotic duty as well as having a personal benefit. As with its Free Trade rival, the new political culture of Protectionism found expression in elements of popular culture such as boys' adventure stories, and adventure stories and some kinds of historical romance more generally.

So, by the 1900s a clear political divide had appeared, between two rival political visions each with their own associated popular culture and iconography. The protectionist and imperialist one was the challenge to the orthodoxy of the mid-Victorian period. The fully articulated politics and culture of Free Trade and consumption were a response to this, with the older ideals of the 1840s that had been set out in the early historiography being revived and adapted and their record and values defended (Howe 1998). Most people on both sides of this argument were moderates but initially the debate was very fierce and polarised. One reason for this was because of the leading part played by Joseph Chamberlain, a uniquely polarising and divisive figure.

The political debate of the 1900 was a genuine clash of two social and political ideals which both had an apparent economic doctrine at their core. This did not mean though that this was an argument about economic policy, any more than it had done in the 1840s. Rather it was that two contrasting sets of social ideals led to certain conclusions with economic aspects or implications: was the ultimate purpose of productive human activity production or consumption? Should human social and political life be understood in terms of cooperation or competition? Were individuals and their well-being and flourishing the ultimate measure (even if aggregated) or was the relative wealth and power of a defined collective such as a nation or Empire?

The debate was fought in the fields of imagery, and popular fiction as much as politics and public campaigning. It had a kind of religious aspect because both sides connected their stance to values that had a transcendent or transhistorical character. It was fought at the level of metapolitics, of feeling and sentiments, even more than at the level of explicit political and policy debate much less academic argument or political theory. This is one reason why the politics of the 1900s had such an intransigent and polarised quality. After the Great War, some of this passion declined, and the meta-political aspect of the contest became less marked, on both sides. The debate however continued and figured prominently in the politics of the 1920s.

In that decade, the Protectionist and Imperialist cause and movement, with which the Conservative Party was now fully aligned, despite its shattering defeat in 1906, gained a renewed impetus. The widespread belief was that the experience of the War showed that the old ideal of Free Trade, which Campbell-Bannerman and others had articulated in the 1900s, was defunct. However, the Free Trade ideal still retained a hold on both the Liberal Party and the newly emerged Labour Party. This became clear in the election of 1923 when Stanley Baldwin, having won an absolute majority in 1922, called fresh elections to seek a mandate for a shift to protectionism. Both Labour and the Liberals opposed this and reasserted the Free Trade ideal and the result was a hung Parliament with the Conservatives losing 86 seats net. (They lost 109 but gained 23). This was the last election in which Free Trade was a central issue. The result showed that the massive expansion of the electorate in 1918 had not significantly reduced popular support for Free Trade and the associated policies. In terms of shares of the electorate, the Conservatives gained 38%, the Labour Party 31% and the Liberals (reunited by the threat to Free Trade after their disastrous split in 1916) 29%. Thus, the balance of opinion as indicated by these votes was 60–38% in favour of Free Trade over Protection. The same rough ratio was repeated in subsequent sections in 1924 and 1929—in the latter the vote shares were Conservative 38%, Labour 37% and Liberals 23%.

However, as Trentmann describes, the popular culture and politics of Free Trade were fading. Arguments about trade policy were acquiring a technical and purely economic quality and no longer counterposed two distinct sets of social, cultural, and political values. The issue of Free Trade versus Protectionism/Imperialism had become one of Free Trade versus Protectionism. The now dominant question in politics was that of socialism versus capitalism, or private enterprise versus a planned economy, with specific questions such as how to deal with Britain's already high levels of unemployment seen through that lens. In the 1920s, there were reiterated articulations of the kind of popular politics of Free Trade found before 1914, such as J. M. Robertson's *The Political Economy of Free Trade* and the same author's *The Economics of Progress* but these turned out to be the end of a tradition (Robertson 1918, 1928).

In 1931 the realignment of politics around the new issue and the demise of the popular culture of Free Trade were decisively confirmed. In that year the National Government (a thinly disguised Conservative administration) gained a crushing victory, winning 67.2% of the vote. Of that total 6.5% went to the rump Liberal Party of Herbert Samuel but the rest went to parties that supported some form of protection. Subsequently, at the Ottawa Conference, Britain finally abandoned Free Trade as an ideal and free trade as a policy and adopted Imperial Preference. Samuel and the Liberals left the government over the issue which shows that for them this was still a definitive question but, as the voting pattern showed, their kind of politics was now marginalised in the new political alignment. Following 1931 both Conservatives and Labour moved towards different versions of a neo-mercantilist economic policy, one of a national capitalism in the Conservatives' case (capitalism in one country as one might put it) and a national-based democratic socialism in the Labour one (Edgerton 2019).

This may be fascinating to those who have an interest in history but why should anyone else care? The reason lies in the way that the ultimate victory of protectionism and neo-mercantilism played out and the current and alarming developments in politics worldwide. In 1931, it seemed that the case made before 1914 by Joseph Chamberlain and the Tariff Reformers had finally triumphed. It proved however to be a Pyrrhic victory. The case for protectionism had always been associated with a particular vision of Britain's nature as a state and its geopolitical position, one that gave the British Empire a central place. In the 1930s this seemed a realistic vision——the Empire was at its maximum extent at that point. However, the coherence of the Empire as a geopolitical entity had already been fatally undermined, by a series of major strategic misjudgments in the 1920s and the emergence of serious anti-colonial resistance, particularly in India. The other problem was that the kind of global imperial role and consequent economic policy that was envisaged depended upon the cooperation of the United States. From the 1890s, onwards the protectionist and imperialist element in UK politics and society had mostly had a fascination with the US and the prospects for some kind of Anglo-Saxon union that would dominate the world (Bell 2011, 2020). In fact, this was a total fantasy and one that was not reciprocated on the American side. The reality was that the US was a geopolitical competitor and, for historical and ideological reasons, implacably opposed to the European empires, above all the British ones. In the 1930s this did not matter so much or become apparent because of the policy of so-called isolationism followed by the US at that time. However, the course of events in World War II, and the full engagement of the US with world affairs thereafter revealed this imperial and protectionist vision for the fantasy it was. The British Empire was finally dismantled in the 1960s. Meanwhile, the other side of the vision that had seemingly triumphed in 1931 also faded away, more slowly but just as certainly, because it did not comport with either the way global business developed after the 1960s or the strategic goals and policies of the major player, the United States.

Consequently, after 1945 British governments of both parties continued to pursue a policy of a 'national capitalism/social democracy' but they did so within the global context of a system or regime of international trade that was shaped by the United States, through a series of international trade agreements under the aegis of GATT. This was supplemented after the early 1960s by the choice of a closer economic alignment with Western Europe, through membership of the Common Market (the EEC as it then was). As this process continued the project of national-based capitalism that had inspired the Protectionist vision became less and less feasible.

The system that was created both in Europe and globally (particularly after the collapse of the rival system in 1989–90) was one of free trade on the basis of harmonised regulations. As an economic policy free trade thus became associated with a structure or system of extensive and detailed rules and regulations many of which were increasingly supranational and which bound national governments in various ways, regardless of what their voters preferred. The system of rules and regulations at both national and supranational level also supports an economic system dominated by large corporate businesses and concentrated private power with an intimate connection to government. The collapse of the Bretton Woods monetary system in 1971 and the subsequent abandoning of most controls on capital movement along with a move to floating exchange rates means that finance and asset management have come to play a central economic role in many parts of the world.

This order is now clearly in crisis and is rapidly unravelling. Just as the end of the Belle Epoque saw a reaction against the trade system of the mid-Victorian era and its associated geopolitical order with the revival of protectionism and the growth of imperialism and rise of new powers, so we are seeing a similar kind of reaction now. The US-led international order faces increasingly serious and organised challenges from rising powers, particularly China but also India, Russia, Brazil and parts of the Middle East. The trade system consolidated by the creation of the WTO is clearly coming apart and we are seeing a recession from globalisation and economic integration, with the rise of 'reshoring' and the shortening and simplifying of supply chains. Politically there is a revival of what I have called 'national collectivism' a kind of politics that combines an active economic role for government with strong nationalism and cultural traditionalism of a certain kind. As in the 1900s, this is found everywhere but most dramatically in the core country of the world order—Britain then, the United States now. All of this poses a threat to liberal values in one country after another but it is not clear how liberals of the classic variety should respond. Clearly, they should resist the rising trend in politics, of nationalism and neo-mercantilism, for all the reasons Campbell-Bannerman set out all those years ago. Today, as then, that kind of politics and its associated culture stands opposed to the essence of liberalism. It does not follow though that they should become ardent defenders of the status quo and its economic and political order.

There are two reasons for that conclusion. The first is the pragmatic one that the existing system that grew up after 1945 and was consolidated after 1989 is not going to survive. Defending a system that has lost legitimacy is a losing proposition, no matter how much elite opinion may disagree. Just as in the history of the earlier periods it is the popular culture associated with a particular kind of policy settlement and the values that culture incorporates and expresses that produce legitimacy and therefore consent. The second, more principled reason is this. The regime we have is certainly better than the protectionist or other current alternatives but that should not conceal the ways that it is unsatisfactory from a liberal point of view and departs from the kind of vision so ably articulated in the political and popular culture that Trentmann describes. It is a vision of a world dominated by expert, technocratic management rather than popular liberation and self-government, of managed and regulated and controlled trade and exchange rather than Free Trade. The social vision is of a top-down order with benefits coming from the enforcement of enlightened rules and structures as designed by a kind of clerisy. This is a new kind of Enlightened Despotism and is different from the sort of vision found in the popular culture and politics of Free Trade as found in late nineteenth and early twentieth century Britain (and indeed in other countries). To tie the wider fortunes of liberalism to this would not only mean being bound to a sinking ship, it would betray a key part of what liberalism historically was and has been.

What we need is a rediscovery of the old yet still radical vision of earlier generations of liberals. This means a kind of popular politics and popular culture of the kind Trentmann describes, one that puts forward a comprehensive social and cultural ideal. As in the 1840s or the years after 1880, this would not be a purely economic doctrine, where the goal or payout would be economic efficiency and higher GDP, even if these were an aspect of it. Instead, the need is to connect the idea of the free exchange of goods between people in all parts of the world as a social and economic activity with all of the other social ideals that go along with it, just as it was in the classical doctrine of Free Trade. This means things such as international peace and reduction of armaments, a different vision of the international rule of law to the currently dominant top-down one that sees it as generated by treaties, a social ideal of personal self-government and responsibility, the principle of voluntary cooperation and collective action as a way to address challenges and social problems, limited and decentralised government, popular culture of the 'democratic intellect', and a focus on improving the conditions of life through unplanned cooperation rather than competition for power between nations (in reality between rival elites). Just as in the 1880s and 1890s, this means metapolitics, the articulation of a more general and pre-political sensibility and outlook on the world, one formed and expressed in ways of acting in everyday life and though mundane and domestic activities such as consumption and work. The raw materials for this are everywhere, just as they were when Richard Cobden and John Bright launched the campaign for Free Trade in the 1830s.

References.

Avebury L (1904) Free trade. Macmillan, London
Bell D (2011) The idea of greater Britain: empire and the future of world order, 1860–1900. Princeton University Press, Princeton, NJ
Bell D (2020) Dreamworlds of race: empire and the utopian destiny of Anglo-America. Princeton University Press, Princeton, NJ
Chang HJ (2002) Kicking away the ladder: development strategies in historical perspective. Anthem Press, London
Cunningham W (1882) The growth of English industry and commerce in modern times: the mercantile system. Cambridge University Press, Cambridge

Cunningham W (1904) The rise and decline of the free trade movement. C J Clay, London

Edgerton D (2019) The rise and fall of the British nation: a twentieth century history. Penguin, London

Edsall NC (1987) Richard Cobden: independent radical. Harvard University Press, Cambridge, Mass

Fawcett H (1879) Free trade and protection: an enquiry into the causes which have retarded the general adoption of free trade since its introduction into England. MacMillan, London

Hilton B (1988) The age of atonement: the influence of evangelicalism on social and economic thought, 1785–1865. Clarendon Press, Oxford

Hinde W (1987) Richard Cobden: a Victorian outsider. Yale University Press, New Haven, CT

Hobson JA (1919) Richard Cobden: the international man. T Fisher Unwin, London

Holland B (1913) The fall of protection, 1840–1850. Edward Arnold, London

Howe A (1998) Free trade and liberal England 1846–1946. Oxford University Press, Oxford

Irwin DA (1996) Against the tide: an intellectual history of free trade. Princeton University Press, Princeton

Irwin DA, Chepeliev MG (2021) The economic consequences of sir Robert peel: a quantitative assessment of the repeal of the corn laws. Econ J 131(640):3322–3337

Mongredien A (1881) History of the free trade movement in England. G P Putnam, New York

Mongredien A (1871) England's foreign policy: an enquiry as to whether we should continue a policy of intervention or adopt a policy of isolation. Stanford, London

Morley J (1881) The life of Richard Cobden (T. Fisher Unwin, London, 1903 1st pub. 1881)

Prentice A (1853) History of the anti-corn law league, 2 vols. W & F G Cash, London

Rea R (1920) The triumph of free trade and other essays and speeches. Macmillan, London

Robertson JM (1918) The economics of progress. T. Fisher Unwin, London

Robertson JM (1928) The political economy of free trade. P. S. King, London

Smith GA (1969) The free trade movement and its results, 1st pub. 1903. Books For Libraries Press, New York

Somerville A (1853) Free trade and the league: a biographic history of the pioneers of freedom of opinion, commercial enterprise, and civilisation. In: Britain from the times of serfdom to the age of free trade in manufactures, food and navigation. James Ainsworth, Manchester

Trentmann F (2008) Free trade nation: commerce, consumption, and civil society in modern Britain. Oxford University Press, Oxford

Free Trade and Austro-libertarianism

Walter E. Block

The present paper is an attempt to make the case on behalf of free trade[1] using the lenses of Austrian economics and libertarian political philosophy.

First, what is Austrian economics? It has nothing to do with the economics of that European country. Instead, it stems from the fact that the first practitioners of this discipline were all located there: Carl Menger, Eugen von Bohm-Bawerk, Ludwig von Mises, Friedrich Hayek, Joseph Schumpeter, and Friedrich von Weiser.[2] This school of thought diverges from mainstream or neoclassical economics in a whole host of dimensions, but two of them stand

---

[1] Milton Friedman once publicly stated (paraphrase): "Thanks to economists, all of us ever since Adam Smith and even before, tariffs are now, probably, one tenth of a percent lower than they otherwise would be. And with that we have paid for our salaries at least 10,000 fold." This insight of his made me proud to be an economist and, as such, to be able to write the present essay. There are so few of us dismal scientists, and we are able to do so much good for overall society.

[2] Their main contributions to Austrianism, their magnum opuses, are as follows: Menger (1871), Bohm-Bawerk (1909), Mises (1949), Hayek (1941), Schumpeter (1942) and Wieser (1893). I would be remiss in this regard if I neglected to mention Rothbard (1962), who was Mises's most notable American student and follower.

I wish to thank Matthew Manzella for an excellent copy editing job. All remaining errors and infelicities are of course my own responsibility.

W. E. Block (✉)
Loyola University New Orleans, 6363 St. Charles Avenue, Box 15, Miller Hall 318, New Orleans, LA 70118, USA
e-mail: wblock@loyno.edu
URL: https://walterblock.substack.com/

© The Author(s), under exclusive license to Springer Nature Switzerland AG 2025
M. Rangeley and D. Hannan (eds.), *Free Trade in the Twenty-First Century*, https://doi.org/10.1007/978-3-031-67656-7_7

out as of relevance to our main focus in this paper, free trade: praxeology and monopoly theory. We deal with these below when we consider objections to the arguments for free trade. Austrians diverge from both Keynesians and Chicago school monetarists on the business cycle,[3] for example, but this is not directly related to free trade. The protectionist Smoot-Hawley tariff worsened the Great Depression, but from a philosophical perspective, this is a distinct issue. Similarly, Austrians are far stronger critics of socialism than mainstream economists, but this, too, is peripheral to free trade.[4]

Next, what is libertarianism, and how does it impact free trade? This political economic philosophy is predicated upon two basic foundations. The first is the non-aggression principle (NAP),[5] which maintains that just law prohibits the use of initiatory violence. The second, the opposite side of the coin from the first, is private property rights based on homesteading[6] and on "capitalist acts between consenting adults" in the immortal words of Nozick (1974, p. 163), such as buying, selling, trading, gift giving, gambling, bartering, investing, borrowing, lending, etc. On the basis of these two doctrines, we can rule out as illegal such crimes as murder, rape, theft, kidnapping, arson, fraud, etc. Since freely trading with someone else falls under none of these prohibited acts, doing so is legitimate, according to libertarian law.

Now for the economics of the matter. It is important, first, to distinguish between absolute advantage and comparative advantage. Consider the simple two goods, two countries, and absolute advantage model. Canada can produce 100 units of maple syrup in a given time period, but only 5 units of bananas. Costa Rica, for some reason or other, can harvest 10 units of the northern good, but 200 units of the southern one. See Table 1.

We assume that no trade takes place, and posit that a unit of each good is equivalent in value to the other good and thus the two can be added together. Then, we arrive at the result that the Canadian GDP is 105, Costa Rican GDP is 210, and the world GDP, consisting of that of the only two nations, is $315 = 105 + 210$. As well, there are now 110 maple syrup units in existence

---

[3] See on this Keynes (1936), Friedman and Schwartz (1963), Rothbard (1963)

[4] A neo-classical supporter of socialism is Samuelson (1961) who predicted that the USSR would eventually catch up to, and then surpass, the economy of the U.S. For a rejoinder, see Skousen (1997). For strong critics of socialism, see Boettke (2001), Bylund et al. (2022), Ebeling (1993), Hayek (1948), Hoff (1981), Hoppe (1989, 2019) and Mises (1922, 1977).

[5] For a critique of this basic principle, paradoxically from a strong libertarian source, see Huemer (2019). For a rebuttal, Block (2023)

[6] Block (1990, 2002a, b), Block and Edelstein (2012), Block and Nelson (2015), Block and Yeatts (1999–2000), Block vs Epstein (2005), Bylund (2005, 2012), Gordon (2019a, b), Grotius (1625), Hoppe (1993, 2011), Kinsella (2003, 2006a, b, 2007, 2009a, b), Locke (1948), McMaken (2016), Paul (1987), Pufendorf (1673), Rothbard (1969, 1973, 32), Rozeff (2005) and Watner (1982).

Table 1 Absolute advantage, no trade

	Canada	Costa Rica	GDP
Maple syrup	100	10	110
Bananas	5	200	205
Product	105	210	315

Table 2 Absolute advantage, with trade

With trade	Canada	Costa Rica	Product
Maple syrup	200	0	200
Bananas	0	400	400
GDP	200	400	600

along with 205 units of bananas, for a grand total, also, of 315, this time the sum of 110 + 205.

We now incorporate trade into the analysis. We assume that each country will specialize in what it does best, and devote not one but both time periods allotted to it. We also postulate that there are no increasing or decreasing returns, so that a doubling of the time, effort, land, and inputs, will yield exactly twice as much of these two goods as before. Given these simplifying assumptions, we then arrive at Table 2.

That is to say, Canada produces 200 maple syrups but no bananas, while Costa Rica goes in the other direction with 400 bananas and no maple syrup. The GDP of Canada rises from 105 to 200, and that of Costa Rica catapults from 210 to 400. Instead of there being 110 maple syrups, there are 200. In like manner, the number of bananas rises from 205 to 400. The number of both goods and world GDP, moves from 315 to 600. This simplified model can only tell us that the collective, consisting of both countries, is now far better off than before. As to which country registers how much of the gain, that depends upon the bargaining skills of each. Suffice it to say that neither country can possibly be worse off than before; otherwise, they would not have agreed to the new arrangements and would have persisted with the previous situation.

By the way, Canada is a cold country.[7] How did they produce any bananas at all in the first instance, given that this item needs warm temperatures? Simple: they built gigantic, very expensive, hothouses. Similarly, Costa Rica has far warmer temperatures and maple trees do not survive in the heat. How did they pull that one off? Simple: gigantic, very expensive refrigerators,

---

[7] Upon one rare occasion to be sure, the temperature in the province of Alberta fell below that which exists on Mars. That is truly chilly. See on this xx.

Table 3 Comparative advantage, no trade

	Computers	Wheat	GDP
US	10	100	110
Japan	200	120	320
Product	210	220	430

Table 4 Comparatve advantage, with trade

With trade	Computers	Wheat	GDP
US	0	200	200
Japan	400	0	400
Product	400	200	600

hundreds of feet high. Yes, yes, this is all silly, but, makes an elementary point about absolute advantage. You do not need a radical free enterprise Austrian economist, not even a mainstreamer, to see the benefits of free trade under the above assumptions. Even the most rabid protectionist may well favor free trade in such a case.[8]

Let us now consider the case for comparative advantage (Table 3).[9]

We again utilize the simplified two-country, two-product model, with the same type of assumptions about trade, adding up items, etc. However, in this case, we no longer assume equality: one country is more efficient at producing one item, and the other can more effectively manufacture the second one. Now, we assume that the super duper Japanese are better at producing both goods than the inept Americans.

When trade is introduced, US GDP rises from 110 to 200, and that of the island nation from 320 to 400. There are now more computers in the world, 400 instead of 210, a gain of 190. It cannot be denied that there is a loss of 20 units of wheat, from 220 to 200, but in terms of human welfare, at least as measured by GDP, there has been a gain, of 170, from 430 to 600. Again, if either country does not like this result for any reason, they are free not to

---

[8] But maybe not. After all, what happens to jobs in the Canadian banana industry, and in the Costa Rican refrigerator plants, after free trade is introduced? Devastation ensues! The unemployment rate in both venues will be 100%. Perhaps, the interventionists in both countries will argue, we ought to keep at least some of these "inefficient" enterprises functioning, lest the other nation tries to hold us up with withdrawing supplies in other to jack up the price of their wares. The only way to do this would be, of course, either to directly subsidize Canadian banana and Costa Rican maple syrup industries, or, maintain some tariffs, not necessarily to go all the way back in the direction of self-sufficiency, but at least part of the way, as a sort of insurance policy. Needless to say, private investors could also do this out of their own pockets, but the socialist anti-traders would never rely on any such initiative. For them, if there is even the hint of a scintilla of a problem far off into the horizon, government, not entrepreneurs, must be wheeled in to solve it.

[9] Brandly (2002), Johnsson (2004), Murphy (2004), Ricardo (1821) and Schmidt (2013).

take part in the openings that free trade provides. They can eschew the gains made possible by specialization and the division of labor.

Let us try one more example in an attempt to cement this understanding. A lawyer earns $2000 per day by engaging in his law practice. However, work with me here, for every day of doing so, it is necessary that he spends an entire day, also, typing up the notes generated by that day of work. He is a pretty good typist and could hire out for $200 per day if he so chose. So, after two days of work, he earns $2200. However, if he hires a typist who is equally skilled in this endeavor, he must pay her the same $200 per day. If he does, he can spend both days, lawyering it up. What does his balance sheet look like if he does just that? It is $2000 + $2000 − $200 − $200 for a grand total of $3600. This sure beats the $2200 he earns when he does not avail himself of specialization and the division of labor. Even though he can type just as effectively as the typist, it still behooves him to hire her; that will free him up to do what he can do even better: function as an attorney.

A reduction ad absurdum.

The case against free trade is invariably articulated with national boundaries in mind. Those so and so's in that their foreign country are "takin' errr jobs!" goes the usual cry. But that is to confuse economics and politics. The same can be said internally to a country. For example, us Louisianans resent them Thar folk in California. They grow oranges better than we do. Let us set up a tariff, or, better yet, a prohibition against the importation of their evil citrus fruit. Yes, the Supreme Court would ban any such effort, based on the U.S. Constitution, but that just shows that the powers that be are ranged against us in the Pelican State. But we can go further than that, much further. Those rascals in Baton Rouge are undercutting us folk in New Orleans, and, indeed, everyone else in Louisiana is exploiting us. Let us prohibit the entry of any goods to Big Easy. Let us become self-sufficient![10] Ditto for the Garden District in the middle of the Crescent City: let us keep ourselves pure; let us not import anything from the French Quarter. You can now readily see where we are going with this. The XYZ block in the Garden District can now inveigh against every other city block in this neighborhood. Where will it end? Right down to the individual level. Every person in the entire world should be forbidden to trade with every other, which would be the logical ending point of this process. We should all be compelled to grow our own food, medicate ourselves, engage in our own entertainment, etc. Of course, if anything like this system were ever God forbid implemented, probably 99% + of us would perish. We owe our very lives to specialization and the division

---

[10] Those people in Brooklyn are particularly egregious. No decent person should have any commercial relations with any of them, ever.

of labor, to trade, whether at the city block level, the neighborhood, the city, the state, or the country. Protectionists thus in effect have a death wish, on behalf of the entire human race. Yes, this sounds harsh to me, even as I was writing it, but the truth is the truth.

Now that we have offered the case in free trade, let us deal with, and refute, several objections to it.

"Buy local".

Another variation on this theme is that we should all "buy local." We should "buy local" is the motto of those who suffer from this economic fallacy.[11] Why should we do any such thing? Why, in order to save money, or save the planet, or, just because! Does this mean that Americans should not listen to Mozart, since he produced his product a long time ago, away from that country? That Costa Ricans should not use maple syrup on their pancakes? That Canadians should eschew bananas? Should none of us purchase expensive automobiles, in order to "save money?" As for the planet, the main danger to it comes from socialism, and war, not from free trade.

The Infant Industries Argument.[12]

This objection to full free trade is only a partial one. Advocates of it accept open borders for goods, labor, and investments, but only in the long run. An exception must be made, they contend for infant industries. What is an infant industry? It is one that is just getting started but has to contend with the competition from extant firms located in another country in which this industry is already well-established. This latter can take advantage of the economies of scale both in and of itself, and, also, in terms of suppliers. The usual case trotted out in this context is the 13 colonies in the late eighteenth century, the infant, versus the well-established industries in England, in terms of manufacturing, based on its industrial revolution. So, is it economically viable for the new nation to set up tariff protections for its "infants" or should this country be forever in the thrall of its former mother country? The answer for those who support this objection to free trade is of course the former.

What are the difficulties with this train of thought?

One is that there are several "infants" who are over a century old. Once an industry is able to garner protectionist support, it is able, also, to attract supporters who protect its status. Another is that every industry, bar none, was at one time an "infant." If infants are to be protected, this would apply, then, to all industries, without exception. So the infant industry argument

---

[11] On this see Carden (2008a, b), Desrochers and Shimizu (2012) and Norberg (2017).
[12] Taussig (1915), is widely "credited" with being the father of the infant industry argument. See also his Taussig (1888) work. Critics of viewpoint include Baldwin (1969), Brandly (2002), Johnson (1970), Mises (1983), Murphy (2003, 2005) and Rothbard (2005).

is revealed not as an exception to free trade and economic freedom, but an attack on its very roots. Another problem with it is that it violates libertarian strictures. Yes, infant children must be helped, coddled, supported, subsidized, diapered, fed, etc. But why should this apply to adult investors who are trying to get their commercial "baby" off to a good start. Should they not be required to subsidize its "birth" themselves? If it succeeds, they and they alone, at least in the free society, will garner benefits from this enterprise. To compel others, strangers, to pay for it with a subsidy, or to be dissuaded from purchasing from "adult" companies, is a violation of their rights.

Yet another support for tariffs is a rather indirect one. Given that there are governmentally imposed misallocations of resources in the domestic country, and/or "market failures," a tax on imports from other nations may sometimes operate in the direction of reducing or even eliminating these aforementioned difficulties. I acknowledge that this is indeed a possibility.[13] But I am not unduly concerned with this justification, since I am implicitly assuming a full free enterprise regime in the domestic country, and it is impossible under such circumstances for there to be any such problem.[14]

Part and parcel of this phenomenon is the supposed "market failure" of monopoly. The pro-tariff argument is the fear that a foreign monopolist will corner the market for an item in which it has a comparative or absolute advantage in, and then proceed to jack up the price to the stratosphere. The domestic country, in order to deal with this threat, would be justified in imposing a tariff or even a quota, against all outsiders. The specific example often mentioned in this context is energy. We must have energy independence, it is asserted, in order to protect ourselves from this threat. Another case in point is the so-called monopoly of John D. Rockefeller and his Standard Oil company.

Take the latter first. Standard Oil did so well not because it had any monopoly "power"[15] but due to the fact that it was more efficient at refining oil (McGee, 1958). Why, then, to take the former, why is the neoclassical

---

[13] Although all tariffs, without exception, violate the NAP of libertarianism.
[14] This is a roundabout way of saying that I also reject the notion of "market failure." Here is where Austrian economics comes in. One of the unique attributes of this school of thought is that there is no such thing as a "market failure." See on this Anderson (1998), Barnett et al. (2005), Block (2002), Callahan (2000), Cowen (1988), DiLorenzo (2011), Guillory (2005), Higgs (1995), Hoppe (2003), MacKenzie (2002), Rothbard (1985), Simpson (2005), Tucker (1989), Westley (2002) and Woods (2009a, 2009b).
[15] For the Austrian demonstration that there is no such thing as a monopolist in the free market, see Anderson et al. (2001), Armentano (1972, 1982, 1989, 1999), Armstrong (1982), Barnett et al. (2005, 2007), Block (1977, 1982, 1994), Block and Barnett (2009), Boudreaux and Costea (2003), DiLorenzo (1992, 1996), DiLorenzo and High (1988), Henderson (2013), High (1984–1985), Hull (2005), McChesney (1991), McGee (1958), Rothbard (2004), Shugart (1987), Smith (1983) and Tucker (1998a, b).

analysis of monopoly fallacious? The core error is interpersonal comparisons of utility. What the mainstream economists assert is that the monopolist "withholds" a given amount of his product[16] and that the costs to him, thereof, is less than the value placed on it by the consumer. This generates the dread "deadweight loss" of monopoly, the supposed proof of its inefficiency. But to make this claim is to assert that one person's costs are less than an entirely different person's gains, and if this is not the invalid doctrine of interpersonal comparisons of utility, then nothing is.

Immigration

There are three factors of production that cross international borders: goods, investments, and labor. So far, we have limited ourselves to the first two of these. It is now time to address the third.

This one has led to a sharp divergence amongst libertarians between those who favor completely open borders,[17] and those who wish to restrict immigration to any degree at all.[18]

The argument of the latter position is clear. There are criminals outside our borders; murderers, rapists, thieves. It is hardly libertarian to allow such folk into the country. They will commit mayhem. They will violate the NAP of libertarianism. There are some, from countries in the Middle East, who when they see a woman in a mini-skirt, or dressed at the beach in a bikini, interpret such entirely legitimate behavior as a rights violation. They stand ready to punish her, with rape, for daring to violate all that is good and proper. Do we really want such criminals in our midst? The libertarians who favor immigration regulations answer with a loud and vociferous "No!".

There is one situation, and only one, that could convert these libertarians into espousing the open borders position. Suppose it was relatively easy to catch such miscreants, even before they engaged in any such criminal activity at all. Then, they would be summarily clapped into prison, caught while in the act of committing a crime, but before they actually did so, such that no rights, none at all, were abrogated. They would be guilty only of attempted crimes, not actual ones in which victims were negatively impacted in any way.

---

[16] The exact amount depends upon demand elasticities. There is no supply curve for the "monopolist."
[17] Babka (2016), Berg (2010), Block (1998, 2004, 2011a, b, 2013, 2016), Block and Callahan (2003), Boudreaux (2002, 2013) Caplan (2012, 2013, 2014), Ebeling (2015a, b), Ebeling and Hornberger (1995), Esplugas and Lora (2010), Fisher (2010), Friedman (1995, 2006, 2012), Gregory and Block (2007), Henderson (2012), Hornberger (2014, 2015), Hudson (1986), Huemer (2012), Krepelka (2010), Lee (2015a, b), Niskanen (2006), Nowrasteh (2012, 2015), Richman (2010, 2013, 2014a, b, c, d, e, 2015a, b, 2016), Salin (2000, chap. 11), Schooland (2002a, b), Shikha (2014), Simon (1989, 1998), Somin (2014), Todea (2010) and Wilkinson (2008, 2010).
[18] Brimelow (1995), De Soto (1998), Hoppe (1999, 2001a, b, 2002, 2004, 2006, 2014, 2015a, b, c, d), Hospers (1998), Kinsella (2005, 2009a, 2009b), Mosquito (2015a, b, c, d, e, f, g, 2016), Kinsella (2005), Reece (2015), Rockwell (2015), Rothbard (1994), Ruark (2014), Taylor (1998).

Now, ordinarily, holding criminals in prison is a costly affair. But that is when governments are in charge of these facilities. Under private enterprise, they would be a paying proposition.[19] Then, in effect, criminal immigrants would be a positive resource. It would be as if a bunch of cows or sheep crossed our borders. There would be a profit in welcoming them, imprisoning them, in effect enslaving them. Let us return to the real world, and leave off our brief visit to this imaginary one.[20]

The open borders libertarians, too, do not exactly relish foreign criminals.[21] Why then, are they against border regulations, even those who are not anarcho-capitalists, and thus oppose all government activity?

There are two reasons. First, an uninvited immigrant need not violate any rights, any rights whatsoever, and, then, to bar him from the country would be to violate his rights, anathema to libertarians. Consider the following. An immigrant arrives in the US. He is from Africa, or Asia, or, indeed, from Mars. He lands his spaceship or helicopter in Wyoming, in the middle of the Rocky Mountains, or in Alaska, in either case in never before homesteaded terrain. Now, according to Locke (1948) the libertarian Godfather of justification in land titles, the first person who homesteads territory is its rightful owner. That person, in this case, is our Martian. Consider the following scenario. The Martian is peacefully cutting down trees, digging up rocks, and putting in a crop of corn. He is approached by a policeman,[22] who says to him: "What are you doing here, sir?"[23] The response by the Martian: "Thanks for asking, sir.[24] Why, I am homesteading virgin land, in the spirit of your John Locke." Comes the rejoinder by the cop[25] "Sorry, you'll have to leave, go back from whence you came. Your activities are incompatible with our immigration law." And now, the word from the Martian: "But, sir, which libertarian law have I broken?" The man from the red planet gets the last word since the gendarme simply has no answer to this query.

Hans Hoppe in his numerous publications on the subject has a response for the police officer: the government really owns this contested land in trust for all the tax payers of the country. This is highly problematic. First

---

[19] We can deduce from the positive price of slaves that it is possible to compel labor from workers at a profit at least under certain conditions.

[20] In defense of this intellectual excursion, it helps us to pinpoint the case in favor of immigration regulations to exclude criminals. We want to exclude them because many of these conditions are unrealistic.

[21] Nor domestic ones either, to be sure.

[22] Hopefully, a private one, an adherent to the libertarian philosophy.

[23] Everyone is polite in this little conversation.

[24] I told you, politeness!

[25] I'm not polite. Just the two of them.

of all, this scholar is a distinguished anarcho-capitalist. Secondly, after John Locke and Murray Rothbard, he has probably done more good work on the libertarian theory of homesteading than any other person on the planet. It is entirely out of keeping with the brilliant analyses he has done on this subject to claim that the US government is really the owner of this virgin land whether on its own hook or on behalf of anyone else. This is untouched territory. No person, before this Martian, has even touched it, nor, even, come within miles of it. This attempt fails, totally.

What, then, is the anarcho-capitalist analysis? First, it does not want to entirely jettison libertarian theory on the matter in order to save ourselves from criminal immigrants.[26] It wants to have its cake and eat it too: it wants to fully protect libertarian theory, and, also, protect us from criminal immigrants, or even nice ones, if there are too many of them.

How, pray tell, can this be accomplished? Simple.[27] Privatize every single square inch of the country, including all waterways (Block and Nelson 2015). Then, when an unwanted Martian or anyone else lands somewhere and starts homesteading, they can be declared guilty of trespassing on private property, and removed. This, needless, to say, would be entirely compatible with libertarian theory.

There is only one possible fly in the ointment. Some land and water are economically sub-marginal. That is, it would cost more to bring them into ownership via homesteading, than the present discounted value of owning them. Thus, no profit-seeking individual would undertake anything of the sort. Moreover, just because they are sub-marginal to the extant population, does not mean they would also be considered in this regard by desperate Martians. The only solution to this vexing problem would be private charity. If we as a society fear these immigrants let us invest in these economically unjustified, but politically and socially justified, homesteading of these marginal lands. In that way, we can close this particular loophole, and, still, remain steadfast, unlike Hoppe, in our support of basic libertarian principles.

References

Anderson WL (1998) Market failure? Mises Institute. October 8, 1998. http://www.mises.org/story/53

---

[26] What about not a million, not a billion, not a trillion, not a quadrillion, but a quintillion Martian immigrants. They are all civilized. Not a one of them is a criminal. Still, we earthlings might not fully relish their moving in amongst us. There would not even be standing room for everyone.

[27] Ok, maybe, not so simple.

Anderson W, Block WE, DiLorenzo TJ, Mercer I, Snyman L, Westley C (2001) The microsoft corporation in collision with Antitrust Law. J Social Polit Econ Stud 26(1, Winter):287–302

Armentano DT (1972) The myths of antitrust. Arlington House, New Rochelle, NY

Armentano DT (1982) Antitrust and monopoly: anatomy of a policy failure. Wiley, New York

Armentano DT (1989) Antitrust reform: predatory practices and the competitive process. Rev Aust Econ 3:61–74. http://www.mises.org/journals/rae/pdf/rae3_1_4.pdf

Armentano DT (1999) Antitrust: the case for repeal, 2nd edn. Mises Institute, Auburn AL

Armstrong Don (1982) Competition vs. Monopoly, Vancouver: the fraser institute

Arnold R (1987) Competition versus monopoly: combines policy in perspective. Rev Austrian Econ 1:231–232. https://doi.org/10.1007/BF0153934

Babka J (2016) I want Lew Rockwell to be libertarian on immigration. Zero Aggression Project. January 19, 2016. https://www.zeroaggressionproject.org/jim-babka/lew-rockwell-be-libertarian-immigration/

Baldwin RE (1969) The case against Infant-Industry tariff protection. J Polit Econ 77(3) (May–June). https://doi.org/10.1086/259517

Barnett WII, Block WE, Saliba M (2007) Predatory pricing. Corp Ownership Control 4(4, Summer):401–406

Berg C (2010) Open the borders. Policy 26(1, Autumn):3–7

Block WE (1977) Austrian monopoly theory—a critique. J Liber Stud I 4(Fall):271–279

Block WE (1982) Amending the combines investigation act. The Fraser Institute, Vancouver

Block WE (1990) Earning happiness through homesteading unowned land: a comment on 'buying misery with federal land' by Richard Stroup. J Social Polit Econ Stud 15(2, Summer):237–253

Block WE (1994) Total repeal of anti-trust legislation: a critique of Bork, Brozen and Posner. Rev Aust Econ 8(1):35–70

Block WE (1998) A libertarian case for free immigration. J Libert Stud Interdisc Rev 13(2, summer):167–186. http://www.mises.org/journals/jls/13_2/13_2_4.pdf

Block WE (2002) All government is excessive: a rejoinder to 'in defense of excessive government' by Dwight Lee. J Libert Stud 16(3):35–82. http://www.mises.org/journals/jls/16_3/16_3_3.pdf

Block WE (2002a) Homesteading city streets; an exercise in managerial theory. Plan Market 5(1, September):18–23. http://www-pam.usc.edu/volume5/v5i1a2s1.html; http://www-pam.usc.edu/

Block WE (2002b) On reparations to blacks for slavery. Human Rights Rev 3(4, July–September):53–73

Block WE (2004) 'The state was a mistake.' Book review of Hoppe, Han-Hermann, democracy, The God that failed: the economics and politics of monarchy, democracy and natural order. Mises Institute, May 25, 2001. http://www.mises.org/fulstory.asp?control=1522

Block WE (2011a) Hoppe, Kinsella and Rothbard II on Immigration: a critique. J Libert Stud 22:593–623. http://mises.org/journals/jls/22_1/22_1_29.pdf

Block WE (2011b) Rejoinder to Hoppe on immigration. J Libert Studies 22:771–792. http://mises.org/journals/jls/22_1/22_1_38.pdf

Block WE (2013) Rejoinder to Todea on the 'open' contract of immigration. Sci J Hum Stud 8(5, March):52–55

Block WE (2016) Contra Hoppe and Brat on immigration. Manage Educ Sci Technol J. http://www.mest.meste.org/MEST_Najava_clanaka.html

Block WE (2023) Defending absolutist libertarianism. In: The emergence of a tradition: essays in honor of Jesús Huerta de Soto, vol II. Palgrave MacMillan, pp 45–52

Block W, Barnett W (2009) Monopsony theory. Am Rev Polit Econ 7(½, June):67–109. http://www.arpejournal.com/ARPEvolume7number1-2/Block-Barnett.pdf

Block WE, Callahan G (2003) Is there a right to immigration? A libertarian perspective. Human Rights Rev 5(1, October–December):46–71. http://www.walterblock.com/publications/block-callahan_right-immigrate-2003.pdf

Block WE, Edelstein MR (2012) Popsicle sticks and homesteading land for nature preserves. Roman Econ Bus Rev 7(1, Spring):7–13

Block W, Epstein R (2005) Debate on eminent domain. NYU J Law Liberty 1(3):1144–1169

Block WE, Nelson PL (2015) Water capitalism: the case for privatizing oceans, rivers, lakes, and aquifers. Lexington Books; Rowman and Littlefield, New York City, N.Y. https://mises.org/library/case-privatizing-oceans-and-rivers

Block W, Yeatts G (1999–2000) The economics and ethics of land reform: a critique of the pontifical council for justice and peace's 'toward a better distribution of land: the challenge of Agrarian reform. J Nat Resour Environ Law 15(1):37–69

Boettke PJ (2001) Calculation and coordination: essays on socialism and transitional political economy. Routledge, London. http://www.mises.org/etexts/cc.pdf

Bohm-Bawerk E (1890) Capital and interest. MacMillan and Co, London

Böhm-Bawerk E (1909 1959) Capital and Interest. 3 vols, South Holland, IL: Libertarian Press

Boudreaux DJ, DiLorenzo TJ (1992) The protectionist roots of antitrust. Rev Aust Econ 6(2):81–96

Boudreaux D (2002) Absorbing immigrants: does America have the space and resources to allow open borders? The Freeman, 1 (June). http://fee.org/freeman/absorbing-immigrants/

Boudreaux D (2013) Immigration: the practice of principle. Café Hayek, June 22, 2013. http://cafehayek.com/2013/06/immigration-the-practice-of-the-principle.html

Brandly M (2002) A primer on trade. Mises Institute, November 4, 2002

Brimelow P (1995) Alien nation: common sense about America's immigration disaster. Random House, New York, NY

Bylund PL, Lingle C, Packard M (2022) Politicised revisionism: comment on Lopes. Cambridge J Econ 46(3, May 2022):609–612. https://doi.org/10.1093/cje/beac012

Bylund P (2005) Man and matter: a philosophical inquiry into the justification of ownership in land from the basis of self-ownership. Master thesis, Lund University. http://www.lunduniversity.lu.se/o.o.i.s?id=24965&postid=1330482

Bylund P (2012) Man and matter: how the former gains ownership of the latter. Libert Papers 4(1). http://libertarianpapers.org/articles/2012/lp-4-1-5.pdf

Callahan G (2000) Market failure again? Mises Institute, April 4, 2000. http://www.mises.org/story/407

Caplan B (2012) Why should we restrict immigration? Cato J 32(1, winter). http://object.cato.org/sites/cato.org/files/serials/files/cato-journal/2012/1/cj32n1-2.pdf

Caplan B (2013) My path to open borders. Open Borders: The Case, January 2, 2013. http://openborders.info/blog/my-path-to-open-borders/

Caplan B (2014) America should open its borders: my opening statement for the reason immigration debate. April 23, 2014. http://econlog.econlib.org/archives/2014/04/america_should.html

Carden A (2008a) Should we buy only locally grown produce?" Mises Institute, July 15, 2008. https://mises.org/library/should-we-buy-only-locally-grown-produce

Carden A (2008b) The Locavore's dilemma: local food, continued. Mises Institute, August 18, 2008. https://mises.org/library/locavores-dilemma-local-food-continued

Costea D (2003) A critique of mises's theory of monopoly prices. Q J Aust Econ 6(3, Fall):47–62. http://www.mises.org/journals/qjae/pdf/qjae6_3_3.pdf

Cowen T (ed) (1988) The theory of market failure: a critical examination. George Mason University Press, Fairfax, VA

de Soto JH (1998) A libertarian theory of free immigration. J Libert Stud 13(2, Summer):187–197

Desrochers P, Shimizu H (2012) The Locavore's dilemma: in praise of the 10,000-mile diet. PublicAffairs, New York

DiLorenzo TJ (1996) The myth of natural monopoly. Rev Aust Econ 9(2):43–58. http://www.mises.org/journals/rae/pdf/rae9_2_3.pdf

DiLorenzo T (2011) A note on the canard of 'asymmetric information' as a source of market failure. Q J Aust Econ 14(2):249–255

DiLorenzo T, High J (1988) Antitrust and competition, historically considered. Econ Inq 26(1, July):423–435

Ebeling RM (1993) Economic calculation under socialism: Ludwig von Mises and his predecessors. In: The meaning of Ludwig von Mises. Kluwer Academic Press, Norwell, MA, pp 56–101

Ebeling RM, Hornberger JG (eds) (1995) The case for free trade and open immigration. Future of Freedom Foundation

Ebeling R (2015a) Freedom to move: personal liberty or government control, part I. Epic Times, July 20, 2015. http://www.epictimes.com/richardebeling/2015/07/freedom-to-move-personal-liberty-or-government-control-part-i/

Ebeling R (2015b) Practicing freedom: markets, marriage, and migration. Epic Times, August 3, 2015

Esplugas A, Manuel L (2010) Immigrants: intruders or guests? A reply to Hoppe and Kinsella. J Libert Stud 22:185–218. http://mises.org/journals/jls/22_1/22_1_10.pdf

Fisher M (2010) How ending birthright citizenship would change immigration. The Wire, August 11, 2010. http://www.thewire.com/politics/2010/08/how-ending-birthright-citizenship-would-change-immigration/23397/

Friedman DD (1995) Open the gates. In: The machinery of freedom: a guide to radical capitalism. Open Court, La Salle, Ill

Friedman D (2006) Welfare and immigration—the other half of the argument. Ideas, April 1, 2006. http://www.daviddfriedman.com/Libertarian/Welfare_and_Immigration.html

Friedman D (2012) Immigrants and welfare. November 15

Friedman M, Schwartz AJ (1963) A monetary history of the United States, 1867–1960. Princeton University Press. http://www.jstor.org/stable/j.ctt7s1vp

Gordon D (2019a) Locke vs. Cohen vs. Rothbard on homesteading. Mises Wire. November 8, 2019. https://mises.org/wire/locke-vs-cohen-vs-rothbard-homesteading

Gordon D (2019b) Violence, homesteading, and the origins of private property. Mises Wire, December 13, 2019

Gregory A, Block WE (2007) On immigration: reply to Hoppe. J Libert Stud 21(3, Fall):25–42. http://mises.org/journals/jls/21_3/21_3_2.pdf

Grotius H (1625) The rights of war and peace, 1901 edn. M. Walter Dunne, New York

Guillory G (2005) What are you calling failure? Mises Institute. May 5, 2005. http://www.mises.org/story/1806

Hayek FA (1935a) Socialist calculation debate: the present state of the debate. In: Collectivist economic planning: critical studies on the possibility of socialism. Routledge and Kegan Paul, London, pp 201–243

Hayek FA (1935b) The nature and history of the debate. In: Hayek FA (ed) Collectivist economic planning: critical studies on the possibility of socialism. Routledge and Kegan Paul, London, pp 1–40

Hayek FA (1940) Socialist calculation: the competitive 'solution.' Economica 7(May):125–149

Hayek FA (1941) The pure theory of capital. Midway, Chicago, IL

Hayek FA (1948) Socialist calculation I, II, & III. University of Chicago Press, Chicago

Henderson D (2012) Tear down these walls. The Freeman, May 30, 2012. http://fee.org/freeman/tear-down-these-walls/

Henderson DR (2013) The robber barons: neither robbers nor barons. Library of Economics and Liberty, March 4, 2013. http://www.econlib.org/cgi-bin/printarticle2.pl?file=Columns/y2013/Hendersonbarons.html

Higgs R (1995) The myth of 'failed' policies. Free Market 13(6, June). http://www.mises.org/freemarket_detail.asp?control=239&sortorder=articledate

High J (1985) Bork's paradox: static vs dynamic efficiency in antitrust analysis. Contemp Policy Issues 3:21–34

Hoff TJB (1981) Economic calculation in a socialist society. Liberty Press, Indianapolis

Hoppe H-H (1989) A theory of socialism and capitalism. Kluwer Academic Publishers, Boston

Hoppe H-H (1993) The economics and ethics of private property: studies in political economy and philosophy. Kluwer, Boston

Hoppe H-H (1999) On free immigration and forced immigration. Lewrockwell.com. https://www.lewrockwell.com/1970/01/hans-hermann-hoppe/on-free-immigration-and-forced-integration/

Hoppe Hans-Hermann (2001a) Secession, the State, and the immigration problem. Lewrockwell.com, May 16, 2001. http://archive.lewrockwell.com/orig/hermann-hoppe3.html

Hoppe H-H (2001B) Democracy, the God that failed: the economics and politics of monarchy, democracy and natural order. Transaction Publishers, New Brunswick, NJ

Hoppe H-H (2002) Natural order, the state, and the immigration problem. J Libert Stud 16(1, Winter):75–97. http://mises.org/journals/jls/16_1/16_1_5.pdf

Hoppe H-H (ed) (2003) The myth of national defense: essays on the theory and history of security production. The Ludwig von Mises Institute, Auburn, AL

Hoppe H-H (2004) In the free market, may a businessman hire any immigrant he chooses? Lewrockwell.com, September 22. http://archive.lewrockwell.com/hoppe/hoppe10b.html

Hoppe H-H (2006) On free immigration and forced integration. Lew Rockwell, April 4, 2006. http://archive.lewrockwell.com/hoppe/hoppe1.html

Hoppe H-H (2011) Of private, common, and public property and the rationale for total privatization. Libert Papers 3(1):1–13. http://libertarianpapers.org/2011/1-hoppe-private-common-and-public-property/

Hoppe H-H (2014) Immigration libertarianism. Lewrockwell.com, October 18, 2014. https://www.lewrockwell.com/2014/10/hans-hermann-hoppe/open-borders/

Hoppe H-H (2015a). Free immigration is forced integration. Lewrockwell.com, July 10, 2015. https://www.lewrockwell.com/2015/07/hans-hermann-hoppe/free-immigration/

Hoppe H-H (2015b) Immigration and libertarianism. Lewrockwell.com, July 11, 2015. https://www.lewrockwell.com/2015/07/hans-hermann-hoppe/open-borders-2/

Hoppe H-H (2019) Why socialism must fail. Mises Wire, July 8, 2019. https://mises.org/wire/why-socialism-must-fail?utm_source=Mises+Institute+Subscriptions&utm_campaign=e9fd7241c6-EMAIL_CAMPAIGN_9_21_2018_9_59_COPY_01&utm_medium=email&utm_term=0_8b52b2e1c0-e9fd7241c6-227976965

Hornberger JG (2014) End immigration socialism. Future of Freedom Foundation, September 22, 2014. http://fff.org/2014/09/22/end-immigration-socialism/

Hornberger JG (2015) There is only one libertarian position on immigration. Future of Freedom Foundation, August 25, 2015. http://fff.org/2015/08/25/one-libertarian-position-immigration/

Hospers J (1998) A libertarian argument against opening borders. J Libert Stud 13(2). https://mises.org/library/libertarian-argument-against-opening-borders-0

Hudson JL (1986) The philosophy of immigration. J Libert Stud 8(1, Winter):51–62. http://www.mises.org/journals/jls/8_1/8_1_5.pdf

Huemer M (2012) Is there a right to immigration? Social Theory Pract 36(3):429–461. http://spot.colorado.edu/~huemer/immigration.htm

Huemer M (2013) Citizenism and open borders. Open Borders: The Case, February 18, 2013. http://openborders.info/blog/citizenism-and-open-borders/

Huemer M (2019) NAPs Are for Babies. Fake Nous, September 21, 2019

Hull G (ed) (2005) The abolition of antitrust. Transaction Publishers, New Brunswick, NJ

Johnson HG (1970) A new view of the infant industry argument. In: McDougall A, Snape RH (eds) Studies in international economics: Monash conference papers. North-Holland, Amsterdam

Johnsson RCB (2004) On Ricardo and free trade. Mises Institute, January 12, 2004

Keynes JM ([1936] 2017) The general theory of employment, interest and money. Wordsworth Editions, Herts, UK

Kinsella SN (2003) A libertarian theory of contract: title transfer, binding promises, and inalienability. J Libert Stud 17(2, Spring):11–37. http://www.mises.org/journals/jls/17_2/17_2_2.pdf

Kinsella S (2005) A simple libertarian argument against unrestricted immigration and open borders. Lewrockwell.com, September 1, 2005. http://archive.lewrockwell.com/kinsella/kinsella18.html

Kinsella SN (2006a) Thoughts on intellectual property, scarcity, labor-ownership, metaphors, and lockean homesteading. Mises Wire, May 26, 2006. https://mises.org/wire/thoughts-intellectual-property-scarcity-labor-ownership-metaphors-and-lockean-homesteading

Kinsella SN (2006b) How we come to own ourselves. Mises Institute, September 7, 2006

Kinsella SN (2007) Thoughts on the latecomer and homesteading ideas; or, why the very idea of "ownership" implies that only libertarian principles are justifiable. Mises Wire, August 15, 2007

Kinsella SN (2009a) What libertarianism is. Mises Institute, August 21, 2009. https://mises.org/library/what-libertarianism

Kinsella SN (2009b) Homesteading, abandonment, and unowned land in the civil law. Mises Institute, May 22, 2009. http://blog.mises.org/10004/homesteading-abandonment-and-unowned-land-in-the-civil-law/

Krepelka J (2010) A pure libertarian theory of immigration. J Libert Stud 22:35–52. http://mises.org/journals/jls/22_1/22_1_3.pdf

Lee J (2015a) Confusing public and private: the nonsensical private property argument against open borders. Open Borders: The Case, March 31, 2015. http://openborders.info/blog/confusing-public-private-nonsensical-private-property-argument-open-borders/

Lee J (2015b) The claim that open borders inevitably leads to homogeneity is incredibly weak. Open Borders: The Case, July 14, 2015. http://openborders.info/blog/claim-open-borders-inevitably-leads-homogeneity-incredibly-weak/

Locke J (1948) An essay concerning the true origin, extent and end of civil government. In: Barker E (ed) Social contract. Oxford University Press, New York, pp 17–19

MacKenzie DW (2002) The market failure myth. Mises Institute, August 26, 2002

McChesney F (1991) Antitrust and regulation: Chicago's contradictory views. Cato J 10. https://www.cato.org/sites/cato.org/files/serials/files/cato-journal/1991/1/cj10n3-10.pdf

McGee JS (1958) Predatory price cutting: the standard oil (New Jersey) case. J Law Econ 1(October):137–169. https://www.journals.uchicago.edu/toc/jle/1958/1

McMaken R (2016) How the feds botched the Frontier homestead acts. Mises Institute, October 19, 2016. https://mises.org/wire/how-feds-botched-frontier-homestead-acts

Menger C (1871) Principles of economics. New York: New York University Press

Menger C (1976) Principles of economics. Translated by James Dingwall and Bert F. Hoselitz. The Free Press, New York (online edition, The Mises Institute, 2004)

Mosquito B (2015a) Hoppe's realistic libertarianism. August 5, 2015. http://bionicmosquito.blogspot.ca/2015/08/hoppes-realistic-libertarianism.html

Mosquito B (2015b) Hoppe and immigration. August 9, 2015. http://bionicmosquito.blogspot.ca/2015/08/hoppe-and-immigration.html

Mosquito B (2015c) Dances with elephants. August 12, 2015

Mosquito B (2015d) Open borders: case study. November 5, 2015

Mosquito B (2015e) Why culture matters. November 17 2015

Mosquito B (2015f) Libertarian open borders. November 21 2015

Mosquito B (2015g) Borders neither open or closed: richman gets it right. November 22, 2015. http://bionicmosquito.blogspot.ca/2015/11/borders-neither-open-or-closed-richman.html

Mosquito B (2016) The real action is in the reaction of the opposition. January 11, 2016. https://www.lewrockwell.com/2016/01/bionic-mosquito/open-borders-saul-alinsky/

Murphy RN (2003) Some subtler arguments for tariffs. Mises Institute, December 9, 2003

Murphy RP (2004) Can trade bring poverty? Mises Institute, December 24, 2004. http://www.mises.org/article.aspx?Id=1699

Murphy RN (2005) The infant industry argument. Mises Institute, January 2, 2005

Niskanen W (2006) Build a wall around the welfare state, not around the country. Cato Policy Report (September/October)

Norberg J (2017) Destroyed a major myth fueling the 'buy local' craze. Uploaded in March 15, 2017. Youtube video, 1:11 mins. https://www.youtube.com/watch?v=_mBgUqqnsyw

Nowrasteh A (2012) Could our immigration laws prevent the next google? Huffington Post, January 27, 2012 (updated 28 March 2012). http://www.huffingtonpost.com/alex-nowrasteh/post_2887_b_1232305.html

Nowrasteh A (2015) Alex Nowrasteh critiques donald trump's immigration plan. The Federalist, September 4, 2015. http://thefederalist.com/2015/09/04/alex-nowrasteh-critiques-donald-trumps-immigration-plan/

Nozick R (1974) Anarchy, state and utopia. Basic Books, New York

Paul EF (1987) Property rights and eminent domain. Transaction Publishers, Livingston, New Jersey

Pufendorf S (1673) Natural law and the law of nations (De officio hominis et civis prout ipsi praescribuntur lege naturali) De officio hominis et civis juxta legem naturalem libri duo. 2 vols. Hein, Buffalo, NJ (reprint of New York, Oxford U. Pr., 1927a)

Reece M (2015) The pragmatic libertarian case against open borders. The Zeroth Position, November 24, 2015. https://reece.liberty.me/the-pragmatic-libertarian-case-against-open-borders/

Ricardo D (1821) The principles of political economy and taxation, 3rd ed., London: J. M. Dent

Ricardo D (1912) The principles of political economy & taxation. J.M. Dent & Sons Ltd.; E.P. Dutton., New York. https://archive.org/details/principlesofpoli00ricauoft

Richman S (2010) Border control bogey; what's next? Internal passports. Foundation For Economic Education, July 2, 2010. http://fee.org/freeman/border-control-bogey/#axzz2TOf3I1IZ

Richman S (2013) What the immigration bill overlooks. Future of Freedom Foundation, July 9, 2013. http://fff.org/explore-freedom/article/what-the-immigration-bill-overlooks/

Richman S (2014a) TGIF: in praise of 'thick' libertarianism. Future of Freedom Foundation, April 4, 2014

Richman S (2014b) Libertarianism is more than just rejecting force: the 'thick' and 'thin' of libertarian philosophy. Reason, April 6, 2014. http://reason.com/archives/2014/04/06/a-libertarian-opposition-to-racism

Richman S (2014c) TGIF: libertarianism rightly conceived. Future of Freedom Foundation, May 2, 2014

Richman S (2014d) What social animals owe each other. Future of Freedom Foundation, July 1, 2014. http://fff.org/explore-freedom/article/what-social-animals-owe-each-other/

Richman S (2014e) Let the immigrants stay. Future of Freedom Foundation, July 9, 2014

Richman S (2015a) TGIF: gun control and immigration restrictions are enemies of liberty. Free Association, October 23, 2015. http://sheldonfreeassociation.blogspot.ca/2015/10/tgif-gun-control-and-immigration.html

Richman S (2015b) TGIF: let the refugees in. Free Association, November 20, 2015

Richman S (2016) Immigrants are less criminal than natural-born Americans. Reason, January 14, 2016. https://reason.com/blog/2016/01/14/immigrants-are-less-criminal-than-natura

Rockwell L (2015) Open borders are an assault on private property. Mises Daily, November 16, 2015. https://mises.org/library/open-borders-are-assault-private-property

Rothbard MN (1962) Man economy and state: a treatise on economic principles. Van Nostrand, Princeton, New Jersey. The Muses Institute. http://www.mises.org/rothbard/mes.asp

Rothbard MN (1963) America's great depression. Van Nostrand, Princeton, NJ

Rothbard MN (1969) Confiscation and the homestead principle. Libert Forum 1(6, June 15). https://www.panarchy.org/rothbard/confiscation.html

Rothbard MN (1973) For a new liberty. Macmillan, New York. http://mises.org/rothbard/newlibertywhole.asp

Rothbard M (1994) Nations by consent: decomposing the nation-state. J Libert Studi 11(1, 1994). https://mises.org/library/nations-consent-decomposing-nation-state-0; http://mises.org/journals/jls/11_1/11_1_1.pdf

Rothbard MN (1985) Airport congestion: a case of market failure? The Ludwig von Mises Institute, Auburn, AL. http://www.mises.org/econsense/ch52.asp

Rothbard MN (1998) The ethics of liberty. New York University Press, New York. https://cdn.mises.org/The%20Ethics%20of%20Liberty%2020191108.pdf

Rothbard MN (2004) Man, economy and state, Auburn AL: Ludwig von Mises Institute, Scholar's Edition; http://www.mises.org/rothbard/mes.asp

Rothbard MN (2005) Protectionism and the destruction of prosperity. The Mises Institute, Auburn, AL. http://mises.org/rothbard/protectionism.asp

Rozeff Michael S (2005) Original appropriation and its critics. Lew Rockwell. September 1, 2005

Ruark E (2014) The (Il)logic of open border libertarians. In: Federation for American immigration reform, May 21 2014. http://www.fairus.org/DocServer/research-pub/The_%28Il%29Logic_of_Open_Border_Libertarians-2.pdf

Salin P (2000) L'immigration dans une société libre" (Immigration in a free society). In: Libéralisme. Odile Jacob, Paris

Samuelson P (1961) Economics. McGraw-Hill, New York

Schmidt S (2013) Understanding comparative advantage. Mises Institute. February 22, 2013

Schoolland K (2002a) Immigration: an abolitionist case. Ideas Liberty (Jan 2002):10–14. http://fee.org/files/doclib/schoolland0102.pdf

Schoolland K (2002b) Why open immigration? In: World conference of the international society for individual liberty. México, Puerto Vallarta. July 29 2002. Speech. http://www.jonathangullible.com/content/why-open-immigration

Schumpeter JA (1942) Capitalism, socialism and democracy. Harper & Brothers, New York

Shikha D (2014) On immigration, Obama may be cynical, but he's not breaking the law. Washington Examiner. August 7, 2014. http://www.washingtonexaminer.com/on-immigration-obama-may-be-cynical-but-hes-not-breaking-the-law/article/2551807%22%20target=%22_blank

Shugart II, William F (1987) Don't revise the clayton act, scrap it! Cato J 6:925

Simon J (1989) The economic consequences of immigration. Basil Blackwell, Oxford

Simon J (1998) Are there grounds for limiting immigration?" J Libert Stud 13(2, Summer):137–152. http://mises.org/journals/jls/13_2/13_2_2.pdf

Simpson B (2005) Markets don't fail. Lexington Books, New York, N.Y.

Skousen M (1997) The perseverance of Paul Samuelson's economics. J Econ Perspect 11(2, Spring):137–152

Smith Jr, Fred L (1983) Why not abolish antitrust? Regulation 23 (Jan–Feb). http://cei.org/op-eds-and-articles/why-not-abolish-antitrust

Somin I (2014) Obama, immigration, and the rule of law. Washington Post. November 20 2014. https://www.washingtonpost.com/news/volokh-conspiracy/wp/2014/11/20/obama-immigration-and-the-rule-of-law/

Taussig FW (1888) The tariff history of the United States. G.P. Putnam's Sons, New York

Taussig FW (1915) Some aspects of the tariff question. Harvard University Press

Taylor J (ed) (1998) The real American dilemma: race, immigration, and the future of America. American Renaissance, Oakton, VA

Todea DV (2010) A libertarian account of freedom of movement and open borders. Sci J Hum Stud 2(2). http://www.academia.edu/1151049/A_libertarian_account_of_freedom_of_movement_and_open_borders

Tucker J (1998a) Controversy: are antitrust laws immoral? J Markets Moral 1(1, March):75–82. http://www.acton.org/publications/mandm/mandm_controversy_35.php

Tucker J (1998b) Controversy: are antitrust laws immoral? A response to Kenneth G. Elzinga. J Markets Moral 1(1, March):90–94. http://www.acton.org/publications/mandm/mandm_controversy_37.php

von Mises L ([1949] 1998) Human action, scholars' edition. Auburn: Mises Institute. http://mises.org/resources/3250. http://www.mises.org/humanaction.asp

von Mises L (1977) A critique of interventionism. Arlington House, New Rochelle, NY. http://www.mises.org/etexts/mises/interventionism/contents.asp

von Mises L (1981) Socialism: an economic and sociological analysis. Translated by J. Kahane. Indianapolis: Liberty Fund. http://mises.org/books/socialism/contents.aspx

von Mises L (1983) Nation, state and economy. Translated by Leland B. Yeager. New York University Press, New York. http://mises.org/nsande/pt1iich2-b.asp

Watner C (1982) The proprietary theory of justice in the libertarian tradition. J Libert Stud 6(3–4, Summer/Fall):289–316. http://mises.org/journals/jls/6_3/6_3_6.pdf

Westley C (2002) The myth of market failure. Mises Institute. June 14, 2002. http://www.mises.org/story/982

Wieser F (1889) Natural value. Translated by Christian A. Malloch. University of Prague, Prague

Wieser F (1893) Social economics, A. Ford Hinrich, trans., New York: Augustus M. Kelley

Wilkinson W (2008) Milton Friedman's argument for illegal immigration. In: The fly bottle: the sweet release of reason. June 11 2008. http://www.willwilkinson.net/flybottle/2008/06/11/milton-friedmans-argument-for-illegal-immigration/

Wilkinson W (2010) Liberalism and birthright citizenship. In: The fly bottle: the sweet release of reason. August 9, 2010. http://www.willwilkinson.net/flybottle/2010/08/09/liberalism-and-birthright-citizenship/

William BII, Block WE, Saliba M (2005) Perfect competition: a case of 'market-failure.' Corp Ownership Control 2(4, Summer):70–75

Woods TE Jr (2009a) Krugman failure, not market failure. Lew Rockwell. June 19, 2009. http://www.lewrockwell.com/woods/woods116.html

Woods TE Jr (2009) Response to the 'market failure' drones. Mises Institute. June 10, 2009. http://mises.org/story/3503

Ludwig von Mises on Trade, Human Development, and Human Progress

Mark Thornton

Introduction

Most of what is written on the topic of international trade typically involves issues such as tariff rates, the technical issues of trade relations, and the negotiations within multinational trading blocs. Even when hostile, this research implicitly reveals the importance of the gains from trade. Here, we take the opportunity to step back and examine the panorama of human progress and its determinants.

This essay provides a pedagogical view of the history of human progress based on the writings of the great Austrian economist, Ludwig von Mises (1881–1973). Mises wrote on the entire gambit of economic topics, including methodology, theory, comparative economic systems, monetary economics, policy analysis, ideologies, and business cycle theory. Of his dozens of books and important articles, there is no single publication devoted solely to his analysis of trade.

Trade was integral to all his work, including his decisive contribution to the Socialist Calculation Debate. Indeed, as we shall see, trade is the

---

The author is pleased to acknowledge the research assistance of Liana Shapiro and Judy Thommesen as well as the feedback and helpful comments by Jonathan Newman, Joseph Salerno and participants of the Free Trade session at the Austrian Economics Research Conference 2024.

M. Thornton (✉)
Ludwig von Mises Institute, 518 West Magnolia Avenue, Auburn, AL 36832-4501, USA
e-mail: mthornton@mises.org

basis of his "social theory" and from this perspective, the history of human progress. Here, we draw on his writings to provide a pedagogical framework to illuminate two important contributions on the topic of trade.

The first contribution is his analysis of the role of trade in the very long-term development of human progress. Here, human development is in terms of the emergence and advancement of social institutions such as property rights, language, letters and numbers, transportation, money, and culture. These developments are driven by trade, but as they occur, they also facilitate both a greater volume and more complex forms of trade, with the result being human progress, as indicated by living standards, life expectancy, and population.

It would be easy to confuse human development with evolution, as both are complex and take time. However, evolution is biological and dependent on the environment, while development is a process driven by rational individual thought. Mises suggests that human development is specifically dependent on the ability to think conceptually about the mutual benefits from trade, broadly conceived, and new ways to improve and facilitate the trading process.

Mises's second contribution is depicted here as a short-run model of policy dynamics along the complete free trade-protectionism spectrum, again, broadly considered. The model described here is labeled the Bilateral Political Feedback Mechanism (BPFM). This mechanism connects domestic economic policy, international trade policy, and foreign policy. The connections are established by policy reaction functions from economic policy analysis and well-known political interaction processes from public choice theory. Disregarding these dynamics and compartmentalization of the three types of policy, *periculo tuo*, guarantees a self-defeating policy dynamic. This short-run model drives the direction and rate of change in the long run model, at the margin.

Social Theory and the History of Human Progress

Mises is famous for many contributions in such areas as monetary economics and the theory of socialism. However, he is perhaps *infamous* for at least two methodological contributions: the method of *praxeology* and his clear demarcation between theory and history. These contributions are foundational for understanding Mises's social theory and the development and progress of humanity.

Praxeology begins with the axiom that individuals engage in deliberate acts to achieve their goals. It proceeds with the logical deductions and obvious implications of the axiom. Action directed at goals implies the use of resources. Given that these means are scarce relative to goals, this implies that the individual must place a relative *value* on each end to make choices and act.

Individuals can conceive of technology that employing resources in certain ways will lead to the attainment of desired outcomes. Reasoning, the characteristic feature that differentiates man from plants and animals, is used to formulate such technologies, to evaluate them, and to act.

Mises's praxeology extends this methodological approach from the economic to the study of non-economic human activity, so that it can be applied to a wide scope of human activity. For example, Thornton (2004) demonstrated that we should expect the same type of results as markets in non-market academic research production if all activities are governed by voluntary exchanges based on private property rights, even when such production is devoid of a "market test." This suggests that we can generalize the results of all human activity that is voluntary and based on private property rights. This would include all market and social activities, which are based on trade, broadly considered, but would exclude coercion of various types.

Mises's understanding of history is simply that the historian who gathers and arranges the various facts of the past, must employ some theory of human action. This theory, loosely conceived, is essential for collecting from the totality of facts and for the arrangement of those facts from among the limitless possible variations. While there is some good agreement on the facts to be collected (from the residual facts), the arrangement and therefore the interpretation of the facts involves the historian's scope of topic, period, and especially the historian's purpose and ideology.

This is where the arrangement of facts and therefore the "interpretation" of the facts can be naturally led astray. For example, the eradication of a disease is often linked in "history" to a "hero," such as the discoverer of a medicine or vaccine, a policy intervention, or a technological advance. In fact, the eradication might have been more correctly described as the result of the tedious progress of material conditions, such as improved diet, increased leisure time, and improved living and sanitary conditions, and the intricate development of the capital structure and knowledge base. All these improved capacities are made possible by trade over time, and without such improvements there would be no hero to emerge. In this manner, the earnest and capable historian might present history at odds with what Mises was suggesting.

To summarize: Mises's view is that history involves interpretation, not *just* the facts. He starts with the common trait of reasonable rationality shared by humans globally and historically, as described below. This sets the tightest boundaries on the range of possible historical interpretations. Mises (1949, p. 859) thought that good historical knowledge was indispensable for those who wanted to make the world a better place to live, but that "history speaks only to those people who know how to interpret it."

Mises's "social theory" provides an interpretation of history. It is a generalized and a longer form of history that is distilled based on the roles of trade and the division of labor on human development and progress. Mises is hardly unique in emphasizing the importance of trade and comparative advantage. For example, for a much more detailed analysis of the role of trade, and the subsequent specialization and division of labor on human development, see Rothbard (1971 [2000]).

In the first chapter of the *Wealth of Nations*, Smith (1776) highlighted the latter in the pin factory example, but without suggesting who had divided the labor in the first place or why they did so. Smith also demoted the role of the former with the more Darwinian phrase; "propensity to truck, barter, and exchange," which implies a genetic trait or tendency, rather than a rational individual choice and profit driven entrepreneurial actions. In so doing, Smith left only the *suggestion* that rational behavior was responsible for the phenomenon.

Mises is not suggesting a new, more robust, or extreme form of rationality, or even what Hayek called "constructivist rationalism." In the simplest terms, Mises rejects the top-down leadership approach to human progress. His bottom-up approach based on individual rational action is a pervasive and persistent force that explains the extremely fast pace of human progress since the dawn of trade, as described here.

At some point in more recent pre-historical times, humans began to transition away from an animalistic, clan-centered existence. This existence was based on hunting, gathering, and warlike clashes between wandering groups. The transition was obviously haphazard, but was in the direction of sedentary agriculture, animal husbandry, and larger groups. A larger, more stationary clan-group would suggest the development of property rights, enhancements to the specialization and division of labor, and intraclan trade.

The success of this approach would suggest rational replication, clan merging and clustering, and thus the stimulation of dispute adjudication processes. Contact would further suggest inter-settlement trade and production based on comparative advantage between settlement locations. We can further imagine that all these processes would stimulate the development of language, rules of behavior, the use of symbols and numbers, money, transport, storage devices, etc.

Figure 1 depicts the progress of human development over time and is for illustration, not descriptive purposes. The important point is that trade induces developments, and each development necessarily promotes a greater potential for trade and human progress. Each new development, as labeled in the figure, is then subject to on-going improvements over time. The entire trade and development process is the result of pursuing rational self-interest. Even under relatively primitive conditions, it is still descriptive of the concept of human society.

Professor Salerno (1990) has shown that in terms of "social theory" Mises was, uniquely, a rationalist. Here, the purposeful and rational human framework of individual choices generates beneficial social results and even the development of social institutions. These may appear evolutionary or haphazard, but they occur in a cauldron of a multiplicity of individual actions, interactions, and a dependable and self-regulating process of profit and loss.

Here, institutions that make up the "social fabric," including property rights and the understanding of trading rules, are the foundation of society.

Human Progress Over Time:
The Impact of Trade

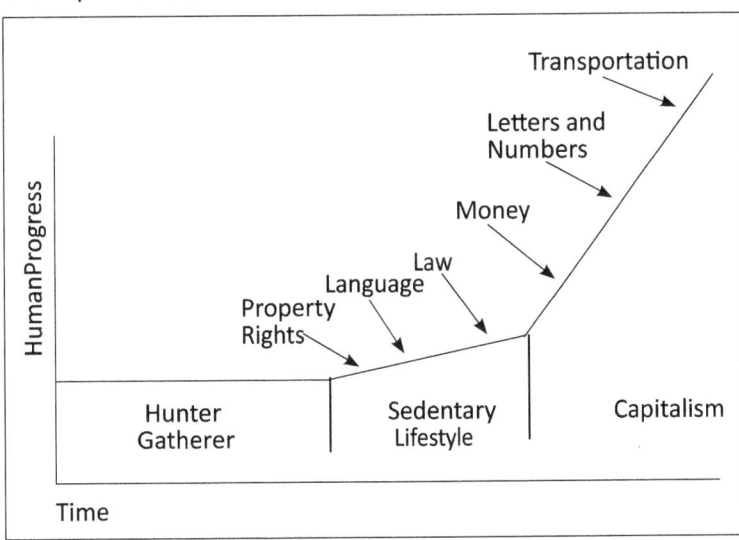

Fig. 1 Human progress over time: the impact of trade

They are not the result of a mythical "social contract," an undesigned spontaneous order, or a democratic vote, but comes from the "bottom-up" social process. Salerno (p. 26) concludes that:

> Mises's argument that law, normative rules of conduct, and social institutions are at one and the same time the product of a long evolutionary process and the outcome of attempts by individual human beings to rationally and purposively adjust their behavior to the requirements of social cooperation under division of labor.

Indeed, to highlight his perspective, Mises viewed *Laissez Faire* as a mere slogan and the "market process" as a metaphor. Market activity is neither soulless, unconscious, mechanical, nor automatic, but is based on plan*s* of many interacting individuals, each with their own ends, resources, information, and incentives. The forces of supply and demand do consistently bring about harmonious results, but that does not make it correct to say the market is automatic, mechanical, robotic, or non-human.

Mises flipped this *academic perspective* of the market upside down. His description of the market is like a living organism but consists of a multitude of individuals, each with their own plans and independent activities.[1] The academic perspective views government decision-makers as enlightened planners, with personality, empathy, if not superpowers, who are always working hard for the greater public purpose, whereas the market is a soulless, unthinking, uncaring, automaton. Mises (1944) turns this notion of good government on its head and pinned it down to the real-world necessities of political system rules, bureaucratic "red tape," and budget constraints. Here, the government is not some enlightened, problem-solving guardian angel, but simply a needed objective functionary to adjudicate disputes between individuals.

Mises's view of government is that of a symbiotic relationship where government draws out resources from the economy to carry out its assigned functions. From this perspective, government has no independent purpose, but Mises recognized the potential danger of government becoming independent and parasitic and thereby a threat to its host. This is addressed in the next section, but to quote Mises (1949 [1998], p. 726, emphasis in the *original*):

---

[1] Similarly, before the word "economy" came into use, proto-Austrian economist Richard Cantillon (1730 [1755]) deployed the word "circulation" for the construct; where individuals, resources, goods, and money circulated. This terminology was no doubt influenced by the discovery of the circulatory theory of blood by William Harvey one hundred years earlier.

The issue is not *automatism versus conscious action*; it is *autonomous action of each individual* [in the market] *versus the exclusive action of the government*. It is *freedom versus government omnipotence*.

Given the long history of pompous government officials and policy debacles and in contrast to the rather consistent harmonious results found in the marketplace, we can understand Mises's perspective and his rationale for highlighting those phrases in the quote. However, it is critical to note that Mises can abstract away this aberrant behavior from his social theory and the linkage between trade and human development and progress. We will see in the next section that this aberrant behavior is what drives the Bilateral Policy Feedback Mechanism in the destructive direction.

Mises hardly stands alone with his social theory. In fact, Professor Dorobăt (2015a) found an important precursor to Mises's rationalist social theory in Destutt de Tracy's *Treatise on Political Economy* (1817), the classic treatment of social rationalism, of which Mises's *Human Action* is the deepest modern presentation. The parallels between Mises and de Tracy extend from the nature and cause of the benefits of trade, to the policies that undermine and destroy it, and the resulting catastrophic consequences. Dorobăt summarizes her analysis thusly:

> Notwithstanding these benefits of social cooperation, both De Tracy and Mises acknowledge with regret that men have many times in history tried to hamper its development through numerous economic and military conflicts.... At the same time, both Mises and De Tracy reveal that the progressive intensification of division of labor and international cooperation remain the surest ways to offset these anti-social initiatives. (p. 450)

Once fully described and understood, Mises's social theory provides an understanding of the history of human development and progress. It seems to be like the theory of evolution of plants and animals, but instead of adaptation to external conditions, human development is endogenous with little physical change, but with monumental changes in mental technologies. The resulting "social institutions," such as law, language, and money represent human development. These are uniquely human and drive forward human progress.

The Bilateral Policy Feedback Mechanism (BPFM)

This model depicts the relationship between the two policy endpoints of the Full Free Trade Doctrine on the one hand, and Total War on the other. The policy dynamics of the model depend on the relationship between domestic economic policy, international trade policy, and foreign policy.

Policy at any one level has well-known effects and causal political connections to the other levels suggesting that "rational" policy should consider the implications of policy at one level on the other levels. Most notably, enacting substantive domestic intervention in the economy can create incentives and political pressure for protectionist policies, which in turn can produce antagonistic foreign policy.

Table 1 shows the Full Free Trade Doctrine (FFTD) on the left designating that free trade is the guiding principle of policy at all three levels. This would include policies conducive to peace between countries, free trade between countries, and a domestic free market economy. This policy doctrine widens the scope of trade and interaction globally and domestically. It maximizes trade and human progress and is the most fertile ground for social development. This position puts the greatest possible upward momentum on the trend growth of progress in Fig. 1, especially if domestic policy is reciprocated by other States.

Policy movements away from the FFTD toward government control and belligerence can begin at any level, but generally start with domestic policies of government intervention. Such policies create belligerence at home, typically by creating a higher price for a product, industry, or resources, such as a particular type of labor. It typically also involves some restriction in output and higher prices for consumers. This government intervention generates an artificial rent or profit for protected groups and harms others domestically.

Table 1 Bilateral policy feedback mechanism (BPFM)

	Full free trade doctrine (free market, free trade and political neutrality)	War (absence of free trade doctrine)
Domestic policies	No regulations	Full regulations
	No union	All labor ionized
	No monopolies	Supported monopolies
Border policies	No protectionism	Legal protectionism
Foriegn policies	No trading blocs	Active trading blocs
	No trade sanctions	Full trade sanctions
	No trade wars	Constant trade wars
	Free and peaceful relations	Total war

As is well known, this will stimulate the purchase of cheaper foreign produced goods as consumers try to protect themselves against higher domestic prices. The political response is to compensate the losers with their own protections, but that only broadens and intensifies the negative economic effects. The primary response is a new form of protection from foreign competition at the border, with tariffs, quotas, and import prohibitions. Such protectionism then creates substantive foreign policy if, as might be expected, other countries reciprocate. In the BPFM, this can ultimately result in war in Table 1.

International protectionism creates foreign policy, diminished trade, and puts downward momentum pressure on the trend growth of trade and human progress. War virtually stops international trade between combatants, increases inefficient domestic production, and puts sharp downward pressure on human development and the trend growth of human progress. In the limit, it displaces human society, collapses human development, and can reverse human progress, if not (in the age of nuclear weapons) extinguish humanity.

The individual components of the model and the political processes or pressures that connect them are well known to economists, policy experts, and even those well acquainted with market activity and government intervention, such as entrepreneurs. Therefore, our concentration here will be on highlighting important aspects of Mises's thought that are most relevant for understanding the mechanisms that motivate and drive the model, rather than the plethora of policies involved and all their expected outcomes and dynamic pathways.

Protectionism is Restrictionism

According to Mises, in terms of understanding the basic implications of the FFTD and the BPFM model, all protectionism is restrictionism and all restrictionism is contrary to the FFTD. Restrictionism reduces production and therefore consumption for all. The artificial "windfall" profits given to protected groups are dissipated by rent seeking competition in the long run. However, such irrational and inefficient policies remain long after their initial purpose because of political inertia. This political inertia is partially explained by the political and economic pathways between the three levels of policy and partially by ideological lethargy.

Therefore, the belief that protectionism stimulates production is an illusion; protectionism necessarily reduces production, trade, and consumption. As Mises (1949, p. 736) explained, any interference with production, including protectionist policies had a clear outcome:

> The effect of its interference is that people are prevented from using their knowledge and abilities, their labor, and their material means of production in the way in which they would earn the highest returns and satisfy their needs as much as possible. Such interference makes people poorer and less satisfied.

Protectionism is just a subset of government interference, as it is simply interference at the border. In fact, to highlight this point, Mises notes that the best proof of the general thesis against government interference is the case of protectionism on the international level. For Mises and most every economist worth their salt, the classical economists in general and David Ricardo, in particular, settled this issue once and forever. Protectionism or "mercantilism" was an irrational economic policy while trade based on comparative advantage was mutually beneficial.

Mises's bottom-up approach warns against all government intervention into the free market economy, not just for their direct deleterious effects, but also because of the potential for those adverse consequences to create political momentum for further government interventions and for protectionist measures at the border as a supposed cure. Ever the pragmatist, Mises would have been open to protectionism if it was a rational policy, and he suggested that alternative policies could be used to achieve the same public purposes without restricting trade.

The Creation of Foreign Policy

A necessary condition for long run stability of a nation's free trade policy is the necessity of eliminating the potential for any belligerence resulting from foreign policy, to eliminate nationalist sentiment in policy making, and most especially for policy to abstain from any colonialist and imperialist objectives, or even well-meaning objectives to help foreign people. These types of impulses create pathways that eventually lead to war and the destruction of all the benefits of free trade.

Protectionism at the border and the likely countermeasures by other nations is what establishes a significant role for foreign policy and foreign policy opens the possibility of trade wars, economic sanctions, and war itself: the ultimate form of destruction. Given that the Full Free Trade Doctrine (political neutrality, free trade, and a free market economy) can be adopted as policy at any time, there is no rationale for foreign policy as it has come to be known.

Ludwig von Mises's closest student, Murray Rothbard (1981), reminds us that Mises was a radical liberal in terms of policies that relate to free trade. Mises's attacks on European colonialism and imperialism reveal the extent of his radicalism. He noted that Europeans worried about the aftermath of colonialism and imperialism, but mostly because of the military technology and ideological blunders that the Europeans had themselves introduced into their former possessions. Mises opposed colonialism and imperialism in principle because it was just other words for conflict, war, and the oppression of other people.

The most extreme example of Mises's radicalism relates to Bolshevism and the Soviet Union. He opposed efforts to prevent communist infiltration and propaganda or to prevent others from interacting with the Russians or prevent Russians from doing what they wanted in their country and the satellite nations. His only major stipulation was to abstain from subsidizing the communists, which the United States did, *ut plurimum quantum*. In fact, Dempster et al. (2023) show that only the various forms of intervention by the Allies in WWI can explain Lenin's highly unlikely rise to power and the Communist conquest of Russia.

Free Trade Organizations and Trading Blocs

There is also no significant reason to engage in trade negotiations because a nation establishes its own independent trade policy that maximizes its self-interest. Dorobăt (2015b) shows that Mises demonstrated that for a nation to achieve free trade it must align its domestic economic policy with pure free market principles. Anything less than a dedication to domestic free market policies would guarantee a destructive foreign and trade policy and open the potential for international conflict. International organizations, like the World Trade Organization (WTO), are merely extensions of domestic policy, and so, they are in fact nearly powerless to achieve free trade when domestic policies are belligerent, i.e., anti-free market, and they are completely unnecessary when a country adopts free market domestic policies.

Despite some victories, the failure of the WTO to achieve full free trade is testament to this view. Trading blocs are also just another manifestation of belligerent policies, and this would include NAFTA, the European Union, and the Trans-Pacific Partnership. Such organizations are dangerous in that they are much more conducive to starting trade wars than they are in establishing free trade policy and indeed have the potential to escalate the scope of conflict.

Mises is clearly thinking global which objective analysis requires to meet scientific standards, at least as a first step. He goes on to note that to achieve rational policy, in the form of the FFTD, it must be remembered that the economic problem is not a material or technological problem, but an ideological one. Success will require "intellectual, spiritual, and moral" renewal. A rationally oriented nation can pursue an independent FFTD policy and maximize its national product, but that misses Mises's larger point. The goal for Mises is global free trade, maximizing the progress of human society and the elimination of conflict and war, and in so doing, driving the role of the State down to an absolute, insignificant minimum.

The spiritual component is not described in detail, but it no doubt involves the individual thinking like a member of the entire group where each is interested in the survival, continuity, and potential of the species. From the current decrepit and degenerate state of political thinking and social ideology (driven by nationalistic ideology), it does seem that only a global spiritual renewal movement could achieve this type of progress.

Friends of Free Trade

Mises follows in the past of the primary historical advocates of free trade policy. Claude-Frédéric Bastiat (1801–1850) was a prominent leader of the French Liberal School of economics and one of the most effective essayists arguing for free trade policy. Bastiat's parable of the negative railroad, for example, unmasked by satire the realities of protectionist trade policies as irrational and conflict maximizing.

Here a stop along the border required disembarking and conveyance of passengers and freight creating jobs for hotels, warehouses, and porters of all sorts. Bastiat (1845) argued that if such a break in the railroad created jobs and helped the local economy, that perhaps the railroad could be broken at regular intervals, so that hotels and warehouses could be set up all along the way. Readers will no doubt realize that the artificial jobs at the border and the potential jobs along the "broken" railway are losses, not gains to the domestic economy.

In a similar fashion, Mises makes the theoretical point that the distinction between domestic and foreign trade does not exist. He wrote: "there is no basis for seeking a fundamental difference between the effects of freedom in domestic trade and in foreign trade. If the mobility of capital and labor internally differs only in degree from their mobility between countries, then economic theory can also make no fundamental distinction between the two" (Mises 1983, p. 92). Mises, like Bastiat, was explicit that free trade policy is a unilateral program and need not requires reciprocity to demonstrate its obvious economic advantages to any nation that pursues it.

The two great political campaigners for free trade of all-time were Richard Cobden (1804–1865) and John Bright (1811–1889). Both were British Radicals and Liberal politicians. In addition to free trade and liberal, i.e., free market policies in general, both were outspoken advocates for peace with other nations and they were against government intervention in the economy, including popular policies supposedly designed to help workers and the poor.

These two men are credited with the Repeal of the Corn Laws in 1846, the hallmark policy of the free trade tradition. The Corn Laws protected British and Irish farmers and kept grain prices and the cost of food high. Repeal meant a substantial and quick drop in food prices and resource movement that made the economy more efficient and productive, although Irish farm labor suffered terribly because of the falling grain prices.

The two also worked on another free trade proposal that resulted in the Cobden–Chevalier Treaty of 1860. Michel Chevalier (1806–79) was a French liberal economist who supported free trade. The resulting treaty was named after the two primary negotiators. The treaty ended a long period of war and protectionism between the two countries, greatly reduced tariffs and increased trade between the two empires and resulted in a lasting peace between them.

Summary and Conclusion

Working largely based on the analysis of Professors Salerno and Dorobăt, the writing of Ludwig von Mises on the topic of trade was examined. From this, two prominent theories that inform rational policy choice were extracted and illustrated. The first is that human progress, economic and otherwise, is highly dependent on human development broadly defined as the introduction and improvements in human institutions, such as language, law, and money. Mises's social theory is that society is based on trade and that human development is spurred on by trade.

The second contribution illustrated here is that domestic economic policy, international trade policy, and foreign policy are mutually dependent. That is, the stability of a nation's "free trade" policy is reliant on having a free market domestic economy and a non-interventionist foreign policy. Likewise, a highly interventionist domestic and foreign policy is supportive of a protectionist trade policy and all that follows from that. The combination of the two contributions helps rationalize policy choice.

If the goal of policy is human progress, then the Full Free Trade Doctrine should be adopted, entailing a free market economy, unilateral free trade policy, and a policy of neutrality with other nations. This policy maximizes human progress and development and is indicative of the citizenry's self-confidence and empathy toward their fellow man. If some different goal is to be pursued, such as nationalism, patriotism, or a personality cult, and various carrots and sticks are required to achieve that goal, then it will require, in turn, an interventionist domestic economy, a protectionist trade policy, and a belligerent foreign policy to reward supporters and harm and threaten non-supporters. This policy choice reduces human progress and development, and likely has much worse consequences, and is indicative of a social disorder or delusion.

References

Bastiat CF (1845) "Must free trade be reciprocal?" This article, originally titled "Reciprocity," is excerpted from The Bastiat Collection (2011); and it appeared originally in *Economic Sophisms*

Cantillon R (1730 [1755]) An essay on the nature of commerce in general

Dempster GM, Ekelund RB, Thornton M (2023) Understanding the timing and outcome of the Russian Revolution: a public choice approach. J Public Finance Public Choice. https://doi.org/10.1332/251569121X16827529522153

Dorobăt CE (2015a) Division of labor and society: the social rationalism of Mises and Destutt De Tracy. Q J Aust Econ 18(4, Winter):436–455

Dorobăt CE (2015b) 'Foreign policy and domestic policy are but one system': Mises on international organizations and the world trade organization. Independ Rev 19(3, Winter):357–378

Robitaille C (2019) Ludwig von Mises, sociology, and metatheory. Q J Aust Econ 22(2, Summer)

Rothbard MN (1971 [2000]) "Freedom, inequality, primitivism, and the division of labor," reprinted in *Egalitarianism as a Revolt Against Nature and other Essays*, Ludwig von Mises Institute

Rothbard MN (1976) Praxeology: the methodology of austrian economics. In: Dolan E (ed) The foundations of modern Austrian economics. New York University Press. https://mises.org/mises-daily/praxeology-methodology-austrian-economics

Rothbard MN (1981) The Laissez-Faire radical: a quest for the historical Mises. J Libert Stud 5(3):237–253

Sahlins M (1972) Stone age economics. Routledge, New York
Salerno JT (1990) Ludwig von Mises as a social rationalist. Rev Aust Econ 4:26–54. https://cdn.mises.org/Ludwig%20von%20Mises%20as%20Social%20Rationalist_0.pdf
Smith A (1976 [1759]) The theory of moral sentiments. Oxford University Press, New York
Smith A (1976 [1776]) An inquiry into the nature and causes of the wealth of nations. Oxford University Press, New York
Thornton M (2004) Does academic publishing pass a real market test? Public Choice 120(1& 2):41–61
Thornton M (2009) Cantillon and the invisible hand. Q J Aust Econ 12(2):27–46. https://cdn.mises.org/qjae12_2_3.pdf
von Mises L (1944) Bureaucracy
von Mises L (1949 [1998]) Human action: a treatise on economics. Yale University Press
von Mises L (2002) The ultimate foundation of economic science: an essay on method, 2nd edn. Foundation for Economic Education, Irvington-on-Hudson, NY, pp 68–69

The Viewpoints of Senior Policy-Makers

The International Trading System: A Practitioner's Perspective

Tim Groser

Introduction

This essay is indeed a trade policy practitioner's perspective—drawing on the author's five decades of professional work in the field as a trade negotiator, international facilitator and decision-maker as Minister of Trade. No attempt is made here to examine either the basic economic theory underlying free trade or to consider the vast supporting set of empirical studies that broadly validate that body of theory. For the purposes of this essay, it is sufficient to recall that titan of mid-twentieth century economics and Nobel Prize laureate, Paul Samuelson, when once asked to name the most powerful and non-trivial theory in economics, responded immediately—'Ricardo's theory of comparative advantage'.

Two hundred years on, a large minority, possibly even a majority, of politicians, media commentators and lobbyists have still not received Ricardo's memo about the benefits of 'free trade'. Their populist political successors never will receive that memo because it is counter-intuitive in terms of the politics they wish to preach. There will always be a huge political market for

---

The Hon Tim Groser has been New Zealand's Chief Trade Negotiator in the last successful multilateral Trade Round, the Uruguay Round, initiator of the first step of the TPP process with Singapore and chief negotiator, WTO Ambassador and Chairman of the DDA Agriculture Negotiations and Trade Minister 2008–15. He was Ambassador to the United States 2016–18.

T. Groser (✉)
Wellington, New Zealand
e-mail: tim.groser@gmail.com

'protecting local jobs' and railing against 'unfair trade'.[1] Practitioners like the author have to work with the political material we have, not what we might wish it to be. Right now, we are in retreat, mustering defensive strategies, while advancing where we can.

Changing Views on Trade

The 'International Trading System' (a simple working definition is provided below) has brought extraordinary benefits to people around the world over the last seventy-five years. It is now under enormous political stress. In the space of a few brief years, we seem to have leapt from a roughly two decade (1990–2010) period of 'hyper-globalisation' to an increasingly fragmented global political economy. There are other evocative adjectives that may point to a darker future—'friend-shoring' (the antithesis of the bedrock principle of non-discrimination[2] and 'de-globalisation' for example.

But the jury is still out on that. In every case, it will come down to the degree of 'friend-shoring' or 'de-globalisation'. All systems and decisions can tolerate exceptions and inconsistencies; some are even necessary. To use the metaphor of President Biden's National Security Adviser, Jake Sullivan, of course the rest of the world can live with a 'small yard and a high fence'[3]—but we are not yet sure what its final dimensions will be. At the moment, that includes as a 'threat to the security of the United States', minute amounts of imports into the US of NZ steel—100% owned by an Australian steel company (Bluescope) operating in New Zealand. This has gone on for five years since the author was Ambassador to the United States. By any measure, this is absurd.

The very concept of economic inter-dependence, seen until recently as a positive fact economically with the additional benefit of acting as a constraint[4] against conflict, is now seen in certain important quarters as a net

---

[1] The scope of what is labelled 'unfair trade' being constantly enlarged beyond the respectable guard-rails that have always existed in international trade agreements to deal with, for example, predatory pricing.

[2] Article I of the General Agreement on Tariffs and Trade (still the core of the WTO) is formally called 'the General Most Favoured Nation [MFN] Treatment'—the non-discrimination principle under-writing the entire multilateral trading system. In a perverse reversal of its common sense meaning, the 'most' favoured nation tariff rate applied to the imports of all WTO members, unless of course they are eligible for lower preferential rates through their membership of a preferential trading agreement such as the EU, USMCA or CPTPP.

[3] An area of the US economy 'fenced off' for security reasons from a pure efficiency-derived view of US economic interests.

[4] An area of the US economy 'fenced off' for security reasons from a pure efficiency-derived view of US economic interests.

negative, compromising a country's national security. And let it be said: for all people, over all time, security, if threatened, will always trump economics. The question is whether the anti-globalists are right with respect to the basic proposition that high economic inter-dependence has <u>undermined</u> countries' security.

The benefits of growing economic ties, inexorably linked with the political process of progressive trade liberalisation, are so well known, they should not need repeating once again. But when a broad political or economic idea of foundational importance such as 'democracy', 'freedom of speech' or 'free trade' is under attack—and each is under attack today in the (political) West— it is essential to repeat to today's generation what the existing system has helped achieve and thus what is at stake.

Of the many excellent summaries that one could draw on to make this point, the author chooses here that of Bradford DeLong—'*Slouching Towards Utopia: An Economic History of the Twentieth Century*'. His analysis includes massive global reduction in extreme poverty—down from approximately 70% in 1870 to less than 10% today.[5] Per capita prosperity has grown at least twenty times higher in real terms. Associated with this vast wealth creation process, almost all metrics one could use to measure 'social' progress have improved out of sight—extraordinary declines in infant mortality, spread of education, food security, better housing among them.

Of course, huge improvements in technology drove all of these positive developments. The 'slicing and dicing' of the production process and the consequent growth of global supply chains, and the extraordinary productivity gains from moving to container shipping are all explained by technology. But malignant politics can always hamper the uptake of benign technology. These changes could not have occurred on anything like the same positive scale without a generally more liberal trade and investment regime to facilitate the adoption of these technologies. The few countries that chose to stand outside this process of global economic integration such as North Korea are perfect laboratory tests of the alternative hypothesis of 'self-sufficiency'.

Consider the tired cliché of the 'progressives' in so many of our countries who are opposed to what we call for shorthand purposes 'globalisation'— namely 'a rising tide does not lift all boats'. The best riposte is that of a distinguished American trade expert, Alan Wolff, who observed that this is correct—a rising tide does not indeed lift all boats, but a stagnant swamp lifts none.[6]

---

[5] Compiled from his introductory chapter: 'My Grand Narrative'.
[6] Alan Wolff, Peterson Institute, 23 May 2023.

In the real world, no broad policy prescription—this applies way beyond the field of trade policy—can ever meet the test that it must work in all circumstances, for all people and for all time. Equally, the very successes of global progress enumerated above carry the seeds of new, more sophisticated problems. The challenge of climate change is the most obvious and important. The huge increase in global population—from around 1.6 billion in 1900 to some 8 billion today, and the increasing average life expectancy of humanity—has greatly increased global emissions. What conclusion should we draw from these data points: that these gargantuan demographic improvements are not improvements at all, but represent a net negative - that we would have been better off were fewer people alive 'enjoying' lower average life expectancy? This sounds like a death wish to the author. Looking forward to, say 2050. If India, Indonesia, Nigeria and others wish to aspire to a middle class standard of living (with the further increase in global emissions historically associated with that) that they should be denied that right?

The broad answer, in the best tradition of liberal thought, is obvious: we now need new policies, new technologies and new approaches to try to mitigate the problems created by these successes. Domestic policies need to be developed to try to help at least some of those 'boats' anchored to the bottom which did not 'rise up' with the tide of growing wealth. Internationally, we need to coordinate an unprecedented technological and investment strategy to counter the relentless growth of emissions without destroying food security and living standards in our societies which rely on intensive energy usage. Solutions, none of them perfect, exist, but this is not the focus here, which is to defend the generally open global trading system and analyse the growing threats to it.

The Open Trading System: A Brief Description

World trade does not take place within a single system of rules, but rather within a series of overlapping systems of extraordinary complexity. The epicentre is of course the price system—the hundreds of millions of prices of internationally available goods and services that buyers and sellers can use and compare. These prices are unified by various international currency clearing systems and a bewildering proliferation of institutions and 'rules' that greatly influence all international transactions. The system is constantly evolving but, at least until recently, in a generally stable way.

The institution at the heart of this is the WTO (World Trade Organisation). The creation of the WTO at the conclusion of the last successful 'round' of multilateral negotiations, the Uruguay Round, was a somewhat less dramatic step forward than might appear. The creation of the WTO in 1994 is better considered an important evolutionary step forward from the GATT.

The core of the WTO—metaphorically call it '80%' of the WTO—was and remains the existing GATT, or 'General Agreement on Tariffs and Trade'. This extraordinarily important exercise in international cooperation started life in 1947 (a survivor from the failed attempt to get the US Congress to endorse the ITO, or International Trade Organisation). Technically a 'Contract', the GATT was initially focussed on industrial trade and goods amongst developed economies. It evolved over eight series ('Rounds') of multilateral negotiations into something approaching a true international organisation. We have more to say on the WTO later.

A huge variety of technical and political institutions, all with overlapping membership, support the WTO system. There are some 140 separate institutions that have observer status to the WTO committees and bodies. They include the FAO (Food and Agriculture Organisation), WIPO (World Intellectual Property Organisation), the OECD, the IMF, the WCO (World Customs Organisation), the WHO (World Health Organisation), and many others beside. It is certainly a system of great complexity, but long-standing practitioners generally see far more coherence, than incoherence, in the way it works in practice. At the end of the day, these other institutions are all politically owned by (different) sub-sets of WTO Member economies.

The second 'level' of the international trading system is the numerous bilateral/plurilateral[7] trade agreements. They are often grouped under the (increasingly misleading) title of RTAs (regional trade agreements). Broadly, they provide more favourable treatment for trade between their members than would be the case if such trade were governed solely by the WTO system. According to the WTO, as at 1 August 2023, some 360 regional trade agreements were in force. Yet, and as elaborated below, these are all based on WTO Agreements—and not simply the technical provisions that permit such agreements.[8]

It should be acknowledged, however, that the word 'regional' is being increasingly stretched. The UK, the world's fifth largest economy, has just joined CPTPP (The Comprehensive and Progressive Agreement for Trans-Pacific Partnership). Last time we looked, the UK was not situated in the Pacific, the Asia Pacific or the Indo-Pacific by any geographic description.

---

[7] 'plurilateral' simply meaning more than two Members.
[8] Article XXIV in the GATT (goods), Article V in the GATS (services).

The importance of these RTAs varies enormously from the EU (an agreement that goes well beyond the original 'customs union' of the EEC[9]) and the USMCA (the North American agreement that replaced the original.

NAFTA and which unifies the trade regimes of the US, Mexico and Canada) through to barely relevant and often redundant bilateral agreements.[10]

The first thing to note—and this is widely ignored—is that this vast array of 'RTAs' complements and does not supplant the WTO. In most cases, many of the vital provisions of RTAs use the WTO frameworks as the basis of their rules systems. The EU, for example, has about 40 trade agreements with non-EU countries, the FTA with New Zealand being the most recent example as at time of writing. A good number of those 40 trade agreements have specific provisions dealing with, amongst other matters, the rules governing the imposition of anti-dumping duties.[11] Those provisions 'elaborate' anti-dumping procedures in often useful but finally marginal ways. Critically, the EU does not have a set of different rules, institutions or expert officials responsible for interpreting and applying anti-dumping for each individual trade agreement. The heart of the EU anti-dumping system is a system designed to be consistent with the relevant WTO agreement[12] and jurisprudence developed over decades in GATT and WTO dispute settlement decisions on anti-dumping measures, as indeed it should be. All the anti-dumping agreements contained in the EU's 40-odd RTAs derive from that.

This is not some minor or purely technical point. It underlines in yet another way the enormous significance of the WTO system to global trade. First, it should be borne in mind that there is no FTA (by any name) between the EU and the US. There is no FTA between the UK and the US. There is no FTA in goods between China and the EU, or between Japan (the world's third largest economy) and the US. The trillions of dollars invested in global supply chains and hundreds of millions of jobs bound up in these giant trade and investment relationships rests on the WTO system. Second, where important trading relationships are governed by additional rules and procedures of RTAs, those RTAs simply would not function in a practical way without the

---

[9] European Economic Community.
[10] There is, for example, a bilateral FTA between NZ and Malaysia—the author was Trade Minister when it was completed. This preceded the two countries' participation in TPP and then CPTPP. If it exists in a strict legal system, no practitioner of today is even aware of its existence. It has been superseded by CPTPP.
[11] Anti-dumping duties are intended to counter predatory pricing, usually called 'unfair' trade in popular political debate.
[12] Formally, the 'Agreement on Implementation of Article VI of the General Agreement on Tariffs and Trade 1994'—known by all practitioners as 'the Anti-Dumping Agreement'.

WTO-based frameworks contained in them. In that sense, the huge number of RTAs do not comprise an alternative 'system' for international trade—they supplement the multilateral system with deeper processes and usually lower tariff rates.

The most important political conclusion that can be drawn from this is also the most obvious. It may well be impossible, for reasons elaborated later, for the WTO to move forward to address the many problems of international trade in anything other than baby steps taken at a glacial pace.[13] But this is far from the most important matter facing the international trading system today. The key issue is to prevent further backward slippage into protectionism and fragmentation. By some large order of political magnitude, it is far more important to defend the '*acquis*' of the past than worry about the large difficulties of moving forward.

The Root of the Problem Facing the International Trading System

'It is political'—one might say rather casually but accurately. An equally predictable, and again accurate, statement would be to say that there is no one factor that can explain this rather rapid *volte-face* in moving from widespread acceptance of hyper-globalisation ('the end of history' in its most extreme form[14]) to advocacy of deliberate deglobalisation and 'de-coupling' economies from one another. In certain important political cultures, to be labelled a 'globalist' is both a term of abuse and worse—an accusation of being an extraordinarily naïve individual. The extraordinary thing about this evolution of opinion on trade is the speed with which the underlying political debate has moved.

---

[13] The signal 'achievement' of the last WTO Ministerial Meeting (MC12), to judge from the numerous commentaries on it, was the Agreement on Fisheries Subsidies; the other 'deliverables' were Declarations and Work Programs. The Fisheries Subsidies Agreement was an important and positive development but as Chair of the 'Rules Group', the author used to chair those negotiations in Geneva over 20 years ago and many key issues have been kicked forward beyond MC12 to future negotiations. The world is moving faster than this, leaving the WTO behind.

[14] See Fukuyama' highly influential books and articles of the mid 1990s describing the then apparent triumph of liberal democracy and the convergence of opinion in country after country on what seemed like a common economic and possibly political pathway. Much less extreme versions were widely accepted views that we were moving to a G2 world—a world where China and the US would establish key understandings on a few issues to allow the rest of the world to move forward. While not popular in the EU, this certainly seemed to explain the success of the Paris Agreement as recently as 2015. Its essential pre-cursor agreement was the agreement between President Obama and President Xi on an approach to climate change (the operational core of which was the hybrid NDC, or National Determined Contribution, applicable to all countries, but taking account of their individual circumstances) which was announced at the APEC Leaders Meeting in Beijing in 2014.

Most of the key factors are also linked. In an excellent study of Chinese economic policy conducted in 2019, clear evidence was presented to justify its title—'*The State Strikes Back: The End of Economic Reform in China?*'[15] While the economic evidence for this is known only to deep specialists, the public interested in international affairs is certainly generally aware of the companion concept of 'wolf warrior' foreign policy adopted by China's spokespersons around that time.

Yet was this a development <u>independent</u> of a sharp shift in Washington's attitude to China? The formalisation of President Trump's 'America First' policy was contained in the 2017 NSS (National Security Statement—the most important unclassified strategic document of the United States on security matters). This document, specifically accusing China (and Russia) of attempting to <u>erode</u> American security and prosperity,[16] stated explicitly that this required the United States to rethink policies of engagement policies of the past. It concluded that for the most part, the premise of engagement 'proved out to be false'.[17]

Unilateral tariff increases on selected imports from China then flowed quite logically from this very different strategic perspective. There has been no fundamental shift in US policy under the succeeding Democratic Administration and in some senses has been taken further, although the debate over 'de-coupling' or 'de-risking' from China is not a stable debate.

Other factors feed into this swift change undermining support for the multilateral system and freer trade. For example, the author shares the views of a minority of trade analysts who believe that some of the decisions taken at the transition from the GATT to the WTO represented gross over-reach by international negotiators. This would require a separate essay but briefly stated, it was, for example, beautiful in theory, but unwise in practice, to impose a legally binding 'two-court' process of global dispute settlement in place of the far more pragmatic GATT Article XXII/XXIII dispute settlement system that, in formal terms, simply 'recommended' to the losing party to a

---

[15] Professor Nicholas Lardy, Peterson Institute for International Economics—the author's favourite Washington think tank.

[16] Note that this is not an absolute, not a relative, accusation. Up until then, American intellectuals may generally have accepted that the 'rise of the others' (Japan, Germany, China et al.) would in time erode the relative importance of the United States in global terms, but this was an indirect consequence of the success of 'the others' and therefore not a fundamental problem. The accusation here in the NSS is different: that China has been seeking not just to enhance its own prosperity in a relative sense to the existing hegemonic power, but to make Americans poorer in absolute terms in some type of binary zero-sum game.

[17] These are the exact words from the 2017 NSS.

dispute that they bring their policies into conformity with the legal framework.[18] It might have been wise had the key negotiators of the DSU reflected more closely on an old moral principle—'beware of trying to do too much good'.

The concept of a 'Supreme Court' for the global trading system got rather ahead of itself[19] and the real politics behind national sovereignty. Legal idealists would of course strongly disagree with this, even though the system they designed is today completely non-operational.[20] Not having a functioning legislative, nor any executive branch, left an unchecked judiciary which blundered into its own destruction—with the best of intentions and elegant high-level justifications, of course.

The Central Role of the United States

At the heart of these negative developments lies domestic political change in the world's most important country, the United States. Far from this being an attack on the US, this is rather an acknowledgement of how much we owe to the United States for its extraordinary leadership in the post-war era. Arguably, that leadership represented the most benign dictatorship that any hegemonic power had previously shown over millennia.

The cynics who dismiss this as an exercise in self-interest by the United States are missing the point. Most certainly the post-war liberal system governing world trade was in the far sighted interests of the United States, provided those 'self-interests' are defined correctly and not in narrow and

---

[18] As the great American legal expert and trade theorist, Robert Hudec argued in many publications, no legal system can be designed that is, in practice, immune from what he called 'legal failure'. The actual 'failure' rate of the old GATT Dispute Settlement system was, by this standard, a relative but not complete success. Did it really need 'fixing' with such a rigid 'solution'? The old cliché 'if it ain't broke, it don't need fixing' might just have applied.

[19] Technically, this statement is incorrect. Article IX.2 of the Marrakesh Agreement indicates that authoritative interpretations of WTO Agreements is exclusively the responsibility of the WTO Membership. The membership has never exercised that over-weening responsibility, and it has been obvious from the start that it would never would or ever could politically. An elaborate chain of command linking the Panels, the Appellate Body, the DSU (Dispute Settlement Understanding) and the DSB (Dispute Settlement Body) was established. Whatever the textbook theory of legal scholars may have been, the magisterial decisions of certain Appellate Body findings left too little room for political flexibility.

[20] No appointments to the Appellate Body are possible in the current impasse; WTO Members losing the initial case are 'appealing into the void'. Under EU and Canadian leadership, a compromise of sorts exists for participants, but this is light years from the central, binding system envisaged by the authors of the new Dispute Settlement system. There is a complicated negotiating history behind this, involving huge pressure to remove US unilateralism (S.301 of the Trade Act 1974) and this was part of the deal. This cannot be summarised adequately in this brief essay.

short-term political terms. Equally, instead of that system imposing a punitive peace on the defeated Axis powers, it permitted the economic recovery of Japan and Germany and, with respect to Continental Europe, sacrificed immediate and important US agriculture export interests to help consolidate cooperation via the original Common Agriculture Policy—a policy vital politically to the formation of the then EEC. The inherent discrimination in the European integration process was tolerated by the United States (the only country with the power that could have stopped it) because it was part of the process of rebuilding Europe and reaching for peace. That, it could be said, is a rather grander vision than worrying about compromising 'free trade'.

This wider American perspective, forged by a deeper understanding by the then American decision-makers of the fundamental strategic interests of the American people, was probably never understood in Peoria or the swing States of the Electoral College system. Advocating such a perspective in today's US domestic political consensus would be to run the grave risk of being labelled a 'globalist'.

In 2018, Robert Kagan, an important American public intellectual, published a brief book with the prescient title '*The Jungle Grows Back: America and Our Imperiled World*'. In this essay, Kagan stated:

> Less than 80 years ago, liberalism outside a few centres of power, was on its death bed…The dramatic change of course after 1945 was not due to some sudden triumph of our better angels or embrace of Enlightenment principles that had been around for centuries. Nor was it the natural unfolding of Universal History in the direction of liberalism. Liberal ideas triumphed because for the first time, they had power behind them: the United States.

Kagan also makes the point that there is (historically speaking) nothing remotely original about the slogan 'America First'—numerous American leaders back to President Harding a century ago used precisely the same slogan. What was different in the post-war era was that the American political system decided collectively that deep global involvement was necessary to preserve American interests. As Kagan concluded: '*That was never the American view before the Cold War, and it is not the view today*'.[21]

Switching to the present and the unmistakable signs of weakness in the pro-trade coalition inside the United States, however uncomfortable it may be for those committed to 'free trade',[22] and the institutions that support

---

[21] Hudec, op cit, p. 14.

[22] The author considers that no rational person should support a literal concept of 'free trade'. After all, Adam Smith himself said: '*People of the same trade seldom meet together, even for merriment and*

it, it is essential to understand that President Trump did not create 'protectionism'. The problem today has deep historical roots, beyond the scope of this brief essay.[23] Rather, President Trump gave voice to its modern manifestation and was arguably carried into office, against all but one pollster predictions in 2016, by deep public concern over trade in those few States whose Electoral College Votes cannot be counted with predictive confidence months in advance of the actual Presidential Election.

The global community should have seen this more clearly many years previously—in 1999 at the celebrated 'Battle at Seattle'. This was the WTO Ministerial Meeting that was meant to launch 'The Seattle Round' of multilateral trade negotiations.[24] It was a catastrophic failure. One would have to wait until 2009 and the Copenhagen Climate Change Summit to see a similar diplomatic fiasco with the same underlying cause: gross wishful thinking on the part of those primarily responsible for the strategy married to a deep commitment to the 'too big to fail' concept (i.e. gather enough important people together at an international meeting and the fear of failure will drive them to a consensus). This is a political theory that has been tested successfully to destruction many times but somehow lives on to fight another losing battle.

The anti-trade coalition present in Seattle to stop the WTO in its tracks was an extraordinary array of dissidents ranging from the lunatic left (there was a group entitled 'Grannies against Globalisation') and anarchist groups attacking Starbucks, through to organisations on the far populist right (the deeply conservative former Presidential candidate Pat Buchanan was there). There were various religious groups with unfathomable concerns about the WTO. In the political middle, there were a series of respectable NGOs with various environmental and other concerns along with the American Trade Union movement (AFL-CIO).

The author, together with the former Prime Minister of New Zealand and then Ambassador to the United States (James Bolger) went down to the street demonstration to talk to some Longshoremen protesting against trade (sic). We asked them what they did for a living—pretending to them that we were

---

diversion, but the conversation ends in a conspiracy against the public, or some contrivance to raise prices'. 'Free Trade' should best be considered 'a worthy direction of travel' and needs many well-designed political and legal guard-rails to qualify it.

[23] Consult, for example, the magisterial history of Professor Doug Irwin on US Trade Policy: '*Clashing over Commerce: a History of US Trade Policy*'. One quote from the Introduction makes the point— '...trade policy has been the source of bitter political conflict throughout American history' (p. 1).

[24] The negotiating roots of this are not central to the purposes of this essay but pertain to the 'Continuation Clause' of the Uruguay Round and the need to build on the progress achieved only five years earlier.

Australians (as generations of New Zealand men have done when in dodgy situations beyond our shores) and, as 'Australians',[25] we claimed we did not understand what Longshoremen did for a living. They patiently explained to these cretins from 'Down Under', that American Longshoremen were part of the US import and export economy. We left them with the obvious retort—'so you're against international trade then?'.

The WTO limped on politically through this large setback and eventually a consensus to launch a new Round of multilateral negotiations was reached in Doha in 2001. Unfortunately, it relied on a terrorist massacre of over 3,000 Americans and other nationals on September 11 to propel delegates a matter of days later in Doha to come together as a demonstration of effective international solidarity in the face of this outrage targeted at the United States. To help paper over many cracks on matters of substance, the Round was linguistically, and thus politically, re-shaped. It was not a 'Round' in the traditional negotiating sense, but an 'Agenda' and it would be focussed not on liberalisation but 'development'. Words matter.[26] This was a hostage to fortune—probably a necessary one to get the negotiations launched, but it had its negative consequences of implicitly drawing a false distinction between 'development' and trade liberalisation.

Only a year later, the Doha Development Agenda, as it was called, crashed, but did not yet burn, in Cancun at the 5th WTO Ministerial Conference. As always, while there were numerous problems in a variety of different dossiers that would have needed to move forward,[27] the proximate cause of failure was an impasse over agriculture. Some important advances were made here and there following the collapse of negotiations in Cancun in 2003 but insufficient to produce a comprehensive result and thus conclusion to the negotiations. In international politics, it is always exceedingly difficult to procure a Certificate of Death either for failed negotiations or for international institutions or 'groups' that have clearly lost their raison d'être decades

---

[25] Australians and New Zealanders, surely the citizens of the two independent countries that most closely resemble each other, have a long history of dark humour about each other. A typical trans-Tasman joke is 'what do you call an Australian in a suit? Answer: 'The Defendant'. Clearly, the butt of these highly flexible jokes can be reversed in terms of rules of origin.

[26] The IPEF (Indo Pacific Economic **Framework**) is a classic example. In an Op Ed published in the Wall St Journal a few weeks before the US authorities announced IPEF, by a large coincidence the author had proposed an 'Indo-Pacific Economic **Agreement**'. What's in a word? Plenty. Agreement implied trade liberalisation commitments; Framework did not.

[27] The author had responsibility for a number of issues in his capacity as Chair of the Rules Group (subsidies, anti-dumping, RTAs) but none of those issues would have got in the way of an agreement had there been a consensus on an agriculture text. After the failure in Cancun, the author was invited to resign as Chair of the Rules Group and take over responsibility as Chair of the Agriculture negotiations. A text was finally agreed in July 2004 in Geneva entitled 'The Framework Agreement on Agriculture'.

ago. The US declared the talks were dead in 2015, but some vague echo of the agenda lives on in Geneva under the chairperson's (the Director General of the WTO) responsibility.

The Bicycle Theory of International Trade Revisited

A cliché that was very popular in the late 1980s during the Uruguay Round, but which seems to have been forgotten, deserves to be resuscitated. It is the 'bicycle theory of international trade'. The theory posited that the international trading system was like a bicycle—it could not stand in one place for very long; sooner or later it would have to move forwards or risk slipping backwards.

Geneva is replete with many highly skilled trick cyclists who, to extend the analogy, are capable of making extraordinarily small adjustments of weight and rapid adjustments to the three levers at their disposal (the handlebars, pedals and wheels), and thus keep the enterprise pretty much standing still at the traffic lights—waiting for the lights to go green. But it was clear by, say, 2015–2018, with no sign of the WTO lights shifting to green/go, Geneva's trick cyclists were starting to show they were politically exhausted. Without any significant movement forward, the WTO bicycle has clearly started to slip backwards.

The most consequential of these backward steps relates to the WTO Dispute Settlement System. There are many different expressions, some rather poetic, of an old principle that without an operationally effective remedy, rights do not exist. The entire Dispute Settlement System of the WTO had been set up to 'strengthen' compliance with legal findings and thus, in theory, strengthen the force of the legal obligations of Members and the rights that flowed from those obligations to others expecting each individual WTO Member to act consistent with their obligations.

However, when legal theory is on a collision course with political facts on the ground over an issue that is of systemic importance, there should be no surprise as to which force will finally prevail over the other. Dissatisfaction with certain important Appellate Body findings started to increase in severity within the United States, the chief architect historically of the entire multilateral trading system. Those who do not understand that in international politics power matters and matters fundamentally will continue to make grave political mistakes. The Obama Administration took the decision in 2011 to block the re-appointment—somewhat ironically an American expert—of one of the seven member Appellate Body.[28]

The next illustration of pent-up frustration by the United States was a decision taken in 2016 to block the appointment of a new Member (this time, not an American). This was, one could say, a procedural nuclear missile launched at the system. For technical reasons, it has taken time to work its way through the system. But the practical reality is that the WTO no longer has a fully functioning dispute settlement system—at least in the form envisaged by the agreement establishing it (the Marrakesh Agreement).

This cannot be reduced to a simple morality tale: US—bad; everyone else—good. There are huge imbalances in the WTO system and far too many to be enumerated, let alone analysed, in this brief essay. What is clear, at least to the author, is there cannot be a lasting 'fix' to such a fundamental aspect of the WTO system without effectively addressing a whole range of issues that feed in politically to this issue.

Even those countries with the strongest possible interest in the primacy of the multilateral system have their own Plan B: RTAs (FTAs, 'Economic Partnership Agreements' and such like). It is not only nature that abhors a vacuum. With the WTO system moving forward with baby steps taken at a glacial pace, the incentive to use non-multilateral frameworks to make progress on pressing trade issues has only grown over time.

Is Plan B Evolving into Plan A? Case Study: CPTPP

We focus here on one of the most important: TPP, which, following the withdrawal of the United States, has evolved into CPTPP—the 'Comprehensive and Progressive Agreement for Trans-Pacific Partnership'. Its title may not be concise, but it has been carefully (and successfully) designed for political markets. Nobody other than a tiny number of officials, trade lawyers and a sprinkling of other academics has ever read a trade agreement[29]; titles convey political messaging and therefore matter. The addition of the words 'comprehensive and progressive' to the title, along with a few minor textual adjustments, helped some of the centre-left Governments, facing opposition

---

[28] Briefly, the Appellate Body can be thought of as a 'bench' (of 7 members), three of which are chosen to adjudicate on a review of the original 'panel' report, if so requested.

[29] Senator Milliken Chairman of the US Senate Finance Committee hearing on the GATT in 1951 famously said—'Anyone who reads GATT is likely to have his sanity impaired'. Senate Hearings p. 92.

within their stakeholders to trade liberalisation, move forward with TPP, cheap at the price.

The author has written elsewhere on the long historical negotiating history of TPP,[30] which was initiated by two small countries (Singapore and New Zealand) both sceptical that the proposed 'Seattle Round' would be launched—in spite of their strong record of support for the multilateral system. The key and more recent development was of course the withdrawal of the United States by President Trump, following clear signs of his Democratic Presidential rival, Senator Hilary Clinton, distancing herself and thus the Democrats from this US led initiative.

Among the many basic political conclusions that can be drawn from this withdrawal, it shows that the serious erosion of support within the United States for advancing open trade policies is not explained finally by problems within the WTO and the multilateral framework. That is part of the problem but by no means explains its dimensions. The problem is more fundamental than that. It reflects a loss of confidence on the part of the most politically important advocate of open trade with open trade policies. There now seems a strong bipartisan position within the US Congress for rejecting <u>any</u> form of advancing the frontier of trade liberalisation.[31] This matters because of the unique role of the United States historically in designing and protecting the liberal rules based system—refer again to the perceptive earlier quotation of Kagan on the importance of power.

Many excellent analyses can be found from high-powered academic works[32] through to many general but high-quality analyses in the pages of the Economist, Financial Times, Wall St Journal and other responsible publications. Among the (linked) factors that seem to explain the loss of support are numerous metrics that show the 'end of the American dream'—often defined as the idea that if you worked hard and played by the rules you would end up better off and more financially secure than your parents. There are dramatic data points showing the decline of manufacturing as a share of US non-farm employment. Economists can show conclusively that this is a global, not a US phenomenon: the share of <u>global</u> manufacturing activity to global GDP (more accurately, 'Global Value Added') declined from 27% in 1970 to

---

[30] Review of World Trade, Cambridge University Press (forthcoming).
[31] The apparent retreat in the 'Trade Pillar' of the US response to TPP—the IPEF (Indo-Pacific Economic Framework) is yet another signal to this effect.
[32] See for example the recent paper by Subramanian, Kessler and Properzi 'Trade hyperglobalization is dead. Long live……?, Peterson Institute, November 2023.

about 9% in 2009, after which it plateaued[33]; we are witnessing here productivity and technology effects, not the demise of manufacturing globally. This, after all, parallels the dramatic decline of employment in agriculture in every developed economy in an earlier period of global economic history.[34]

What is clear is that while the 'problem' does not exist in aggregate (the United States does not have 'an unemployment problem', at least in the last ten years), its political impact locally has been a very different matter. The so-called 'rust belt' of the United States is real, even if shoots of recovery are now being seen in many parts of it. Linked to the Electoral College voting system of the United States, the political impact of the decimation of industrial jobs in those few districts that are functionally relevant to the outcome of a Presidential Election, trade became a major and divisive issue, even if objectively it can be shown that technology was far more important.

China's Rise: Its Political Impact

This intersected with the extraordinary rise of China and the successful entry of China in 2001 into the WTO. Let us briefly analyse this question since it is central to the global outlook on trade, and arguably beyond trade to the broader geopolitical outlook.

First, the rise of China has been so well documented over the last 10–15 years[35] that there is no need to describe it here. However, to recall just one aspect of this remarkable process of wealth creation that lifted hundreds of millions of people out of grinding poverty in China itself, as recently as 2017, China ranked only 76th globally in terms of per capita income. If measured in purchasing power parity terms, China's per capita income was then still around 25% of US per capita income.[36]

In the field of trade, China simply exploded as the world leading exporter over a remarkably brief period. This was super-charged 'export-led growth'. This process of relative 'catch up' is hardly likely to stop here. And of course,

---

[33] Subramanian op cit.

[34] In 1920 in the US, there were three non-agriculture workers to every two people working in agriculture; half a century later this ratio was 22:1. This data point implies economic success, not economic or political failure, but one would have been foolish to try explaining that to past rural political populists who believed that 'real wealth' or 'real jobs' came only from the land. Nor is there anything 'American' about this political phenomenon—comparable examples abound in the political and economic history of European countries.

[35] Among the many early analyses that could be cited is the epic narrative by the British 'Marxist', Martin Jacques, with its catchy title—'When China Rules the World: The Rise of the Middle Kingdom and the End of the Western World', 2009.

[36] Lardy, *op cit*, p. 41.

there is every reason to believe the same painful political process to unfold with the world's largest country by population, these days—India. China was not a major 'problem' politically in the world trading system until it started to matter and pose a competitive threat to developed country economies. India is starting to matter too and has massive 'water in the tariff' to fall back on,[37] expect trouble in the future.

There is now a bipartisan consensus in the United States that it was a mistake to let China into the WTO. This is usually summarised politically as a mistake to 'open our market' to China and its unfair, state-dominated economy. This is, of course, a political mine-field of immense strategic importance and few people want to wander through a mine-field. However, this is not an option for those of us who seek to defend the generally open global trading system.

First fact most overlooked: the US did not 'open' its market to imports from China at all when, after 15 years of negotiation, China entered the WTO. Contrary to widespread belief, there was no liberalisation of US import barriers applied to imports of Chinese origin as a consequence of that decision. Broadly speaking, what changed (in terms of imports from China) was the security of China's access to the US market. For over 20 years, the US Congress had gone through an annual ritual of providing China with a waiver that allowed China to continue to enjoy the US MFN tariffs (i.e. what tariffs Japan, the EU and every other WTO Member who did not enjoy preferential access into the US paid[38]).

For this to be considered a major enabler of Chinese export growth, one would have to believe that the greater political security of WTO membership, removing the need for the annual ritual (which had never failed to produce the goods) was an important factor behind investment in the Chinese export machine. It probably had some effect along these lines, but it is hard to sustain an argument that it was a large factor. In considering the competitive pressure China put on certain American industries as its export machine moved to a higher gear, it is also important to keep in mind the crucial role of multinational companies, including massive American companies like Apple, play in the China export story. If one uses the more sophisticated concept of 'trade in value added', many of these 'Chinese' exports alleged to have 'hollowed out' American manufacturing, contained huge proportions

---

[37] For technicians, this is the difference between applied and bound MFN tariffs. It implies that India has vast scope to increase protection against competitive imports in a perfectly 'legal' way in terms of its WTO obligations. There are, of course, remedies, but it is not difficult to concoct an explosive trade cocktail out of these elements in, say, 10 years' time.
[38] Namely, the waiver of the 1974 Jackson-Vanik amendment which had intended to restrict the trade benefits the United States offered to Communist countries.

of American inputs which is changing as China develops more sophisticated technologies, of course.

In spite of a deep conviction that Chinese state controlled companies are the root of the competitive challenge to the United States and thus the centre of the political problem, all the evidence suggests something closer to the opposite. Chinese SOEs (state-owned companies) are generally mediocre exporters (because being state controlled, they are, almost by definition, hopeless allocators of capital and generally inefficient[39]). In 2020, they were responsible for around 10% of Chinese exports—something closer to 45% of Chinese exports were from foreign multinational companies, often American. This also helped middle class Americans (consumers) by keeping downward pressure on inflation.

What did of course change was the Chinese import regime. The entry of China into the WTO resulted in China accepting obligations to liberalise extensively its trade regime, opening up the vast and growing Chinese consumer market to imports from all Member countries of the WTO. Some WTO members, and the author's country was the first developed country to do so, then proceeded to negotiate comprehensive FTAs with China on the back of the strategic decision of the Chinese authorities to engage in trade liberalisation. The combination of increasingly liberal trade access, Chinese economic growth, and growing FDI flows into China produced the situation we have today: China is the largest export market for well over 100 countries in the world.

The debate over 'unfair' trading practices is a complex one to unpick. The first-order issue defines the field of 'unfair' practices. Does it include lower wages and lower statutory labour standards in poor countries compared with rich countries? In that case, although there are no operational WTO rules on the matter, did China some decades ago, by having low total factor productivity and therefore low wages, enjoy an 'unfair' advantage over countries with superior labour conditions, higher productivity and higher wages?[40] Whatever the answer may have been 15–20 years ago, the subsequent rapid rise of China's wages—a direct consequence of its economic successes—have vastly reduced its ability to expand exports on the basis of what is called by technicians 'low wage cost arbitrage'. There are numerous empirical studies that support this view—but all this is a little too sophisticated for the hustings.[41]

---

[39] In 2016, according to China's own Finance Ministry, more than 40% of state enterprises were losing money. Lardy, op cit, p. 55.
[40] Put aside the deeper problem with this view: the absurd implication that 'poor' countries can and should have the same 'high' wages and high standard first-world labour conditions as rich countries.
[41] For example, one study estimates that an upper bound of the number of US manufacturing jobs that were lost as a result of Chinese competition 1999-2015 were about two million (out of a

What does seem clear is that shortly after entering the WTO, China systematically engaged in what is called 'financial repression' and Central Bank sterilisation policies designed to keep its exchange rate undervalued. Huge surpluses were accumulated in the early years of the twenty-first century. What would have been expected if market forces had been allowed to operate—an appreciation of the RMB—did not occur. Unquestionably, this accentuated China's relative export competitiveness.

But again, the more sophisticated conclusion is that this is not a 'China story'. The asymmetry in global rules around structural current account deficits and surpluses has been debated ever since Harry Dexter White and John Maynard Keynes of the US and UK Treasuries negotiated the outlines of the post-war liberal global trade and payments system in the 1940s.[42] This is, in short, a systemic problem of the global system and is unlikely ever to be resolved through negotiation.

What is clear is that the problem of deliberate undervaluation of the Chinese currency relative to any basket of currencies disappeared some 10–15 years later. The IMF (the unquestioned global authority over the matter) formally concluded in 2015 'substantial real effective appreciation has brought the renminbi to a level that is no longer undervalued'.[43]

With respect to China's observance of WTO rules—the author is slowly trying to trace a pathway through this political mine-field—we have a similar problem. The actual record of compliance of China with formal WTO Dispute Settlement rulings is more than respectable. Before the WTO system blew up politically, one American (Republican) expert analysed the 12 WTO cases the United States pursued through the courts (there were other disputes settled through bilateral negotiations). He found that in all cases China had taken some action to comply with judicial findings they had lost. There is an ongoing argument amongst US trade lawyers about one or two of them but in no case did the US authorities use the legal remedy provided for failure to comply.[44]

---

workforce of about 150 m which 'churns' constantly). In terms of annual labour market churn (every year, more than 50 million Americans are looking for jobs, changing jobs and joining or leaving the US workforce), the author, Adam Posen, President of the Peterson Institute, concludes '...*this amounts to a sliver of the average churn of the US labor market*' ('America's Self-Defeating Economic Retreat', May/June 2021).

[42] See, for example, 'Sterling-Dollar Diplomacy in Current Perspective', Richard Gardner. Written in 1957, it remains a classic account of one of the world's most eventful negotiations. It did not, however, settle the issue of an asymmetrical adjustment system, albeit in those days for a system of fixed exchange rates until the collapse of the Bretton Woods system in the early 1970s. A more modern (2013) account is 'The Battle of Bretton Woods', Benn Steil.

[43] Lardy, op cit, p. 38.

[44] The Article 22 Suspension Process. See Philip Levy 'Was Letting China into the WTO a Mistake? Why There Were No Better Alternatives', Foreign Affairs, April 2018.

Again, this is all far too technical to impact on the broader political debate around a central issue of global politics. This is what happens when elites abandon the field of careful, measured analysis and leave it free for the populists to spread their anti-trade messages. What seems reasonably clear is that China has, at worst, a reasonably satisfactory record of conforming to international rules and norms where they exist. Where they do not exist, then Houston we do indeed have a problem. And as the international trading system continues to evolve in ways that the stasis in the WTO cannot match (its signal failure, for example, to lead the definition of global rules for digital trade) that problem can only increase in dimension and therefore political impact.

The Case for Optimism

The main long-term reason for optimism is based on decades of practical experience—open markets perform better than closed markets and those who opt for protectionist policies fall behind. However, to rely simply on rationality prevailing in the long term is a big call applied to any field of global or domestic politics.

Fortunately, there are well functioning coalitions of countries, including some very significant economies that are doing a great deal to uphold the generally open trading system. This includes the EU and the UK: there are no important differences post-Brexit between the two of them in working to uphold the WTO. Regionally, there are numerous RTAs linking countries who support the open trading system. Even without the United States, TPP (with the addition of its two adjectives, 'Comprehensive & Progressive', to help the Centre Left) is one of the most important. As noted previously, the entry of the UK has changed its character from a regional agreement to potentially an alternative sub-set of global trade rules. A whole range of countries are now applying to join and more expected to in the future. Most important is the application of China. It is quite possible that the EU and CPTPP Members may explore options to advance new rules and norms on emerging trade policy issues if the WTO remains stuck in the mud like the Russian motorised armed convoy outside Kyiv in 2021.

The WTO itself will not be able to move forward in a non-trivial way until the United States returns to Geneva in a real, committed sense—it is not enough for USTR to be the ghost at the table on the shores of Lac Leman. This is not going to happen any time soon. But that is not, as has been argued in this paper, the main issue. The main issue is for the WTO Membership, led by those economies in Europe, Latin America and the Asia Pacific, and hopefully with at least the tacit support of USTR in Geneva, to fight to preserve the '*acquis*' of the past successful 8 Rounds of multilateral trade negotiations since that is vital to their trading economies. It would be grossly pessimistic to expect a wholesale retreat from the pillars of the international trading system and we should expect to see continued creative 'work-arounds' developed for that end.

We come back, however, to the political central role of the United States. As at time of writing, the likely candidate of the Republican Party, a certain Donald J Trump, is espousing overt protectionism: a unilateral increase in tariffs that would break almost every binding the US has in the multilateral system. This would, if he becomes President once again and actually implements it, cause a huge decrease in the competitiveness over vast swathes of the US economy. A minimum of 50% of imports into the United States are imports of intermediate goods—products used in the subsequent production of final goods for sale either in the domestic markets or as US exports.

Nor would this be confined to trade in goods—it would cross over into services which is some 70% of the economy. Take a trivial example: sheets. Presumably, given what has happened over the past 75 years to the US textile industry, vast hotel chains in the United States which use tens of thousands of bedding sheets every day get their sheets from Bangladesh, Egypt and other import sources. If they have to pay a 10% impost on the cost of those sheets, their costs go up. Any reader sufficiently motivated to read this far into the essay will be able to predict the second round effects of such a cost increase on inflation (hotel prices) and the competitiveness of the US tourist market.

This trivial example would be multiplied across the US economy in millions of higher cost transactions. A unilateral and WTO-illegal impost of this nature would then cause retaliation against US exports by the more powerful countries. We have seen this movie before: the Smoot Hawley Tariff Act of 1929. A new political leader with the name of Hawley has mounted the political stage today, Senator Josh Hawley. He is a leading advocate of unilateral increases in tariffs. This proves not only that God exists, but She has a wicked sense of humour.

The phrase 'never bet against America' is however a phrase the author, a strong pro-American, believes in. We do not know if Churchill was serious or just joking when he famously said that one can '…always depend on the United States to make the right choice – once the Americans have exhausted the alternatives'.[45] Where the United States is today on trade is not a stable

---

[45] There are variants of this observation.

equilibrium. In the meantime, we can identify a few core concepts of any way forward, when the domestic political wheel turns again in Washington.

First, we cannot move forward at the global level without the full commitment of the United States. It is not that solutions do not exist to key concerns of the United States around the Security Exceptions Clause, the future of the Appellate Body, the extreme interpretations of many emerging economies to the principle of 'Special & Differential Treatment' that takes far too little account of their far stronger competitive position in the twenty-first century, and many other matters besides.[46] But the United States would have to 'own' politically whatever solution set was found both to address past systemic failures and future solutions to emerging trade policy problems.

Second, objectively, the United States needs effective rules (and observance of the norms that lie beneath the rules) more today than at any time in its post-war history. 75 years ago, the United States could have formulated an entirely different system based on 'it's my way or the highway' thinking, not the enlightened liberal rules-based system they championed. That option is not open to the United States today. However, one describes the evolving shape of geopolitics, we are no longer living in that unipolar world and the United States would benefit more than ever before in the post-war era from strong global rules—provided the US was the main driver of those changes. The US would receive huge support from its many allies, friends and partners if, at some future point, it committed itself to such a project.

Third, one should not forget that there is a certain 'fickleness' to the trade debate in US history, making long-term projections of the future of US trade policy a very dicey proposition.[47] The tone of this essay is dark and, the author would argue, for good reason. However, it is instructive to look at what happened politically the last time a Trade Agreement went to the US Congress and Members of Congress had to put real money (i.e. their votes), not cheap anti-trade rhetoric, on the table. The last time this happened, and it was during the Trump Presidency, was in December 2019 when the USMCA, the successor of the NAFTA Agreement unifying the trade regimes of the

---

[46] For example, Alan Wolff, a former US Deputy Director General of the WTO, has written a number of excellent articles and a book ('Revitalising the World Trading System') containing many powerful suggestions.

[47] As recently as 2019, a study entitled 'Making Foreign Policy Work for the Middle Class', Carnegie Endowment for International Peace (the authors included Jake Sullivan, the current US National Security Adviser) noted that polls that year 76% of Democrats and 71% of Republicans '…responded that US involvement in the global economy is a good thing'. Purists would always pick away at such high level ambiguous statements ('What does that mean?'); those who have been politicians and stood for office in a democracy know that is about as much material you get to work with to try to carry the public with you on sound policy.

three North American economies (Mexico, Canada, the United States) was put to the US Congress.

Briefly the background to this was that the President had denounced the NAFTA as 'the worst ever trade agreement' and threatened to end it; a renegotiation then began; perhaps around 80% of the 'worst ever trade agreement' was carried forward into the new agreement, some politically adroit changes to the rest of the NAFTA provisions were agreed and *voilà*!—we now have the 'best trade agreement ever'. From the ugly (Trade) duckling to beautiful swan in the blink of a politician's eye: the House of Representatives voted in favour of this entirely sensible trade agreement with 385 votes with a mere 41 votes against it. Only a resolution to support motherhood and apple-pie would have attracted stronger Congressional support. Lesson: do not entirely rule out Congress getting behind other, politically savvy trade agreements.

Finally, it is likely that we will need an external shock to galvanise a change in mood inside the US political community. Consistent with the insight of Nassim Taleb, author of many outstanding books and articles on black swan/tail end events, it is by definition impossible to forecast what those external shocks might be. The only certainty is that if and when this 'exogenous shock' comes to nudge the United States back into a better place in terms of American leadership, it won't have anything to do with an intellectual awakening of the merits of Ricardo's theory of comparative advantage.

In the meantime, those of us who support the generally open trading system (and secretly admire Ricardo, Cobden and the other heroes of open trade while being terrified of being accused as a 'globalist') will continue to do what we can to avoid yet further erosion of a system under threat and which has so many benefits to so much of mankind, contrary to the fantasies of most of its critics. Additionally, we should be ready to take what opportunities we can to advance it, waiting for Godot, in the form of the US Congress, to arrive.

Why Free Trade Is Difficult to Achieve in Practice

Syed Kamall

How Markets Work

Much academic research looks at how a particular phenomenon works in the real world works and seeks to explain how it works in theory, sometimes by constructing models (Ouliaris, 2011). Many economic courses teach students about the perfect competition model to explain how markets work. This assumes that:

- all firms sell identical products
- sellers cannot influence the market price for their product or service
- a seller's market share has no influence on prices
- buyers and sellers have the same complete or perfect information, referred to as symmetric information
- firms can enter or exit the market without cost (Hayes 2024).

Under this model, sellers increase or decrease the volume of products they make as the market price changes in order to maximise their profit. The perfect competition model assumes that no individual seller is able to affect the overall market price, no matter how many or how few products they make. It also assumes that if the total output of all firms changes, this leads

---

S. Kamall (✉)
St Mary's University, Twickenham, UK
e-mail: syed.kamall@stmarys.ac.uk

to an increase or decrease in the total supply to the market, which in turn leads to changes in the market price.

Having made all these assumptions, the teacher or textbook then admits that markets are not perfect and that buyers do not have perfect information, before introducing models of imperfect competition:

- **Monopolistic competition** where many companies offer similar competing products or services, differentiated by pricing and marketing
- **Oligopolies** with a small number of firms who together dominate and control the market.
- **Monopoly** where only one firm dominates the market controlling supply, demand and prices. There is no close substitute for that product, and the entry barrier is very high.
- **Monopsony** where the market is dominated by a single buyer.

Despite admitting that markets are not perfect, when markets deviate from the textbook model of perfect competition or do not produce the desired outcomes, economists refer to these deviations as *market failures*, which are then used to justify interventions by government. (Booth 2008). Arguably, it is the model of the market that has failed since the market did not produce:

i. the outcomes predicted by the model; or
ii. the outcomes desired by economists or policy makers.

Now it could be argued that *market failure* is a valid term since the market 'failed' to produce the desired outcome, but equally it could be argued that the person using the term *market failure* has failed to understand how markets work.

The Austrian School

The Austrian school of economics is sceptical of models of the economy, especially those based on mathematical equations. Instead, Austrian economists adopt a subjective bottom-up approach, known as methodological individualism, based on '*the insight that every individual chooses and acts purposively, i.e. in pursuit of his [or her] purposes and in accordance with his [or her] perception of his options for achieving them*' (White 2003).

Every day there are hundreds, thousands, millions and billions of transactions that occur between willing sellers and willing buyers 'acting purposively'

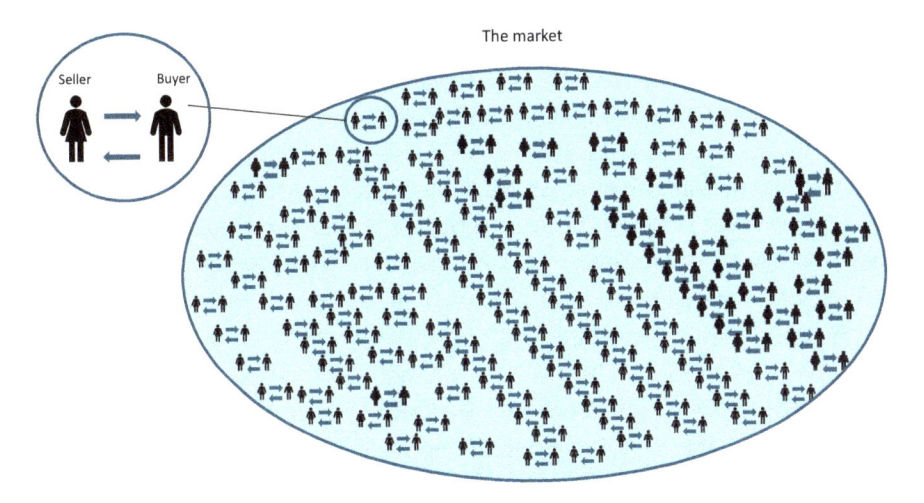

Fig. 1 The spontaneous order of the market

for mutual benefit. The effect of adding up or aggregating these transactions leads to the spontaneous order of the market, as shown in Fig. 1.

In other words, markets are the sums of smaller individual decisions and actions. Markets are not perfect and are asymmetric, i.e. buyers and sellers do not have the same information. Even though markets are not perfect they are seen to lead to "*a more efficient allocation of societal resources than any design could achieve*" (Petsoulas 2001). Kirzner (1997) suggested that "*Entrepreneurial discovery is at the centre of the real-world market process. Knowledge is neither perfect nor is it available from some central pool which can be tapped: it is naturally dispersed and is uncovered by entrepreneurs competing one with another to find better ways of satisfying consumers.*"

For Kirzner, entrepreneurial discovery "*represents the alert becoming aware of what has been overlooked*" i.e. spotting economic opportunities that others cannot yet see, such as the need for new goods or services. By assessing information about the market, entrepreneurs seek to supply a product or service that is different to competitors. In response, competitors seek to improve their product and service to compete on quality or price or both. It is this competition of supply and customers willingness to buy the products or services that sets the market price. An entrepreneur is portrayed as somewhat of a hero since she or he bears the risk of an uncertain future by taking responsibility for the success or failure of their chosen strategy. The Austrian view of the entrepreneur encompasses not just innovators and inventors, but also business owners and investors. There is some disagreement over whether intermediaries or middlemen are entrepreneurs, but since they too spot asymmetries and market opportunities, it can be argued that they too are entrepreneurs.

Inevitably, there are criticisms of Kirzner's thesis. For example, in suggesting that entrepreneurs are *"aware of what has been overlooked"* Kirzner is said to believe *"that entrepreneurial alertness cannot be taught"* (Laplume 2017). Critics argue that market research, customer surveys and even lessons in entrepreneurship can help individuals to recognise business opportunities. However, it could also be argued that knowing that market research was needed in the first place is part of the entrepreneurial process.

Also, alertness is not necessarily enough to be an entrepreneur. Many people may see the same opportunity, but the entrepreneur is the person willing to take the risk, borrow money for their venture, mortgage their home, live off their savings, forego a salary, etc. So even though an individual may be alert to a business opportunity, they may decide that it is not worth the risk or that they cannot put their family through the economic uncertainty and possible pain. While some people see risk akin to gambling, Carosa (2010) suggests that entrepreneurs are 'calculated risk takers'.

Some critics such as Marks (2010) argue that entrepreneurs are not that risk-averse, since they may come from wealthy families where a relative is able to lend or give their lucky child a large sum of money to start a new business. This is certainly true for some entrepreneurs but not all come from wealthy backgrounds. There are many stories of entrepreneurs scrimping and saving before ultimately becoming successful. In fact, limited opportunities may actually drive entrepreneurial activity. For example, immigrants sometimes start their own businesses after encountering discrimination in applying for jobs.

Even if these criticisms are valid, Kirzner's thesis that by balancing supply and demand, entrepreneurs play a pivotal role in the economy is still valid.

International Trade

The theory of international trade is usually based on the idea of comparative advantage. Smith (1776) proposed the idea of absolute advantage which suggested that if producers in one country were better at making a specific good, the country would be better off specialising in that good and selling it for export to earn money to buy a product that producers in another country were more efficient in making. To take a highly simplified example, if UK bakers are more efficient at making bread and French producers are more efficient at making cheese, then the UK would be better off specialising in producing bread and selling it to French customers while France would be better off making cheese and selling some to UK consumers. In this case, the

UK has an absolute advantage in making bread, while France has an absolute advantage in making cheese and both countries are better off trading with each other.

But what happens if one country has an absolute advantage in making both products? Ricardo (1817) proposed a simplistic scenario looking at two countries, UK and Portugal, which both produced the same two goods (wine and cloth). Comparative advantage suggests that both countries would benefit from manufacturing the product they are best at producing and importing the other product from the other country, even if one of the countries is better at producing both products.[1]

However, methodological individualism offers another explanation for international trade, i.e. buyers and sellers are not always in the same country. Transactions between a seller in one country and a buyer in another country is considered as international trade. The Encyclopaedia Britannica defines international trade '*as economic transactions that are made between countries*' (Anderson, 2024). When journalists and academics write about international trade, just as Adam Smith and David Ricardo did before them, they usually write about trade between two countries such as between the UK and USA or trade with trade blocs such as trade between the UK and the European Union. However, methodological individualism of the Austrian School would view international trade between two countries as the aggregate of transactions between individual buyers and sellers in Country A trading with buyers and sellers in Country B.

Trade Barriers

In response to sellers and buyers willing to trade with each other whether within a country or across international borders, governments face a choice. They can either get out of the way, often referred to as *laissez-faire* or they can get in the way. Free trade is said to occur when governments get out of the way of a trade between a buyer in one country and a seller in another country. However, in practice, governments tend to get in the way of international trade in the form of trade barriers. These trade barriers are referred to as tariff and non-tariff barriers.

- A tariff barrier is an import tax that the government of a country—where the buyer is based—levies on the product or service being imported, which

---

[1] A more detailed explanations of absolute and comparative advantage can be found at: https://www.econlib.org/library/Topics/Details/comparativeadvantage.html.

increases the price that the buyer pays. Often if the importer is not the final customer or end user, the importer will probably pass this tax onto the end consumer making the product or service more expensive. Some countries may also charge a tax on goods or services being exported.
- A non-tariff barrier is a regulation or rule that governs the products and services that can be imported and sold in a specific country or trade bloc. Governments may erect barriers in response to political pressure or to protect consumers. This will be discussed below.

Trade without these barriers is often described as frictionless trade. However, even with no trade barriers, there would still be some friction due to additional costs known as transaction costs.

Transaction Costs and Intrafirm Trade

Some international trade is conducted within the same firm, i.e. between two subsidiaries of a multinational enterprise (MNE). Such trade is known as intrafirm trade and arises since the act of buying and selling products and services usually incurs costs in addition to the cost of production. These additional costs are known as transaction costs. There are numerous types of transaction costs, but a few examples are:

- Costs of transporting a good to the market and to the customer
- Costs of buyers finding the seller of product or service buyer they are seeking
- Costs of sellers finding buyers
- Buyers or sellers' fees or fees paid to intermediaries
- Tariff and non-tariff barriers
- Bargaining costs
- Decision costs
- Enforcement costs.

Coase (1937) proposed the idea that firms exist because "*outside the firm, price movements direct production, which is co-ordinated through a series of exchange transactions on the market. Within a firm, these market transactions are eliminated and in place of the complicated market structure with exchange transactions is substituted the entrepreneur-co-ordinator, who directs production.*" In other words, firms exist where it is cheaper to internalise transaction costs than engage in external market transactions. Alviarez and Saad (2022) estimate '*exports of manufactured goods from U.S. parents to their cross -border* network of affiliates account for 20 percent of total U.S. exports, and intra-firm imports by foreign-controlled U.S. affiliates from their foreign parent groups account for 20-25 percent of total U.S. imports.'

Trade Agreements

Governments of countries or trade blocs sign trade deals between each other to reduce barriers to trade. A trade deal signed between the governments of two countries or between a trade bloc and a country or between two trade blocs is known as a bilateral deal. A trade deal signed between more than two countries is referred to as a plurilateral deal. Trade deals are sometimes referred to as free trade agreements (FTAs) but while they may lead to freer trade between buyers and sellers in one country and buyers and sellers in another, they are not completely free trade. They are more accurately described as preferential trade agreements (PTAs) where governments of a signatory country offer individuals and firms from other signatory countries preferential access to their markets on a reciprocal basis. In other words, trade is liberalised in some sectors but not all.

For many free traders, an ideal trade agreement would be a single piece of paper which says something along the lines:

1. The government of country A will open all markets to products and services from sellers in country B.
2. The government of country B will open all markets to products and services from sellers in country A.
3. The government of country A will not prevent individuals or firms in country A from buying products and services from sellers in country B.
4. The government of country B will not prevent individuals or firms in country B from buying products and services from sellers in country A.

Such free trade agreements are considered idealistic and do not exist for a number of reasons which will be explored below. Also, there are always some products or services that governments would seek to prevent from being traded such as illegal drugs, weapons of torture and alcohol.

Trade agreements between governments of many countries are known as plurilateral or multilateral trade agreements. The system of multilateral trade is governed by the World Trade Organisation (WTO) which currently has 164 member countries. The difference between plurilateral and multilateral is explained by Herdegen (2016), i.e. "*Multilateral agreements are binding on all WTO Members and must be ratified, together with the WTO Agreement, as* a whole. Plurilateral agreements are optional in character and only obligate those members which choose to ratify them".

Now that we have looked at the basic tenets of free trade, we should now look at how the governance of international multilateral trade evolved in the twentieth century.

Governance of Global Trade

Bretton Woods Institutions

In the years between the First and Second World Wars, especially after the Wall Street Crash of 1929 and the Great Depression of the 1930s, governments around the world engaged in protectionist measures by:

- imposing higher tariffs on imports
- devaluing their currencies—which made exports cheaper but also meant that imports became more expensive
- preferring imports of goods and services from some countries over others, i.e. discriminatory trade
- imposing or increasing capital controls, i.e. the amount of money that could be taken or transferred from one country to another.

The impact of these policies on world trade can be seen in Fig. 2.

These measures threatened to destabilise the global economy. In response, the allied countries led by the USA decided that economic cooperation was the best way to achieve post-war peace and prosperity (US Office of the Historian, n.d.).

According to Hoekman (2018): "*The genesis of the multilateral trading system was the interwar experience of beggar-thy-neighbor protectionism and capital controls put in place by governments ... to stimulate domestic economic activity and employment. Following the ... Smoot–Hawley Tariff Act, [in 1930] which raised average US tariffs from thirty-eight to fifty-two percent, US trading partners imposed retaliatory trade restrictions. A domino effect resulted: As trade flows were diverted to other markets, protectionist measures were taken there, and further retaliation ensued. Even before World War II was over, political leaders sought to establish international institutions to reduce the probability of a repeat performance.*"

In response, US and UK officials led by Harry Dexter White, Special Assistant Secretary of the US Treasury, and British economist John Maynard

Down the plughole
World trade 1929-33, $B

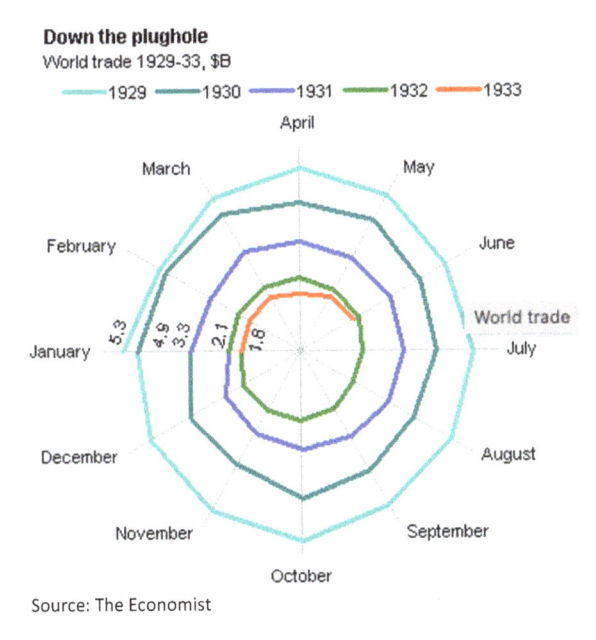

Fig. 2 The decline of world trade 1929 to 1933. *Source* League of Nations' World Economic Survey 1932–33

Keynes, who was an advisor to the British Treasury, proposed international (governmental) organisations to offer financial assistance to countries to dissuade them from adopting protectionist policies. Since their proposals differed, a series of meetings began in 1942 to agree a joint approach. In 1944, the United Nations Monetary and Financial Conference was held in Bretton Woods, New Hampshire, USA attended by delegates from 44 countries. In Bretton Woods, delegates agreed to create:

- the **International Monetary Fund (IMF)** to supervise a system of exchange rates linked to the dollar (IMF 2022)
- the **International Bank for Reconstruction and Development (IBRD)**, commonly known as the **World Bank**, to provide financial assistance for post-war reconstruction and to support development of less developed countries (World Bank, n.d.).

These are referred to as the Bretton Woods institutions. The delegates also proposed setting up a third international organization to facilitate international trade, but no agreement was reached.

After the war, negotiations began to find agreement on managing international trade. In 1947, representatives of 23 countries meeting in Geneva:

Name of the Round or Location	Dates	Value of Trade Involved (roughly)	No. of Countries Participating	Notable Outcomes
Geneva	1947	$10 billion	23	45,000 tariff cuts -- average 35 percent cut
Annecy (France)	1949	n/a	13	tariff reductions
Torquauy (England)	1950-51	n/a	38	tariff reductions
Geneva	1956	$2.5 billion	26	tariff reductions
Dillon Round	1960-61	$4.9 billion	26	tariff reductions
Kennedy Round	1962-67	$40 billion	62	35 percent average cut on industrial goods; commitments on use of anti-dumping laws
Tokyo Round	1973-79	$155 billion	102	34 percent average cut on industrial goods; commitments on non-tariff measures
Uruguay Round	1986-93	$3.7 trillion	123	services trade and intellectual property included; "built-in agenda" on agriculture, WTO institution created
Doha Round	2001-	n/a	148+	fully incorporates services and agriculture, trade facilitation, development agenda

Fig. 3 GATT and WTO rounds. *Source* Hinrich Foundation Unger (2017)

- agreed to a draft charter for a new International Trade Organization (ITO)
- concluded a General Agreement on Tariffs and Trade (GATT) to reduce tariffs and imperial preferences, and as an interim measure until the ITO charter was ratified.

In 1948, 53 countries signed the Havana Charter in 1948 to create a new International Trade Organization (ITO). However, the charter was never ratified by the US Congress, killing off the ITO. But all was not lost. Without a formal international organisation to manage trade relations, governments negotiated a further seven rounds of GATT up to 1993. A list of the various rounds is shown in Fig. 3. After nearly 50 years as an interim measure, GATT was absorbed into the World Trade Organization in 1995.

The Kennedy Round and Non-Tariff Barriers

The early rounds leading up to the Kennedy Round focused on reducing in tariffs. The reductions in tariffs are shown in Fig. 4.

In the Kennedy Round negotiations from 1964 to 1967, discussions began to seek agreement on non-tariff barriers (NTBs) including:

- antidumping measures
- quantitative restrictions.

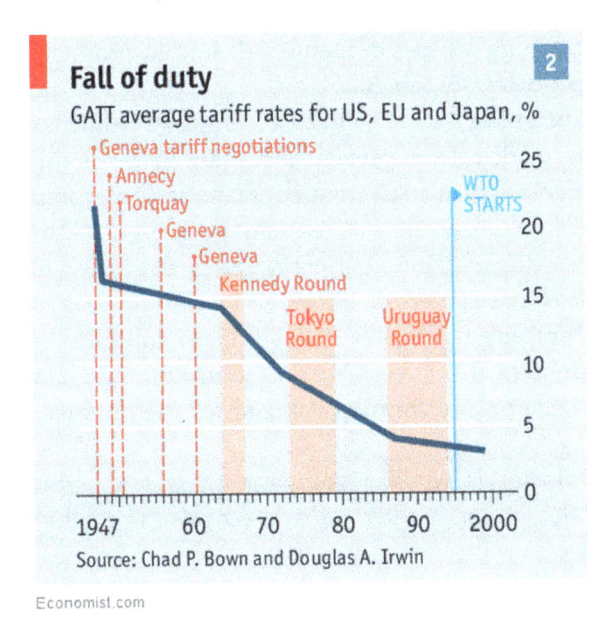

Fig. 4 GATT rounds and the reduction of tariffs. *Source* The Economist

Anti-dumping Measures

Dumping is said to occur when an exporter sells a product at a cheaper price in another country than in the home market of the producer. Under Article VI of *GATT*:

> a product is to be considered as being dumped, i.e. introduced into … another country at less than its normal value, if the export price of the product exported from one country to another, is less than the comparable price … for the like product when destined for consumption in the exporting country. (WTO 2024a)

Companies may sell their products at a lower price—sometimes less than the cost of making the product to—gain market share. However, companies may also do this to get rid of excess stock or older models. In this case, they may be considered to be dumped in an overseas market. Some companies consider this a legitimate business practice which benefits consumers. Under WTO rules, dumping is not illegal unless the government of the country where the importer is based can prove that dumping harms domestic competitors (Barone 2021). There are four types of dumping:

1. **Sporadic dumping** where companies sell unsold products in an overseas market. This occurs occasionally.
2. **Predatory dumping** occurs where a company deliberately sells goods in a foreign market at a price lower than in its home market. This allows companies to increase market share at the expense of competitors. European manufacturers of telecommunications network equipment have accused Chinese manufacturers of giving away their products to gain market share (Bases 2013)
3. **Persistent dumping** happens when a company continues to sells products at a lower price in the foreign market than domestic competitors. This may happen due to a continuing demand for the product in the overseas market.
4. **Reverse dumping** is when a company charges a higher price for its products in the foreign market and a lower price in the local market.

Quantitative Restrictions

Governments sometimes restrict the amount of a specific product that can be imported or exported. Under Article XI of GATT:

> No prohibitions or restrictions other than duties, taxes or other charges, whether … through quotas, import or export licences or other measures, shall be instituted or maintained by any contracting party on the importation of any product of the territory of any other contracting party or on the exportation or sale for export of any product destined for the territory of any other contracting party. (WTO 2024b)

However, there were exceptions including:

(a) temporary export bans or restrictions where there is a critical shortage of foodstuffs or other essential products;
(b) import and export bans or restrictions related to standards or regulations for the classification, grading or marketing of commodities in international trade
(c) Import restrictions on agricultural or fisheries products: Where the government of the importing country
   i. restricts the sale of the same or similar domestic products
   ii. wants to reduce a temporary surplus of the same or similar domestic products

iii. restricts the volume of production of any animal product that is dependent on the imported commodity.

This did not stop other quantitative restrictions. In 1981, the US government asked the Japanese government to voluntarily cap the exports of Japanese-made cars to the US, due to concerns about the uncompetitiveness of US car manufacturers (Berry et al. 1999). Such agreements are known as voluntary export restraints (VERs). These VERs were later phased out, partly due to the fact that this encouraged Japanese car makers to open factories in the US to avoid VERs while cars made in Japan under a US brand were subject to the VER. They also kept the price of cars artificially higher than they would have been in a more competitive markets.

Tokyo Round Agreement on Technical Barriers to Trade (TBT)

After the Kennedy Round in 1967, the GATT secretariat suggested further liberalisation of non-tariff barriers, which led to the Tokyo Round negotiations between 1973 and 1979 where further tariff cuts were agreed. Some participants also came to an agreement on technical barriers to trade (TBTs) to:

- "*[recognise] the … contribution that international standards and certification systems can make … by improving efficiency of production and facilitating … international trade*"
- "*encourage the development of … international standards and certification systems*"
- "*ensure that technical regulations and standards, including packaging, marking and labelling requirements, and methods for certifying … technical regulations and standards do not create unnecessary obstacles to international trade.*"

Once again, there were some exceptions which allowed countries to raise barriers:

- "*to ensure the quality of its exports*"
- "*for the protection of human, animal or plant life or health, of the environment*"
- to prevent "*deceptive practices*" as long as these measures were not a "*disguised restriction on international trade*"
- "*for the protection of … [an] … essential security interest*" (WTO 2024c).

Uruguay Round

The Uruguay Round from 1986 to 1993 took twice as long as originally intended and at times negotiators thought it might fail. In the end, there was agreement on reducing more tariff and non-tariff barriers as well as on an agenda and timetables for future negotiations on most areas of trade not already covered by GATT. The Uruguay Round also agreed to create the World Trade Organisation to govern global trade.

Three of the most notable areas of agreement were on:

- sanitary and phytosanitary (SPS) measures
- intellectual property rights (IPR)
- measures affecting trade in services.

Sanitary and Phytosanitary (SPS) Measures

The agreement on the *Application of Sanitary and Phytosanitary Measures* set basic rules for food safety and animal and plant health standards. While countries are allowed to set their own standards, the regulations state that countries or trade blocs setting such measures:

> … shall ensure that any sanitary or phytosanitary measure is applied only to the extent necessary to protect human, animal or plant life or health, is based on scientific principles and is not maintained without sufficient scientific evidence …

Where there is insufficient scientific evidence, a WTO Member "*may provisionally adopt sanitary or phytosanitary measures on the basis of available pertinent information, including that from … relevant international organizations as well as from sanitary or phytosanitary measures applied by other Members … [but].. shall seek to obtain the additional information necessary for a more objective assessment of risk and review the sanitary or phytosanitary measure … within a reasonable period of time*" (WTO 2024d).

However, there is still some dispute over the scientific advice behind some SPS measures. For example, Ganesan (2022) explains how the EU blocked imports of Basmati rice from India on the basis of maximum residue limits (MRLs) event though the MRL is not a scientific toxicological safety standard, but is in fact a trading standard adopted by the EU.

Intellectual Property Rights (IPR)

The negotiations led to the signing of the agreement on Trade-Related Aspects of Intellectual Property Rights (TRIPS). There are two main types of IPRs.

- Copyright and related rights
- Industrial property.

Copyright and Related Rights

These include "*the rights of authors of literary and artistic works ... [which] ... are protected by copyright, for a minimum period of 50 years after the death of the author.*" This includes so-called "*neighbouring rights*" which protect "*the rights of performers ... recordings and broadcasting. The main social purpose of protection of copyright and related rights is to encourage and reward creative work*" (WTO 2024e).

Industrial Property

There are two main areas of Industrial property.

- distinctive signs, i.e. trademarks and geographical indications (where products from a specific geographical location have a reputation due to that origin)
- other types of industrial property such as patents, industrial designs and trade secrets (WIPO, n.d).

Trade in Services

A new General Agreement on Trade in Services (GATS) was also agreed to apply to all service sectors, except.

- "*services supplied in the exercise of governmental authority*", i.e. services supplied on a non-commercial or non-market basis, such as government social security schemes and other public services, such as health or education, which in many countries are provided on a non-market basis (WTO 2024f).

- some Air Transport Services measures, since "*negotiators recognised … that international air transport was governed by … over 3,500 bilateral agreements, each based on … balanced and reciprocal … rights between states … and … [due to the existing] … the multilateral framework provided by ICAO and IATA*" (IATA 1999).

The World Trade Organisation and the Doha Round

The first major negotiating round of the WTO was the Doha Round for Development launched in 2001. The negotiations cover twenty areas of trade, including agriculture, services trade, market access for non-agricultural products and some intellectual property issues. (Lester 2016). The round has yet to be concluded and was suspended in 2006 (WTO 2006), but in 2013 all members signed up to the Bali Package which was described as "*the first major agreement among WTO members since it was formed in 1995*" (WTO, 2013). This package included development-related agreements on:

- trade facilitation by reducing regulatory barriers to allow goods to flow through ports quicker
- food security
- duty-free, quota-free access for firms from least developed countries to export to richer countries' markets.
- reducing export subsidies in agriculture
- improving market access for cotton products from least developed countries.

In 2015, the Doha Round was declared dead (Financial Times 2015) calling into question the future of the WTO. However, in June 2022, the WTO was said to have '*stepped back from the abyss of irrelevance*' when all 164 member countries signed agreements on:

- a waiver on COVID-19 vaccines
- new disciplines on fisheries subsidies
- food security
- extending a moratorium on tariffs on e-commerce (Bacchus 2023).

Commentators have suggested a number of reasons why the Doha Round was not successfully concluded including:

- giving each member country one-vote and seeking consensus made it more difficult to achieve agreement
- the deal on the table was not good enough for the more powerful countries
- the deal on the table did not include enough concessions from richer countries towards poorer nations
- seeking agreement by a single undertaking, i.e. nothing is agreed until everything is agreed, means that there are more trade-offs and that smaller nations can hold up talks
- the shifts eastwards in relative economic fortunes
- the 'rise of the rest' vs 'the west', i.e. non-western countries are more assertive in standing up to western nations.
- China's share of global trade increasing from less than 2.5 per cent in 1997 to 12 per cent in 2022 (IMF 2023)
- agreement being required from more countries as a result of WTO membership growing from 128 member countries in 1995 to 164 today
- a wider diversity of interests, commitments and capacities of member countries due to increased membership
- the collapse of world trade following the financial crisis in 2008 and COVID in 2020/1
- the impact of COVID on supply chains and global trade, including the uneven distribution of vaccines, saw an increase in onshoring, near shoring and protectionism changing the dynamics of international trade.

Other Trade Agreements

While the Doha Round did not lead to the agreements that were hoped for when negotiations began in 2001, bilateral and plurilateral trade agreement continue to be negotiated and signed. The WTO has facilitated two sector-specific plurilateral agreements.

- In 2015, 52 WTO members signed the **Information Technology Agreement Expansion (ITA 2)** agreement which updated the original ITA that was signed in 1997. This eliminated import tariffs on around 200 information technology products, many of which did not exist when the ITA was signed in 1997.
- In 2021, 70 WTO members signed the **Services Domestic Regulation** agreeing common rules on domestic regulation to make trade in services easier.

In addition, as of 1 January 2024, there were 361 regional trade agreements (RTAs), which are defined as trade agreements between two or more countries (WTO 2024g).

Free Trade Versus Real Trade

As a result of the various GATT and WTO rounds, we can see, trade negotiations have become increasingly technical and take many years, which presents challenges for free traders. In addition, while tariffs have fallen over GATT's lifetime, Fig. 5 shows that non-tariff barriers have increased.

In order to understand why trade is not as open and free as free traders would like, it would be helpful to look at the governance of global trade from the perspective of two theories of political science:

- Political choice theory
- Principal agent theory.

Political Choice Theory and Global Trade

A central tenet of economics is that individuals are mainly motivated by self-interest and maximising their sense of well-being. Individuals will differ on their notion of self-interest, and while most people will be concerned about

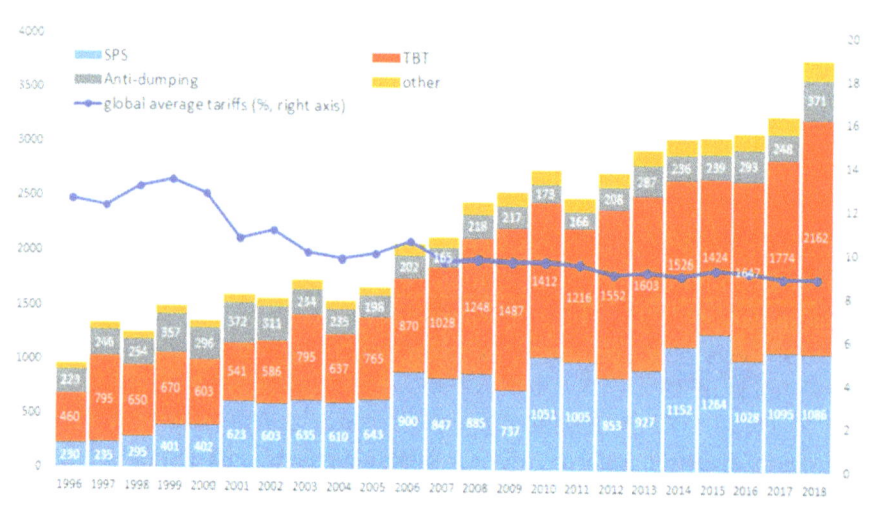

Fig. 5 Falling tariffs, rising non-tariff barriers. *Source* Cho et al. (2020)

others when making decisions in the marketplace, they are assumed to be mainly concerned about themselves.

Public choice theory, according to Shughart II (2023), "*applies the theories and methods of economics to the analysis of political behaviour ... [and] ... like the economic model of rational behaviour on which it rests, assumes that ... the motivations of people in the political process are no different from those of people in the ... housing, or car market ... As such, voters ... [support] candidates ... they think will make them personally better off; bureaucrats strive to advance their own careers; and politicians seek election or re-election to office. Public choice, in other words, simply transfers the rational actor model of economic theory to the realm of politics.*"

While those who argue for government intervention see government as neutral, altruistic and acting in the public interest, public choice theorists ask questions including:

- What influences and motivates officials and politicians in their decision-making?
- What is the public interest?
- Does everyone agree on what is in the public interest?

James Buchanan, who received a Nobel Prize for his work on public choice theory, described public choice as "*politics without romance.*"

When Weck-Hannemann (2001) applied public choice to international trade, she found that:

- tariff and non-tariff barriers are determined by the demand for, and supply of, protection on a political market.
- often domestic industry owners, managers and workers unite to lobby for import barriers, which yield rents (rent-seeking).
- those arguing for protectionism are often few in number but are well organised.
- calls for protectionism are more likely to be heeded:
  - the more concentrated the industry is; and
  - for declining industries and sectors with low-wage employees.
- describing protectionist measures as asking for protection from 'foreign cut-throat firms' appeals to voters and politicians.
- while consumers benefit from low import tariffs and increased competition, their interests are often outweighed domestic competitors arguing for import barriers.
- domestic competitors call for nontariff barriers

- to offset reductions in tariffs (after trade negotiations); and
- as a complement to tariffs.

One of the reasons that lobbyists for trade barriers are successful is because while trade liberalisation leads to gains for consumers, it is also seen to lead to concentrated losses for domestic companies and workers. The millions of consumers who may gain from free trade outnumber those who lose out, but they are dispersed, rarely meet each other and are not an organised movement. While those who lose out are often concentrated in the same geographical locations or the same industries. There have been suggestions that '*those who win should compensate those who lose*' USTIC (2022). For example, the European Union created the Globalisation Adjustment Fund in 2007 '*to help workers negatively affected by globalisation find new jobs*' (Claeys and Sapir 2018).

These factors help to explain why complete free trade is politically difficult to achieve in practice.

While the early rounds of GATT made progress on reducing tariffs over many years, it seems that it is now politically more difficult to get agreement on further trade liberalisation. While this could be partly explained by negotiators tackling the low hanging fruit in the early GATT rounds, principal agent theory offers a further explanation.

Principal Agent Theory and Global Trade

Principal agent theory looks at the problems that occur when an individual or organisation (referred to as the principal) delegates tasks to another person or organisation (referred to as the agent). The principal delegates the tasks for three main reasons:

- **specialisation** where the agent has the skills for the task delegated to it
- **depoliticisation** so that decisions are made on technical and less on political grounds
- **deniability** since delegation removes accountability and responsibility from the principal.

However, agents do not always act in accordance to the wishes of the principals resulting in what is termed as agency slack. In the case of GATT and later WTO negotiations, governments delegated responsibility for negotiating trade agreements to officials as illustrated in Fig. 6

Elsig (2011) explains the change in the dynamics of GATT and WTO negotiations by disaggregating both principals and agents to study chains

Why Free Trade Is Difficult to Achieve in Practice   179

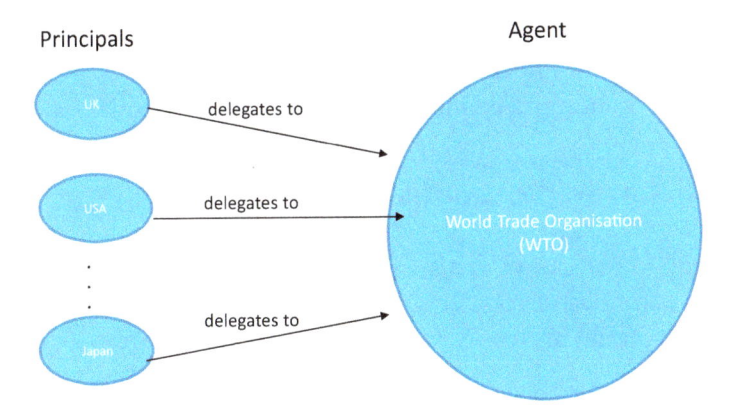

Fig. 6 Principal agent theory with countries as principals and the WTO as the agent

of delegations, as shown in Fig. 7. He found that GATT's first DG Eric Wyndham:

- shaped negotiations
- initially chaired every Kennedy Round sub-Committee
- and his secretariat staff had a '*privileged position*' but the role and influence of GATT officials changed over time.

One WTO official interviewed was quoted as saying '*As a young professional during the Tokyo Round I could do more against the will of members than today as a Director.*' So, while in the early years of GATT, the Secretariat and especially the Director General had more influence over negotiations, over time the ambassadors of countries took more interest in their negotiators and

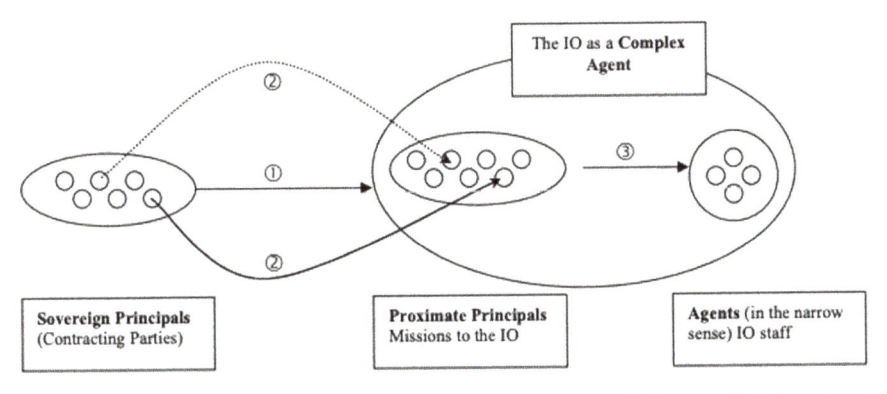

Fig. 7 Disaggregating principals and agents to understand chains of delegation in the World Trade Organisation (WTO). *Source* Elsig (2011)

negotiations to make sure their national interests were being pursued. This increased interest by ambassadors was due to governments of WTO/GATT member states wanting to maintain control over their negotiators.

The Politics of Trade Negotiations

In delegating responsibility to trade negotiators, it is important to understand the incentives for negotiators. Before trade negotiations begin, negotiators for the various governments will draw up a list of offensive interests and defensive interests.

Offensive Interests

Let us consider a simple bilateral negotiation between two countries, Country A and Country B. The offensive interests of Country A will be those sectors in Country B that the businesses and government in Country A want to see open to Country A's firms. Likewise, Country B negotiators will also draw up its list of offensive interests, i.e. those sectors in Country A where it wants firms from Country B to be able to sell their goods and services.

Defensive Interests

Continuing with the example of the simple trade negotiations, Country A's defensive interests are those sectors in Country A that domestic businesses and the government want to keep closed to foreign competition. Country B will also have its own list of defensive interests.

Bargaining Chips

In some cases, Country A may have no domestic producers of a good or service produced by firms in Country B, but it will still resist reducing tariff or non-tariff barriers to the imports of these goods or services from Country B, i.e. a defensive interest. Often, this is because the negotiators of Country A will use opening of these sectors as leverage to open up a sector in Country B to exports from Country A. In these cases, tariff and non-tariff barriers are no longer about protecting domestic competitors but about having a bargaining chip. For example, there are few if any growers of citrus fruit in the UK due to its climate, but the UK government still levies tariffs on imports of citrus fruit from other countries. While consumers would benefit from lower prices if the tariffs were reduced or abolished, the UK keeps these tariffs to use as bargaining chips in trade negotiations.

Safety Measure or Non-tariff Barrier?

As discussed above, the Tokyo and Uruguay Rounds addressed technical barriers to trade, including product standards. Under WTO/GATT rules, governments may maintain non-tariff barriers for reasons of safety, prevent deceptive practices or national security. While non-tariff barriers based on safety are supposed to be based on scientific evidence, in practice we now have a situation where one country's safety standard is another's non-tariff barrier. There are many examples of this, especially around sanitary and phytosanitary standards (SPS). In 2007, the EU banned imports of so-called 'chlorinated chickens'. In practice, this referred to the practice of rinsing chicken with chlorine-based chemicals for hygiene reasons. As Sen (n.d.) has pointed out there is "*little scientific evidence ... that ... rinsing is harmful for human[s] ... US residents have consumed chicken processed by such means for decades without any proven adverse effects. Interestingly, ... even European food products sometimes have chlorine contents higher than the prescribed EU limits.*"

In the EU and UK, food containing genetically modified organisms (GMOs) must be labelled as such. There is not sufficient scientific evidence to ban GMO foods, so the labels are to provide information to consumers who may prefer to avoid such food. However, US politicians, negotiators and academics claim that such labelling is a non-tariff barrier (Runge et al. 2001).

Behind the Border Issues

Even though trade negotiators may agree to open their countries' markets to foreign firms, foreign firms may still face so-called behind the border issues. These include:

- difficulty of registering or obtaining licences to operate (Sadikov 2007)
- poor infrastructure making it difficult for foreign firms to get their good to domestic consumers
- sector-specific government departments discriminating against foreign firms, even though the trade ministry of a country may have agreed to open that sector to non-domestic firms

- state or local governments treating domestic forms more favourably even though the national or federal government agreed to reduce barriers to foreign firms (Wajda-Lichy 2014).

Summary of International Trade in Theory and in Practice

As we can see there are many factors that lead to international trade not being completely free trade. The contrast between economics and trade theories and international trade in practice are summarised as Table 1.

Table 1 Trade in theory and in practice

	Theory	Practice
Markets	• Perfect markets • Perfect competition and symmetrical information	• Spontaneous order of markets • Imperfect competition and asymmetric information
Trade gains	• Society or nation gains from trade-liberalisation	• Dispersed winners/concentrated losers • Difficult/impossible to compensate losers
Ease of trade	• Frictionless exchange	• Information, transaction and bargaining costs
Governments and negotiators	• Benign and omniscient government maximising economic welfare • Comparative or absolute advantage	• Politics and public choice theory • Trade barriers are bargaining chips • Pursue offensive interests & focus on exports • Protect defensive interests & minimise imports • Focus on exports more than gain to consumers of imports
Protectionism	• Damages domestic economy	• 'can be interpreted as a rational policy for decision makers in a democracy'

Conclusion

This chapter has looked at economics and trade in theory as well as the politics and the evolution of the governance of international trade in practice. While national and international markets can be seen as an aggregation of the billions of transactions that take place between willing buyers and willing sellers, governments can either get in the way or erect barriers. Public choice and principal agent theories explain some of the politics behind protectionism and why further liberalisation is proving more difficult to achieve.

In practice, global trade has grown—since the General Agreement on Trade and Tariffs (GATT) was initially signed in 1947—as a result of the reduction of tariff barriers and many non-tariff barriers. However, with successive GATT rounds and more WTO member countries, it has become harder to achieve multilateral agreements, leading to the collapse of the WTO Doha Round. The politics of international trade has inhibited trade from being truly free or as most free traders would prefer.

This is partly due to the fact that while businesses like to trade, trade negotiators like to negotiate. This leads to trade negotiators seeking to keep as many bargaining chips as possible to open overseas markets while protecting domestic markets, even where consumers would gain by reducing import barriers. This also explains why governments resist engaging in unilateral free trade, i.e. opening up their domestic market without reciprocal access granted by other countries.

To be fair to negotiators, many (but not all) businesses claim to be in favour of free trade when they are attempting to enter an overseas market but seem less keen when they face increased competition in their domestic market. In addition, while tariffs on most goods have fallen massively, removing non-tariff barriers is proving difficult due to how they are perceived. One country's safety standard is another country's non-tariff barrier. In addition, the gains from trade are not obvious to everyone since the act of trade liberalisation often leads to dispersed gains and concentrated losses. Those who lose out may be fewer than those who gain, but they are better organised and more vocal.

This does not mean that the world will inevitably become increasingly protectionist. However, understanding the politics of international trade highlighted by both principal agent theory and the public choice school help to explain why complete free trade will be difficult to achieve in practice, even when economic and international trade theory suggest that we would all be better off with free trade.

References

Alviarez V, Saad A (2022) Multinational production and intra-firm trade. Inter-American Development Bank. IDB Working Paper Series, DB-WP-1369. https://publications.iadb.org/publications/english/viewer/Multinational-Production-and-Intra-firm-Trade.pdf

Anderson K (2024) World Trade Organization. Encyclopaedia Britannica. https://www.britannica.com/topic/World-Trade-Organization

Bacchus (2023) The future of the WTO. Multilateral or plurilateral? Policy Analysis No. 947. Cato Institute. https://www.cato.org/policy-analysis/future-wto

Barone A (2021) Dumping: Price discrimination in trade, attitudes and examples. Investopedia. https://www.investopedia.com/terms/d/dumping.asp

Bases B (2013) EU cites Chinese telecoms Huawei and ZTE for trade violations. Reuters. https://www.reuters.com/article/trade-eu-idINDEE94H01U20130518/

Berry S, Levinsohn J, Pakes A (1999) Voluntary export restraints on automobiles: evaluating a trade policy. Am Econ Rev 89(3):400–430. http://www.jstor.org/stable/117026

Booth P (2008) Market failure: a failed paradigm. Econ Aff 28(4):72–74. https://doi.org/10.1111/j.1468-0270.2008.00865.x

Carosa C (2010) Why successful entrepreneurs need to be calculated risk takers. Forbes. https://www.forbes.com/sites/chriscarosa/2020/08/07/why-successful-entrepreneurs-need-to-be-calculated-risk-takers/?sh=359f95ca2f5b

Cho J, Hong E, Yoo J, Cheong I (2020) The impact of global protectionism on port logistics demand. Sustainability 12:1444. https://doi.org/10.3390/su12041444

Coase RH (1937) The nature of the firm. Economica 4:386–405. https://doi.org/10.1111/j.1468-0335.1937.tb00002.x

Claeys G, Sapir A (2018) The European globalisation adjustment fund: easing the pain from trade? Policy Contribution Issue n°05. Breugel. https://www.bruegel.org/sites/default/files/wp-content/uploads/2018/03/PC-05_2018.pdf

Elsig M (2011) Principal–agent theory and the World Trade Organization: complex agency and 'missing delegation.' Eur J Int Rel 17(3):495–517. https://doi.org/10.1177/1354066109351078

Financial Times (2015) The Doha round finally dies a merciful death. https://www.ft.com/content/9cb1ab9e-a7e2-11e5-955c-1e1d6de94879

Ganesan S (2022) India's Rice Trade SPS barriers from EU—with special reference to pesticide MRLs. Crop Care Federation of India. https://cropcarefed.in/wp-content/uploads/India-Rice-Trade-and-SPS-Barriers-from-EU.-Final-Rev_19-Aug-2022.pdf

Hayes A (2024) Perfect competition: examples and how it works. Investopedia. https://www.investopedia.com/terms/p/perfectcompetition.asp#:~:text=his%20college%20dorm.-,What%20Is%20Perfect%20Competition%3F,and%20companies%20cannot%20determine%20prices

Hoekman B (2018) Global trade governance. In: Weiss TG, Wilkinson R (eds) International organization and global governance. Routledge

IATA (1999) Liberalisation of air transport and the gats. IATA Discussion Paper. International Air Transport Association. https://www.wto.org/english/tratop_e/serv_e/iacposit41.pdf

IMF (2022) The IMF in history. International Monetary Fund. https://www.imf.org/en/About/Timeline

IMF (2023) Regional economic outlook. Asia and Pacific: challenges to sustaining growth and disinflation. International Monetary Fund. https://www.imf.org/en/Publications/REO/APAC/Issues/2023/09/27/regional-economic-outlook-for-asia-and-pacific-october-2023

Kirzner I (1997) How markets work disequilibrium, entrepreneurship and discovery. Institute of Economic Affairs. https://iea.org.uk/wp-content/uploads/2016/07/upldbook104pdf.pdf

Laplume A (2017) *Kirzner's alertness theory of entrepreneurship*. Blogspot.com. https://entrepreneurshiptheories.blogspot.com/2017/08/kirznerian-entrepreneurship.html

Lester S (2016) Is the Doha round over? the WTO's negotiating agenda for 2016 and beyond. Free trade bulletin No. 64. Cato Institute. https://www.cato.org/sites/cato.org/files/pubs/pdf/ftb64.pdf

Marks G (2010) Entrepreneurs are great, but it's mom and dad who gave them their start. The Guardian. https://www.theguardian.com/business/2021/jan/31/small-business-entrepreneurs-success-parents

Ouliaris S (2011) Finance and development. Finance and Development. F&D. https://www.imf.org/external/pubs/ft/fandd/2011/06/basics.htm

Petsoulas C (2001) Hayek's liberalism and its origins his idea of spontaneous order and the Scottish enlightenment Hayek's liberalism and its origins. Routledge. http://pombo.free.fr/petsoulas2001.pdf

Ricardo D (1817) On the principles of political economy and taxation. John Murray, London

Runge CF, Bagnara G, Jackson LA (2001) Differing U.S. and European perspectives on GMOs: Political, economic and cultural issues. Estey Cent J Int Law Trade Policy 2(2):221–234. https://www.iatp.org/sites/default/files/Differing_US_and_European_Perspectives_on_GMOs.htm#:~:text=If%20labelling%20strategies%20implicitly%20define,from%20entering%20the%20European%20market

Sadikov, A. (2007) *Border and Behind-the-Border Trade Barriers and Country Exports* IMF Working Paper Policy WP/07/292. December. Available at: https://www.imf.org/external/pubs/ft/wp/2007/wp07292.pdf

Sen (n.d.) Chickening out? chlorinated chicken and trade. Linklaters. https://www.linklaters.com/en/insights/blogs/tradelinks/chickening-out-chlorinated-chicken-and-trade

Shughart II WF (2023) Public choice. Econlib. The Library of Economics and Liberty. Liberty Fund. https://www.econlib.org/library/Enc/PublicChoice.html

Smith A (1776) An inquiry into the nature and causes of the wealth of nations. https://www.gutenberg.org/files/3300/3300-h/3300-h.htm

Unger M (2017) GATT rounds: who, what, when. Hinrich Foundation. https://www.hinrichfoundation.com/research/tradevistas/wto/gatt-rounds/

United States International Trade Commission (2022) Distributional effects of trade and trade policy on U.S. workers. Publication Number: 5374: Investigation Number: 332–587. https://www.usitc.gov/publications/332/pub5374.pdf

US Office of the Historian (n.d.) Bretton Woods-GATT, 1941–1947. https://history.state.gov/milestones/1937-1945/bretton-woods

Wajda-Lichy M (2014) Traditional protectionism versus behind-the-border barriers in the post-crisis era: experience of three groups of countries: the EU, NAFTA and BRICS. J Int Stud 7(2):141–151. https://doi.org/10.14254/2071-8330.2014/7-2/12

Weck-Hannemann H (2001) Globalization as a challenge for public choice theory. Public Choice 106(1/2):77–92

White LH (2003) The methodology of the Austrian school economists. Ludwig Mises Institite. https://cdn.mises.org/methfinb.pdf

WIPO (n.d.) Geographical indications. World Intellectual Property Organisation. https://www.wipo.int/geo_indications/en/

World Bank (n.d.) History. https://www.worldbank.org/en/archive/history

World Trade Organisation (2006) Talks suspended. 'Today there are only losers'. https://www.wto.org/english/news_e/news06_e/mod06_summary_24july_e.htm

World Trade Organisation (2013) Days 3, 4 and 5: round-the-clock consultations produce 'Bali Package'. https://www.wto.org/english/news_e/news13_e/mc9sum_07dec13_e.htm

World Trade Organisation (2024a) Agreement on implementation of article VI of the General Agreement on Tariffs and Trade. https://www.wto.org/english/docs_e/legal_e/kennedy_e.pdf

World Trade Organisation (2024b) Article XI General elimination of quantitative restrictions. https://www.wto.org/english/res_e/publications_e/ai17_e/gatt1994_art11_gatt47.pdf

World Trade Organisation (2024c) Agreement on technical barriers to trade. https://www.wto.org/english/docs_e/legal_e/tokyo_tbt_e.pdf

World Trade Organisation (2024d) The WTO agreement on the application of sanitary and phytosanitary measures (SPS Agreement). https://www.wto.org/english/tratop_e/sps_e/spsagr_e.htm

World Trade Organisation (2024e) What are intellectual property rights? https://www.wto.org/english/tratop_e/trips_e/intel1_e.htm

World Trade Organisation (2024f) The general agreement on trade in services (GATS): objectives, coverage and disciplines. https://www.wto.org/english/tratop_e/serv_e/gatsqa_e.htm

World Trade Organisation (2024g) Regional trade agreements. https://www.wto.org/english/tratop_e/region_e/region_e.htm

Free Trade: A Ministerial Perspective

Lord Peter Lilley

Introduction

The theoretical case for free trade was made over two centuries ago, largely by British economists—Adam Smith and David Ricardo—and brilliantly popularised during the nineteenth century by Frederic Bastiat in France, Henry George in America and Richard Cobden in Britain. The latter gave free trade not just an economic, but religious, significance—declaring that "free trade is God's diplomacy". Since then a broad consensus has existed between the political parties in Britain in favour of free trade in theory[1] though, in practice, governments have often bowed to protectionist lobbies. British experience in recent decades, throughout which I have been fortunate enough to play a part, illustrates how those theoretical arguments and pragmatic compromises play out in practice.

In the early 1990s, the UK was involved in negotiating the Uruguay Round—the last successful multi-lateral trade agreement which halved tariffs between industrialised countries and created the World Trade Organisation

---

[1] The Liberal Party was the quintessentially free trading party in the nineteenth century, but it was a Conservative Prime Minister—Lord Salisbury—who said (to Margot Asquith, wife of the Liberal leader): *"Have you ever known a man with a first-rate intellect in this country who was a protectionist? ... Free trade will always win against protection here"*.

L. P. Lilley (✉)
Cambridge, England
e-mail: lilleyp@parliament.uk

(WTO). At the same time, the UK also took a leading part in creating the European Single Market—which went further in removing non-tariff barriers than any previous agreement. As it happens, I was the UK Secretary for Trade and Industry involved in key negotiations on the Uruguay Round and responsible for implementing the Single Market programme.

More recently, Brexit has meant that the UK has had to learn afresh how to negotiate trade agreements with third countries and with the EU itself and to consider which (if any) tariffs to retain on imports from the rest of the world.

In this chapter, I reflect on those four decades of experience, debate and discussion with other participants especially about aspects of trade negotiations on which economics textbooks rarely dwell.

Trade Negotiations in Theory and Practice

In theory, trade negotiations should be simple.

Most negotiations, about matters other than trade, involve a country sacrificing something of value to it in exchange for something of greater value. But trade negotiations involve each country stopping doing something (protecting uncompetitive industries) which is overall harmful to it,[2] in exchange for something beneficial (easier access to the other country's market). So trade negotiations should just involve each country saying: "I will remove all my protectionist measures if you remove all yours". Couldn't be simpler!

Needless to say, in practice trade negotiations are not like that. They can be tough, long and complex. Why is that? The main factor making trade deals difficult is that the hardest negotiations are not *between* countries but *within* each country—between governments keen to liberalise trade and lobbies supporting domestic industries determined to retain tariffs, quotas or technical barriers behind which they have been sheltered from foreign competition.

The reason there is protection in the first place is because powerful domestic lobbies had the clout, coupled with plausible arguments, to persuade politicians to enact protective measures. They have been able to do so for two reasons.

---

[2] As Henry George pointed out: "*In time of war, we blockade our enemies in order to prevent them from importing goods. In time of peace, we do to ourselves by tariffs what we do to our enemy in time of war*".

First, as Bastiat pointed out, because: "Protection concentrates at a single point the good it does, while the [greater] harm that it inflicts is diffused over a wide area." It is easier to organise support for protectionist measures which give a particular sector substantial and identifiable benefits than to mobilise opposition to it, since the costs imposed on the rest of the country by protection—higher prices, reduced choice, lower quality and slower growth—though greater overall, are less identifiable and less per head when diffused over the general population. Moreover, free trade negotiations are about removing protections for specific industries which are already in place. Persuading an industry to give up that protection is even harder than resisting its introduction in the first place—especially as the industry may have become, or fear it has become, less competitive behind that protection than it was originally.

Second, because the arguments in favour of protection (it supports jobs, prevents wages being undercut, etc.), however fallacious, are plausible; whereas arguments against protection (that it diverts resources to areas where a country lacks comparative advantage, prevents competition stimulating productivity, increases prices, reduces quality, restricts choice and undermines economic growth)—though economically powerful—are not self-evident to non-economists.

That twofold asymmetry is why the case for unilateral free trade—though intellectually persuasive—is rarely politically triumphant. Even Britain, which unilaterally abolished the corn laws to allow in cheap food and proclaimed the doctrine of free trade, retained import duties averaging higher than those of France for much of the nineteenth century[3]—albeit primarily for revenue raising purposes on imported non-essentials like wine, spirits, tea, coffee, tobacco and sugar—rather than on manufactured goods.

In the unusual circumstances following Brexit, the UK did have to consider whether to remove protectionist measures that it had been obliged to adopt when a member of the EU or even, as some advocated, to abolish all tariffs and pursue a policy of unilateral free trade. The UK did unilaterally abolish tariffs on 100 product lines—notably those on products which were produced (uncompetitively, hence the need for protection) in other EU countries but not in the UK. The option of moving to unilateral free trade was rejected in part to retain some protectionist measures to use as bargaining chips in trade negotiations with countries outside the EU.

Removal of protective measures becomes possible in the context of trade negotiations because they give governments a lever they did not possess when

---

[3] John Vincent Nye, 'The Myth of Free-Trade Britain and Fortress France' Journal of Economic History, March 1991, vol. 51, issue 1, pp 23–46.

protection was conceded—the prospect of less costly access to an overseas market. So the domestic political challenge for each government during trade negotiations is to mobilise domestic support for reducing protection from those who may gain from greater access to foreign markets and, with their help, to stir up the general public who may have been largely unaware of the costs protection imposes on them.

That contest within a country—between those who gain from retaining protection and those who will benefit from access to overseas markets allied with the diffuse majority who lose from protectionism—is often far more important and difficult than the negotiations between governments.

More recently, the UK has been negotiating trade agreements post-Brexit. Even in the case of those with Australia and New Zealand, which enjoy great public sympathy in the UK and with which Britain had free trade prior to joining the European Common Market, the most difficult problem has been overcoming domestic lobbies who resisted every reduction in protection built up during EU membership.

In addition to those fundamental, but often overlooked, negotiations *within* countries, the negotiations between states may be made more difficult than the simple theory suggests, by external factors.

Negotiations will inevitably be more difficult if one or both parties do not accept the free trade argument that the harm done by protection exceeds the benefits.[4] They will only agree to remove protection if convinced that the benefits of reciprocal market access exceed the supposed economic or political cost of forgoing existing protection.

Even where governments accept the case for free trade, some have political cultures dominated by legal or military mindsets which assume all negotiations involve winners and losers. So, to be seen to "win", they make as few concessions as possible even if those concessions—reducing protection—would make their country better off.

Where those mindsets do not initially prevail, the negotiating process can itself develop such attitudes. As Shanker Singham points out: "The very language that trade negotiators use, describing tariff reductions as concessions and utilising the so-called request/offer process reinforces the rhetoric of

---

[4] Some negotiators may be influenced by more recent critiques of orthodox free trade theory e.g. *Where Ricardo and Mill Rebut and Confirm Arguments of Mainstream Economists Supporting Globalisation* Paul Samuelson Journal of Economic Perspectives (Summer 2004) and *Kicking Away the Ladder: Development Strategy in Historical Perspective* (2002) Ha-Joon Chang. The former applies mainly to countries as large as the USA and China. The latter is comprehensively rebutted by *Free Trade and Prosperity—How Openness Helps Developing Countries Grow Richer and Combat Poverty* Arvind Panagariya OUP 2019.

mercantilism and strengthens the hand of producer lobbies in negotiations"[5] as does current jargon like "aggressive and defensive objectives".

Negotiations can drag on simply because officials have no interest in reaching speedy conclusions. The Abbott Government in Australia, conscious that its predecessor had not concluded a single trade agreement, told its negotiators not to strive for perfection but to conclude the best possible agreement within twelve months. They succeeded in completing three within a year—with China, Japan and South Korea.

The nature of negotiations changes when non-trade issues are involved—for instance, immigration, human rights, security and defence.

Immigration is usually a matter for each government's individual decision, though simplifying visa arrangements for business visits can form part of trade deals. But negotiations between India and the UK have been prolonged because they include the issue of the large inflow of Indian immigrants for work purposes and dealing with the many overstayers in the UK.

Under the Lisbon Treaty, the EU is required to address human rights in its trade deals which can prolong negotiations (as in the EU/Canada deal, which took seven years to ratify). Fears that this would rule out an agreement with India seem to have been set aside since current EU negotiations with India make no mention of such clauses. The UK does not insist on such clauses, which gives it an advantage in trade negotiations with India.

Multi-lateral, Bi-lateral, Pluri-Lateral and Regional Integration Deals

Although the main obstacles to negotiating freer trade are domestic to each country, how tough, long and substantive trade negotiations are also depends on: the number of countries involved in multi-lateral deals, the number of bi-lateral negotiations needed in the absence of multi-lateral agreements, the economic and geographical diversity of countries involved in any negotiation, and the range of issues covered.

The large number of countries involved in multi-lateral GATT Rounds—reaching 123 in the Uruguay Round—might be thought to make agreement, requiring unanimity, almost impossible. Agreement did take over seven years. In practice, the negotiations were made manageable by groups of states with similar interests acting together—like the Cairns Group of agricultural exporters. Multi-lateral deals had the advantage of comprehensive

---

[5] *A General Theory of Trade and Competition p. 21.* Shanker Singham. Cameron May (2007).

coverage of the whole GATT/WTO membership. And successive Rounds were immensely successful in bringing goods tariffs down from an average of around 22% in 1947 to 5% after the Uruguay Round and a comparable reduction in use of quotas and subsidies.

Nonetheless, the Doha Round failed to reach agreement—since when bi-lateral and regional free trade deals have proliferated. In theory, bi-lateral deals should individually be easier to conclude and can go deeper in removing non-tariff barriers. But, e.g. the Canada/EU deal (albeit including 28 countries on the EU side) took as long as the Uruguay Round to complete. Moreover, a huge number of bi-lateral deals would be required to liberalise the amount of trade covered by GATT/WTO rounds. And the proliferation of deals means traders face a confusing matrix of differing terms and rules.

Regional trade agreements can avoid some of the complexity of multiple bi-lateral deals and, where they involve economies with similar levels of development, can involve deeper and wider liberalisation.

To extend deeper liberalisation beyond bi-lateral agreements one encouraging option is "pluri-lateral" agreements, covering specific aspects of trade (like digital services), initially between a group of countries but open to others to join.

Lessons of the Uruguay Round, Single Market and Post-Brexit Trade Deals

Although the European Commission took the lead in the Uruguay Round negotiations, Britain participated directly along with other Member States both in setting the Commission's mandate and because negotiations included issues which were not then part of the EU competence. I was involved for a couple of years, including the crucial week of ministerial-level negotiations in Brussels when many issues were resolved but which ended in temporary deadlock.

Prior to the Brussels negotiations and each morning during them, EU Member States had to reach agreement on the European negotiating position. These internal negotiations between 14 Member States were at least as difficult as the subsequent negotiations with the 100 or more other countries participating in the Round. They resembled and reflected the internal debates I mentioned above.

Differences between States reflected different economic interests, different attitudes towards protection and different negotiating cultures. Whereas the UK and northern states tended to be in favour of maximal free trade,

France and most southern states were inclined to retain protection where possible. The free traders tended to see the negotiations as win-win; the more protectionist states saw negotiations as a zero-sum game, winners versus losers.

To try to bridge these differences my French counterpart and I met ahead of the Brussels negotiations. He raised a specific French demand for a cultural carve out to allow France to give priority to making and broadcasting French films. To the horror of my officials, I promised not to oppose this. Officials felt this offended against the purest doctrine of free trade even though it did not harm UK commercial interests. This was a minor issue but an example of how the adversarial negotiating process can harden attitudes even among officials committed to free trade. I wanted to avoid making the perfect the enemy of the good. (Also, like many British people, I am a fan of French cinema and delighted that French taxpayers should subsidise it for us!)

Agriculture was the most contentious issue between Member States and then between Europe and America which temporarily derailed the Brussels talks. They subsequently resolved their differences in the Blair Accords enabling the multi-lateral negotiations to proceed to completion. As discussed below, agriculture is invariably the most difficult issue in trade negotiations.

The final outcome of the Uruguay Round was an immense success. It halved tariffs between industrialised countries; it reached agreement to shift agricultural subsidies away from production to supporting farmers' incomes; it covered intellectual property rights for the first time and set up the WTO to steer future negotiations.

Given its success, why was Uruguay the last successful multi-lateral trade round? The subsequent Doha Round ran into the sand. It was billed as the "Development Round" with the aim of promoting trade and growth of developing countries. In previous Rounds, they had not been required to match the tariff cuts agreed by the developed countries, but they benefitted from the Most Favoured Nation principle requiring states to extend their lowest tariff to all other GATT members. The one successful outcome of Doha was an agreement to phase out export subsidies (which often meant dumping agricultural surpluses and depressing the prices farmers in developing nations received). This went ahead despite failure of the Round.

Part of the reason Doha failed was that Uruguay had dealt with the less difficult issues. Most non-agricultural tariffs had been abolished or reduced to low levels and leaving only those to which states are most attached (like the 10% EU tariff on cars). Further progress in liberalising trade therefore meant tackling non-tariff barriers which tend to be much more complex and varied.

The world therefore moved to bi-lateral deals and regional integration—like the EU Single Market.

The Single Market

The most ambitious programme of regional integration was the European Community's Single Market plan. Formulated in 1985, its aim was to remove non-tariff barriers by 1992. The approach was initially based on mutual recognition of standards for goods: any product which met the standards of one member state must be accepted as suitable for sale in all other member states. This principle had been promulgated by the European Court "Cassis de Dijon" ruling in 1979.[6] But the Court left member states the right to enforce national rules impeding trade if they were necessary for "fiscal supervision, the protection of public health, the fairness of commercial transactions and the defence of the consumer". This made it unclear where mutual recognition applied and blunted its impact. The Single Market programme involved agreeing minimum standards in certain areas for health, fairness and consumer protection making it possible to apply the principle of mutual recognition across the board.

The programme generated less opposition from protectionist lobbies than normal trade deals. There were disputes where proposed minimum standards were, or were perceived to be, designed to protect domestic industry. For example, British makers of lawnmowers suspected that a German proposal for a very low noise threshold was intended to benefit German manufacturers rather than to protect the hearing of users or tranquillity of suburban gardens. And my predecessor as Trade Secretary, fearing plans to standardise light bulb fittings, declared pugnaciously: "We must bayonet them, or they will screw us!" But these issues were resolved without too much hassle. In subsequent decades, the EU moved more towards harmonisation and standardisation of policies. However, the success of the mutual recognition principle suggests that it should provide a good basis for future international deals to reduce non-tariff barriers. It is the attractive basis of the CPTPP[7] to which UK is adhering.

---

[6] The Court ruled that "*In the absence of common rules, obstacles to movement within the Community resulting from disparities between the national laws relating to the marketing of a product must be accepted*" ONLY "*in so far as those provisions may be recognized as being necessary in order to satisfy mandatory requirements relating in particular to the effectiveness of fiscal supervision, the protection of public health, the fairness of commercial transactions and the defence of the consumer.*"

[7] Comprehensive and Progressive Trade and Prosperity Pact—often called the Pacific Trade Pact.

Free Trade: A Ministerial Perspective

During the Uruguay Round and the Single Market process, I made enthusiastic speeches about how both would boost UK exports. A quarter of a century later it was possible to assess their actual impact on trade. A comparison of the growth in UK goods exports to the 14 member states initially comprising the Single Market and to the 111 countries with which the UK traded on WTO terms without any bi-lateral trade deal showed markedly different outcomes.[8]

UK goods exports to the Single Market14 rose by 23% an annual rate of 0.9%—not even keeping up with growth of their GDP. By contrast, UK goods exports to the 111 countries with which it traded on WTO terms increased by 92% or 2.9% pa. At first sight that was surprising. The conventional wisdom had been that non-tariff barriers (which the Single Market aimed to remove), were a greater impediment to trade than tariffs (halved by the Uruguay Round). However, it would be wrong to conclude that the Single Market programme was a failure or had trivial impact.

Mutual recognition undoubtedly made it less costly for manufacturers to supply the European market. Instead of having to produce up to 14 (later 28) different ranges of their products to meet different national standards, they could sell the same range in every country in the Single Market. But this was as true for American and Japanese companies selling to Europe as it was for British or German companies selling within Europe. So it did not give British or other European manufacturers any advantage relative to their non-European competitors.

What it did mean is that the advantage of lower costs from greater standardisation of model ranges was passed on to consumers thanks to competition.

Failure to foresee this benefit or even recognise it in retrospect illustrates how politicians (me included) tend to see free trade deals in mercantilist terms—how much they boost a country's exports—making us blind to the at least equally important benefit of lower prices for consumers.

Novel Arguments Against Removing Protection

During the Uruguay Round, all the classical arguments for retaining protection were deployed: that removing protection would mean loss of jobs and strategic industrial capacity and undermine the balance of payments; that without a secure and profitable home market the industry would be unable

---

[8] *It's quite OK to walk away* by Michael Burrage. Civitas 2017.

to spread its costs and finance research enough to be internationally competitive; and that it is unfair and impossible to compete with countries where pay is much lower.

More recently, as Britain has to negotiate bi-lateral trade deals in its own right, a new range of arguments has emerged. Trade is now less often seen as "God's diplomacy"—bringing potentially hostile countries into a mutually beneficial relationship. Instead, trade is often treated as something Britain should only do freely with countries whose policies meet our approval. Withholding the right to trade freely is seen as expressing our virtuous disapproval or a means of imposing our policies on others. Absence of trade is rhetorically the default position! This approach is propounded by intellectuals, NGOs, academics, politicians and others who are not directly involved in trade. But their support is welcomed by, and powerfully reinforces, protectionist lobbies.

Those taking this position particularly oppose extending free trade to countries which do not practice adequately high standards in human rights, political freedom, labour law, environment, biodiversity, greenhouse gas emissions and animal welfare.

In the case of human and political rights, interference in another country's internal affairs can only be justified if the wrong is so egregious that other states have a "duty to protect" its citizens. But trade sanctions can only be effective if multi-lateral. Failings in human or political rights cannot justify retaining protectionist measures which were designed to protect our own industries not to influence the other state.

The environmental, biodiversity and labour standards adopted by other countries are primarily a matter for their internal polity. It is usually poorer countries whose policies are deemed inadequate. This may be because they cannot afford higher standards or lack administrative capacity. Other countries may wish to contribute to the costs of, e.g. protecting rain forests. But penalising developing countries for not matching the standards of richer countries smacks of liberal imperialism.

In a few areas, the arguments against using trade policy to penalise different standards are less clear cut. For example, countries which penalise domestic emissions of greenhouse gases may render their energy intensive industries uncompetitive so that they migrate to countries relying on fossil fuels. In which case the aim of reducing global emissions will be thwarted. Hence, the pressure for Carbon Border Adjustment Mechanisms, though these may be hideously complex to administer. Another area is animal welfare standards—a high profile issue in a nation of animal lovers like Britain. The concern is that high standards impose such additional costs on farmers that they may lose out to imports from countries with lower standards. If so, fewer animals in total will benefit from higher welfare standards. In theory that could justify retaining protection against imports. But in practice, the argument is used to oppose imports from countries whose practices are little different from those permitted in the UK.

Agriculture—The Most Difficult Issue

Agricultural issues are invariably the most difficult to resolve in trade negotiations. So reductions in agricultural tariffs, quotas and subsidies lag way behind those in manufacturing.

Surprisingly, agricultural lobbies remain as strong, or stronger, in rich countries with few farmers than in developing countries where most people work on the land. In the UK, only 1% of people are involved in agriculture, in the USA, 1.7%, and in the EU, 4.2%. Yet farmers in rich countries secure subsidies and protection far exceeding those which manufacturing and service industries have managed to retain.

For example, the EU still spends 35% of its total budget on agriculture and fishing. The simple average of EU tariffs on agricultural products is 14.9% with some exceeding 150%, whereas those on manufactured products average 4.3%.[9]

Although Brexit provided the opportunity to reduce subsidies (accounting for 25% of value added in farming) and the punitive tariffs and quotas on food imports inherited from the EU, they have been largely maintained. Reducing agricultural protection in free trade deals with non-EU countries has proved the most contentious aspect of those deals within the UK.

It would be understandable if the agricultural interest were dominant in developing countries where half or more of the population may be employed in farming. Paradoxically, that is often far from the case. Many developing countries have operated schemes where farmers, far from being subsidised, are obliged to sell surplus product to state marketing Boards at well below the market price. The Boards then sell the produce to town dwellers or for export at world prices. So, farmers are effectively subsidising the minority of their compatriots who live in towns. I asked one African Minister why this was so? He replied succinctly: "Because you can't riot in the countryside!" The threat of rioting in towns, which are the seat of government, is far more serious. Also, developing countries' main priority is (rightly) to industrialise rather than to protect agriculture. Maybe fear of urban riots explains why

---

[9] WTO EU Trade Policy Review.

Britain chose to abolish the Corn Laws in 1846 to allow imports of cheap food even though farm workers outnumbered those in towns and landowners were a powerful force in Parliament.

Why do developed countries, where few now work on the land, retain such high subsidies and protection. One reason is that, precisely because agriculture as a share of the economy and food as a share of consumers expenditure are so much smaller, the cost of agricultural subsidies and protection is more affordable than in the past.

That would explain why one of the few countries to have unilaterally abolished agricultural subsidies and protection is New Zealand which, while being comparatively wealthy, has a large farming sector. It simply found the cost of subsidies, and the inefficiencies fostered by protection, unaffordable. (When I congratulated Mike Moore, the former Labour Prime Minister responsible for this bold decision, he replied ruefully: "It may explain why I was the shortest serving PM in New Zealand's history!" But his country has never reinstated protection.)

Another factor which became vividly apparent during debates on post-Brexit trade deals is the widespread romantic nostalgia for a rural past and love of the countryside. This has been a feature of British culture since the industrial revolution when Blake contrasted "England's green and pleasant land" with the "dark satanic mills".[10] There is a similar nostalgia in Europe, America and Japan.

It is reinforced by fashionable environmentalism often coupled with bourgeois disdain for working class desire for cheaper food. In one Parliamentary debate there were 16 references to "cheap" food—every one of them derogatory. I observed that: "Listening to this debate, I felt that the House had been transported back to the nineteenth century debates on the Corn Laws. Then, as now, landowners, supported by romantic believers in an unchanging rural England—argued that we should prevent the import of cheap food, protect the labouring classes from their predilection for it and that if we did not, it would mean our farming industry would be destroyed, our fields remain untilled, and our agricultural capacity permanently diminished."[11]

Alas, whereas opponents of the Corn Laws won, this time the government was forced to accept protectionist amendments.

---

[10] *Jerusalem* by William Blake 1804 which has become almost a second national anthem.
[11] Lords Hansard 22nd Sept 2020.

Are Trade Deals Worth the Effort?

Although successive trade agreements have reduced the level of tariffs and quotas, protectionists have fought with undiminished vigour to retain those that remain. The case for protection has been hydra headed—new arguments emerging as old ones are rebutted. Most protectionist measures are small compared with movements of exchange rates. Yet strangely, the latter arouse far less industry lobbying. Maybe that is because exchange rate changes give rise to equal and opposite costs and benefits to importers and exporters. Also they are not seen as the result of government policy and therefore amenable to political lobbying. And they may be assumed to be temporary.

Recently, trade negotiations have been accompanied by attempts to quantify their benefits. Invariably the estimates are puzzlingly small. The official British assessment of its deals with Australia and Japan were that, despite expecting both to increase trade by over 50%, they would add respectively just 0.08% and 0.07% to UK GDP. Even the Trade and Cooperation Agreement giving tariff and quota free trade between the UK and EU (accounting for half of UK goods trade) was valued by the EU[12] at just 0.75% of GDP for the UK compared to trading on WTO terms. Parliament undoubtedly assumed a much higher figure when it was panicked into legislating to prevent the government leaving without a deal.

Such tiny figures might suggest that further trade deals are scarcely worth the effort. But they do not include potential dynamic benefits of open trade which are intrinsically unquantifiable. Moreover, Singham and Abbott[13] emphasise the full benefits of openness come when trade liberalisation and internal competitive reforms are aligned. Future deals are likely to focus more on services which constitute by far the largest share of developed economies' GDP and on removing internal barriers to trade and competition. They will be well worth pursuing.

---

[12] https://economy-finance.ec.europa.eu/system/files/2021-02/ip144_en_1.pdf. European Economic Forecast Winter 2021 Box 2.1 on p. 14.
[13] *Trade, Competition and Domestic Regulatory Policy*. Shanker Singham and Alden Abbott. Routledge 2023.

My Experiences of Global Trade Negotiations

Liz Truss

I am a free trader at heart. I've always believed in freedom. And when I studied economics at university, I learned how important economic freedom was. And then I studied trade economics and I saw how free trade benefited all parties.

Prior to entering politics, my career was in the oil and gas and telecoms industries—trading these vital goods and services around the world. So when Boris Johnson gave me the opportunity in July 2019 to do deals on a national level as Secretary of State for International Trade, I leapt at the opportunity.

What I hadn't realised is how trade would divide today's Conservative Party—much as it had done at several pivotal points in the party's history, under Peel over the repeal of the Corn Laws in the nineteenth century and then in the early twentieth century with splits over protectionist tariff reform promoted by Joseph Chamberlain. This was partly because the UK had not been responsible for trade decisions throughout my lifetime during our more than four decades' membership of the European Community and European Union. Trade had therefore become part of the overall Brexit debate and the cracks were thus papered up.

After Britain voted to leave the EU in 2016, these cracks became apparent. There were those who wanted to cleave as closely to the EU as possible, not allow concerns about China to damage domestic priorities and carry on with business as usual. Then there were others, of whom I was one, who felt we

L. Truss (✉)
Oxford, England
e-mail: contact@elizabethtruss.com

owed it to the public to deliver on the referendum result and the promise of the 2019 manifesto and make Britain a truly independent, successful nation.

I saw trade as a key area where we could boost the economy, lay out Global Britain's stall and lead the world in promoting free trade and free enterprise.

As with the Corn Laws that divided the Conservative Party in the nineteenth century, not everyone agreed. There were those with protectionist instincts who wanted the UK to simply replicate the trade policies of the EU— including their Meursing table (of commodity codes to calculate agricultural tariffs) which had over 500 different classifications of biscuit!

New reasons to oppose free trade had emerged: farming practices, animal welfare, the environment, the NHS, sharp practices of pharmaceutical companies… not to mention the fact that most of those who had never wanted to leave the EU in the first place did not want us to do anything that would see us diverge from EU regulatory practices.

Boris Johnson was reluctant to resolve these differences up front. Instead, I had a series of battles to get the mandates for the UK's new free trade agreements I wanted to negotiate agreed to. And even once they were resolved, Cabinet ministers would relitigate decisions and stop progress.

There was a relentlessly negative backdrop from the leftist media about the UK's ability to do trade deals. Our competence was questioned. There were predictions that we wouldn't be able to get as good deals as the EU. These points were all proved to be wrong. In fact, Department for International Trade officials did a heroic job. Yet it did not change any of the naysayers' minds.

The Brexit Withdrawal Agreement with the EU was largely out of my hands, but it occupied the full efforts of the first months of Boris Johnson's Government, as he sought to succeed where Theresa May had failed. Eventually, after some tough negotiations and bruising parliamentary battles, he had his deal. We then had effectively until the end of 2020 to secure the EU-UK future partnership, including trading arrangements. This negotiation was not one for which I had responsibility and was instead conducted by David (later Lord) Frost.

A fundamental mistake the Government made early on was not treating the U.S. and the EU as parallel deals and playing them off against each other. Europe's farmers, especially the Irish, were very dependent on the British market. Opening up to American agriculture would have been very damaging to them. You need to build all the leverage you can during a negotiation, wherever you can find it. The threat of the UK being in the U.S. regulatory orbit would also have spooked the EU. I advocated a list of "pain" that we could inflict on them if we didn't get what we wanted.

Sadly it was not used. The Government laid down our arms in the EU negotiations by offering tariff-free access both ways for agricultural products, rather than negotiating hard line by line. This was a mistake. Every trade negotiator knows agriculture is the hardest part of any deal because all countries have a protectionist farming lobby. The balance of trade was in the EU's favour because they exported much more to us than we did to them. We should have traded off reducing tariffs for something else in turn. We may have ended up with a zero-tariff relationship, but we could have secured more in return. I found myself in alliance with the National Farmers' Union and the Agriculture Secretary—a rare moment of common cause.

Despite the pugnacious "Get Brexit Done" mantra of that time, Michael Gove, who was by then Chancellor of the Duchy of Lancaster (a senior minister in the Cabinet Office) and his close ally Dominic Cummings, the Prime Minister's chief adviser, were not keen to pursue an ambitious trade agenda. They wanted to focus on simply rolling over existing EU trade deals and play down the possibility of new agreements with other potential major trading partners. They had protectionist instincts and were worried the EU could cause us major pain. The power of the Treasury and the wider establishment, which had spent more than forty years under the EU comfort blanket, was significant. It was a strategy for risk mitigation, not one that was going to drive economic growth.

I wanted to get on with what I saw as the biggest prize and what should have been our priority— a new trade deal with the United States. Even the Treasury's economists had deemed it the number one economic opportunity of Brexit! This would take time and in order to achieve results before the next general election— and indeed the next U.S. presidential election— we would need to get going fast. My belief had always been that we should have started these talks years before, in parallel with negotiating the Withdrawal Agreement, using it as leverage to get a better deal from the EU. That hadn't happened, but I still believed we could have made up for lost time.

This was an argument I had from the moment I was appointed International Trade Secretary in July 2019. At that time, we had in Donald Trump a U.S. President who had talked about a U.S.-UK Free Trade Agreement on many occasions and was evidently sincere in his desire to reach what he called "a very big trade deal." With a presidential election due the following year in which a less favourable candidate could be elected, there was a narrow window to get something done, and I was determined we should use it.

My first official meeting as International Trade Secretary was with the U.S. Ambassador to London, Woody Johnson, where I made clear the deal was my top priority. Woody was beyond enthusiastic and determined to do all he could to assist. The following week, I travelled to Washington for talks with my counterparts, the U.S. Trade Representative, Bob Lighthizer, and the Secretary of Commerce, Wilbur Ross. Lighthizer is a tough negotiator and not a free trader. One of his early roles was negotiating with the Soviet Union on grain quotas under President Reagan. But he was likeable, conservative and I could work with him.

I wasted no time in getting down to business and we had some substantive discussions, somewhat to the surprise of my officials, who had tried to play down expectations of anything more than a round of courtesy meetings. While in Washington, I made a speech at the Heritage Foundation in which I quoted Ronald Reagan's 1980 campaign slogan, declaring that as far as a trade agreement was concerned, "The Time Is Now." This got a negative reaction from Number 10 apparatchiks.

In September, I was back in the United States for the UN General Assembly where I met ministers from around the world. I was not scheduled to attend Boris's meeting with Trump. This was despite the fact that Trump would be accompanied by a large delegation, including Lighthizer, Vice President Mike Pence, Secretary of State Mike Pompeo, and about half the U.S. Cabinet. Boris, as was the wont of the Whitehall machine, was the only politician listed to attend from the British side, accompanied by Foreign Office officials.

I was keen to attend to talk about trade and was also concerned about U.S. threats to slap tariffs on Scotch whisky (which they alas did do the following month). So after attending an early morning business reception with Boris at Hudson Yards, I chased him down a fire escape, grabbed him by the shoulders, and demanded to come. He agreed and further official protests were duly elbowed aside.

At the meeting itself, which took place in the basement of the UN building, I sat alongside British officials on one side of the Prime Minister, while on the President's left sat Vice President Pence and Bob Lighthizer. With a large media presence recording the event, Trump opened the meeting by telling Boris:

> We're going to be discussing trade. We can quadruple our trade with the UK, we can really do a big job. Bob Lighthizer is here, our trade representative. Your trade representative is here, and they're already scheduled today to continue negotiations. But we can have substantially more trade with the UK and we look forward to doing that.

In his remarks, Boris also expressed his hope that we could make "a lot of progress quite fast on trade," before going on to talk briefly about other issues and field questions from journalists about events relating to Brexit back in the UK.

Once the media had left, Trump was even more loquacious about the opportunities for a trade deal. He was enthusiastic and entertaining and clearly very enamoured with Boris. He repeated that we could "quadruple" trade between the U.S. and the UK and said that we would outdo Germany. He urged Lighthizer and me to get on with talks. Lighthizer made some hardball comments, as usual, but I said we were ready to go.

Every time Trump talked trade, however, Boris kept trying to move the conversation to Iran and the Joint Comprehensive Plan of Action nuclear deal. This clearly was not a ripe avenue as there was a fundamental disagreement. I'm not sure if this focus on Iran was a result of the Foreign Office brief or whether it was because of the negativity in Downing Street towards the whole prospect of a trade deal.

I have no doubt that we could have done a trade deal with Trump. We missed that opportunity. Unfortunately, as well as the protectionists in the Cabinet, many in Number 10 seemed to want to hold Trump at arm's length for political reasons. The UK media provided universally negative coverage of Trump and leftists in the Conservative Party were keen to insult him at every opportunity. My view was that he was the leader of the free world and an important ally.

I found it deeply frustrating. Here was a U.S. President who was keen to do a trade deal with the UK. No more "back of the queue," as President Obama infamously threatened while visiting the UK in the run-up to the 2016 referendum. At the margins of that very same UN meeting, Trump and the Japanese Prime Minister had signed a new trade agreement. In time we could have done that too. It might not have been perfect, but it would certainly have been beneficial to both our countries and would have strengthened our hand in negotiations with the EU and others around the world. Ultimately, we threw away that opportunity.

Boris, I believe, had instincts that were closer to my own. Whenever I pinned him down to give a clear direction on this issue, he backed my position. But (as I would discover for myself in due course) the Prime Minister has to deal with endless demands for meetings and calls with foreign leaders, public events, media appearances and so on. It is impossible to give constant direction to every area of policy, however important.

When it came to trade, protectionists like Gove and Cummings wanted to focus on the EU deal and change as little as possible. They actively sought to thwart me in my attempts to pursue a more ambitious policy with the U.S. and elsewhere. There were delaying tactics and bogus nonsense was spouted in Cabinet sub-committees about Brazilian rainforests. I am all for saving rainforests but it was nonsense to suggest that my proposed trade agreements were threatening them. I knew if I could get the Prime Minister in a room where he had to make a firm decision, he would make the right one. In Greenwich in February 2020, Boris made a powerful and unequivocal commitment to expanding free trade. But despite such pronouncements, it became a daily battle to stop the machine from sliding back into obstruction.

There was also a clear degree of reluctance on the part of our diplomats to push trade with the Americans. This was part of a wider systemic problem that our Embassy in Washington and the Foreign Office were much more in tune with the leftist Democratic establishment than with the Republican Party and those on the right. And if they had to deal with Republicans, they would rather it was the Bushes than the Trumps.

I finally managed to get Boris to sign off on starting trade talks with the U.S. when he was holed up at St Thomas's Hospital in London while recovering from COVID in April 2020. I knew he would have his mobile phone on him and be free of nefarious Downing Street influences. We then kicked off negotiations by video in May and these continued for the next few months. However, with the U.S. election looming, talks were paused after the fourth round of negotiations in October 2020. They never resumed. We had started too late.

We did eventually get the whisky tariff removed in the summer of 2021, with my Special Adviser Sophie Jarvis in particular having pushed hard on a political level in talks with the new Democrat administration. Indeed, we secured a deal before the EU did, much to the annoyance of officials in the European Commission. But with Joe Biden as President, it was made quite clear that a trade deal with the United Kingdom was no longer a priority. We had missed the boat.

As well as working on the U.S., I had to secure continuity trade deals with sixty-eight nations before the end of December 2020, when our EU exit would be implemented and our existing deals with those countries would end. Having not been an independent trading country for nearly fifty years, there was work to be done just to get the negotiators in place and build up the necessary capacity. This was particularly the case given that dozens of such agreements would have to be negotiated in parallel.

Many of these agreements were airily dismissed as "rolling over" the existing deals we had as an EU member, as though it were simply a matter of cutting and pasting them into a new document. It was ironic that the same Brexit-sceptics who had previously said it would be impossible for the UK to benefit from the same terms of trade as an individual country outside the EU now took it for granted that we would.

It was not an easy matter to get countries to agree to the same terms of trade they already had with the EU. In particular, they could not reduce the size of the import quota for a particular product— for example, butter. Therefore in any agreement with the UK, they were effectively having to give additional market access for that product.

Every country has its sensitive sectors it wants to protect—like Singapore's financial services or Canada's dairy industry. And lots of countries also tried to use the opportunity to get new market access to the UK for everything from strawberries to rice to chicken. The ministerial team, the negotiating teams and I were involved in an unprecedented flurry of negotiations to secure these deals. Many of these came down to the wire, and there were tricky moments during each of them. But by December the finalised agreements had begun to pile up.

On December 3, we signed a deal with North Macedonia, followed by one with Egypt on December 5, and then a significant one with Norway and Iceland on December 8, the same day as we signed an agreement with Kenya. The following day we signed the UK-Canada deal, followed by Singapore the day after that, then Vietnam on the eleventh, Switzerland on the fourteenth, Mexico on the fifteenth, and Moldova on Christmas Eve. In the week after Christmas, it was perhaps appropriate that we had Turkey left over to sign, and did so on December 29. In total, we had concluded trade deals covering sixty-eight countries by the end of the year—a real Herculean achievement by the negotiators at the Department for International Trade.

The most important deal done that year was with Japan, the third largest economy in the world and a key UK ally. In September 2019, I had kicked off the process in Tokyo with Foreign Minister Toshimitsu Motegi. We were both agreed that we wanted to go further than the existing EU deal and included more terms on digital trade and business visas to deepen our close economic relationship. The sticking point was on the issue of quotas, most specifically on blue cheese. When Motegi visited London for talks in August 2020, he told me it was impossible to keep the same level of access for British blue cheeses like Stilton. This is because the Japanese Diet (Parliament) had specifically ruled out expanding the quota. It is one of the ironies of trade negotiations that deals worth billions can potentially be blown off course by a single product. Eventually, we managed to find a solution that guaranteed our exporters access.

The UK-Japan Comprehensive Economic Partnership Agreement (CEPA) was the first major trade deal signed by the United Kingdom as an independent trading nation. It pointed the way to other deals in future and demonstrated that we were able to secure better and more bespoke terms for British exports than we had done as members of the EU. When I went to Tokyo to sign the final agreement in October 2020, I brought Motegi a pot of Stilton. It has now become a running joke. In celebration of the deal, I was afforded the honour of feeding the carp at the Foreign Office building, a privilege that had most recently been extended to President Trump.

The deal also had a wider strategic significance, pointing the way towards our eventual membership in the Comprehensive and Progressive Trans-Pacific Partnership (CPTPP), a trade agreement among eleven nations. This was important in order to take on China and its unscrupulous trade practices. In order to get into the CPTPP, we needed to agree trade deals from scratch with two of its existing members, Australia and New Zealand.

I went on my first visit to Australia in December 2019. I toured Sydney Harbour promoting British exports and met all the key political players in Canberra including new Prime Minister Scott Morrison. There was clearly a massive desire in Australia to get a trade deal done. I gave a press conference with my Australian counterpart, Simon Birmingham, during which I suggested that part of a trade deal could be making it easier for Brits and Aussies to travel and work in each other's countries.

It was the night of the Midwinter Ball in Canberra, an annual event which that year featured a tropical theme, right down to the guests wearing garlands. That night it served as a victory lap for Morrison for recently winning the election he'd been expected to lose. After the ball, I headed back to the UK High Commissioner's residence where I was staying before heading off to board a flight for Tokyo at 4:30 a.m. during which I was able to sleep off the evening.

It was only when I arrived in Japan that I learned Number 10 was outraged that I had been promoting the free movement of people with Australia. I was duly slapped down for proposing to make it easier to live and work in Australia for young Britons and in Britain for young Australians. This was completely different from free movement of people across the European Union, which put no checks or controls on people entering Britain from the EU when we had been members. (In fact, the final deal did enable young Brits under the age of thirty-five to travel freely to Australia and be able to work without having to labour on a farm.)

By the time negotiations formally started, the COVID-19 pandemic had taken hold, so we did our kick-off video aboard the *Cutty Sark*, the historic tea clipper in Greenwich. There were months of talks and various sticking points, including whether there would eventually be tariff-free access to all products that included beef and lamb and the removal of the farm work requirement for Brits going to Australia. It quickly became clear that our biggest problem was not with Australia, but with certain colleagues in the British Government who didn't want us to diverge from the EU and didn't want to have free trade with Australia.

The arguments put about by these people were ludicrous. All we were talking about was giving Australia the same access to the UK beef and lamb market that the EU enjoyed, but with a huge time delay of fifteen years. (This was the access that Australia had before Britain had joined the EU.) It was already the case that neither Australian nor New Zealand farmers used their lamb quotas, and given that meat prices were far higher in Asia than Europe, it seemed unlikely that Australian producers would want to undercut themselves. I suspect some of the objection was from the Irish, who exported a lot of beef to the UK and were probably concerned about Australian beef cutting into that.

Throughout the process, the agricultural lobby and their friends in the protectionist environmental lobby tried to claim we shouldn't do a deal with Australia because they had low animal welfare standards. This wasn't true. Aside from that, Australia is a sovereign nation not subject to British law. But this didn't stop misinformation being spread. One adviser to DEFRA, Henry Dimbleby, had to apologise for emailing me graphic pictures of Australian veterinary practices that were designed to prevent parasitic disease.

There were many leaks about the arguments around animal welfare and the Australian trade deal in the press. Even at the last minute, Gove tried to stop the deal from happening in a Cabinet sub-committee meeting. I pointed out that we had given away quota-free access to the EU and he'd seemed perfectly happy with that. We were merely giving Australia the same terms but with a fifteen-year delay, which in any case was much less of a threat, what with Australia being on the other side of the world. Boris finally opined. Who had been on our side over the years? Who had fought alongside us to defend freedom? It certainly hadn't been some of the member states of the EU. After what Australia had done for us at Gallipoli, we should do the deal.

I believed that to get this deal done, I was going to have to force the pace because of all the internal opposition. The G7 Summit in June 2021 provided the perfect opportunity, as Australian Prime Minister Scott Morrison would be in the UK. I knew Boris would not be able to resist doing a deal. I just needed to get the ducks in a row. I saw Morrison at a barbeque at Stoke Lodge, the official London residence of the Australian High Commissioner, then George Brandis. Apart from telling me he was a descendent of a Cornish yarn thief, we discussed what would be needed to make the deal work. I was still holding regular video calls with Dan Tehan, my Australian counterpart.

The scene was set for Boris's dinner with Morrison the next night. All they had to do was agree the level of beef and lamb quotas over the transition period. This proved a confusing evening and it was very hard to get a read-out of what had actually been agreed. The team worked through the night to prepare the text of the Agreement in Principle.

In the morning, I then had to go to breakfast with Boris and Morrison and sort out a few things. Namely that this would be a "single pocket" negotiation and the UK would not need to make any more concessions to get into CPTPP. We also had to agree to the details of the quotas. The Cabinet meeting scheduled for that Tuesday morning was delayed while this haggling was going on and there was a farcical scene where a Downing Street staffer got stuck in a double door as the protagonists roamed around the building. At several points, Morrison threatened to get on his plane and leave London. Eventually, it was all nailed down. We had agreement in principle.

The UK-Australia trade deal is an example of what can be achieved between two close allies with huge economic and social benefits to both. With young people able to travel freely between the two countries and services freely exchanged from legal services to banking to tariff-free access to goods, this is what trade should be about. Once we had done the Australia deal, the Kiwis did not want to be left out, and we were able to get agreement in principle with New Zealand four months later in October.

The Japan, Australia and New Zealand deals were all critical to the UK's accession to the CPTPP. With them done, all we had to do was get the text agreed. I faced the usual barrage of internal opposition from Gove and his allies in Cabinet who did not want the CPTPP deal to go ahead. But again we faced them down and got it through. I formally submitted the United Kingdom's membership application in February 2021 and began the negotiations that resulted in our successfully joining this major trading bloc in 2023. As well as being an important economic opportunity for the United Kingdom, CPTPP was also an important geopolitical alliance for taking on China.

At the Department for International Trade, I was unceasing in my pursuit of trade deals with countries around the world. But there was indeed one country with which I had no desire to deepen our relationship. Despite constant pressure from Number 10, I was determined not to make China a priority.

In my early years in politics, I had subscribed to the conventional belief that free trade by itself would expand and entrench freedom, that if we traded more with China, the country would move in the right direction. My doubts over this grew over my time in government. I had already seen some evidence of restrictive trade practices while I was Environment Secretary, with shipments into China being blocked for arbitrary reasons that were clearly political.

I also remembered my rather surreal trip around that time to what I called the "Potemkin dairy" in China. I was taken to a massive dairy plant full of shiny steel machines, where I was shown around under the watchful eye of the ever-present Chinese Communist Party functionaries. They were very proud of this state-of-the-art facility but there didn't seem to be anything happening. No actual production was taking place. It was very strange—and not exactly evidence of a normally functioning industrial sector.

It was in 2018 that the last remaining scales fell from my eyes. That was the year President Xi Jinping abolished his term limit and had himself effectively declared president for life. It gave the lie to the theory that increased engagement with the West and greater trading relations would automatically lead to greater democratisation and political liberalisation.

It was clear that China was subverting the international trading system to their own benefit, including through intellectual property violations and illegal subsidies for key commodities like steel. I agreed with the stance taken by the Trump administration and my counterpart, Bob Lighthizer. For this reason, I was firmly against any moves to seek a closer trading relationship with Beijing. I kept being urged by Number 10 to set up a meeting of the Joint Economic Trade Commission with China, but I used every delaying tactic I could think of to keep this at the bottom of my in-tray and avoid spending any time on it.

I also supported stripping Chinese telecom giant Huawei out of the UK phone network as soon as the issue came to light. I had a row with Cummings about this. He said we wouldn't meet our 2025 target for broadband availability if we took their equipment out of the network. Yet again the UK's long-term security was being trumped by short-term economic interests. Later on, under pressure from the United States security establishment, we ended up having to do it anyway.

A free market can only exist when you have trust and a consensus on the fundamental conditions necessary for it to operate. That means an acceptance and defence of lawful property rights and the freedom of individuals and companies to work without facing unjustified coercion. Slavery has no place in a free market. If goods produced with slave labour are being flooded into a market where everyone else subscribes to basic human freedoms, that is not my definition of a fair system or a truly free market. The fundamental question should always be whether the existence of a trading relationship enhances freedom and democracy or undermines it. In the case of countries whose entire system is built on exploitation of their people and hostility to Western ideas of freedom, the answer should be obvious.

On this basis, I believe it was a huge mistake for the West to have allowed China into the World Trade Organisation and to have opened up ever greater economic ties. Not only has this failed to improve human rights and democracy for people in China, but it has hugely boosted the global power of a country that is actively hostile to us and our interests. Regrettably the WTO has been powerless to change this.

China frequently levels hostile trade sanctions against supposed trading partners—for example, in 2020 when Beijing imposed tariffs on a range of Australian imports in apparent retaliation for the Australian Prime Minister's call for an independent investigation into the origins of COVID-19.

In the absence of credible institutional restraints, we must accept that we cannot regulate the behaviour of hostile economic actors. Instead we should seek to limit our trading relationships to those who share our values and our belief in economic and personal freedom. We need to develop a trading network of allies in the free world—and shut out our enemies.

I have described my conception of this new trading bloc as akin to an economic NATO. Recent events in the world have made that allusion more pertinent than ever. In the same way that Western countries have clubbed together to impose punitive sanctions on Russia, they should band together and decide what we are and are not prepared to do in terms of trade with China.

During the Cold War, Western allies cooperated closely to decide how to deal with the Soviet Union. There was a sense of shared interest in the name of freedom against those who sought to undermine us. That model strikes me as being ripe for being rejuvenated for the circumstances in which we find ourselves today.

But for countries which do share values and a belief in freedom, free trade has indisputable mutual benefits. Trade with Australia is booming after the trade agreement came into force and we should be looking to do similar deals with allies such as Canada. The failure thus far of the UK to do a trade deal with India has been a massive missed opportunity. It is an example of something we see far too often in British politics: the fact that you get criticised more for doing something than doing nothing results too often results in inaction.

Despite the portents of doom from sceptical quarters over the UK's decision to leave the European Union, with predictions of trade drying up and the UK becoming an isolated protectionist island, none of this has come to pass. While the COVID-19 pandemic undoubtedly had an impact on trade flows, the House of Commons Library cites UK exports of goods and services to the EU as having been just under £300 billion in 2019, and by 2022 exceeding pre-pandemic levels, reaching £340 billion.

It is essential that we continue to reject the idea that there ought to be regulatory alignment between countries trading with each other and that things must be produced in exactly the same way. So long as they are given the necessary information to make an informed decision, it should be up to consumers to make their own choices about the purchases they make. Every year millions of Britons visit the U.S. and eat hormone-injected beef or chicken that has been chlorine-washed. Why shouldn't they have the option of purchasing the same products at home?

As a sovereign nation, we should be free to tighten or loosen regulations on the production of goods in the UK as we see fit. For example, if manufacturers are struggling to compete as a result of punitive net zero policies, we need to review those policies. People voted for Brexit in 2016 in order to take back control from Brussels of our laws, our regulations and our trade policy. It would be patently absurd for the UK to keep its laws and regulations aligned with those of the EU now that we are outside its orbit.

Revising Globalising

Tony Abbott

At the beginning of 2020, taken as a whole, the world had never been more free, more fair, more safe, and more rich for more people than ever before, thanks to globalisation under the Pax Americana; because in all of human history, there'd never been a time when goods, people and ideas could move more freely around the world. Partly, this was due to technological improvement, partly to the prestige of liberal democratic and free market ideals after the collapse of Soviet communism, partly to increased immigration at a time when the West, at least, had (rightly) become almost completely colour-blind; but mostly, this was thanks to several decades' absence of major conflict, under strong and mostly high-minded US global leadership, assisted by the rest of the Anglosphere, and the countries of NATO.

Since the pandemic, though, there has been a significant fall in global well-being. With mostly closed borders and often closed workplaces, the pandemic response badly interrupted the flow of goods, the delivery of services and the daily lives of billions of people. With normal life severely disrupted for the best part of two years, economic growth stalled and human well-being declined as an inevitable consequence of all the restrictions imposed in a bid to defeat a virus. The pandemic has been succeeded by the first European war between two major countries in seven decades; a dire incursion into Israel with the high risk of general conflagration in the Middle East; and a growing challenge from communist China to US global pre-eminence.

T. Abbott (✉)
Forestville, Australia
e-mail: tony.abbott@aph.gov.au

© The Author(s), under exclusive license to Springer Nature Switzerland AG 2025
M. Rangeley and D. Hannan (eds.), *Free Trade in the Twenty-First Century*, https://doi.org/10.1007/978-3-031-67656-7_13

This has expressed itself in the bullying of China's neighbours, even India; global influence-peddling via soft loans, bribery and efforts to subvert the Chinese diaspora; technology theft and market manipulation; and, above all, the steadily escalating siege of Taiwan through grey zone intimidation backed by the threat of overwhelming military force.

There is now growing global re-polarisation into two blocs: one, broadly liberal democratic and with varying degrees of closeness to the United States; the other revisionist and dictatorial, with China, Russia and Iran in an alliance of convenience against America and the global order it created; and with the "global south" trying to stand aloof from the tension while also taking advantage of it. This has changed the calculus on the benefits that would normally flow from freer trade and fewer restrictions on the movement of people and ideas.

A further complication has been growing political disruption, in Western countries especially, as freer trade has decimated many established industries, and mass immigration has unsettled many societies. Globalisation and the spread of technology has also meant equalisation: with some countries (like Japan, South Korea, Taiwan and Singapore—those that have substantially adopted market economics under the rule of law) approaching or even exceeding North Atlantic living standards; and others such as China, India and Indonesia vastly increasing their individual economic well-being, their overall economic strength, and ultimately their military power.

All this requires some rethinking of how freer trade should be pursued in practice, without negating the importance of freer trade in-principle, as a way to maximise wealth and to build trust between people and countries.

There is no doubt that after 1945, driven by the bitter lessons of two world wars and the "beggar thy neighbour" tariff polices that exacerbated the Great Depression, there was a strong consensus in favour of freer trade among the policy intellectuals of the victorious democracies. This expressed itself in the General Agreement on Trade and Tariffs and the creation of the World Trade Organisation, dedicated to lowering tariff and non-tariff barriers to economic interactions across national borders. The creation of the European Economic Community, subsequently the European Union (now a project of political union rather than fully free trade between its members), was an expression of this, despite the EEC/EU's protectionism against non-members.

This push towards removing, on an across-the-board basis, formal barriers to cross-border economic interactions, peaked at about the time China was admitted to the WTO in 2001, and its subsequent rapid emergence as the "workshop of the world". The 2008 breakdown of the Doha round of negotiations under the GATT, due to sectoral concerns within more developed countries about competition from lower wage and lower regulation economies, signalled the end of multi-lateral free trade measures.

Since then, freer trade has mainly been pursued via bi-lateral and plurilateral agreements (such as the Trans-Pacific Partnership) that have invariably had important foreign policy and geo-political dimensions. Indeed, the TPP was originally conceived as the economic arm of President Barack Obama's "tilt" to Asia, in response to growing concerns about the assertiveness of China. It was then torpedoed by the "rust-belt" politics of the 2016 US election campaign, only to be resurrected by Japan and Australia as something well worth doing even without US participation.

My introduction to the complexities of bi-lateral trade talks was as health minister in the Howard government between 2003 and 2007, during the negotiation of a trade deal with the US. The Australian Pharmaceutical Benefits scheme, which dispenses approved medicines to patients at a fixed, subsidised price, had long been an irritant to American Big Pharma, that disliked the Australian health department's bargaining power as bulk purchaser on behalf of some 20 million potential consumers. Consequently, US trade negotiators pushed hard for a change in Australia's patent laws, which only protected US drug companies' products for five years, before the PBS could offer patients cheaper generic brands that required much lower taxpayer subsidy. Had this bid been conceded, extra Australian health spending would have padded the profits of US Pharma, to no local patient benefit (although the US maintained that it would boost health R&D by increasing the returns on patented medicines).

In the end, Australian resistance didn't become a deal-breaker, mostly because President George W Bush wanted a deal, as a way of further reinforcing the US-Australia strategic partnership. The 2005 US-Australia FTA, that largely eliminated tariffs on exports between the two countries, increased quotas for Australian agricultural exports to the US, and created a special class of visa for Australian professionals to work in the US was an important economic advance. A by-product, though, was my initiation into the reality of trade negotiations, that usually turn out to be about harmonising systems as much as reducing and abolishing tariffs and quotas; and are always fiercely contested by domestic vested interests on the basis of short-term gain or loss.

Also in my time as health minister, Australia and New Zealand were unable to agree on a mutually acceptable standard for some blood products because different national jurisdictions were unable to compromise, as they saw it, on either price or quality (even though the 1983 Closer Economic Relations agreement was probably the world's most comprehensive bi-lateral FTA, between two countries that might once have been joined in a single federal Commonwealth). Perhaps obdurate officialdom on both sides of the Tasman was also an element here.

On becoming prime minister in 2013, I sought to resolve the free trade talks with our three biggest trade partners, China, Japan and South Korea, that had been spluttering on for the best part of a decade. There had been interminable negotiating rounds that, at least during the term of the previous Labour government, had been complicated by Australia's desire to include workplace and environmental standards into any agreement. My view was that labour and environmental standards in other countries were essentially their own business and that the purpose of trade talks was to remove restrictions on inter-country commerce (as well as boosting relations more generally).

I also suspected that it might be human nature for some officials to gain more satisfaction from on-going overseas travel opportunities than from bringing negotiations to a close. To that end, I gave trade minister Andrew Robb a 12 month deadline to get all three done; and also suggested that rather than letting the best be the enemy of the good, we should focus on finding the best deals that our partners had done with anyone else, and then aggregate them in a deal with us.

As PM, it wasn't normally my job to get involved in negotiating detail; more to establish the best "mood music" at national leader level, because no deal is ever done between sovereign countries unless their leaders want it. More generally, with other national leaders, I tried to begin a personal interaction on the best possible basis, by saying something that was undeniably true, that I could say in good conscience, that they would definitely like to hear; and that others would not normally have said to them, either through national pride or more pressing business. In this, I'd been impressed by the observation of Joe Biden, in a meeting with some Australian visitors, responding thus to my quoting Tip O'Neill's legendary line that "all politics is local": "I'll go one better than that", said the then VP, "all politics is personal". Heeding Biden's advice certainly helped Australia's trade talks.

Hence, to China's President Xi Jinping, I praised the remarkable achievement of the Chinese government in moving half a billion people from the third world to the middle class in scarcely a generation; the largest and fastest advance in human well-being, I said, in all history. To Japan's Shinzo Abe, I noted that, since 1945, Japan had been an absolutely exemplary international citizen and observed that other countries (cue China) shouldn't try to use more distant history as a weapon against it. And to Korea's President Park Geun-hye, I apologised for the former government's cancellation of an order for self-propelled artillery and promised that I'd try to find some other military procurement to make amends.

I don't claim that these forays sealed any deals. Our negotiating success came from Minister Robb's indefatigable energy and the sustained work of some fine officials led by then-chief trade negotiator Jan Adams; but I'm sure Australia's willingness to be helpful to other national leaders, wherever and whenever the opportunity arose, didn't hurt. An example was the sustained navy, air-force and undersea efforts Australia made after March 2014 to locate the missing airliner MH370, that had disappeared into the southern Indian Ocean with over 150 Chinese citizens on board.

At the start of my 2014 trade trip to Japan, South Korea and China, our most seasoned official cautioned that the trip to China would start the day I arrived in Japan and the trip to Japan would end the day I left China. It was sage advice about the geo-political ramifications of trade. He continued that a good outcome in Japan could mean either a very good, or a very bad outcome in China, depending upon whether the Chinese decided upon punishment or reward. As it happened, on this occasion, they decided to try to out-do their rival in the warmth of the engagement.

Our China deal gave 95 per cent of Australian exports tariff free access to the Chinese market and also increased to $1 billion the threshold before Chinese investment into Australia attracted Foreign Investment Review Board scrutiny. There is little doubt that it helped to boost further two way trade, that had already been running at close to $150 billion a year. Of course until about 2015, prior to the Chinese militarisation of the South China Sea, the crackdown on internal dissent, and the effective scrapping of "one country two systems" for Hong Kong, it was easier to be confident that a measure of economic liberalisation in China would eventually lead to some political freedom too. As it turned out, the conclusion of the China trade talks in November 2014, and President Xi's address to the Australian parliament, with the English version declaring the China would be "fully democratic" by mid-century, may have marked the high tide of Western engagement with the Middle Kingdom.

Our trade deal with Japan built on the earlier 1957 trade treaty that had been the foundation for Australia's 1960s resources boom. Like the deal with South Korea, finalised at much the same time, it eventually eliminated tariffs and quotas on about 95 per cent of Australia's merchandise exports, with improved access to Japan's highly protected rice market; and gave Japan, also, a $1 billion threshold for inward investment before FIRB scrutiny was required. For his part, PM Abe wanted to establish an even stronger basis for the Japan-Australia relationship than trade, and was even willing to provide

Australia with its next generation submarine, a potential strategic partnership that South Australian parochialism regrettably later scuttled.

For years, I'd regarded India as a potential strategic partner, as well as a somewhat neglected economic one. I emphasised that India was the world's "emerging democratic superpower" during Prime Minister Narendra Modi's post-G20 visit here in November 2014. I'd intended to visit India in late 2015, when I'm sure a trade deal would have been finalised. My successor, though, was less India-focussed; and the eventual deal had to wait until 2022, after I'd become Australian trade envoy to India under the Morrison government.

In that capacity, making the most of the standing of a former head of government, I'd helped to re-start largely stalled negotiations, via a personal call on Modi, stressing the importance of a deal as an economic complement to the Quad security partnership linking India with the US and Japan (with which Australia already had trade deals) and also Australia; in a potentially era-shaping show of democratic solidarity.

I stressed this geo-political dimension in numerous meetings with Indian ministers; and also suggested that the best way to proceed might simply be to get the list of our countries' exports to each other and to substitute much lower tariffs and much larger quotas for the current figures. While both countries' main ministers, Piyush Goyal and Dan Tehan, were keen to get a deal done; in the end, it was the Indian PM's determination to drive his officials that actually made it happen.

Even though the deal was expressed to be "interim" or "early harvest", it was the first India had done with a major economy in over a decade and the most comprehensive it had ever done. Under the deal, 85 per cent, rising to 90 per cent of Australia's goods exports to India, and 96 per cent rising to 100 per cent of India's exports to Australia, would be tariff free.

In 2020, based on my record as a trade-focussed PM, I was appointed a honorary adviser to the UK Board of Trade, a consultative group that had been in existence, on and off, since the 1600s reporting to the Secretary of State, or President of the Board of Trade. Such advisors have no specific role, other than to offer counsel in quarterly meetings, but are expected to use their good offices generally to promote Britain's trade. As an Australian, I had no qualms about doing so: first, because I regard the countries of the Anglosphere as being hardly "foreign", except in a juridical sense; and second, because an economically strong and successful "global Britain" is overwhelmingly in Australia's national interest.

Other than to roll over existing deals between the EU and its trade partners, the first big post-Brexit deal that the then-UK trade minister, Liz

Truss, wanted to do: was with Australia. I'd previously said that a trade deal between Australia and the UK should be reducible to one page, given our two countries' shared values, history, and heritage. Essentially, I'd said, it should provide that goods exports between us should be entirely tariff and quota free; that UK and Australian standards and credentials should be mutually recognised in both countries; and that each other's citizens should be recognised as locals for the purposes of living, working and doing business. In effect, it should be a relationship without borders and a distinction without any institutionalised difference.

Unsurprisingly, that is not quite how it turned out in practice, given the vested interests involved. After four decades of EU protectionism, the UK farm lobby was especially vociferous and highly influential within the Conservative government. Apart from public advocacy in favour of a deal, stressing that UK agriculture tended to be "boutique" while Australia's was largely "commodity", and hence were more complementary than competitive, my role was mostly stressing to ministers and prime ministers that if Britain and Australia were incapable of doing a very wide-ranging deal then no one could. Occasionally, both ministers were in contact seeking help with the alleged intransigence of the other side. Eventually, it did require face-to-face settlement between prime ministers Scott Morrison and Boris Johnson on the basis that tariffs and quotas on Australian beef and lamb exports would be phased out over ten years. Even so, with (eventually) almost completely free trade in goods, it was, the Australian government declared, our "most ambitious free trade agreement with any country other than New Zealand".

Because economic interaction is largely determined on the basis of price, quality and convenience, realistic access to a wider range of goods and services, via freer trade, is unambiguously good for consumers. On the other hand, more foreign competition will eventually hurt less efficient domestic producers even though, in both the exporting and the importing country, overall economic well-being would improve.

Economic well-being, though, is not governments' or nations' only consideration. It certainly isn't the main consideration for the current Beijing government, which regards prosperity as a means to securing its own longevity rather than a good in itself; and regards economic success as the key to building its military power. What is now much more obvious than even a decade back is that Beijing never really believed in competitive markets; just competitive countries. And at least to Beijing, a measure of market freedom was simply a means to making China more formidable as a strategic competitor. To that end, Beijing often goes through the motions of cooperating with the West on issues like climate change, for instance, but only because what is supposedly needed to deal with it, impacts much more heavily on the West's strength than on China's.

It has to be recognised that, in practice, while freer trade with China has been good for consumers everywhere, it is been a key factor in the relative de-industrialisation of many advanced economies. Over the past three decades, large swathes of the West's manufacturing, electronics and IT industries have moved offshore, first to China and then to other countries that have managed to combine increasingly sophisticated technology with wages that are still substantially below the West's. While this has advanced overall global prosperity, it is also increased China's relative economic strength and made many Western countries dependent on China for critical intermediate goods. These days, the sophisticated manufactures of the West often include imported components, many from China. This wouldn't matter in a peaceful, harmonious world but in a world of renewed great power competition, it matters very much indeed.

China has used subsidies, bribes and government-controlled businesses to manipulate the global market in vital commodities such as rare earths and nickel. And it has showed a readiness to turn on-and-off-like-a-tap access to these, plus trade more generally, to advance its foreign policy and strategic objectives. To the Chinese party state, and to other dictatorial and totalitarian regimes, trade is politics by other means. Their businesses are under government direction, actual or potential, in a way that liberal democratic countries' businesses would simply never accept. Hence, the freer trade that in other circumstances would be in everyone's interests is not in Western interests, if it gives the West's strategic competitors a technological edge or makes the West dependent on potentially hostile countries for critical supply chains.

As the on-going Russian war against Ukraine has demonstrated, success—even survival—depends on access to superior technology and to a sustained supply of war fighting materiel, as well on good leadership, a just cause and high morale. At least until "the lion finally lies down with the lamb", countries that wish to maintain their freedom and their independence in the face of powerful potential adversaries must maintain trained and motivated armed forces and the industrial base needed to sustain them. This requires secure access to critical raw materials, a substantial domestic industrial base and a science and technology sector that is mindful of with whom it is sharing. In that sense, trade and other interactions between liberal democratic allies and their potential adversaries need to be carefully managed and certainly shouldn't be fully free right now.

What this means in practice is not that the West and China should fully decouple but that the Western allies should be far more stringent about sharing STEM research and high technology, and should rapidly develop secure sources of strategic minerals and rare earths, while still trading resources and most consumer goods. The case for higher tariffs on Chinese goods, for instance, in order to protect key manufacturing sectors in economies such as the US and the UK, is now much stronger than it was a decade ago; even compelling. Almost by definition, this is economically suboptimal; but it is becoming essential if freedom is to be preserved; and in the end, it is better to be poorer and freer than richer and at risk of being militarily overwhelmed.

Australia's trade deal didn't stop China subsequently banning some $20 billion in our exports (on spurious quality grounds) as punishment for calling for an independent investigation into the origins of the Wuhan virus. Formally abrogating that deal right now might be gratuitously offensive but the obvious need to reduce and, if possible eliminate, exposure to China in critical supply chains means that no such agreement would be reached today. Likewise, it would be an act of appeasement to admit China to the TPP, given its bad faith on trade and the obvious motivation of its bid to complicate Taiwan's much more credible case for TPP membership.

This is not an argument against globalisation and in favour of polarisation. Rather, with polarisation a fact of life and with only one of the key antagonists holding that freer trade is desirable in itself, it is an argument for free trade with our friends but not our enemies; for globalising more selectively; for pursuing globalisation only with countries that are broadly like-minded. It is not an argument for reversing globalisation, but for revising it.

In this era of renewed great power competition, at least some economic nationalism is necessary for economic security. As Australia discovered during the pandemic, when a normally well-disposed European government seized a vaccine shipment that we'd ordered and paid for, there are some things countries always need to have on hand in sufficient quantities, or be able to produce for themselves; other things that we might be ready to rely on our friends for; and still others that we're happy to obtain from anywhere in the world. We need to consider what should be on-shored, what might be friend-shored, and what could be off-shored. It would be a rare country today, that did not want at least some capacity to produce munitions or medicines. Maybe it is not necessary to be able to produce planes or missiles, but a country under any threat at all would certainly want the capacity to repair them and to produce the munitions they need in large quantities.

The one country that could, over time, substitute for China as a source of high quality, low cost consumer goods—and that is already a substantial strategic counterweight to China—is India. India is a democracy under the rule of law, that has substantially assimilated a British inheritance, however problematic that has been in the past. On Ukraine, India has mostly declined publicly to criticise Russian aggression and to join trade sanctions, due to its need for oil and gas and weapons' spares. Still, it is hard to find a single informed Indian who fails to acknowledge the sheer evil in Russia's assault.

Confirming India in the liberal democratic orbit, not just though reinforcing the Quad, but through the pursuit of all possible bi-lateral partnerships should be among the key strategic objectives of every Western country. If there is to be a "leader of the free world" a century hence, that is as likely to be the Indian prime minister as the American president.

To this end, a key immediate goal should be the finalisation of a free trade deal between India and the UK. There is a considerable community of values between both countries, from Britain's past role in the sub-continent, and the vast Indian diaspora now in Britain. Large Indian businesses such as Tata and Infosys have a big presence in Britain. It would be a tragic missed opportunity, if anxieties about even higher immigration, or short-term vested interests, were to jeopardise an economic (and ultimately strategic) deal between a traditional bulwark of the West and the rising democratic superpower. In the end, such a deal eluded a distracted British Conservative government (notwithstanding the first British PM from a sub-continental background) but it's reportedly on the "to do" list of its Labour successor. The sooner this can happen, the better for the security and the prosperity of everyone.

Free Trade Under Siege: Analyzing Contemporary Trade Policies

Barbara Kolm and Miguel Del Valle

Introduction

In 1776, Adam Smith wrote *The Wealth of Nations*. The book, almost a thousand pages long, introduced two innovative ideas, among many: the self-regulatory nature of markets and the advantages of trade. In contrast to contemporary economists, who advocated for self-sufficiency and with whom Smith bitterly disagreed, Smith advocated for trade between countries. In *The Wealth of Nations*, he outlined the case for trade between countries. According to Smith, self-sufficiency was pointless; trade could make society better off: "If a foreign country can supply us with a commodity cheaper than we ourselves can make it, better buy it of them with some part of the produce of our own industry, employed in a way in which we have some advantage." (Smith 1909).

Smith's successors would further develop his arguments on trade. David Ricardo, an economist and Member of Parliament, drew on Smith's arguments to develop the doctrine of comparative advantage. In *Principles of Political Economy and Taxation*, Ricardo postulated that countries were better off by producing what they could do best and buying the rest from other countries. Ricardo posited that countries should eschew their inefficient production and focus on what they do best—"not in comparison to other

B. Kolm (✉) · M. Del Valle
Austrian Economics Center, Vienna, Austria
e-mail: b.kolm@austriancenter.com

countries, but rather what they do best relative to other things they do" (Frieden 2020, p. 32):

> England may be so circumstanced, that to produce the cloth may require the labour of 100 men for one year; and if she attempted to make the wine, it might require the labour of 120 men for the same time. England would therefore find it her interest to import wine, and to purchase it by the exportation of cloth. To produce the wine in Portugal, might require only the labour of eighty men for one year, and to produce the cloth in the same country, might require the labour of ninety men for the same time. It would therefore be advantageous for her to export wine in exchange for cloth. This exchange might even take place, notwithstanding that the commodity imported by Portugal could be produced there with less labour than in England. Though she could make the cloth with the labour of ninety men, she would import it from a country where it required the labour of 100 men to produce it, because it would be advantageous to her rather to employ her capital in the production of wine, for which she would obtain more cloth from England, than she could produce by diverting a portion of her capital from the cultivation of vines to the manufacture of cloth. (Ricardo 1817/2001, p. 89)

Free trade follows logically from these postulates. If a country gains from selling what it does best and buying the rest, then barriers to trade lead to an inefficient outcome. Policies that restrict trade prevent countries from selling the goods that they produce best and force countries "to manufacture goods that are not in its comparative advantage to produce." (Frieden 2020, p. 32) Therefore, protectionist measures—such as tariffs and quotas—lead to inefficiency: inefficient domestic production and an increase in the price of goods (finished goods and inputs to production).

Smith's arguments took around 70 years to take hold. It was only in 1846 that the British Parliament repealed the Corn Laws, "the country's major agricultural tariffs." (Frieden 2020, p. 32) Although the theoretical case for free trade was overwhelming, "only Britain and the Low Countries actually pursued free trade" (Frieden 2020, p. 32). Why Britain? Britain's adoption of free trade was a natural consequence of its superior industrial capabilities. The technologies introduced by the Industrial Revolution gave a considerable advantage to British manufacturers. "By the 1820s British factories could undercut competitors in virtually every market." (Frieden 2020, p. 3) Unsurprisingly, British manufacturers were among the first ones in Western Europe to advocate for the removal of trade barriers. The removal of trade barriers meant that British manufacturers "could lower their costs directly by importing cheaper raw materials, and indirectly because cheaper imported food would allow factory owners to pay lower wages without reducing worker's standard of living." (Frieden 2020, p. 3) The adoption of free trade policies also meant access to new markets: British manufacturers could sell overseas. And "if foreigners earned more by selling to Britain, they would be able to buy more British goods and if foreigners could buy all the manufactures they needed from low-cost British producers, they would have less need to develop their own industries." (Frieden 2020, p. 3)

Other countries would follow suit and open up their economies but only "gradually and partially." (Frieden 2020, p. 32) Some would adopt protectionist measures (in the form of barriers to imports), mostly "targeted and not broadly applied" (Frieden 2020, p. 67), as means to develop their fledging industries. Friedrich List, a nineteenth century German political economist, advocated for *industrialization by protection* a doctrine that postulated that free trade, despite being the ultimate objective of a country, was only feasible once a nation had fully developed its industry. Temporary trade protection was necessary to "equalize trade relations between countries." (Frieden 2020, p. 65) Supporters of industrialization by protection argued that a country needed time to industrialize; with time the country's industry would become efficient, and protection could be removed: "In order to allow freedom of trade to operate naturally, the less advanced nations must be first raised by artificial means to that stage of cultivation to which the English nation has been artificially elevated." (List 1916, p. 107)

These protectionists pointed to Britain as an example of the need for protective barriers: the United Kingdom had removed protective barriers only after achieving industrialization. Additionally, "national security demanded industrial self-sufficiency." (Frieden 2020, p. 65) Even some classical economists, such as John Stuart Mill, accepted the argument that "early industries needed government support." (Frieden 2020, p. 65) However, Mill and the neoclassicals always thought of protection of fledging industries as a temporary measure "more to be tolerated than embraced." (Frieden 2020, p. 65)

Free trade would not go unchallenged by the citizenry as not everyone benefitted from economic integration. "Societies that abandoned less productive economic activities often also abandoned those trapped in them." (Frieden 2020, p. 26) "Whole industries, regions and classes were made redundant, and those on the losing side of specialization and economic integration were less willing to accept a hands-off government that did nothing to ease their sufferings." (Frieden 2020, p. 26) But despite opposition, free trade prevailed and the world entered into a golden age of globalization. "By 1913, all major nations were exporting far more of what they produced, and importing far more of what they consumed, than they had in 1870." (Frieden

2020, p. 68) This however would come to an end with the onset of the First World War and would only resume in the 80s:

> The golden age of the first globalization, 1850-1914, came to an end with World War I. The disruptions of the war itself were followed by six decades of relatively turbulent times in the world economy. In the 1920s monetary problems led to the imposition of tariff controls and limits on capital movements. The Communist takeover isolated the Russian Empire from the world economy. The world Depression of the 1930s led to further disintegration of the world economy as nations lost faith in free markets and strove to solve their problems through protection, capital controls, and currency devaluations. After the disruptions of World War II, there was further fragmentation of the world economy with the creation of a raft of new Communist regimes, and the breakup of much of the British Empire into independent states. Only in the 1980s did a new era of globalization emerge, with worldwide moves towards freer trade in goods and capital amongst democracies, combined with the ending of Communist rule, or its transformation into Communism in name only as in China. (Clark 2007, p. 319)

The world of today resembles the world of back then. The global economy is largely integrated and much of what we consume is imported and much of what we produce is exported. Cultural trends traverse across countries and continents irrespective of national borders. The world is connected to an unprecedented scale and so globalization and free trade seem like the norm and not the exception. Even nominally communist states are well integrated into the world economy. China, being the quintessential example, is the top trading partner to more than 120 countries (Green 2023), exporting around 3.38 trillion of dollars and importing 2.56 trillions of dollars in 2023.

Today, just like back then, free trade is belittled by its enemies on both sides of the political spectrum. Politicians run on political platforms that denounce free trade as a rapacious system that has created a set of winners and losers: the economic elites have seen their fortunes soar, while craftsmen, "tradespeople and factory workers have seen the jobs they love shipped thousands and thousands of miles away." (Trump 2016b) In his famous speech of 2016 in Monessen, Pennsylvania, President Trump made the case for tariffs as a necessary measure to protect the forsaken American industry and its workers. For him and for many others, the workers' loyalty had been repaid with betrayal. Politicians had aggressively pursued a policy of globalization, moving jobs, wealth and factories overseas, enriching themselves and their donors in the process while leaving millions of workers "with nothing but poverty and heartache" (Trump 2016b).

After his election, Trump would go on and impose tariffs on a series of goods. To this year, 2024, some of the tariffs remain in place.

Why Managed Trade and Protectionism is Harmful to a Country in the Long Run

Theoretical Arguments

Tariffs can be thought of taxes on imports, levied to discourage the consumption of foreign goods and to encourage the production, and therefore, consumption of domestic goods. Superficially, tariffs might seem desirable. After all, they provide jobs and strengthen the domestic industry of a country making it less reliant on foreign countries and raise, just like any other tax, revenue for the country levying the tariffs. However, this is one half of the story. By raising tariffs, consumers have to pay higher prices. Directly, as tariffs might be levied on finished goods; or, indirectly as the cost of goods might rise due an increase in the prices of inputs or raw materials. Even if producers and the government are better off by the enactment of tariffs, it might be the case that society as a whole is worse off as consumers no longer have access to cheap goods. In fact, once you take into consideration that the countries, whose goods are tariffed, are likely to retaliate, both consumers and producers, now caught in the crossfire of a trade war, are worse off than before. There are other indeterminable consequences of levying tariffs: a policy of tariffs might dampen competition among manufacturers and therefore stifle innovation in the long run. Tariffs might as well divert a country from its comparative advantage. "By making protected activities artificially profitable, trade protection diverts resources to inefficient activities" (Frieden 2020, p. 66) in which countries might not have a comparative advantage.

In autarky, a society with no international trade, consumers and producers reach an equilibrium where supply equals demand.

Surplus, for both consumers and producers, is represented by the shaded areas in the triangles (Fig. 1).

Trade might introduce goods at a lower price. Therefore, the quantity traded in an economy open to trade is higher than in an autarkic economy. Figure 2 shows that at a lower price (PW or price world), the quantity traded is higher than in autarky. With trade, the quantity traded is CT, the point where world price meets domestic demand.

However, domestic producers produce less. Domestic producers producing at world price will only produce QT.

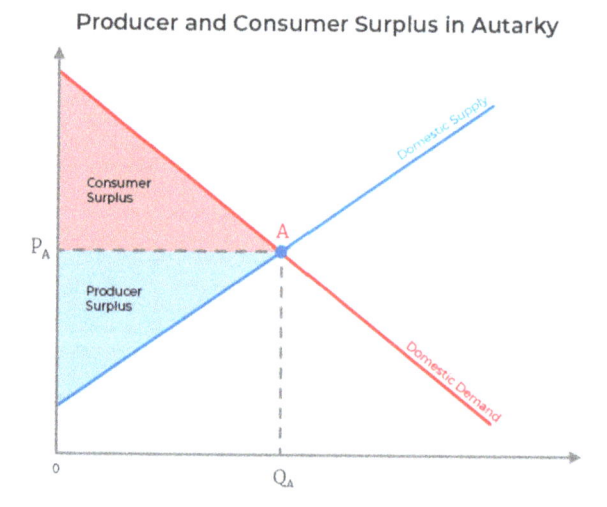

Fig. 1 Producer and consumer surplus in Autarky (*Source* Jaki King for MIT Opencourseware)

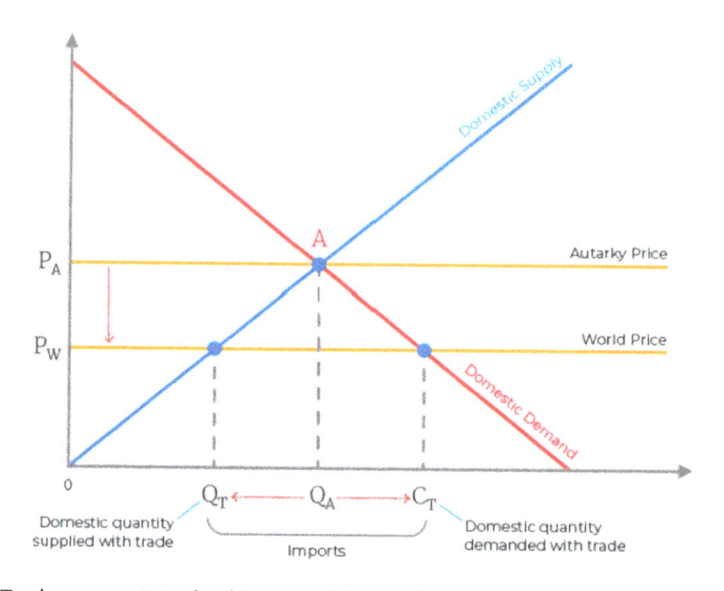

Fig. 2 Trade versus Autarky (*Source* Jaki King for MIT Opencourseware)

Trade alters consumer and producer surplus.

In autarky, consumer surplus is represented by W. Now, with a lower price (P_w) and a higher quantity (CT), consumers have a higher surplus represented by the shaded areas W, X and Z.

Domestic producers, however, have a lower surplus, represented by Y. Since they went from producing QA to QT (Fig. 3).

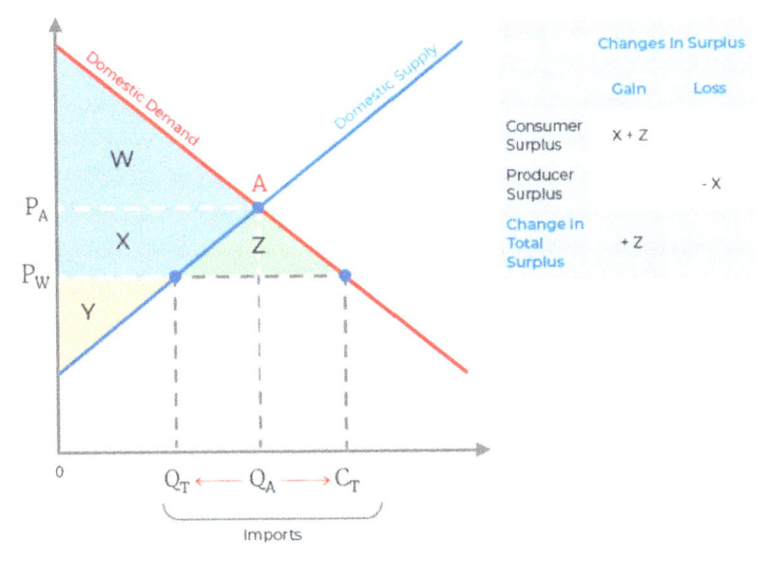

Fig. 3 Trade alters consumer and producer surplus (*Source* Jaki King for MIT Opencourseware)

Despite a decrease in producer surplus, society is better off by trading. The decrease in producer surplus is offset by an increase in consumer surplus. The net increase in societal surplus is represented by Z.

Tariffs, however, distort this by increasing, artificially and deliberately, the world price (PW) from PW to PT (price with tariffs). At PT, domestic producers are willing to produce more but domestic consumers are willing to consume less.

Consumers at PT are only going to consume $C2$. They moved from $C1$ to $C2$.

Producers at PT are going to produce $Q2$. They moved from $Q1$ to $Q2$ (Fig. 4).

Consumer surplus decreases while producer surplus increases. With a higher price and a higher quantity, producer surplus will get the area labeled as A.

Consumers will lose A along with the areas B, C, D (formerly part of Z).

Government, however, will be better off by levying tariffs on goods. The shaded area labeled C is their surplus or revenue (Fig. 5).

The aforementioned example relies on the neoclassical assumptions of no labor market frictions, inelastic labor supply and other assumptions which ensure that the aggregate economy is always at full employment so even if producers are worse off, the model assumes that labor and capital will reallocate to other profitable sectors (Acemoglu et al. 2014, p. 3). However, in

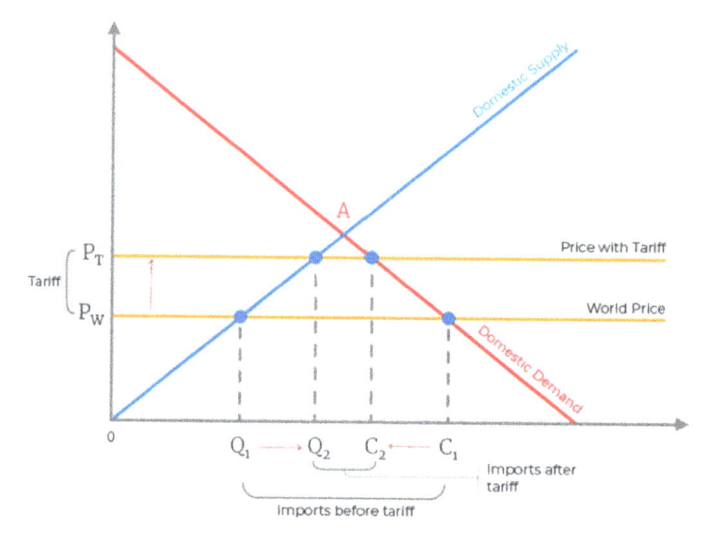

Fig. 4 Influence of tariffs (*Source* Jaki King for MIT Opencourseware)

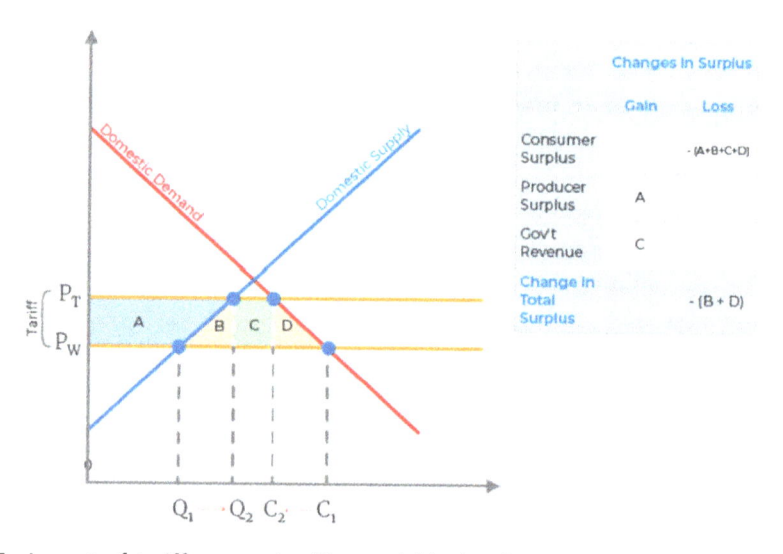

Fig. 5 Impact of tariff on surplus (*Source* Jaki King for MIT Opencourseware)

the real world, a world "with imperfections in labor and other markets, there is no guarantee that reallocation effects will be sufficient to restore employment to the same level" (Acemoglu et al. 2014, p. 3). Shu and Steinwender (2018) have pointed out that trade liberalization doesn't have the same effect everywhere. Its effects are resented distinctively in the emerging and in the developed world. While trade liberalization seems to spur productivity and innovation in emerging countries (Shu and Steinwender 2018), the impact of trade in developed countries is mixed. "In developed countries, export opportunities and access to imported intermediates tend to encourage innovation, but the evidence on import competition is mixed, especially for firms in the United States. At the firm level, the positive effects of trade on innovation are more pronounced at the initially more productive firms while the negative effects are more pronounced at the initially less productive firms." (Shu and Steinwender 2018, p. 1)

In the long run, there are other undesirable and unquantifiable effects of tariffs. An increase in prices is not the only drawback of prices of tariffs. Tariffs disincentivize innovation by removing real competition from the market. Industries protected by tariffs don't have to face market pressures, an element that spurs competition, and therefore have no need to innovate. Competition is a natural feature of markets. Joseph Schumpeter coined the term "Creative Destruction" to emphasize the dynamic nature of the market: creative destruction is a process "that incessantly revolutionizes the economic structure from within, incessantly destroying the old one, incessantly creating a new one. This process of Creative Destruction is the essential fact about capitalism." The creation of cartels is another possible and undesirable effect of tariffs: large corporations may collude to limit the supply of goods and keep prices artificially high at the expense of consumers.

Empirical Evidence

On the midst of Trump's presidential term, 2018, his administration "imposed substantial tariffs on Chinese imports and selective goods from other countries" (Autor et al. 2024, p. 1). Trump had advocated early on in his campaign for tariffs as means "to bring back jobs to America" (Trump 2016b).

On account of this, the Trump administration launched investigations to "address a wide variety of unfair acts, policies, and practices of the US trading partners" (Office of the United States Trade Representative 2018, p. 3). On the grounds of threats to national security (Section 232) and unfair trade practices (section 201), the US levied a series of tariffs on imports in 2018. Tariffs' objectives were threefold: economic, political, and electoral.

Economics

The explicit economic objective of tariffs was to bring back jobs to the United States. Robert Lighthizer, United States Representative and architect of American trade policy during Trump's presidency, argued, and continues to argue, that tariffs are a necessary measure to protect the American manufacturing industry: the China tariffs are means to "ensure that domestic manufacturers won't be undercut by Chinese importers" (Lighthizer 2022). For Lighthizer, Chinese manufacturing has grown at the expense of the American manufacturing: "China has used unfair trade practices to destroy various US industries. This has led to lower wages, increased income inequality, and the breakdown of many American communities." (Lighthizer 2022) Additionally, the trade "tariffs are a necessary measure to counter the US-China trade deficit—more than $350 billion annually. The deficit's unabated increase over decades has transferred trillions of dollars of American wealth to China" (Lighthizer 2022). For him, the revival of American manufacturing depends on the government's ability to lure companies into re-relocating into the US and tariffs provide the incentives to do so. Bereft of tariffs, American companies manufacturing in China would simply "avoid costly long-term investments in American manufacturing capacity" (Lighthizer 2022) and continue manufacturing in China.

Politics

On the one hand, these are an attempt to slow China's "global economic and military pre-eminence" (Lighthizer 2022): "Fearing that China is inexorably poised to become the world's leading economy, policy makers in the United States have embraced tariffs, investment restrictions, export controls and massive domestic subsidies" (Packard and Lincicome 2023, p. 1). On the other hand, tariffs act as a punishment and an attempt to bring China, "America's primary geopolitical adversary" (Lighthizer 2022), to the negotiation table. Tariffs act as a punishment, insofar as they were a response to decades of Chinese outright criminal practices and other unfair trade policies. (Packard and Lincicome 2023)

First, China conducts "state-sponsored cyber espionage into the US commercial networks in order to steal trade secrets and abuse intellectual property" (Packard and Lincicome 2023, p. 3). Next, "China uses hidden industrial policy and foreign discrimination, including via its numerous state-owned enterprises (SOEs) that hurt American competitors" (Packard and Lincicome 2023, p. 3). Next, China pressures US companies to transfer their technology "to Chinese companies as a condition of accessing the Chinese market." (Packard and Lincicome 2023, p. 3)

In Peter Navarro's words, director of the Office of Trade and Manufacturing Policy Electoral, an office directed to "defend and serve American workers and domestic manufacturers while advising the President on policies to increase economic growth, decrease the trade deficit, and strengthen the United States manufacturing and defense industrial bases," the tariffs were a crackdown on China's "Seven Deadly Sins:" cyber hacking, intellectual property theft, forced technology transfer, currency manipulation, illegal export subsidies, predatory state-owned enterprises and the killing of Americans with deadly fentanyl. (Navarro 2022).

Elections

Throughout both campaigns 2016 and 2020, Trump used his platform to lambast the negative consequences of foreign trade. The trade policy touted by Trump conveyed solidarity "with voters in import-competing sectors and locations." (Autor et al. 2024, p. 1) After all, growing Chinese imports had a negative effect on the US manufacturing employment. Acemoglu, Autor and Dorn estimate that the rise in import competition from China over 1999 to 2011 amounted to "net job losses of 2.0 to 2.4 million stemming from the rise in import competition from China over the period 1999 to 2011." (Acemoglu 2014, Abstract)

Tariffs were an electoral success, a political wash and an economic gaffe.

Tariffs remain a popular measure among the population. In 2020, the Steelworkers Union pledged the Biden administration to keep the steel tariffs in place. Tariffs, according to the union had proved a major success: it had bolstered the industry and provided jobs. Gina Raimondo, Biden's Department of Commerce Secretary, declared that tariffs on steel and aluminum "helped save American jobs in steel and aluminum industries." This is consistent with the findings of Autor, Beck, Dorn and Hanson: the tariff war appears to have been a political success for the Republican Party. "Residents of regions more exposed to import tariffs became less likely to identify as Democrats, more likely to vote to reelect Donald Trump in 2020, and more likely to elect Republicans to Congress. Foreign retaliatory tariffs only modestly weakened that support." (Autor et al. 2024, p. 2) The effect, however, was uneven: the metallurgic industry benefitted from tariffs, while agricultural sectors experienced net job losses as a consequence of China's retaliatory tariffs "partly mitigated by compensatory US agricultural subsidies." (Autor et al. 2024, p. 1)

Despite their political success, tariffs weren't able to exercise much political leverage over China. The trade war with China stopped with a truce signed by Washington and Beijing. Both China and the US agreed to forgo additional tariffs and China, as part of the Phase One Agreement, "agreed to purchase large quantities of American exports over a two-year period and promised to make certain structural changes to its economic practices." (Packard and Lincicome 2023, p. 4) The Phase One Agreement did not achieve its goals: "China purchased only 58 percent of the total US goods and services exports over 2020–2021 that it had committed to." (Bown 2022) Beijing, however, blamed COVID-19 for its inability to fulfill its obligations. There is little evidence that tariffs altered Beijing's trade practices. Charlene Barshefsky, former US trade representative asserted that China "did not change their economic model one iota." (Davis and Wei 2022) In fact, it seems that "China has doubled down on the state-led economic model the Trump administration had set out to change: Chinese authorities increased their use of subsidies—including cash infusions, discounted loans and cheap land—to dominate high-technology industries." (Davis and Wei 2022)

The economic performance of tariffs was lackluster at best. Autor et al. (2024) concluded that the imports enacted by the Trump's administration were unable to bring back many jobs to the US: "import tariffs on Chinese and other foreign goods had neither a sizable nor significant effect on US employment in regions with newly-protected sectors." (Autor et al. 2024, p. 1) However, the retaliatory tariffs, caused by the subsequent trade war, had clear negative employment impacts particularly in agriculture, and these harms were only partially "mitigated by compensatory subsidies." (Autor et al. 2024, p. 2) The tariff's inability to reach its desired goal can be explained by producers finding alternative sources of foreign imports (i.e., importing products from countries not targeted by tariffs). However, Autor et al. (2024) conclude that "it remains an open question whether import protection that failed to generate substantial job gains during the trade war might spur job creation over longer time horizons."

Why Free Trade Benefits a Country: The Case of China

History is ripe with examples about the advantages of free trade. However, one of the most instructive examples is the liberalization of the Chinese economy in the 70s and its further accession into the WTO. In the 70s,

China was among the poorest nations in the world. Civil war and mismanagement by central authorities had torn the country apart. Mao Zedong's vision of self-reliance destroyed agriculture, devastated the economy "and led to mass starvation as people's communes were established and resources were forcibly shifted from farming to heavy industry." (Dorn 2023) The death of Mao and subsequent rise of Deng Xiaoping enabled a series of reforms that would turn the country away from central planning and toward a market-oriented economy.

Contrary to his predecessor, Mao, Den Xiaoping's approach was not quixotic but pragmatic in nature. Improving the lives of the Chinese was paramount even if it came at the expense of ideology. If the markets could help alleviate decades of suffering, it was worth to turn away from utopian standards and turn to the market as means to develop. After all, Xiaoping famously said "it doesn't matter if a cat is black or white, as long as it catches mice."

The path to change was gradual, nonetheless radical. Deng Xiaoping during his address to Central Work Conference in December 1978 called citizens to "emancipate the mind, seek the truth from facts and unite as one in looking to the future." Deng's words were a radical departure from Maoism and the "two whatevers" that had defined Hua Guofeng, Mao's successor, approach ("Whatever Mao said, whatever Mao did"). Deng's speech was an invitation to reshape society. This was however a daunting task. After all, the Chinese economy was derivative of the Soviet model: collectivized agriculture, centralized planning, state ownership of banks and commerce.

After 1978, a series of reforms that would radically alter the fate of the Chinese Society were put in place. These reforms would kick-start the "Chinese economic miracle, a remarkable thirty-two-year period, through 2010, during which GDP grew at an annual rate of 10 percent." (Naughton 2022, p. 722) Reforms were slow but they would allow "China to take advantage of its factor endowments and structural conditions and spur economic growth." (Naughton 2022, p. 722) Change would come gradually. In the words of Deng Xiaoping, change was to be undertaken with utmost care like "crossing the river by feeling the stones."

The first challenge that China had to face was their own policies. "China was mired in a vicious cycle of shortage, poverty, and inefficiency." (Naughton 2022, p. 727) The command economy had created a completely inefficient system. Labor and capital were misallocated and every solution that had been attempted had created further problems. Reform was further stalled due to "ideological commitment to socialist institutions" (Naughton 2022, p. 727):

one of China's biggest problems was that central planners were fixated on self-sufficiency. "For decades, the country had been following a capital-intensive development strategy, giving priority to the development of the most capital-intensive industries, including steel, machinery, and armaments." (Naughton 2022, p. 727) China, however, was a country with abundant labor resources. It was in its best interest to capitalize on labor.

Early reform attempts started in 1978 after Chinese heads of state, including Deng Xiaoping and Hua Guofeng, visited the neighboring capital countries. They were especially surprised by industrial and prosperous Japan, which had sustained growth for decades. Moreover, they were disabused of their misunderstanding of the capitalist world: the capitalist workers were not impoverished, society was well ordered, and workers were well educated (Naughton 2022, p. 730). As Gregory Clark asserted: "Marx and Engels, trumpeting their gloomy prognostications in *The Communist Manifesto* in 1848, could not have been more wrong about the fate of unskilled workers." (Clark 2007, 294) Unskilled labor had reaped more gains from industrialization than any other group. (Clark 2007, 294)

Impressed by what they had seen in the capitalist world, "Vice premier Gu Mu led a team to five countries in Western Europe and briefed top leaders in June 1978 for over seven hours, galvanizing opinion to support reform and further opening [the country]." (Naughton 2022, p. 730) The visits confirmed the need for reform and the possibility of rapid growth, and the necessity of doing business with capitalist powers. (Naughton 2022, p. 730) The first reforms attempted to import technology. However, these early attempts failed despite the will by the Chinese to industrialize and the will of lenders and manufacturers in neighboring capitalist countries to sell to the Chinese government. China was not yet ready for industrialization. Despite these initial failures, Chinese policy makers were not discouraged and decided to relax controls, decentralize decision making and expand autonomy.

Expanding autonomy and abandoning the import technology program, which had done nothing but to "extract resources from the countryside and pump them into capital-intensive industry" (Naughton 2022, p. 736), allowed the Chinese economy to flourish. Citizens were unconstrained by regulation and its ideological underpinnings and free to pursue more rewarding paths. The entrepreneurial Chinese spirit emerged immediately. Change in rural property rights along with newly gained control of their cropping and labor allocation decisions, allowed farmers to increase their output. Trade would play a much bigger role in reshaping Chinese society. "Market opening accelerated structural change that moved resources toward more productive uses." (Brandt 2022, p. 812) China would sign its first exporting contracts in the 70s, exporting blue jeans. Thirty years later, China was exporting laptops. A key to success was China's ability to capitalize on their comparative advantage, cheap labor and profit from it. By the early 90s, China had become one of the major Foreign Direct Investments (FDI) recipients in the world. "Overseas firms, eager to capitalize on low Chinese costs, promoted domestic supply chains to feed their Chinese assembly plants." These Foreign-invested firms occupied a vital role in China as they not only provided jobs but they brought with them the much needed "technology, production and organizational skills, managerial know-how and expertise" (Brandt 2022, p. 813) that powered Chinese capacity to manufacture cutting edge internationally competitive products. (Brandt 2022, p. 813)

In 1992, Deng Xiaoping declared: "development is the only hard truth." This symbolized China's departure from their prior ideological rigidity. Change had already taken place and Chinese society had been transformed. However, another economic boom awaited Chinese society. Chinese accession into the World Trade Organization (WTO) propelled an already flourishing economy into new heights or more precisely it launched the economy overseas. "If pre-WTO opening was concerned primarily with bringing in foreign investment, post-WTO opening was driven by the concept of 'going abroad'." (Yao 2018, p. 76)

The Chinese economy would have to be reshaped for China to be accepted into the WTO. In 2000, Long Yongtu, China's Chief Representative of Trade Negotiations wrote: "planned economies have never been part of economic globalization. China's economy must become a market economy in order to become part of the global economic system." (Yongtu 2000, as cited in Dorn 2023) Chinese policy makers understood that the process to enter into the WTO would be taxing: Chinese state-owned enterprises would face harsher competition as lowering tariffs would lead to an increase in imports of agricultural and industrial products. Zgu Rongji at a 1999 press conference had declared: "If China wants to join the WTO … then China must play by the rules of the game. China cannot do that without making concessions … such concessions might bring about a very huge impact on China's national impact on some state-owned enterprises, and also on China's market. But … we will be able to stand such impact. And the competition arising from such impact will also promote a more rapid and more healthy development of China's national economy." (Rongji 1999, as cited in O'Hanlon 2016)

China had already undertaken gradual unilateral steps to liberalize its international trade in the 1980s (Drysdale and Hardwick 2018, pp. 554–555). Entry into the WTO, however, would require China to further reform its trade practices: markets became increasingly open, barriers to trade were dropped and businesses practices homologized to international standards. "From the 1990s until China's accession to the World Trade Organization (WTO) in 2001, the average import tariff for all agricultural products was reduced from 42.2 percent, in 1992, to 23.6 percent in 1998 and 21 percent in 2001. Tariff rates fell to 12 percent in 2004, making China one of the most free agricultural trading nations in the world." (Huang and Rozelle 2018, 496) Furthermore, "China committed to lower its average industrial tariff rate to 8.9 percent, to remove all license requirements and import quotas on manufactured goods before 2005 and (with a small number of exceptions) to abolish the "designated trading" system (whereby the central government permitted selected domestic companies to trade certain commodities internationally)." (Drysdale and Hardwick 2018, pp. 554–555)

Concessions made by the Chinese were indeed harsh, but they were immediately rewarded. On one hand, from 2001 to 2008, China's "export growth averaged 29 percent per annum—more than quadrupling its total amount over the seven-year period." (Yao 2018, p. 76) On the other hand, an unintended consequence of China's entry into the WTO was the amendment of "domestic laws, regulations and traditional management methods that were in conflict with international rules." (Huang and Rozelle 2018, 496) Domestically these amendments led to a more efficient allocation of resources, improvements in business practices and the eradication of vested interests of a group of managers appointed under previous administrations.

China's entry into the WTO kick-started a period of unprecedented growth. Key indicators across all areas (trade, GDP, GNI, FDI, employment) attested the salutary consequences of liberalization and trade in China. In 2001, China rose to the rank of lower-middle-income country (according to the World Bank Criteria). Only ten years later, in 2010 China would rise to the rank of upper-middle-income country (Fig. 6).

From 2000 to 2012, the Chinese economy grew at double digits. Government revenues grew at an annual rate of 22% (Wong 2018, p. 274). In 2016, China's total imports amounted to US$1.6 trillion, accounting for 11% of world imports. In 2001, the total volume of imports and exports was equivalent to 38.5% of GDP and reached a high of 64.2% in 2006. During the period 2002–12, private enterprises' share in industrial output increased from 60 to 76% and continued a 3.3 percentage point contribution to economic growth (Wang 2018, pp. 178–180).

China's share of world manufacturing exports expanded from 5% in 2001 to 17% in 2016. From 2001 to 2010, China's total exports and imports increased by 5.9 and 5.7 times, respectively, and its total GDP more than doubled (Drysdale and Hardwick 2018, p. 550). As a percentage of GDP,

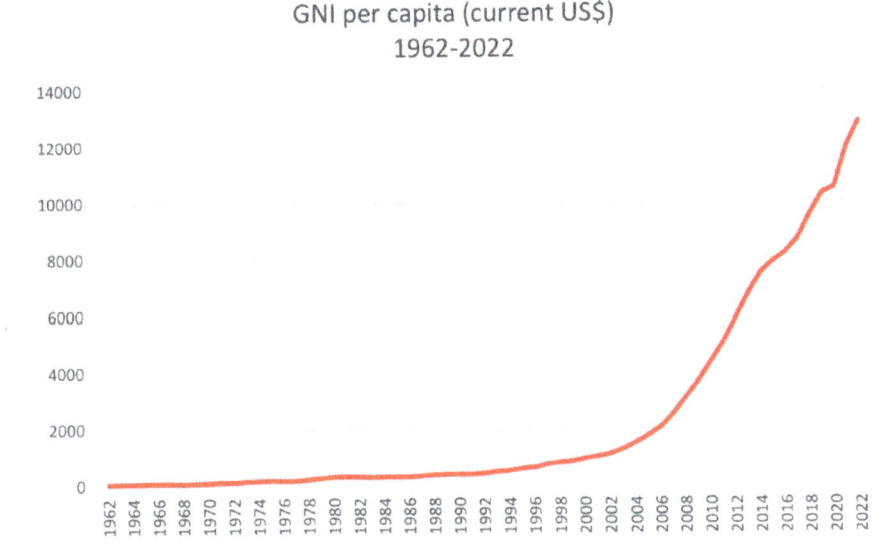

GNI per capita (current US$)
1962-2022

Source: World Bank national accounts data, and OECD National Accounts data files.
https://data.worldbank.org/indicator/NY.GNP.PCAP.CD?locations=CN

Fig. 6 GNI per capita (current US$) 1962–2022

Chinese exports have surpassed American exports since 1984. In 2021, exports in China represent 19.94% of its GDP, while exports in the US represented only 10.89% (Fig. 7).

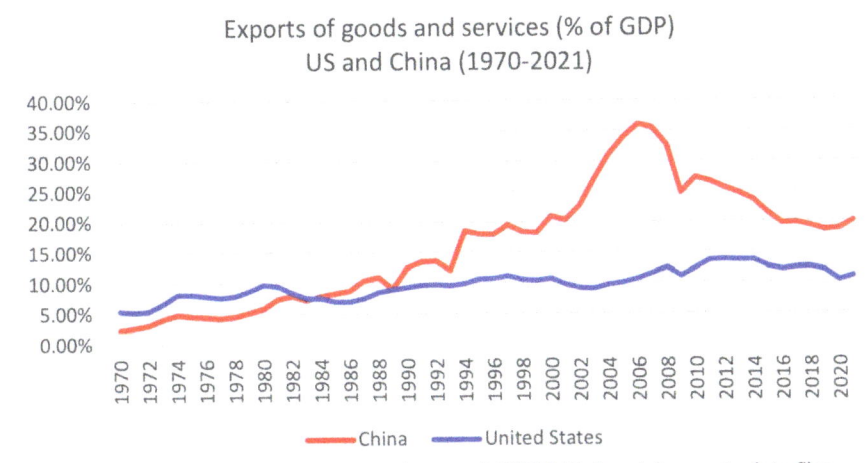

Exports of goods and services (% of GDP)
US and China (1970-2021)

Source: World Bank national accounts data, and OECD National Accounts data files.

https://data.worldbank.org/indicator/NE.EXP.GNFS.ZS

Fig. 7 Exports of goods and services (% of GDP) US and China (1970–2021)

As trade flourished, so did China. Economic growth led to urbanization and urbanization led, in turn, to an increase in production and trade. Public services and infrastructure improved as a consequence of economic growth, all sponsored by the post-WTO economic reforms.

It is worthwhile to consider that the "Chinese economic miracle" is all but a miracle. It is the textbook example of the power of markets and improvements that follow suit once central planning is eschewed and individuals are allowed to take their own decisions and pursue profit as they see fit. The effective allocation of labor and capital was the inevitable consequence of the liberalization of the economy. Once Chinese policy makers abandoned ideological rigidity, China was able to take advantage of its factor endowments and dramatically accelerate economic growth. China's integration into the market is responsible for its ascendancy. As James A. pointed out: China could not have become the world's second-largest economy without allowing the market to play a decisive role in allocating resources and without integrating itself into the global trading system. "China's reforms coincided with an era of increasing globalization, which was characterized by a more open global trading environment resulting from significant reduction in tariffs and other forms of trade protection." (Drysdale and Hardwick 2018, p. 545) Today the opposite seems to take place. In these turbulent times, looking at the Chinese example could serve as a guide for policy makers.

Current and Potential International Trade Issues

"Decoupling" and "De-Risking" from China

Sino-American relations have soured in the past couple of years. This is one of the top geopolitical issues facing the world today. "How the two countries manage this relationship will greatly affect global peace, prosperity, and stability in the twenty-first century." (Packard and Lincicome 2023, p. 2) A deterioration of the Sino-American relations and the COVID-19 pandemic, with its disastrous consequences for global supply chains, has prompted policy makers in Europe and the United States to rethink international trade arrangements. Consequently, conceptual frameworks such as "Decoupling" or "De-Risking" from China have been developed.

De-risking and decoupling are used interchangeably. The difference lies on the scope, or the degree of disengagement pursued. In this context, decoupling entails complete economic disentanglement from another country. More radical proponents of decoupling advocate not only for halting trade, but also investment, and migration. (Packard 2023) De-risking involves a degree disentanglement, but its goal is to end exclusive reliance on another country and consequently to diversify economic dependence. Put briefly, if the objective of de-risking is to diversify, the objective of decoupling is to withdraw. "Unlike decoupling, de-risking seeks to continue basic trade and investment activities—once the risks have been dealt with." (Capri 2023) In practice, much decoupling has been diversification (Lehner 2023). And "some actions taken under the banner of de-risking may inadvertently lead to a form of decoupling." (Benson and Sicilia 2023) Therefore, the terms are used interchangeably save for diplomacy where the authorized term is "de-risking."

President Trump made job repatriation a centerpiece of his campaign. According to the former president, China had grown, through questionable practices, at the expense of the US. In 2016, at a rally in Fort Wayne, Indiana, Trump accused China of committing "the greatest theft in the history of the world." (Trump 2016a) Trump's abrasive attitude toward China was new, however wariness of Chinese behavior was not. The Obama administration had already grown disillusioned of Beijing's behavior during its second term. Underhanded Chinese state-led policies such as cyber economic espionage on the US firms; poor enforcement of intellectual property rights; extensive use of industrial policies; and interventionist policies to devalue the renminbi had cast doubts in the mind of the Obama administration officials about China's willingness for reform. In the eve of the Obama administration, Penny Pritzker, then the US commerce secretary, addressed the threat of technology sensitive to national security flowing to China. The Trump administration would inherit the problem and opt for a brazen confrontation against China, by 2015 the second largest economy in the world.

US policy makers had bet that China's accession into the WTO would liberalize not only China's economic institutions but also its political institutions. Henry Rowen, chairman of the Reagan administration's National Intelligence Council, forecasted in 1999 that China would "join the club of nations well along the road to democracy" in 2015, when he expected its per capita GDP to reach $7000. China would reach the mark in 2013, signs of democracy, however, were nowhere to be seen. The underlying assumption, bolstered by "the end of history optimism," was that political transformation would ensue after economic transformation. In 2000, Bill Clinton asserted that economic transformation in China would unleash forces that no totalitarian regime could manage to:

> Yes, China is still a one-party state, restricting rights of free speech and religious expression, doing things from time to time that frustrate us and even anger us.

But by forcing China to slash subsidies and tariffs that protect inefficient industries, which the Communist Party has long used to exercise day-to-day control, by letting our high-tech companies in to bring the Internet and the information revolution to China, we will be unleashing forces that no totalitarian operation rooted in the last century's industrial society can control. (Clinton 2000b)

Optimism didn't last long. By the end of the Obama administration, American policy makers were increasingly concerned about Chinese duplicitous practices.

Decoupling undoubtedly recalls Trump's tariffs and his administration's allegedly unprovoked attempts to hedge against China. However, it wasn't Trump who started the decoupling wars. Black and Morrison (2021) argue that China started the decoupling in 2005: "China's strategy began in 2005, with the launch of its Medium- and Long-Term Plan for Science and Technology Development (2006–2020), or MLP, in which the government called for increasing domestic content in eleven sectors to 30% by 2020 through import substitution, a practice through meant to replace foreign imports with domestic production." The Made in China 2025 plan (MIC 2025), launched in 2015, and updated this percentages to 40% by 2020 and 70% by 2025 in 10 sectors. MIC 2025 also set market-share goals for domestic corporations. Thereafter, domestic corporations were meant to capture a designated share of the market. For example, "the plan envisioned that Chinese makers of electric vehicles and energy equipment would capture 80% and 90% of the domestic market, respectively" (Black and Morrison 2021). Chinese policies like the MLP or the MIC 25, now updated to MIC 35, put a heavy burden on foreign companies. And while foreign companies can hedge against domestic-content targets (which demand an increase in domestic production by import substitution) via increasing manufacturing in China, foreign producers are helpless against high market-share targets, which ensure that indigenous firms will dominate the Chinese market (Black and Morrison 2021).

There is no consensus on how to decouple from China. At the extremes are separationists, who argue for complete decoupling, and cooperationists, who advocate for continuing engagement as any attempt to decouple would lead to retaliation from China. Few policy makers advocate for such policies of complete engagement or disengagement. Most policy makers advocate for some middle ground: enacting tariffs, repatriating jobs, reshoring supply chains and relocating industries that key to national security.

To engage or to hedge is the question that both China and the US have to address. Meetings between leaders give some hope for possible cooperation (Bessler 2021). However, it is unlikely that the situation will ameliorate.

Partly, due to China's unwillingness to change its questionable business practices. Partly, due to a difference in expectations: the US has long awaited a reform of the Chinese political institutions. However, the Chinese Communist Party doesn't envision a China without a CCP. This difference in expectations has also led to deep distrust between the countries and their ulterior motives. China's claim over independent Taiwan exemplifies China's disregard for rule of law and its reluctance to abide to international law. Finally, China's emergence as an economic and military superpower represents a challenge to the US and its "rules-based" world order. China may be getting closer to establishing political and economic blocs capable of rivaling the US-led West. Politically, China's increasing cooperation with Russia, North Korea and Iran is raising concerns both East and West. Antti Hakkanen, Finland's Defense Minister, labeled this incipient coalition a "long-term threat to European countries." Economically, China's Belt and Road Initiative (BRI) aims to establish "key economic ties to developing states and control critical minerals and resources." (Cordesman 2023, p. 3) If successful, the Chinese may succeed in creating "a rival economic bloc that could function and grow outside the 'rules-based order' democracies created after World War II." (Cordesman 2023, p. 3)

The Biden administration's approach to decoupling is in line with the previous one even if the tone is softer. The administration has emphasized the importance of "de-risking" as means to build "resilient effective supply chains" and to avoid being the "subject to the coercion of any other country." (Martin 2023) These are understandable objectives. After all, the global pandemic and the war in Ukraine evidenced the need to hedge against unforeseen events. However, evidence casts doubt on the veracity of the Biden administration's rationale for "de-risking." Evidence points toward growing suspicion, competition and increasing tensions as the main drivers behind both countries' attempts to decouple or de-risk.

Direct confrontation remains unlikely. Nonetheless, both countries feel that "they have grown overly dependent on each other" (Black and Morrison 2021) and that trade is now a zero-sum game, where one country will inevitably grow at the expense of the other. In this spirit both countries have set their overt and covert decoupling strategies. Whether the USA, a liberal democracy, will manage to do so remains a relevant question. The CCP has the leverage to implement their MLP and MIC plans, which set domestic and market-share goals. However, the USA is not an authoritarian state. Its success in decoupling from China largely depends on the market reactions to American policies and the benevolence of certain producers willing to move production out of China.

The task will be incredibly difficult and taxing for the US. China is a formidable competitor to contend with. It is a manufacturing behemoth with a colossal workforce and market and the largest trading partner of almost 120 countries, including the US and allies such as Japan, South Korea and Germany. In 2018, it accounted for 28% of all global production. After all, China "has become 'the world's factory' not just because it has abundant labor but because that labor force is increasingly higher skilled and includes more than 200 million people who can flexibly move across producers as demand fluctuates." (Black and Morrison 2021)

For the US, decoupling would require American companies to forego the massive investments they have made in Chinese plants and supply chains. Many American companies are heavily dependent on Chinese manufacturing: American companies' supply chains are deeply imbedded in China. Executives don't "want to see the time, effort, and investment they've put into developing a presence in China go to waste." (Black and Morrison 2021) An anonymous executive quoted in Harvard Business Review stated: "We spent 13 years getting into China. It is impossible for us to just pull out." (Black and Morrison 2021)

Then, even if companies were willing to forego their investments, they wouldn't have a place to move their manufacturing. There is currently no match for Chinese manufacturing. According to Stewart Black and Morrison (2021): few other countries can match the quality of Chinese workers at a comparable cost. As Apple's CEO, Tim Cook, noted "China has moved into very advanced manufacturing, so you find in China the intersection of craftsman kind of skill and sophisticated robotics and…computer science… That intersection, which is very rare to find anywhere…is very important to our business because of the precision and quality level that we like." (Black and Morrison 2021) Besides a highly trained labor force, China offers "a well-financed infrastructure, a great safety and quality control regimen, excellent transportation and communication points." (Black and Morrison 2021)

The decoupling wars will have disastrous consequences for firms. Some will be able to bear the brunt of losses, others will be able to adapt. However, some will inevitably be forced to close and consequently capital, know-how, expertise and jobs will be lost in the process. Few companies have the capital to set up new plants or to enlarge existing ones. Perhaps, the decoupling wars are a look into the future. As the world becomes more uncertain and increasingly polarized, companies will have to assess for potential political and geopolitical and to prepare for potential contingencies.

EU and US Industrial Policy Schemes

The past couple of years have deeply shaken the foundations of the rules-based order upon which the world was supposedly cemented. The COVID-19 pandemic and the subsequent war in Ukraine have exposed the flaws in infrastructure, supply chains, policies and even of the international system. This has consequently compelled countries to implement industrial policy schemes, aimed at supporting industries that are deemed strategic.

Industrial policy is nothing new. It didn't arise as a consequence of the challenges of the past years. Over 170 years ago, Friedrich List and his contemporaries had already argued "that national security demanded industrial self-sufficiency." (Frieden 2020, p. 36) Prior to this, Alexander Hamilton had already outlined something akin to industrial policy in his *Report on the Subject of Manufactures*. In practice, it had been embraced much earlier.

The US, a champion of free trade, has, in theory, been averse to such policies. However, it has often embraced them. As Wade (2020) noted: "the most effective US industrial policy is to make the rest of the world believe that the US does not do industrial policy." The New Deal, the WW2 mobilization and the Space Race are examples of the US engaging in industrial policy (Berman and Siripupapu 2023). American policies differ from those of the EU. They are less conspicuous as they exist in other forms: grants, subsidies, government contracts, and financing through federal and subnational institutions (Berman and Siripupapu 2023). The EU, on the other hand, has more overt industrial policies: "Today, the French government is still a major shareholder of the automaker Renault, while the aerospace giant Airbus is the result of a collaborative effort by the British, French, Spanish and German governments." (Berman and Siripupapu 2023)

The threats posed by China, Russia and global warming have compelled both, the US and the EU, to draft and propose a slew of legislations aimed at countering possible contingencies. These legislations, however, remain controversial as they interfere with the market, increase the scope of government, and consequently shake the international order and delegitimize free trade "by which mainstream economists saw economic development as the result of free-market policies such as the privatization of state enterprises and promotion of free trade." (Berman and Siripupapu 2023)

Proponents of industrial policy argue that there are certain goods (military equipment and medical supplies) that ought to be produced domestically. National security warrants the production of such goods at home even if a loss in efficiency is incurred or a higher price is paid. According to them, the expertise and know-how in these high-value industries are a key asset that must not be outsourced, lest it falls in the wrong hands. This follows from their argument that the market, in some, cases fails to structure the economy in the national interest (Berman and Siripupapu 2023).

Despite their disagreements when it comes to environmental, social and governance policies, both the EU and the US have common goals like addressing the military and economic threat that Russia and China represent. Collaboration between the US and the EU may obviate the need for industrial policy.

As Clark Packard and Scott Lincicome have noted, the threats are real and should be addressed. However, a careful cost and benefit analysis of the consequences of industrial policy should be performed before any policy is enacted. A defective policy can easily stifle innovation and competitiveness. Industrial policy can easily destroy the same industries it purports to protect.

Case Study: Trade Between China and US

Modern Chinese history is a history of contrasts, of shadow and light, of despair and hope. A history to learn from. While Mao's China is and will be for the years to come the quintessential example of the dangers of communism and central planning. Modern China is an example of the merits of markets.

China's 2001 accession into the WTO, turned the inward country, once dirt-poor, into a manufacturing giant. Opening up the economy allowed China to capitalize its strengths, (abundant labor resources; huge land plots; and sea access) and to modernize its economy in the process. The USA played no minor role in it. President Bill Clinton would continually lecture lawmakers and Americans about the benefits of China's entry into the WTO. American lawmakers were divided on the issue. Proponents of China's entry into the WTO considered that China's accession would economically benefit the whole world and liberalize China's authoritarian regime in the process:

> By joining the WTO, China is not simply agreeing to import more of our products, it is agreeing to import one of democracy's most cherished values, economic freedom," Mr. Clinton said. "When individuals have the power not just to dream, but to realize their dreams, they will demand a greater say. (Clinton 2000a)

Opponents argued that China's accession would turn China into an export powerhouse and propel the Asian country to a dominant world trade position, after which no manufacturing job in [the US] would be safe (Lighthizer

1997). Opponents, additionally, argued that China was not a real market economy, its admission into the WTO was unwarranted and ultimately dangerous to the market economies.

Proponents were right, Sino-American trade and diplomatic relationships were to flourish. China was posed to become an economic superpower. But the honeymoon didn't last long. The Obama administration expressed doubts about China's willingness to play by the international rules. A reprimand came during Obama's second term when the US secretary of commerce expressed concerns about sensitive technology falling into Chinese hands. Duplicitous practices by China had long predated this reprimand and had been outlined before China's entry into the WTO. In 2005, China had already outlined a series of policies aimed at "eliminating its dependence on foreign countries and corporations for critical technology and products; facilitating the domestic dominance of indigenous firms; and leveraging that dominance into global competitiveness." (Black and Morrison 2021) These policies were coupled with other practices such as state subsidies; and currency manipulation-practices condemned by the WTO. It would take almost a decade for the US to retaliate against those practices. In 2018, the Trump administration enacted a series of tariffs on Chinese imports citing concerns of national security and unfair trade practices. America's enactment of tariffs angered Beijing and provoked retaliation.

Despite animosities, both nations continue to trade. The United States is China's main trading partner. And China is among the US top three trading partners. In 2022, "China was the top supplier of goods to the United States, accounting for 16.5 percent of total goods imports." (Office of the United States Trade Representative 2024) "In 2022, both the US exports to China and imports from China continued to grow for a third year in a row. The US exports totaled $153.8 billion, an increase of 1.6% ($2.4 billion) from 2021; the US imports from China totaled $536.8 billion, an increase of 6.3% ($31.8 billion)." (Office of Technology Evaluation 2022) Economic interdependence extends beyond trade: as of January 2023 China holds $859.4 billion of US debt "making it one of the United States' major creditors." (Benson and Sicilia 2023)

This raises the question whether the two largest economies can do without the other. Achieving decoupling or a "hard economic break" between the world's two largest economies seems almost impossible. A breakup of such magnitude would lead to significant economic losses for both countries. That is not to say that the US should not address China's duplicitous practices. "There are legitimate concerns about numerous international trade and investment policies pursued by Beijing, its increasingly brutal human rights practices, and its geopolitical bellicosity and coziness with Russia and rogue regimes, which all demand attention." (Packard and Lincicome 2023, p. 2)

However, the US should pursue another approach. There is evidence that Washington's current policies such as tariffs, investment restrictions and export controls have failed to alter Beijing's behavior. US Trade Representative, Katherine Thai, declared before the House Ways and Means Committee that despite multiple commitments from China, real change had remained elusive (Tai 2022). In fact, even the Phase One Agreement, through which China has failed to deliver. American attempts to counter China have angered Beijing, whose targeted retaliatory tariffs have harmed the American sector—harm that has been only partly mitigated by compensatory US agricultural subsidies (Autor 2024). This illustrates a sad reality about trade wars: politically connected the US companies and unions profit from them, while innocent bystanders are caught in the crossfire (Packard and Lincicome 2023, p. 7).

The US should be avoid emulating Beijing's practices. Policy makers that advocate matching China's economic interventionism, as means to counter Chinese influence, may be doing so based on a misleading understanding of the Chinese economy. "The Chinese economy today is not the powerhouse many believe it to be." In fact, it is beleaguered by current problems and future problems that await them—problems "created in no small part by China's shift away from economic liberalization." (Packard and Lincicome 2023, p. 2) Currently, the Asian giant faces a real state crisis, a stagnant tech industry—a once dynamic and growing sector of the economy but paralyzed by Xi Jinping's heavy interventionism—and inefficient State Operated Enterprises—"the International Monetary Fund (IMF) estimates that Chinese SOEs are about 20 percent less productive than private sector competitors in the same market." (Packard and Lincicome 2023, p. 3) In the short run, Beijing's interventionist policies may have managed to bolster the economy, hurting US competitor firms in the process. However, in the long run, interventionism will be a greater liability due to a loss in efficiency and reputational damage caused by disregarding the rule of law.

Instead, the US should employ more efficient tools to counter China's behavior. Tailored policies would be better than the "blanket tariff regime currently employed by the US administration." (Packard and Lincicome 2023, p. 10) Espousing the protectionist and decoupling principles could cost the US dearly. Up until now, the US was the unwavering champion of the principles of liberalism. Its commitment to freedom played no minor part in turning the country into an intellectual, cultural, economic and industrial powerhouse. The American commitment to rule of law and liberal tradition has fostered economic growth and innovation. Forsaking this legacy could stifle innovation.

The trade war has negatively affected and will affect people in the future. It is a reminder of the consequences of intervening in markets. The trade war is the inevitable consequence of subordinating markets to political concerns and the whimsies of politicians. Politicians' misguided efforts to fundamentally change Beijing's mercantilism and nationalism have achieved nothing in China, yet have brought despair at home.

Given the tensions between Washington and Beijing, the fact that trade has managed to grow for the last three years is surprising. Despite this, some fractures are showing. In mid-February 2024, the US imports from Mexico outgrew imports from China for the first time in over 20 years. "Mexico surpassing China as America's top trade partner signals a significant shift in global commerce dynamics." (Sheidlower and Gaines 2024) The US has also increased trade with other countries: US businesses and consumers have been buying more from European countries, South Korea, India, Mexico and Vietnam (Sheidlower and Gaines 2024). This might be a direct consequence from Trump's trade war and Biden's subsequent attempts at "de-risking" and reshoring. "The Biden administration has continued pushing companies to 'reshore' by returning manufacturing to the US or 'friend-shore' to trade with allies." (Sheidlower and Gaines 2024) Whether the trend will continue remains an open question.

Chapter Conclusion

The optimism that characterized the early 2000s is long gone. China's accession into the WTO has not spurred the liberalization of its political institutions, once heralded by US policy makers. Contrary to what was expected, the regime has grown more authoritarian and has blatantly disregarded international laws.

In the face of it, the US policy makers can either mimic Chinese behavior and carry out industrial policies and interventionism or they can bet on trade and innovation as means to develop and grow. Today trade is taken for granted. But history shows us that globalization is not the natural state of things. "In 1914, it took only a few months for the entire edifice of globalization to collapse. World War One broke out in August 1914 and swept away the foundations of the preexisting global economic order." (Frieden 2020, xiv)

This is a reminder that globalization is a choice, not the natural state of things. "It is a choice made by governments that consciously decide to reduce barriers to trade and investment, adopt new policies toward international money and finance, and chart fresh economic courses." (Frieden 2020, xv) If globalization is to stay, it needs the support of governments. However, governments will support the principles of free trade as long as there is domestic political support: "globalization needs supportive governments, and supportive governments need domestic political support. International economic affairs depend on political backing from powerful countries and from powerful groups in those countries. The integrated world economy before 1914 rested on government actions to sustain it; when these policies became unpopular, they could not be maintained, and with them fell the international economic order." (Frieden 2020, xv) Today's global economy, just like back then, depends on domestic political support.

In these times, the history of the Soviet Union is a cautionary tale of the consequences of ideology, looking inward and economic isolation. The Soviets had brilliant scientists capable of contending with American scientific prowess, but they were always a step behind the US.

Ideology-bound and inward-looking the Soviets were never able to catch-up with their American counterparts. And incapable of catching up and developing in-house new technologies, the Soviets resorted to cartoonish behaviors to develop their industries: "tapping into spy networks including American engineers" (Krammer 2023) and building replicas of whatever the US built. The US, on the contrary, bet on freedom and collaboration as means to develop. Their bet has paid off with dividends.

Today countries face the same conundrum. It seems that China has chosen a policy of underhandedness reminiscent of that of the Soviet Union: intellectual property theft and espionage. On the other side, the US and Europe at a crossroads. They can bet on free trade and cooperation as means to develop and innovate or on protectionist measures and industrial policy schemes to safeguard their economy. Whichever policies are enacted today will shape the future these nations and their citizens. It seems that China has followed a path akin to that of the defunct Soviet Union. Perhaps, it might not be too late think to why the Soviet Union is defunct and what led to its demise.

References

Acemoglu D, Autor D, Dorn D, Hanson G, Price B (2014) Import competition and the great U.S. employment sag of the 2000s. J Law Econ S1(34):141–198. https://doi.org/10.3386/w20395

Autor D, Beck A, Dorn D, Hanson G (2024) Help for the heartland? The employment and electoral effects of the trump tariffs in the United States. National Bureau of Economic Research, working paper series 32082, Jan 2024. https://doi.org/10.3386/w32082

Benson E, Sicilia G (2023) A closer look at de-risking. CSIS, 20 Dec 2023. https://www.csis.org/analysis/closer-look-de-risking

Berman N, Siripupapu A (2023) Is industrial policy making a comeback? Council on Foreign Relations, 18 Sept 2023. https://www.cfr.org/backgrounder/industrial-policy-making-comeback

Bessler M (2023) The drive to decouple: new perspectives on Asia. CSIS, 24 Jan 2023. https://www.csis.org/blogs/new-perspectives-asia/drive-decouple

Black JS, Morrison AJ (2021) The strategic challenges of decoupling from China. Harvard Bus Rev. https://hbr.org/2021/05/the-strategic-challenges-of-decoupling

Bown CP (2022) US-China phase one tracker: China's purchases of us goods|PIIE. Peterson Institute for International Economics, 19 July 2022. https://www.piie.com/research/piie-charts/us-china-phase-one-tracker-chinas-purchases-us-goods

Brandt L, Rawski TG (2022) China's great boom as a historical process, 1st edn, vol 2. In: Ma D, Von Glahn R (eds) The Cambridge economic history of China. Cambridge University Press, pp 775–828

Capri A (2023) The difference between decoupling and de-risking: article. Hinrich Foundation, 12 Dec 2023. https://www.hinrichfoundation.com/research/article/trade-and-geopolitics/china-decoupling-vs-de-risking/

Clark G (2007) Farewell to alms: a brief economic history of the world. Princeton University Press, Princeton, New Jersey

Clinton BJ (2001) President Clinton's speech at the Paul H. Nitze school of advanced international studies of the Johns Hopkins University. Institute for Agriculture and Trade Policy, Baltimore, Maryland. https://www.iatp.org/sites/default/files/Full_Text_of_Clintons_Speech_on_China_Trade_Bi.htm

Clinton BJ (2000b) Remarks by the president at democratic leadership council retreat. US Gov Info, New York. https://www.govinfo.gov/content/pkg/WCPD-2000-05-29/pdf/WCPD-2000-05-29-Pg1178.pdf

Cordesman AH (2023) China's emergence as a superpower. Center for Strategic and International Studies, 15 Aug 2023. https://www.csis.org/analysis/chinas-emergence-superpower

Davis B, Wei L (2022) Who won the U.S.-China trade war? Wall Street J https://www.wsj.com/articles/who-won-the-u-s-china-trade-war-11653059611

Davis R (2018) When the world opened the gates of China. Wall Street J. https://www.wsj.com/articles/when-the-world-opened-the-gates-of-china-1532701482

Dorn JA (2023) China's post-1978 economic development and entry into the global trading system. Cato Institute, 10 Oct 2023. https://www.cato.org/publications/chinas-post-1978-economic-development-entry-global-trading-system#growing-out-plan

Drysdale P, Hardwick S (2018) China and the global trading system: then and now, 1st edn. In: Fang C, Garnaut R, Song L (eds) China's 40 years of reform and development 1978–2018. Australian University Press, pp 545–574

Frieden JA (2020) Global capitalism: its fall and rise in the twentieth century, and its stumbles in the twenty-first. W.W. Norton & Company, New York

Green MA (2023) China is the top trading partner to more than 120 countries. Wilson Center, 17 Jan 2023. https://www.wilsoncenter.org/blog-post/china-top-trading-partner-more-120-countries#:~:text=China%20is%20the%20largest%20trading,trader%20with%20Russia%E2%80%94and%20Ukraine

Huang J, Rozelle S (2018) China's 40 years of agricultural development and reform, 1st edn. In: Fang C, Garnaut R, Song L (eds) China's 40 years of reform and development 1978–2018. Australian University Press, pp 545–574

Krammer SM (2023) Chip war: the fight for the world's most critical technology. J Int Bus Policy 6(4):541–45. https://doi.org/10.1057/s42214-023-00173-0

Lehner UC (2023) To decouple, or to de-risk? That is the question. Washington International Trade Association, 7 July 2023. https://www.wita.org/blogs/decouple-or-derisk/

Lighthizer RE (1997) What did Asian donors want? The New York Times, 25 Feb 1997. https://www.nytimes.com/1997/02/25/opinion/what-did-asian-donors-want.html

Lighthizer R (2022) Biden's China tariff cuts would hurt the U.S. Wall Street J. https://www.wsj.com/articles/bidens-china-tariff-cuts-would-hurt-the-u-s-inflation-trade-deficit-national-security-consumers-beijing-economy-11658175481

List F (1916) The national system of political economy (S. S. Lloyd, Trans.). Longmans, Green & Co., New York

Martin E (2023) US wants to 'de-risk,' not decouple, from China, Biden Aide Jake Sullivan Says. Bloomberg.com, 27 Apr 2023. https://www.bloomberg.com/news/articles/2023-04-27/us-wants-to-de-risk-not-decouple-from-china-biden-aide-says

Navarro P (2022) Bring back the tariffs. The American Mind, 15 Apr 2022. https://americanmind.org/features/beating-china/bring-back-the-tariffs/

Naughton B (2022) The Chinese economy in the reform era, 1st edn, vol 2. In: Ma D, Von Glahn R (eds) The Cambridge economic history of China. Cambridge University Press, pp 722–774

Office of the United States Trade Representative. "Countries & Regions." Office of the United States Trade Representative. Accessed 14 Mar 2024. https://ustr.gov/countries-regions#:~:text=U.S.%20goods%20imports%20from%20the,per cent%20of%20total%20goods%20imports

O'Hanlon ME (2016) Issues in China's WTO accession. Brookings, 28 July 2016. https://www.brookings.edu/articles/issues-in-chinas-wto-accession/

Office of the United States Trade Representative . President Trump Announces Strong Actions to Address China's Unfair Trade, Office of the United States Trade Representative, https://ustr.gov/about-us/policy-offices/press-office/press-releases/2018/march/president-trump-announces-strong (2018).

Office of Technology Evaluation. Rep. (2022) U.S. trade with China. https://www.bis.doc.gov/index.php/country-papers/3268-2022-statistical-analysis-of-us-trade-with-china/file.

Packard C, Lincicome S (2023) Working paper. Course correction charting a more effective approach to U.S.-China trade policy analysis no. 946. CATO Institute, 9 May 2023. https://www.cato.org/policy-analysis/course-correction

Packard C (2023) The high costs of a 'hard' decoupling from China. Cato.org, 22 June 2023. https://www.cato.org/blog/high-costs-hard-decoupling-china

Principles of microeconomics: economics. MIT OpenCourseWare. Accessed 19 Feb 2024. https://ocw.mit.edu/courses/14-01-principles-of-microeconomics-fall-2018/

Ricardo D (2001) On the principles of political economy and taxation. Batoche Books, Kitchener, Ontario. Original work published in 1817.

Sheidlower N, Gaines C (2024) The US is now buying more from Mexico than China for the first time in 20 years. Business Insider, 9 Feb 2024. https://www.businessinsider.com/mexico-us-top-trading-partner-china-economic-nearshoring-trade-agreement-2024-2

Shu P, Steinwender C (2018) The impact of trade liberalization on firm productivity and innovation. Nat Bureau Econ Res Innov Policy Econ 19:39–68. https://doi.org/10.3386/w24715

Smith AW (1909) The wealth of nations. Collier and Sons, New York, NY

Testimony of Ambassador Katherine tai before the house ways & means committee hearing on the president's 2022 trade policy agenda (2022). https://ustr.gov/about-us/policy-offices/press-office/speeches-and-remarks/2022/march/testimony-ambassador-katherine-tai-house-ways-means-committee-hearing-presidents-2022-trade-policy

Trump DJ (2016a) Donald Trump speaks during a campaign stop at the Allen county war memorial coliseum. POLITICO, Indiana. https://www.politico.com/blogs/2016-gop-primary-live-updates-and-results/2016/05/trump-china-rape-america-222689

Trump DJ (2016b) Donald Trump's speech on trade in Alumisource, a metals recycling facility in Monessen, PA, 28 June 2016

The U.S.-China WTO agreement will help promote reform, accountability, and openness in China. White House Archives, 8 Mar 2000. The White House. https://clintonwhitehouse4.archives.gov/WH/New/html/20000308_2.html

Wade RH (2020) Global growth, inequality, and poverty, 6th edn. In: Global political economy. Oxford University Press, Oxford

Wang X (2018) China's macroeconomics in the 40 years of reform, 1st edn. In: Fang C, Garnaut R, Song L (eds) China's 40 years of reform and development 1978–2018. Australian University Press, pp 167–186

Wong C (2018) An update on fiscal reform, 1st edn. In: Fang C, Garnaut R, Song L (eds) China's 40 years of reform and development 1978–2018. Australian University Press, pp 271–290

Yao Y (2018) The political economy causes of China's economic success, 1st edn. In: Fang C, Garnaut R, Song L (eds) China's 40 years of reform and development 1978–2018. Australian University Press, pp 75–92

Mrs. Thatcher's Prescient Bruges Speech

Daniele Capezzone

Foreword

I take the liberty of challenging the readers of these pages with a game, a test: read (if they don't know it), or reread (if they already know it) the gigantic speech that Margaret Thatcher held in Bruges on 20 September 1988, now almost thirty-six years ago.

Here's the test: try and remove those expressions that inevitably reveal the year in which the speech was delivered. For example, imagine replacing "European Community" with "European Union". I am almost certain that, with this little adjustment, the speech will seem as if it was thought, written and read no later than this very day. What's more: it will appear to you as a possible beacon in the fog.

In (our) liquid, or rather gaseous, times, in which everything flies away and seems to vanish almost instantly, the magic of some principles as solid as rock lies right here: despite the passing of decades, these ideas remain very much alive and are still capable of guiding us, indicating a criterion and a path.

Mind you, I understand how politics requires tactical exercises from our current leaders: even more so in a historical phase in which, with rare exceptions, government seasons tend to last less and less. However, precisely for this reason, and possibly also to reverse this trend, the space of tactics should be restrained to the benefit of that of strategy, of underlying visions, of powerful

---

D. Capezzone (✉)
Milan, Italy
e-mail: d.capezzone@gmail.com

ideas. In the absence of this, what does politics risk being reduced to? To a mixture of fight between gangs and talent shows, of brawl and light entertainment: so light—at times—that we don't even remember about it the next morning.

This is why this chapter is not just a tribute to Lady Thatcher and her prescient and anticipatory vision. I detest—in current affairs journalism—the use and abuse of the term *prophecy*: any improviser, and even some poor peddler of lies, if by chance gets a prediction right, is immediately described as a "prophet". It is a laughing matter! But here the word "prophecy" is absolutely appropriate. Margaret Thatcher had long warned against the drift which Brussels was unfortunately heading for, and above all—without excesses, without provocations, without exaggerations—she had offered a reasonable alternative scheme.

Upon closer inspection, this aspect of method is also odd and far from incidental. The iron Lady's haters have always presented her, and continue undeterred to do so, as a strict and inflexible ideologist, a woman prone to confrontation and indeed eager to metaphorically hit her opponents with her bag. On the contrary, if you reread this text of hers without prejudice, you will also appreciate its pragmatism, its reasonableness, the constant indication of really feasible paths, the constant offering of a *pars construens*. I'm about to write an adjective that I generally tend to mistrust, which would draw towards me the just mentioned Thatchers's bag: it is a *moderate* text.

We'll get there. Just as we will get—and the comparison will not do justice to the times we live in today—to the quality of the discussion that Thatcher tried to trigger, as opposed to the sense of asphyxia and claustrophobia fostered by the current discussions on Europe. One might say: but what are we talking about today? Why so much time and energy devoted to aspects that are all in all marginal and insubstantial? Why do we tire ourselves out in little squabbles? The following pages offer us another possible discussion: a bitter clash (or perhaps a great point of contact) on principles, ideas and prospects.

Particularly on the economic side, the Bruges speech has the value of a compass from two points of view.

Firstly, looking outwards, therefore beyond the geographical borders of Europe (a different concept from the European Union, obviously): "It would be a betrayal if, while breaking down constraints on trade within Europe, the Community were to erect greater external protection. We must ensure that our approach to world trade is consistent with the liberalization we preach at home". Thus wrote Lady Thatcher. And instead, there is a protectionist wind of uncooperative behaviour and retreat blowing everywhere. Today it is almost impossible not to come across, almost everywhere (even on the right!), political personalities who are sceptical towards the potential of the free market, of the free circulation of goods, services and capital.

Secondly, looking towards Europe (and even more so towards the European Union): "The Treaty of Rome itself was intended as a Charter for Economic Liberty. But that it is not how it has always been read, still less applied". Words spoken in 1988: and the worst—from this point of view, as we will see—was yet to come.

But let's take a step forward in time and reach June 2016, the date of a potentially great opportunity.

Brexit: A Missed Opportunity on Both Sides

Together with a friend of mine, the journalist Federico Punzi, in 2017 we published an Italian book about Brexit: the title was "Brexit. The challenge", and it was a reaction to the main "narrative" which went on describing Brexit in terms of anathema and superstition.

We have tried to put down in black and white the other side of the story. From the British point of view, explaining that Brexit might mean taking back control of the main political decisions about economy and immigration, and making Britain a global superhub capable of attracting resources and investments.

And also from a European point of view, arguing that the future negotiations between London and Brussels may offer an extraordinary opportunity to trigger a European renegotiation. The Brexit process should have been considered as an opportunity to prevent the introduction of a sort of "superstate", a Franco-German project designed in Berlin, in Paris and in Brussels, and then imposed to all of the others.

Some years later, there is a painful truth to cope with: perhaps that a wonderful opportunity has been missed and spoilt on both sides.

In Britain, yielding to the left-wing pressure, several Conservative governments have considered Brexit in terms of damage limitation, in terms of a political "harm reduction". On the contrary, after getting out of a building on fire, the UK might finally do what was (and is) perfectly in the interest of the British people: make Britain a global superhub, capable of attracting resources and investments, of cutting taxes and red tape, of securing the better deals with any possible partner on the global scene.

But also on the European side of the field, something different should have happened. The time had come to understand that too much time had been spent and wasted on the institutional aspect of the EU architecture. For decades, many have focused their attention on institutional tools, forgetting the political will and courage to carry out real economic (and pro-market) reforms. They have mixed up the means with the purpose. Let me quote once again Mrs Thatcher and what she presciently explained in her Bruges Speech in 1988: "The Community is not an end in itself. Nor it is an institutional device to be constantly modified according to the dictates of some abstract intellectual concept. Nor must it be ossified by endless regulation. The European Community is a practical means by which Europe can ensure the future prosperity and security of its people in a world in which there are many other powerful nations and groups of nations. We Europeans cannot afford to waste our energies on internal disputes or arcane institutional debates".

This was (and is) the main reason, from our perspective, why we must absolutely reject every EU project of deeper and excessive political integration: that would be the "final cage", the final attempt to impose an absurd strait-jacket of uniformity from Portugal to Finland. We must make clear that we need free competition between different models, a willing cooperation (and a virtuous challenge) between fiscal and legal systems, and not a single and unique solution imposed to everyone.

We should learn from the Brexit experience, or from what the Brexit experience should have meant. Of course, not all of the EU countries can now afford a sort of leap in the dark. Many countries are not in the same economic position as the United Kingdom, unfortunately: they are not the fourth military global power, their economic systems are not strong enough, and many of them are overwhelmed by massive sovereign debt.

But the time has come to outline different scenarios about the EU, and to design a coping strategy. No one can honestly take for granted that what has not worked so far will be working in the future. And (that should be the main political lesson to learn, in my opinion), we should offer a constructive proposal to the mass of disappointed and disaffected electors. Instead of "judging" them, we should offer them something better. A great part of the European electorate is looking forward to listening not only to a criticism of the EU, but also to a positive and constructive platform. It would be essential that rational and reforming movements and personalities should promote this kind of public conversation. And a consequent political challenge.

Unfortunately, this is still not happening in Brussels, let alone in so many European capitals, where a lot of political leaders refuse to come to terms with reality. Ironically, they go on describing themselves as "realist". But the opposite is true: here in the EU, the only unrealistic attitude is thinking that going on with the same doctors and with the same treatments which have already sickened the patient, might work (for some mysterious reason) in future.

In particular, concerning the EU situation, my point is: we need a network of countries and political movements to keep together all those who, across Europe, are against the EU status quo. To cite an example, we may push for three main points for a European renegotiation process, which might cater for the remaining EU members:

1. Push for a multi-speed/multi-tier European Union in which members can join in or abstain from programmes that suit or don't suit them;
2. Prevent a euro-area Finance Secretary, with the mission of "harmonizing", that is to say building the "final cage". On the contrary, we need fiscal competition between states and territories;
3. Pass a sort of sovereignty bill in as many European countries as possible, stating that EU rules may prevail, unless they are overturned by national Parliaments (or repealed by Constitutional Courts, as it happens in Germany). The best thing would be that National Parliaments should be given a general opt-out option on what comes from Brussels.

The EU must not be a cage. It should be a means by which we can achieve our purposes of democracy, free market, full respect for the taxpayers.

The Key Point: No to a European Superstate

The heart of Bruges Speech is exactly here. Let's put it in the *construens* version first. What is Thatcher telling us, I believe, rereading her thirty-six years later? She's telling us that the main community failure was to forget the best part (perhaps the only one that can still be saved and relaunched) of the European project: the economic freedom and the building of a large market. Upon closer inspection, this is precisely the part that would be worth working on even today. If there was a glimmer of clarity, the EU should start running with resolution, abandoning the crazy idea of a single Minister of Finance, every demand for fiscal homogenization, every idea of centralization of expenditure and economic decisions in Brussels, and choose the way of a virtuous competition between states and territories. The old world does not exist any longer. There is a huge economic and commercial arena in which people fight to seize opportunities, to capitalize on the "opportunity", in a Machiavellian way and above all to make their territory a welcoming "airport" for capital, investments and money.

The EU should become—and it would mean a lot, not a little—"just" a platform of services. Offering programmes and projects to those who want them, it would allow each country to choose for itself the most suitable formula and degree of involvement. Giving up the claims on political integration. The Eurolyrists will shout: "But this is a project of Europe *à la carte*". There is no doubt about it: and in a restaurant, in fact, it is always better to be able to freely choose among different courses rather than having a set menu forced on you. Especially by a French or German chef.

Let's look at the same question from a *destruens* perspective. What is it that Thatcher didn't want already in 1988? She didn't want the prospect of a European superstate. She didn't want some excessive political integration. She didn't want verticalisation or centralization at the head of Brussels, let alone detached from a factual possibility of parliamentary and popular control. And she didn't want—she said it explicitly—the *dirigisme* that came out of the British door to re-enter the European window: "And certainly we in Britain would fight attempts to introduce collectivism and corporatism at the European level—although what people wish to do in their own countries is a matter for them".

This brings about some options that we must keep in mind:

Flexibility (more possible solutions, more degrees of integration and collaboration) versus strictness (a single solution equal for all imposed on 27 states);
Pragmatism and successive approximations versus ideology and forced unanimity decided *ex ante*;
Democracy and control (parliamentary and popular) against any temptation to correct, sterilize and bypass the will of citizens;
Competitive federalism versus homogenizing federalism.

A significant passage is when Thatcher emphasizes the historical differences between the European states (each endowed with an identity and characteristics that cannot be erased in the name of the laboratory construction of a non-existent "*homo europaeus*") and the United States (which was born with a sense of purpose projected entirely forward and linked to the new constitution imagined by the Founding Fathers). It is no accident that for our continent, Lady Thatcher insists on the need not to attribute excessively broad and ultimately discretionary and highly political functions to an appointed bureaucracy. Furthermore, she emphasizes the paradox of wanting to focus here on an obsessive centralization of power precisely coinciding with the crisis and imminent collapse (we are in September 1988, let's not forget) of a hyper-centralized system *par excellence* like the Soviet one.

Clear Thatcherite Principles as an Embankment Against the Waves of Confusion and Political Inconsistency

Some years ago, it was Allister Heath, the bright commentator and editor of *The Sunday Telegraph*, to put things in the right context. In the Western world, our parents—and ourselves too, when we were young—used to choose between simple, clear, binary and alternative options. On the one hand, as consumers: every night between two or three TV channels, for example. On the other hand, as voters and electors: between Labour and Conservatives, Democratic or Republicans, socialists or free marketeers, etc.

Now, on the contrary, we have come into the Amazon era, into the Netflix age, and everyone has got used to getting what they want, when they want, in their extremely personalized and individually tailored version. Every single nuance, every single shade can be demanded.

The very same revolution has been coming to politics: it is what Allister Heath calls "pick and mix political age". So, I'm sorry to inform you that it won't be easy to find ideal consistency and logical reasoning, let alone simple, clear, binary and alternative options. You're likely to face incoherent ideas, ultraspin politics, (sometimes) lack of knowledge, hybrid solutions as a rule (not as an exception). It is going to be the political and cultural triumph of the conjunction "but": "I am a free marketeer but…", "I believe in free trade but…", "on the one hand, but on the other hand…"; perhaps too many hands…

That's why I think we should cross out these "buts" and start once again from some clear principles, just like the ones written in Mrs Thatcher's Bruges Speech.

Let me remind you a quotation, when she makes the moral case for free trade without any "but": "We shouldn't be protectionist (…). The expansion of the world economy requires us to continue the process of removing barriers to trade".

I think that, 36 years later, our Western countries should start from here: no trade barriers, no embargoes, no restrictions.

Let me underline a cultural (not only political) point: we should consider these Thatcherite principles as an embankment against the waves of confusion and political inconsistency, as a compass to look at in times of uncertainty and lack of vision. In a political dimension, you may have to forge a compromise: but you should not forget principles.

Competitive Federalism vs Centralizing Federalism

The *Brahmins*, the hieratic caste of the mainstream media, the *ayatollahs* of European centralisation, the so-called experts (the same who failed to understand Brexit, Trump, the elections in a quantity of countries, and nevertheless are still lecturing us), in their usual patronizing tone, have been offering for years their solemn pronouncement, as a modern version of the Delphis Oracle: the nation-state has died, it is an obsolete notion. End of the matter.

As it regularly happens, they turned out to be wrong. The nation-state is still alive, and someone may raise the suspect that it's them who are obsolete, if not yet dead (still talking as they are…).

In their oracular statements, they have been making at least three logical mistakes.

First: in an environment of popular resentment, in an atmosphere of rage towards politicians and traditional institutions, many electors are inclined to trust only the levels of government on which they can directly exercise their control.

Second: most of the existing supranational and transnational institutions (from the EU to the United Nations) are in the middle of an existential crisis, dominated by non-elected bureaucracies and untransparent procedures, which are not likely to attract popular trust and support.

Third: in the Western electorate, as David Goodhart explained some years ago, we are witnessing a comeback (even a revenge, perhaps) of the *Somewheres* and a retreat of the *Anywheres*. If you are tied to a territory, to some traditions, you are less likely to accept the idea that fundamental decisions might be made far in time and in space from you, from your concrete chance to ask politicians to account for that.

In the presence of such conditions, why on earth should nation-states have disappeared?

Anyway, as classical liberals and free marketeers, we know very well how nuanced and complex things are (and will be). On the one hand, we may enjoy the show of this humiliation of the *Brahmins*: we had warned them that every attempt to wipe out the dimension of nationhood was a cultural and political mistake. Moreover, we are well aware that the precious gifts—which we inherited—of political liberty and electoral democracies have been produced just by modern nation-states. Mankind (or peoplekind, as the Orwellian soldiers of political correctness recently tried to rename all of us…) has not produced anything better, so far.

But, on the other hand, we know that there is another side to the story. We cannot deny that nation-states have often given rise to and inspired and harboured statist, protectionist, interventionist, centralizing economic policies. So many people (on the left and also on the right side of the political spectrum, unfortunately…) believe in a more assertive economic role of the state. To them, the nation-state is the perfect tool to impose high taxes, high public spending, a positive prejudice towards public initiative and nationalizations, and a negative bias against private business.

So, to settle the conundrum, we must take a political risk, and make the most of our awareness of the contradictions we must face.

As an embankment against the waves, we should choose the very same notion of competition which we praise in the free market, and bring it into the institutional arena. The key concept is: let's make free nations compete (inside and outside the existing international institutions) so that lower-taxes and lower-regulation systems can act as a model for the others. The time has come to encourage (for example, inside the EU) not a *centralizing federalism,* with Brussels imposing an autopilot on 27 countries, a monstrous straitjacket of uniformity, but a sort of *competitive federalism,* to see which model performs better from a legal, fiscal and regulatory point of view.

Thirty-six years later, Mrs Thatcher's prescient *Bruges Speech* still remains a cornerstone and an inspiration, the best option for the future, a willing cooperation between sovereign states. From this perspective, instead of wasting time on the abstract details of the EU institutional architecture, we could finally focus our efforts on the political will to carry through effective reforms in every single nation.

All over the world, the blessed race of fiscal competition has finally started: now, it's up to every single state to be part of this global contest to grab resources, high-skilled talents, investment, opportunities. It would be mad, on the contrary, to choose a forced homogenization, paving the way for Brussels to level up taxes and regulation.

In this perspective, nation-states can prove—once again—to be the least dangerous, the least intrusive among the existing institutional schemes. As players of a new global competition, they can help us get over two historic "divorces": the divorce between nationalism and classical liberalism, and the divorce between nationalism and individualism.

A Kind of Post-COVID-19 (and Post-war) Socialism

Let's now look at current events. Both within the Community and then within the European Union, a bitter battle has always been fought between manic regulators and personalities with a more liberal and pro-market position. The bitter truth is that the latter ones have been overcome, crushed, defeated. I would even say humiliated, and not just because of the torrent of micro-rules aiming at regulating every aspect of human life that the various EU institutions, with sadistic fervour, persist in producing. There has been a vast literature on the prescriptive delirium of Brussels for decades, starting with the unforgettable topic of the bending of bananas. All of this naturally denotes an illiberal mentality, reveals an unbearably high normative claim, but—upon closer inspection—it is almost folklore.

The biggest problem is another one, and it is the increasingly systematic "European" reappearance of Soviet-style five-year plans. It is here that the state-control sickness appears in all its gravity, I would say at a full-blown, contagious and probably no longer curable stage. In a world that changes incessantly, only wild and hallucinated organizers can think of planning interventions (moreover from the "centre", i.e. from Brussels) on 27 very different countries, and—what's more—spread over very extended periods of time (4, 5 and 7 years). And yet this is what incredibly keeps on happening.

Among the least reasonable and careful people, aware of the mutability and uncertainty in which we are immersed, the opposite would be done: they would make sure (both at a European and national level) to create an entrepreneur-friendly environment, i.e. one with a low fiscal and regulatory pressure and with a high rate of normative and tax favour towards companies with the rest left to the market players. But no: the fatal conceit leads planners to consider themselves so visionary and enlightened that they can foresee everything from the centre and for a very long time.

Anyone who is not disconnected from reality would consider this claim madness. Not even the most far-sighted of politicians (European or national) can really know which sectors will prove to be driving sectors in 7–8 years and which will instead come to a standstill or be in crisis. Therefore, wisdom would suggest not to overdo with *dirigisme:* it is better to focus on keeping taxes and bureaucratic oppression low, leaving freedom of action to businesses and consumers, in short to the protagonists of supply and demand.

In fact, the opposite regularly happens. Thatcher explained it very well—I would say prophetically—at the end of the 1980s. But unfortunately, in recent years, on the one hand COVID-19 and on the other hand the war events have triggered off a kind of insidious new "socialism" (post-COVID-19 and post-war exactly), with gigantic plans that aim at an unnatural and very artificial "transformation", at a diabolic "reorganization" of the economy and its priorities.

The demiurges, the high priests stationed in Brussels (and their national fifth columns) feel entitled to choose the winners and losers of the future. As if they were emperors in a 2.0 Colosseum, they raise their thumbs up or down and decree the life or death of a gladiator. Worse: tragicomically, they pretend to tell the gladiator how he should recycle himself. In the case of the National Recovery and Resilience Plan (NRRP) and much more dangerously with the package conceived in the last European parliament by Commissioner Frans Timmermans, we would be required to become green and/or digital, with a surreal level of detachment from people's real lives.

But do we really think that, causing 60 or 70 thousand jobs lost in the automotive sector in Italy alone between now and 2035, for example due to the ban on petrol and diesel engines, all those people will have to become web designers or social media managers? I'm obviously making it extreme and caricaturing in a polemic spirit, but if someone were touched by such thoughts, well-built male nurses should urgently take care of him.

The question is: we hear many (meritorious!) voices fighting against one crazy idea or the other, for example in the green sector. But it is difficult to see a movement that puts together an overall contrast strategy and that, inductively (i.e. starting from the actual protests and tracing a point of principle), comes up with a political line of frontal contrast to this *neo-dirigisme*.

To be even clearer: it is not just a matter of contesting individual issues dear, e.g. to eco-fundamentalism (interventions on homes, cars, fishing, agriculture, rearing, packaging and so on), nor is the case to move the *dirigiste* temptation in another direction. As if the public choice of desirable economic goals became more acceptable simply by changing the direction of state or superstate interference. No: the point is to challenge at the root the public decision-maker's claim to guide the economy, to direct industrial policy, to "reward" and "punish". It is a diabolic ambition in general, but in times of perpetual changes and unpredictability as a distinguishing feature of our era, this act of hubris is evidence of a special obtuseness. Illness—as we know—for which there is no effective treatment.

The Dangers of Excessive Political Integration: The Risks of the Approach Suggested by Mario Draghi

Let's start again from Thatcher's quote from the Bruges Speech that I have already made in the first part of this chapter: "My third guiding principle is the need for Community policies which encourage enterprise. If Europe is to flourish and create jobs of the future, enterprise is the key. The basic framework is there: the Treaty of Rome itself was intended as a Charter for Economic Liberty. But that is not how it has always been read, still less applied. The lesson of the economic history of Europe in the 70s and 80s is that central planning and detailed control do not work, and that personal endeavour and initiative do. That a state-controlled economy is a recipe for low growth and that free enterprise within a framework of law brings better results".

Without controversy or harshness, the pragmatic reflections of Thatcher's Speech seem to me—so far—the best response to the constructivist and strongly integrationist acceleration proposed today by many personalities, including the former governor of the ECB and then former Italian Prime Minister Mario Draghi.

As it is known, some are naming Draghi for important European positions after the June 2024 elections; in any case, in recent months, the outgoing president of the EU Commission Ursula von der Leyen has asked the former Italian Prime Minister to write a report on competitiveness.

The fact is that—in a series of public occasions—Draghi has appeared to be a champion of the greatest possible integration. He is also in favour of a decision-making power of spending and allocation of resources strongly centred on community institutions, except that he has also mentioned the need to collect further resources in another way. Clearly, this leads either to the involvement of resources and private wealth in EU-megaplans (which is not reassuring), or to new debt (via Eurobonds or in another way). Such policy, in addition to encountering the well-known opposition of half of Europe, would inevitably lead to an acceleration in the logic of a European nation-building, or—euphemisms aside—to a dangerous approach to the superstate.

Far from us to caricature disrespectfully the opinions that do not convince us. But a cold and realistic look should lead the Eurolyrics themselves to be more cautious in their line of integration imposed from above.

From an institutional point of view, it appears to put under the administration of an external commissioner national governments and parliaments by moving the heart of decisions towards institutions not subject to direct popular scrutiny. This is a dangerous move. And so it is from an economic point of view. It also seems to consider channelling private wealth towards megaplans of public origin. It risks fuelling significatively the belief in a non-democratic drift in which the decisions are made over the heads of citizens and even over those of their representatives.

It's sad to have to remember elementary notions such as the etymon of the word "democracy", but it is never a good idea to separate the exercise of the *kratos* from what should always be its source, namely the *demos*. When this was done in Italy, from 2011 onwards, by governments that were certainly legitimate—as receivers of parliamentary trust according to the Constitution—but politically disconnected from the will expressed by the voters at the polls, it was an operation that—in the medium term—further took away credibility from politics without fuelling trust in the institutions, seen by growing segments of public opinion as distant, self-regarding entities insensitive to popular will.

Thinking of transferring this method from the national to the community level does not seem like a good idea at all. Or rather: inevitably, a drift of this type will emphasize—rather than dampen—the distrust of many Europeans towards the EU institutions. It would be worth thinking about it: the game can get out of control not only to the sorcerer's apprentices, but also to the more experienced, authoritative and proven sorcerers.

Giving Hope and Perspective to Middle-Class People

The global establishment (mainstream politicians, mainstream media, "experts", etc.) failed to understand Brexit, they failed to understand Trump, and so they were totally unprepared to figure out what was going to happen at home. The real point that the traditional élites failed to consider is an immense middle-class (and lower middle-class) whose living standards have been stagnating for years. So many people may have kept their jobs: but, in spite of that, they feel poorer and less secure, and they are also fed up with an immigration crisis which has got out of hand. And—what is more—they have been kept out of the official "agenda" of the public conversation: their fears and worries have been rejected and brushed aside for years. So, in many countries, populist forces have become the instrument of their revenge.

But—please—don't forget to look at the electors: an immense middle-class whose living standards have been stagnating for years, and whose fears and anxieties have been dismissed by the "intelligentsia". For so many years (consider the Italian case, for example) the electors have not been allowed to choose freely their government: they have been forced to accept technocratic juntas. In addition, they have been constantly lectured and patronised with the usual mantras: "more Europe, more immigration".

It was natural that they should grab the elections as an opportunity to take revenge against the political establishment and to reject the dogma of the tyranny and of the infallibility of the EU. That's why old parties often lose badly in spite of their control of the traditional media.

Looking to the future, and considering the next years, it won't be easy to imagine an alternative, principled, conservative, small-government centre-right option in many Western countries. From a cultural point of view, this would be extremely needed. And someone should offer a constructive proposal to this mass of disappointed and disaffected electors. Instead of "judging" them, they should be offered something better in order to channel all this social anger.

Agriculture and Green, the Damage of Dirigisme (and Double Standards)

The months behind us in this spring 2024 have seen—intertwined together like wicker wood—two burning issues: on the one hand agriculture, with massive demonstrations by producers against EU policies; on the other hand, the formidable and ultra-*dirigiste* green agenda imposed by Brussels.

It is really interesting to show how the principles asserted in one case were contradicted in the second, staging a spectacular double standard. First, for decades, European agriculture was removed from the market through a system of duties and subsidies. Second, not infrequently, people from the same left-wing or technocratic or traditional establishment circles began to argue against this approach, using—sometimes—classical liberal and pro-market arguments. But immediately afterwards—here's the turnabout—the dirigiste toolbox was taken back into hand to promote the green transition and impose it according to (super)statist planning logic.

To cut a long story short: blows have suddenly rained down on farmers' heads to force them towards organic farming, complete with classical liberal sermons against the old system of subsidies and duties. But at the same time, the logic of subsidies (and above all of political choice!) was revived to impose electric cars and renewable energy. It is this short circuit that has contributed to aggravate a significant portion of public opinion, as well as taking away the credibility of politicians and commentators capable—overnight—of overturning criteria and arguments (liberal or statist, anti-subsidies or pro-subsidies), depending on the cause to be promoted, or the category to be punished.

Someone will say: but this is how "industrial policy" is carried out, this is how "a market is created". To begin with—from a theoretical point of view—it seems ridiculous to think of opening new markets using subsidies imposed from above. But above all—from a practical point of view—it is foolish to think that in order for something to work, in this case to facilitate an exchange of goods and services, public intervention is necessary (it makes no difference whether it is from state or a superstate), with a corresponding a priori selection of winners and losers.

It could be summarized as a bullying attitude: they could choose between the green and the collapse of the market. They have chosen the green, and they will also have the collapse of the market.

In the EU, Regulatory (and Anti-Market) Madness Affects Everything, Even Artificial Intelligence

For that matters, the signs of the usual ultra-regulatory, anti-market and anti-innovation approach never end.

For example, I promise to read better and with greater attention (threatening for the size, and perhaps not only for that) the 458 pages of the AI Act, the new European regulations on artificial intelligence.

At very first sight, there are some elements of common sense, starting from the distinction between high or low risk activities, which in the first case are subject to more thorough checks, and in the second to transparency duties. Other Chinese-style activities (facial recognition, "social score", etc.) are obviously prohibited. And so far so good.

But—I confess—getting to the heart of every single regulation seems to me a lunatic or even alien attitude. The question is that 458 pages are a bundle from super-lawyers which not only confirms the European passion for every new possible regulatory cage, but projects it into a dimension in which—in the short run—that same regulation will be realistically outdated by ever changing reality.

We always get there, to the well-known trio: "America innovates, China replicates, Europe regulates", which expresses—alas—a deep-rooted aptitude. It is no coincidence that in the AI sector, as well as in that of social media and most advanced multimedia communication, there are no European "champions". It is not hard to guess why.

Conclusion: Offer a Flexible Approach. Doing Some Things Together, in Moderation, with a Pragmatic Attitude and Without Imposing Unnatural Homogenization. Free Cooperation Between Sovereign Nations

And so we have reached the conclusion of Margaret Thatcher's reasoning. Let's give her the word again: "I am the first to say that on many great issues the countries of Europe should speak with a single voice. I want to see us work more closely on the things we can do better together than alone. Europe is stronger when we do so, whether it be in trade, in defence or in our relations with the rest of the world. But working more closely together does not require power to be centralized in Brussels or decisions to be taken by an appointed bureaucracy. Indeed, it is ironic that just when those countries such as the Soviet Union, which have tried to run everything from the centre, are learning that success depends on dispersing power and decisions away from the centre, there are some in the Community who seem to want to move in the opposite direction. We have not successfully rolled back the frontiers of the state in Britain, only to see them re-imposed at a European level with a European superstate exercising a new dominance from Brussels".

She was three times right. The first time, on the collapse of the Soviet Union (her speech dates back to September 1988); the second time, on the risk that someone in Brussels tended (and still tends, more or less consciously) to imitate that catastrophic model of centralization; the third time, in suggesting a pragmatic, flexible and feasible path: that of free cooperation between sovereign nations, willing to cooperate intensively in some areas but without giving up their autonomy and virtuous competition between states and territories. The essence lies in this clear conclusion: "Let Europe be a family of nations, understanding each other better, appreciating each other more, doing more together but relishing our national identity no less that our common European endeavour".

As I wrote before, the EU, realistically, could provide a service platform. That is, offering projects and programmes to those who want them, allowing each member state to decide the most appropriate level of involvement for itself and its needs. Leaving aside—therefore—the claims of excessive and too rapid political integration. The most dogmatic Eurolyrics will protest: "But it is too little". No, dear gentlemen, that would already be a lot: and a wise and cautious politician should never go beyond the threshold of what is reasonably acceptable to his fellow citizens in a specific historical moment.

The Case for Free Trade—Why We Need to Keep Making It

Douglas Carswell

Many of the most important ideas we have about how the world works must have once seemed contrary to common sense.

Take the theory of evolution as an example. The idea that the wings of a bird, bat or butterfly might be the product not of divine design, but of natural selection, must have seemed almost fanciful to many at first. Until Charles Darwin put forward his theory in *On the Origin of Species* in 1859, belief in some form of creationism was the norm for most of human history.

Then, there is heliocentricism, the technical term for the idea that the Earth revolves around the Sun. First mooted by the ancient Greeks in the third century BC, it remained a minority view until well after Copernicus in the sixteenth century.

So, too, with free trade, the idea that you become rich by allowing yourself to be dependent on what others produce is so counterintuitive, it, too, needed to be 'discovered', in this case by two eighteenth century thinkers, Adam Smith and David Ricardo.

While Darwin and Copernicus' ideas went on to gain widespread acceptance, 200 years after David Ricardo, his insights still do not seem to be widely accepted.

Evolution, of course, happens whether humans had a theory about it or not. The Earth, too, spins around the Sun, whether people living on it appreciate the fact or otherwise. Unfortunately, when there is scepticism free trade,

D. Carswell (✉)
Jackson, MS, USA
e-mail: carswell@mspolicy.org

it can mean bad policies which make it much less likely to occur. There needs to be some level of belief in the benefits of free trade for it to happen.

Over the past half century or so, global trade has grown rapidly. World trade today is now 45 times greater than it was in 1950.[1] The value of imports and exports relative to output rose in almost every country around the world. Indeed, it is one of the reasons why output expanded.

Global trade grew particularly rapidly after 1990, with the collapse of the Soviet block and the opening up of China. This enabled one billion people to escape extreme poverty.[2] Indeed, poorer countries benefited more from this growth in global trade, and during the first decade of this century, per-capita incomes in developing economies grew 3.5 percentage points faster than in developed economies.

In 1990, 4 out of every 10 people on the planet lived in extreme poverty. Today, fewer than 1 in 10 do.[3]

This, you might imagine, would give us all the evidence we need that free trade works. Far from validating Ricardo's insights about comparative advantage, the growth of global supply chains has prompted many to advocate abandoning it.

Globalisation, they say, has caused deindustrialisation in the West. Jobs in manufacturing, we are told, have moved overseas.

American leaders on either side of the aisle once lined up to support the World Trade Organisation and the North American Free Trade Area. Today, they are just as likely to suggest that opening our markets to low-cost Asian producers has been a mistake.

As President, Donald Trump imposed tariffs on a range of imports, notably steel. His successor, Joe Biden, has kept them, at times suggesting that he might raise them further. Biden has moved in an even more protectionist direction, promising to veto a Japanese acquisition of Pittsburgh-based US Steel, and providing massive subsidies for US companies to move manufacturing operations to the US.

Across the Atlantic, the European Union remains a protectionist trade block, using not only tariffs to keep out cheap imports, but regulatory barriers, too (US food imports, for example, are often excluded on the basis of spurious health concerns.)

---

[1] https://www.wto.org/english/res_e/statis_e/trade_evolution_e/evolution_trade_wto_e.htm#:~:text=Trade%20Growth&text=World%20trade%20volume%20today%20is,400%20times%20from%201950%20levels.

[2] https://www.worldbank.org/en/topic/trade/brief/trade-has-been-a-powerful-driver-of-economic-development-and-poverty-reduction#:~:text=From%201990%20to%202017%2C%20developing,36%20percent%20to%209%20percent.

[3] https://www.brookings.edu/wp-content/uploads/2022/02/Evolution-of-global-poverty.pdf.

China, meanwhile, has adopted under President Xi an overtly mercantile approach in its dealings with much of the world, using trade access, cheap imports and government loans as leverage to advance a geopolitical agenda.

It is now thirty years since the last multilateral global trade deal was completed, the Uruguay Round. At the same time, according to the World Bank, the number of trade restrictions is on the rise, often done under the guise of seeking to secure supply chains.[4]

Cumulatively, this is all now starting to have an impact on global trade. There has been a dramatic slowdown in the rate at which global trade has grown since the 1990s. The danger is that as we drift towards protectionism, growth will disappear altogether, if not actually decline.

We need to tackle head on the myth that globalisation has caused deindustrialisation in the West.

American industrial production today is close to an all-time high. US industrial production now is twice what it was in the early 1980s, and four times what it was when JFK was in the White House.

Across the Atlantic, the European Union might not have grown as rapidly, but even there industrial output has risen. The value of German industrial production in 2022 ($752 billion) is not far off double what it was in 2000 ($400 Billion).[5] UK manufacturing output rose from $180 billion in 1990 to $260 billion by 2022.[6]

To be sure, the nature of industrial output might have changed significantly. Certain industries in particular places might have declined as others expanded, but overall, the West has never made more than it does today.

When people talk about deindustrialisation, they are not talking about a fall in industrial output (There has not been one). What they perhaps mean is that manufacturing industry is a less important part of overall output. This is certainly true.

Manufacturing fell as a share of overall output in Germany between 1990 and 2022 from 24 to 18%.[7] In the UK, it fell over the same period from 16 to

---

[4] https://blogs.worldbank.org/en/voices/how-can-we-reinvigorate-international-trade#:~:text=The%20number%20of%20export%20bans,measures%20reduce%20global%20economic%20efficiency.

[5] https://www.macrotrends.net/global-metrics/countries/DEU/germany/manufacturing-output#:~:text=Germany%20manufacturing%20output%20for%202022,a%204.52%25%20decline%20from%202018.

[6] https://www.macrotrends.net/global-metrics/countries/GBR/united-kingdom/manufacturing-output.

[7] https://www.macrotrends.net/global-metrics/countries/DEU/germany/manufacturing-output#:~:text=Germany%20manufacturing%20output%20for%202022,a%204.52%25%20decline%20from%202018.

8%.[8] Manufacturing might be less important overall to Western economies, but Western economies nonetheless manufacture more than before.

Another reason why people believe the deindustrialisation fallacy is that the number of people employed in industry has fallen.

The number of manufacturing jobs in American peaked in 1979.[9] Since then, there has been a fall of about a third in the total number of manufacturing jobs, with a particularly fast fall in the first decade of the twentieth century.

But is it right to blame global trade for this?

What has happened in manufacturing over the past thirty years is perhaps similar to what once happened in agriculture. Back in the day, a large chunk of the work force worked on the land. Today, less than 2% of the US work force works in agriculture, yet farm output has never been higher.[10]

Manufacturing jobs have disappeared not because everything is now being made in China, Mexico or Asia. Those jobs have largely disappeared because US (and European) manufacturing is now so much more productive that not as many people are needed to produce far more.

While manufacturing jobs might have disappeared, the overall number of jobs in America has never been higher. The fall in manufacturing jobs has been more than offset by the growth in jobs in financial services, healthcare, repairs and professional services.

In 1970, there were fewer than 100 million jobs in America. Today, there are well over twice as many jobs.[11] For every job in old industries that might have disappeared, a greater number of new jobs have sprung up to replace them, often requiring fewer hours and paying better wages.

Is that really true, you might wonder?

Often, we are told, well paid work in manufacturing is being replaced by minimum wage work that leaves many people struggling to make ends meet.

"Not so!" say the anti-globalists. "Free trade has actually made Americans poorer".

Claims as to the impoverishing effects of globalisation often point out that median household incomes in American have not grown rapidly, rising from $61,000 in 1990 to $74,000 in 2022.[12] That is still an increase, albeit

---

[8] https://www.macrotrends.net/global-metrics/countries/GBR/united-kingdom/manufacturing-output.
[9] https://fred.stlouisfed.org/series/manemp.
[10] https://www.statista.com/statistics/270072/distribution-of-the-workforce-across-economic-sectors-in-the-united-states/.
[11] https://united-states.reaproject.org/analysis/comparative-trends-analysis/total_employment/tools/0/0/#:~:text=During%20this%2054%2Dyear%20period,of%20121%2C388%2C800%2C%20or%20133.32%25.
[12] https://www.statista.com/statistics/200838/median-household-income-in-the-united-states/.

nothing like as rapid as the increase that happened in the decades after the Second World War.

Is this really proof that global trade has impoverished America? It is worth examining the data in a little more detail.

While median household incomes have not risen so sharply, per-capita income over that same period in America has. In per-capita terms, Americans are on average about three times richer than they were in 1990.[13]

One of the reasons why median household incomes in America have not risen as rapidly as per-capita income, is that the number of households in America has increased faster than the population due to demographic changes.

This, not the impact of global trade, accounts for why median household income, which divided by households, grows faster than per-capita income, which divides by population.

Look at US per person income and the rate of growth has been remarkable. In 1990, per-capita income was $19,000. By 2022, it was $68,000.[14]

Far from stagnation, globalisation has coincidence with a period of rapid income growth across America and much of the Western world.

So why is it, despite all the evidence in favour of free trade, that there is so much scepticism about it? Why does the protectionist mindset persist?

Part of the problem is that self-sufficiency seems so reassuring. There is something romantic about the idea of being able to produce all that we need ourselves.

In Britain, agrarian protectionists in Parliament talk about the need to secure food supply lines. In the United States, politicians talk about the need to grow more of what we eat locally.

Both have it 180 degrees wrong. The best way to ensure a dependable supply of food is to have access to multiple supply chains, not necessarily the shortest ones.

This is not just a theory. We know this from what happened in the past.

Back in premodern Europe, localised famines were a not uncommon occurrence. This was because there would be the occasional localised crop failures. An unusually wet or dry summer, or an outbreak of crop disease, might ruin the harvest. Before there was transportation and trade, a poor harvest where you lived meant there was not enough good to go around, and people starved.

It was only once Europe created the conditions that allowed a regional trade in agricultural goods that famine became a thing of the past. Today,

---

[13] https://fred.stlouisfed.org/series/A792RC0A052NBEA.
[14] https://fred.stlouisfed.org/series/A792RC0A052NBEA.

a particularly dry summer in Britain or Germany might make strawberries or lettuce a little more costly. No one starves because farmers have a poor harvest. Trade means that shortages in one location can be offset by supplies from further afield, not only across Europe, but around the world.[15]

It is trade that ensures the security of supply.

Another reason why free trade is often so underappreciated is that the benefits are often not obvious.

Millions of mums and dads might pay a few dollars less each year to cloth their kids with the removal of tariffs on textiles. But removing those tariffs might have immediate consequences for those working in textile mills that might lose their jobs. The disruptive effects of free trade can seem obvious, the enriching effects are more subtle.

As a Member of Parliament in the run up to the Brexit vote in Britain, I once spent a morning with a camera crew in a supermarket trying to explain to a TV audience the benefits of free trade. I filled the shopping trolley with grapes from Brazil, Israel avocadoes, cheese from France and lamb from New Zealand.

It was imports like these from around the whole world, I said to the camera, that allowed my constituents to eat affordable food from all over the world.

Since the Brexit vote, many of those that opposed it at the time and who have struggled to come to terms with the result ever since, have advanced an alternative narrative. The Brexit vote, they insist, was some sort of atavistic rejection of globalisation. They have been so effective at rewriting history that today it is easy to overlook just how committed the Brexiteers actually were to free trade at the time.

Brexit was not a vote against globalisation or free trade with the world. It was an attempt to embrace it by leaving a sclerotic European regional trade block, and opening the UK economy to the world.

What shocked me after the Brexit vote was how few UK government officials put in charge of trade policy had any sympathy for this view.

Appointed a non-executive at the newly created Department of International Trade, I had a ring side seat as Britain's post-Brexit ministers and officials began to formulate a distinctly UK trade policy for the first time in forty years. It because painfully obvious very early on that it was officials, not the voters, that needed to hear the message I had tried to deliver using my supermarket shopping trolley.

---

[15] Read Matt Ridley's The Rational Optimist for more on this.

Those I worked with seemed remarkable resistant to the idea that improved access to cheap imports would be a win for the UK.

For trade officials, a win meant more exports, not imports. With an almost comically mercantile mindset, they talked endlessly about export promotion.

At a time when the cost of living in Britain was rising rapidly, one might have imagined that officials would be anxious to ensure UK households had access to more low-cost imports. Instead, UK trade negotiators seemed determined to retain UK import tariffs, even on products that the UK did not produce at all.

"Why" I would often ask "could we not simply eliminate such and such an import tariff?"

Retaining import tariffs, I was just as frequently informed, gave us "leverage" in our trade negotiations. If we were prepared to remove taxes that we imposed on UK consumers when buying something from overseas, I was informed, where would be the quid pro quo from the other side?

With this mindset, the UK's post-Brexit trade negotiations stopped being about trade liberalisation, and rapidly became an exercise in trying to bureaucratise trade instead.

UK negotiators would create 'chapters' in their trade deal making, into which they would insert—without any political direction to do so—issues that we tangential to trade. There would be sections on sustainability, inclusion and gender equality.

A basic free trade deal between say, Australia and the UK ought to be fairly straight forward; remove all tariffs, so that neither country is penalising its own citizens for wanting to buy from the other country and then have a system of mutual standard recognition such that if a product is approved for sale in one country, it is automatically approved in the other.

Instead the deal has provisions to "transition towards a circular economy". One section in the agreement is all about encouraging people to "reuse and repair" manufactured goods, and encourage "resource efficient design".

Those might all be desirable outcomes, but what on earth has any of it got to do with free trade?

When I once challenged one of our top officials about this, they explained that such considerations were essential in order to get approval for the deal in Parliament. I would have thought such considerations would be up to ministers, not their officials.

Watching trade agreements being hammered out, I got the clear impression that what I was looking at was less a bold, post-Brexit move towards trade liberalisation, and instead the establishment of a permission-based trade system.

Instead of embracing mutual standard recognition, UK officials interpreted that as a requirement for bureaucratic alignment. An approach to trade was supposed to diminish the power of officials ended up placing them centre stage.

This mindset by UK officials in charge of trade negotiations goes a long way to explaining why post-Brexit Britain has yet to take full advantage of trade opportunities outside the European Union.

In light of all this, and given the volume of trade between the UK and the US that already occurs without a trade deal, I even started to wonder US-UK trade deal was actually desirable after all.

Perhaps there has never been a time when most people, or even many people, understood or appreciated the theory of free trade. Perhaps there has always been scepticism about the idea that imports make you rich. But what mattered most of all was that the policy making elite subscribed to the idea. Not everyone needed to have heard of Ricardo, but provided the administrative elite understood that more imports and exports were desirable, it did not really matter.

My experience with the Department of International Trade makes me wonder if that supposed 'administrative elite' is now the problem, rather than a reliable redoubt that could always be counted on to steer trade policy in the right direction.

What should policy makers be aiming to do to advance free trade? Another Uruguay round? Should we embark on some decades long multilateral trade talks?

No. What any country such as Britain or the US want to advance free trade in a world still sceptical about it, should follow a straightforward approach.

Step one, Britain, or the United States (or preferably both!) should offer each other a trade deal that eliminates all tariffs. Step two, rather than produce a lengthy trade deal that stipulates under what conditions items X can or cannot be sold, have a deal that simply says if it is legal to buy and sell a product in one country, it should be legal to buy and sell it in the other (unless specifically prohibited by law).

In other words, no tariffs and no additional regulatory compliance to access the overseas market.

"But that would mean allowing American chlorinated chicken to be sold in UK supermarkets!" some will scream.

Indeed. How many Europeans happy to tell you of their concerns about US chicken would actually avoid eating US food in the United States? So long as UK consumers could clearly see on the packaging in the supermarket that the product was from America, it would be up to them to decide if they were willing to run the risk of eating a US chicken fillet.

But it is not only products that should be sellable in each other's countries. Under such a deal, it should be made easier to sell services between jurisdictions. With the service sector of the economy increasingly important, why only allow in tangible imports?

If someone is a certified doctor in New Zealand or the United States, why not enable them to practise in the UK? And why stop at doctors? With a few adjustments, it ought to be possible for an architect that knows how to design buildings in one country to practise in another.

Tragically, none of Britain's post-Brexit trade deals seeks this sort of simplicity. The officials have got in the way. But there is one trade deal that mercifully UK trade negotiators had little influence over.

The Comprehensive and Progressive Agreement for Trans-Pacific Partnership (CPTPP) is a free trade agreement between Australia, Canada, Japan, Vietnam and several other fast growing Pacific states.

In what might just turn out to have been an extraordinarily fortuitous move, Liam Fox and then Liz Truss as trade ministers managed to submit an application for Britain to join. This meant that the UK became part of a free trade club, the rules of which had largely been decided before our involvement. The ability of UK officials to over bureaucratize the entire enterprise has been mercifully diminished.

By being part of CPTPP, the UK has not only joined a free trade group that includes some of the most dynamic economies on the planet. The idea is that everyone in the group trades freely with one another.

CPTPP has chapters on tariffs and market access, intellectual property, financial services and even government procurement. That is to say, it has all that you should expect from a free trade agreement that actually liberalises trade, and now of the sort of nonsense British trade officials are inclined to insert into a trade deal.

Provided our new Pacific trade partners do not let UK officials rewrite the rules, the UK will find herself part of an ever expanding arrangement that allows free trade. As well as being a model for UK officials to follow, CPTPP offers America a ready-made Pacific trade club, without China, that she ought to be willing to join.

What else, other than being part of CPTPP, should free traders call for?

The UK ought to unilaterally abolish all tariffs. That is not to say that the tariff rate should be set a zero. There should be no tariffs and no tariff setting bureaucracy at all. UK customs tax receipts currently generate about Pounds

4.8 billion in revenue. By removing that tax on imports, the UK government would be passing on the benefit to consumers, and stimulating more growth.

There is an argument that in some instances tariffs might need to be phased out over time to allow players in protected markets time to adjust. In order to protect UK and European sugar producers, for example, the UK as part of the European Union has long imposed a tax on cane sugar imports from abroad and maintained a quota system. Eliminating those tariffs and quotas on sugar imports would reduce the cost of food and help UK consumers, and needs to be done.

However, a case could be made that eliminating of sugar tariffs and quotas should be phased in over a period of two or three years in order to give UK beet farmers time to adjust. Either way, full elimination needs to be the end result.

In certain areas, the UK ought to be prepared to—unilaterally if necessary—allow goods to be sold if they have been approved for sale in other Western states.

Take for instance, pharmaceuticals. The instinct of trade officials is to create a system of regulatory convergence, with UK medicine regulators mirroring what EU regulators, or US regulators are doing. But why do that at all?

Why not simply say that if a medicine has been approved by either the UK regulatory agency, or the America Food and Drug Administrator, or the European Medicines Agency, it is approved for sale in the UK? If the drug is good to treat Hans in Germany or Hank in Pennsylvania, why not Harry in Suffolk?

Perhaps under such a system, free trade might even stimulate a little regulatory competition? If the FDA keeps one kind of lifesaving treatment off the market in America due to over caution, the UK regulator might focus on fast track approving it. It was, after all, precisely this kind of approach that allow Britain to deliver the world's first anti-Covid vaccine.

However impolite it might sound to say it, perhaps the reality is that free trade is an essentially Anglosphere phenomenon.

Following the fall of the Soviet Union, many assumed that all countries would converge towards free trade and the free market model. China's admission to the World Trade Organization at the turn of the century only reinforced this sense of inevitability about the liberal international order.

Two decades on, it is clear that China has not embraced free trade, and is if anything growing more Ming-like in her mercantilism. India, another emerging economic powerhouse, might be growing, but there is precious little evidence that she is becoming more inclined to open up her markets.

Japan, the first Asian power to achieve lift off, might resemble Western states in many ways. Beneath the veneer, she remains an essential protected, corporatist economy. Her recent growth rates reflect this.

Far from converging towards a Western free trade model, countries like Turkey, Brazil and Russia seem to be moving away from it.

To what extent is the West moving away from the Western model of free trade and open markets? The European Union seems to owe much to the German tradition of the "zollverein", a customs union creates a free trade area in order to establish a goal of political union.

If free trade has a future around the world, it is unlikely to be because every country comes to an agreement on it around a table. Instead, it would to emerge—rather like the Gold Standard in the nineteenth century—because a few Anglosphere countries practised it.

Victorian Britain never set out to create a global currency system that enabled free trade and prosperity. But by doing what she did, Britain created an economic order that others were happy to become part of. If Britain and America practise free trade today, through CPTPP and unilaterally, they might once again create an open economic order that others will strive to be part of.

Let Free Trade Work Its Magic in the UK: Lord Moynihan of Chelsea, OBE

Jon Moynihan

Openness To Trade—making it easy for other countries to sell their Goods and Services to us, and doing our best to persuade them to make it easy for us to sell *our* Goods and Services to *them*—is unequivocally important for facilitating the growth of a country's GDP; an important determinant of economic growth (Bergh and Nilsson 2013). As the OECD stated (in 2010) (OECD, Ilo, World Bank, WTO, Final Report 2010): "*the large body of empirical work on the topic strongly supports the theoretical presumption that trade liberalization reduces poverty on average, and in the long run*". I review that body of empirical work in more detail, further on in this chapter.

Free Trade, the consequence of Openness to Trade, is one of the most studied issues in economic theory, starting with Adam Smith's work in the eighteenth century; through to the insights of Ricardo and Bastiat in the 19th; and now, in the present day, we see almost all economists who study the matter praising, and conversant with, the importance of Free Trade to economic growth. (Why many such economists simultaneously praise the free trade-phobic EU is just one of life's many little mysteries). Recent in-depth reviews of the power of opening up an economy to Free Trade confirm that adopting a Free Trade approach can have a big positive impact on economic growth. Post-Brexit, with Britain now opening up to global trade, its GDP growth—were we to take proper advantage of our opportunities—can accelerate significantly, just as Britain's GDP grew rapidly in the second half of

J. Moynihan (✉)
London, United Kingdom
e-mail: moynihanj@parliament.uk

the nineteenth century after the abolition of the Corn Laws (which led to the UK becoming, at the time, the world's largest and most successful economy in the world).

Popular nationalists, EU-philes and anti-globalists; all of them work hard to obscure the clarity of this position. A further negative complication: even those who support Free Trade talk about the advantages of improved trade in terms of how much we increase our *exports;* they ignore the even bigger benefit of Free Trade that comes from the better and cheaper Goods and Services that, with Free Trade, we can *import* for our citizens' enjoyment and consumption.

One further dimension to that complexity: there is a general lack of understanding of the difference between trade in Goods, and trade in Services; and how different the UK is, in its profile for these two kinds of exports, relative to the EU. The particular point there, as regards the UK, is that about 80% of its economy is in Services—the highest percentage among the developed economies (https://www.ons.gov.uk/economy/nationalaccounts/balanceofpayments/bulletins/uktrade/January2024#monthly-trade-in-services), and very different from all the other EU countries. Commensurate with that, the UK is the second largest exporter of Services in the world—behind only the US. In 2022/23, our Services exports rose by about 14%[1]—and can be expected to have done similarly well for the year 2023 (Trade Secretary welcomes record year for Services export 2023). As far as increasing exports is concerned, the key desideratum is therefore, primarily, a matter of finding markets for our *Services*, not so much for our *Goods*. This then takes us to a further key point: our Services are less suited for exports to the EU than they are to the rest of the world (which contains, for example, many English-speaking economies, and countries that, English-speaking or not, base their legal system on Common Law, not the EU's Napoleonic Law).

The arguments in the UK for and against Free Trade have suffered recently from the ideological battle within the UK around Brexit. Many of those who would in theory be expected to advocate Britain opening its economy up to the world—most economists in the UK; other eminent economists in transnational bodies and in prominent American universities—instead argue muddle-headedly yet fiercely against Britain being allowed to conduct its own Trade Policy, claiming that the EU is a beacon of Free Trade (rather than the protectionist cartel that it actually is—even when it comes to Services and professional standards within the EU). They argue that EU standards,

---

[1] In chained volume measures.

UNSEEN SUCCESS – SERVICES
G7 Countries, Service Exports Q4 2018=100

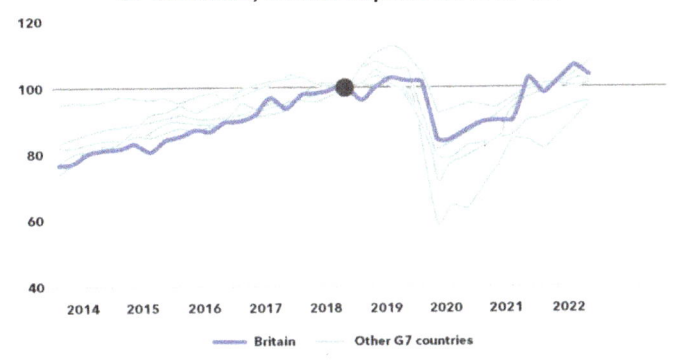

Chart 1 Over the past decade, and commencing properly post-2016, Britain has enjoyed one of the best performances in G7 countries in exports of Services: *Source* The Economist (https://www.economist.com/britain/2023/05/09/britains-services-exports-are-booming-despite-brexit-why2023) (OECD; ONS)

and directives from Brussels, are primarily for consumer protection, rather than acknowledging what in the main they are—carefully constructed protectionist non-tariff barriers, designed to fend off outside competitors at the expense of their own consumer citizens.

In the post-Brexit environment, the British Services sector has already, according to the Economist, "*enjoyed one of the best performances in the G7*", see Chart 1.

According to the research by the Resolution Foundation (Hale and Fry 2023), the UK's exports of Services have grown 3.6% more than a typical OECD country since the trade and cooperation agreement with the EU came into force in early 2021—even after accounting for the UK's sectoral makeup (https://www.economist.com/britain/2023/05/09/britains-services-exports-are-booming-despite-brexit-why2023). Goods exports, on the other hand, have not done so well (Chart 2).

So, post-Brexit, things looks positive for Britain's Services exports, and as the Resolution Trust tell us, Services are more than two thirds of British Exports by value added (https://www.resolutionfoundation.org/press-releases/services-account-for-a-record-share-of-britains-exports-but-they-are-increasingly-concentrated-in-london/).

What are the best policies for ensuring that our Services export success goes up a further notch, and that—possibly even more important—we allow in the low-priced imports that our citizenry could be enjoying? The following sections review these issues:

UNSEEN SUCCESS – GOODS
G7 Countries, Service Exports Q4 2018=100

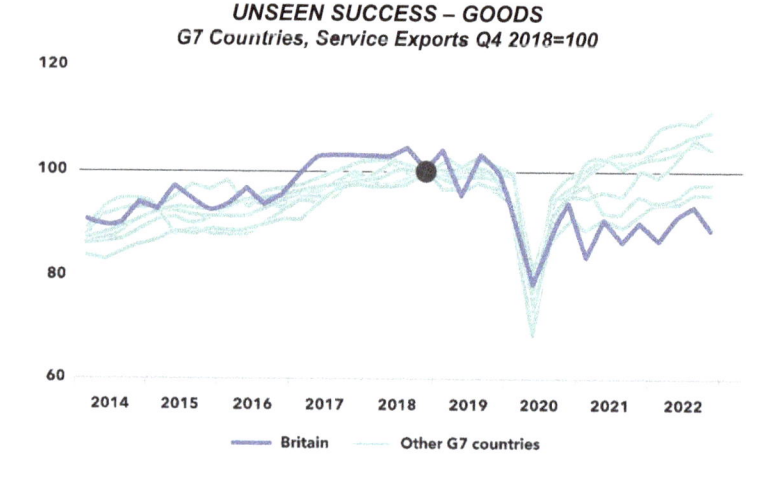

Chart 2 Goods exports seemed by 2022 had not recovered to pre-Covid levels, unlike other G7 countries: *Source* The Economist (https://www.economist.com/britain/2023/05/09/britains-services-exports-are-booming-despite-brexit-why2023) (OECD; ONS)

1. Economic theory demonstrates why, and practical experience proves, that Openness to Trade accelerates economic growth
2. Britain's future economy, as we now pursue our own trade policy, can benefit greatly from opening itself up to the world
3. To benefit properly from opening up its economy, Britain must recognise protectionism for what it is, and avoid it. Now that we have left the EU, we must avoid replicating its cartel-like protectionist behaviour
4. The UK should focus instead not just on developing its capabilities in high-value sectors, but also on exploiting any sectors where it has Competitive and Comparative Advantage.

1. Economic theory demonstrates why, and practical experience proves, that openness to trade accelerates economic growth

In recent years, academics around the world have focused mightily on understanding the potential and actual benefits of Free Trade. The current focus on trade openness is something of an interesting throwback to the eighteenth and nineteenth centuries, when the power of the reasoning in works by economists such as Adam Smith, David Ricardo, and Frédéric Bastiat led to an eventual breakthrough for Free Trade in the UK—the abolition of the Corn Laws. As reviewed earlier, that abolition in turn led to unparalleled growth in the British economy; the country's economy grew so fast that Britain became, and for many decades remained, the largest and most successful economy in the world.

As the 19th Century went on, many large economies followed Britain's Free Trade lead. However, by the twentieth century, things were changing, and at the beginning of the Great Depression of the 1930s the imposition of the Smoot-Hawley Tariff Act in the US, and other trade barriers, resulted in a catastrophic collapse in world trade, and consequent relative immiseration among the populations of many countries (including the US). All over the world, tariff and non-tariff barriers—protectionism in general—sprang up, and persisted for many decades. Particularly in developing countries, the majority of economies did not start opening up again for half a century or more; quite a few not before the 1990s. The change back to open trade, slowly as it did come, was originally precipitated by an event that occurred much earlier than the 1990s. This was the formation and activities of the General Agreement on Trade and Tariffs (GATT), from 1948 on, which led to a slow, cautious opening of economies—some sooner than others—over the following decades. GATT was probably one of the finest achievements of the modern economics profession, slowly rolling back the disaster of the pre-war protectionist era; but it took several decades for it to bear fruit. There were, at first, a few cases of opening up in the 1970s; then more widely in the 1980s; and then, with the great opening up of China and India in the early 1990s, the commencement of a period of enormous enrichment of populations around the world, as billions of world citizens, formerly living in poverty, started to receive better wages and living conditions, thanks to the application of the capitalist model in those countries, and the willingness of Western countries to buy their Goods. This was helped particularly by GATT being made more operational through the establishment of the WTO in 1995—helped by the resistance of many countries to the pressure created by the continued presence of protectionist trade cartels around the world, and despite ongoing populist protests against "Globalisation".

We have, over the past couple of decades, and until very recently, had a relatively benign period of Free Trade, a situation that many around the world constantly work hard to improve even further.[2] Britain, in particular, has exited the protectionist EU, which, also, has dropped its tariffs by a significant amount in recent decades (but the EU still to this day maintains, and

---

[2] The split of the world into two geopolitical camps, with the "Western" powers aligned against China, Russia, Iran, North Korea and similar countries, poses a large challenge to further global trade liberalisation. But there is no reason why trade liberty should not continue to develop among those "Western" Powers, and other states.

effects, many 'non-tariff barriers'—often, as discussed previously, under the hypocritical guise of 'standards').

The UK is now poised to take a leading role in, and benefit greatly from, this era of global trade, although we need to resume and increase our traditional global leadership role in advocating Free Trade—which we can do better now, because having left the EU, we again sit in our own independent seat at the WTO table. Constant protectionist counterattacks, attempting to reverse trade freedom, proliferate around the world—as described in a recent Economist special report, *Homeland Economics* (https://www.economist.com/weeklyedition/2022-10-08). It is essential that Free Trade advocates fight protectionism wherever it occurs.

Adam Smith is universally acknowledged as having laid the foundations of classic free-market economic theory, and in particular as having moved the world from a "Mercantilist" economic system to a Free Trade one. In his time, the predominantly Mercantilist approach believed that the way for a country's economy to flourish was in essence to sell as many Goods as possible to other countries, while inhibiting those countries, as well as it could, from selling anything back. Smith's "Liberal Markets" approach is grounded on his more general analysis as to how economies can grow through specialisation, and by frustration of monopolistic behaviour; for example, famine in a country can occur, as happened in 19th Century Ireland (which at that time was part of Britain), if other countries are prevented by tariffs from selling affordable grain into that country.

Ricardo refined Smith's ideas with what is often claimed as one of the most important (and counterintuitive) economic ideas ever; the theory of Comparative Advantage (https://en.wikipedia.org/wiki/Comparative_advantage). This says that country X should produce Goods and Services only when it can do so at a lower opportunity cost *relative to the other Goods and Services it can produce*. In other words—and this is the part that most people find surprising—it should import products from sector A in country Y, even it if could itself make sector A products more cheaply than Y, *whenever X's economy contains another sector, B, where X's advantage over Y is even greater*. Observing this rule moves country X up the value chain to whatever place it can as a country add the most value.

When the world follows that rule, there are two consequences. First, every country can find some demand for its Goods and Services, even when it can be outperformed *across the board*, in absolute terms, by other nations. Second, even in those cases when a given country's own productivity does not improve, any increase in the productivity of *other* countries will make it wealthier.

"Absolute Advantage", alternatively called "Competitive Advantage"—the ability to produce a Good or Service better or cheaper than other countries—is of course *also* key for a country to develop, and was the foundation of Adam Smith's original argument for Free Trade (*Of Treaties of Commerce* (https://en.wikipedia.org/wiki/The_Wealth_of_Nations)). Ricardo's concept of "Comparative Advantage" goes beyond that, in saying that even those countries that are superior to other countries in *all* economic sectors will still want to trade with other countries, in order to move resources from one sector within the home country to another, higher value added one; to move capital and people out of those sectors where Comparative Advantage is least, and into those where it is most. Doing that calls for mobility of capital and labour within the country. Any difficulties in hiring and firing, imposed by taxes or regulation, will inhibit that. Artificial costs placed on housing (for example: shortages; stamp duty) prevent people from moving to where the jobs in the most advantageous sector are—so the large impositions of stamp duty on houses for the past decade in the UK will have been particularly damaging in that respect.

A final point about Ricardo's theory, whose high-level concept is these days pretty much universally accepted among economists: it further underlines the benefits a country can get from Free Trade agreements.

How are Competitive and Comparative Advantage created? There are for each country some basic foundations that can underpin a country's building, and exploiting, such advantages. The UK is replete with such foundations, for example our fortune in having the English Language and Common Law; and then our reasonably good education system, our excellent science base, our entrepreneurial national spirit.

Beyond these basic foundations, we can see Competitive and Comparative Advantage being built up in business ecosystems, where clusters of capability reinforce each other and create formidable advantages. One random example would be 'Motorsport Valley', the Oxfordshire/Midlands cluster of high-tech companies that feed the Formula 1 racing industry (Johnson 2019). In this ecosystem, a combination of expertise, manufacturing capability, and suppliers both large and small, have led to such a formidable interlocking set of capabilities that a full 7 of the world's 10 Formula 1 competitors are located within an hour of Oxfordshire; and as can be appreciated, such dominance in this area has enormous downstream benefits to other related industries. Jaguar Land Rover, in nearby Birmingham, benefits from this hi-tech nearby presence, for example.

Again, Silicon Fen (https://en.wikipedia.org/wiki/Silicon_Fen), located around Cambridge and benefiting from Cambridge University's science competence, has created enormous economic success and growth for the UK. With over one thousand high-tech companies established in 1992–1997, that ecosystem has continued to grow and develop, now boasting over five thousand tech companies, in fields such as biotech, AI, chips, Fintech (McDermott 2022). A similar science cluster has more recently sprung up around Oxford (https://oxfordcluster.com/). Tech hotspots have sprung up in London (Silicon Roundabout), Birmingham, Manchester, Edinburgh; the UK consequently emerging as a global tech hub (https://www.technomads.io/blog/uk-tech-ecosystem-evolution-the-global-talent-visas-impact).

Parenthetically: the problem with any focus on Competitive Advantage is that it quickly develops into a yen for an Industrial Policy. Governments can, certainly, support creation of Competitive Advantage by working to have well-educated citizens; by encouraging a great science base; cheap energy; low taxes. Governments can also, unfortunately, waste a colossal amount of money pursuing the chimera of "Industrial Policy". "Picking Winners"; doling out subsidies (whether to entire sub-sectors as is the case with Green Energy companies, or individual companies in the UK—the list grows longer with each passing month); or anointing specific products (e.g. heat pumps, EVs) that are then allowed to have a monopoly in the marketplace.

And since Competitive and Comparative Advantage comes from ecosystems, attacking sectors in the supply chain, whether downstream or upstream, also damages possibilities for Competitive, and thus also Comparative Advantage. The attack on hydrocarbons therefore creates a major problem for the UK; the closure of Britain's last Ammonia plant (https://www.nfuonline.com/updates-and-information/cf-fertilisers-announces-closure-of-billingham-ammonia-plant/) and of Grangemouth, Scotland's last Oil Refinery (Cook and Bonar 2023) will inevitably have calamitous knock-on downstream effects on the UK's economy and exporting ability; all leading to loss of advantage in advanced sectors. (This is not to argue for subsidies for those plants, but rather for removal of the newly introduced punitive taxes and regulations that played a large part in driving them out of existence.)

It can be seen from the above that Competitive Advantage and Comparative Advantage go hand-in-hand: development of the former can be facilitated by, and its advantages more fully realised by, the latter.

At the time that Ricardo propounded the concept of Comparative Advantage (1818), Britain—thanks originally to the commercialisation and industrialisation of Arkwright's Water Frame—had a comparative advantage in textiles, as compared to agriculture, where it did not. It took decades after Ricardo's death for his arguments to bear fruit, so powerful was—is—the instinct to protectionism: but eventually, the repeal of the Corn Laws led to a major, largely wealth creating, shift in Britain's economy, away from agriculture and towards textiles and other manufacturing.

Bastiat, one of the most fluid and amusing of economic writers, focused in particular on the flaws of protectionism. His misfortune was to be born and live in France, where protectionism flourished in his time—just as it does now. But his ideas received much greater appreciation in Britain, where they were highly influential on Cobden, the father of Corn Law abolition. The repeal of those laws in 1846 ushered in the golden era of Free Trade for Britain. An excellent short review of this period, leading all the way through to the 1930s when it all started to go wrong, can be found in the first chapter of Radomir Tylecote's *"The New Trade Route"* (Tylecote 2021).

As mentioned earlier, the whole topic of Free Trade has become, somewhat absurdly, embroiled in the Brexit discussion. Remainers still hanker and argue for a return to the EU's customs union and/or Single Market. One of their chief bolsters for this argument is the so-called "Gravity Theory" of trade; this theory says, formally, that the amount of trade you would/should find yourself easily doing with another country can be expressed mathematically as a combination of (a) the size of that country's economy, and (b) the square of its distance from your own country. An apparently reasonable idea (although somewhat doctrinaire[3]); but one that—in the modern era, and particularly for a country with 80% of its economy in Services—is, increasingly, dead wrong.

In the modern era, starting after the Second World War and with an accelerating trend ever since, the face of global trade has changed dramatically. In the period 1945 to 1980, despite GATT, most countries around the world practised some form of protectionism. At the same time, the costs of trade were expensive, particularly for Goods as opposed to Services, and particularly when it came to trade with distant countries. Frankel and Romer (1999), using data for the period up to 1985, were among the more influential of the early authors studying the issue. They identified that countries with a larger amount of exports and imports as a per cent of their GDP tended to have higher income per capita, but they could not find arguments for there being a correlative cause. They ended up focusing on geography (specifically, nearness of one country to another) as a determinant of trade success. Their

---

[3] It is inspired by the gravitational law in Newtonian physics where the gravitational force between two objects is proportional to their masses and inversely proportional to the distance between them. There is no particular scientific reason why Newtonian Physics should translate one-to-one to the laws of Trade Economics.

work seems, unfortunately, to have led to something of an obsession, among modern economists, with the aforementioned Gravity Theory.

Frankel and Romer had created their analysis using data from a now long-lost era. In the period that they plucked that data from, the distance-abolishing Internet had not arrived. Containerisation (with its enormous potential for transporting Goods cheaply from far-off countries such as China) had not been invented. Digital trade had never even been thought of, let alone becoming the enormous economic force that it now is. Neither China nor India had liberalised. All Frankel and Romer's data that they used to prove the Gravity Model was data only from that earlier, very different, period—as can be seen from the fact that almost all of their data series ended in the mid-1990s. Yet as noted, from 1985 to 1995 a dramatic transformation of trade liberalisation had begun to take place across the world (not to mention the arrival of a little something that people started out by calling The World Wide Web), resulting in massive changes to global trade post-1995. Most of modern trade liberalisation, as with China and India, started either towards the end of, or often after, the 1985–95 period. Even Frankel and Romer emphasised that their conclusions on the gravitational power of propinquity were weak, but in any event we can confidently say that in the new world of containerisation, digitisation, internet, information, AI and global trade liberalisation (and especially as illustrated by the enormous trade success of so many countries—China, India, Vietnam, Bangladesh, and on—as they have found ways to sell their Goods to very faraway countries), the Gravity Model is superannuated and irrelevant to the modern world (Moynihan 2017).

This outdated "Gravity" theory, however continues to have an enormous influence on establishment trade economists—in no small part, it seems to me, because it is so convenient for their obsession to return the UK to the EU, an obsession that bemusingly still grips so many influential economists.

To properly examine the impact and implications of the new liberal trade order, one really has to use post-1995 data. Douglas Irwin (2019) has written one of the most quoted and up-to-date survey papers. He noted that, as I have mentioned earlier, review papers that used sample periods ending in the early 90 s, such as Rodriguez and Rodrik (2000a), tended to end up with conclusions that were ambivalent about the benefits of trade policy on economic growth for a country. He then reviewed papers that used later data, and came to very different conclusions. In his summing-up:

> the findings from recent research have been remarkably consistent. . . . There appears to be a measurable economic payoff from more level trade policies . . . . the results are fairly uniform across methods of analysis, different indicators of

trade policy and other dimensions . . . . Economic growth is roughly 1 to 1.5 percentage points higher than the benchmark, after trade reform . . . Several studies suggest that this gain cumulated to about 10 to 20% higher income after a decade.

Think about what an enormous impact on the size of an economy and improved growth level of that sort would bring—growth that would be over and above the addition of growth from small government, small tax and low regulation. Irwin gives examples of countries that reformed, such as Indonesia, where after trade reforms:

Indonesia's per capita GDP soared . . . 40% higher than the estimated counterfactual after five years, and 76% higher after 10 years . . . these results are robust to placebo testing.

Pretty impressive.

One important caveat is that, as can be guessed from the above, Irwin's review is mostly a review of developing, not developed countries. There is no reason to believe that his result is not generalisable; but (for example) Barro, having also found that countries embracing Free Trade grew faster, was pessimistic that developed countries could, despite their past growth, henceforth expect to grow more than 2% per capita per annum (Barro 1996). This belief, is, however now some 20 years later, robustly demolished by the undeniable examples of recent economic progress in such countries as Switzerland, Norway, the US, Singapore, Taiwan and South Korea (And of course, even just 2% per capita growth per annum would at this time be an achievement gratefully embraced by the larger EU countries, and indeed by us in the UK, in a world where achievement of anything greater than 1% sustained growth per annum currently seems questionable for any of us Western European economies.)

Going beyond Irwin's and Barro's reviews, there have been a number of other surveys—Kim and Lin (2009), Singh (2010) and others—that equally robustly demonstrate the positive impact, in the modern trade era, of trade liberalisation on growth.

For a summary of this important and excellent news about the power of Openness to Trade, Palumbo and Ianoco, quoted before, provide a table (Chart 3) of multiple studies of the early 2000s. They all find (apart from Rodriguez and Rodrik, discussed above, who were neutral) a positive impact on growth from trade openness.

Our own analyses show the same. Using the Fraser Institute's measure of trade freedom (based on the size of trade tax revenue, mean tariff rate and

Chart 3 There have been hundreds of studies of the impact of trade openness

Palumbo and Ianoco's Summary of Reviews of Trade Openness

Study	Method	Effect of trade openness on economic growth:
Burg and Krueger (2003)	Literature review of more than 100 studies	Positive effect of trade openness on growth. Also, trade reduces poverty by increasing growth
Hallaert (2006)	Literature review of approximately 50 studies	Positive effect of trade openness on growth
Cline (2004)	Literature review of more than 100 studies	Positive effect of trade openness on growth. Trade reduces poverty by increasing growth
Baldwin (2003)	Literature review of more than 30 studies	Positive effect of trade openness on growth
Winters (2004)	Literature review of approximately 50 studies	Positive effect of trade openness on growth
Rodriguez and Rodrik (2000)	Literature review of over 100 studies	No effect
Srinivasan and Bhagwati (2001)	Literature review of more than 50 studies	Positive effect of trade openness on growth

Palumbo and Ianoco summarised 7 different meta-reviews of these studies
All but one found a positive impact
Source: Palumbo and Ianoco: In Defence of Classical Liberalism: An Economic Analysis (Iacono and Palumbo (2021))

standard deviation of tariff rates) at the beginning of each 5-year period from 1975 to 2019 (i.e. for the 5-year periods starting in 1975, 1980, 1985, etc.), for the 23 OECD countries considered in the previous chapters, we found a positive association (Chart 4, over the page) between the level of trade barriers and the subsequent economic growth over those 5-year periods. The lower the barriers, the higher the growth.

The chart, apart from showing that Trade Liberalism creates growth, also shows how by the Fraser Institutes' measure, in 2000, the UK had one of the most liberal tariff policies in the OECD. Its growth rate was slightly above the level predicted by our regression. By 2015 our policies were worse—middle of the pack—and our growth rate had dropped commensurately, to lower than the already poor predicted level.

The order of magnitude of the impact of Trade Freedom is such that *if* the UK could improve from its 2015 position, enough to get back to where it was in 2000 (which would still make it not quite as liberal in Free Trade

TRADE FREEDOM VERSUS GDP GROWTH
1975-2019

[Scatter plot showing average annual growth in real GDP during 5-year period (%) on the y-axis, ranging from -6 to 10, versus Tariffs level index at the beginning of 5-year period (1975, 1980, ..., 2015) on the x-axis, ranging from 4 (High tariffs) to 11 (Low tariffs). Data points for UK, 2000 and UK, 2015 are highlighted. Linear Regression Line: Growth = -0.05 + 0.28 (Tariffs Index), R Squared = 0.02, Confidence level: 95%]

Chart 4 Trade Liberalism leads to economic growth: *Source* Fraser Institute (https://www.fraserinstitute.org/economic-freedom/map?geozone=world&page=map&year=2021), Penn World Tables (https://www.rug.nl/ggdc/productivity/pwt/?lang=en), moyniteam analysis

as, say, Singapore), then its GDP growth rate would—if it followed the result implied by the regression line—increase by over 0.3% annually. So, Trade Freedom is an important driver of economic growth.

2. **Britain's economy, as we now pursue our own trade policy, can benefit greatly from further opening itself up to the world**

The world, in our post-Covid era, is certainly something of a puzzling place when it comes to Trade. If the prior decades saw a golden opening up of trade around the world, there now seems to be a bipolar global model emerging, creating barriers that will reduce economic growth all round.[4] Russia and China on one side use a mostly mercantilist approach to trade (and are seeking to wrap as many other countries as possible into their embrace). On the other side is the "Free World", with many different approaches; but with a worrying, not insignificant, number of its member countries in retreat from the Clinton-era NAFTA, WTO, generally open GATT approach. The US has not as yet particularly resiled from the Trump era "America First" rhetoric, although the US economy is, with some exceptions, not massively protectionist—even after both a Trump and a Biden administration. Both, however, embraced America First-style language; while the EU, even though it has

---

[4] This is not to argue this bipolar model can be avoided, given the emergence of bandit countries that are increasingly difficult to trade with, and that threaten the security of Western nations.

UK MAIN GOODS TRADING PARTNERS
1960 vs 1980

Imports, 1960	% imports	Imports, 1980	% imports	Exports, 1960	% exports	Exports, 1980	% exports
1 United States	16%	1 United States	12%	1 United States	10%	1 Germany	11%
2 Canada	11%	2 Germany	11%	2 Australia	7%	2 United States	10%
3 Australia	9%	3 France	8%	3 Canada	6%	3 Netherlands	8%
4 New Zealand	8%	4 Netherlands	7%	4 Germany	5%	4 France	8%
5 Germany	5%	5 Belgium-Luxemburg	5%	5 South Africa	4%	5 Ireland	6%
6 Netherlands	5%	6 Italy	5%	6 India	4%	6 Belgium-Luxemburg	6%
7 Sweden	5%	7 Saudi Arabia	4%	7 Sweden	4%	7 Italy	4%
8 Kuwait	4%	8 Switzerland	4%	8 Netherlands	3%	8 Sweden	3%
9 India	3%	9 Ireland	4%	9 New Zealand	3%	9 Switzerland	3%
10 Denmark	3%	10 Japan	3%	10 Ireland	3%	10 Nigeria	3%

Commonwealth countries and the United States

Countries in the European Economic Community before 1980, and Switzerland

Chart 5 The geographical pattern of the UK trade shifted towards the single market after joining the European Economic Community in 1973: *Source* International Monetary Fund (https://data.imf.org/?sk=9d6028d4f14a464ca2f259b2cd424b85&sid=1409151240976)

gradually lowered tariffs over recent decades, a forest of non-tariff barriers to prevent other countries from having much success in selling into the EU (Burrage 2016).

When the UK joined the Common Market, in 1973 we were required to lodge ourselves inside—behind—its tariff wall. This automatically destroyed large swathes of existing commerce that we had with Commonwealth countries—whether Australia, Canada, New Zealand, or the many other less developed (at the time) Commonwealth countries. Trade with all these countries steadily diminished, as Britain ended up essentially required to buy from within the EU —in particular its agricultural products. In 1970, the UK's Goods exports to the Common Market (later to become the EU) were 22%, and to the Commonwealth 19%, of its total. By 2019, thanks to the protectionist barriers of the EU, the Commonwealth had been increasingly shut out of trade with the UK: Goods exports[5] to the EU were 46% of the total, while to the Commonwealth: 9% (Brown 2021). As can be seen in Chart 5, next page, even by 1980 (just 7 years after joining), a massive shift in trade patterns had occurred.

Why, as Chart 5 shows, were exports affected by that shift just as badly as imports? The answer is that because we joined the EU, which puts up barriers against the rest of the world, the rest of the world in turn put up retaliatory barriers against us. So, we could not have quite as cosy a trade relationship as

---

[5] Remember: British exports are, by value added, almost 70% Services; so only around 30% Goods.

we had, previously, with the US (for example). And as can be seen from the chart, once the UK joined the Common Market, trade with Australia, New Zealand and Canada fell off a cliff.

All this was, frankly, a tragedy.

While EU tariff levels have dropped considerably in size since the 1970s, so that in theory non-EU countries have in recent years been able to sell their Goods more easily to the EU (and, so long as we keep our own tariffs low, to the UK), the EU has created non-tariff barriers that are more formidable than the original tariff barriers. The Single Market approach uses the sneaky device of highly detailed specifications for products and produce, and detailed local required qualifications for a swathe of markets ("The Licence Raj"), with mandatory requirements, for any company exporting to the EU, to have local offices, companies and officers. Thus, products (as well as Services) from outside the EU are kept out.

In food trade, the EU, and the ongoing legion of its supporters in the UK, have created a faux moral panic regarding such issues as "chlorine-washed chicken" from the US. Does the US have mass outbreaks of disease from its populace's eating "chlorine-washed chicken"? Not that anyone has noticed. Is chicken less delicious in the US than in the UK? As visitors to the US in their tens of thousands will aver, far from it. But the idea has been allowed to take hold that Britain would suffer enormous harm from the revolting ingestion of chlorine (almost as much as when we brush our teeth in the UK with our chlorinated water, forsooth), if we were to allow cheap American chickens to be sold in the UK. I happen to be typing these words in the US, having by coincidence just consumed a chicken dinner. It was delicious (more so than in the UK, I would say), and healthy, and the chicken was cheaper than in the UK. I am massively confident that, chlorine-washed or not, I will suffer no intestinal harm from having consumed that chicken. The only harm that Britons are suffering on the chicken front is to their bank balances—from having to pay more for their chicken than if we had a deal to have the US supply some to us. (Some 35% of all chicken consumed in the UK is, by the way, imported—a great deal of that expensively, from the EU.) Again, because we still live in an EU mindset, our trade negotiators have kiboshed a trade deal with Canada over the issue of hormone-fed beef—another faux moral outrage issue (the real reason behind the ban has to be the desire to protect our own beef farmers from foreign competition and offering better beef at lower prices) (Seddon and Whannel 2024).

Britain is now, post-EU, in the process of establishing a new era of trade freedom. For the first time in 50 years, we can strike our own trade deals, ones that benefit the UK; not deals negotiated by the EU, with the UK as a captive member (as has been the case up till now); not deals that end up containing detailed clauses that are structured around the specific protectionist concerns of one or many of the 27 other countries of the EU. Often, the details of how such clauses came to be agreed to, with the country we sought to trade with, were the result of the EU demanding, on behalf of one of its members, undesirable concessions—many of which were specifically contrary to the UK's needs and interests, yet for which a price was extracted by the other side— also contrary to the UK's interests! Each of the 27 EU countries has specialist desires and needs, and each think in protectionist terms. All 27 countries' protectionist concerns are, necessarily, reflected in EU trade deals, which are therefore of far less benefit to the UK than our own tailored deals can be, now that we are able to negotiate a separate deal, one that has not needed to accommodate those 27 countries' multifold needs.

To reiterate what we should be trying to achieve with our trade: the common, superficially arrived at, understanding is as discussed that we are trying to maximise our exports while minimising what we import (the Mercantilist approach). But as was demonstrated by Smith, Ricardo, Bastiat and Cobden; and from the evident impact of their ideas in creating the glorious era of Free Trade in the second half of the nineteenth century, it is actually the opposite that is the case. What our most important overall objective should be is trade freedom—particularly for *imports*—to deliver Goods and Services, regardless of source, that are the best possible for our citizens, at the cheapest prices.

What that means, of course, is lowering tariffs and non-tariff barriers as much as possible. The prime advantage of trade deals to the people of the UK will be in getting cheap Goods and Services from abroad, with access for British Goods and Services into markets abroad as a beneficial by-product of that.[6] Ever wondered why, in so many cases, that which sells for dollars in the US sells for the same amount, but in pounds, in the UK (example: a Play Station, $499 on amazon.com, £479 on amazon.co.uk)? Ever wondered why Argentinian beef, famous around the world, and enjoyed so cheaply and copiously by Argentinians, is not available, equally delicious and equally cheaply, in the UK? Ever wondered why Australian wheat, so abundantly and inexpensively produced, is not sold more here? All these examples, each the result of trade protectionism, impact the cost of living crisis for ordinary people in

---

[6] Note that substitution by cheaper Goods from abroad for more expensive home-made Goods actually *lowers* GDP—but in a good way. (And much of such cheaper imports substitute for other, more expensive, imports—as with the example given of chickens.) Exports do, of course, increase GDP, and a jolly good thing too.

the UK. With the right trade deals, each could be lowering the cost of living for our citizens.

Who is to blame for the failure to overcome the protectionist barriers that constrain those Goods? ***The answer is in the main us, the UK***: still in thrall to the EU view of the world, we impose import charges, and sometimes quotas, on these and so many other Goods, and provide protection for our domestic producers. Thus, we increase the cost of living for the UK consumer.

For the past almost 50 years, we were required to impose protectionist costs, because we had no independent trade policy; we had to follow the EU's. Now that we (very recently) are out of the EU, we have had to spend much of the (relatively short) time that has since elapsed in replicating (necessarily, so as not to have to take a large step backwards) the trade deals, not always so terrific for us, that the EU had with various countries. Only recently, and in particular with the CPTPP deal signed mid-2023, have we started to go beyond those deals. (For the past few years, entering the CPTPP was said to be unachievable: now it has been achieved, the expected effect is now alleged to be insignificant. The same was said about how we would struggle to replicate EU trade deals—but we have, and in some cases we have improved them (Webb 2024); we will continue to do so. The impact of all these deals will, over time, be significant.) Organisations such as the (Remainer and left-wing) OBR have asserted, by torturing the data in the most improbable manner, that we will lose 4% of GDP as a result of Brexit (/), but that we will only improve GDP 0.08% from joining CPTPP (a trading area that is equally large as the EU). (James Forder has effectively rebutted such negative claims about the CPTTP (Forder 2023)). As regards the former claim, how on earth can it be true that we lose 4% from leaving one trading block (note, by the way: the assumptions in the OBR's calculation assumed we wouldn't do a tariff-free deal with the EU. But we have; yet the OBR has failed to update its assumptions), and gain less than 0.1% from getting access to a market of equal size?

As Patrick Minford has pointed out (Minford and Meenagh 2020), the Treasury went even worse than the OBR, with a forecast of a 7.7% reduction in GDP from Brexit (when our trade with the EU is only 12% of GDP!). As Minford has shown, if more reasonable assumptions were fed into the Treasury's exact same model, that 7.7% shrinkage reverses to a 4% *gain* in GDP (as well as a reduction in consumer prices of 8%[7]).

---

[7] Page 24 op.cit.

It is certainly true that the EU has done its very best to punish the UK for leaving the EU, temporarily imposing all sorts of constraints (ones which punish its own citizens as much as they do the UK). All these problems will disappear fairly quickly, as the EU's hissy-fit over our leaving subsides:

- Disruption in the first few days of Brexit on the **Dover/Calais crossing**, leading to long lines of trucks backed up from Dover (this did not last more than a few days, so can now be seen as having been merely a toddler's tantrum by France)
- Aggressive behaviour by the **fishing fleets of France** (a two week wonder) (Barnes 2021)
- Forcing UK citizens to **queue up in non-EU lines,** despite the software being present to allow us e-passport entry (this restriction is not followed in all EU countries, thus proving that those who do restrict, merely do it to attemptedly punish); again, a more polarised, but almost certainly finite, tantrum that will eventually be rescinded as each such country realises it costs them more to use humans rather than machines, with no benefit to them, and a difficult-to-deny appearance of petulance (Gower et al. 2023)
- Forcing UK citizens travelling to or from the EU in countries such as France to **not stay more than 90 days** (these restrictions are gradually disappearing as, again, these countries realise that it is themselves who are punished by these restrictions, since the excluded Brits then spend their money back home rather than in that country) (Hinchliffe and Samuel 2023)
- **Pet restrictions**, whose justification necessitates, apparently, the intriguing hypothesis that rabies is endemic in the UK (in distinction from the actuality, that it is in Continental Europe where *La Rage*—in more senses than one—is found). Again, these restrictions are bound to be removed within a few years (Goss 2023)
- Multiple petty restrictions and costs on **exports from the UK, particularly low-ticket ones, to the EU countries** (Chapman 2021). (This is being worked around with advanced and welcome digital apps, created by such commercial shippers as DHL, and the government in the form of the DBT, for companies exporting to the EU). Most exporters of low-ticket Goods, having found and employed the workarounds, no longer complain about this
- Cutting off **trade between Northern Ireland and Mainland UK**[8] (Trimble 2022). The surrender of Northern Ireland, and its subjugation,

---

[8] A totally unnecessary and damaging concession by the UK, apparently conceded originally by the Remain-disposed Theresa May. Its major repercussions (possibly intended by both sides) include the

to the EU, is one of the most sordid events in the Brexit saga and is the one blow to trade that is, so far, *not* going away. Politicians, from May to Johnson to Sunak, are responsible for this entirely unnecessary and damaging situation. It eventually can and must be reversed: but we need a government that will fight hard to get rid of it. Until then, this is one appalling and entirely self-inflicted negative outcome of Brexit, whose damaging nature we have to acknowledge.

It is, however, very evident that one-by-one (apart from the final point above) these restrictions are dropping away, as different EU countries come to realise that each restriction, satisfying to the EU bureaucracy and politicians as it may at the time, is harming the member countries of the EU more than it harms the UK.

Once these barriers have been dropped, that in turn will result in even greater volume of trade, and general international activity, between the EU and the UK—but at no detriment to the UK's growing exports to the rest of the world.

We now face the ongoing task to create Free Trade deals, whether with the EU or the rest of the world, that are good for the UK and its people—utilising our until recently absent, but now established and growing, ability to negotiate and conclude our own deals. (The Department for Business and Trade is rapidly gaining a reputation for responsiveness and expertise. This will lead to great success, so long as its political masters continue to champion the Free Trade agenda.[9])

In setting out to sign trade deals, we should first never forget that the objective of a trade deal is to be true to the theories of Competitive and above all Comparative Advantage, whereby we seek out deals that will provide great, cheap Goods and Services for the UK's citizens, and where using our good relationships with these countries will also, as a result of such accommodation, persuade them to agree in turn that we can sell UK Goods and Services to them, with as few barriers as possible.

Secondly, when we turn to helping our businesses export to the rest of the world, it is essential that we realise how different the UK economy is from that of the EU, and in particular that some 80% of our economy is in

---

fact that whenever mainland UK diverges from EU law, so as to improve our economy, we have to leave Northern Ireland behind—so as a result we do little diverging—so our economy suffers.

[9] An energetic Free Trade approach (albeit one that has contained regrettable protectionist elements, such as with the recent deal with Australia) has, since Brexit, been pursued by the successive Ministers and Secretaries of State—Truss, Trevelyan, Badenoch. The Trade Champion Crawford Falconer has been highly influential within DTI. The more recent installation of EU-phile Lord Cameron as Foreign Secretary is more annoying/concerning.

Services. The EU's internal market regulations did not cover Services, but, as Burrage showed (2016), that did not result in our seeing terrific growth of our world-class Services to the EU, because most of the large established national providers of Services within the EU had collaborated with Brussels and their own national governments to construct a thicket of non-tariff barriers—for example, as mentioned earlier, requirements to establish local offices; multiple local professional qualifications; complex local regulations.

Outside the EU, it is a different story. As discussed, one of the pretty much tear-inducing consequences of our joining the Common Market in the 1970s was that it ripped us away from our ties with the Commonwealth. The Commonwealth, overall now a larger economy than the whole of the EU (and growing annually far faster than the EU) is a prime potential market for Britain's Services—and also, of course, for its Goods.

The Commonwealth is a key market for British Services in part because so many of those countries use British Common Law. British-created systems of accounting and auditing; the British language for business. This is an enormous competitive advantage that we are lucky enough to have inherited; one is left wondering what might have happened to our economic relations with these Commonwealth countries during the past 50 years, had we not ripped up our ties with them on joining the Common Market. Water under the bridge (though not necessarily forgotten by those Commonwealth countries): but we now have the opportunity to painstakingly repair those ties. The CPTPP is our first major opportunity to do that.

A further opportunity exists as we seek to get a visa program with India that helps them get skilled Indian workers into the UK (note: in accordance with the Comparative Advantage argument, this is a good thing for our economy); we need to understand how to persuade India, in return, to open up its markets to British Services (again, in accordance with the theory of Comparative Advantage, this would be a good thing for India's citizens).

To give an illustrative example, from which many analogies flow: as travelled readers will have noted, a tiny but telling emblem of our continued—not totally destroyed—relationship with the Commonwealth is the small but influential fact that dozens of Commonwealth (and indeed some non-Commonwealth) countries, from Malaysia to Guyana, to Uganda and Botswana, on to Vanuatu, all use the square three-pin plug—a feature that signals that the entire electricity ecosystem of each country uses 240 V-type. That apparently small yet vital fact means, in turn, that products and services developed for the UK's own electricity ecosystem (from generation, to transmission, to delivery) also fit neatly with each of these countries' own needs. This example points us to a better appreciation of the many different and important common standards and technologies that we still share with most Commonwealth countries.

Turning to the US, Prime Minister Rishi Sunak's trip there in June 2023 achieved some relatively minor but still valuable agreements to open up markets between the US and the UK—an achievement that could not have been accomplished while we were within the EU. This points the way to a future where digital services such as AI could be an enormous export for the UK around the world. And the DIT's ingenious pursuit of, and success with, trade deals at the level of individual States within the USA—seven State-level deals, and counting, have now been signed (https://www.gov.uk/government/news/uk-and-florida-sign-pact-to-boost-trade)—thus bypassing the Biden Administration's self-harming reluctance to do a deal with us—will result in cumulatively closer trade ties with the more dynamic states of the US, and thus greater trade between the UK and the US. A US-wide trade deal is still elusive—but much less so than if we were in the EU.

Again, the whole argument as to what kind of trade deals we can accomplish as a standalone trading power in the world, outside the EU, is bedevilled by the politics of Brexit (and of the Northern Ireland situation described earlier). Some Brexiteers say we are now certainly going to be an exporting superpower. Many Remainers, having a mercantilist view (even if they do not realise it), take the opposite tack, and sneer that tiny Britain will be helpless before the trading juggernauts of the EU, America and China. When it comes to Trade deals, Biden's people, in their ignorance, seem to see some sort of Manichean choice between the EU and the UK and thus drag their feet when it comes to doing a deal with us.

The fact is that we will, primarily, do as well at exports as our domestic producers of Goods and Services manage to succeed, by their own efforts, in doing; aided by our country's growing ability to negotiate useful trade deals. (Remainers, apparently more interested in showing their abiding love for the EU than acknowledging good work by our own DBT, jibed just a couple of years ago that it would take us many years to replicate existing EU deals around the world; but as already mentioned, these replicate deals are now more or less all done already—while more and more have been, or will be, improved, to a greater or lesser degree, from what those EU deals offered us (Webb 2024)). We are already seeing significant export benefits, whether from our new independence, or because of a new mindset among the British Business Community. 2022 saw a 23% increase in exports to the Commonwealth (Ward 2023)—whose trade statistics with us, see Chart 6 opposite, are growing very rapidly—and a 27% increase in exports to Brazil (https://assets.publishing.service.gov.uk/media/65f95aeed977c2001f9b807b/brazil-trade-and-investment-factsheet-2024-03-21.pdf). Just two (admittedly outlier, but nevertheless indicative) examples.

IMPORTS & EXPORTS FROM AND TO THE COMMONWEALTH 1999-2022

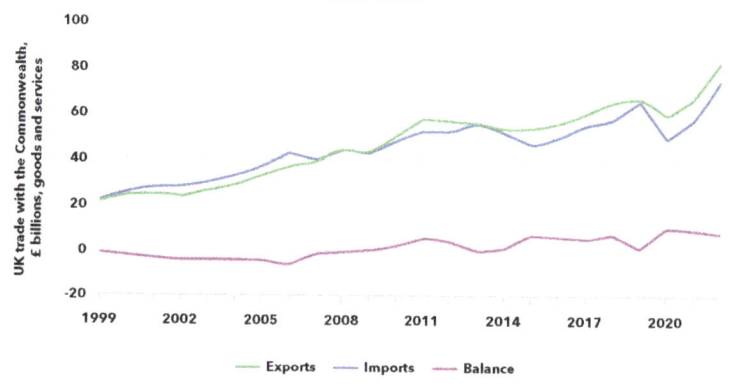

Chart 6 The countries of the Commonwealth are becoming more and more valuable trading partners: *Source* ONS, Pink Book 2023 (Ward 2023)

The Commonwealth, collectively a huge market, is, as discussed, currently only some 10% of the UK's overall trade: the percentage could be far larger if the DBT continues to work on creating far greater and better trade deals, and as our exporting companies exploit the opportunities created by those deals.

As Chart 7, over the page, shows, exports to the EU have not declined commensurately with our growth in exports to non-EU countries (McBride 2023). This is because EU countries buy Goods and Services from Britain because they want them, and because they are pretty much used to having those Goods and Services, and expect to keep on purchasing them—whether Brussels pigheadedly puts obstacles in their way or not. As discussed, we have a tariff-free deal with the EU now, and the petty obstacles the EU have been putting in the way of Brexit Britain's exports to them are rapidly disappearing. Now that the DBT is beginning to rack up the wins on trade deals, critics revert to saying these deals will have only a negligible impact on GDP—for example, the Treasury forecast only a 0.2% improvement in the UK's GDP from trade liberalisation; yet Australia has reported an estimated increase of 5% in GDP from its *actual* experience of trade liberation over the past decades.[10] On the one hand, a pessimistic 'modelled' forecast; on the other, the optimistic actuality of experience. And note that our regression, Chart 4 earlier, predicted a 0.3 percentage points increase *per annum*, which is more in line with (although slightly smaller than) the Australian experience.

---

[10] Minford Op. cit p.19.

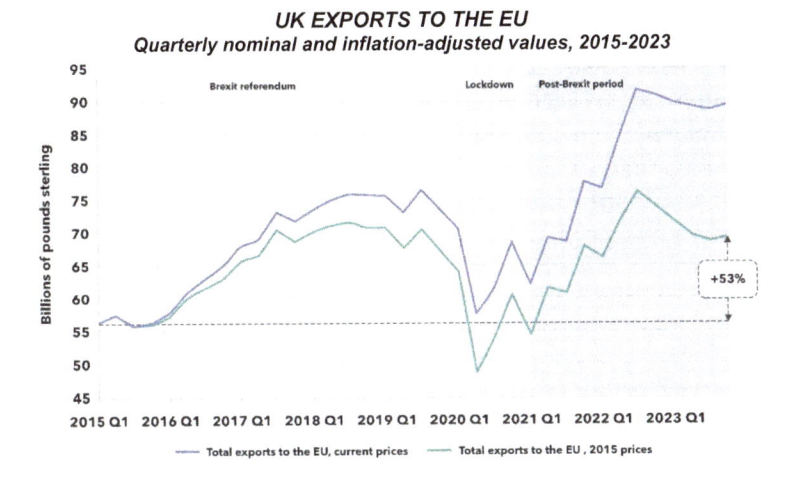

UK EXPORTS TO THE EU
Quarterly nominal and inflation-adjusted values, 2015-2023

Chart 7 Despite gloomy forecasts, the UK's trade with the EU has not collapsed: *Source* Office for National Statistics (https://www.ons.gov.uk/economy/nationalaccounts/balanceofpayments/bulletins/uktrade/January2024#monthly-trade-in-services; https://www.ons.gov.uk/economy/inflationandpriceindices/timeseries/l522/mm23), moyniteam analysis

Overall, if our trade negotiators continue to keep a cool head; are prepared to drop British tariff and non-tariff barriers to imports from other countries; and can focus on ensuring deals that ease the way for Services exports (for example, by mutual recognition of professional qualifications, mutual legal standards, mutual and equivalently recognised regulatory regimes), then very significant growth in our economy can be achieved in the coming years, and major benefits for our citizens realised—in terms of access to cheaper and better Goods—from such Openness to Trade.

3. **To benefit properly from opening up its economy, Britain must recognise protectionism for what it is, and avoid it. Now that we have left the EU, we must not replicate its cartel-like protectionist behaviour**

The prime reason for international trade faltering, and for the growing failure of opportunities for trade to improve the condition of citizens in countries around the world, is growing protectionism around the world.

This comes in many forms. Workers believe that their jobs are being taken from them by someone halfway around the world; farmers believe they should not have to compete with world prices; manufacturers would much rather not compete with better or cheaper products from other countries: all such are therefore content for their country to erect tariff and non-tariff barriers. The EU is a master at putting up barriers, only semi-visible, to trade. The

UK, for nearly 50 years, sat the feet of the master, learning a viewpoint that we now have to cast off.

An example of a classic EU "non-tariff" barrier (though it is in fact a tariff, disguised as a tax, further disguised in obfuscatory wording), is the EU's upcoming "Carbon Border Adjustment Mechanism". This, as the Economist (https://www.economist.com/middle-east-and-africa/2023/09/14/kenya-wants-to-pioneer-a-new-african-approach-to-global-warming) pointed out:

> in effect taxes carbon-intensive imports, (and) is seen in some quarters as a brake on African Industrialisation. A recent study said it might reduce African exports to the EU by 6%. "The EU and US are seeking to destroy our export potential", says Mohammed Amin Adams, Ghana's Minister of State for Finance.

There is no need now for the UK to follow—as it is currently threatening to—the EU's protectionist behaviour: we should ensure that whether in this, or with similar barriers, we go our own way and welcome reciprocal trade from across Africa, with national benefit accruing for both us and them.[11] These are very difficult issues, and politically challenging. That is why Britain took 30 years after Ricardo's compelling treatise in 1817 to abolish the Corn Laws; it is why our recent trade deal with Australia will result in food prices in the UK being higher than they need to be for decades more, because tariffs are not being fully abolished for 15 years. But other countries have adopted the approach of "ripping off the plaster" in abolishing, or massively reducing, barriers to trade. These countries are the ones that have seen the greatest benefits from Free Trade. In the studies listed earlier (Table 1), country after country, such as Indonesia as discussed, saw their GDPs grow rapidly after they took the plunge. New Zealand, essentially a farming country, abolished, under "Rogernomics", all tariffs (in 1984–88). Despite forecasts of doom, New Zealand is now much richer, leading the world in many agricultural products. There are now few New Zealand farmers who would argue for the country going back to its former protectionist ways (Lambie 2005; Farren 2018).

4. Instead, the UK should focus on developing and exploiting Competitive and Comparative Advantage.

---

[11] Instead of putting up such a border tax, we should cease subsidising Green Energy, and thus cease placing the cost of those subsidies onto our domestic producers who could then produce in our country what we increasingly, though unnecessarily, have to import.

If we wish to grow the UK's economy through exploiting the vast opportunities for trade in our Goods and Services around the world, we must work our way towards doing the same as New Zealand and other countries did. For those sectors where we do not have Comparative Advantage, and do not think we can get it, it will be to the benefit of our nation to allow others to provide those Goods and Services to us, rather than producing them ourselves. To the issue of job displacement, it is certainly true that we must (and are currently failing to) control and manage our immigration policy,[12] so that we do not overwhelm the labour market (particularly at the low paid end) with too many workers, nor the country's infrastructure (schools, hospitals, roads and housing). But today, Britain is suffering from labour shortages, not the other way round; we have the opposite situation from what the Remainers gloomily predicted (half a million or more would be thrown out of work, they claimed). We now need to look forward, to a Free Trade economy that focuses on our Competitive and Comparative Advantages. In the second half of the nineteenth century, as trade both into and out of Britain flourished, and in particular as much grain was imported into the UK from around the world rather than being grown in England, agricultural jobs dried up, as less grain was produced—and farmers had to learn to be more productive, so as to compete with overseas producers. Many tens of thousands of workers moved, in consequence, from the country to the towns, fuelling the manufacturing boom. The end result for workers was way higher average wages; and for the economy overall, more jobs. As always, when there is trade liberalisation, just as in any time of technological change, there was (and will be) dislocation of the workforce, involving regrettable individual difficulties and dislocation. But since the alternative is stagnation, and an eventual decline in job opportunities and wages for all, such challenges have to be faced head on.

The concepts of Competitive and Comparative Advantage are not something that calls for passive acceptance—rather, they call for active engagement. Comparative Advantage exists in every country, as discussed earlier. In the UK, the building blocks of Competitive and Comparative Advantage include our language, our common law, our academic and tertiary education excellence, our financial services capability, our fintech leadership, our success in attracting investment for, and hosting, hi-tech startups, and more generally our many Services skills.[13] In order to have continued long-term economic success, we have continually to build new Competitive and Comparative

---

[12] A few pages back, I advocated visas for Indian IT engineers with qualifications. This does not contradict advocating restructuring immigration at the unqualified end.

[13] A recent Financial Times article revealed that our largest sub-sector export was, of all things, Management Consulting. https://www.ft.com/content/8d3ed4d7-6ab3-487d-81ee-3fd337b68538.

Advantage, taking us ever-further up the value chain. Switzerland is a classic example of this. As Switzerland does well in a particular field, its finances improve; over time, its currency appreciates (leading to short-term challenges but long-term benefit); wages go up; imported products become cheaper (because of the high currency). Even just to stand still against competitor countries, let alone find new sectors to excel in competitively, Switzerland must continually upgrade its workforce's capabilities; its infrastructure; its general attractiveness as a country. Switzerland does all of that continually, so that its currency continues to appreciate, its wages continue to rise, and the general standard of living of its citizens continues to grow even further, beyond those of all but a very few countries in the world. This, too, is the path that the UK must look to take, just as other countries, such as Singapore, Chile, Korea and more, are doing.

(Inevitably, this raises the issue for the UK of how to move up the value chain if we have a large swathe of our workforce as poorly-educated as it currently is.[14] Creating productive citizens through an excellent education is entirely possible, as has been shown by the many schools around the UK, such as Michaela, West London Free School, and others, that single-mindedly pursue educational excellence. How to ensure that that same single-mindedness is pursued, and that same excellent educational outcome is delivered, in *all* of our schools, is crucial—but that is a matter that is way beyond the scope of this chapter; it requires a book of its own).

In any event, the road to success is for us to create the conditions for our economy for the emergence of multiple types of Competitive and Comparative Advantage; and then step back while our businesses build successful enterprises. Unfortunately, under the current government—indeed, throughout this current poor-performing century to date—we instead interfere more and more in the economy, creating massive problems through distortive financial subsidies and incentives, with imposition of equally distortive punishment taxes, disincentives and consumer charges. This approach seems predicated on the assumption that a centralised direction of our economy—"we know best"—will build winners. The remorseless judgement of markets, delivered against the many scores of centrally directed

---

[14] The recent PISA results show the UK, as a direct consequence of the Gove/Gibb reforms, shooting up the ladder of international comparisons, generally and particularly in Maths. But there are two caveats: first, our rise in the tables is purely because other countries' results got worse during Covid, while ours stayed overall the same. Second, our schooling is now a tale of two 'cities'—the first, those schools that have embraced the reforms, and the second, the very large swathes that have not; the latter resulting in still an estimated 40% of our school children leaving school either illiterate or innumerate (15–20% of children are both); unable to function effectively as autonomous citizens in our modern world. https://explore-education-statistics.service.gov.uk/find-statistics/level-2-and-3-attainment-by-young-people-aged-19.

economies over the past century and more, suggests that such an outcome is not going to happen. (It is always worth repeating the immortal Peter Mandelson: "*We thought we were picking winners. In fact the losers were picking us.*") The primary outcome of such interference from the centre will, in fact, be to waste eye-watering amounts of money on fruitless fantasies; to create losers not winners; and meantime to condemn our economy to low-or no-growth. Instead, if we stick to the principles articulated in this chapter, we will usher in a new period of prosperity for our country.

References

"Britain's services exports are booming despite Brexit. Why" The Economist, 9 May 2023. https://www.economist.com/britain/2023/05/09/britains-services-exports-are-booming-despite-brexit-why

"Comparative Advantage" Wikipedia. https://en.wikipedia.org/wiki/Comparative_advantage

"Kenya wants to pioneer a new African approach to global warming". The Economist, 14 Sept 2023. https://www.economist.com/middle-east-and-africa/2023/09/14/kenya-wants-to-pioneer-a-new-african-approach-to-global-warming

"Silicon Fen" Wikipedia. https://en.wikipedia.org/wiki/Silicon_Fen

"The Wealth of Nations" Wikipedia. https://en.wikipedia.org/wiki/The_Wealth_of_Nations

Trade Secretary welcomes record year for services export (2023) Gov.uk. 10 February 2023 Trade Secretary welcomes record year for services exports—GOV.UK (www.gov.uk)

Department for Business and Trade and the Rt Hon Kemi Badenoch MP, "UK and Florida sign pact to boost trade", Gov.uk, 14th Nov 2023. https://www.gov.uk/government/news/uk-and-florida-sign-pact-to-boost-trade

"What next? A special report on the world economy" The Economist, 8 Oct 2022. https://www.economist.com/weeklyedition/2022-10-08

Winters LA (2004) Trade liberalisation and economic performance: an overview. The Econ J 5 Feb 2004. https://onlinelibrary.wiley.com/doi/abs/10.1111/j.0013-0133.2004.00185.x

Brexit Analysis, Office for Budget Responsibility, updated 17 Apr 2023. https://obr.uk/forecasts-in-depth/the-economy-forecast/brexit-analysis/

Bergh A, Nilsson T (2013) Trade openness is an important determinant of economic growth. IFN Working Paper No. 862, 6 Dec 2013. https://papers.ssrn.com/sol3/papers.cfm?abstract_id=2363784

Berg A, Krueger AO (2003) Trade, growth, and poverty: a selective survey. IMF Working Paperer No. 03/30, 28 Feb 2003. https://papers.ssrn.com/sol3/papers.cfm?abstract_id=879105

Balance of Payments, Office for National Statistics. https://www.ons.gov.uk/economy/nationalaccounts/balanceofpayments/datasets/balanceofpaymentsstatisticalbulletintables

Baldwin RE (2003) Openness and growth: what's the empirical relationship?". National Bureau of Economic Research, Working Paper 9578, March 2003. https://www.nber.org/papers/w9578

Barnes J (2021) French fisherman blockade channel tunnel and Calais port over licence row", Daily Telegraph, 26 Nov 2021. https://www.telegraph.co.uk/world-news/2021/11/26/french-fishermen-blockade-channel-tunnel/

Barro RJ (1996) Determinants of economic growth: a cross-country empirical study. National Bureau of Economic Research, Working Paper 5698, Aug 1996. https://www.nber.org/papers/w5698

Cook J, Bonar M (2023) BBC "Grangemouth oil refinery could cease operations by 2025" 22 Nov 2023. https://www.bbc.co.uk/news/uk-scotland-tayside-central-67497023

Brown T (2021) Renewing the UK's trading relationship with commonwealth countries. House of Lords Library, 2 July 2021. https://lordslibrary.parliament.uk/renewing-the-uks-trading-relationship-with-commonwealth-countries/

Burrage M (2016) Myth & Paradox of the single market: how the trade benefits of the EU membership have been mis-sold", Civitas, Jan 2016. https://www.civitas.org.uk/email-resources/myth-and-paradox.pdf

Chapman B (2021) Brexit: one in four small export businesses have stopped selling to the EU, poll finds, Independent, 29 Mar 2021. https://www.independent.co.uk/news/business/brexit-small-businesses-exports-sales-b1824008.html

Cline WR (2004) Trade policy and global poverty. Peterson Institute for International Economics Number, pp 379. Oct 2004. https://ideas.repec.org/b/iie/ppress/379.html

Direction of Trade Statistics (DOTS), International Monetary Fund. https://data.imf.org/?sk=9d6028d4f14a464ca2f259b2cd424b85&sid=1409151240976

Tylecote R (2021) The new trade route: the story of the IEA, Brexit and the UK's new approach to global trade, IEA. https://iea.org.uk/publications/the-new-trade-route-the-story-of-the-iea-brexit-and-the-uks-new-approach-to-global-trade/

Economic Freedom Ranking. https://www.fraserinstitute.org/economic-freedom/map?geozone=world&page=map&year=2021

Farren M (2018) Subsidies prevent farmers from reaching their full potential. The Hill 15 Oct 2018. https://thehill.com/opinion/finance/411379-subsidies-prevent-farmers-from-reaching-their-full-potential/

Forder J (2023) The benefits of joining the CPTPP go far beyond the headline figures. Institute for Economic Affairs, 31 Mar 2023. https://iea.org.uk/the-benefits-of-joining-the-cptpp-go-far-beyond-the-headline-figures/

Frankel JA, Romer DH (1999) Does trade cause growth?. Amer. Econ. Rev. 89(3). https://www.aeaweb.org/articles?id=10.1257/aer.89.3.379

Hale S, Fry E (2023) Open for business? UK trade performance since leaving the EU. 28 Feb 2023. https://economy2030.resolutionfoundation.org/reports/open-for-business/

Goss L (2023) Dog-friendly holidays in Europe: how post-Brexit rules affect your trip. Daily Telegraph, 3 Aug 2023. https://www.telegraph.co.uk/travel/advice/does-brexit-mean-pet-passports-travelling-dog-cat/

Gower M, Fella S, Jozepa I (2023) After Brexit: visiting, working and living in the EU. House of Commons Library, 28 Nov 2023. https://commonslibrary.parliament.uk/research-briefings/cbp-9157/

Hallaert J-J (2006) A history of empirical literature on the relationship between trade and growth. Mondes en Développement 34(135). https://papers.ssrn.com/sol3/papers.cfm?abstract_id=1671544

Hinchliffe R, Samuel H (2023) Punished enough by Brexit: France could relax 90-day rule for British second home owners. Daily Telegraph, 13 Nov 2023. https://www.telegraph.co.uk/money/property/second-homes/france-brexit-visa-rule-relax-british-second-homes/

CPIH Index OO: All Items 2015=100, Office for National Statistics. https://www.ons.gov.uk/economy/inflationandpriceindices/timeseries/l522/mm23

Irwin DA (2019) Does trade reform promote economic growth? A review of recent evidence. Working Paper 25927, June 2019. https://www.nber.org/system/files/working_papers/w25927/w25927.pdf

Johnson W (2019) Motorsport valley: the biggest hub of motor racing in the world. Inside the Motorsport Valley 26 July 2019. https://medium.com/inside-the-motorsport-valley-the-biggest-hub-of/the-motorsport-valley-the-biggest-hub-of-motor-racing-in-the-world-ab13e16e4d36

Kim D-H, Lin S-C (2009) Trade and growth at different stages of economic development. EconPapers, J Developm Stud 45(8):1211–1224. https://econpapers.repec.org/article/tafjdevst/v_3a45_3ay_3a2009_3ai_3a8_3ap_3a1211-1224.htm

Lambie T (2005) Miracle down under: how new zealand farmers prosper without subsidies or protection. CATO Institute 7 Feb 2005. https://www.cato.org/free-trade-bulletin/miracle-down-under-how-new-zealand-farmers-prosper-without-subsidies-or

McBride C (2023) Has Brexit really harmed UK trade? Countering the office for budget responsibility's claims, institute for Economic Affairs, 6 Nov 2023. https://iea.org.uk/publications/has-brexit-really-harmed-uk-trade-countering-the-office-of-budgetary-responsibilitys-claims/

McDermott K (2022) A guide to the Silicon Fen tech sector" Growth Business 20 July 2022. https://growthbusiness.co.uk/a-guide-to-the-silicon-fen-tech-sector-20192/

Moynihan J (2017) Gravity models, free trade and game theory: how the bien pensant 'experts' of the Remain camp allowed their prejudices to distort their thinking. Brexit Central, 16 June 2017 https://brexitcentral.com/gravity-models-remain-prejudices-distort/

Tech Nomads "UK Tech Ecosystem Evolution: The Global Talent Visa's Impact". https://www.technomads.io/blog/uk-tech-ecosystem-evolution-the-global-talent-visas-impact

OECD, ILO, World Bank, WTO, Final Report (2010) Seizing the benefits of trade for employment and growth. 11 Nov 2010. https://www2.oecd.org/g20/summits/seoul/46353240.pdf

Office for National Statistics Service Industries: Key Economic Indicators UK Parliament 23 June (2023). https://www.ons.gov.uk/economy/nationalaccounts/balanceofpayments/bulletins/uktrade/January2024#monthly-trade-in-services

Oxford Cluster. https://oxfordcluster.com/

Iacono C, Palumbo M (2021) In Defense of Classical Liberalism: An Economic Analysis. ISBN: 1500963933. https://www.amazon.co.uk/Defense-Classical-Liberalism-Economic-Analysis/dp/1500963933

Minford P, Meenagh D (2020) After Brexit, What Next:" Trade, Regulation and Economic Growth". ISBN: 978-1839103087, https://www.amazon.com/After-Brexit-What-Next-Regulation/dp/1839103086

Penn World Table version 10.01, Groningen Growth and Development Centre, Faculty of Economics and Business. https://www.rug.nl/ggdc/productivity/pwt/?lang=en

Resolution Foundation "Services account for a record share of Britain's exports – but they are increasingly concentrated in London". https://www.resolutionfoundation.org/press-releases/services-account-for-a-record-share-of-britains-exports-but-they-are-increasingly-concentrated-in-london/

Rodriguez F, Rodrik D (2000a) Trade policy and economic growth: a skeptic's guide to cross-national evidence. National Bureau of Economic Research, Working Paper 7081, Apr 1999. https://www.nber.org/papers/w7081

Rodriguez F, Rodrik D (2000b) Trade policy and economic growth: a skeptic's guide to cross-national evidence. Working Paper 7081, National Bureau of Economic Research, Apr 1999. https://www.nber.org/papers/w7081

Singh T (2010) Does international trade cause economic growth? A survey. Wiley Online Library, 25 Nov 2010. https://onlinelibrary.wiley.com/doi/abs/10.1111/j.1467-9701.2010.01243.x

Srinivasan TN, Bhagwati J (2001) Outward-orientation and development: are revisionists right?". Economic Growth Center, Yale University, Sept 1999 http://www.econ.yale.edu/growth_pdf/cdp806.pdf

NFU The Voice of British Farming "CF Fertilisers announces closure of Billingham ammonia plant" 26 July 2023. https://www.nfuonline.com/updates-and-information/cf-fertilisers-announces-closure-of-billingham-ammonia-plant/

Department for Business & Trade, Trade and Investment Fact Sheets. https://assets.publishing.service.gov.uk/media/65f95aeed977c2001f9b807b/brazil-trade-and-investment-factsheet-2024-03-21.pdf

Trimble D (2022) Ditch the protocol: the EU threat to Northern Ireland. Briefings for Britain, 5 Feb 2022. https://www.briefingsforbritain.co.uk/ditch-the-protocol-the-eu-threat-to-northern-ireland/

Ward M (2023) Statistics on UK trade with the commonwealth. House of Commons Library, 6 Nov 2023. https://commonslibrary.parliament.uk/research-briefings/cbp-8282/

Webb D (2024) Progress on UK free trade agreement negotiations. House of Commons Library, 8 Apr 2024. https://commonslibrary.parliament.uk/research-briefings/cbp-9314/

Seddon P, Whannel K (2024) UK halts trade negotiation with Canada over hormones in beef ban. BBC, 26 Jan 2024. https://www.bbc.co.uk/news/uk-politics-68098177

Monetary Economics and Global Trade

The Monetary System of Free Trade

Keith Weiner

Preface to This Chapter

Commodities are traded by weight. The principal issue is fair dealing. The buyer and seller are agreeing on a certain mass of iron ore or coffee beans, at a price. If the seller delivers a reduced amount, then he is breaching the agreement, if not committing fraud. Alternatively, if the buyer goes into the seller's warehouse and takes more than agreed, then he is stealing from the seller.

Simple theft or breach is a minor issue. But now suppose that the government imposes a *mass policy*, in which it keeps changing the definition of a kilogram. The amount that the seller delivers to the buyer would change with each new policy update. Sellers would lobby for decreases in the meaning of a kg, and buyers would fight for a larger kg.

Or apply this idea to a *length policy*. The definition of a meter would change, and when it did, the amount of material on every roll of fabric would change. The size of your property would change. Even the taxes on your house could be revised, based on the new calculation of the area under roof.

Would this optimize the economy somehow? Obviously not. Only the lobbyists would win.

K. Weiner (✉)
Scottsdale, USA
e-mail: keith@monetary-metals.com

The same principle occurs with money itself. No one would suggest cheating with the units of measure of mass and length. But nearly everyone believes in cheating for the units of measure of economic value—the dollar and pound. These were once units of weight (of precious metals). They now bear no relationship to a weight of gold or anything else.

Changing value is cheating. It is a big problem for trade, both domestic and international. As John Maynard Keynes (Keynes 1919) observed:

> As the inflation proceeds and the real value of the currency fluctuates wildly from month to month, all permanent relations between debtors and creditors, which form the ultimate foundation of capitalism, become so utterly disordered as to be almost meaningless; and the process of wealth-getting degenerates into a gamble and a lottery.

Production and trade do not occur automatically. Indeed throughout most of history, and throughout much of the world even today, bad systems restrict, impair, reduce, and stop it altogether. A system built on an irredeemable currency, which is designed for chronic reduction in the value of the currency, is a bad system. The result of impeding production is always impoverishment and misery, often brutality and war.

In this chapter, we discuss the problems with fiat currency and the virtues of a free market in money (i.e., a proper gold standard).

A Free Market in Money is the Prerequisite of a Free Market in Everything Else

The most important question for any productive enterprise is whether the firm is creating or destroying wealth.[1] If, for some reason, management cannot recognize that it is destroying wealth then the firm is doomed. It may go through a frenetic period, of hiring more people, buying more raw materials, and even selling finished goods. But, it will eventually deplete its capital, and then go out of business.

Suppose the problem were not limited to one firm, and the root cause was not incompetent management. Instead, the system somehow distorted the measurement of profit and loss. Viewed through this defective lens, losses appeared to be profits. In this case, it is not just one firm that will go under.

---

[1] In 1970, Milton Friedman argued that if individuals wish to give their own money to charitable causes, then they may do so, but it is problematic if managers of corporations attempt to do so (Friedman 1970).

There may be a period of frenetic booming activity—or multiple such periods. But eventually, the entire society could collapse.

The very theory of monetary policy is that, by changing the value of the monetary unit, the central bank can boost employment or Gross Domestic Product (GDP). However, in reality, it is merely distorting the measurement of profit and loss, of determining whether wealth is created or destroyed. It is true that increasing wealth-destroying activities can temporarily boost employment or economic activity. This gain is ephemeral, and it is akin to feeding sugar to a child. After the high wears off, there are consequences.

For example, the reduction of real capital employed in the economy puts downward pressure on wages. Inevitably, people want the government to enact legislation to try to compensate. So they enact a minimum wage statutes (or increase the minimum wage).

Unfortunately, minimum wage statues add to the unemployment problem. The next intrusion is for the government to pay a basic income to those whose jobs are destroyed by the monetary distortion (or the consequent statutory minimum wage). This is a further drain on the remaining productive capital.

The largest firms, with the biggest balance sheets, are best able to replace lost capital by selling more equity or raising more debt. Therefore, they are gifted the opportunity to acquire smaller rivals. This leads to concentration of industry in fewer and fewer corporations which grow larger and larger. Government then attempts to compensate for this trend by enacting antitrust regulation.

Solving the problem of the concentration of assets in the biggest corporations, which began with monetary policy and then was extended by regulations, is like trying to put out a fire by spraying gasoline on it. Regulatory compliance is a cost that large corporations are more easily able to absorb, compared to their small rivals.

What began as one intrusion into the free market—forcing people to use a fiat currency, and manipulating its value—inexorably degrades into a less and less free market, with more and more government control. As Ayn Rand described it (Rand 1966):

> A mixed economy is a mixture of freedom and controls—with no principles, rules, or theories to define either. Since the introduction of controls necessitates and leads to further controls, it is an unstable, explosive mixture which, ultimately, has to repeal the controls or collapse into dictatorship.

The problem is compounded in international trade.

Each country seeks advantage—a temporary sugar high—by manipulating the value of its currency. This competitive debasement is not only to try to boost GDP, but also exports. It is a perverse sort of advantage. It is, at best, a temporary boost in exports at the immediate expense of imports and hence quality of life for the people. And then impoverishment of the people, as their capital is eroded.

People are aware that debasement is a policy. The more nimble and clever ones seek to trade the trend, for their own profit. A "gamble and a lottery" indeed!

The speculators (i.e., Keynes' "gamblers") enter into the *carry trade*.[2] That is, they borrow a currency whose interest rate is lower than others and hence likely to lose value relative to others. Then, they exchange this currency for one with a higher interest rate on offer. They are not only betting on the currency devaluation, but taking the interest rate differential as additional profit. This brings *hot money flows* into emerging markets, which do not have the capacity to productively deploy so much capital. Much of this capital ends up in *malinvestment*. Later, the flow reverses, starving these economies of capital, and on top of that with a plunging currency.

Another problem arises from the fact that the whole international monetary order is based on one global reserve currency. Those who control the issuance of this currency have nearly absolute power. No one should be given the means to control billions of people.

In 1971, US Treasury Secretary John Connolly said to the European finance ministers "the dollar is our currency, but it's your problem" (Wikipedia 2024). His snide remark surely came because he felt that he possessed an awesome power.

This is no basis for free trade between nations. Discoordination, both within a country and internationally, is the result of a fiat currency regime.

A Fiat Currency is Central Planning of Credit

Monetary policy is not acting directly on the value of the currency. If this were possible, central banks would not have struggled and failed to hit their 2% inflation targets during the post-financial-crisis period up until the Covid lockdown, as shown in Fig. 1, a graph of the Consumer Price Index.

It is interesting that (U.S.) inflation even hit just about zero in 2015.

Monetary policy operates primarily by controlling the interest rate paid on 1-day deposits. This all but dictates short-term rates such as the 1-week

---

[2] As Investopedia says, "A carry trade is typically based on borrowing in a low-interest rate currency and converting the borrowed amount into another currency." (Chen 2022).

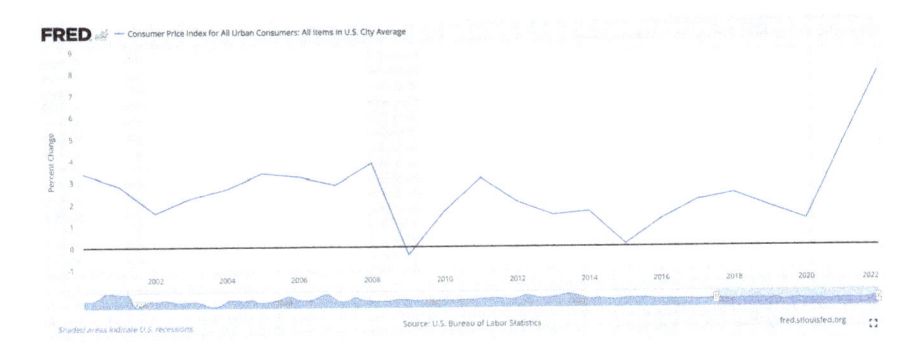

Fig. 1 Consumer price index

and 1-month rates. The effect is lessened for longer maturities (and the yield curve can invert, which provides additional perverse incentives).

How do central bank officials determine what interest rate to set? Do they even have the means to know? This one price affects all other prices in the economy, hence all production and trade.

To administer interest rates is to centrally plan credit.

The Soviet Union tried to centrally plan wheat production. Wheat is a simple product. You just plant seeds in fertile soil, wait for sun and rain. And harvest. It has an annual cycle. Yet the Soviet Union starved. (Wikipedia 2024a).

Credit is the most complex product in the economy. It operates by numerous mechanisms, some of which are not well understood. It has a cycle that can be years or decades. Most economists realize that central planning of wheat cannot work, yet they still persist in believing that central planning of credit could work, if only the central bank used the right formula, such as inflation targeting (Sarwat Undated) or nominal GDP targeting (Bhandari 2017).

Central planners, including central banks, do not know the right interest rate. They cannot know it, as only a market can determine it. But a market in interest rates is precisely what the central bank negates with its monetary policy.

The central bank administers the short-term rate. There is a market for longer-dated credit maturities. It goes through the motions of price discovery. However, prices in this market ultimately depend on the administered rate because financial institutions can borrow at the administered rate to buy long-dated bonds. The mechanism which sets the price (and hence interest rate) on long-dated bonds is more complex than simple arbitrage between the central bank rate and the bond rate. But the administered rate is a key input into long-term rates.[3]

We are left to conclude that bureaucrats administer the short-term rate, and the long-term rate generally follows.

a. An Irredeemable Currency Necessarily Suffers Unstable Exchange and Interest Rates

Credit is far more complex than wheat. But, even with wheat, we can see the consequences of fixing its price. If the price is too low, then production is immediately disincentivized and people will soon starve. Since no one wants to starve, they are forced to plant private gardens, which is the devolution of the division of labor. If food shortages become acute, then crime becomes rampant, and people can be marched off to war.

With credit, the consequences of mispricing may not become obvious for years or decades. Consequences include capital consumption and capital destruction, currency trading, and rampant speculation. Most people end up impoverished, though a few lucky winners take serious amounts of wealth from the gyrating markets. As Keynes said, in the preceding paragraph to the one cited earlier (Keynes 1919), "while the process impoverishes many, it actually enriches some."

To put this in more mathematical terms, the process involves *positive feedback* and *resonance*. A stable system is characterized by *negative feedback*. This is when any excursion tends to cause forces that push it back. For example, if the apple harvest is poor, the price will skyrocket. In the grocery store, people see apples suddenly much more expensive than pears. Most will switch their custom to pears. The bad harvest caused the price to rise, but the high price caused buying to fall. There is negative feedback.

The *carry trade* has positive feedback. The first speculator to notice the interest rate disparity shorts a currency to exchange it for another, and buys assets denominated in that currency. The carry currency drops down in value by a tick. The emerging market currency ticks up, as well as the price of assets in that country. This draws the attention of the next trader.

Eventually, the trade is overdone. The value of the emerging market currency rises too high. Or the interest rate on the carry currency rises. The carry trade slams into reverse, and with it, the value of the emerging market currency. Speculators pile on to this trade also.

---

[3] The moral hazard of various lending facilities, plus deposit insurance, certainly encourage a great deal more borrowing short-to-lend-long than would exist in a free market. Hence, a closer tie between long- and short-term interest rates.

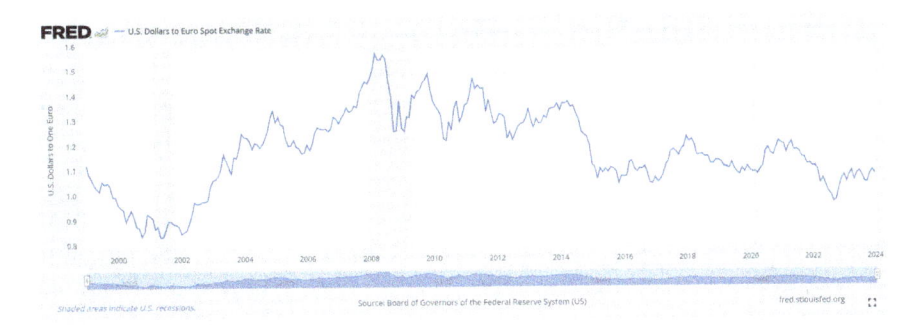

Fig. 2 Euro priced in US dollars

Currency exchange rates are necessarily unstable. Figure 2 is a graph of the second biggest and most liquid currency in the world, as measured in the biggest and most liquid. In 25 years, it has had quite a large range, from $0.80 to $1.60.

Interest rates are more complicated, but there is a positive feedback dynamic here too (Weiner 2013). The interest rate, which is the cost of capital, has a relationship to the return on capital. No business can borrow at a higher rate than it generates. Suppose a firm generates 8% return on capital, then borrowing at 10% interest cause a 2% loss.

Indeed, if a firm had borrowed previously at lower rates, then when its rate goes up it will be forced to sell capital assets. And even if it has cash on the balance sheet to invest, still it must seek the highest return. If government bonds pay more than investing in its own activities, this is a powerful disincentive to invest in growth.

When the interest rate is rising, those enterprises which had borrowed at lower rates have growing margins. The problem is when their plant reaches the end of its life and needs to be replaced. There may not be a business case to borrow and buy new equipment. A protracted rising-rates environment, such as the 1970's, tends to hollow out capital-intensive industries. This gives increased pricing power to the surviving firms. In turn, this causes rising commodity prices.

Rising commodity prices motivates businesses to borrow, not to finance more productive capacity, but to finance growing inventories of raw materials and work-in-progress. Like the carry trade, the trend of rising prices catches the attention of the first firm. Its borrowing—i.e., selling a bond—causes the bond price to tick down, which is the same as the interest rate ticking up. Its increase in the quantity of commodities in holds causes an uptick in commodity prices.

There is positive feedback written all over this. As the interest rate rises, more productive plant is not renewed when it wears out, thus causing higher commodity prices. Higher commodity prices encourage more borrowing to build more inventory buffers. Borrowing to build inventory causes the interest rate to rise.

Positive feedback is characterized by a runaway trend. For example, the nuclear fission reaction. Fission releases heat. The hotter the remaining uranium gets, the more it undergoes fission. This is how a nuclear bomb detonates and causes so much destruction.

The government's interference in the interest rate market introduces *positive feedback* to a market that would otherwise be driven by *negative feedback*.

The central bank may try to control the short-term interest rate, but it can be forced to react to the trend set in motion by this positive-feedback loop.

Another problem is that the bureaucrats get information with a lag. A drunk driver also exhibits this problem. The start of the cycle is that he begins drifting to one side of the road. With a lag, due to the depressing effect of alcohol on the central nervous system, he notices. Then, he overcorrects, due to poor motor control caused by the alcohol. He swerves more and more severely to each side, until he ends his drive upside down in a ditch.

In addition to the information lag, there is another source of delay. The central bank sets interest rates in a politicized process. There are competing factions, some of which want lower rates, some want rates to hold steady, and some want higher rates. The rate-setting committee must process these different views—not only according to their opinion on the economic impact of lower, stagnant, or higher rates—but also according to their assessment of the political repercussions of pleasing one group and frustrating another. And their personal career ambitions may also factor in to the decision.

A system in which corrective responses occur with a delay is subject to resonance. And a politicized process does not always choose the corrective response.

An example of resonance is the infamous Tacoma Narrows Bridge collapse. The valley has heavy winds, but they are gusting periodically, rather than a steady speed. The period of the gusts matched the natural frequency of the bridge, creating a resonance, which amplified the resulting torsion wave (the bridge twisted when hit by each gust). When the amplitude exceeded the strength of the steel, the structure collapsed.

This is how central bank reactions to the positive feedback works.

b. These Risks are Systemically Unhedgeable

Positive feedback combined with resonance can cause wild gyrations. While some financial institutions and producers are nimble and clever and can position themselves to benefit from these trends, most are forced to try to hedge the risk of adverse moves.

Market makers—i.e., financial institutions—are happy to sell them instruments such as *swaps* to hedge currency exchange and interest rate risk. The risk-averse party pays a counterparty to take the risk that the interest rate will move against it. This is an interest rate derivative.

The seller of the *swap* now incurs the risk. The problem is that this firm needs to hedge also. It could buy a similar swap. But the problem is that it cannot make a profit if it has to buy the same hedge as its selling. It may turn to a *swaption*.

A swaption is the right to buy a swap. Similar to a stock option, it is cheaper to buy the option than to buy the underlying instrument. A swaption is a derivative of a *swap*, or a second derivative of the interest rate.

The seller of the *swaption* now incurs the risk that the buyer is protected from. It, too, must seek protection itself. The chain of derivatives can get very complicated and very large. According to the Bank for International Settlements, there were $643 **trillion** worth of derivatives outstanding as of the end of June 2022 (Bank for International Settlements 2022).

The root demand for these derivatives comes from the productive firms who suffer, when currencies or interest rates move adversely. This can often be biased to one side of the trade (e.g., protecting from rising rates, or protection if a hot emerging market currency drops). The speculators also tend to crowd on one side of the trade, based on the trend.

Such hedging demand is unlike, say, the demand for credit itself. The bank can balance its loan book with natural lenders on one side such as wage-earners and retirees, and natural borrowers on the other side such as productive firms.

Demand for currency and interest derivatives is inorganic, it comes from the need for stable liabilities. Both the value of the unit to be paid, and the interest rate on it are subject to volatility that is ultimately caused by government intrusion into money and credit. When the derivatives users are biased to one side, any individual player can hedge this risk, but the system is vulnerable to the risk. Chalk this up as another political pressure for the central planners to consider when setting monetary policy.

c. Irredeemable Currency Necessarily Creates Winners and Losers

Let us return to that quote from Keynes, "the process of wealth-getting degenerates into a gamble and a lottery." that describes the environment created by unstable interest rates. During periods of rising rates, such as 1947–1981, asset prices are soft if not falling. This is because the net present value of a cash flow falls, with each rise in the discount rate (which is the market interest rate). During periods of falling rates, such as 1981–2022, asset prices are strongly rising.

Each time asset prices change, those who can trade nimbly can make money. But their profits comes from other market participants. Changing asset prices (especially rising asset prices) is a process of conversion of one party's capital to another's income. The recipient spends it, consumes it (Weiner 2012).

Consider this example. Joe buys a bond for $1000. The interest rate drops, and he sells it to the next investor for $1200. He has $200 to spend. The buyer would never have consumed his savings, but he willingly hands it over to Joe, who consumes it.

If asset prices are endlessly rising, then this process of conversion is endless. The central bank is not printing real wealth. It is merely causing asset prices to rise. This makes people feel richer, and hence spend more on consumer goods. This so-called "wealth effect" is not real wealth, it is a manipulation of people's perception of wealth. It is, as Keynes said, when "the real value of the currency fluctuates wildly from month to month."

d. Irredeemable Currency Does not Work, Even on its Stated Terms

The stated purpose of monetary policy, at the time the Federal Reserve was established, was to stabilize what was assumed to be a cycle which is intrinsic to free markets. The Federal Reserve Act of 1913 states that the Board of Governors shall (Federal Reserve Act 1913):

> ...maintain long run growth of the monetary and credit aggregates commensurate with the economy's long run potential to increase production, so as to promote effectively the goals of maximum employment, stable prices, and moderate long-term interest rates.

However, it was not due to free markets, but intrusion into the market by governments (even long before 1913). Figure 3 is a graph of the interest rate on the 10-year Treasury from 1790-to 2012.

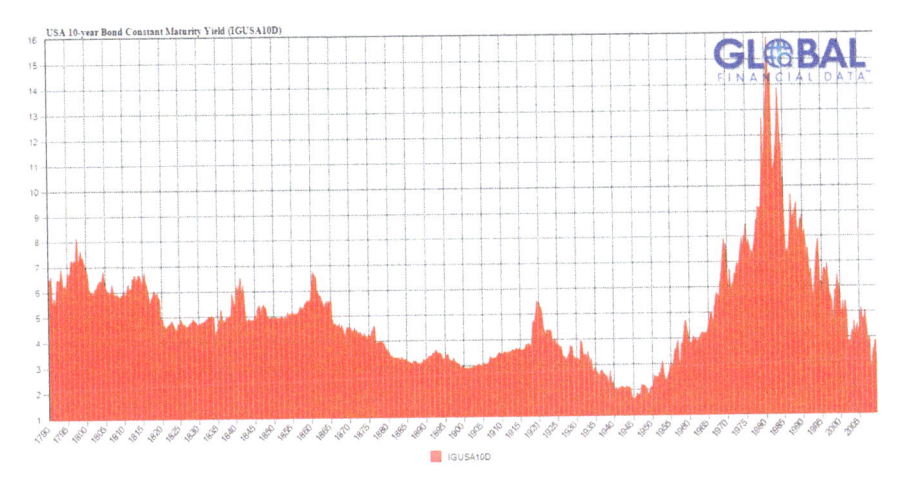

Fig. 3 History of the 10-year treasury rate

This graph shows the interest rate responded to a few dislocations, such as the existential wars of 1812 and 1861. And after 1865, the rate fell because the government forced federally-charted banks to buy Treasury bonds to back the notes they issued, while the government was paying down its debt. With less and less debt to be had by the banks required to have it, the price of Treasury bonds increase (i.e., the interest rate decreased).

But even this fall is small relative to the much bigger spikes and drops which occurred during the Federal Reserve era after 1913. The spike of 1919 was unprecedented (other than during the aforementioned existential crises), but no one could have imagined the Great Depression and what would happen during this dark chapter, much less what happened after World War II through 1981.

If the interest rate is a measure of business demand for credit, and hence the state of the economy, then by this measure the Fed achieved the exact opposite of what it promised to do.

With the passage of the Humphrey–Hawkins Full Employment Act in 1978 (Steelman 2013), the stated purpose of the Fed shifted to promoting full employment balanced somehow with stable prices. According to mainstream theory (CORE Undated), the central bank faces a tradeoff. It can increase the quantity of money, which causes the economy to boom. But that also causes consumer prices to rise.

So Humphrey–Hawkins mandates that the Fed somehow achieve two mutually-exclusive goals. In practice, this gives the Fed latitude to act at its own discretion and point to whichever of these goals rationalizes its policy post-hoc.

It should be clear that employment and rising consumer prices are a false alternative. In a free market (i.e., without fiat currency, central planning, minimum wage laws, and other restrictions on production and trade), there is no such thing as structural unemployment. In a free market, the more people working—i.e., producing—the more goods become abundant.

However, instead of addressing unemployment at the root, the central bank seeks to artificially boost employment with inflation. This has the net effect of depleting the capital base. Since capital is required to employ people, this pushes up unemployment in the longer-term. Even if the central planners can temporarily boost employment hey end up lowering it in the end.

The government achieves neither stable prices nor full employment to begin with, much less by tinkering with the value of the currency, or the price of borrowing it.

e. The Interest Rate Determines the Hurdle Rate of Return on Capital

There is another problem with changes in the interest rate. It drives the return on capital.

Consider a falling interest rate environment. The marginal business opportunity is the one which will be funded, when either projected revenues increase or costs decrease. Interest is a significant component of cost. So when the interest rate drops, many enterprises build more capacity. New hamburger restaurants are opened, and new manufacturing lines to make hamburger grilling equipment are added (which adds to employment).

The net result is that the return on capital invested in these industries is pulled down. It will continue to be pulled down until the greater supply causes prices to fall sufficiently to drive return on capital down to marginally above the new, lower interest rate. Then, the marginal project is not funded, until the next downtick in rates.

Each downtick in the interest rate encourages businesses to go deeper into debt. And, as we see, these more-indebted businesses have lower return on capital and smaller unit margins. This is a picture of businesses becoming brittle. They are more and more vulnerable to reductions in consumer demand and, of course, to rising interest rates.

When the rate rises (as is happening when this chapter was written in November 2023), it goes above the marginal return on capital. What does a business do, when it earns less on its capital than it pays for this capital? It must try to sell off assets, to pay off some debt. If this is happening economy-wide—the interest rate is economy-wide—then asset prices plunge. Many businesses will go through bankruptcy.

This causes higher unemployment, believed to reduce the rate of increase of consumer prices. More importantly, the return on capital must rise to get above the interest rate. The only way for an industry, or an economy, to increase return on capital, is by destroying capacity and hence reducing supply. Lower supply brings higher prices. Higher prices bring higher unit margins. Higher unit margins cause higher return on capital. At least, for the survivors.

In order for higher margins to generate higher return on capital, volumes must hold steady. This is true only for the survivors, when their competitors eventually go under.

Note that even if a business has no debt, it is still in an untenable position if it invests capital to earn a return lower than that offered by Treasury bills. Business has risks, and headaches. T-Bills do not.

R > I is iron an economic law. Return on capital must be above the interest rate, or else capital will be liquidated (Weiner 2023).

f. Irredeemable Currency is Ultimately Headed Toward an Existential Crisis

Thus, interest rates must keep falling. A rising rate would cause mass defaults which would cause bank insolvencies. And, skyrocketing unemployment, which it is the Fed's mandate to prevent.

As described earlier in this chapter, the falling interest rate causes capital consumption by conversion of wealth to income. And by stimulating increases in production capacity when there is no increase in consumer demand. And falling rates has another problem.

What happens when interest gets below zero?

In a normal world (i.e., free market), any business which destroys wealth is shut down. The sooner, the better. But now we are projecting falling rates to its inexorable terminus: negative rates. If a business can borrow at -2%, then it can destroy capital at -1% and still declare a profit. Any profitable activity should be scaled up, the profitable firm should seek to do more of it. Which means that under a negative interest rate, negative returns on capital will be profitable hence those activities will be scaled up.

The return on capital is pulled down, with each downtick in rates. When interest falls sufficiently below zero, then return on capital will be pulled below zero. All during the falling rates, the system is incentivizing the consumption of capital via speculation on assets and malinvestment. It becomes more obvious when interest < 0, because then return on capital is negative, and thus, the destruction of capital becomes obvious to anyone who can read financial statements.

At the same time, the total debt extant is rising exponentially. So there is more and more debt, to be serviced by less and less profit. And then, (operating) profit will go negative.

If debt cannot be serviced out of operating profit, it can only be serviced by more borrowing. Governments have been doing this for a long time, now it will spread to infect the entire productive sector.

We can debate the exact timing and likely sequence of events that will cause the debt, the economy, our currency (and our civilization) to collapse (Weiner 2012). But no matter when and how it plays out, it will be catastrophic.

Free Trade Between Nations Depends on Free Markets Within Nations

It should be axiomatic that trade between nations is cannot be fully free, unless trade within each nation is free. If each nation is busy manipulating its economy, distorting its currency, seeking to achieve internal central planning targets and inevitably corrupting and politicizing the process, then it will extend this dysfunction to external central planning targets.

The nation's trading partners will rightly cry foul—and wrongfully tinker with and extend the scope of their own central planning machinations. If it makes sense to manipulate the currency to achieve goals like boosting GDP and employment, then it makes equal sense to manipulate the currency to boost exports.

Note that boosting exports, and its twin policy minimizing imports, is a policy of subsidizing manufacturers who export their goods, and impoverishing everyone else. Add this on top of a policy of debasing the value of the currency, which subsidizes debtors and impoverishes everyone else.

a. Free Trade is Impossible, if Trade Finance and Settlement Depends on One Nation's Politics

In addition to the problems described above, there is another problem. Production and trade require finance. The iron ore mine in Australia, the port facilities, the ships that carry to China, and the smelter all borrow large sums to build their capacity. The trade itself requires finance, as the ore is delivered to the port, loaded on ships, and sailed over to China, where it is unloaded and put on rail cars to be delivered. This is a large value worth of ore, and it needs finance for the time in transit.

A change in the value of a currency can easily be greater than the profit margins of these businesses. In other words, you borrow a currency to finance a shipment on which you will make 3%, but the currency goes up by 5%.

Another problem is that you owe a payment for goods, which you will make in a few months. If the value of the currency you must pay rises, you can suffer a loss. Alternatively, you are expecting to receive a payment, and in the meantime the currency falls.

This is an intractable problem, but one coping method is to converge on a single currency for finance and trade. This currency is the world's reserve currency, the US dollar.

Thus, US monetary policy inflicts collateral damage on Australian miners, Norwegian shippers, and Chinese smelters with each change in the exchange rate of the dollar and each change in the interest rate of the dollar (which contributes to changes in the exchange rate).

This is not exactly free trade.

b. Issuer can Weaponize it (as 2022–2023)

In 2022, the US weaponized the dollar. I do not refer to confiscating the boats, airplanes, cars, real estate, equities, and US Treasury holdings of Russia due to the war in Ukraine. This was predictable sanctions, imposed by the US and other countries.

Weaponization, here, refers to the massive and prolonged rise in interest rates imposed by the Federal Reserve. The Fed may claim that it is fighting the rapid increases in consumer prices which occurred following the Covid lockdown and supply chain whiplash from unlocking. But this policy has the effect of making dollars scarcer, of drying up liquidity.

Liquidity contracts at the margin, which means outside the borders of the US. Producers all over the world depend on dollar finance. And under this policy, they find it much more expensive to obtain this finance, when they can get it at all. They are struggling, and many will not survive this episode.

Whether or not this is deliberate, a blow "aimed" at China or whichever nation is not the point. This is not about trying to speculate about motives in geopolitics. The point is that the US government has a tool at its disposal which can wreak havoc on the rest of the world.

Mere possession of this tool poses a threat which undermines free trade. Much less the use of this tool.

c. **Triffin's Dilemma: Conflict Between Domestic Monetary Policy and International Need**

Even if this tool is not unlimbered for purposes of inflicting deliberate harm on another nation, it causes harm nevertheless. Economist Robert Triffin described a dilemma, in the 1960's (International Monetary Fund Undated). He posited that domestic policy concerns, such as fighting inflation, conflict with global need for more dollar reserves to support economic growth. The US, he said, would be obliged to run perpetual trade deficits, with whatever consequences may ensure from that.

Picture the discussions that must take place when the Federal Reserve Board of Governors meets. However they may decide, whichever side of this false alternative they may favor at one moment (influenced, no doubt, by lobbyists for various industries) the result could hardly be called free trade between nations.

Gold is the Impartial Money, and the Solution

The foregoing discussion should show clearly why any politicization of the process of setting the quantity of money, the value, the exchange rate, and the interest rate causes intractable problems. These problems cause the domestic market to be unfree, and cause the degree of un-freeness to increase over time. Additionally, they also cause trade between nations to be unfree.

It is in everyone's interest[4] to use a money which is impartial, that is not subject to monetary policy. It is in everyone's interest to use a money which enables a free market to determine its metrics. Gold.

a. **Gold is not Controlled by any Government**

Gold is widely available and widely distributed. Any person or government who wants it, can get some. Gold ore deposits, unlike certain other minerals, are widely dispersed. Anyone who wants to mine for it can attempt to do so. But gold is hard to find in commercially viable deposits. It has been mined for millennia, but never that much at any one time.

---

[4] The US dollar system harms the rest of the world. Because of zero-sum thinking, many people assume that if the rest of the world is losing, then America must be winning. They should know that the system, which was dictated to the Allies (and later the defeated Axis) by the US government at Bretton Woods in 1944, was architected by Harry Dexter White. White was later found to be an agent working for the Soviet Union (Wikipedia 2024b). It seems unlikely that he was trying to set up a monetary system to benefit America, but rather to undermine it. Which the system does.

No government, not even the US government, can hope to control gold's quantity, value, or interest rate. Gold stands as a bulwark, to protect wage-earners and savers from the ravages of monetary policy. And peripheral countries from the ravages of US monetary policy.

Naturally, the government and its court-economists long hated gold. They still hate it today.

b. **Extremely High Stocks-to-Flows Insulates Gold from Variation in Mine Output**

In an ordinary commodity, every ton that is produced is consumed. There is very little inventory buffer of an ordinary commodity, such as in storage tanks at major oil distribution centers. Even in a crop such as wheat, which is harvested once or twice a year, there are only inventories sufficient to meet consumer demand until the next harvest.

These inventory buffers are "stocks". The rate that they are produced are "flows". The ratio of stocks to flows for ordinary commodities is very low, measured in months.

If production is slightly higher than normal, perhaps due to a perfect combination of sun and rain, then there is a "glut" in wheat. The price can drop sharply. This is a disincentive to plant the crop, and an incentive for the marginal consumer of plant starches to switch from whatever they normally use to wheat. The glut is quickly worked off, and the price recovers.

This is not applicable to gold. So far as we know, mankind has prized gold for at least 6,200 years (Wikipedia 2024c). Gold is not consumed. Even when it is fashioned into items such as candlesticks, if those items are no longer needed, the gold is melted and recycled into something else. It is too valuable to discard. Most of the gold ever mined in human history is still in human hands.

There is no such thing as a "glut" in gold. The market is ready to absorb whatever the mines produce (World Gold Council 2023), currently about 3600 tons per year, without the price crashing. The total amount of gold estimated to be in human hands is 209,000 tons (World Gold Council 2024).

Therefore, we can calculate the stocks to flows for gold equal to 58 years. This is at least two orders of magnitude greater than that of regular commodities.

This has extraordinary implications.

Consider wheat. It is perishable. No one wants to hold more wheat than he can be certain to sell before it spoils. Or oil. It is toxic and flammable, so requires a specialized storage facility. No one can hold more oil than their storage capacity.

Or would want to. This is because the marginal utility of these commodities rapidly diminishes as quantity rises. When marginal utility is below cost, there are no buyers. Which is price must fall as quantity rises.

With gold, this does not occur. Therefore, gold's marginal utility either does not diminish at all, or if it does, it diminishes at a rate which is many orders of magnitude slower than that of wheat or oil. In other words, people do not have the same kind of limit for holding gold as they do for wheat or oil. In other words, they are willing to accept the Nth + 1 oz of gold on the same terms as they accept the Nth.

This is precisely the behavior you would expect and need for money. No one objects to being paid more money!

We can think of the high stocks to flows as analogous to a physical object having high mass, hence inertia. It takes a great force to push an aircraft carrier. By comparison, a kayak, canoe, rowboat, sailboat, or even a big yacht takes comparatively little force. Gold is like the aircraft carrier, wheat, oil, and the other commodities are like the kayak, canoe, and rowboat.

The amount of gold mined annually is less than 2% of the total amount of gold held in human hands. Changes in one mine's output, or one country's, are small changes at the margin.

This also addresses the concern of a country somehow controlling gold, the way the United States can control the dollar, to impose a monetary policy. There is so much gold out there, it is so broadly distributed, and it would be inconceivable.

c. Irredeemable Currency Lacks a Proper Market Mechanism for Setting Interest Rates

With an irredeemable currency, there is no way around a profound law borne of its mechanics. To own a money balance is to be a creditor. One party's money is another party's liability. Ultimately, every money holder is a creditor to the government. All dollars are either direct or indirect ownership of a government bond.

To have dollars means one of four things. One, you hold a paper Federal Reserve Note. The Fed issues these Notes to finance its purchase of Treasury bonds. The Note holder is a creditor to the Fed, which backs its liability by its asset, the bond. The Fed is a creditor to the Treasury.

Two, you hold a bank balance. You are a creditor to the bank. The bank issues these liabilities to fund its assets, which principally include government bonds and reserves held at the Fed itself.

Three, if you are a bank, you can hold reserves at the Fed. The Fed issues these liabilities to finance the purchase of its assets, Treasury.

Four, you can hold Treasurys' directly.

There is no way to opt out. There is no way to take your money home, to withdraw it, to opt out of the system. You have a (limited) choice of obligors, but you are forced to be a creditor.

This has a particular significance to the process which sets the interest rate, i.e., the price of a bond (which is a strict mathematical inverse of the interest rate). Consider the price of anything else, say apples. If the price of apples rises significantly, then people will switch to other fruits such as pears. Or they may not buy any fruit. Consumers can take their money home. This choice of the consumer is what keeps a ceiling on prices, what checks the desire of grocers to charge more.

Irredeemable currency obliterates this choice for savers.

Suppose a socialist dictatorship abolished currency and private enterprise. People are forced to buy food from a government grocery store, shoes from a government shoe store, etc. The government issues each person a certain number of credits, not only specific to each store such as groceries, but to each category. Credits are forfeit, if not used in the time period.

For example, you get one portion of fruit per week. You go to the store, and the only fruit is apples, and they are bruised and squishy. What choice do you have? You cannot switch to another store, you cannot switch to another fruit, and if you walk out you forfeit your fruit ration for the week.

There is no market, hence no price discovery. Consumers have zero impact on the price of apples. There is no feedback mechanism for them to influence farmers, distributors, or retailers to improve the availability or quality.

Irredeemable currency does this, not to the price of fruit, but to the price of credit (Weiner 2024). This is a profound point, and counterintuitive. It is worth taking the time to think it through all the way.

Gold works differently. To own a gold coin or bar is not to be a creditor, but the opposite. You own a physical, tangible object. No one owes you anything. You have the thing in your hands.

A gold standard with circulating coinage is a free market in money.

In a free market in groceries, you can choose pears over apples, Grocery B over Grocery A, or walk out and not buy anything at all. The same is true in a free market in money. You can choose to put your gold into one kind of bond or another, one bank or another, or walk out and keep your gold coin in your pocket.

Irredeemable currency disenfranchises the saver. However, a free market in money respects the right of every saver to extend credit, or not, to whom, and under what terms and interest rate. This means that the interest rate cannot fall below the marginal time preference of the savers. If it ticks down to that threshold, the savers stop buying bonds, and begin to withdraw their gold. Which forces the bond price to tick down/interest rate to tick up.

There is a profound moral issue here (as whenever freedom is at issue).

Gold enables a proper mechanism for a market to set interest rates. This is the only real alternative to monetary policy, with interest rates administered by a central planning authority.

As discussed earlier, if interest rates are set by governments, then free trade is undermined. Interest rates set by free markets is prerequisite for free trade to occur within national borders, and also prerequisite for free trade among nations.

Yet, arguments in favor of irredeemable currency still persist. Irredeemable currency enables governments to pursue other policies, such as Mercantilism.

The Fallacy of Mercantilism Must Go to the Ash Heap of Bad Ideas

One bad idea has persisted for at least half a millennia. Mercantilism is based on the idea that each nation should seek to get as much money from other nations as possible. This means, in practice, that each nation should try to run a trade surplus. Many policies have been tried, in service of this goal. But one stands out above the others.

Currency debasement.

The logic goes like this: a country whose currency is cheaper will be able to sell goods cheaper than competing countries, hence export goods and import money. Never mind that the money it is importing is worth less—this is supposed to add to GDP and create jobs. A falling currency is supposed to be a competitive advantage.

It would be like believing that shooting yourself in the foot gives you a competitive advantage when running a marathon. So let us break this down.

At first glance, the Mercantilist argument is tempting. Suppose two companies come to the international market with identical goods. Company X is located in South America, doing business in local pesos. Company Y is in Europe, doing business in euros. Assume the peso = euro = $1.00. Both companies make a 10% profit margin, that is, their costs are (about) $0.90. Both companies need to sell their products for a minimum of $0.90 to break even, or $1.00 to make their normal profit.

But what if the peso devalues by 10%. Company X can now sell for $0.90 which is worth 1.0 pesos. It can underprice Company Y, which must charge $1.00.

It would seem to be very simple, devaluation helps Company X win. But this is a good example of what Frédéric Bastiat described (Bastiat 1850):

> There is only one difference between a bad economist and a good one: the bad economist confines himself to the visible effect; the good economist takes into account both the effect that can be seen and those effects that must be foreseen.
> Yet this difference is tremendous; for it almost always happens that when the immediate consequence is favorable, the later consequences are disastrous, and vice versa. Whence it follows that the bad economist pursues a small present good that will be followed by a great evil to come, while the good economist pursues a great good to come, at the risk of a small present evil.

He could have been directing his comment toward a policy of debasing the currency. The immediate effect is a small benefit, but there are a few great evils to come.

First, consider the concept of Terms of Trade. After Company X sells its product, it must buy more raw materials. The more that the peso drops, the smaller the quantity of goods Company X can purchase. The same thing is happening to every company subject to this devalued peso.

To generalize this, the devaluation erodes the capital of every productive enterprise in that country. In a way, it equivalent to removing cash from every bank account and at the same time reducing domestic price, such as the price of labor.

While this is supposed to give an advantage to these companies, in reality is stripping them of vital capital. It takes capital to produce things at scale, and it takes capital to employ people. It is not helping producers to strip their capital away (to be consumed by the government in nonproductive activities, such welfare state, as is always the case with currency devaluations).

a. The Goal is Not to Import the Most Money, Export the Most Goods

Note also the irony that what begins with the goal of importing money necessarily goes astray into devaluing this money. In other words, the country may be importing more units of currency—but each of those units is worth less.

It is importing less economic value, in any event (and as described this is because it is producing and exporting less economic value).

The goal should not be exporting the most goods, but producing the most. Whether the goods produced are consumed domestically, or whether they are exported, to increase production is to increase wealth.

If government wishes to achieve this goal, then it does not do so by intervening. It does so by removing the obstacles that prevent producers from producing. One of which is unstable and falling currency values.

b. The Other Side of a Trade Deficit is a Capital Surplus

There is another fallacy in the Mercantilist philosophy and that is the belief that trade deficits are bad.

There is nothing wrong with a trade deficit per se. Indeed a trade deficit is not really a "deficit". If producers in Country B sell more goods to people in country A, than producers in country A sell to people in country B, this is mis-called a trade "deficit" in country A. The flip side of this "deficit" is typically a capital surplus.

In other words, the producers in B are selling goods to A but not getting goods in return. What are they getting? Country B's producers are investing this surplus in A's producers—either lending to them, or buying their equity. Or, they may be buying real estate or other productive assets in Country A.

This is not a bad thing, for Country A or for Country B.

The rare case is Country A could be destroying its producers. Then, obviously producers in Country B will not reinvest the profits in Country A. They will take the money out. Consumers in Country A will keep buying from abroad (not having domestic goods available) until they run out of money.

To cure this ill, government needs to look deeper into structural issues such as the Rule of Law and respect for the rights of property and contract, regulations that prevent production or make it unduly expensive.

And of course monetary devaluation, devaluing the currency is hardly a way to stop capital flight!

The Key Elements of an International Free Market in Money

Having made the case that a free market in money is necessary, let us look at what this entails.

The first feature is the right to take delivery of the gold metal. As with individuals within a nation, this right safeguards the soundness of the financial institutions and the financial system. It is an important right that everyone has. However, delivering physical gold in exchange for delivery of physical goods is not efficient. Most people, most of the time, will not withdraw their wealth and take home gold coins. Just as most people do not walk out of grocery stories, their shopping unfinished.

So, as in individual decisions, trade between nations may involve sending payment in the form of coins (or more likely bars for such large amounts) by airplane from buyer to seller. It seems likely that a new, emerging international gold standard would begin exactly this way. Russia sells oil to India, India sends gold. India sells spices to Russia, Russia puts many of the same gold bars back on a plane, and flies it to India.

Fairly quickly, one inefficiency becomes obvious. If Russia sells oil worth 1.0 tons of gold to India, and India sells spices worth 0.9 tons to Russia, why should they fly 1000 gold bars one way, and then soon fly 900 bars the other way (assuming kilogram bars). Should not India just send 100 bars?

Shipping gold back and forth not only cost something, it is slow. While the metal is in the logistics process, the money is in limbo, and there is no liquidity for either party. This is by far the greater inefficiency.

The problem seems simple, but it is bigger than it seems. It comes into sharper focus, when we realize that it is not Russia and India, per se, who are selling and buying goods from each other. Perhaps socialist governments buy and sell on behalf of their people. But a free market is composed—not of state actors on behalf of socialized resources—but innumerable companies. It is a Russian oil company, not the Russian government, who sells oil not to the Indian government, but to an Indian power plant. It is an Indian food distributor who sells spices, not the Indian government, and the buyer is not the Russian government but a Russian restaurant chain.

Additionally, the transactions may not take place at the same time. There could be days or weeks in between.

Clearly, a clearing mechanism is necessary.

a. **Settlement**

Let us look at the mechanics. Suppose the Russian oil company sells the oil to the Indian power plant. The Indian power plant initiates a gold payment via its bank, which looks not too dissimilar from sending a wire of dollars today via a bank connected to the SWIFT system. So far as the Indian company is concerned, the bill for the oil is paid.

But, if the gold is not to be put on a plane immediately, then how will this work? The Indian bank credits the Russian oil company's bank the 1,000kg gold. That is, it says in effect "we have the gold, held in trust for you." The Russian bank credits the gold to the oil company's account.

Later—it could be a few hours, days, or weeks, the Russian restaurant receives the spices and initiates payment to the Indian food exporter. The same thing happens. The result is that the Russian bank now holds 900kg gold in trust for the Indian bank, and the Indian bank holds gold for the Russian bank.

They can net off the difference. Then, only the Indian bank is holding only 100kg of gold for the Russian bank.

This example was kept simple, for the sake of clarity of the first point. However, in the real world, it is likely that the Indian power plant does not use the same bank as the Indian food exporter, and the Russian oil company does not use the same bank as the restaurant. What is need is not bilateral settlement, but multilateral.

The most efficient way to provide multilateral settlement is a clearinghouse. All the banks would hold gold at the clearinghouse. And they can settle the differences by transferring gold from one bank's account to another, held at the clearinghouse.

b. Bills

Another kind of clearing is required for supply chains for goods which are in urgent and predictable demand, like wheat.

The farmer grows wheat, which he sells to the miller. The miller grinds the wheat into flour, which he sells to the baker. The baker bakes it into bread, which he sells to the (gold paying) consumer. It seems simple enough, so what is the problem?

Notice that the miller must pay the farmer before he, himself, has been paid. The same problem occurs for the baker. The payments originate from the consumer. They flow in the opposite direction than the goods. That is, the miller must pay the farmer, and the baker must pay the miller, before the consumer pays the baker. Each must pay days or weeks in advance of being paid, in turn.

Keep in mind that these are low-margin businesses, as one would expect in an efficient global economy. This means they deal in goods with high gross value, compared to the small percentage of additional value they each add to the goods.

Such businesses would never have the gold to pay for the gross value of their raw materials weeks or months ahead of the final sale to the consumer.

If there were not some kind of clearing credit system, each business would require sufficient working capital to do just that, to pay for the gross value of the goods it handles. Such an economy would require a lot of physical gold.

It gets worse. Innovation can create new business models. New businesses can insert themselves into the supply chain, resulting in a better experience for consumers. For example, a supermarket provides goods from every kind of producer from dairy to meat to processed foods, to … bread. This means that the baker will not sell bread at retail any more, but become bigger and more efficient and focus on producing a higher quantity of higher-quality bread at lower cost per unit, which it sells to grocers (or distributors).

And this creates a problem. Now, instead of only three producers in the bread supply chain, there are four: farmer, miller, baker, and retailer (perhaps five including the distributor). This means that, absent a clearing system, the need for gold metal just increased by about 33% (67%).

The same thing occurs in every supply chain, as the economy develops and production becomes more roundabout, which means more efficient. Each new business inserted into each supply chain must pay for its input raw materials prior to receiving payment for its output products.

Since the amount of gold is finite, it would be impossible for new businesses to extend and improve efficiency in the supply chain.

An efficient clearing mechanism developed historically. It was the Bills market, which traded gold bills of exchange, otherwise known as Real Bills (Fekete 2002).

A Real Bill is not a loan. There is no lender who gives gold to a borrower in this system. Instead, the party receiving the goods and owing payment endorses the back of the bill, which is his promise to pay. The payee can then pass this on to his creditors. Historically, the market readily accepted Bills. There is no reason why it would not accept them, again.

In our example, the miller endorses the bill of the farmer. Then, the farmer can pay the Bill to his own creditor or vendors. Now, the farmer is out of the credit loop, and the miller owes the farmer's creditor. Next, the baker receives the goods from the miller, and he endorses the miller's bill. The miller can then pay the farmer's creditor, and he is also out of the credit loop. The baker now owes the farmer's creditor. The baker delivers bread to the grocer. The grocer signs the bill. The baker pays the farmer's creditor, and the grocer owes the gold. In the end, the grocer receives the gold from the consumers. The grocer extinguishes the credit, by paying the gold.

This is a key differentiator. The bill is self-liquidating. It is not amortized by operating a productive asset. It is extinguished when the goods are sold to the gold paying consumer.

Historically, the Bills market was an international market. This fits the requirements of free trade among nations, as some nations produce certain goods and others produce others, based on their comparative advantages. All nations needed a market for clearing these credits. And similarly investors from all nations needed access to Bills, which were the highest quality earning assets.

c. Bonds

Production must be financed, especially large-scale production. This means enterprises sell bonds.

One fact is obvious to even casual observers: the dollar is borrowed (far) more than any other currency. As described earlier, this causes problems for borrowers outside the U.S. But it is logical because of a principle known as *Winner Take All*. In each field, one standard is superior, that is, it has advantages unmatched by the others. For this reason, it becomes more widely adopted. The wider adoption becomes an additional advantage. This is a virtuous circle which completes when it wins the market. Think of the Internet Protocol, or for less-technical readers, the use of petrol as an automobile fuel. While there were other networking protocols, and other hydrocarbons would work in a motor, the market has standardized on these.

The same occurs in currencies, if there is more than one. The winner (for many reasons, which are outside the scope of this chapter) was the dollar. This leads us back to all the problems described earlier.

In the freer markets of halcyon days, the winner was not the credit issued and controlled by a government, but a commodity monetary good. Gold.

This does not refer merely to medium of exchange. The dollar is not used as a medium in most countries. It is used as a vehicle for finance. A new hydroelectric project in Ethiopia, a computer chip factory in Taiwan, and a farm in Iowa borrow dollars. This is because the most lenders have dollars, as opposed to birr (the Ethiopian currency) or new Taiwan dollars. Of course, lenders have many reasons for preferring dollars. And one of them is that this is where the most borrowers are.

The driver for Winner Take All is the *Network Effect*.

If one were to make a list of potential replacements for the dollar, only gold has a comparable network effect. Billions of people own it, and have been owning it for millennia. No other irredeemable currency comes close, nor any other commodity.[5]

So every producer from farms, to mines, to manufacturers, to distributors, to fixed infrastructure issues bonds to finance the acquisition or upgrade of productive assets, or large operating expenses which must be paid up front (e.g., in a farm).

And every lender, from individuals to banks and insurance companies, buys bonds to earn a return.

The producers and lenders come together in the bond market (or through banks as intermediaries). They need to agree on basic terms which standardize all bonds. And the most important is in which money or currency is it denominated, with principal and interest payable in that currency.

Gold worked well historically, and will work well again if governments can get out of the way.

Conclusion: Free Trade and Free Market in Money and Credit

In a way, it is a sign of how long it has been since we had a free market in money and credit, and a sign of how far we have deviated from the philosophy of free markets, which it needs to be stated explicitly. International free trade goes hand in hand with free markets in money. The opposite—that international free trade can be built on national socialist currency regimes with central planning of interest rates and manipulation of exchange rates—is an extraordinary statement that would demand extraordinary proof to support it.

It is becoming more obvious that dollar hegemony is not serving the world very well (or indeed even the U.S.) While the actual collapse of the world's reserve currency would be a horrific event, the early warning signs provide an opportunity. People all around the world are looking for new monetary solutions (though they currently think mostly about an alternative irredeemable currency). They may be reached with the idea of a proper gold standard, a free market not controlled by the US government or any other government.

The goal of this chapter is to provide enough clarity on this point, and enough details of how such a system would work, to enable a movement for monetary freedom.

---

[5] Bitcoin is hardly worth a footnote here, as it has little network effect. Its volatile precludes it from use in borrowing, and this lack of usability in finance discourages would-be savers from buying in. It is almost an inverse network effect.

References

Bank for International Settlements (2022) OTC derivatives statistics at end-June 2022. https://www.bis.org/publ/otc_hy2211.htm. Accessed 30 Oct 2023

Bastiat F (1850) What is seen and what is not seen. https://oll.libertyfund.org/pages/wswns. Accessed 15 May 2024

Bhandari P, Frankel J (2017) Nominal GDP targeting for developing countries. https://scholar.harvard.edu/files/frankel/files/ngdpt-_india_researchinecon.pdf. Accessed 15 May 2024

Chen, J (2022) Carry trade: definition, how it works, example, and risks. In: Investopedia. https://www.investopedia.com/carry-trade-definition-4682656. Accessed 15 May 2024

CORE (Undated) Inflation, Unemployment, and Monetary Policy. In the CORE Project. https://www.core-econ.org/the-economy/v1/book/text/15.html

Federal Reserve Act [Chapter 6 of the 62nd Congress; Approved Dec. 23rd, 1913; 38 Stat. 251]. In: GovInfo. https://www.govinfo.gov/content/pkg/COMPS-270/pdf/COMPS-270.pdf. Accessed 15 May 2024

Fekete A (2002) The second greatest story ever told. https://professorfekete.com/articles/AEFMonEcon101Lecture5.pdf. Accessed 15 May 2024

Friedman, M (1970) A Friedman doctrine—the social responsibility of business is to increase its profits. In: The New York Times. https://www.nytimes.com/1970/09/13/archives/a-friedman-doctrine-the-social-responsibility-of-business-is-to.html. Accessed 15 May 2024

International Monetary Fund (Undated). In: Money matters, an IMF exhibit—the importance of global cooperation, system in crisis (1959–1971), part 4 of 7. https://www.imf.org/external/np/exr/center/mm/eng/mm_sc_03.htm. Accessed 15 May 2024

Keynes JM (1919)

Keynes, JM (1919) The economic consequences of the peace. In: Keynes JM (ed) The project Gutenberg e-book of the economic consequences of the peace. https://www.gutenberg.org/cache/epub/15776/pg15776-images.html. Accessed 15 May 2024

Rand, A (1966) The new fascism: rule by consensus. In Capitalism: the unknown ideal

Sarwat, J Inflation (Undated) Targeting: holding the line. https://www.imf.org/external/pubs/ft/fandd/basics/72-inflation-targeting.htm. Accessed 15 May 2024

Steelman, A (2013) Full employment and balanced growth act of 1978 (Humphrey-Hawkins). https://www.federalreservehistory.org/essays/humphrey-hawkins-act. Accessed 15 May 2024

Weiner, K (2012) When gold backwardation becomes permanent. https://monetary-metals.com/when-gold-backwardation-becomes-permanent/. Accessed 15 May 2024

Weiner K (2013) The theory of interest and prices in paper currency. https://keithweinereconomics.com/2013/12/28/the-theory-of-interest-and-prices-in-paper-currency/. Accessed 15 May 2024

Weiner K (2014) We need a declaration of monetary independence. https://www.forbes.com/sites/keithweiner/2014/08/09/we-need-a-declaration-of-monetary-independence/?sh=26b0996b7228. Accessed 15 May 2024

Weiner, K (2015) The gold standard for the 1%. In: Forbes. https://www.forbes.com/sites/keithweiner/2015/01/12/the-gold-standard-for-the-1/?sh=26269faf1778. Accessed 15 May 2024

Weiner, K (2023) Keith Weiner's macroeconomic equation: https://monetary-metals.com/macro-equation/. Accessed 15 May 2024

Wikipedia (2024b) Harry Dexter White. In: Wikipedia. https://en.wikipedia.org/wiki/Harry_Dexter_White. Accessed 15 May 2024

Wikipedia (2024c) Varna necropolis. In: Wikipedia. https://en.wikipedia.org/wiki/Varna_Necropolis. Accessed 15 May 2024

Wikipedia (2024) John Connally. In: Wikipedia. https://en.wikipedia.org/wiki/John_Connally#:~:text=Bush.,currency%2C%20but%20your%20problem.%22. Accessed 15 May 2024

Wikipedia (2024a) Soviet famine of 1930–1933. In: Wikipedia. https://en.wikipedia.org/wiki/Soviet_famine_of_1930%E2%80%931933. Accessed 15 May 2024

World Gold Council (2023) Supply. https://www.gold.org/goldhub/research/gold-demand-trends/gold-demand-trends-full-year-2022/supply. Accessed 15 May 2024

World Gold Council (2024) How much gold has been mined? https://www.gold.org/goldhub/data/how-much-gold. Accessed 15 May 2024

Twin Deficits—How Are They Related?

Alasdair MacLeod

A phenomenon that is often pointed out is that a trade deficit often appears to be accompanied by a government budget deficit. It has been described by some economists as the twin deficit hypothesis. Simplistically, it appears that the expansion of a currency or currency substitute in the form of reserves held at the central bank fuels an excess of imports over exports. In turn, the expansion of currency and bank reserves reflects a shortfall between government revenues and spending—in other words a budget deficit.

Clearly, other factors must be involved. Analysis is complicated by changes in the purchasing power of a currency, particularly in a fiat currency regime, of which the mathematical economists in their accounting treatment take little or no account. Yet, in today's world of fiat currencies, floating exchange rates and the subjectivity of currency relationships with both their purchasing powers and against each other, macroeconomic theory ignores this obvious error.

Instead, and ignoring Frederic Bastiat's maxim that they should not be misled by what is seen and instead consider what is not seen, it is common for economists and commentators to ignore the possibility that there is a relationship between deficits and look at a trade deficit as something to be corrected by direct action, such as the deployment of higher import tariffs and imposing quotas. This was President Trump's trade policy in 2017—2021. The balance on goods—it was always about goods rather than services—was

---

A. MacLeod (✉)
Sidmouth, UK
e-mail: alasdair.macleod@goldmoney.com

© The Author(s), under exclusive license to Springer Nature Switzerland AG 2025
M. Rangeley and D. Hannan (eds.), *Free Trade in the Twenty-First Century*, https://doi.org/10.1007/978-3-031-67656-7_19

a deficit before he took office of $800 billion which increased every year of his tenure to over a trillion dollars. The accumulated total deficit on goods trade during his tenure was $3.7 trillion, during which time the fiscal year budget total was $5.6 trillion, distorted in 2020 by the economic shut-down due to Covid.

When tariffs and quotas reduced China's exports to the US, as if by magic exports appeared to increase from elsewhere, or other imported goods substituted them in the trade balance. Mexico was a significant beneficiary of this trade substitution. Some US multinationals switching their supply chains from China, instead of repatriating them entirely, which was Trump's original policy objective.

Admittedly, this was not the whole picture, not least because they exclude the balance of trade in services. Furthermore, the Federal Government's fiscal year ends in September, while trade figures are calendar. But they do illustrate a point which no one on Trump's economic advisory team seemed prepared to take, that there appeared to be a connection between the two deficits.

This chapter examines the relationship between the two deficits. But the abandonment of a global gold standard based on the post-war Bretton Woods Agreement in 1971 has made this a game of two halves. Before then, there was a high degree of certainty over trade values, reflecting price stability in commodities and the interchangeability of currencies at fixed rates. Since 1971, commodity prices have soared, reflecting loss of purchasing power in currencies no longer anchored to gold. Under gold standards, the relationship between the deficits was easier to identify than it is today. That is where our analysis must start.

The Sound Money Case

So long as credit takes its value from gold, under gold standards there is an inherent stability in prices. By way of contrast, in an unstable fiat currency environment, macroeconomic statistics and assessments are of little value in economic forecasting, as lamentable experience confirms. Many economists proceed as if currency values in terms of their purchasing power do not vary when they are as a matter of fact horribly subjective and prey to significant shifts in value over time. Changes in a fiat currency's value are down to the collective faith in it, as much if not more than in changes in its quantity.

For this reason, a starting point for assessing trade imbalances and their relationship with other economic disparities, particularly a government's budget deficit, must be under the conditions of an internationally accepted sound money standard, historically the role fulfilled by gold. A precondition for understanding the sound money case is to resuscitate Say's Law, which before it was traduced by Keynes in his *General Theory*, defined the basis of the division of labour to the satisfaction of all economists.

Before the days of welfare states, it was unarguably true that we all produced to consume. In other words, consumption was firmly tied to production which came first. And importantly, the ability of governments to corrupt the production–consumption relationship was limited by the requirement to maintain a stable exchange rate with gold, albeit through the medium of the US dollar.

With respect to trade, Say's Law has important implications. In our model of free markets and sound money conditions, endogenous changes in a national economic condition cannot affect the balance of trade fundamentally, except to the extent that shifts in the relationship between consumption and savings alter prices for foreign consumers, leading to a potential for goods arbitrage. In consequence, as markets and international trade become increasingly efficient the price consequences of bank credit cycles become less disruptive. This was certainly the experience in the United Kingdom in the nineteenth century as Fig. 1 illustrates.

At the commencement of the Napoleonic Wars, the suspension of the gold standard led to a substantial inflation of prices, driven by wartime government spending in a fiat currency environment. Having been suspended by the Bank Restriction Act of 1797, the gold standard was legally restored in 1821 when the Bank restriction Act was rescinded. After Waterloo, government military spending was greatly reduced, and the new gold sovereign was launched in 1817 preparatory to full convertibility. The deflationary consequences were severe, returning wholesale prices to pre-war levels. For the next

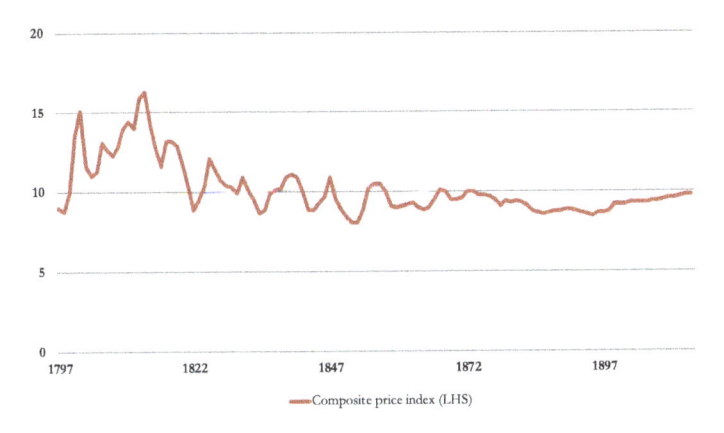

Fig. 1 UK wholesale prices 1797–1913. *Source* ONS, Chronicle of Britain

thirty years, the cycle of bank credit expansion and contraction led to wholesale prices oscillating around an index level of about 10 on the chart, which diminished due to two factors. The first was the gradual perfection of the commercial banking system as a whole, and the second was the spreading adoption of gold standards with Britain's European trade partners. Together, these factors naturally led to greater price stability.

The free trade position with minimal government spending and a balanced budget which were the British Government's policies at the time are relatively easy to understand. In free trade conditions, consumers benefit from the comparative advantage of choosing goods and services from whomever and from wherever their preferences take them. The same is true for manufacturers sourcing raw materials, manufacturing equipment and part-assembled products. Indeed, free trade particularly within the colonies and dominions was crucial for the economic advancement of Britain, which rapidly became the dominant global force despite a diminutive population estimated at about 9,000,000 in 1801 (Ashton 1955).

Under a gold exchange system, it is an iron rule that imports have to be paid for in gold or gold substitutes acceptable between transacting parties. A gold substitute is credit which is readily exchangeable for gold coin or bullion at a predetermined fixed weight. In practice, gold only changes hands if there are sufficient interest rate differentials between jurisdictions, otherwise one form of substitute is exchanged for another at a rate determined by the ratio of their gold values by weight (Macleod 1877). So long as a nation's currency unit is priced in gold by weight and freely exchangeable for gold, the currency aspect of trade settlement is not an issue, and currency exchange rates are fixed by their common reference to gold.

The base case for trade is that imports should be paid for by exports. In practice, it is never this simple because commercial banking systems can vary the quantity of credit in circulation. Trade finance is generally self-extinguishing, but a more general expansion in the quantity of bank credit in favour of payments to importers or exporters could allow a deficit on the balance of trade to arise. But so long as the expansion of bank credit does not lead to more than moderate gold outflows or inflows, and so long as the expansion of bank credit is not aimed at financing excess consumption, trade can be expected to return to a balance over time. It will not undermine the purchasing power of commercial bank credit, which allowing for specific bank credit risk is firmly tied to the value of the currency. The key is that the issuing authority for the currency must maintain the gold cover for its currency liabilities, guaranteeing the value link with currency and bank credit. This is achieved by separating the issue function from central banking entirely and handing interest rate policy to the issuer under instructions to use interest rates solely to manage the gold reserves.

These were precisely the conditions that prevailed under working gold standards before the First World War, allowing for the errors in the 1844 Bank Charter Act with respect to interest rate management objectives.

As noted above, most of commercial bank credit created for trade finance is self-extinguishing. Credit advanced for the purposes of financing the shipment and transfer of ownership of goods is paid back on delivery, or at least when the value of imported goods is realised for the importer. But a temporary trade deficit arising out of an expansion of industrial investment, when it leads to imported raw materials, machinery and part-assembled goods is normal at a time of relative economic expansion.

Other factors aside, a trade imbalance might initially arise due to different rates of economic expansion between nations, being the consequence of different rates of investment in production. Capital investment is funded by an expansion of credit either as debt or equity, to be substantially offset by consumer savings, which is consumption deferred. In time, increasing capital investment tends to lead to better values for consumer goods, thereby offsetting demand for imported substitutes. The same factors lead to increased exports of goods and services benefitting foreign consumers in turn. But so long as bank credit is not created as a substitute for consumer saving, thereby leading to excess consumption, allowing for timing differences imports and exports are bound to offset one another.

This gives us a clue as to how the twin deficit phenomenon arises, whereby a trade deficit appears to develop at approximately the same time as a budget deficit. In a free market and sound money trade model, changes in the level of commercial bank credit do not lead to permanent trade imbalances. It is the expansion of the currency that leads to a trade deficit. And it is the inflation of the currency, particularly when it is fiat which funds a government's budget deficit, which is responsible.

As noted above, if bank credit is expanded for non-productive purposes, then that leads to trade deficits to the extent that it finances excess consumer purchases. But under sound money conditions, consumers tend not to borrow excessively for consumption, restricting debt to what they can afford to repay. This was the origin of Dickens's Micawberism about how spending in excess of one's income led to misery, written in 1849 when Britain's gold standard had firmly crystalised consumer attitudes at the time.

To summarise the conditions of sound money and free trade unhampered by government intervention, we can express it in the following accounting identity:

> Trade Deficit Budget Deficit---(Savings---Capital Investment).

This is the basis of the twin deficit hypothesis. If there is no change in savings and capital investment, then through credit creation by the currency issuer to finance a government's budget deficit a similar trade deficit is bound to arise. It is a conclusion reinforced by Say's Law defining the relationship between domestic production and consumption through the division of labour, because government demand not met by revenue funded by private sector production can only lead to an increase in imports over exports.

The Consequences of Tariffs

Admittedly, the sound money and free trade model is an ideal, which assumes that the state does not intervene in trade matters. In practice, this has almost never been the case. Before the evolution of other taxes, customs and excise duties on imported goods were an important source of government revenue. In the eighteenth and nineteenth centuries, these duties discriminated in favour of European nations' own colonies against foreign interests. The political lure of trade tariffs was and remains protectionism, giving trade advantages to settlers encouraged to emigrate to a nation's colonies. The protectionist benefits of being in a group of colonies evolved into pure protectionism of vested interests in the wake of the First World War, which set back the trend towards the economic integration of the world economy.

As a result of the Great War, America changed from being a net international debtor to the world's largest creditor. It loaned dollars to Germany, so that Germany could pay its reparations to France and other European Allies. And they in turn could pay their war debts to America. Consequently, the dollar's importance rose eclipsing that of sterling, and the world's most important financial centre shifted from London to New York.

Previously, most significant economies had been on gold standards, but these were abandoned by all the European combatants while America only joined the Allies three years after it started. With its proportionately lower war spending, America was able to retain her gold standard. The growing disparity between gold-backed dollars with unbacked European currencies led to obvious currency and trade tensions. Making it worse for the Europeans, their war debts were paid out of depreciating currencies into one hard one—the dollar being freely convertible into gold.

Reparations, war debts and the repayment of billions of dollars of private foreign investment loans all hinged on the free movement of goods and services, which required export surpluses to the US to allow debtors to repay gold or dollars. By hyperinflating their currencies, Germany, Austria, Hungary and Poland obtained a significant price advantage for their compensating exports to America. And naturally, American vested interests pushed for tariffs against this "unfair" competition.

In 1921, the Emergency Tariff Act to aid agriculture followed by the Fordney–McCumber Tariff Act in 1921 was the legislative result of political pressures, putting great stress on the international financial structure. Between them, these tariff acts raised tariffs by an average of 55%. The largest creditor with the largest economy and the world's largest gold reserves now made it harder for its debtors to meet their obligations. Inevitably, other governments took similar measures in response by erecting their own import tariffs and quotas. Domestic content regulations, export subsidies, foreign exchange controls and other mercantilist mechanisms followed.

The nationalism that swept the world after the Great War demonstrated itself in a widening range of trade barriers and subsidies. In many countries, the post-war price collapse in agricultural prices encouraged farmers to demand special protection from their governments to avoid having to adjust to the new economic realities, the expansion of mechanisation and more efficient farming methods—all leading to falling farm product prices. The demand for protection from foreign suppliers was met with wide-ranging tariffs and domestic subsidies that prolonged the readjustment of agriculture to market conditions.

Tariffs are an addictive solution, in that they put off dealing with the economic adjustments necessary for businesses to remain competitive. So it was that the Smoot–Hawley Tariff Act of 1930 doubled down on the tariff precedents of the 1921 Acts and those that followed.

Like Fordney–McCumber, Smoot–Hawley was highly protectionist. Average tariffs on dutiable imports were raised from anything between 38 and 60%. Inevitably, other countries responded with tariff increases of their own. And the contraction of global trade that resulted backfired badly against the US, deepening her depression when bank credit was being wiped out by multiple bank failures.

The Wall Street crash and the depression which followed probably did more to destroy free markets and free trade between them than any other event. The expansion of credit by the newly created Federal Reserve Board in the 1920s led to a stock and bank lending bubble, responsible for the crash that followed. The new President, Herbert Hoover was an avid interventionist, unlike Calvin Coolidge his predecessor who was strictly laissez-faire. It was Hoover who signed Smoot–Hawley into law in 1930. Faced with collapsing collateral values and misguided interventionism by the Hoover administration, some 9000 banks were wiped out leading to a severe contraction of bank credit as deposits became worthless. It is a story well told: what is less understood is the error of blaming free trade policies, and increased interventionism under Franklin Roosevelt with his New Deal became the norm.

Doubtless, before these tariff wars and when currencies were still credible gold substitutes, the link between the balance of trade and the balance on a government's budget could be easily understood, particularly when the benefits of both were so obvious. But that was in a sound money environment. Government intervention in the economy, however, it is argued on protectionist grounds, becomes a slippery slope towards intervention in all other private sector affairs. The experience of anti-trade policies such as tariffs and quotas at best reduces the efficient functioning of an economy and at worst has been a road to economic decline.

Trade in an Unsound Money Economy

Sound money and free markets are not today's conditions. The erosion of them can be traced back to the social consequences of the First World War, which ended the golden era of the industrial revolution. Driven by vested interests and creeping socialism, sound money became progressively undermined until in 1971 the feeble Bretton Woods Agreement, designed to give prominence to the dollar as the international gold substitute, finally collapsed. Since then, American propaganda has expunged gold from the monetary system, replacing it with her fiat dollar, whose value depends totally on faith in its credibility.

Markets have become increasingly regulated and the classical view of economic actors entering into transactions purely on the basis of the customer always being king has been long forgotten by government economists. It is the height of irony that today's increasingly unstable conditions have only served to enhance mathematical analysis of economic and credit relations when the instability of mediums of exchange render these calculations entirely useless.

With respect to demonstrating the twin deficit hypothesis in fiat currency conditions, the impermanence of value introduces additional difficulties. To

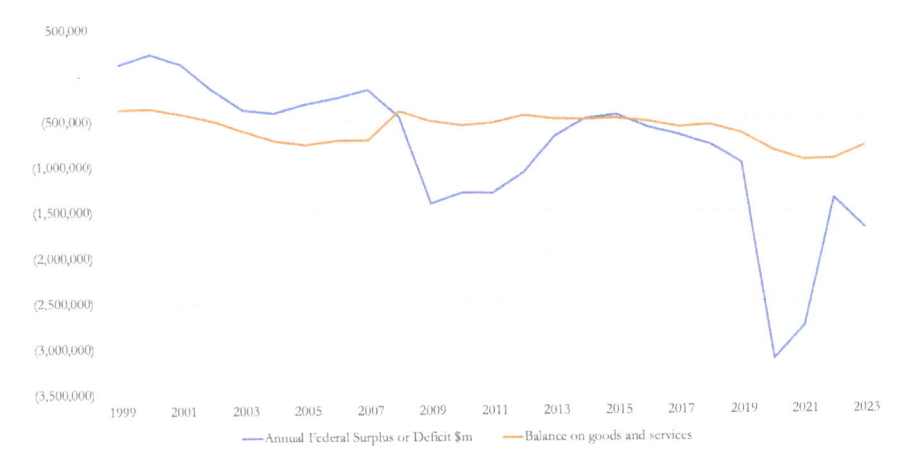

Fig. 2 US Budget balance versus trade balance $m

a casual observer, the hypothesis is no longer meaningful. But Fig. 2 of the two deficits shows that there still appears to be some correlation.

There are some significant distortions illustrated in the chart. Trade figures are calendar year, while budgets are fiscal year to end-September. The sharp increase in the budget deficit in 2009—2011 was a temporary distortion due to the financial crisis. And the record budget deficits of 2020—2021 were due to Covid shutdowns, while imports were suppressed by the chaos in international logistics that followed.

Furthermore, just as increases in money supply take time to work through into consumer prices, there is an unquantifiable delay between excess government spending and its effect on the balance of trade. But in the broadest sense, we can see that since 1998 there does exist a twin deficit phenomenon. But to nail it properly, we need to look further at the relationship in a fiat currency context. First, let us remind ourselves of the accounting identity linking the two deficits.

$$\text{Trade Deficit} \cong \text{Budget Deficit} - (\text{Savings} - \text{Capital Investment}).$$

In the context of the current fiat currency regime, we need to examine the consequences of changes in savings and investment.

The Role of Savings in Trade

Savings are consumption deferred. In other words, they are credit put aside with a view to funding future consumption. As Keynes pointed out, an increase in savings leads to a reduction in immediate consumption. Variations in the rate of savings affects consumer demand, and therefore has an impact on prices.

Say's Law tells us that we produce to consume, and that domestic production is broadly tied to demand. That is a generalisation which baldly stated takes no account of a propensity to save. But clearly, the greater the portion of income consumers on average allocate to future consumption, the greater is the level of goods and services circulating relative to immediate demand. A surplus of product arises, which tends to drive the general level of prices lower. And when domestic prices become lower, the propensity to import goods declines. This was the bit that inflationist Keynes did not like, calling it the paradox of thrift (Keynes 1936).

The expansion of credit, in large part engineered by monetary policy in a fiat currency environment is contra to this effect. It is rarely expressed quite in this way by the monetary authorities, but monetary policy effectively aims to achieve a balance whereby credit is expanded allowing for changes in the savings level, so that the general level of prices rises modestly—currently agreed internationally to be a targeted 2% per annum. But some nations have a greater propensity to save than others. Japan, for instance, has a persistently high savings rate, which allows the Bank of Japan to expand its liabilities (currency plus other elements of its base money) without their expansion feeding so easily into higher consumer demand. It has allowed the Japanese government to run consistently large budget deficits without those deficits being reflected in the trade position, due to the national propensity to save thereby capping domestic prices.

The same cannot be said of the United States and United Kingdom, which not only have a generally low propensity to save but continually accumulates consumer debt. Consequently, the lower savings rates in these consumption-driven nations tend to fuel twin deficits.

Capital Investment

The twin deficit hypothesis posits that an increase in capital investment increases the trade deficit.

Returning to our accounting identity,

Trade Deficit ≅ Budget Deficit---Savings---Capital Investment),

We can see that unless savings increase to fund capital investment, the trade deficit must increase relative to the budget deficit. The way to understand the real world impact of capital investment is that it is spent on materials, goods and services creating demand additional to domestic production, just as immediate consumer spending creates demand.

The eventual outcome of private sector investment differs from that of immediate consumption because capital investment is almost always productive in outcome. In time, returns on investment can be expected to emerge from increases in both product quality and quantity designed to satisfy evolving consumer tastes, usually at more competitive values. While capital investment initially increases a trade deficit relative to the budget deficit, other things being equal it should result in the trade gap subsequently being narrowed through import replacement and/or increased exports, all else being equal.

Capital investment by a government is not often productive in the sense of producing wanted goods. The spending of it puts funds in consumer pockets and therefore leads to a rise in imports with little or no offsetting factors. It is the starkest example of how investment can lead to an increased trade deficit.

Distortions from Inflation

Sticking with our fiat currency case, the consequence of a budget deficit not funded out of savings is currency debasement. But if a budget deficit is funded out of savings diverted from deployment in the private sector, it is at the expense of capital investment for private sector production, limiting the scope for economic progress. But being non-productive in nature, the budget deficit is still inflationary because it is unmatched by production.

Alternatively, if the budget deficit is funded by an increase in savings, consumer spending is accordingly subdued, and price inflation moderates due to the processes outlined above. This effect is particularly noticeable in savings-driven economies, such as China and Japan, where consumer price inflation is considerably less than in consumption-driven economies. Furthermore, according to twin deficit theory, if savings are great enough they can turn a budget deficit into a trade surplus—again, the examples of Japan and China prove this point.

The cleanest demonstration of the twin deficit phenomenon is the sound money example, because in that case the purchasing power of circulating credit is stable. We must now consider the situation under fiat currency regimes when the purchasing power of circulating credit declines.

If the assessment of a currency's value in the foreign exchanges coincides with the assessment in domestic markets, then a decline in purchasing power will be closely reflected in the exchange rate. However, this is rarely the case, with foreign exchanges sometimes anticipating a fall in a currency's purchasing power relative to other currencies, in which case imported goods gain no price advantage. If, however, a currency is overvalued imported goods do get a price advantage, likely to increase the trade deficit relative to the budget deficit. Clearly, the relative valuations given to fiat currencies in foreign exchange markets do have an impact.

By making imported goods relatively expensive, trade tariffs and import quotas become even more tempting to policy planners as a means of limiting a trade deficit, when the free market remedy is simply to reduce the budget deficit. Instead, the excess of government spending financed by the expansion of its central bank's base money coincides with import restrictions to drive up manufacturers' input prices and consumer prices alike. Put another way, if imports are restricted in a fiat currency regime, the consequences feed into higher prices relative to the rest of the world, ultimately undermining the currency's purchasing power on the foreign exchanges.

In general terms, we can see that the difference between the twin deficit phenomenon in the free market sound money case, and that of the interventionist fiat currency system of today is that the latter has a propensity towards rising prices, reflected in a falling purchasing power for a fiat currency.

The Evolution of Twin Deficits and the Ghost of Triffin

Since 1971, after the Bretton Woods Agreement was suspended, governments have used the freedom gained to inflate their currencies under the guise of targeting a 2% inflation rate. The expansion of currency and credit has been considerably greater than the officially calculated consequences, principally due to the financialisation of the advanced economies.

At the same time, mounting regulations and the legacy of unionised labour increased time to production for manufactured and semi-manufactured goods, making it considerably cheaper to export production to greenfield sites in the Far East where factories could be up and running in considerably less time. Advanced automation techniques allowed plentiful low-skilled labour to be rapidly trained and deployed to produce high-quality goods for western markets. This led to significantly lower costs of production, which with just-in-time inventory management techniques led to the evolution of highly efficient global supply chains. Speculative demand for commodities was diverted into new derivative substitutes, ensuring price moderation for raw materials.

The successful attributes of this post-Breton Woods arrangement led to increasing pressure for trade to be freed from the constraints of the General Agreement on Tariffs and Trade (GATT) which was established in 1947. Accordingly, following the Uruguay Round in 1994 the World Trade organisation (WTO) took responsibility for overseeing global trade agreements. The new WTO arrangement gradually reduced barriers to the development of global trade whereby East Asia, including China, would become the principal manufacturers of goods for consumers in the advanced economies.

To a superficial observer, it was this development which became responsible for US trade deficits, and not a theory linking them to the US Government's budget deficits. But that ignores the relationship between trade deficits and the balance of payments, as opposed to the balance of trade. It has been a deliberate act of US policy to run budget deficits to produce the currency for foreign ownership, so that the dollar operates as the undisputed global reserve currency. This has ensured that dollars paid to foreign importers are not sold for their local currencies but bought from importers by their national central and commercial banks to add to their balances. Inward portfolio investment also served to bolster the dollar. And because these foreign interests deposit their dollars in US banks and buy US Treasury debt, budget deficits have been funded without undermining the dollar on the foreign exchanges and the dollar has remained stable against other currencies despite an unfavourable trade balance.

It is a relationship which was explained to US Congress in 1960 by economist Robert Triffin and has gone down in history as the Triffin dilemma. Triffin described it as the US running destructive domestic economic policies in the long run to ensure that there would be ample dollars available to fulfil its role as the world's reserve currency. He predicted that it would lead to a currency crisis eventually. Indeed, it resulted in the failure of the London gold pool in the late 1960s and ultimately the abandonment of the Bretton Woods Agreement in 1971. Since then, the subsequent fiat dollar regime has led to a massive expansion of dollars in foreign hands.

In effect, the twin deficits are locked in together, further proof of the enduring relationship between them. But unless the US Government is prepared to return its budget to balance, it will continue to lead to a trade deficit and for that deficit having to be covered by continuing foreign demand for dollars.

The ghost of Robert Triffin hovers over us, predicting that this situation faces yet another test in time. The conditions which led to the financialisation of advanced economies and the exporting of goods production are changing, which could lead to such an event. The Covid crisis of 2020 exposed the fragility of extended global supply chains, and businesses are reassessing them accordingly. Political pressures in America are pointing in the same autarkic direction. If pressure for increasing trade tariffs returns, and the trade deficit is successfully restricted, we have seen from this analysis that it will be at the cost of higher domestic US consumer prices, undermining the dollar's value on the foreign exchanges. Just as foreign holders began dumping dollars for gold in the late 1960s, they could begin to reduce their colossal dollar holdings in another Triffin event.

Conclusions

Having examined the twin deficit hypothesis in free market and sound money conditions, it has been demonstrated that adjusted for differences in savings and capital investment rates there is a strong link between budget and trade deficits. The key to understanding why this is the case is to understand that domestic production is the source of consumption, inextricably linked through the division of labour summarised in Say's Law.

In practice, the relationship between the two deficits is modified by trade tariffs. These became highly weaponised in the 1920s, following the First World War. And the post-Bretton Woods fiat currency regime has introduced further distortions. Nevertheless, though heavily disguised it is clear that the existence of twin deficits remains a valid hypothesis.

References

Ashton TS (1955) An economic history of England—the 18th century. Methuen O Co., London
Keynes JM (1936) The general theory of employment, interest and money. MacMillan Cambridge University Press
Macleod HD (1877) The elements of banking. Green & Co., Longmans

Big Players and the Volatility of Exchange Rates

Roger Koppl and Marta Podemska-Mikluch

Introduction

Imagine you're an aspiring entrepreneur planning to open a coffee shop in Berlin and keen on importing specialty coffee beans from Brazil. You called suppliers in Brazil to ask about prices; then, you looked up the Brazilian real/ euro exchange-rate online to run your business plan calculations. Your plans looked promising, so family and friends support you by investing in your venture. You're about to place your first order when, suddenly, the value of the euro drops relative to the Brazilian real. Now, those same coffee beans are far more expensive, throwing your plans into disarray.

This is the challenge of volatile exchange rates. When countries independently set their monetary policy, the value of a currency fluctuates in response to the changes in its supply and demand.

This chapter explores the causes and consequences of exchange-rate volatility. The chapter opens with a brief overview of the origins of floating exchange rates, followed by an analysis of the causes of volatility in exchange rates. In looking at the causes of volatility, we distinguish between market and non-market factors and pay special attention to the role played by Big

---

R. Koppl (✉)
Syracuse University, Syracuse, NY, USA
e-mail: rkoppl@syr.edu

M. Podemska-Mikluch
Gustavus Adolphus College, Saint Peter, MN, USA
e-mail: mpodemsk@gustavus.edu

Players—institutions characterized by significant market influence, insensitivity to profit and loss, and discretionary actions. While we do not make any specific policy recommendations, the chapter highlights the importance of public awareness about the institutions that either support or hinder a free society, as summarized in the concluding section.

International Trade as Trade

Trade is a fundamental force of human progress, allowing societies to move beyond subsistence living. By facilitating cooperation and exchange, trade enables individuals and communities to specialize—to engage in the division of labor. When we specialize, the total amount of knowledge in society increases; we no longer need to know all the same basic things necessary for survival. Specialization allows for more problems to be solved, driving improvements in living standards, e.g., when freed from handwashing by a washing machine, moms can read books to their children instead.[1] Specialization and division of labor allow for more efficient use of resources and a greater variety of products and services. By exchanging surplus goods and services, communities have been able to support larger populations and develop more complex social structures. Trade has enabled economic development, cultural exchange, and the advancement of civilizations.

In societies characterized by frequent trade, a relatively refined division of labor, and clear property rules, monetary calculation is a crucial tool for decision-making. It involves evaluating the value, costs, and benefits of various economic activities. Monetary calculation is instrumental for individuals and businesses in making informed choices about production, investment, and trade. Market prices play a key role in this process, signaling the relative scarcity and perceived value of goods and services.

International trade is a trade that transcends political borders. The essence of trade—creating value through the exchange of goods and services—remains the same in an international context. Nonetheless, political boundaries introduce additional complexity in the form of differing national currencies and varied regulatory environments. While domestic trade within a country operates under a single currency and uniform legal system, international trade requires navigating multiple currencies and legal frameworks. This complication necessitates the exchange of currencies, understanding

---

[1] https://www.ted.com/talks/hans_rosling_the_magic_washing_machine?utm_campaign=tedspread&utm_medium=referral&utm_source=tedcomshare.

different regulatory standards, and sometimes dealing with tariffs and trade barriers.

A significant challenge in international trade is managing fluctuating exchange rates. These rates, which represent the value of one currency in terms of another, are crucial in determining the cost and feasibility of cross-border trade. Volatile exchange rates can disrupt monetary calculations, making it challenging for businesses to plan and coordinate their international activities. Such volatility can impede the spontaneous coordination of economic plans across borders, as it becomes more difficult to predict costs, revenues, and investment returns.

To navigate these challenges, businesses engaged in international trade often adopt advanced financial analysis and risk management strategies. They may use financial instruments like forward contracts, options, and derivatives to hedge against currency fluctuations and lock in favorable exchange rates. Additionally, multinational companies might strategically position their production or sourcing in countries with stable economic conditions or currencies to minimize exchange-rate risks. These measures are crucial for businesses to effectively manage the uncertainties of international trade and capitalize on its opportunities.

How Exchange Rates Are Determined

Recall our coffee shop example. You want to open a coffee shop in Berlin specializing in coffees from Brazil. You have euros. But to buy coffee in Brazil, you need Brazilian money. You need Brazilian reals. How are you going to get them? You will, of course, *buy* them. This humdrum logic shows that Brazil reals are *commodities*. Just as you might use some of your euros to buy gasoline, you can use some of your euros to buy Brazilian money. We say that you are buying "foreign exchange." Just as you must pay, say, €1.8 per liter of gasoline, you must pay, say, €0.20 per Brazilian real. Now think of it from the other side. If you buy reals, someone in Brazil is selling them. They are giving reals in exchange for euros. They must want to buy something in the Eurozone. Perhaps a Brazilian entrepreneur wants to open a wine bar in São Paulo specializing in Italian wines. To get Italian wines, our Brazilian entrepreneur will have to *buy* euros. If you must pay €0.20 per Brazilian real, they must pay R$5 per euro.

If there were only two currencies in the world, the euro and the real, we could say that the supply of euros *is* the demand for reals and the demand for euros *is* the supply of reals. But, of course, there are many currencies, which complicates the picture. We have so far ignored another complication, which is the costs of intermediation. You don't go to Brazil and ask random strangers if they'd like to buy euros. You go to a financial intermediary such as a bank and get your Reals from them.

The bank will require you to pay a little more than €0.20 per Brazilian real while requiring Brazilians to pay a little more than R$5 per euro. You could almost say that there are "really" *three* exchange rates when "the" exchange is €0.20 per real. First, there is the benchmark rate of €0.20 per real. Second, there is the less favorable price of, say, €0.225 per real (or about R$4.44 per euro) that ultimate demanders of reals must pay. Third, there is the similarly unfavorable price of, say, €0.175 per real (or about R$5.71 per euro) that ultimate suppliers of real must accept. The €0.05 difference between the price of €0.225 for the buyer of reals and the price of €0.175 for the seller covers the intermediary's costs plus a surplus. We can express the same relationships with "the" exchange rate given in reals per euro. First, there is the benchmark rate of R$5 per euro. Second, there is the somewhat less favorable price of R$4.44 per euro that ultimate suppliers of euros must accept. Third, there is the similarly unfavorable price of R$5.71 per euro that ultimate demanders of euros must pay. The R$1.27 difference between the price of R$5.714 for the buyer and the price of R$4.444 for the seller covers the costs of the intermediary plus a surplus.[2] Because there are many intermediaries, many types of demanders and suppliers, purchases of different magnitudes, and so on, there are really many exchange rates clustered about a benchmark value reported by the financial press.

In the imaginary world of totally unfettered, free-market competition, the difference between the price to ultimate demanders of a currency and the price for ultimate suppliers would be just the size needed to cover the intermediary's costs. That's true, at least, if we include in those costs the return on their investment they could have gotten in some other area. This "opportunity cost" of invested capital is sometimes called "normal profit." Adam Smith spoke of the "ordinary profits of stock," where "stock" meant invested capital. If intermediaries were enjoying profits above this "ordinary" level, new intermediaries would enter the market to compete away some of that surplus. If intermediaries had profits below the "ordinary" level, some incumbent intermediaries would exit the market allowing the surplus to grow to a more acceptable level for the remaining intermediaries.

---

[2] We should not expect the difference in euros, 0.05, to be one fifth of the difference in reals, 1.27. Instead, as a little algebra reveals, $1/x - 1/y = (y - x)/xy$. Plugging in 0.175 for x and 0.225 for y (and rounding to two decimal places) we find that $0.05/(0.175)(0.225) = 1.27$. Thus, our computed values of €0.05 and R$1.27 are consistent and correct.

Microeconomics textbooks say that in the "equilibrium" situation just described "economic profits" are zero. The idea is that a surplus that doesn't get competed away is not a "profit," but "interest," or a "rent," depending on context. In the language of microeconomic textbooks, then, the only "normal" profit is zero. This way of speaking follows from the decision to use the word "profit" or, when clarification is needed, "economic profit" only for surpluses that will be competed away. That way of defining "profit" helps college students think more clearly about things like profit, interest, and competition. In everyday language, however, the word "profit" often gets a broader meaning.

Recognizing the basic supply-and-demand relationship at work in currency markets helps us to understand how currency values are determined and fluctuate in response to various economic factors.

Origins of Floating Exchange Rates

Floating exchange rates are a relatively new phenomenon, especially when viewed in the context of the long history of international trade. For much of this history, trade was conducted using commodities like gold or silver. In the nineteenth century, most countries adopted a gold standard by fixing the price of domestic currency to gold. The period from 1880 to 1914 became known as the classical gold standard. It coincided with strong economic growth and relatively free trade in goods, labor, and capital. The gold standard broke down in 1914 when the pressure of war pushed governments to inflate the value of their currencies. While the gold standard was reintroduced after the war, adherence to it was inconsistent in the 1920s and 1930s (White 2012).

At the conclusion of World War II, a new global monetary system was created at the Bretton Woods Conference. In the Bretton Woods system, most countries used U.S. dollars to settle their international balances. At the same time, the United States guaranteed that their dollar holdings could be exchanged for gold at a fixed, predetermined rate. From the outset, the Bretton Woods exchange-rate system was fraught with conflicting goals (White 2012). It sought to accomplish three objectives: establish fixed exchange rates similar to the classical gold standard, allow central banks the freedom to enact independent national monetary policies, and promote free trade and capital mobility.

Achieving all three objectives simultaneously turned out to be impossible.[3] Take, for example, a fixed exchange rate between the United States and Canada, along with free trade that allows goods and payments to flow freely across the border. In this scenario, the American price level must align with the Canadian price level: the U.S. dollar should buy the same goods as what its exchange rate with Canadian dollars suggests it should.[4] Yet, independent monetary policies imply independent national price levels. Therefore, one of the three objectives has to be surrendered.

In the first years after the war, the Bretton Woods system maintained independent monetary policies and fixed exchange rates. This was possible because the third element, free trade, and the flow of capital across borders, was suppressed. European countries kept wartime exchange controls well into the 1950s, limiting the exchange of currency, which effectively restricted free trade and the flow of capital. As the wartime controls were eventually lifted in the late 1950s, the fixity of exchange rates began to break (White 2012). Countries with inflationary tendencies saw a decline in the purchasing power of their currencies and had to devalue their currencies against the U.S. dollar. On the other hand, those countries where the inflation was lower than in the United States had to increase the exchange value of their currency against the dollar. Ultimately, the Bretton Woods system collapsed, largely due to the Federal Reserve System's expansionary monetary policies in the United States. The breakdown of the Bretton Woods system introduced a new era of fiat money and floating exchange rates. No longer constrained by the commodity standard, economies became more susceptible to inflation.

---

[3] This conundrum is known as "the impossible trinity" or "trilemma." Economists Robert Mundell and Marcus Fleming independently developed models that demonstrated the impossibility of simultaneously maintaining a fixed foreign exchange rate, free capital movement, and an independent monetary policy (Mundell 1963; Fleming 1962).

[4] At the time of this writing, 1000 US dollars would get you about 1336 Canadian dollars. The idea of "purchasing power parity" is that 1000 US dollars should buy in New York about what 1336 Canadian dollars buy in Toronto. But what do we mean by "about"? In an important article, McCloskey and Zecher (1976) explain that we have "purchasing power parity" if the integration of prices between New York and Toronto is the same as that between New York and Chicago. For each pair of cities, some things will be more expensive and others less. But the exchange rate is establishing international "parity" in "purchasing power" if Toronto is not more out of whack with New York than Chicago is.

Volatility in Exchange Rates

Real and nominal exchange rates became volatile after the world abandoned the Bretton Woods system of fixed exchange rates in the early 1970s. Without the constraints of fixed exchange rates, countries resorted to expansionary monetary policy. As one study found, the average inflation rate under commodity standards was just 1.75% per year, compared to 9.17% under fiat money (Rolnick and Weber 1997).

In a market where competition is atomistic and rules are stable, individuals and businesses can focus on their specialized knowledge to make informed decisions (Koppl 2014). The system naturally filters out poor judgments through losses and filters in good judgment through profits. This filtering mechanism of profit and loss conduces to efficient outcomes. Under such conditions, the prices of financial assets such as stocks and foreign exchange tend to reflect all available information. (We ignore the important question of just what information is "available" and to whom.) The "Efficient Market Hypothesis" assumes the tendency is fully realized. In that case, one could "explain" asset prices by assuming tomorrow's price will equal today's price plus or minus a strictly random "error" term.[5] To the extent that foreign exchange markets are informationally efficient in a regime of floating exchange rates, all available information will be already priced into current exchange rates.

Koppl and Yeager (1996) have shown, however, that the market filter of profit and loss is disrupted by "Big Players." A Big Player is defined by three key traits: first, its actions have a significant impact on the market in question; second, it operates without being strictly guided by profit and loss considerations; and third, its actions are discretionary, not rule-based (Koppl 2002, 120).

Big Players disrupt the market by reducing the reliability of expectations; this disruption unfolds in two distinct ways (Koppl 2002, 120). First, Big Players increase the difficulty for people to anticipate the consequences of their actions (Koppl and Yeager 1996). Unlike market firms, Big Players are not disciplined by the market forces of profit and loss. Their arbitrary and unpredictable actions can disrupt confidence. For example, an activist central bank can affect market conditions in ways that are hard to anticipate, introducing uncertainty. In the presence of Big Players, entrepreneurs shift

---

[5] We are alluding to "martingale models" of asset prices. In these models, very roughly, stock prices move up and down in a completely random manner. This statement is too crude. For example, it is not the stock's *price* that moves randomly, but the value of a portfolio in which dividends are reinvested in the same asset. But our too-crude summary may nevertheless convey the spirit of such models. See LeRoy (1989).

their focus from economic fundamentals to predicting unpredictable policy changes.

Second, Big Players are less likely to allow markets to weed out the players who are bad at forecasting and more likely to weed out traders who are good at forecasting (Butos and Koppl 1993; Koppl and Langlois 1994). In the presence of Big Players, investors are more likely to follow the crowd and make decisions based on prevailing market sentiment, whether optimistic or pessimistic. As a result, market confidence becomes more volatile and is driven by arbitrary shifts in optimism and pessimism.

The theory of Big Players has been tested with data from a significant episode in Russian nineteenth-century monetary history (Koppl and Yeager 1996; Broussard and Koppl 1999; Koppl and Nardone 2001), the 1950s–1980s monetary policy of the United States Federal Reserve (Gilanshah and Koppl 2005), and Slovenia (Koppl and Mramor 2003).

The episode in Russian monetary history provides an especially clear illustration of the consequences of Big Player influence. The ruble was a fiat currency known as the "credit ruble" from the Crimean War of 1853–1856 when Russia went off silver until 1897 when the ruble was tied to gold. This period had a revealing episode in which a finance minister who was a strict non-interventionist was followed by a finance minister who was an unusually energetic interventionist in foreign exchange markets. Nikolai Bunge was finance minister from 1881 through 1886. He was a principled opponent of interference in the foreign exchange market. He let the ruble sell for whatever price it was taken to by the autonomous influences of supply and demand. His successor, Ivan Vyshnegradsky, served from 1887 through 1891. Unlike his predecessor, Vyshnegradsky was an interventionist. Koppl and Yeager (1996, p. 372) described him as "more energetic" than Bunge.

Figure 1, reproduced from Koppl and Yeager (1996), shows the difference in behavior of the ruble under these two finance ministers. The statistical analyses of Koppl and Yeager (1996), Broussard and Koppl (1999), and Koppl and Nardone (2001) support the impression given by the figure: The ruble was more volatile and irregular in its behavior under Vyshnegradsky than under Bunge. The interventionist finance minister did not stabilize the ruble but contributed to swings in its value in foreign exchange markets.

We should not be surprised by that intervention created volatility under Vyshnegradsky. As we have seen, currencies are commodities on foreign exchange markets. And exchange rates are prices. If it is generally best to let prices be determined by the unfettered interaction of supply and demand, then it is generally best to allow exchange rates to be determined the same way. Official interventions are attempts to move exchange rates away from

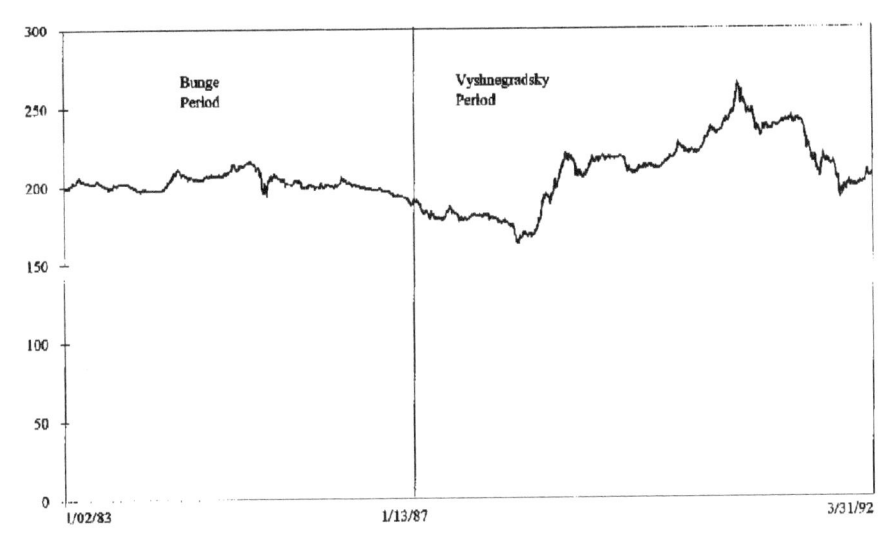

Fig. 1 Ruble exchange rate: German marks per 100 rubles of bank notes

their supply-and-demand levels. They are attempts to second-guess and override supply and demand. Such attempts to second-guess and override usually go awry in other markets. Why wouldn't they go awry in currency markets?

European Central Bank and the Swiss Franc

In macroeconomic textbooks, discretionary monetary policy is presented as a tool for combating instability in money demand. But what causes this instability? Koppl (2002, 184–194) suggests that its discretion produces instability, suggesting that we need less of it, not more. Similarly, Wagner (2012) argues that turbulence is a natural feature of social life. The author argues that the inherent incompleteness of intertemporal coordination creates turbulence in economic processes. This turbulence can be mitigated either by individual liberty and private ordering or through state policy and public ordering. Noting the incompleteness of knowledge, Wagner concludes that it is liberty, not policy, that calms (but does not eliminate!) turbulence. Private ordering allows for experimentation and discovery, leading to better coordination and less turbulence in economic processes. In contrast, using power to impose policy impedes the assembly of knowledge, in effect, increasing rather than calming turbulence.

And yet, the use of power is common and likely on the rise. Elsewhere, Wagner speaks of entanglement between the private and public sectors (Wagner 2016, 2023). For example, in the American financial system, large banks take on more risk because they know that profits are privatized while losses are socialized (Smith et al. 2011). Entanglement contributes to the rise of Big Players as it lowers the importance of profit and loss considerations.

Can the growth of entanglement and Big Players be reversed?

The end of the Bretton Woods system in 1971 led to a period of economic uncertainty, prompting European leaders to create a new solution. In 1979, they established the European Monetary System (EMS), which anchored exchange rates to the European Currency Unit (ECU), serving as a precursor to the eventual formation of the Eurozone. While the common currency stabilized exchange rates among the 20 Eurozone countries, it did not shield them from volatility when trading with non-euro countries.

This became evident on January 15, 2015, when the Swiss National Bank abruptly ended its fixed exchange rate with the euro. In 2011, the Swiss National Bank pegged the Swiss franc to the euro at a rate of 1.20 to counteract the massive inflow of safe-haven funds during the European debt crisis (Lleo and Ziemba 2017). The peg was abandoned in anticipation of the European Central Bank's announcement of a large-scale quantitative easing program. The unpegging of the Swiss franc from the euro had widespread economic consequences in Switzerland, the Eurozone, and beyond. All major sectors, money management, tourism, and exports, were impacted. For example, Swiss ski resorts were forced to lower rates as the unpegging made their prices twice those in France and Austria.

The unpegging also negatively impacted Central and Eastern Europe. In Central and Eastern European countries like Austria, Hungary, and Poland, mortgages denominated in Swiss francs became popular in the early 2000s, when Swiss interest rates were as low as 1.5% (Vassileva 2020; Frum 2015). The Swiss franc had been gaining strength since 2007, but it was the Swiss National Bank's 2015 decision to detach it from the euro that led to a dramatic increase in its value, surprising foreign exchange markets.

In 2023, the European Union's top court ruled in favor of Polish borrowers who had taken out mortgages in Swiss francs (Wlodarczak-Semczuk 2023). The Swiss franc rose sharply against the Polish zloty after Switzerland abandoned fixed exchange rates, which increased mortgage payments on franc-denominated mortgages. The court ruled that if the terms of such a loan had been determined to be excessive (and thus unenforceable) the mortgage-issuing bank could not turnaround and impose on the mortgage holder its costs of capital on such foreign-currency loans. In short, the banks were left holding the bag. In consequence, banks might likely consider increasing fees and the cost of borrowing, which could negatively affect already vulnerable consumer spending (Frum 2015). The unfortunate "solution" has been to create cheap mortgages for first-time homebuyers (Krasuski 2023). This "solution" is unfortunate because it discourages mortgage lending, thereby making it harder to become a homeowner and not easier.

Conclusions

We have seen that exchange-rate volatility may throw entrepreneurial plans into "disarray" and that Big Players such as central banks and finance ministers can contribute to exchange-rate volatility. Recall that Big Players act on discretion; they do not follow any strict rules. Only rule-following government actors such as central banks and finance ministers can moderate exchange-rate volatility and enable reasonably prescient entrepreneurial expectations. For this reason, we support the "rule of law" in money and finance.

In politics, the term "rule of law" usually means something like being "tough on crime." We are using it here in a very different sense. In its proper sense in legal theory, the "rule of law" means, "in the first place, the absolute supremacy or predominance of regular law as opposed to the influence of arbitrary power, and excludes the existence of arbitrariness, of prerogative, or even of wide discretionary authority on the part of the government" (Dicey [1915, 1982). In other words, no discretion. Hayek (1944) speaks of "government in all its actions" being "bound by rules fixed and announced beforehand—rules which make it possible to foresee with fair certainty how the authority will use its coercive powers in given circumstances and to plan one's individual affairs on the basis of this knowledge" (see also Fallon 1997). We are playing by the same rules, and we know what those rules are.

Exchange-rate volatility is technical issue involving much study and the crunching of many numbers. And yet, there is an unexpectedly simple bottom line to it all. Governments induce needless and wasteful volatility by acting as Big Players, that is, by violating the rule of law. To improve the performance of foreign exchange markets, governments should do the thing they hate the most: leave it alone.

References

Broussard JP, Koppl R (1999) Big players and the Russian rouble: explaining volatility dynamics. Manag Financ 25(1):49–63. https://doi.org/10.1108/03074359910765858

Butos W, Koppl R (1993) Hayekian expectations: theory and empirical applications. Const Polit Econ 4(3):303–329

Dicey AV ([1915] 1982) Introduction to the study of the law of the constitution. Liberty Classics, Indianapolis, IN

Fallon RH (1997) 'The rule of law' as a concept in constitutional discourse. Columbia Law Rev 97(1):1–56. https://doi.org/10.2307/1123446

Fleming JM (1962) Domestic financial policies under fixed and under floating exchange rates. Staff Papers (International Monetary Fund) 9(3):369–380. https://doi.org/10.2307/3866091

Frum D (2015) The world's next mortgage crisis? The Atlantic, 29 Jan 2015. https://www.theatlantic.com/international/archive/2015/01/europe-mortgage-crisis-switzerland-franc/384958/

Gilanshah CB,, Koppl R (2005) Big players and money demand. In: Modern applications of Austrian thought. Routledge

Hayek FA (1944) The road to serfdom. University of Chicago Press

Koppl (2014) From crisis to confidence: macroeconomics after the crash, 1st edn. London Publishing Partnership

Koppl R (2002) Big players and the economic theory of expectations. Palgrave Macmillan, Houndmills, Basingstoke, Hampshire, New York

Koppl R, Langlois RN (1994) When do ideas matter? A study in the natural selection of social games. Adv Austrian Econ 1:81–104

Koppl R, Mramor D (2003) Big players in Slovenia. Rev Austrian Econ 16(2):253–269. https://doi.org/10.1023/A:1024549025380

Koppl R, Nardone C (2001) The angular distribution of asset returns in delay space. Discret Dyn Nat Soc 6(2):101–120

Koppl R, Yeager LB (1996) Big players and herding in asset markets: the case of the Russian Ruble. Explor Econ Hist 33(3):367–383. https://doi.org/10.1006/exeh.1996.0020

Krasuski K (2023) Polish lawmakers pass plan offering cheap mortgages for first-time homebuyers. Bloomberg.Com, 26 May 2023. https://www.bloomberg.com/news/articles/2023-05-26/polish-lawmakers-pass-housing-plan-for-cheap-mortgages-from-july

LeRoy SF (1989) Efficient capital markets and martingales. J Econ Liter 27(4):1583–1621

Lleo S, Ziemba WT (2017) The swiss black swan unpegging bad scenario: the losers and the winners. In: Guerard JB (ed) Portfolio construction, measurement, and efficiency: essays in honor of Jack Treynor, 389–420. Springer International Publishing, Cham. https://doi.org/10.1007/978-3-319-33976-4_17

McCloskey DN, Richard Zecher J (1976) How the gold standard worked, 1880–1913. In: Frenkel JA, Johnson HG (eds) The monetary approach to the balance of payments. University of Toronto Press, Toronto, pp 357–385

Mundell RA (1963) Capital mobility and stabilization policy under fixed and flexible exchange rates. Can J Econ Polit Sci 29(4):475–485. https://doi.org/10.2307/139336

Rolnick AJ, Weber WE (1997) Money, inflation, and output under fiat and commodity standards. J Polit Econ 105(6):1308–1321. https://doi.org/10.1086/516394

Smith A, Wagner RE, Yandle B (2011) A theory of entangled political economy, with application to TARP and NRA. Publ Choice 148(1–2):45–66

Vassileva R (2020) Monetary appreciation and foreign currency mortgages: lessons from the 2015 Swiss franc surge. Euro Rev Private Law 28(1). https://kluwerlawonline.com/api/Product/CitationPDFURL?file=Journals\ERPL\ERPL2020008.pdf

Wagner RE (2012) Viennese Kaleidics: why it's liberty more than policy that calms turbulence. Rev Austrian Econ 25(4):283–297

Wagner RE (2016) Politics as a peculiar business: public choice in a system of entangled political economy. Edward Elgar, Cheltenham

Wagner RE (2023) Social science, administrative science, and entangled political economy. In: Novak M, Podemska-Mikluch M, Wagner RE (eds) Realism, ideology, and the convulsions of democracy, 1–16. Studies in public choice. Springer Nature Switzerland, Cham. https://doi.org/10.1007/978-3-031-39458-4_1

White LH (2012) The clash of economic ideas: policy debates and experiments of the last hundred years. Cambridge University Press, Cambridge

Wlodarczak-Semczuk A (2023) EU top court backs consumers in polish FX mortgage case. Reuters, 15 June 2023, sec. Finance. https://www.reuters.com/business/finance/eu-top-court-backs-consumers-polish-fx-mortgage-case-2023-06-15/

Fix Money Fix the World

Dominic Frisby

The idea of "patient zero" is the trope of many a film about a virus or pandemic. Patient zero is where the virus started: the metaphorical Wuhan bat (or lab, as now seems to be the case). Our hero has to reach patient zero either to get the antidote or to eliminate it. Patient zero is how he saves the world.

I have long argued that, if we are to "save the world", that is to fix our badly broken economies, then there is a patient zero: our system of money.

Fix money and you fix the world, runs the mantra. Fortunately, the free market is already taking care of things.

Why Do We Need Free Trade Anyway?

In his book Rational Optimist: How Prosperity Evolves, Matt Ridley argues that Homo sapiens overtook the stronger Neanderthals and, indeed, the rest of the animal kingdom, to become the dominant species on earth, by doing something no other animal does—by exchanging things. "There was a point in human pre-history," he says, when "people for the first time began to exchange things with each other, and that once they started doing so, culture

D. Frisby (✉)
London, UK
e-mail: frizzers@gmail.com

suddenly became cumulative, and the great headlong experiment of human economic "progress" began. Exchange is to cultural evolution as sex is to biological evolution."

This applies not just to the exchange of objects, but the exchange of ideas, knowledge and information, of skills and services—just about anything. "If I catch the food, you cook it" means that I could specialise in catching—and become better at it—while you specialise in cooking and become better at that. With my superior catching and your superior cooking, we both now enjoy considerably better lifestyles. Mankind also progresses through the subsequent improvement of catching and cooking techniques, which are then passed on to the next generation.

There is an exchange taking place right now. You are reading my material. I benefit from your eyeballs and the increased awareness of my work that every writer so desperately craves. You are benefiting from my words in that you might find entertainment, interest or wisdom in them.

We are only able to do what we do today because of what was done in the past. It is only because of the cumulative work of millions of people—from Steve Jobs to Alan Turing to Shakespeare to millions of people who I'll never know or even hear of—that I am able to write this essay on this Mac. I don't know how to build a Mac, I don't know how to extract the oil necessary to manufacture its component parts; I can't make paper or ink or printing presses, yet, because of the cumulative effects of the exchanges of millions of people, I'm now able to exchange my work—itself the product of studying the work of many others—with you.

The collective intelligence of mankind is far, far greater than what can be held in the mind of even the brightest individual that ever lived. That collective intelligence keeps on growing. There is no limit to it. 'The extraordinary thing about exchange,' says Ridley, 'is that it breeds: the more of it you do, the more of it you can do. And it calls forth innovation.' The more we exchange, the more we progress. This accumulation of intelligence over generations has led to a situation where, even a hundred years ago, to quote the French philosopher Ernest Renan, 'The simplest schoolboy is now familiar with truths for which Archimedes would have sacrificed his life'.

But the reverse applies as well. The less we exchange, the less we progress. Exchange is limited under oppressive, totalitarian or bureaucratic regimes, which is why they are overtaken by freer neighbours. When we stop exchanging altogether, there is regression. 10,000 years ago, as Ridley argues, rising seas cut off Tasmania from mainland Australia. Isolated, the possibilities for exchange diminished. Technologically, the Tasmanian people actually regressed.

It follows, therefore, that for individuals, families, communities, nations—indeed mankind—to prosper and progress, conditions need to be as conducive as possible for trade and exchange. It really is that simple. That should be the primary agenda of every policy maker and leader in the world: to create an environment conducive to exchange. This means a marketplace where, from tax to tariff to bureaucracy, there are as few barriers to exchange as possible. It means a marketplace where there is trust and confidence. It means a market in which ownership of property is secure. It means a marketplace where participants can operate without coercion or crime; where good practice is rewarded with success and bad practice meets with failure. It also means a marketplace whose medium of exchange—money—is dependable.

I'm talking, of course, about a free market.

Government Money

In the ideal free market, of course, market participants can choose what they use as money. Today we don't really get to make that choice, however, largely for reasons related to taxation. We use national currencies, issued by the government and backed by the law: you must accept national currencies in settlement of debts.

What's more, the central bank, when it sets interest rates, decides the price of money. Governments do not set the price of bananas. The market does—and does so effectively. But the price of money, the most important commodity of all, is set by a government body, usually a committee of twelve experts. That body, be it the Federal Reserve, the European Central Bank, the Bank of England or Japan is often lent on by politicians with their own agenda (usually getting re-elected).

As long as we use national currencies, also known as fiat currency, markets will never be properly free. Money has become a political tool and, as a result, misallocation of capital and price distortion are everywhere.

House prices are a good example. We'll leave aside the (unnecessarily) high costs of land with planning permission and of building regulations, both of which lead to higher prices, and focus here on the monetary causes of high house prices. Interest rates have not reflected real inflation for decades, because they do not take money supply into account—"expanding—i.e. inflating—the money supply with the consequence of higher prices" was the original definition of inflation. House prices themselves are not included in government measures of inflation, nor are financial assets, yet both of these attract vast quantities of newly-created money in the form of debt. Official inflation measures only track the prices of certain goods and services, which are largely prone to the deflationary forces of improved productivity and globalisation. Many of the goods tracked by inflation measures can be made cheaply in China, for example, and that helps keep official inflation low. Even when that is no longer the case, such as when supply chains were impacted during the Covid lockdowns and prices rose, central banks proved reluctant and slow to raise rates. As rates have been so low for so long, the cost of debt has been cheap and led to increased borrowing. This borrowing led to an increase of money, especially in the housing market and prices duly rose to levels that bear little relation to earnings. The effects of this influx of new money into a market which is limited in how much it can expand because of restrictive planning laws has been that houses have become unaffordable and bear little relation to actual build costs, never mind earnings. Since 1971 in the UK, for example, average house prices have risen by 70 times, while average wages have only increased by 22 times. House prices therefore have risen by three and a half times as much as earnings. Increased immigration has exacerbated this: the extra competition for work drives down wages but increases demand for housing.

Before the imposition of national currencies in the fiat era, which began in the twentieth century, metal was money—gold, silver, nickel and copper. Indeed the words for money and silver are interchangeable in some 50 or more languages—from Scottish (airgid) to Spanish (plata) to Swahili (fedha). The English pound sterling was once a pound of sterling silver. In Western Europe, this ended shortly after the onset of the First World War. Fearing runs on their gold, the British, French and German governments all came off their gold standards enabling them to devalue their money in order to help them cover the costs of the war. There were attempts to rejoin the gold standard in the 1920s, but by the early- to mid-1930s these were all abandoned.

After World War Two, the US remained on a gold standard, albeit a hypocritical one as US citizens were not allowed to own gold, and other nations fixed their currencies to the dollar. Known as the Bretton Woods Agreement, this eventually fell apart with the Nixon Shock of 1971, when President Nixon ended US dollar convertibility with gold. So began the fiat era.

The Shortcomings of National Currencies

Money is fundamental to trade and exchange. No trade or exchange is possible without it. But let us consider for a moment what money actually is.

This mnemonic rhyme was common in old economic textbooks.

Money is a matter of functions four:
A medium, a measure, a standard and a store.

Money is a medium of exchange; a store of value; a unit of account and a standard of deferred payment. We shall look at each of those four functions in turn, starting with medium of exchange.

The internet has proved the most fantastic medium by which to exchange: to communicate, to swap ideas, to trade goods and services, especially digital goods and services, and more. It has a huge reach. It is cheap, frictionless, global and, almost, borderless. What a facilitator it has been. I can communicate with pretty much anyone in the world instantaneously. I in the UK could partner with somebody in Africa, set up a company in Asia, selling goods and services in Australia and America, and no one need ever leave their desk. But if I want to cross borders in the real world, this is a time-consuming process, requiring transportation, visas, passports, security checks and all the rest of it.

While I can send messages, documents, videos or music to any part of the world, sending money can be more problematic. It can be a slow, burdensome and expensive process, requiring forms, forex conversion, customs declarations, money laundering enquiries, multiple bank processes and more. Unlike the internet, the money we use—national currencies (dollars, euros and pounds)—fiat money, in other words, is not borderless.

Even the US dollar, which is the reserve currency of the world, has limitations. Try opening a US dollar account outside of the US. It is problematic. If you are living in remote, rural Africa or Asia, it is well-nigh impossible. It is hard enough getting a bank account in your own currency.

Often it is not possible to send money at all. You might live in a part of the world in which, for reasons ranging from international sanctions to totalitarian government to untrustworthy banks, it is not possible to send money internationally at all.

You might not be able to get a bank account. In the west, we take financial inclusion for granted, but globally there are still close to 1.5 billion people who are unbanked. That is something like 20% of the adult global population which is excluded and with whom we, effectively, cannot trade and exchange goods or services. With no bank account, cash is the only form of money they can make or take payment in, so they are confined to trading with people in their immediate vicinity. How are such people supposed to improve their lot under such restrictive circumstances?

But even for the financially included, there are limitations. If I wanted to send a payment to someone else in the world who operates with a different currency of, say, £1, via a bank, the costs are prohibitive. There are all sorts of reasons why I might want to do this: to pay for a small good or service, a tip, a bet. But it is very difficult to send small payments such as this internationally through the banking system. Services such as Revolut make it easier, but these have all sorts of shortcomings (not least the risks of account hacking and lack of consumer protection—I wrote an article last year about a friend who had her Revolut account hacked and I was flooded with emails from people who had had a similar experience and were unable to get their money back.) If I want to send a micropayment of, say, one-tenth of a cent, it is just impossible.

But industries based around micropayments are a huge area of potential growth. Imagine if, instead of getting a like for your YouTube video or Twitter, Instagram or Facebook post, somebody could tip you the equivalent of 1/10th of a cent. A meaningless amount to the person paying it, but a million 1/10th cents, instead of a million likes, is ten thousand bucks. Not bad. But beyond content monetisation, there is so much economic growth waiting to happen, especially in a world of artificial intelligence and the internet of things: streaming, apps, games, in-app and in-game purchases, rewards, donations, tipping, credit card verification, identity verification, Wi-Fi access, public document access, libraries, parking, phone calls, public transport, pay-per-use in cloud computing or application programming interface (API)—when apps talk to each other—exchange of or access to information via the internet of things, content licencing, ad-free browsing, access to news and journalism, paying freelancers. It's a big list. The problem is money. National currencies do not enable the micropayment economy, they are a barrier to it.

In summary, while national currencies work reasonably as a medium of exchange within a nation, across borders they are limited, so that, rather than facilitate trade, they create barriers to it. They exclude the unbanked. They are not good for micropayments. Large payments are expensive and time-consuming.

Whether good currencies like the Swiss franc and the Singapore dollar, or bad ones like the Turkish lira and the Argentine peso: national currencies are inadequate for the new borderless medium that is the internet.

That final comment brings up another important point. What if you "lose" the geographical lottery and are from somewhere with a poor national currency? Straight away you are held back, before you have even got to market.

National Currencies are a Rotten Store of Value

As well as being a medium of exchange, money should also be a store of wealth. Indeed, I would argue that it is essential to an honest, functioning society that money fulfils this function and retains its purchasing power. If I work, I expend energy. The money I receive in exchange for my labour is, in effect, stored energy. The amount of energy stored should endure for as long as I need it to, and not be eroded away.

Over the course of the nineteenth century, when the UK was on a gold standard, money was an effective store of value. The purchasing power of the pound more than doubled, as this chart of consumer prices shows. (As consumer prices fall, the purchasing power of money increases, so when this chart falls, the purchasing power of money goes up).

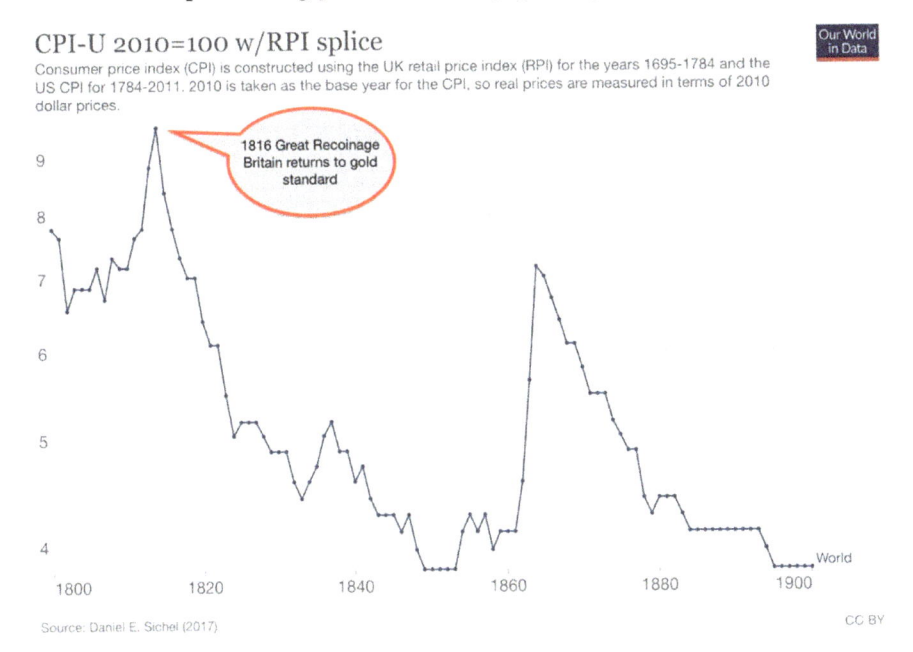

CPI-U 2010=100 w/RPI splice

Consumer price index (CPI) is constructed using the UK retail price index (RPI) for the years 1695-1784 and the US CPI for 1784-2011. 2010 is taken as the base year for the CPI, so real prices are measured in terms of 2010 dollar prices.

1816 Great Recoinage Britain returns to gold standard

Source: Daniel E. Sichel (2017)

Prime Minister William Pitt took Britain off the gold standard in 1797 to try and preserve depleted gold reserves (he had exhausted them by sending gold sovereigns abroad, known as the Golden Cavalry of St George, to fund Napoleon's enemies).

Prime Minister Robert Banks Jenkinson restored the standard in 1816 with the Great Recoinage and over the next 30 years prices went from above 9 on the index to below 4. Consumer prices fell by almost 60%. The purchasing power of money more than doubled. It was a good time to be a worker earning pay. The consequence was the rapid growth of the British middle class.

Prices rose again with the American Civil War. Once it was over, over the next 40 years they would fall again, until 1914.

This next chart shows consumer prices going all the way back to the formation of the Bank of England in 1694. When money was tied to gold, consumer prices rose and fell, as you would expect them to, but broadly speaking they stayed within a range. It is only since the twentieth century when countries started to abandon gold that money began to lose its purchasing power so rapidly. This was especially the case since 1971 and the Nixon Shock, when the US President untied the dollar, and effectively the world, from gold. Look how prices turned up after 1971.

We think inflation and the loss of the purchasing power of money is normal. Until 1971, it wasn't.

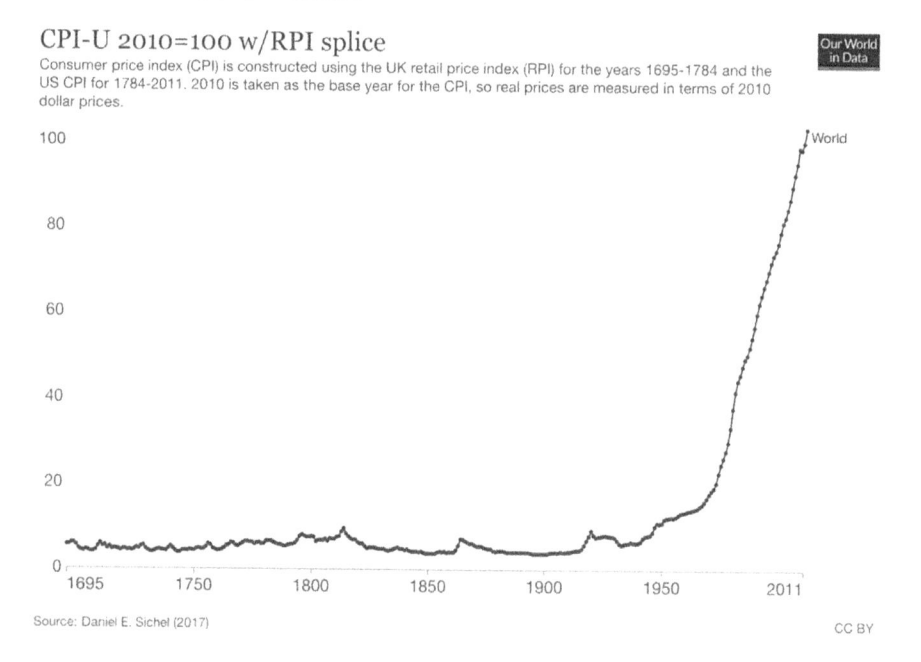

CPI-U 2010=100 w/RPI splice

Consumer price index (CPI) is constructed using the UK retail price index (RPI) for the years 1695-1784 and the US CPI for 1784-2011. 2010 is taken as the base year for the CPI, so real prices are measured in terms of 2010 dollar prices.

Source: Daniel E. Sichel (2017)

Gold worked well as a store of value. Modern national currencies—fiat money—on the other hand fail terribly. Please cast your eye over the table below.[1] It shows the price of various items in the UK in 1970 compared to their price today.

---

[1] The Flying Frisby. (July 5, 2022). What Really Causes Inflation? Here's... https://www.theflyingfrisby.com/p/what-really-causes-inflation-heres. Accessed March 24, 2024.

Fix Money Fix the World

It's amazing just how much things have risen in price.

	1970	Today	Multiple	Fixed supply?
Average salary (before tax)	£1,456	£31,980	22×	No
Average house	£4,057	£278,000	69×	Yes + debt
Ford Cortina	£882	£28,500 (Ford Mondeo)	32×	No + debt
Range Rover	£1,998	From £83,525	42×	No + debt
Pint of beer	15p	> £5	33×	No + tax
Pint of milk	6p	70p	12×	No
Gallon of petrol	31p	> £7	23×	No + tax
12 eggs	18p	£3	20×	No
Washing machine	£90	£400	4×	No
Phone call (1976—6 min local)	10p	0	–	No

Average wages have gone up by 22 times, give or take, over the last 50 years. However, there have been huge deflationary forces at work, which have driven down the cost of labour. The increased competition brought about by cheap immigrant or outsourced labour, for example, has driven down wages to an enormous extent. So has more women entering the workforce: the workforce has expanded, meaning more competition for jobs, which has driven down prices. Great if you're an employer, but not so great for the employees.

While there is no shortage of labour supply, with houses, however, the story is different. House prices have gone up almost 70 times over the same period—three and a half times as much as wages. If wages had gone up by as much as house prices over the period, the average salary in the UK would be around £100,000.

The key observations about these high prices are, first, that the supply of housing, thanks to planning laws, is more limited than the supply of labour. Second, and probably more importantly, we use debt—mortgages—to buy houses. We don't usually use debt to pay for labour. It is paid out of cashflow.

New debt entering the market—newly-created money in other words—has pushed up house prices in a way that could not have happened if this was a cash market.

A similar dynamic has been at play in the car market. Cars are obviously a lot better today than they were in the 1970s, but their supply is not as finite as housing, while the impact of improved productivity in car manufacture should have had a deflationary effect.

Yet we see the average car—a Ford Cortina in 1970, a Ford Mondeo today—is 32 times more expensive, while the luxury car that is the Range Rover is over 40 times dearer. The reason? We use finance to buy cars. Cheap debt has pushed up car prices too.

Cheap debt—i.e. easy money creation—enables more money to enter a market. More money in a market means higher prices.

I had a message from a reader yesterday, and it is of relevance. The UK government is increasing the subsidy on nursery and preschool fees for most families. My reader found this welcome. He was paying more on nursery than for his mortgage. But all of sudden the nursery has increased its fees by 28%—in one go. Other parents at other nurseries said similar things had happened. Thanks to government subsidy more money has entered this market, and so prices have gone up. It doesn't matter where the money comes from—whether via debt, taxes, subsidy, printing and QE, earnings, or from abroad—the more money there is in a market, the higher prices will go.

On the other hand, we don't use finance to buy bread, milk or eggs, we pay cash. Meanwhile, the production techniques for each have dramatically improved. With improved productivity, and neither debt nor limited supply to push up prices, basic, low-end staple food costs have fallen relative to wages. With sound money, they would have fallen by a lot more.

This same dynamic doesn't apply to beer costs. Why? In recent times the extra cost of serving beer in a Covid-compliant manner has driven up prices, but the main villain has been increased alcohol duty. Cost of government in other words. The actual cost of making beer, before all the add-ons, is quite low. The same goes for fuel. Cheap, easy-to-produce oil may be rarer than it was in the 1970s, but oil production techniques have improved. In any case, around 70% of the cost of petrol at the pump is the cost of government (taxes and duties).

When we look at the cost of washing machines, we see the other big factor at play: globalisation. On the whole, we don't use finance to buy washing machines and they have been prone to the deflationary force of improved productivity and globalisation. Washing machine buyers benefit from China's cheap labour and the export of its deflation. And so washing machine prices have "only" quadrupled.

And what about the cost of phone calls? If you want to see the deflationary forces of improved technology at work, look no further than the cost of communication. Even in a world of rampant money printing it has gone to almost nothing. There's the scalability of digital tech for you right there.

Once upon a time, a local call cost me 10p for three minutes. Now I can make a video call anywhere in the world where there is internet access and the cost is nothing.

Modern national currencies are a rotten store of value. This creates all sorts of mal-incentives at every level of society, not least short-termism.

Money is a Political Tool

Under a fiat money system, digital debt-based fiat money to give it its full name, increased money supply is inevitable. It is built into the system: the supply of money, whether through the issuance of debt, money printing or Quantitative Easing, never stops growing. Only an enormous credit contraction reverses this, and policy makers never allow such a thing to happen. At any sign of the slightest contraction in credit, they step in with lower rates and other incentives to stimulate borrowing, or the government borrows and prints itself, as with Quantitative Easing.

With fiat money, it is just the speed of the loss of purchasing power that changes. Under fiscally prudent governments, such as Switzerland—a rare thing—the rate of decline will be slower. When interest rates are high, the rate of credit expansion and thus purchasing power erosion will be slower. Under imprudent rulership, however, the decline in purchasing power accelerates. The pound has lost a third of its purchasing power just since 2020, according to figures from Truflation.[2] Measured in the constant that is gold, the pound has lost 90% of its purchasing power just this century.[3] Turkey and Argentina have seen much faster rates of decline.

Thus people who hold government money are having their purchasing power and wealth stolen from them in this process. Never mind that this is insidious, unjust and immoral, what are the effects?

Over time, because of the extraordinary incremental effects of compounding, the consequence is colossal wealth inequality. Those on salaries, fixed incomes or with savings are disproportionately affected. That might be the very old or the young who see the effective purchasing power of the salaries eroded. Those with assets, especially houses, on the other hand, benefit. Assets rise in value to reflect the new money in circulation. But those wanting to buy a house—the young, especially—are priced out. They can't

---

[2] Truflation Twitter. https://twitter.com/truflation/status/1722294156503208413?s=20. Accessed March 24, 2024.
[3] Gold was £150/oz in 1999. Today it is over £1,500/oz.

afford to buy. To enjoy the basic middle-class existence enjoyed by previous generations, now takes two salaries instead of one and a lot more debt.

As a result, leaving aside the psychological damage, the young put off starting families, they have smaller families, later in life. When people are asked why they have fewer children, and why, the most commonly given reason is cost. The consequence of fiat money in the west has been declining family size in the west and population decline.

When they do buy, they usually end up unable to buy where they grew up, meaning a loss of touch with their families, their traditions and their roots. The effect is to dramatically widen wealth gaps—it is the cause of today's intergenerational wealth gap, for example, and the injustice of this inequality means anger, social tension and unrest. It erodes trust and confidence in the system. We are seeing all these things happening around us in real time.

Sound money is an essential bedrock of society. Since the Nixon Shock of 1971 when the US, and with it the world, finally abandoned the gold standard, that bedrock has gone.

While money and money creation remain in the hands of government, this process is, as I say, inevitable. Politicians use money as a political tool to gain votes or popularity, to engender economic stimulus where they think it is needed, to devalue their debt obligations, and to enable their deficit spending where they are unable to balance books. It is a lot easier than imposing taxes, which are more directly felt.

It means citizens are beholden to their governments for the purchasing power of money. Money and state should be separated.

In the case of the US dollar, the global reserve currency, global citizens are beholden to the US government and its monetary policy. While US monetary policy is determined by the Federal Reserve Bank, it is often lent on by the US government which often has its own agenda: anything from domestic borrowing costs to engineering popularity before an election to personal career risk of the policy maker can determine decisions. After Russia invaded Ukraine the US dollar became an important weapon in the conflict, used to freeze Russia out of the banking system. It means that international US dollar users, for example in South America or parts of Africa, become beholden to US domestic monetary policy. That is not ideal for a global reserve currency.

With national currencies, money is not just money—a tool for trade and exchange, a store of wealth—but a political tool.

Surely, however, world trade, if it is to be truly free, needs international money that is not subject to the US or any other political machinations. It needs money that is apolitical and independent. Why should users in Warsaw, Winchester, Wellington or Wurzburg suffer for policy set in Washington?

Finally, we have the last two functions of money: standard and measure. A measure needs to be constant to be an effective unit of account. If the measure keeps changing, it is as good as useless. Fiat money, because of the ever-increasing supply and erosion of its purchasing power, fails in this regard. It is inconstant. Statisticians and economists resort to "inflation-adjusted dollars", but not everybody agrees as to what inflation actually is, never mind the inflation rate. It is not an effective measure or unit of account.

Gold, on the other hand, is about as constant a substance as you will find. It does not decay or tarnish. It has been around since accretion compressed the dust in our solar system to form the planets, and is exactly as it was then. You can't debase it. New mine supply increases at the same rate as population growth. It makes for a far better unit of account, particularly when measuring relative costs over time, than fiat.

The same goes for standard, whether referring to standard of deferred payment (which, as a definition, in many ways gets subsumed under the other three categories of money—medium, measure and store) or standard as in basis of the money system (as in gold standard). Fiat money falls short. Its constant erosion means it fails in both cases.

The bottom line is that when one body in a society has the unique power to create money at no cost to itself then it is inevitable that that body will grow disproportionately large within that society. This is the reason the state has grown so large and invasive in the west and it is antithetical to free markets.

Indeed, as this chart from Matthew Lesh of the Institute of Economic Affairs demonstrates, areas of our economy in which the state gets heavily involved have become extremely expensive. Where it stays away remains cheap.

United Kingdom Price Changes: 2000 to 2023

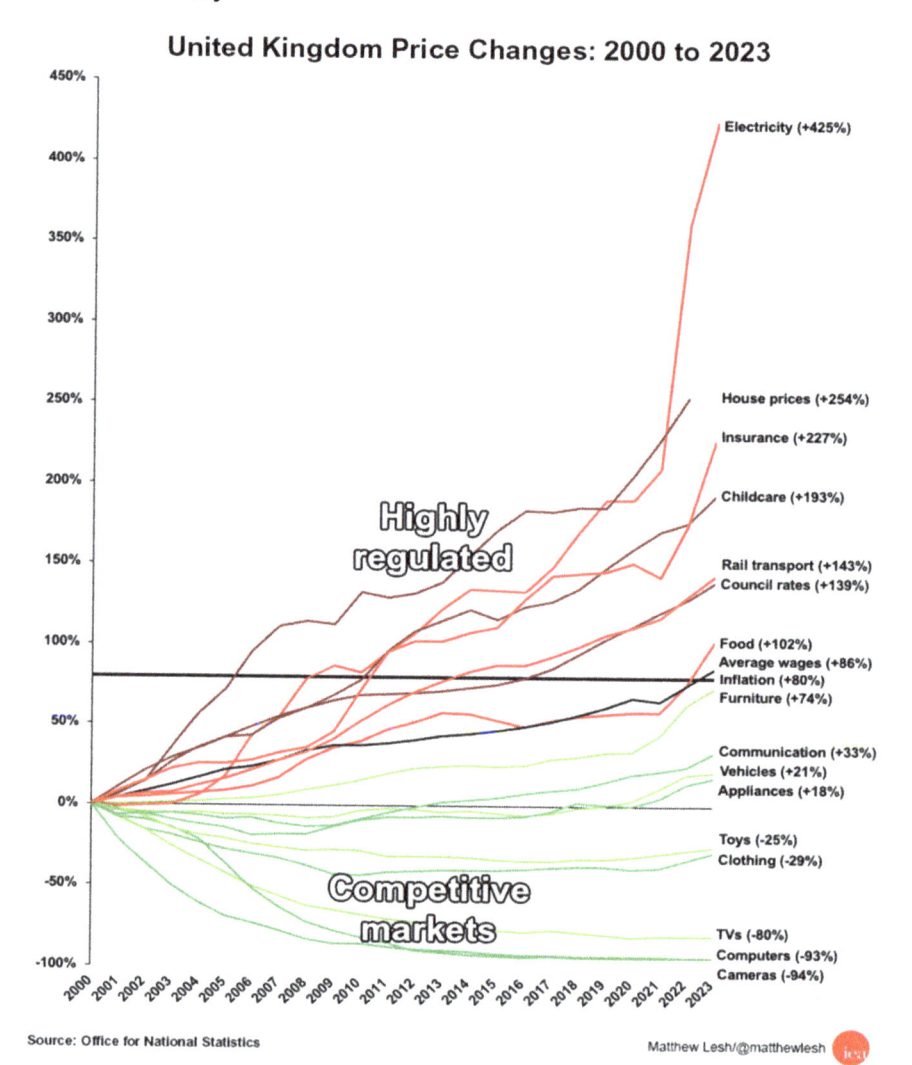

- Electricity (+425%)
- House prices (+254%)
- Insurance (+227%)
- Childcare (+193%)
- Rail transport (+143%)
- Council rates (+139%)
- Food (+102%)
- Average wages (+86%)
- Inflation (+80%)
- Furniture (+74%)
- Communication (+33%)
- Vehicles (+21%)
- Appliances (+18%)
- Toys (-25%)
- Clothing (-29%)
- TVs (-80%)
- Computers (-93%)
- Cameras (-94%)

Highly regulated / **Competitive markets**

Source: Office for National Statistics. Matthew Lesh/@matthewlesh

An occasional glass of red wine might even be good for your health. Too much, however, and your liver fails. So it is with government: a little bit of state might be good for economic health. Too much, however, and the outcome is very different.

With national currencies, money is not just money—a tool for trade and exchange, a store of wealth—but a political tool. We need to separate money and state.

Is Metal the Solution?

"In the long run, the aggregate of decisions of individual businessmen, exercising individual judgement, in a free economy, even if often mistaken, is less likely to do harm than the centralized decisions of a government; and certainly is likely to be counteracted faster," said John James Cowperthwaite, the former Financial Secretary of Hong Kong.

It is not for me nor anyone else to prescribe what should be money. It is for the market and those operating in it. In the pre-digital age, when left alone, markets have always gravitated to metal, with gold as the main store of value, and silver, nickel and copper as medium of exchange.

The beauty of metal is that, first, governments can't print it. Metal is independent and thus resistant to inflation. It has intrinsic value because of its scarcity, its utility and beauty. This value is recognised the world over and provides a stable foundation that underpins it as money. Metal is uniform and fungible: an ounce of gold is an ounce of gold, wherever or whenever you are. It doesn't change. An ounce of pebbles, for example, is different everywhere you go. Metal is durable—meaning it can withstand repeated handling and endure many years. It is divisible, so can be made into smaller units allowing for precise transactions. The difference in value of relative metals—gold, silver, nickel and copper—allows for further divisibility. Metal carries a certain amount of prestige, particularly in the case of gold and silver. Finally, metal is portable. Coinage, invented in Ancient Lydia some 2700 years ago, proved a brilliant technology, perhaps the greatest fintech of all time, given we are still using it all these years later. It allowed for economic mobility, people could carry their wealth with them in certifiable, measurable amounts, which increased the possibilities for trade, exchange and progress.

No wonder metal proved so effective as money.

But in this digital age, does metal have much of a future as money? As store of value, gold certainly still has a role to play. That is why the period from 2022 to 2024, as I write this, has seen central banks accumulating gold at the fastest rates since the 1960s and why gold remains such a popular choice among investors. As the world de-dollarises, in an age of increasing global tension and insecurity, central banks still need an effective store of value that is nobody else's liability. Hence gold.

In early 2024 a story broke that Russia paid Iran $2 billion in gold bullion for Shahed-136 drones used in attacks on Ukrainian cities.[4] It flew that gold

---

[4] V. The Telegraph (2024, February 7). Russia paid billions in gold bullion for Shahed drones in Ukraine war. https://www.telegraph.co.uk/world-news/2024/02/07/russia-paid-billions-gold-bullion-shahed-drones-ukraine-war/. Accessed March 24, 2024.

to Iran by plane. While that transaction might have worked for those two nations, the idea of having to ship gold every time you want to send a high-value transaction over distance makes it extremely unlikely that gold or metal will find common, everyday use. One possibility is for gold to be stored in a safe vault and for ownership of that gold to be transferred. But this requires trusted third parties which are not always available.

Commodity money has little use in the digital age.

Money, Language and Communication

You might call it the cable that changed history.

In the mid-nineteenth century, there were various attempts to lay cables across the Atlantic Ocean between Britain and the US. It took several failures and numerous bankruptcies over ten years before they got it right. But eventually they did and on July 27 1866 Queen Victoria broadcast a message to US President Johnson, which read:

> Osborne, July 27, 1866
> To the President of the United States, Washington
> The Queen congratulates the President on the successful completion of an undertaking which she hopes may serve as an additional bond of Union between the United States and England.

> Johnson replied:
> Executive Mansion

> Washington, July 30, 1866
> To Her Majesty the Queen of the United Kingdom of Great Britain and Ireland
> The President of the United States acknowledges with profound gratification the receipt of Her Majesty's dispatch and cordially reciprocates the hope that the cable which now unites the Eastern and Western hemispheres may serve to strengthen and perpetuate peace and amity between the governments of England and the Republic of the United States.
> (Signed) Andrew Johnson.

To send a message by ship could take ten days or more. Now it was a matter of minutes. So somebody came up with the slogan "two weeks to two minutes".

Transmission speeds improved rapidly. Morse code became words. It was soon possible to send multiple messages at once. By the end of the nineteenth century, Britain, France, Germany and the US were all linked by cable. Personal, commercial and political relations were altered for all time.

Back then gold was money, of course, as were paper notes representing gold. But you couldn't send gold down the cable, however, nor paper. You could, however, send a promise.

Within a fortnight of Queen Victoria's message, that's what two parties who trusted each other did. An exchange rate between the dollar and the pound was agreed and then published in the New York Times on August 10. That is why, to this day, the pound-dollar exchange rate, GBPUSD, is known as cable.

"All money is a matter of belief," said Adam Smith. He had a point. Look at a twenty-pound note (if you still use them) and you will see the words "I promise to pay the bearer". Money is promissory. Of course, promises disappear. Gold doesn't. The two are quite different forms of money: one is belief, the other is real.

Nevertheless, since the dawn of civilisation, we have been using promissory money. In Ancient Mesopotamia, man used mud tokens—a cone or a sphere—representing sheep or barley, baked inside clay balls to log debts owed. Over time, he found it more efficient, rather than bake tokens in balls, to inscribe pictures of the tokens in the mud for the same purpose. That is how the first system of writing came about.

In Ancient China, man recorded his debts on bits of leather. After the invention of printing, he started using paper.

Today, the promises are recorded and exchanged between trusted third parties on computers.

Millions, probably billions of promises are sent across the internet every second, transferring as quick as words, probably quicker. Not only does (promissory) money evolve with communication technology, but it is often the spur, the impetus for communication technology to evolve.

What is money, then, but a form of communication?

What we do often says more about us than what we say. What we do with our money says even more. What we do with our money communicates value, not just between buyer and seller, but across the economy. What is the price of this thing? What is its value? The answer is constantly being sent and received, digested and acted upon; and so does the economy constantly, incrementally evolve and develop with each new signal: the how, why and when, of what needs producing and where.

Money then is like a language. Constantly evolving and changing. Nobody is really in charge, not even central bankers. Our fiat system wasn't really planned. It has just constantly evolved, with billions of people contributing in their own different ways simply by using it. The architects of fiat money did not plan what we have today, they just used it to get out of a tight fiscal spot—extenuating circumstances at the time.

Similarly, nobody planned the language we speak today. Language is hard to plan and regulate, try as many have over the years—and still do. It just constantly evolves and develops, according to the use and needs of billions. The English we speak today is a long way from the English of Chaucer, Shakespeare or Dickens. There are probably fewer words, certainly fewer tenses. Grammar is simpler. Yet it is far more widely spoken. The network has grown.

Mandarin may have three or four times more native speakers, but English is more widely spoken: most people have it as their second language. There may well come a time when everybody in the world speaks it. It is the dominant linguistic network.

Meanwhile, other languages fade away. Cornish has gone. Few now speak Welsh or Gaelic. The local dialects of France and Italy are disappearing. Similarly, there is no doubt a plethora of African, Asian and American languages that are on the way out, if they haven't already gone.

The question to ask is this: how scalable is the language? English has the potential to become the default language of the world. It's almost inevitable at this point. Despite having more native speakers, that's unlikely to be the case with Mandarin. It's certainly not going to happen to Gaelic, Neapolitan or Swahili.

National currencies have the same problem. They are not scalable. They are limited by national borders. The US dollar is the global reserve currency. You can send that over the internet. But, as we have discussed, it is hard for people who aren't American to get US dollar bank accounts. Foreign exchange fees are expensive. Money transfers can take several days sometimes. Billions remain unbanked and thus excluded from the financial system altogether. The dollar is a national currency that is used internationally. A country – and several do—could use it as their national currency, but they would be importing US monetary policy too, and so subjecting themselves to US political whims. Which is why most countries with their own political agenda issue their own currencies.

Thus, though "international", as a national currency, the US dollar is limited by its national borders and its politics. The same goes for any national currency.

But language is not limited by national borders—or at least English isn't.

How many different monies have there been in history? Shells, whale teeth, metals, paper, cigarettes, mackerel packs, cognac, Zimbabwe dollars, reichsmarks, denarii, farthings, shillings, altcoins. Most have died. Most of those which haven't yet died, will die. Only gold goes on, immutable and permanent.

Metal is scalable in that its value is understood globally and over time. But, as with transatlantic cables, you can't send metal or gold over the internet. Only golden promises between trusted parties.

What is needed is an apolitical system of money—a system of money that does not involve government. A system of money that is widely recognised, which can be used across borders on the internet, just as we send messages, whether for tiny payments or for large sums. This money must be inclusive so that anyone can use it, and it must preserve its purchasing power over time. It must be immutable and immune to interference, especially by governments or bad actors. It must be scalable. If only there were such a system. If only there was an apolitical, borderless currency for the borderless medium that is the internet.

Where the market needs, the market provides.

Money for the Internet

In 2008, in reaction to the money printing and bail-outs that had taken place following the Global Financial Crisis, Satoshi Nakamoto announced his invention, bitcoin, on an out-of-way mailing list with the words, "I've been working on a new electronic cash system. It might make sense to get some just in case it catches on." Here we are in spring 2024 and the market cap of bitcoin now exceeds one trillion dollars. By market cap bitcoin is the 13th largest currency in the world.[5] The value of bitcoin exceeds the value of all the silver in the world. With silver's historical association with money, this is a huge milestone to have reached.

Many have dismissed it as a bubble. They have usually not properly done their research. Bitcoin is volatile, as all new tech is. It has had no fewer than six 80% corrections in its evolution. But if it was a bubble, it would long since have disappeared. Today something like 300 million people use it, whether as currency, savings vehicle or tool for speculation, close to 4% of the global population, one in every 27 people worldwide. That user base is growing all the time, unlike those of national currencies, which are static.

---

[5] Fiat Market Cap. https://fiatmarketcap.com/. Accessed March 24, 2024.

The Governor of the Bank of England, Andrew Bailey, is among those who have turned his back on it, dismissing it on numerous occasions. The UK's Financial Conduct Authority banned retail investors from owning bitcoin derivatives, such as bitcoin ETFs. This was when the bitcoin price was US$10,000. Today it is $70,000. Here was an enormous opportunity for British people and for British industry that short-sighted policy makers removed. With sterling now overtaken, it has proved Bank of England's Kodak moment.[6]

Bitcoin was originally designed to be cash for the internet. A digital replication of the process by which person A can hand cash directly to person B with no middleman involved. In coding this system, Nakamoto solved a number of problems that computer programmers had been wrestling with for decades: among them double spending and the Byzantine Generals problem (neither of which we need to go into now). Nakamoto's solution was his breakthrough technology, a decentralised ledger, known as the blockchain. It got the programming world extremely excited. It was now possible to send tiny or vast amounts of money across the internet without the need for third parties such as banks or credit card companies, just as you would hand cash to someone next to you.

Bitcoin has since grown into something much bigger. Unlike pounds or dollars, this money is not issued by a government. It is apolitical money. Instead, it is issued by an international network of computers, according to an open source protocol set in computer code. Its value is determined by the market: what people are prepared to buy it for. Unlike national currencies, participation is entirely voluntary.

What backs this money is an extraordinary amount of computer power. A network of computers maintains the blockchain and processes transactions. Anyone can put their computer to work doing this. In return, computers are rewarded with bitcoins. The process is known as mining. As bitcoin has evolved, this network of computers has grown very powerful. It is the largest computer network in the world, orders of magnitude larger than the combined size of the clouds that Amazon, Google, and Microsoft have built over the last 15–20 years. Bitcoin's hash rate hit an all-time high of 500 exahashes last month. There are tens of thousands of computers at work—verifying, auditing, processing. It is quite something: an incorruptible machine driven by mathematics.

---

[6] Kodak was one of the world's most successful and innovative companies, and one of the first companies to develop a digital camera. But it decided to turn against the technology for fear it would undermine its existing film business. It went bust as a result.

Bitcoin's inflation rate is set in code, and guaranteed by that computer power. The supply is finite. This distinguishes it from national currencies where money supply growth is inevitable. It cannot be manipulated. Governments cannot tinker with bitcoin's money supply with political objectives in mind and create more of it. The 21 million coin maximum is set. A finite and limited supply means bitcoin's value is likely to increase. (It also means that, in time, it will prove an effective unit of account). Like gold, this is a deflationary system of money (prices get cheaper in bitcoin), unlike national currencies which, as we have seen, are inherently inflationary (prices go up). This is why bitcoin has proved such an effective savings vehicle and store of value: the world's best-performing asset of the past 15 years.

Each bitcoin is divisible to 8 decimal places—100 million times—with the smallest denomination being the satoshi or sat. There are thus 100 million satoshis to a bitcoin.

One US dollar would be around 2500 sats, and one cent about 25 sats. This means you can send micropayments, which amount to 1/25th of one cent. I have verified this myself and sent micropayments of one sat—or 1/25th of a cent. It costs nothing. Try getting a bank to process a payment of that size.

Meanwhile, last week, somebody transferred the bitcoin equivalent of $1.3bn for a fee of $2.[7] No forms, permits or declarations were required to effect the transaction.

If you like, you can send that kind of money over the weekend, when the banks are shut. You can send to anyone anywhere, huge value transactions or tiny value transactions, and the transfer is frictionless and almost instantaneous.

We are starting to see businesses keep their treasury in bitcoin. The most famous example is Nasdaq-listed Microstrategy Inc. The reasoning of Chairman, Michael Saylor, behind this change of strategy was that his company was losing 5–10% annually to currency depreciation. Therefore, he had to grow by 10% per annum just to stay flat. Instead of share buybacks, Microstrategy now issues stock and buys bitcoin. Since adopting a bitcoin standard in 2020, the share price has appreciated by over 1000%. The market cap of the corporation has grown by even greater multiples. Bitcoin rewards early adopters. Other corporations will see Microstrategy's performance and surely follow suit.

---

[7] V. Simply Bitcoin TV Twitter. https://twitter.com/SimplyBitcoinTV/status/1761284919635096042?s=20. Accessed March 24, 2024.

Nations too might adopt a bitcoin standard. El Salvador already has. Despite receiving considerable criticism, and the ire of the IMF, El Salvador's national balance sheet has dramatically improved as a result.

The evolution of bitcoin has been a voluntary, market-driven phenomenon. The market has, by itself, found a solution to the fiat money problem. None of it is as a result of government planning. Here is a money communication network backed instead by mathematical proof and the most powerful and resilient computer network ever known to man. Technically, bitcoin is a superior form of money to government currency, as both medium of exchange and store of value. Eventually, unit of account or standard of deferred payment will follow. Technology is destiny. As a technologically superior, borderless system of money, it has a potential to scale that no national currency can compete with.

If money is language, then bitcoin is English. There may be more people who have Mandarin as their first language than English, but it is English that will become the global standard by virtue of the fact that so many have it as their second language. English is more scalable.

Bitcoin's attraction is its appreciating price. While fiat continues to lose purchasing power, this attraction will endure, making bitcoin adoption inevitable. National currencies will either have to adapt and copy the bitcoin model of limited supply or die.

We are entering an era of Hayekian competing currencies. There are national currencies, there are cryptocurrencies, there are private currencies, such as air miles and rewards points, there are even, with stable coins, private companies effectively issuing national currencies. In such a world, the best currencies will win. Some governments will embrace the best currencies and the best practices, others will see them as a threat and try to ban or regulate them out of existence. The citizens of those nations will lose out as a result.

But there was a problem. And the market has given us the solution.

Bibliography

Adams C (2012) Fight, flight, fraud: the story of taxation. Algora Publishing
Carswell D (2012) The end of politics and the birth of iDemocracy. Biteback Publishing.
Frisby D (2013) Life after the state. Unbound
Frisby D (2014) Bitcoin: the future of money? Unbound
Frisby D (2014) Daylight robbery: how tax shaped our past and will change our future. Penguin Books

Hayek FA (1990) Denationalisation of money: the argument refined, 3rd edn. Institute of Economic Affairs

Lesh M (2024) Graphic content: how red tape is fueling the cost of living crisis. Institute of Economic Affairs

Nakamoto S (2008) Bitcoin: a peer-to-peer electronic cash system

Ridley M (2010) The rational optimist: how prosperity evolves. Harper

Turk J (2012) The collapse of the dollar and how to profit from it: make a fortune by investing in gold and other hard assets. Doubleday

Truflation Twitter. https://twitter.com/truflation/status/1722294156503208413?s=20. Accessed 24 Mar 2024

The Flying Frisby (2022) What really causes inflation? Here's... https://www.theflyingfrisby.com/p/what-really-causes-inflation-heres. Accessed 24 Mar 2024

The Telegraph (2024) Russia paid billions in gold bullion for Shahed drones in Ukraine war. https://www.telegraph.co.uk/world-news/2024/02/07/russia-paid-billions-gold-bullion-shahed-drones-ukraine-war/. Accessed 24 Mar 2024

Economic Policy and Trade: The Good, The Bad and The Ugly

Free Trade in the Nordic Countries

Hannes H. Gissurarson

Introduction

In 1018, more than a thousand years ago, Swedish farmers attended an assembly at Uppsala in the centre of the country, as was their wont. Icelandic chronicler Snorri Sturluson described the meeting two hundred years later in his history of Norway. The farmers were dissatisfied because King Olav of the Swedes refused to make peace with his namesake, King Olav the Fat of Norway. When this was brought up at the meeting, the Swedish king was enraged whereupon Earl Rognvald Ulfsson from West Gothia intervened. He recalled that the present Norwegian king had made several peace offers. 'He recounted what a problem it was for the Western Goths to be without all the things from Norway which would supplement their own produce, and at the same time to be exposed to their attacks and raids whenever the king of Norway mustered an army and invaded them.' This was an early statement of the case for free trade: The farmers in West Gothia, close to the border with Norway, needed things 'which would supplement their own produce'. Moreover, they did not want to be exposed to attacks and raids. Upon hearing this, King Olav of the Swedes became even more angry and said that under no circumstances should peace be made with the fat man of Norway. But then the respected old Lawspeaker Thorgny stood up and told the king that he was causing trouble by a war against Norway. 'Should you be unwilling to accept

H. H. Gissurarson (✉)
Reykjavik, Iceland
e-mail: Hannesgi@hi.is

what we demand, then we shall mount an attack against you and kill you and not put up with hostility and lawlessness from you. This is what our forefathers before us have done. They threw five kings into a bog at Mulathing who had become completely full of arrogance like you with us' (Sturluson 2016 [*c.* 1230], pp. 73–74). The people at the assembly reinforced his words with the clashing of weapons and a great din. King Olav of the Swedes grudgingly realised that he had to relent. He promised to make peace with Norway so that the farmers in West Gothia could continue to trade with the farmers on the other side of the border.

The Nordic Political Tradition

In Snorri Sturluson's chronicles, a clear distinction was made between good and bad kings. The good kings respected the ancient law, as accepted and interpreted in popular assemblies. Such assemblies were common to all the Germanic nations and described centuries earlier by the Roman historian Tacitus (1999 [98], Chap. XI). Neither did the good king increase the tax burden, and they allowed the farmers peacefully to produce their goods and trade with one another, or to 'supplement their produce', as Earl Rognvald had put it. The bad kings on the other hand went against time-tested rules and institutions, imposed new taxes on the population and conscripted the farmers and their sons for military adventures home and abroad. Telling was the contrast drawn by Snorri between the first king of Norway, Harold Finehair, and his son, Haakon, foster-son of King Athelstan of England. 'Harold had enslaved and oppressed all people in the land, while Haakon wished everyone well and offered to return the farmers their patrimonies' (Sturluson 2016 [*c.* 1230], p. 88).[1] Snorri, writing in the 1220s and 1230, was observing the attempts by Norwegian kings to extend their power and to replace customary law with royal decrees. Against these new ideas, he upheld the old Nordic traditions of government by the consent of assemblies and the right of rebellion: The king was bound by the law just like his subjects and he could be deposed (and even killed) if he broke the social contract implicit in the law, as Lawspeaker Thorgny had insisted. Perhaps Snorri deserved even more than St. Thomas Aquinas (Acton 1985 [1877], p. 34) to be called 'the First Whig'. Indeed, the leader of the Swedish conservative-liberal party, Prime Minister Bildt (1986), invoked the example of Lawspeaker Thorgny, as described by Snorri: 'A strong sense of justice is not unique to our country.

---

[1] In Icelandic, old and new, there are no family names, Sturluson only meaning that Snorri was the son of Sturla. Therefore, he should be called Snorri rather than Sturluson.

But its role has been important in a country which has never seen slavery or serfdom and where every young student has read the words of Lawspeaker Thorgny.'

In the late Middle Ages, the five Nordic countries were for some of the time divided into three kingdoms, Norway, with Iceland as a tributary, Denmark, and Sweden, which ruled Finland as a part of her realm. From 1380, Denmark, Norway, and Iceland were unified under one monarch, and between 1397 and 1523 the five Nordic countries formed a personal union, the Kalmar Union, under the Danish king, although each country maintained its own law and customs. Although the ancient farmers' assemblies disappeared and were replaced by aristocratic state councils and later by diets of the estates, the population continued to resist attempts by the kings to extend their power. In England, King John had been forced to issue Magna Carta in 1215, and in Denmark, King Erik V. had to issue a royal charter in 1282, promising to impose taxes according to established rules and not to imprison people arbitrarily. Similar provisions were in the royal charters of 1320, 1326 and 1376, and starting in 1448 it became the custom for each Danish king to issue a charter upon assuming the throne. Similar charters were also issued in Sweden, notably by King Magnus Eriksson in 1319: taxes were to be limited and non-arbitrary. In Sweden, it also soon became a custom for each king to issue a charter at the beginning of his reign. The limits on royal power in the Nordic countries were noted elsewhere. The French philosopher Montesquieu observed (2018 [1648], Bk. XI, Chap. 6): 'It suffices to read the excellent work by Tacitus on the ways of the Germans to see that the English got from them the idea of their political government. This elegant system was discovered in the woods.' He added (Bk. XVII, Chap. 5) that the nations of Scandinavia 'have been the resource of liberty in Europe, which is to say of almost all there is of it today among men'.

Chydenius: A Pioneer of Free Trade

In late seventeenth century, however, the Danish and the Swedish kings succeeded in assuming absolute power, in 1660 in Denmark and in 1680 in Sweden, with the difference, however, that in Sweden the Diet of the Estates was not abolished; it consisted of four estates, the nobility, the clergy, the burghers and, exceptionally for Europe, the farmers. Both kings followed mercantilist policies, restricting competition from abroad in the interest of domestic merchants and manufacturers. They also restricted or even prohibited the import of corn (Heckscher 1935, II, p. 93). In the Great Northern

War of 1700–1721, Sweden was defeated by an alliance of Russia, Denmark, and Poland, and lost many of her Baltic possessions. The result was that the position of the king weakened, whereas the Diet of the Estates, the *Riksdag*, gained more power. An 'Era of Freedom' began, as it has been called. Soon, two parties emerged in the Diet, the 'Hats' who sought to restore Sweden to her former glory, and the 'Caps' who wanted peace. In 1765, the clergy in Ostrobothnia in Central Finland elected from their ranks a Swedish-speaking Finn, Pastor Anders Chydenius. He was a supporter of the 'Caps' who were now in majority. Once in Stockholm, he published a pamphlet, *The National Gain,* where he criticised the mercantilist policies of Sweden. He could observe its detrimental effects in his local region. The farmers and burghers of Ostrobothnia were forbidden to sell their products, mainly tar and timber, directly to customers in other countries. Trade had to go through Stockholm, on the other side of the Gulf of Bothnia.

In his pamphlet, Chydenius argued (2012a [1765], §5) '*that each individual will of his own accord gravitate towards the locality and the enterprise where he will most effectively increase the national profit*, provided that the laws do not prevent him from doing so' (italics in the original). He added: 'Each individual pursues his own advantage. That inclination is so natural and necessary that every society in the world is based on it: otherwise laws, penalties and rewards would not even exist and the whole human race would perish completely within a short space of time. That work is always best rewarded that is of the greatest value and that most sought after that is best rewarded.' Chydenius based his argument on each individual's need for the goods and services of others (2012a [1765], §2). 'The needs are manifold, and no one has ever been able, without the help of others, to acquire the minimum of necessities, while there is hardly a nation that has no need of another. The Almighty Himself has made our species such that we ought to cooperate. Should such mutual assistance be obstructed within or beyond a nation, it is contrary to nature.' Thus, eleven years before Adam Smith published the *Wealth of Nations* (1904 [1776]), Chydenius had clearly anticipated his argument for free trade. In the Diet, Chydenius was successful in lifting some of the restrictions on trade in the towns of Ostrobothnia, but most of the reforms he suggested had to wait for the nineteenth century to be implemented. Chydenius was also instrumental in abolishing censorship in Sweden. He argued (2012b [1765]) that in a free competition of ideas, truth would win. Since man was a fallible being, also the censor, nobody should be entrusted with deciding what to publish. The Freedom of Information Act which was passed by the Diet was the first of its kind in the world. When

Chydenius was again a member of the Diet in 1778, he campaigned for religious freedom (2012c [1778]) with the result that Sweden passed a Toleration Act in 1781. Even if the Swedish king in 1772 regained absolute power in a coup, he was in sympathy with many of Chydenius' ideas, and the Diet of the Estates was not abolished.

Disciples of Snorri and Adam Smith at Eidsvoll

In the eighteenth century, the Nordic countries were divided into two kingdoms, Sweden with Finland on the one hand and Denmark with Norway and Iceland on the other hand. While nominally Denmark was even more of an absolutist kingdom than Sweden, with almost no limits on royal power, in practice this power was limited by the strong Nordic legal tradition, and by public opinion. It has therefore been called 'opinion-governed absolutism'. The monarch was supposed to listen to his subjects, weigh their arguments and make decisions for the common good, not favouring any special interests. An Icelandic legal expert observes (Lindal 1981, p. 38): 'Kingship asserted itself but was, in one way or another, forced to recognise and to compromise with the older Germanic scheme.' Perhaps the ideal of a Nordic king could be illuminated by the contrast drawn by French philosopher de Jouvenel (1997 [1957], pp. 40–41) between the *dux*, possessing personal authority and stirring others into action, and the *rex*, invested with institutional authority, moderating and adjusting conflicts. For example, a *dux* was General Napoleon Bonaparte riding on a horse at the bridge in Arcola, egging on his soldiers, whereas a *rex* was King Lewis IX sitting under an oak in Vincennes, dispensing justice to his subjects. Most of the Nordic kings belonged to the category of the *rex*.

Slowly, liberal ideas from abroad began to reinforce the liberal Nordic heritage. In May 1762, Peter and Carsten Anker, sons of a wealthy Norwegian merchant, were on a grand tour of Europe, with their tutor and compatriot Andreas Holt. In Glasgow, the three of them called on the Scottish philosopher Adam Smith. Although Smith had not yet published the *Wealth of Nations*, he was already well-known for his *Theory of Moral Sentiments* (1853 [1759]). The three Norwegians and Smith had a lively discussion and almost two years later, in March 1764, they met again in Toulouse in France, when Smith was now travelling with a tutor to the young Duke of Buccleuch. The three Norwegians all became civil servants, Peter Anker in the Danish Foreign Service and Carsten Anker and Andreas Holt in the Danish civil administration, in what now would be called the Ministry of Finance.

Soon after their friend Adam Smith published his book on economics, they arranged for its translation into Danish, and it came out in two volumes in 1779–1780. In a letter to Holt, Smith expressed his pleasure over the translation (Banke 1955). The ideas of the Scottish philosopher probably played a role when the Danish authorities decided in 1787 to abolish the Danish monopoly trade with Iceland which had greatly impeded economic growth on the island for centuries. Moreover, in the Danish realm, including Norway, tariffs were reduced significantly in 1797. The Danish authorities also encouraged comprehensive land reforms: in the beginning of the nineteenth century, two-thirds of Danish farmers had become owners-occupiers compared to only ten per cent in the mid-eighteenth century (Henriksen 1993).

In the first two decades of the nineteenth century, the Nordic countries underwent dramatic political changes. In 1809, Sweden lost Finland to Russia which resulted in a coup against the Swedish king who was deposed and expelled, with an elderly uncle replacing him and a French general being chosen as his successor. The coup was led by a liberal, Count Georg Adlersparre, who was much influenced by Chydenius, but also by Adam Smith, whose *Wealth of Nations* he partly translated into Swedish. A new constitution for Sweden (or 'Instrument of Government' as it was called) was adopted in 1809, guaranteeing freedom of the press, of religion, and of assembly, as well as the protection of private property, while some royal prerogatives and aristocratic privileges were retained. In 1814, Sweden was promised Norway by the European powers as a compensation for the loss of Finland. But the Norwegians refused to be pawns in a chess game. They wanted an independent state. A Constituent Assembly was convened at Eidsvoll, a manor house near the capital, Oslo (then named Christiania). In the spring of 1814, it adopted a liberal constitution, guaranteeing freedom of the press, and of assembly, and economic freedom: 'New and constant restrictions in the liberty of trades must not be allowed to anybody for the future' (§101). While the Swedes subsequently forced the Norwegians to enter into a personal union with the Swedish king, the Eidsvoll Constitution was retained, with minor changes. It is the second oldest constitution still in force, after the American one. The meeting place, Eidsvoll, was owned and provided by Adam Smith's old friend and disciple Carsten Anker, who could not however himself attend, as he was representing Norway in the United Kingdom. But he undoubtedly had some influence on drafting the constitution, also through his cousin, landowner Peder Anker, who was a delegate and later Prime Minister of Norway. Another delegate, pastor Wergeland (1830, p. 111), wrote that the constitution was 'based on the liberal and now generally accepted principles that the political philosophers have established', by which he presumably meant John Locke, David Hume, Adam Smith, and the American Founding Fathers. But the ancient Nordic traditions of government by consent and legal certainty also influenced the constitution. The constitution's main author, lawyer Christian Magnus Falsen, mentioned the account by Snorri Sturluson of the reign of King Hakon the Good. The Norwegians were returning to their roots, Falsen argued. As in King Hakon's time, the new Constitution vested the legislative power in the people, he claimed (Castberg 1949, p. 71). Yet another Eidsvoll delegate, the industrialist Jacob Aall, later translated Snorri's history of Norway into Norwegian (Aall 1838–1839).

Liberal Statesmen: Gripenstedt and Schweigaard

It had taken two dramatic defeats to break the power of the Swedish kings, the loss of the Baltic possessions in 1721, and the loss of Finland in 1809. Consequently, the Swedes turned from warfare to trade. The motto became, in the words of the poet Esaias Tegnér, to conquer inside the borders of Sweden what had been lost outside, by harnessing the forces of nature. In the decades after the adoption of the 1809 constitution, the king and the Diet of the Estates repeatedly engaged in power struggles, but in 1848 a committed liberal, Baron Johan August Gripenstedt, was appointed Minister without Portfolio and between 1856 and 1866 he was Minister of Finance and the most influential person in Sweden, supported by another liberal, Baron Louis Gerard De Geer, Minister of Justice in 1858–1870. Under Gripenstedt's leadership, Sweden made a peaceful liberal revolution. Private property rights were secured. Regulations hampering the timber and iron industries were lifted. The guilds were abolished. Institutions of capitalism such as limited companies and banks were established. Freedom of the press and religion were expanded. Women won the right to own property, attend schools and have a career. Controls on the internal movement of people were abolished. In 1865, Gripenstedt even made Sweden a member of the free trade treaty between France and Great Britain. In the same year, the old Diet of the Estates was replaced by a modern parliament which convened for the first time in 1867. Gripenstedt was a disciple of Bastiat, and on 4 June 1857, he told a sceptical audience that soon Sweden would abolish poverty and ignorance, through free trade, the full use of the nation's potential, specialisation and innovation: 'We can with certainty predict a development to which perhaps no other country in Europe can equal. This requires, however, that the resources we have, but which still for the most part lie dormant, unexploited, are duly utilized.' His speech was dismissed as 'flower paintings', but in fact, in the period from 1870 to 1970 Sweden went from being one of the poorest countries of Western Europe to being one of the richest, after Switzerland and Luxembourg (Norberg 2023).

The task facing the Norwegians after establishing a sovereign state in a personal union with Sweden, having been governed from Copenhagen since 1380, was to build a nation. The most influential nation builder in Norway was Anton Martin Schweigaard, a child prodigy from a modest background who had in 1835 taken up teaching of Jurisprudence and Economics at the University of Oslo (Christiania), to become a Professor in 1840. He was a committed liberal who had as a young man published a pamphlet (1836) in defence of free trade. In 1842 he became a member of the Norwegian Parliament, and he was its most prominent and powerful member until he retired in 1869. His friend and fellow liberal Frederik Stang was Prime Minister from 1861 to 1880. Together, Schweigaard and Stang practically ruled Norway from 1845 to 1880, significantly liberalising the economy. In 1842–1866, all restrictions on internal trade were lifted, and in 1866 all artisan privileges were abolished. Protective tariffs were greatly reduced or abolished, and the government built roads, canals, bridges, railways, and telegraph wires. In 1875, Norway joined the Scandinavian Monetary Union which Sweden and Denmark had founded two years earlier. The three Scandinavian *kronor* or *kroner* were equivalent and freely interchangeable in the three countries, and all were based on the gold standard. (In practice, although not formally, the same applied to the Icelandic *kronur*, first issued in 1885.) Schweigaard also did his utmost to promote the ideal of Norwegians as a nation of seafarers. In 1840, he exclaimed: 'Make the Norwegian shipping as free as possible! This argument cannot be repeated too often and not strongly enough to anybody that sees Norway as a shipping nation. The widest horizons are revealing themselves!' (Fasting 2013, p. 49). At the end of the nineteenth century, Norway had the fourth-largest merchant fleet in the world. Schweigaard was however, like Stang in Norway and Gripenstedt and De Geer in Sweden, a pragmatic rather than a dogmatic liberal (Sørensen 1988). His guiding principles were free trade and private property, whereas he saw an important role for government in facilitating commerce. In this, he was a faithful student of Adam Smith and David Hume. In his *Wealth of Nations*, Smith mentioned roads, bridges, canals, and harbours, all of which would facilitate commerce (1904 [1776], p. 216). Hume also thought that some tasks could not be left to private initiative. 'Thus, bridges are built; harbours open'd; ramparts rais'd; canals form'd; fleets equip'd, and armies disciplin'd, every where, by the care of government' (1896 [1739], p. 539).

Norwegian liberalism was not confined to urban elites. It had its own Norwegian traits, best represented by two extraordinary individuals. In 1796, a poor farmer's son, Hans Nielsen Hauge, had a religious vision whereupon he travelled around Norway, preaching and building up a large following. Imprisoned several times for violating a ban on lay preaching, Hauge was also a successful entrepreneur who invested in real estate, farms, and copper mines, owned nine ships, built grain mills, paper mills, and textile mills, distilled salt, produced fishing gear, established a printing house, a brick factory and trade stations along the coast of Southern Norway, and acted as a banker to his followers. He believed that people could best serve God by producing profits. 'Those who will not work should rather not eat,' he said. 'I will, however, build Factories, be involved in Trade, work in the help of Crafts, and when Time and Energy allows, preferably cultivate the Land' (Grytten 2021, p. 25). Some of the liberal Eidsvoll men were Haugians. Another very Norwegian character was the farmer Søren Pedersen Jaabæk who was member of parliament between 1845 and 1891. An intelligent autodidact, he was a relentless critic of public profligacy, voting against all proposals to extend government activities (earning him the nickname Neibæk, as in Norwegian 'yes' is 'jaa' and 'no' is 'nei'). He proudly exclaimed: 'I consider myself to be a disciple of Adam Smith and Frédéric Bastiat' (Petterson 1982). Perhaps the Norwegian urban establishment did not appreciate him, but the farmers did.

Liberalism in Iceland and Finland

The pioneer of Icelandic liberalism in the nineteenth century, Jon Sigurdsson, was also the leader of Iceland's struggle for independence. He argued (1848) for national self-determination on three grounds: that Iceland had since the establishment of a Commonwealth in 930 been a sovereign country, but from 1262 in a personal union with first the Norwegian and then the Danish king; that the Icelanders were a distinct nation, speaking their own language and sharing a long history; and that they generally knew better than officials in Copenhagen what was in their own interest. The third argument was of course the liberal argument for decentralisation, or, if you will, the Catholic principle of subsidiarity. Jon was also a firm supporter of free trade. 'We have advanced the most when we have travelled widely and traded with other countries, but with many countries, not only with just one,' he observed (1842, pp. 146–147). He once said in a letter (1866) to his brother who had expressed doubts about free trade: 'You think that someone will absorb us. Let them all absorb us in the sense that they trade with us and do business with us. Freedom is not about living alone and not having anything to do with others. I doubt that Simeon Stylites or Diogenes were freer than any other unfettered people. True enough, freedom comes mostly from within, but no freedom relevant in society is realized except in exchanges, and they are therefore necessary for freedom.' Jon was mainly influenced by French economist Jean-Baptiste Say and English philosopher John Stuart Mill, whereas the author of the first book in Icelandic on economics (1880), Pastor Arnljotur Olafsson, was a disciple of Bastiat. Two milestones in the liberalisation of the Icelandic economy were the abolition of the last restrictions on free trade with other countries in 1855, and the adoption of a liberal Constitution, modelled on the Danish Constitution, in 1874. The fisheries in which Iceland had a comparative advantage replaced agriculture as the dominant economic sector. The islanders began their long and arduous journey to prosperity.

Finland was like Iceland a Nordic outlier. She had been ruled as a part of Sweden until Russia seized her in 1809 and turned her into a Grand Duchy under the Russian Tsar. The Finnish legal tradition was therefore Nordic in origin, and as in Sweden, the farmers were represented in the Finnish Diet of the Estates, alongside the nobility, clergy, and burghers. In the nineteenth century, strong voices were raised in defence of free trade, not least after Finnish scholars rediscovered their compatriot Anders Chydenius. They also stressed the tradition of liberty under the law, for example, Johan Jakob Nordström, Professor of Constitutional Law at the University of Helsinki (then the Imperial Alexander University). The influential journalist Carl Quist wrote: 'The cheaper a product can be obtained, the cheaper its purchase will be, it may now be produced anywhere, within the country or abroad, on this or on the other side of the sea, by the nearest neighbors or by the antipodes. And, as the profit of the individual is also that of the nation, the nation in its entirety can only benefit from an unrestricted free trade system' (Grandell 2021, p. 243). Finland got her own currency in 1860, the *markka*. It was tied to a silver standard in 1865, and moved to a gold standard in 1878. In the 1860s, mercantilism was abandoned, limited companies were founded, railways were laid, banks were established, wood processing in which Finland had a comparative advantage became important. When the Russian Emperor first summoned the Diet of the Estates in 1863, liberals turned out to be in the majority in two of the four estates, the nobility and the burghers. In 1879, freedom of trade was greatly extended (Grandell 2021, p. 250). Questions about free trade and protectionism were however long overshadowed by two contentious issues: the relationship with Russia, and the co-existence of a Finnish-speaking majority and a Swedish-speaking minority which had under

Swedish rule formed somewhat of an overclass. Some Finns wanted to accommodate their mighty neighbour, while others sought to defy the Russian bear. Some Finns wanted to make Finnish the only recognised national language, under the slogan 'One Nation, One Language', while the Swedish-speaking minority resisted this.

Grundtvig and Civil Society

In Denmark, economic liberalism remained strong in the nineteenth century, whereas the fortunes of political liberalism varied. In 1848, the Danish king renounced his absolute power, and a liberal constitution was adopted by a Constituent Assembly in 1849. A remarkable Danish pastor, poet and philosopher, Nikolaj F. S. Grundtvig, was a member of the Constituent Assembly where he expressed his conviction that the constitution being drafted should essentially be a restatement in modern terms of ancient Nordic legal principles. Grundtvig warned against socialist ideas coming from abroad:

> However, in drawing up this sound basic law, we must at the same time beware of any provisions that may seem beneficial today but damaging tomorrow. Indeed, we must be particularly on guard against all grandiloquent forms of speech, which are always unclear and, when it comes to it, can often do harm but never any good. Thus in a basic law we must not turn the practice of authority into a duty to feed and clothe the people; on the contrary, it is the people who must feed and clothe the authority. Nor must we make it a civic duty for the rich to feed and clothe the poor, for all experience teaches us that this turns the entire people into paupers who can feed and clothe neither themselves nor one another (Grundtvig 2019c [1848], p. 234).

Ultimately, Grundtvig did not vote for the final draft of the Constitution, because it was too good to be rejected and too bad to be accepted, he said, its main defect being restricted franchise to the upper house of the new parliament. Grundtvig was like some of the Eidsvoll men in Norway influenced by Snorri Sturluson whose history of Norway he translated into Danish, with a perceptive introduction (1818). He followed the German philosopher Johann Gottfried von Herder in believing that there was such a thing as a national spirit, expressed in language, literature, folkways, folk songs, legends and myths. The Danish spirit was a Nordic spirit, and in his epic poem, 'Northern Mythology' (2011 [1832], p. 49), Grundtvig exclaimed:

Freedom our watchword must be in the North!
Freedom for Loki as well as for Thor.

Loke and Thor were heathen gods, *Aesir*. Loki was a clever rogue and slanderer whereas Thor was a hero and fighter. Grundtvig was here emphasising the need for free speech, also for those who hold unpopular opinions or belong to a minority. But the main message of this work, and many others by Grundtvig, was that the Danes should reaffirm their identity as a Nordic nation. An important part of it was Grundtvig's idea of people's high schools which should provide common people with basic education, but also to instil in them a pride in their culture, self-reliance and hard work. Their task was twofold, to build the individuals and the nation.

In the mid-nineteenth century, the Danes were preoccupied with the Schleswig question. Since the Middle Ages, the Danish king had also been Duke of Schleswig and Holstein. The Northern half of Schleswig spoke Danish and considered themselves to be Danes. The Southern half spoke German, whereas all of Holstein spoke German. Holstein was a member of the German Confederation, but not Schleswig. The so-called National Liberals in Denmark wanted to abandon Holstein, but to annex the whole of Schleswig, thus forcing her German speakers, about half the population, to become Danish citizens. The German Confederation vehemently opposed this. They regarded Schleswig as an integral part of Germany. Grundtvig was almost the only person in either Denmark or Germany to hold the liberal position that the inhabitants of Schleswig should choose themselves whether to be Danes or Germans: 'The land of Denmark stretches only so far as the language is spoken, and certainly no farther than people wish to speak Danish, in other words, somewhere that no one knows in the middle of the duchy of Schleswig' (Grundtvig [1848] 2019a, p. 111). He expressed the same idea in a poem ([1848], 2019b, p. 230):

Of a 'people' all are members
Who regard themselves as such,
Those whose mother-tongue sounds sweetest,
And their fatherland love much.

Denmark fought two wars over Schleswig against an alliance of German states, in 1848–1851, when the main European powers forced the Germans to accept Danish rule in the two duchies, and in 1864 when she was heavily defeated by the Prussians and their allies, and lost the two duchies.

This was the second heavy blow to Denmark, after the loss of Norway fifty years earlier. Now she had become almost a pure nation-state, albeit with some small possessions left in the North Atlantic and the Caribbean. But not least under Grundtvig's influence, the Danes turned defeat into a victory by liberalising the economy and encouraging the growth of civil society. They reacted like the Swedes to the loss of the Baltic possessions and then of Finland. Their attitude was summed up by the admonition of the Danish poet Hans Peter Holst to 'turn an external loss into an internal gain'. Farmers, often educated in Grundtvigian high schools, formed cooperatives based on mutual gain, and when cheap grain from the United States flooded European markets, the Danish response was not protectionism, but rather an adjustment to new conditions, substituting livestock for grain, with Denmark becoming a major supplier of cheese, butter and pork, mostly to the large British market. This was a development that had begun earlier, with agricultural reforms in the late eighteenth and early nineteenth centuries, not least with innovations by landowners and agricultural entrepreneurs (Lampe et al. 2019). The farmers' cooperatives then adopted those innovations and provided the social integration of farmers. They were rather an effect than a cause. By 'maintaining free trade, the Danes adhered to a national tradition of liberalism, a reflection of a small economy without any domestic mineral resources', an economic historian comments (Henriksen 1993, p. 156). In 1920, Grundtvig's sensible proposal for a solution of the Schleswig problem was also implemented: The population of Schleswig was allowed to choose in plebiscites between Denmark and Germany in two regions, the Northern part choosing Denmark and the Southern part of Germany, with the result that the Danish-German border was moved southwards. Grundtvig's influence was also felt in the other Nordic countries and undoubtedly contributed to the social cohesion, high level of trust and great strength of civil society which facilitated economic progress in all of them. In a conversation with Copenhagen Mayor Ernst Kaper in 1940, shortly after the Nazis had occupied Denmark, a German officer spoke admiringly about the self-discipline of the Danes. Kaper retorted: 'This is not discipline; it is culture' (Kaper 1944, p. 283).

Swedish Liberalism in the Era of Social Democracy

In early twentieth century, suddenly there were five sovereign Nordic countries. Norway seceded from Sweden in 1905 and became an independent kingdom. Finland seceded from Russia in 1917 and became a republic. Iceland amicably parted ways with Denmark in 1918, becoming first a kingdom in a personal union with the Danish king and then a republic in 1944. Although the world moved towards protectionism in the late nineteenth century, Denmark and Norway maintained free trade, not least because the United Kingdom was their main customer. Sweden had however in the late nineteenth century introduced protective tariffs on corn. But in the early twentieth century, a new challenge emerged to the liberal Nordic heritage, the Social Democrats. Like the kings of the past, they wanted to extend the power of government, and like the kings, they asserted that in this they had only in mind the public interest. The difference was that they thought of themselves as being chosen by the grace of the People, and not like the kings of the past by the grace of God. Although all the Nordic countries managed to stay out of the First World War (even Finland, although she was a Grand Duchy under the Russian Tsar), they were subject to the same rupture of trade as other European countries. The Scandinavian Monetary Union broke up at the beginning of the war, and efforts afterwards to restore it failed. Social Democrats took power in all three Scandinavian countries in the 1920s and 1930s and dominated politics for the next fifty years. The durability of their rule was extraordinary. In Denmark, they led the government for 37 of the 49 years between 1924 and 1973. In Norway, they led the government for 41 of the 53 years between 1928 and 1981. In Sweden, they led the government for 49 of the 56 years between 1920 and 1976. In Denmark and Sweden, the Social Democrats tried to be moderate and flexible, while they were more radical in Norway. They were ambivalent about free trade rather than against it. Like the kings of the absolutist period, they were however in all three countries constrained by the Nordic liberal tradition. They even sometimes claimed to be a part of it. In a speech on Grundtvig's 150th anniversary in 1933, a leading Danish Social Democrat said: 'The reason why the Danish people cannot be infected by Nazism and fascism is not least Grundtvig's mighty effort to educate the people' (Korsgaard 2015, p. 327). The famous expression coined by the Swedish Social Democrats to describe their ideal, the People's Home, *folkhemmet*, was certainly also about national unity rather than class struggle.

In Sweden, two prominent economists, Gustav Cassel and Eli F. Heckscher, were strong supporters of free trade. 'Either an economic sector is profitable, and then it does not need tariff protection; or it is not profitable, and then it does not deserve tariff protection,' Heckscher observed (Norberg 1998, p. 232). In the 1930s, Cassel (1934) and Heckscher (1934) also presented cogent arguments against central economic planning, in many ways anticipating Hayek's *Road to Serfdom* (1944). Probably they had some moderating influence on leading Social Democrats in Sweden and the other

Nordic countries. However, Cassel's ablest student Gunnar Myrdal was a firm believer in social engineering on a large scale. In the 1930s, he was, for example, a forceful advocate of sterilisation. It was necessary to 'circumscribe the reproductive freedom of the slightly feeble-minded' (Myrdal et al. 1934, p. 223). A sterilisation bill was passed by the Swedish parliament in 1934, and between 1935 and 1975, 62,888 individuals were subjected to sterilisation, mostly women. Now this is regarded as a grotesque mistake, and the Swedish state has paid out compensation to the victims (Spektorowski et al. 2004). In the 1940s, Myrdal became convinced that after the Second World War, the United States would plunge into a depression. Often wrong, but never in doubt, he devoted a book (1944) to this prognosis. Accordingly, as Minister of Trade in 1945–1947 he made a huge trade deal with the Soviet Union, with generous credit provisions. This turned out to be a costly blunder. There was no depression. Swedish companies met little problems in selling their products in Western Europe. When Myrdal faced a storm of protest, and harsh personal criticism for his pro-Soviet position, he resigned in anger and left politics. Nevertheless, with Cassel and Heckscher departed, in the 1950s and 1960s economic liberalism found few articulate spokesmen in Sweden. The eloquent political theorist Herbert Tingsten had in 1944 been convinced by Hayek that central economic planning might lead to a police state. But at the founding meeting in 1947 of Hayek's liberal debating club, the Mont Pelerin Society, he had a row with Ludwig von Mises. Mises had categorically rejected income redistribution as a possible part of the liberal agenda. Tingsten angrily strode out and muttered to himself: 'If this is liberalism, then I am still a socialist' (1963, p. 334). He attended no further meetings of the Society. The prominent economist Bertil Ohlin who became leader of the Liberal Party was also influenced by Hayek's book, but did not join the Mont Pelerin Society: He did not want to be identified with 'old liberalism'. Instead, he presented his 'social liberalism' to the Swedes (1936). Both Tingsten and Ohlin remained however ardent defenders of free trade.

Norwegian Liberalism in the Era of Social Democracy

In twentieth-century Norway, policy makers and economists tended to be much more sceptical about free trade and capitalism than in the other Nordic countries, doubtlessly under the influence of Professor Ragnar Frisch and his 'Oslo School'. Frisch was a man of the Hard Left, first supporting the Labour Party, later the Socialist People's Party. He was, like Myrdal in Sweden, convinced that the United States would plunge into a depression after the Second World War. In 1947, he wrote that the United States would be 'a textbook example about the terrible convulsions modern capitalism would go through when it was allowed to develop freely' (Søeilen 1998, p. 54). His closest associate at the University of Oslo, Leif Johansen, was a member of the Norwegian Communist Party and a lifelong supporter of the Soviet Union. In 1960, Johansen publicly presented the 'calculation of the century': When would the Soviet Union overtake the United States in GDP and in GDP per capita? His answer was: in GDP 10–11 years and in GDP per capita 17–18 years (Thalberg 2000). Frisch went even further. In 1961, he wrote: 'The blinkers will fall once and for all at the end of the 1960s (perhaps before). At this time the Soviets will have surpassed the US in industrial production. But then it will be too late for the West to see the truth' (Sæther et al. 2014, p. 63). Under the influence of Frisch and his disciples, many of whom became civil servants or Labour Party politicians, or both, Norway kept strict restrictions on foreign trade longer than the other Scandinavian countries, although she reluctantly had to abolish some of them when she accepted Marshall aid from the United States and joined the Organisation of European Economic Cooperation, OEEC (later the Organisation of Economic Cooperation and Development, OECD), and the General Agreement on Tariffs and Trade, GATT. This 'saved the country from the worst excesses of a regime bent on economic planning' (Sæther et al. 2014, p. 59).

Frisch and Johansen were not Keynesians who wanted to save capitalism by reforming it. They wanted to replace capitalism not with classical socialism, but with an economic system where regulators held almost all the power. They tended to ignore or dismiss the knowledge problem, although a Norwegian economist and writer, Trygve Hoff, had written a book (1938) explaining it: how the regulators were unable to accumulate and process all the knowledge necessary to adjust economic activities. For example, one of Frisch's disciples, Odd Aukrust, in 1948 wrote to another of Frisch's disciples, Petter Jacob Bjerve, that now total consumption had turned out to be much larger than the planners had foreseen. He had suggested that these numbers should be concealed. 'I can just see the right-wing press exclaim: Here total national income has been underestimated by a billion, while some still think that one can govern by detailed planning' (Søeilen 1998, p. 72). Of course, Aukrust later was appointed Director of Research at Statistics Norway. The recipient of the letter, Bjerve, later became Director of Statistics Norway and then went into politics, serving as Finance Minister from 1960–1963. He said as late as 1981 that it was widely accepted that 'public servants managed resource allocation better than the interest rate mechanism' (Eriksen et al. 2007,

p. 18). The record hardly bears Bjerve out, however. The relevant period to study is from 1950 until the mid-1970s, before the oil boom. Then, the average annual economic growth in Norway was similar to that in the other Nordic countries, but crucially, the investment ratio was around 30, much higher than in the other two Scandinavian countries, Sweden and Denmark, where it was around 20. 'Year after year Norwegians sacrificed better living (consumption) to pay extra for only average growth rates' (Sæther et al. 2014, p. 67).

Trade in North and South

Although the Nordic spirit (as Grundtvig would put it) was and is relatively liberal, it also has had a puritanical streak, where puritanism could be described somewhat facetiously as the haunting fear that someone somewhere might be happy (Mencken, 1949, Chap. 30). A manifestation of such puritanism was the strength of the temperance movements in all the Nordic countries except Denmark. Those movements campaigned not only for private moderation but also for a total nationwide ban on producing and selling alcohol. In Sweden, such a proposal was narrowly defeated in a 1922 referendum, but prohibition was imposed in Finland in 1919–1932, in Norway in 1917–1927, and in Iceland in 1915–1935. It did not achieve its stated goal of reducing demand for alcohol, whereas smugglers and bootleggers thrived. But in Norway and Iceland, prohibition also had an ironic and unintended consequence. Both countries exported a lot of fish to the wine-growing countries of Southern Europe, Spain, Portugal, and Italy where Catholics were allowed during Lent to eat fish but not meat. These countries found the import ban on their products unacceptable and threatened to retaliate and ban fish imports from Norway and Iceland. In 1922, both Norway and Iceland bowed to pressure and allowed the import of wine, although both countries retained the ban on distilled beverages for a while. In Finland, trade with Southern Europe was less of a concern, but as the failure of prohibition became evident, public opinion changed and the ban was abolished. Upon abandoning prohibition, all three countries (and Sweden as well) established state monopolies for selling wines and hard liquor, whereas such beverages were and are freely available over the counter in Denmark.

In the early twentieth century, Denmark was one of the few countries in the world, with the United Kingdom, which did not abandon free trade. The party supported by most Danish farmers, *Venstre* (which literally means the Left), was strongly in favour of free trade. Its longtime leader, Thomas

Madsen-Mygdal, Prime Minister from 1926 to 1929, fervently believed in free competition to encourage hard work and eliminate mistakes: 'Let that fall which cannot stand,' was his refrain. Many members of the Conservative Party were also sympathetic to economic liberalism (Kurrild-Klitgaard 2015). In Denmark, like Sweden, Hayek's *Road to Serfdom* prompted a lively discussion about democracy and socialism. Two eminent Danish economists became members of Hayek's Mont Pelerin Society, Thorkil Kristensen and Carl Iversen, but they drifted, like Bertil Ohlin and Herbert Tingsten in Sweden, from classical to social liberalism. Despite vast outlays on welfare under the Social Democrats, the Danish economy nevertheless remained open and relatively free.

In Iceland, the conservative-liberal Right was unified in the Independence Party, founded in 1929 by Jon Thorlaksson, a disciple of Gustav Cassel, whereas the Left was divided, with a strong communist element. Jon was in many ways similar to Denmark's Madsen-Mygdal. But in the Great Depression, stringent import, currency and investment controls were imposed in Iceland by centre-left governments. Icelandic farmers, unlike their Danish colleagues, were protectionists, barely surviving on a windswept, inhospitable island and fearing competition from more fertile regions of the world. Because rural districts were vastly over-represented in the Icelandic Parliament they long held power. The economic controls were however slowly removed in three major steps, in 1950, 1960, and 1970 (when Iceland joined EFTA, the European Free Trade Area, which had been founded by the United Kingdom, Sweden, Denmark, and Norway in 1960), and after developing a sustainable and profitable system of utilising her fertile fishing grounds, Iceland prospered (Gissurarson 2015).

Finland used the opportunity after Russia's defeat in her 1904–1905 war against Japan to abolish the old Diet of the Estates in 1906, establish a modern parliament and introduce universal suffrage, also for women. Language remained a contentious issue in Finnish politics, but soon another contentious issue presented itself: socialism. After Finland declared independence from Russia in late 1917, a short but violent civil war was fought where the Right defeated the Left. In 1919 a republican constitution was adopted. The two presidential candidates were both representatives of the conservative-liberal European tradition (Gissurarson 2020), General Carl Gustaf Mannerheim and Law Professor Kaarlo Juho Ståhlberg. Mannerheim had led the forces of the Right in the civil war, but both he and Ståhlberg were steeped in the Fenno-Swedish legal tradition. Ståhlberg who was elected as President had drafted the constitution. Mannerheim later became President.

The language problem was solved by ensuring the rights of the Swedish-speaking minority. Autonomy was also granted to the Swedish-speaking inhabitants of the Åland Islands. In connection with the Second World War Finland fought three wars, first defending herself against a Soviet attack in the Winter War of 1939–1940, then trying to regain lost territory in a war against the Soviet Union in 1941–1944 and then again driving out the German forces from the country in 1944. After the war, Finland was burdened with huge war reparations to the Soviet Union. Because of Soviet opposition, she could not participate in the Marshall plan. Nevertheless, Finland maintained an open economy, upheld the rule of law and prospered, like the other Nordic countries.

Conclusions

Free trade can hardly be discussed in isolation from the institutional framework establishing and maintaining it. It requires the rule of law, at least to some extent, to bring about what David Hume called the 'performance of promises', as essential to the free and just order according to him as the 'stability of possession' and 'its translation by consent'. The Nordic countries developed this framework long ago: as early as 1018, the farmers of West Gothia in Sweden demanded freedom to trade with the Norwegian farmers across the border. The Nordic countries have also provided good examples of the peaceful resolution of political conflicts between countries, crucial to free trade: the autonomy in Finland of the Swedish-speaking Åland islanders after 1917 and the change of the Danish-German border according to plebiscites in 1920. In the late twentieth century, the five Nordic countries were all staunch supporters of international free trade, not only in the OEEC, later the OECD, and GATT, but also in EFTA, and in the European Union which was joined by three of the five Nordic countries, Sweden, Denmark, and Finland, while the remaining two, Norway and Iceland, are members of the EEA, European Economic Area, participating in the European internal market, but without all the political and legal obligations which follow from full membership of the EU. In all the Nordic countries in late twentieth century, the intellectual and political hegemony of Social Democrats was broken. It came to be recognised that the success of the Nordic countries was not because but rather in spite of social democracy. It was based on three main pillars, the rule of law, free trade, and social cohesion. Indeed, the economies of the five Nordic countries are relatively free. In 2021, all five Nordic economies were in the freest quartile of the world. Denmark comes

7th, Iceland 14th, Finland and Sweden tie in the 17th place, and Norway comes 29th, of the 165 jurisdictions surveyed (Gwartney et al. 2023). It is no coincidence that small economies are often free and prosperous. It is because they tend to be open. Paradoxically, the economic integration of the world economy, or 'globalisation', may have facilitated political disintegration or rather the proliferation of small states: they are able to enjoy the benefits of the division of labour and free trade, while maintaining their distinct political structures.

It is sometimes said that if goods cannot cross borders, soldiers will. The great truth in this is of course the contrast between trying to get something from others by offering an acceptable price for it and seizing it by force. It is the contrast between trade and warfare, between the views of Earl Rognvald on the one hand and King Olav of the Swedes on the other hand. The two leading Nordic countries Sweden and Denmark demonstrate the blessings bestowed on countries which turn from warfare to trade. But the Nordic countries may also provide other interesting examples in international relations. Why is the conflict between Russia and Ukraine about borders not resolved by allowing plebiscites in the contested areas, as was done in Schleswig in 1920? And if Russia finds Ukraine's possible membership of the EU and of NATO, the North Atlantic Treaty Organisation, so unacceptable that she is willing to go to war against Ukraine to stop it, would a possible way out be for Ukraine to become member of the EEA like Norway and Iceland? Moreover, is not the autonomy of the Åland Islands a model for the treatment of small minorities within the borders of bigger countries, such as the Palestinians on the West Bank of Jordan? There would be enormous possibilities for free trade between the Arab countries and Israel, with all the Arab oil money and the extensive technical knowledge in Israel on how to deal with arid regions. Perhaps the Nordic countries should in the near future not try only to promote free trade directly, as they are indeed doing, but also indirectly by suggesting peaceful solutions of political conflicts, based on their own experience and heritage.

References

Aall J (1838–1839) Snorre Sturlesons Norske kongers sagaer, I–III. Guldberg, Christiania

Acton J (1985 [1877]) The history of freedom in christianity. In: Fears JR (ed) Selected writings of lord acton, vol I. Liberty Fund, Indianapolis IN

Banke N (1955) Om Adam Smiths Forbindelse med Norge og Danmark. Nationaløkonomisk Tidskrift 93:170–178

Bildt C (1986) Frihetens parti. Moderata samlingspartiet, Stockholm
Cassel G (1934) From protectionism through planned economy to dictatorship. International Conciliation 16(1934–1935):307–325
Castberg F (1949) Norsk livssyn og samfunnsliv. Aschehoug, Oslo
Chydenius A (2012a [1765]) The national gain. In: Jonasson M, Hyttinen P (eds) Anticipating the wealth of nations: the selected works of Anders Chydenius, 1729–1803. Routledge, London, pp 142–165
Chydenius A (2012b [1765]) Memorial on the freedom of printing. In: Jonasson M, Hyttinen P (eds) Anticipating the wealth of nations: the selected works of Anders Chydenius, 1729–1803. Routledge, London, pp 219–225
Chydenius A (2012c [1779]) Memorial regarding freedom of religion. In: Jonasson M, Hyttinen P (eds) Anticipating the wealth of nations: the selected works of Anders Chydenius, 1729–1803. Routledge, London, pp 317–322
Constitution (1814) The constitution of the Kingdom of Norway. Jacob Lehmann, Christiania
de Jouvenel B (1997 [1957]) Sovereignty. An inquiry into the political good. Liberty Fund, Indianapolis IN
Eriksen IE, Hanisch TJ, Sæther A (2007) The rise and fall of the Oslo School. Nordic J. Polit. Econ. 33(1):1–31
Fasting M (2013) Torkel Aschehoug and Norwegian historical economic thought. Anthem Press, London
Gissurarson HH (2015) The Icelandic fisheries: sustainable and profitable. University of Iceland Press, Reykjavik
Gissurarson HH (2020) Twenty-four conservative-liberal thinkers, vols I–II. New Direction, Brussels
Grandell J (2021) Classical liberalism in Finland. Econ Watch J 18(2):235–256
Grundtvig NFS (2011 [1832]) Nordic mythology, extract. In: Broadbridge E, Warren C, Jonas U (eds) The school for life. N. F. S. Grundtvig on education for the people. Aarhus University Press, Aarhus, 43–50
Grundtvig NFS (1818) Norges Konge-Krønike af Snorro Sturlesøn, vol 1. Schultziske Officin, Kiøbenhavn
Grundtvig NFS (2019a [1848]) Speech to the Schleswig aid society on 14 March 1848. In: Broadbridge E, Korsgaard O (eds) The common good. N. F. S. Grundtvig as politician and contemporary historian. Aarhus University Press, Aarhus, 251–255
Grundtvig NFS (2019b [1848]) "Of the people" is our watchword. In: Broadbridge E, Korsgaard O (eds) The common good. N. F. S. Grundtvig as Politician and Contemporary Historian. Aarhus University Press, Aarhus, 230–231
Grundtvig NFS (2019c [1848]) On the concept of 'basic law' and the state constitution in Denmark. In: Broadbridge E, Korsgaard O (eds) The common good. N. F. S. Grundtvig as politician and contemporary historian. Aarhus University Press, Aarhus, 232–237

Grytten OH (2021) The entrepreneurial legacy of Hans Nielsen Hauge. In: Grytten OH, Liland T (eds) In the legacy of Hans Nielsen Hauge. Bodoni, Bergen, pp 19–38

Gwartney J, Lawson R, Murphy R (2023) Economic freedom of the world: 2023 annual report. Fraser Institute, Vancouver BC

Hayek FA (1944) The road to serfdom. Routledge, London

Heckscher EF (1934) Planned economy past and present. Index IX(5):91–105

Heckscher EF (1935) Mercantilism, vols. I–II (1931). George Allen & Unwin, London

Henriksen I (1993) The transformation of Danish agriculture 1870–1914. In: Persson KG (ed) The economic development of Denmark and Norway since 1870. Edward Elgar, Aldershot, pp 153–178

Hoff T (1938) Økonomisk kalkulasjon i socialistiske samfund. Aschehoug, Oslo

Hume D (1896 [1739]) A treatise of human nature. Clarendon Press, Oxford

Kaper E (1944) Efterladte Memoireblade. Liv og virke. Nordisk forlag, København

Korsgaard O (2015) Grundtvig's idea of a people's high school. In: Hall JA, Korsgaard O, Pedersen OK (eds) Building the nation: N.F.S. Grundtvig and Danish National Identity. Djøf Publishing, Copenhagen

Kurrild-Klitgaard P (2015) Classical liberalism and modern political economy in Denmark. Econ J Watch 12(3):400–431

Lampe M, Sharp P (2019) A land of milk and butter: how elites created the modern Danish dairy industry. University of Chicago Press, Chicago

Lindal S (1981) Early democratic traditions in the Nordic countries. In: Allardt E (ed) Nordic democracy: ideas, issues, and institutions in politics, economy, education, social and cultural affairs of Denmark, Finland, Iceland, Norway, and Sweden. Det danske Selskab, Copenhagen, pp 15–41

Mencken HL (1949) A Mencken Chrestomathy. Albert Knopf, New York

Montesquieu CL (2018 [1648]) The spirit of the law. Cambridge University Press, Cambridge

Myrdal A, Myrdal G (1934) Kris I befolkningsfrågan. Albert Bonniers Förlag, Stockholm

Myrdal G (1944) Varning för fredsoptimismen. Albert Bonniers Förlag, Stockholm

Norberg J (1998) Den svenska liberalismens historia. Timbro, Stockholm

Norberg J (2023) The mirage of Swedish socialism. The economic history of a welfare state. Fraser Institute, Vancouver

Ohlin B (1936) Fri eller dirigerad economi. Folkpartiets ungdomsförbund, Stockholm

Olafsson A (1880) Audfraedi. Hid islenska bokmenntafelag, Reykjavik

Petterson PB (1982) Liberaleren fra Lista. Et nytt blikk på Søren Jaabæk (1814–1894). Ideer om frihet 2

Sigurdsson J (1842) Um Skola a Islandi. Ny Felagsrit 2:67–167

Sigurdsson J (1848) Hugvekja til Islendinga. Ny Felagsrit 8:11–16

Sigurdsson J (1866) Letter to Jens Sigurdsson 3 October. Lbs. 2591 4to. Icelandic National Library

Smith A (1853 [1759]) The theory of moral sentiments. Henry G. Bohn, London

Smith A (1904 [1776]) An inquiry into the nature and causes of the wealth of nations. Methuen, London

Spektorowski A, Mizrachi E (2004) Eugenics and the welfare state in Sweden: the politics of social margins and the idea of a productive society. J Contemp Hist 39(3):33–352

Sturluson S (2016 [*c.* 1230]) Heimskringla, vol I. Viking Society for Northern Research, London

Sæther A, Eriksen IE (2014) Ragnar Frisch and the postwar Norwegian economy. Econ J Watch 11(1)

Søeilen E (1998) Fra frischianisme til keynesianisme? En studie av norsk økonomisk politik I lys av økonomisk teori. Doctoral thesis, Høyskolen i Agder

Sørensen Ø (1988) Anton Martin Schweigaards politiske tenkning. Universitetsforlaget, Oslo

Tacitus PC (1999 [98]) Germania. Clarendon Press, Oxford

Thalberg B (2000) Leif Johansen 1930–1982. Norsk Økonomisk Tidsskrift 114:136–137

Tingsten B (1963) Mitt liv, vol III. Norstedt & Söner, Stockholm

Wergeland N (1830) Fortrolige Breve til en Ven, skrevne fra Eidsvoll i Aaret 1814. Malling, Christiania

Old Lessons for the New Protectionists

Phillip W. Magness

In May 1930 over a thousand economists presented a letter to the United States Congress denouncing a then-pending revision to the federal tariff schedule. The signatories warned of the "bitterness which a policy of higher tariffs would inevitably inject into our international relations," accompanied by contractionary repercussions in the American economy.[1] Their misgivings reflected a consensus in the economics profession even as supporters of the proposed bill presented it as a stimulus package against the emerging Great Depression. The economists' plea was not without precedent. A generation earlier, a group of leading British economists rallied against Joseph Chamberlain's 1903 plan to turn the empire toward trade protectionism. Their arguments prevailed, with the electorate delivering a decisive victory for the free trade side in 1906.[2] Political victories built upon the advice of economists are nonetheless uncommon. Even storied campaigns such as the repeal of Britain's Corn Laws in 1846 only succeeded after a decades-long

---

[1] "Economists Against Smoot-Hawley" Reprinted in Econ Journal Watch, 4-3, September 2007.
[2] "Convictions Opposed to Certain Popular Opinions: The 1903 Anti Protectionism Letter Supported by 16 British Economists" Reprinted in Econ Journal Watch, 7-2, May 2010.

P. W. Magness (✉)
David J. Theroux Chair in Political Economy, The Independent Institute, Oakland, USA
e-mail: philwmagness@gmail.com

battle with entrenched landowner interests that benefitted from agricultural protectionism at the expense—and food security—of the nation.

Entrenched interest groups, not the economists, would unfortunately win the day in 1930. The Smoot-Hawley Tariff Act was passed with ease amid rhetoric that promised its ability to insulate American industries from the unfolding depression. To its supporters, the new tariff followed the prescription of Henry Clay's "American System," a nineteenth-century economic doctrine that empowered government with proactive tools to bolster "strategic" industries through domestic subsidies and insulation from international competition.[3] Not coincidentally, a number of observers noticed favors and even money-trading hands between the seekers of preferential rates and members of the congressional committees charged with drafting the legislation. The political scientist E.E. Schattschneider (1935, p. 283) marveled at the unfolding spectacle despite his misgivings about the resulting policy: "(i)f one is permitted to appraise this legislation apart from its economic consequences, it must be rated as one of the most notable political achievements in American history."

The economists' warnings proved to be prescient. By 1933, U.S. exports and imports alike had collapsed. The American tariff measure triggered a trade war abroad as other countries responded with retaliatory tariffs and trade restrictions of their own. At the end of this downward spiral, global trade volume shrank to barely a third of its 1929 level (Rowley et al. 1995, p. 160). As for the lobbying efforts, the promised relief to individual industries never materialized. Most suffered under the collective collapse of trade, and an accompanying rise in input prices. In the assessment of economist Thomas Rustici (2005, p. 76) "every major special interest group promoting Smoot-Hawley ultimately ended up losing because of their efforts."

A curious conundrum emerged in the wake of this disaster. Despite the near-universal acknowledgement of Smoot-Hawley's failures and an electoral sweep in 1932 that ousted several of its architects, the measure became an insurmountable fixture of federal tariff policy. Direct legislative repeal had no viable prospect, and indeed the Smoot-Hawley schedule remains officially on the U.S. statute books almost a century later even as it has been bypassed by other means.

The reason for this situation may be diagnosed in a simple game-theoretic scenario. Interest group behavior in cases of extreme protection such as Smoot-Hawley exhibits the characteristics of a prisoner's dilemma. Each individual tariff beneficiary seeks out protection to obtain strategic advantages

---

[3] See speech of Hamilton Fish, May 21, 1929. *Congressional Record*, 71st Congress, Vol. LXXI-2, p. 1665.

for itself in relation to other industries, banking on the respective inability or unwillingness of other interests to do the same. A legislative coalition then assembles the pieces into a majority through logrolling and tradeoffs, resulting in a comprehensive protectionist schedule wherein no tariff recipient retains an individual upper hand relative to the others. Dismantling the legislative package becomes politically impossible, even under friendly congressional majorities, because the first mover to forego a protectionist rate will face international competition as a price-taker in a still highly protected marketplace for all other industries. Individual industries thereby continue to lobby to retain protectionist tariff rates for themselves in the hopes of maintaining an individualized advantage after the tariff is repealed. They will rationally do so, even as the cumulative tariff package is openly acknowledged to harm all industries. "The very tendencies that have made the legislation bad," observed Schattschneider (1935, p. 283), "have…made it politically invincible."

The tendency of congressional tariff-making to devolve into a special interest free-for-all stands in marked contrast with Madisonian constitutional theory. In matters of trade protection, the "ambition" of one industry does not appear to "counteract ambition." In practice they collude, as was the pattern for much of the nineteenth century United States (Magness 2009; Peart 2018). As the retaliatory collapse of global trade after Smoot-Hawley reveals, no country is immune to the same tendencies.

The protectionist quagmire of 1930 only began to resolve after a flanking move that altered the institutional dynamics of trade policy, first in the United States and then abroad. In 1934, facing no viable routes for a direct repeal of Smoot-Hawley, the U.S. Congress effectively agreed to initiate the gradual cession of its tariff-setting powers to the world of diplomacy. The Reciprocal Trade Agreements Act (RTAA) initiated this sea change by authorizing the executive branch to pursue bilateral and multilateral negotiations for tariff barrier reduction. The negotiated results could then be presented to Congress for a simple vote, effectively working around the codified tariff schedule on a country-by-country basis. Over time, Smoot-Hawley and the retaliatory measures it triggered abroad could be whittled away through negotiations that were comparatively insulated from the legislative interest group politics that emerged around line-by-line revisions to a statutory tariff schedule.

The genius of this shift may be seen in its readjustment of the constituent participants in trade policy negotiations. Codified tariff schedules such as Smoot-Hawley emerged from legislative bargaining in the committee rooms of Congress, with each member incentivized to deliver favorable rates to his or her constituency industries and donors. Although the costs of tariff protectionism fall on consumers at large, their stake in the game is comparatively diffuse vis-à-vis the concentrated industry beneficiaries of a higher protective rate. Of equal significance, international diplomacy is effectively sidelined under these circumstances and relegated to the comparatively cumbersome treaty process. The RTAA upended this status quo by shifting the locus of trade policymaking into the executive branch, as further solidified by subsequent expansions of reciprocal negotiating authority.

As summarized by political scientist I.M. Destler (1986, p. 16), the RTAA may be credited with creating an additional "bargaining" factor in the political equation of trade policy, that of international pressure. The negotiating power of reciprocal trade liberalization creates "something of a political counterweight on the liberal trade side" by increasing the stakes and influence of export interests to a level that counteracts domestic producers through international pressure. This new approach saw quick utilization under U.S. Secretary of State Cordell Hull as a depression-relief strategy to reestablish world trade in the 1930s. In total, the United States negotiated some 32 bilateral agreements under the RTAA before the end of World War II. After the war, the strategy of achieving trade barrier reduction through reciprocal negotiation became the basis for the General Agreement on Trade and Tariffs (GATT) and initiated a pattern of nearly-uninterrupted trade liberalization from the postwar period to the early twenty-first century.

While the economic profession's free trade consensus has never been stronger, recent years have born witness to a resurgence of protectionist ideology on the political left and right. Following cues from U.S. President Donald Trump, the "National Conservative" movement has taken up the task of rehabilitating Henry Clay's "American System" as a forgotten or even suppressed alternative to an allegedly-British free trade paradigm (Lind 2012; Lighthizer 2023). These economic nationalists spin an unambiguously false historical narrative wherein the United States' industrial growth in the nineteenth century is causally attributed to protective tariffs. This argument falls apart under scrutiny, as non-traded sectors of the economy generally matched or exceeded the growth seen in import-competing industries with tariff protection (Irwin 2000). After conveniently ignoring how the "American System" strategy backfired under Smoot-Hawley, advocates of this position seek a return to the high tariff policies of the late nineteenth century with an explicit aim of attaining a positive trade balance through legislation.

On the academic far-left, a separate and burgeoning literature portrays the postwar free trade consensus, and particularly its institutional manifestations such as the 1947 GATT agreement and its successor established in 1995, the

World Trade Organization (WTO), as centerpieces of conscious constructs to entrench an international "capitalist" or "neoliberal" order against what they perceive to be inevitable challenges from Marxian and postcolonial revolutionary movements. Although this strain of academic argument is less wedded to any explicit theory of protectionism, they view the primary institutions of international trade policy as obstacles to other redistributive goals. The free exchange of goods and services is subordinate to normative expressions of "social justice" in this worldview, and its institutional components are cast aside as tools to maintain allegedly "neoliberal" economic exploitation of the "Global South."

The rhetoric of such charges is seldom sustained in evidence, and indeed economic confusion often plagues its scholarship. To use one example, a leading far-left historical account by Quinn Slobodian (2018) almost haplessly depicts the GATT and its successor policies as an ideological extension of the free-market Austrian school of economics, as situated in the allegedly "neoliberal" Mont Pelerin Society. In reality, its lineage traces to the 1944 Bretton Woods conference as the direct outgrowth of the New Deal-initiated RTAA and accompanying proposals for an International Trade Organization by progressive economist John Maynard Keynes.

This left-leaning interpretation differs from the nationalist aims of right-leaning protectionists in terms of its specific political objectives. Insofar as this literature displays explicit hostility to the postwar trade system, it nonetheless advances toward a similar goal of deconstructing the very same institutions that stand in the way of nineteenth century-style tariff-making. A curious feature of both positions is that they reach their desired policies while giving negligible amounts of attention to the implications of currently existing institutional arrangements on the political economy of tariff creation.

The New Protectionists, both left and right, ignore the lessons of 1930 at their peril. Specifically, calls to weaken the institutional framework of postwar trade reciprocity or to reinvigorate legislative primacy in tariff-making risk opening the floodgates to unconstrained special interest group politics of the type that produced Smoot-Hawley and subsequent retaliation. It was neither a free trade conspiracy nor a "neoliberal" institutional imposition that prompted the abandonment of this earlier approach to tariff-making, but rather its own disastrous consequences, as realized through the political-economic quagmire of interest group capture.

The Winners and Losers in a Conventional Trade Model

Trade policy has long been recognized as displaying an acute susceptibility to interest group politics. Tariffs in particular alter the rules of economic exchange in ways that are perceived to advantage specific politically connected industries or even specific factors of production within those industries. In a more colloquial expression, trade restrictions create economic winners and losers. Groups that are able to influence tariff legislation will accordingly seek an advantageous position by securing legislative favors.

A significant component of protection's political economy is thereby determined through the identification of its beneficiaries (Mayer 1984; Magee et al. 1989; Rowley et al. 1995; Rodrik 1995). By delineating the political implications of a basic trade model, we may accordingly see the risks that follow from the weakening of institutional barriers against tariff-creation.[4]

Notably, both left and right-wing variants of New Protectionism misstate the alleged benefits of their policies to labor in the affected sectors. Starting from the famous Heckscher–Ohlin (1919, 1924) trade model, wherein labor and capital are assumed to have inter-sectoral mobility, a country's endowment of each factor determines the goods it exports and imports based on their production's use of the abundant or scarcely endowed factor. For example, a country with a large labor endowment will shift production to the labor-intense good. Under free trade, this good is exported. Given the country's comparatively scarce capital endowment, it will import capital-intense goods.

Our first complication emerges as a direct implication of Stolper and Samuelson's (1941) theorem about the effect of prices on the relative returns to the factors of production. Holding that an increase in the relative price of a good will raise the real return to the factor used intensively in the production of that good and lower the real return of the other factor, free trade will be resisted—and tariffs will be favored—by industries that use a country's scarce factor, be it labor or capital, in their production.

This result is illustrated in a basic two-country model in Fig. 1, assuming a labor-endowed nation, where the introduction of trade induces a production shift from A to B benefiting Good I, the labor-intensive good. The shift reduces the capital-labor ratio, K/L, for both goods, thus:

$$K_1/L_1 \text{ decreases, causing } MP_{L1} = w/p_1 \text{ to increase}$$

---

[4] This section is adapted from Magness (2010). For an extended examination of the political economy of protectionist policies, see the parallel discussion in Hillman (1989).

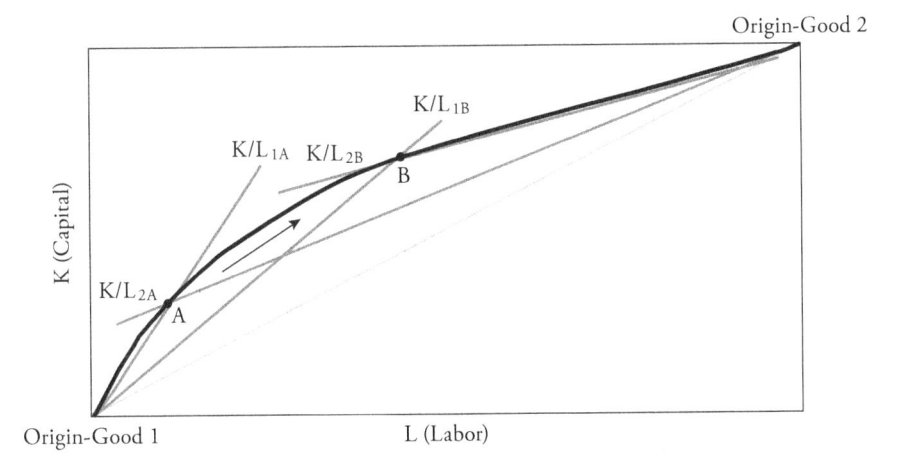

Fig. 1 Effects of the introduction of trade in a labor-endowed country

$$K_2/L_2 \text{ decreases, causing } \text{MP}_{L2} = w/p_2 \text{ to increase}$$

and

$$K_1/L_1 \text{ decreases, causing } \text{MP}_{K1} = r/p_1 \text{ to decrease}$$
$$K_2/L_2 \text{ decreases, causing } \text{MP}_{K2} = r/p_2 \text{ to decrease}$$

where w = wages, r = rental rate on physical capital, p = price, and MP_i – the marginal product of i where $i = L, K$.

Hence, under standard Heckscher-Ohlin assumptions, the intensive factor in this example (L) experiences real-term gains from an increase in the wage–price ratio for both products, while the scarce factor (K) experiences real-term losses in decreasing rental rate-price ratios. Capital owners will thus favor protection while labor favors free trade.

This result changes substantially if the assumptions are altered to restrict factor mobility by making the factors of production industry-specific to certain sectors—a realistic move according to Rowley et al. (1995, p. 73) given that "industry-specific interests and not factor-based coalitions" are typically observed in practice to seek trade protection. Factor specificity in this case, notes Michael Hiscox (2002, p. 594), drives a "wedge between members of the same class employed in different industries."

Holding specific types of physical capital, A and B, to be industry-specific to the production of certain goods (for example, land to agriculture) with only labor exhibiting mobility, the introduction of free trade may be seen to affect both capital owners and labor. Supposing trade increases the price P of Good I, intensive in A, labor in that sector, an outward shift in $P(\text{MP}_{L1})$, also expands the labor allotment in that good's production at the expense of Good II as exhibited in Fig. 2.

- L_1 increases, causing $MP_A = r_A/p_1$ to increase
- L_2 decreases, causing $MP_B = r_B/p_2$ to decrease

Thus, owners of capital B experience real-term losses from trade and will seek protection. Labor's role is more ambiguous though:

- L_1 increases, causing $MP_{L1} = w/p_1$ to decrease
- L_2 decreases, causing $MP_{L2} = w/p_2$ to increase

Whether labor gains or loses from trade (and thus seeks or opposes protection) will accordingly depend on this ambiguity's resolution in a specific case (Ruffin and Jones 1977). Wages in the production of Good I increase with trade, but so does the price of Good I itself by a larger amount, making the real-term impact on wage earners contingent upon their relative consumption levels of Goods 1 and 2.

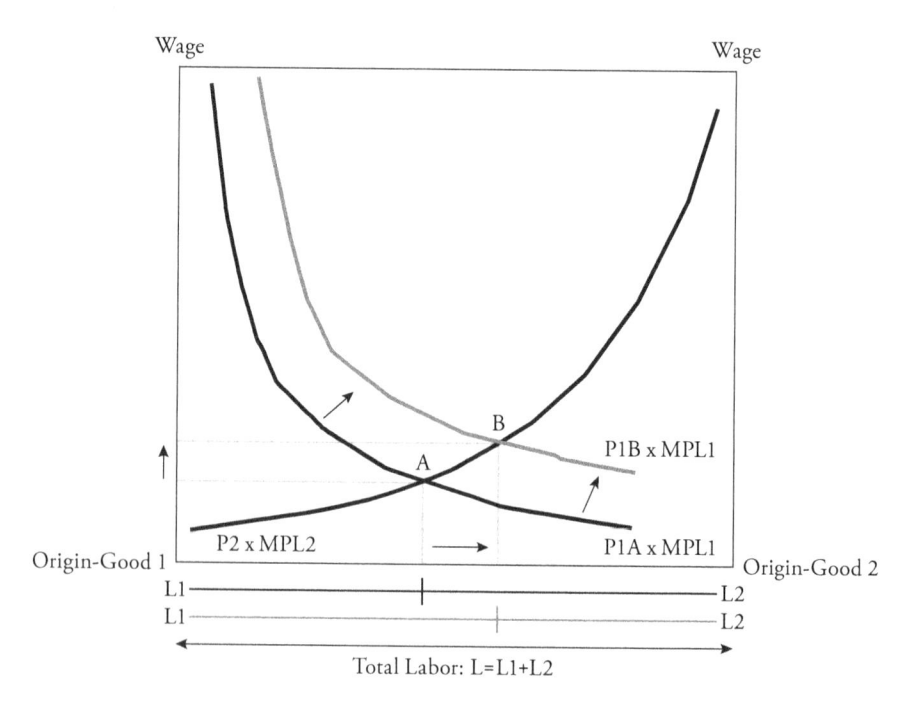

Fig. 2 The ambiguous position of labor under factor specificity

Factor mobility/specificity assumptions have far-reaching implications for the political emergence of tariffs, and thus should be accounted for in attempting to explain the existence of protection. Stated differently, factor mobility suggests that protectionist interests may form in factor-based coalitions across multiple industries, potentially placing labor and capital owners, who find themselves further divided by specificity in capital as well, at odds over the policy. Factor specificity is accordingly more conducive to protectionist interests organizing by industry based on its position relative to the protective policy. Thus a single industry's labor and factor-specific capital owners might both favor protection, though this is by no means certain given labor's consumption preferences.

As a broader consideration, factor mobility/specificity assumptions in the exchange of goods demonstrate the clear presence of economic "winners" and "losers" who arise from the introduction or restriction of trade across borders. They guarantee that trade policy will not emerge in a technocratic vacuum of carefully set rates and strategically identified industrial priorities. Tariffs are a product of a political world inhabited by vested interests and pressure groups that cannot be casually brushed aside.

By practical implication, the strategic selection of prioritized industries under a nationalistic "American System" design will always be confounded by the presence of interest groups, as will any effort to fine-tune or adjust a tariff schedule once it is established. "American System" advocates are thereby guaranteed to lose control of a policy regime that they imagine they can design. All the same, the New Protectionists on the left risk removing the institutional constraints of the GATT and WTO that have otherwise mitigated and dampened a political devolution back to interest group-driven protectionism. When rampant interest group influence is the default policymaking condition, as the political economy of trade predicts it to be, any policy crafted in ignorance of the same condition will succumb to its influence.

Protectionist Interest Group Emergence

The identification of the "winners" and "losers" from tariff protection demonstrates the endemic nature of the interest group problem in trade policy. Taken alone though, it is insufficient to determine which specific groups possess the ability to mobilize and exert influence on the political outcome that emerges. An interest group's position may be fully known from its gains/losses and accurately represented, yet the dynamics of its ability to influence the political process remain. A numerical majority constituency could even find itself unable to defeat a minority interest. This somewhat counterintuitive outcome is the logical prediction of Mancur Olson's (1965) pioneering examination of collective action dynamics in public decision-making.

Olson's framework illustrates that a public-sector interest group's object—government policies that benefit its members collectively—possesses the attributes of a "collective good," to wit: indivisibility and thus non-excludability to beneficiaries who do not contribute to its acquisition. This concept implies that most interest groups will suffer from the same free-rider problems that inhibit collaborative upward pricing between competitive firms in the private sector. Just as any given producer within an industry lacks a rational incentive to "restrict his output in order that there might be a higher price…so it would not be rational for him to sacrifice his time and money to support a lobbying organization."

As a result, the desired "collective goods," and the groups seeking them, will be undersupplied except in small groups, where members constitute a sufficiently large fraction of the beneficiaries to find it in their personal interest to provide "some amount of that collective good."

In practice, this situation favors lobbying from concentrated interests with large individual benefits from the sought policy, whereas diffuse interests with few individual benefits will not organize. Thus, to Olson, asymmetry in group structure will tend to bias collective organization toward groups with certain beneficial attributes and can produce an inefficient result where a concentrated minority obtains collective benefits that impose diffuse costs—including inefficient ones—upon latent unorganized majorities. Conditions of this type often appear in trade and tariff politics where concentrated producer interests exert pressure to obtain the benefits of tariff protection while its costs are dispersed through small price increases onto the general population of consumers (Rowley et al. 1995, pp. 92–93). As a result, tariff schedules emerge that primarily serve politically concentrated interest groups that are in the clear numerical minority but nonetheless succeed in overcoming the free-rider disadvantages of the diffuse majority.

Ultimately, the gains and losses at stake in a protective tariff measure come down to an evaluation of its political rents. Economist Gordon Tullock (1967) was the first to fully develop this aspect of trade protection's political economy when he posed the theory of potential waste in the pursuit of favors through legislative interferences in international trade. Economist Ann Krueger (1974) formalized this activity under the term "rent seeking," which describes the pattern of using political tools to alter the conditions of market exchange to the advantage of one or more constituent interests. Tullock's original model identified the tariff as being exceptionally susceptible to this pattern, and subsequent work has confirmed the potentially severe economic losses that arise from rent-seeking behavior around trade policy (Bhagwati 1982).

Traditional welfare economics identifies the efficiency loss from tariff protection in the "dead weight" or Harberger (1959) efficiency losses caused by the displacement of the consumer surplus, indicated by triangles "b" and "d" in Fig. 3. In contrast, Tullock observed the transfer attributes of the tariff, represented in trapezoid "a," the producer surplus transfer received by protection's beneficiaries through higher prices (and thus their true motive for supporting protection), and rectangle "c," the tariff's revenues, which are available for disbursement in government expenditures that are allocated to successful rent-seeking interests.

The potential of obtaining these transferred resources, Tullock (1967, p. 174) notes, motivates various interests to seek them out from the government itself. In doing so, "one would anticipate that the domestic producers would invest resources in lobbying for the tariff until the marginal return on the last dollar so spent was equal to its likely return producing the transfer." It is thus theoretically possible that rent competition with free entry could potentially waste away the full value of the transfers themselves in diverted expenditures on lobbying.

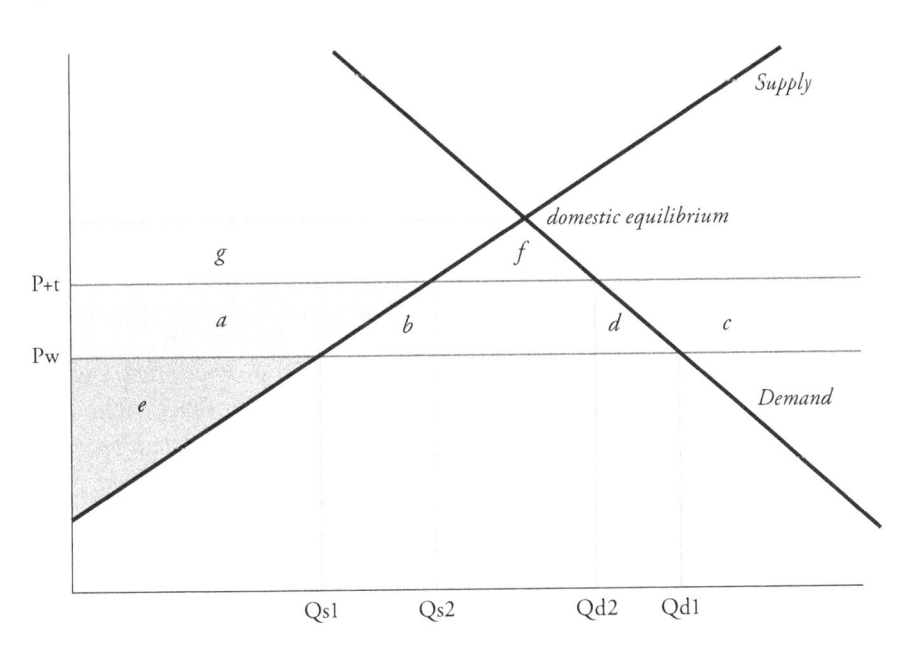

Fig. 3 Political rents after the introduction of a protective tariff

Asymmetrical access to political information, combined with the advantages that small cohesive groups have in controlling free-ridership, often creates conditions where protectionist interests obtain the upper hand in political competition for tariff rents. As long as these advantages hold, we may reasonably expect to see widespread tariff rent-seeking from institutional arrangements that make legislative action the primary process by which trade policy decisions are meted out and codified.

The result is something of a perpetual challenge for free traders as it implies that having stronger economic evidence alone is insufficient to win in the policy arena. Both theoretical and empirical arguments for free trade offer useful tools in explaining its economic benefits as well as showing the corresponding efficiency and deadweight losses associated with tariff protectionism. The determinants of actual trade policy adoption, however, almost always involve competition between interest groups who are largely unphased by such arguments and instead care primarily about their stake in the rents to be gained from a protective policy, no matter how ill-conceived.

The economists lost the battle in 1930 not because of superior arguments from Smoot-Hawley's "American System" enthusiasts. As we have seen, the worst predictions of their petition came true in the years that followed. Instead, they lost for the reasons that Schattschneider identified at the time. Intellectual appeals to free trade never stood a chance in an institutional environment that made tariff rents available for seeking, and that privileged precisely the types of special interests that desired them.

Dismantling the Postwar Trading System

It would be a mistake to conclude that the postwar trade institutions of the GATT and WTO have resolved the historical problem of interest group-induced protectionism. Both arrangements emerged from extended negotiations that did not run completely afoul of protectionist political constituencies at the time of their creation, particularly in the United States and Europe. The GATT included exploitable loopholes modeled on earlier U.S. tariff code provisions that temporarily exempted signatories from multilateral trade barrier reductions on specific items or sectors, most notably amidst allegations of material injury from "dumping" by other countries or claims that fulfilment of an obligation would subject a domestic industry to "serious injury" (also known as "Escape Clause" cases). These provisions carried over into the WTO's litigation framework, and some seven decades of operation have seen them used and abused with regularity, and often in response to domestic pressure groups seeking protection for the reasons delineated in the foregoing sections.

At the same time, the GATT and its WTO successor have provided an important buffer against the worst tendencies of unmitigated protectionism. Rowley et al. (1995, p. 315) describe them as "managed rather than…free trade," albeit "strongly trade-liberalizing" in their overall thrust. In the United States, a nascent postwar effort to resume protectionism was held at bay by the GATT negotiations. Average tariff rates have been held down ever since through multilateral agreements operating under the Most-Favored-Nation principle, even as Smoot-Hawley remains on the statute books. In the same period, GDP per capita has undergone a dramatic and seldom-interrupted increase. While not without shortcomings or continuous vulnerabilities due to their carved-out exceptions, the postwar trade institutions have performed well in holding off a resumption of the Depression-era policies that they largely superseded and rendered moot.

A curious feature of the New Protectionists, both right and left, is that they attribute these features to malicious interest group designs that are often asserted yet seldom in evidence. Both depict the postwar trading system as tools of "globalization," "internationalism," and "neoliberalism," working to the advantage of nameless and faceless business interests. Left-leaning iterations tend to allege the plight of labor as the primary detriment of this system, even as the above-noted political economy of trade illustrates that labor's interests are ambiguous and determined by relative price levels, not sector-wide unity. Right-leaning iterations usually contend that small and domestic manufacturing industries are victimized by trade liberalization, usually ignoring that these same industries have made ample use of lobbying to secure anti-dumping and escape clause carve-outs in the postwar era. Neither narrative maps cleanly onto the observable interest group characteristics of how tariffs and other trade barriers actually form, and much of the accompanying rhetoric seems to operate as a rationalization for rent-seeking behavior.

But therein lies the danger of the New Protectionists' objections to the last seven decades of trade liberalization. The postwar trade institutions, while proven on net, exist in a relatively fragile geopolitical setting, upheld only to the extent that their constituent members abide by their frameworks. Even in the absence of protectionist challenges, the WTO has frequently become mired in political disputes between major powers when exercising its quasi-judicial functions. A retreat from postwar liberalization would cast trade policy into a world that merges the obsolete economic theories behind protectionism with the unconstrained interest group dynamics of tariff creation on the national level under systems of legislative primacy. We saw the repercussions of that exact scenario in 1930 and, for a time, internalized its lessons. The current risk, however, is of amnesia to the same events, overlaid with a mistaken belief that, this time, the interest group politics may somehow be harnessed or mitigated. Such thinking is hopelessly naïve.

Bibliographys

Bhagwati JN (1982) Directly unproductive profit-seeking (DUP) activities. J Polit Econ 90(5):988–1002

Destler IM (1995) American trade politics. Institute for International Economics, Washington, DC, pp 14–15

Harberger AC (1959) Using the resources at hand more effectively. Am Econ Rev 49:134–146

Heckscher E, Ohlin B (1919 & 1924) Translated by Harry Flam and M. June Flanders. In: Heckscher-Ohlin trade theory. MIT Press (1991)

Hillman AL (1989) The political economy of protection. Harwood Academic, Chur, Switzerland

Hiscox MJ (2002) Commerce, coalitions, and factor mobility: evidence from congressional votes on trade legislation. Am Polit Sci Rev 96(3):593–608

Irwin DA (2000) Tariffs and growth in late nineteenth century America. National Bureau of Economic Research, Working Paper 7639

Kreuger AO (1974) The political economy of the rent seeking society. Am Econ Rev 64:291–303

Lighthizer R (2023) No trade is free: changing course, taking on China, and helping America's workers. Broadside Books

Lind M (2012) Land of promise: an economic history of the United States. Harper

Magee SP, Brock WA, Young L (1989) Black hole tariffs and endogenous policy theory. Cambridge University Press, Cambridge

Magness PW (2009) Morrill and the missing industries: strategic lobbying behavior and the tariff, 1858–1861. J Early Republic 29(2):287–329

Magness PW (2010) From tariffs to the income tax: trade protection and revenue in the United States tax system. George Mason University

Mayer W (1984) Endogenous tariff formation. Am Econ Rev 74(5):970–985

Olson M (1965) The logic of collective action. Harvard University Press, Cambridge

Peart D (2018) Lobbyists and the making of US tariff policy, 1816–1861. JHU Press

Rodrik D (1995) Political economy of trade policy. In: Grossman GM, Rogoff K (eds) Handbook of international economics III. Elsevier, Amsterdam

Rowley CK, Thorbecke W, Wagner RE (1995) Trade protection in the United States. Edward Elgar, Aldershot, UK

Ruffin R, Jones RW (1977) Protection and real wages: the neo-classical ambiguity. J Econ Theory 14:337–348

Rustici, T.C., 2005. The economic effects of the Smoot-Hawley Act of 1930 and the beginning of the Great Depression. George Mason University.

Schattschneider EE (1935) Politics, pressures, and the tariff. Prentice Hall, New York

Slobodian Q (2018) Globalists: the end of empire and the birth of neoliberalism. Harvard University Press

Stolper W, Samuelson P (1941) Protection and real wages. Rev Econ Stud 9:58–73

Tullock G (1967) The welfare costs of tariffs, monopolies, and theft. In: Rowley CK (ed) (2004) Virginia political economy, vol 1. Liberty Fund, Indianapolis

Free Trade Is Not Free: Why Deglobalization Is (Unfortunately) Here to Stay

Keith Jakee and Stephen Turner

Introduction

Policy experts around the world have sounded the alarm. After an extended period of increased economic globalization, there are disturbing signs that progress on this front has not only stalled but is now going in reverse. Global exports of goods and services, as a percentage of world GDP, peaked in 2008 and have fallen since then. Foreign direct investment shows a similar trend, reaching a high of 5.3% in 2007 and falling to 1.3% in 2020 (Rajan 2023). Equally important, there is no longer a broad political consensus in favor of more open trade. After the failed Doha Round of world trade negotiations in 2014, there has been no concerted attempt to revitalize the push for trade liberalization. More ominously, the United States and China both seem determined to pull back from their earlier embrace of growing economic interdependence. And, the Covid pandemic revealed all too clearly the risks

---

Forthcoming Chapter in *Free Trade in the Twenty-First Century* Max Rangeley and Lord Daniel Hannan (eds.). 2024. Springer.

K. Jakee (✉)
Wilkes Honors College, Florida Atlantic University, Jupiter, FL, USA
e-mail: kjakee@fau.edu

S. Turner
Danish International Studies, Stockholm, Sweden
e-mail: stephen.turner@disstockholm.se

© The Author(s), under exclusive license to Springer Nature Switzerland AG 2025
M. Rangeley and D. Hannan (eds.), *Free Trade in the Twenty-First Century*,
https://doi.org/10.1007/978-3-031-67656-7_24

of distant and complex supply chains controlled by other, potentially hostile, nations.

In fact, observers are in broad agreement that the trend toward deglobalization will have profoundly negative consequences for the world economy. Over the past 75 years, increased global trade has been the pivotal factor in spreading prosperity and reducing poverty. In 1960, approximately 60% of the world lived in extreme poverty (defined as an individual daily income of less than 2.15 USD); by 2019, the percentage had fallen to just under nine percent (World Bank 2022). Policies in support of trade liberalization transformed the theory of comparative advantage into a tangible reality for many nations. For those nations participating in the globalized economy, their wealth is therefore no longer determined solely by local access to natural resources, plentiful energy, arable land, and navigable waterways. In this global free-trade system, any country can, in principle, prosper by specializing in sectors in which they can compete internationally.

What, then, are the likely effects of deglobalization? The outlook looks grim. We can expect, most importantly, lower global economic growth. Less globalized trade will mean less competition, less innovation, and a drop in long-term trends in global output. For the wealthy nations of the world, slower growth is obviously undesirable, but it does not pose a fundamental threat to survival and human flourishing. GDP per capita for OECD Europe, for example, was approximately 44,000 USD in 2023 (IMF 2023). The situation is starkly different in much of the world. Despite the impressive gains of the last 60 years, widespread poverty continues to plague the globe. According to the World Bank (2022), almost four billion people still live in countries with a GDP per capita of less than 7.00 USD per day. And these are likely to be the countries hardest hit by a reduction in globalized trade.

This disturbing scenario raises an obvious question: How are we to explain the widespread retreat from globalization? Why, in other words, do the world's policymakers seem willing to abandon such a highly effective method for spreading global prosperity? Policy experts have suggested two main lines of argument. Proponents of globalization argue, first, that many policymakers do not understand what is really at stake. They have failed, in other words, to comprehend the pivotal role of free trade in spreading prosperity and fostering global peace and cooperation. The second line of argument is complementary to the first. The global surge in national populism has generated pressure on politicians to respond to the demands of disgruntled voters. The vote for Brexit and the election of Donald Trump are only the most well-known symptoms of this widespread backlash against mainstream political parties (Goodwin and Eatwell 2018).

Both explanations lead to the same conclusion: policymakers are making an egregious error in their retreat from globalization (Posen 2022and 2023; Prasad 2023; Rajan 2023; Subramanian and Freeman 2020). Pointing to the widely acknowledged costs of protectionism, free-trade advocates argue that this policy shift is likely to seriously damage both global cooperation and prosperity. Deglobalization, they seem to argue, will generate only losers. And the poorest, most vulnerable nations of the world will be hit the hardest. To accept—or worse, embrace—deglobalization is thus the result of a deeply flawed analysis that must be corrected before it is too late.

Our main objective is to challenge this broad consensus on the underlying causes of deglobalization. We believe the pro-trade experts have underestimated the importance of shifting parameters underlying international trade, particularly in terms of transaction costs. They have subsequently made a logical error in attributing recent policy decisions rolling back globalism to ignorance or misguided national populism. Our argument proceeds by defining "globalization" and "deglobalization" in the "Empirical Developments in Deglobalization" section. We discuss what we view as the logical error concerning policymakers' intentions that many pundits seem to make in the "The Experts' (Flawed) Analysis of Globalization/Deglobalization" section, and we present our argument concerning transaction costs in the "The Shifting Calculus of Costs and Benefits in a Globalized Economy" section.

Empirical Developments in Deglobalization

"Globalization" typically refers to the substantial increase in world trade, especially from about 1970. International trade grew—in real terms—from 0.45 trillion dollars in the early 1960s to 3.4 trillion dollars by 1990, a factor of seven (Bernhofen et al. 2016: 36). Its path, measured as "trade as a share of total world GDP," continued on a strong upward trajectory until roughly 2008–2009, years which correspond to the Global Financial Crisis. Figure 1 plots "trade as a share of GDP" for the entire world. "Trade" is defined as the addition of a country's exports and imports (as a percentage of GDP), so the vertical dimension in the figure reflects the world average of each country's $\frac{[\text{Exports}_i + \text{Imports}_i]}{\text{Country } i\text{'s GDP}}$. This ratio is also known as the "trade openness index."

The globalization pattern is clearly evident in the "world" data series in Fig. 1. Trade "openness" increased from 25% in 1970 to 61% in 2008. The rise in global supply chains meant that an increasing number of countries

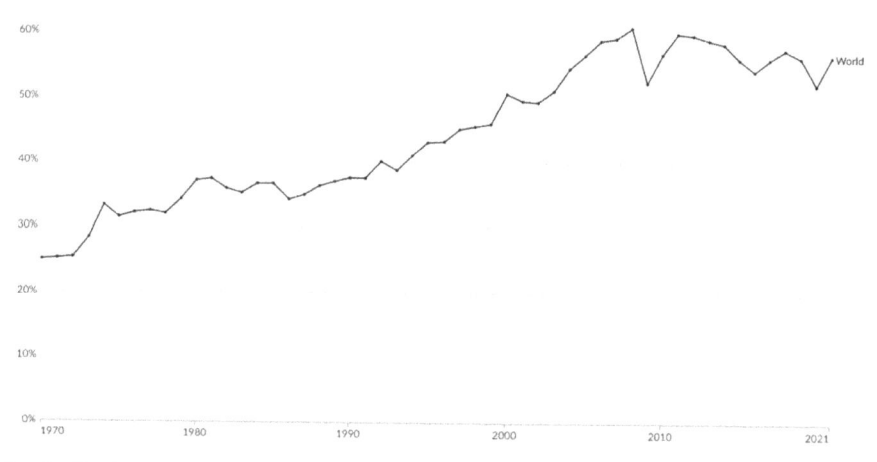

Fig. 1 Trade openness index: world trade/world GDP, 1970 to 2021. *Source* OurWorldInData.org from World Bank and OECD data

could benefit from comparative advantages and specialization: many countries, not least among them China, substantially increased their per capita incomes and many others enjoyed considerably lower-cost consumer products as a result of this increased trade. This scenario largely describes the "win-win" description of foreign trade described by its proponents.

Scholarly attention has focused on two broad causes for increased trade: changes in technology, and changes in trade policy. In simple terms, technological advancements in transportation and communication manifest as reductions in transportation costs. For example, the adoption and growth of shipping containerization, the beginning of which Bernhofen et al. placed in 1966, is often cited as a principal cause (2016: 36). Improved data collection, analysis, and transmission helped launch the revolution in improved logistical control. We return to a critically overlooked aspect of transaction costs in the "The Shifting Calculus of Costs and Benefits in a Globalized Economy" section.

The second broad category responsible for the increase in world trade, liberalized trade policies around the world, is manifested in the proliferation of specific trade agreements, such as the World Trade Organization (WTO) in 1995 (Hanson 2024: 164). These policies provided a framework for negotiating international trade relations and eventually provided the "rules of the game," which nations were meant to follow in this grand international exchange of goods and services. It has been argued this framework encouraged cooperation in trade negotiations among nations (Anderson 2016; Goldstein et al. 2007).

However, the momentum of world trade began to decelerate after the 2008–09 financial crisis. The crisis triggered a global economic downturn, which led to a contraction in demand and trade volumes. As credit conditions tightened, consumer spending plummeted; meanwhile increasing risk aversion reduced investment, and businesses scaled back their production and supply chain activities. The crisis also prompted some countries to adopt protectionist measures to shield domestic industries. Following the initial shock of the financial crisis, the volume of world trade nearly regained its pre-crisis level in 2011. However, while the global economy gradually recovered, the rate of trade growth remained subdued relative to the pre-crisis period: the peak in trade openness therefore remains stalled in 2008.

The term "deglobalization" is largely used in reference to this slowing growth in world trade. While the reduction in absolute levels of trade openness is not large (61% in 2008 versus 56.5% in 2021), it is clear that something substantial has happened to the *momentum* in greater trade openness since 2008. Figure 2, which plots several countries' openness indices, also shows a shift in specific countries after about 2008. While the United States' openness has remained relatively steady in the low- to mid-20% range, several countries' indices, such as China's and Canada's, have fallen precipitously. An exception to this trend is, of course, Mexico, which has experienced increased trade, particularly with the rest of North America. We turn to the pundits' evaluation of that change, as well as ours, in the next section.

Fig. 2 Trade openness index: world trade/world GDP, 1970 to 2021 (world and various countries). *Source* OurWorldInData.org from World Bank and OECD data

The Experts' (Flawed) Analysis of Globalization/Deglobalization

Our argument concerning the flawed analysis of globalization/deglobalization begins by carefully separating three distinct claims that are often collapsed into one. Claim 1 is a straightforward empirical claim: globalization is the most effective way to maximize global economic output. An ancillary point, which is commonly included, implies that globalization is a universal win-win—or "everyone wins"—phenomenon. Deglobalization, in contrast, implies "everyone loses." We are in general agreement with the expert consensus on the first part of Claim 1: free trade is the most effective way to promote growth, reduce poverty, and broadly improve standards of living. We also accept the converse of this claim: a retreat from globalization will lead to negative economic, social, and likely political consequences. The frequently implied claim that "everybody wins" is, however, problematic, a point we return to below.

Claim 2 is a normative, rather than an empirical, claim. At its core, many pro-trade experts seem to imply that because globalization is an effective means to maximize global welfare, policymakers *ought* to universally embrace policies that promote globalization. We will declare ourselves agnostic on this particular moral-philosophic claim, as our principal concern here is not with what policymakers *ought* to do, in some idealized sense.

Our fundamental objection is neither to Claim 1 nor Claim 2, per se. We believe mainstream proponents of globalization routinely conflate (empirical) Claim 1 and (normative) Claim 2 to generate a third (empirical) claim regarding the *motivation* for both pro- and anti-globalization policies: it is this motivational claim that seems to form the basis for their views that current policy, which is moving away from globalization, is flawed. At the core of Claim 3 is the (often implied) stance that—in the past—national policymakers were specifically promoting pro-globalization in order to improve world living standards. From this perspective, *the retreat from globalization can only be understood as an irrational policy error* based on either (i) a failure to fully understand the arguments in Claim 1, or (ii) political pressure from narrow-minded populists who are indifferent to the welfare of the global poor. We reject the empirical Claim 3 and argue such a view misdiagnoses the current policy environment.

Our rejection of Claim 3 is based on "Hume's guillotine" (Hume 1739)—conflating the "ought" with the "is"—which is often considered to be a subspecies of the naturalistic fallacy.[1] Economists should be intimately familiar with Hume's admonition in the guise of the "positive-normative" distinction. Positive (or "empirical") claims, we tell our introductory students, are synonymous with "facts:" these are, in other words, the *is*. In the case of positive *theory*, we attempt to explain the interaction of social phenomena by explaining the nature of "how x impacts (or causes) y," not "how we would like x to impact y." We have no intention of suggesting normative claims are improper or inadmissible, merely that we should not conflate—or worse, disguise—the normative with the positive.

Normative positions are often deeply embedded in—and confused with—positive analyses. A glaring example can be found in public finance theory that preceded the public choice movement. The earlier tradition of public finance routinely obscured the *ought* with the *is* by subtly shifting between the implication that government *ought* to correct market failures to assuming—and widely propagating—the notion that government actually *does* correct market failures (Buchanan 1984). This intellectual sleight-of-hand has generated untold confusion both within, and outside of, economics about the nature of state action. The entire public choice enterprise can be understood as a methodological attempt to re-establish a clearer division between normative and positive models of the state.

Thus, simply identifying that policy x will cause outcome y, where y is deemed valuable, does not mean policymakers will actually pursue policy x, or that they even intended y, had they pursued x. This insight is related to the more familiar "unintended consequences" notion, or the idea that simply because y occurred hardly proves it was intended.[2] In fact, this line of reasoning is considerably more consistent with basic economic intuition—especially that of public choice—than one that assumes past policymakers were actively involved in maximizing some benevolent global utilitarian social welfare function when they adopted increasingly liberal trade policies.

It appears to us that many globalization advocates have committed this logical error, just as scholars and policy analysts did prior to the public choice movement. In the case at hand, the pro-globalists have identified a "good"—an increase in global welfare—and assumed, or implied, that is what

---

[1] Hume's discussion of the matter is found in Book 3, Part 1, Section 1, or in the reference reprint [1896: 469]. The concept is referred to as a "guillotine" because it proposes to sever *descriptive* statements from *prescriptive* ones. Much of the remainder of our explanation on Hume's guillotine is taken from Jakee and Spong (2003: 82–83).

[2] In other words, Hume's problem of confusing the *ought* with the *is* has much in common with Adam Smith's (2007 [1776]) insight concerning "unintended consequences." For a recent treatment of Smith's emphasis on unintended consequences, see Infantino (2020). Such an intellectual overlap should not be altogether surprising, given the close relationship between Smith and Hume (see Rasmussen, 2017).

governments intended to pursue. To be more precise, these experts seem to imply that governments in the postwar era supported pro-trade policies *in order to* maximize something like a global utilitarian welfare function. And, the argument goes, the only reason we would now deviate from such a policy is a misunderstanding of these forces or ill-advised populist pressure.

As noted, we fully endorse the claim that widening trade in the past likely *did* maximize such an imaginary function. The logical error is in assuming this was the actual motivation for pro-globalization policy. Our argument, which we will spell out in the next section, is that maximizing such a global utilitarian welfare function was decidedly *not* what past policymakers intended. Rather, the increase in trade was a *byproduct* of pursuing other—dare we say, less magnanimous—interests.

Put in this context, a number of issues arise in addition to the historical one that asks, "did policymakers *actually* engage in maximizing global utility during the period that globalism was on the rise?" While we return to the historical question in the next section, it is worth raising other logical problems with the "global utility max" claim. First, why would policymakers maximize something like a *global* utilitarian welfare function? Seventy years of public choice analysis would ask whether citizens would vote for such a policy, or whether political leaders actually deliver such a policy.[3]

Second, merely noting this is a utilitarian function raises a well-known problem with that particular ethical rule: *that there can be losers*, as well as winners, in such a "maximized" system. On this matter—and related to public choice concerns—we cannot assume that policymakers would willingly trade away jobs in, say, Detroit factories for improved standards of living among the chronically poor in China. This is a very wide logical gulf to traverse, and it is far from clear that the historical record of actual policy objectives in advanced democracies would support such a claim.

In sum, to point out that global GDP and living standards around the world have been increased by more liberal trade policies does not demonstrate that these welfare improvements were the actual goal of the policymakers. It is our contention that liberalization was largely a byproduct of another set of policies: thus, the massive increase in both trade and living standards was incidental to a different set of policymaking objectives. In the next section, we lay out our view of how the geopolitical landscape has changed, and particularly how underlying costs—and the United States' ability to finance them—have fundamentally changed.

---

[3] For those unfamiliar with public choice, or modern political economy, see Jakee (2022) for a brief introduction and history.

The Shifting Calculus of Costs and Benefits in a Globalized Economy

As noted throughout this chapter, the overall results of increased globalization have been nothing short of astounding. We have witnessed an unprecedented period of global peace, widespread economic growth, and a dramatic reduction in extreme poverty over the last 70 years. And while these developments have benefited hundreds of millions of people around the world, the United States has managed to maintain its global dominance as "the liberal hegemon." From this vantage point, the United States' (former) embrace of globalization appears as the ultimate win-win: not only did the United States remain in a position of world dominance, but countries around the world raised their standards of living. Why, then, are we today witnessing signs the United States is no longer fully committed to this proven framework for global peace and prosperity?

We would argue there is an unacknowledged paradox at the heart of the globalized economy. The wide range of policies that make globalization possible are, in fact, the result of decisions made by sovereign countries in the pursuit of their own national interest. One need not endorse every aspect of the "realist paradigm" in international relations to acknowledge that all nations, regardless of regime type, show a marked tendency to favor the interests of their own citizens over the interests of others (Mearsheimer 2018). While moral philosophers can make compelling arguments for why we *should* value all human life equally, both the historical record and casual observation clearly show that national interests remain a powerful force around the world. It is not that human beings do not care about the welfare of others; it is simply that we tend to care more about "our own people first" (Haidt 2012).[4]

We begin by making three, arguably uncontroversial, assumptions concerning national interests in a globalized world. First, as noted, we assume all countries promote international policies that primarily serve their own national interest. If the pursuit of the national interest inadvertently contributes to the global utility function, that is a beneficial byproduct; it is not the motivation for the policy itself. The second point, which is often obscured by the positive-sum nature of global trade, is to recognize that different nations have distinctive, and sometimes conflicting, interests. Finally, nations differ dramatically in the amount of power they wield in shaping global outcomes.

---

[4] Tullock (1981), incidentally, has an insightful view on such grand, international, redistributions, which starts with the assumption that people are considerably more concerned with the welfare of their fellow citizens than they are with those in distant nations, however impoverished.

The acknowledgement of national interests does not imply, of course, that distinctive national interests must lead to international conflict. In fact, much of the appeal of globalization lies in its potential capacity to transform conflict between nations into mutually beneficial exchange based on specialization and trade. But the reality of shared benefits through trade must not be conflated with the disappearance of distinctive national interests. Many advocates of globalization appear to make this error. The implicit assumption is that because a globalized economy benefits "everyone," all countries have a rational interest in embracing policies that promote globalization.

We argue a country's policy stance on globalization will always be conditional: it is based on a national assessment not only of the benefits—but also the costs—of policies required to promote and maintain globalization. A cost-benefit analysis of this magnitude can, of course, only be based on rough estimates of the short- and long-term consequences of a global trade regime. But our underlying claim does not require great precision in this regard. What matters for our analysis is only that countries have distinctive interests, and that they exercise agency in favoring national interests over those of the so-called global community.

By our account, then, a crucial explanation for the *policy* retreat from globalization—in the case of the United States, in particular—is due to a change in the long-term national calculus regarding the overall costs and benefits of maintaining the globalized economy *from a US policy point of view*. While the pundits are surely correct in viewing the United States as a major beneficiary of a globalized economy, they fail to appreciate the enormous *transaction costs* inherent in maintaining a globalized economy. And, an important set of those costs have been borne overwhelmingly by the United States since WWII. We broadly review the historical role played by the United States in globalization, next.

Some Historical Context

The origins of the "liberal world order," and the remarkable expansion of global trade, can be traced to the end of WWII. Thanks largely to the alliance between the United States and the Soviet Union, the war ended in the total defeat of Germany and Japan. But that alliance of convenience broke down very quickly. Stalin's Red Army, which bore the brunt of the fighting against Hitler's forces, was able to establish the "facts on the ground" in all the countries that had the misfortune of lying east of the Iron Curtain. As Stalin established communist puppet regimes throughout Eastern and

Central Europe, the United States found itself in dire need of reliable allies who could balance the daunting power of the Soviet Union.

Faced with the complex challenges of the Cold War, the United States developed an innovative four-pronged strategy that proved remarkably successful (Ikenberry 2011; Kagan 2012). The United States chose to promote both the political transformation and the economic recovery, of both Germany and Japan. Second, it sponsored the Marshall Plan in a bid to speed the recovery of war-torn Europe.[5] Third, it created a security umbrella for its European allies with the establishment of NATO. Finally, and arguably most importantly, the United States promoted international trade by maintaining global peace and by subsidizing the costs of maritime transport.

Only the United States—with its unrivaled economic and military power—has had *both the objective as well as the capacity* to take on the essential role of the global police (Kagan 2018). *The motivation for bearing these costs was not an altruistic concern for the wellbeing of Europe or the global community.* This American strategy was, in other words, decidedly not designed to maximize some global utilitarian social welfare function, but was predicated on rebuilding Europe and Japan and cultivating enduring partnerships with former enemies and traditional allies. The fact that this policy also promoted a surge in global prosperity was therefore an unintended, and fortuitously benign, byproduct of US national strategy.

The incidental promotion of global trade did have the effect of transforming geopolitical rivals into trusted economic partners. And, by coordinating its NATO partners, the United States hoped to deter the Soviet militarily while preventing the dangerous re-emergence of geopolitical rivalry among its allies. As such, we argue that US support—and direct subsidization—for globalization in the postwar period, and the hyper-globalization of the last 25 years, was the result of a unique geopolitical period in which the national benefits for the United States exceeded the costs of subsidizing that trade.

More recently, however, our analysis suggests the national interests of the United States are no longer tightly aligned with the interests of the global community. From an American calculus, the costs of subsidizing global trade are no longer greater than its own benefits from that trade. For the remainder of this section, we articulate our position concerning the costs and benefits of trade *from a national policy point of view*. This argument relies heavily on the role transaction costs play.

---

[5] However, see Cowen (1985) for a persuasive account of why the Marshall Plan was largely insignificant in real economics terms.

Transaction Costs Defined

While the so-called free-trade regime has made it possible for nations to utilize their comparative advantage, the concept of "free trade" is a misnomer. A large body of economic scholarship—from Coase (1960) to Williamson (1975) and North (1990)—has revealed the decisive impact of "transaction costs" in determining the viability of even the simplest economic exchange. And, global trade is anything but simple. The complex exchanges that take place over vast distances generate different types of transaction costs, including, but not limited to: search and information costs, negotiating costs, contracting costs, monitoring and enforcement costs, transportation and logistics costs, and transaction risk due to product defects, delivery delays, and currency fluctuations.

Even a moment's reflection reveals the myriad ways that trade between nations—which must encompass vast geographical distances and highly divergent cultural norms and legal systems—adds an order of magnitude to the underlying challenge of the most "basic" transaction costs of exchange. We acknowledge that many of the costs in international trade are borne by the firms that participate in the global economy. What is often overlooked, however, is the unique role played by the United States in subsidizing a liberal world order that has not only maintained global peace but has also ensured safe transport on the world's waterways.

Consider, for example, that an important factor in stimulating global trade has been the sharp drop in the cost of maritime transport. Today, about 80% of global trade by volume is transported via sea routes (UNCTAD 2017), and a recent World Bank report estimated that the cost of international maritime shipping has declined by approximately 40% since 1990 (Dappe et al. 2017). This reduction is normally attributed to technological advancements, increased vessel sizes, and improvements in port efficiency.

We have no reason to question the role of improved shipping technology and better port infrastructure in stimulating globalization through the reduction of maritime transport costs. This view, however, neglects one of the very foundations of an expanding global economy: that the huge volume of global trade we have come to take for granted has arisen precisely because of the order and stability associated with the United States' world dominance. Transaction costs, then, will be part of the calculus of not only firms but nations that are contemplating their involvement in world trade. We argue the costs and benefits to the United States—*from a policy perspective*—have fundamentally changed and we turn to those changes next.

Transaction Costs of Maintaining Global Order Are Increasing

We now discuss a short list of costs and benefits that have fundamentally changed the policy calculus for the United States, highlighting three areas: increasing military expenditures, increasing fiscal constraints *within* the United States, and increasing military expenditures by major rivals and changes in technology that have made military operations more costly.

Safe transport for commerce is a basic prerequisite for a globalized economy, and it is the growing cost of maintaining safe transport where we begin our discussion. Prior to the establishment of the liberal world order, a handful of "great powers" maintained navies in order to protect their own commercial fleets and, perhaps, to obstruct (or destroy) the commerce of their rivals. For many decades now, the United States has chosen instead to police the world's waterways on behalf of all nations engaged in global trade. It should be noted, moreover, that the global benefits of this policing role are a textbook definition of a "public good." While it might be worthwhile to consider the inherent problem of the "rest of world" free riding on US efforts in this context, our sole aim here is to point out that the United States—and its taxpayers—have indeed shouldered this burden since the end of WWII.

In fact, building and maintaining a blue water navy that spans the globe is exorbitantly expensive. The cost of this subsidy for maritime transport is therefore substantial. In addition to the costs of ships and personnel, a global naval presence also requires an extensive range of ports and military facilities around the world. At the peak of WWII, control of the world's oceans could be ensured by the US Navy, thanks to its 367 destroyers and 376 frigates (US Navy 2017). Due in part to a long-term strategic shift to large carrier groups, today's navy has a total of only 67 destroyers on active duty. Despite annual defense spending of 877 billion USD in 2023 (or approximately 3.5% of GDP), American naval resources are already stretched very thin (Peterson Foundation 2023; Brands 2024).

Relatedly, it is well-known that the United States spends more than any other country on national defense, which at first glance might seem self-evident: given its large population and its great wealth, the US is unrivaled in its capacity to finance military expenditures. But the scale of US military expenditures completely dwarfs spending in all other countries, including Russia and China. In fact, US spending is greater than the total spending of the next nine countries combined. This point is clearly illustrated in Fig. 3.

Ironically, from a geopolitical perspective, the United States is blessed with a greater degree of "natural security" than probably any nation in history,

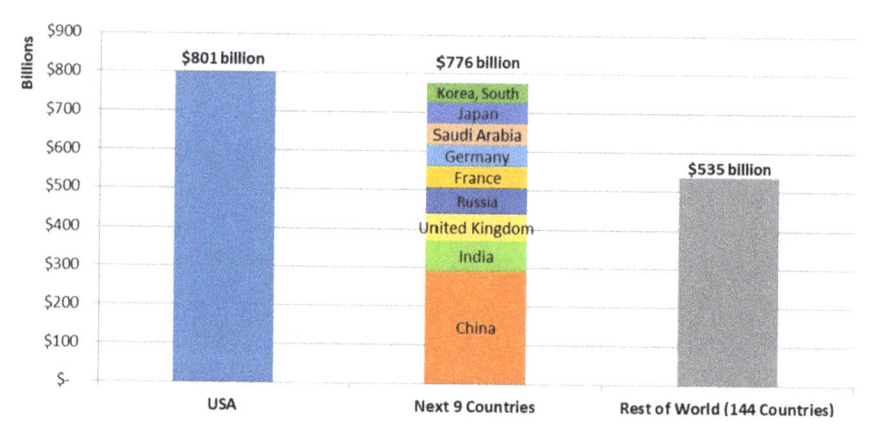

Fig. 3 US versus world military spending (2021). *Source* Institute for policy studies (2022), based on data from SIPRI military expenditures (2022)

owing largely to geography. The NAFTA nations of Canada and Mexico are not only tightly interlinked with the US economy and allied with US interests. Equally important, both nations are extremely weak in military capacity and do not pose a threat to US security. The Atlantic and Pacific Oceans, which form the eastern and western borders, provide an even greater degree of protection. While it is true the United States cannot be fully sheltered from acts of terrorism or long-range air strikes, there is no possibility whatsoever that a hostile nation could invade the homeland with ground forces (Stratfor 2011).

Due to its extraordinarily favorable geopolitical environment, one might assume the United States could radically reduce defense expenditures with little risk to its national security. And yet the US continues to vastly outspend even major powers, such as China and Russia. This tension between massive expenditures and what would seem to be the country's most obvious "defensive" requirements should be striking. This spending paradox is even more puzzling when we consider our next class of "costs" confronting the United States in its maintenance of global order.

Our second set of costs, *the internal cost of financing government activities*, has changed substantially in recent decades. Despite its enormous wealth, the United States has developed a chronic dependence on deficit spending to finance government expenditures (Jakee and Turner 2023).[6] This applies not least to military spending; annual borrowing routinely exceeds total defense

---

[6] This recent work (2023) builds on Buchanan and Wagner (1977) and on earlier work by the present authors (Jakee and Turner 2002). Jakee and Turner (2002) extend Elinor Ostrom's insights (i.e., Ostrom 1998) and model complex government fiscal processes as a "fiscal commons." Analogous to the subset of common pool resources that Ostrom identifies as overexploited, we argue the fiscal

costs. Since 1932, the federal government has only run surpluses in 11 years. The largest deficits (as a percentage of GDP) since WWII, were incurred during the great recession of 2008–2009, peaking at over nine percent of GDP, and then during the Covid crisis, when the deficit soared to over 14% of GDP. What is arguably even more alarming is the *post*-Covid situation: despite the end of the pandemic and a robust economic recovery, the deficit still exceeded six percent of GDP in 2023. There is, moreover, no reason to believe a balanced budget will be achieved at any time in the foreseeable future.

Chronic reliance on budget deficits has led, in turn, to a dramatic increase in the national debt. The Congressional Budget Office predicts an unprecedented surge in debt over the next 30 years, rising from 100 to 166% of GDP, and this figure only counts debt that is "publicly held" (CBO 2024). As the national debt mounts, rising annual interest costs will themselves become a significant factor in aggravating the underlying deficit. In fact, 2024 marks a major watershed in US public finance: from that year, *interest payments* on the national debt will exceed total military expenditure, which has traditionally been the third largest category of federal spending after Social Security and health care. The fact that Social Security and Medicare costs will rise even more dramatically offers little consolation (Wallerstein 2024). The dire CBO projections can be readily seen in Fig. 4.

It is impossible to predict how US policymakers will respond to the unavoidable fiscal crunch that lies ahead, as the prospects for substantial cutbacks in the large entitlement programs appear limited. It is even more difficult to imagine taxes can be raised enough to begin to compensate for the exploding costs of these massive social programs and increasing debt-service costs. If major entitlements cannot be cut substantially—and taxes cannot be raised significantly—something else will have to give. And that something, we argue, is likely to be military expenditures. This is not to suggest that the United States will be dethroned from its position as a dominant military power. Our claim is far more limited. Due to growing fiscal constraints, the United States will likely be forced to reduce, in real terms, the military spending that has subsidized both global security and safe maritime transport.

The third aspect of the increase in transaction costs of maintaining global order *involves escalating military expenditures by major rivals, and changes in technology*. There are, in other words, significant shifts in both military technology and efforts to control the world's waterways. This shift can be seen in the dramatic expansion of China's navy and Russia's ambition to control

---

commons are overexploited because of poor comprehension of the pools themselves, and weak control over access.

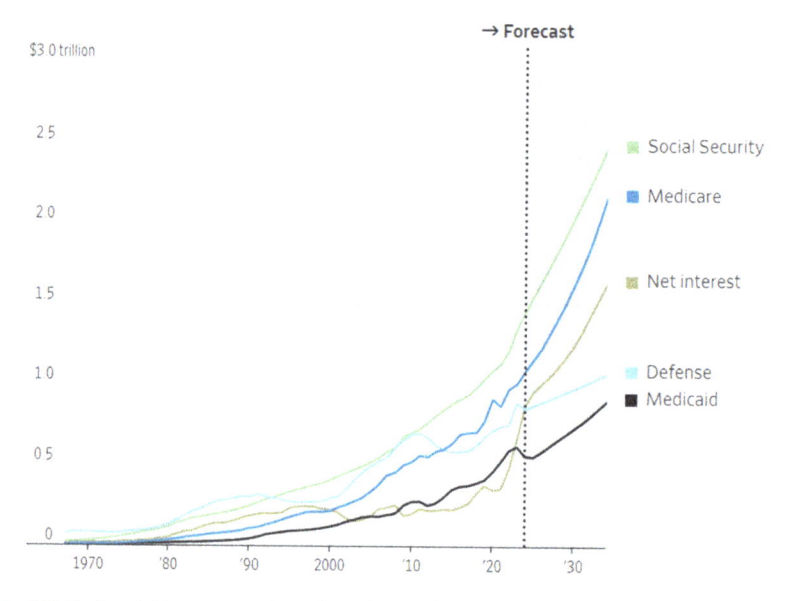

Fig. 4 US Federal Government outlays by major category. *Source* Wallerstein (2024) based on CBO (2024) data

the resource-rich Arctic. We suspect the United States will be increasingly hard-pressed to effectively match its major geopolitical rivals in their own "near abroad." To do so will necessarily further raise the costs of US military operations.

The role of technology in reducing the costs of inflicting global damage is evidenced in the shutdown of the vital Red Sea trade routes beginning in 2023. With the help of low-cost but high-precision missile technology, the Houthi rebels from Yemen have revealed a novel and surprisingly cheap challenge to freedom of navigation (Hookway 2024). The presence of a major US carrier group facilitated devastating bombardments of Houthi positions. However, even the United States' massive advantage in military firepower has proven incapable, at least so far (as of 2024), of reopening the sea lanes.

Benefits of US Subsidization of Global Trade Are Likely Falling

While we have focused largely on the increasing transaction costs of subsidizing the global order that underpins international trade, we would argue the benefits of trade have also changed. In broad terms, it is useful to think of the issues we discuss, next, as recent phenomena that raise the actual costs of trade—to the traders themselves—and hence *lower the net benefits of global trade from a policy perspective*. We distinguish between two categories of risk: random events and the increased risk of geopolitical conflict, or war.

We begin with the claim that "random events" have caused serious disruption to trade flows, and hence have directly raised the cost of trade. In 2021, for example, a large container ship ran aground in the Suez Canal. This single event, in a channel that accounts for almost 10% of global maritime traffic, blocked all transport in the region for six days (Cramer 2022). To take another example, the shipping delays caused by drought in the Panama Canal in 2023 and 2024 are far more serious from a US perspective. Although the Panama Canal accounts for only five percent of global shipping, it accounts for almost 40% of US container traffic. Particularly alarming are the growing concerns that the transit delays here, which trigger higher shipping costs, are not an aberration but are likely to become the new normal (Dahl 2024).

The decisive wake-up call regarding globalization risk was triggered by the mother of all random events: the Covid Pandemic that started in late 2019. Even four years later, it is difficult to grasp the extent to which this novel virus overturned the orthodoxy concerning the wisdom of complex global supply chains and extensive economic interdependence. In calculating the transaction costs of global trade, virtually no one anticipated the possibility that, across the world, factories could be closed, transportation networks could be shut down, and national borders could be sealed off. One of the most striking results of the crisis was the resurgence in policies that prioritized one's own nation over others. All countries, including close allies, adopted policies designed to protect the welfare of their own citizens, with little regard for the so-called "global community." Suddenly the quest for optimal efficiency through extensive specialization and global trade was called into question as the *actual* costs of engaging far-flung international trade increased. National policymakers, not least in the United States, started to look for ways to reduce dependency on foreign suppliers of vital goods.

A second category of risk, the increased possibility of geopolitical conflict, has generated even greater alarm regarding economic interdependence with potentially hostile nations (Copeland 2022). The Russian invasion of Ukraine signaled the brutal "return of history" to the European continent. The war has had a devastating effect on the Ukrainian economy, with GNP falling by an estimated 30% in 2022. But the economic impact extends far beyond Ukraine. Prior to the invasion, Russia and Ukraine ranked among the world's top agricultural exporters. The war, including the blockade of Ukrainian exports in the Black Sea, has led to a sharp drop in exports and, in turn, to significant price increases and food shortages in global markets (Kilfoyle 2023).

The impact on energy prices has been even greater. Over the last two decades, Germany and many other European nations became highly dependent on cheap energy from Russia. At the start of the war, Russia provided more than half of Germany's natural gas, a third of its oil, and almost half of its coal imports. The loss of cheap Russian energy has hit the German economy very hard. According to a recent report, the energy shock has caused the largest postwar decline in living standards and the most severe economic downturn since the 2008 financial crisis (Wintour 2024). As Germany has long served as the locomotive for the broader European economy, a long-term decline in German economic strength would have severe repercussions for the entire EU.

One of the main attractions of globalization was the hope that extensive economic interdependence would eliminate the risk of large-scale warfare. The Russian invasion of Ukraine shattered that illusion. Policymakers are now forced to confront a question that was, until very recently, simply not on the agenda: what are the risks in remaining dependent on both Taiwan and China for a vast range of products, ranging from vital minerals to advanced semiconductors? Starting with President Trump and escalating with President Biden, US economic policy is increasingly focused on reducing dependence on both Taiwan and China (Agrawal 2023).

In concluding our discussion of the changing benefits of world trade, we assume policymakers attempt to assess the likely economic consequences of reducing foreign trade and economic interdependence. The result will vary dramatically from one country to another. While globalization generates economic prosperity by utilizing comparative advantage, specialization, and trade, the contribution of global trade to a given country's prosperity is highly variable. Sweden's prosperity, for example, is inextricably linked to its ability to participate in global markets, which can be seen in Sweden's "trade openness" in Fig. 2 (greater than 80% of GDP). In the absence of global trade, Swedish standards of living would suffer heavily. The picture could hardly be more different for the United States, which is nowhere near as dependent on international trade (barely 20% of GDP), especially beyond its very close neighbors. The United States is therefore unlikely to experience anything like the fall in living standards that many other countries will as it pulls back from more global trade.

Conclusion

Our basic argument, to state it simply, is that mainstream analysis of global economics has been ignoring the considerable transaction costs that must be paid to maintain global peace and ensure safe passage over the world's waterways. For this reason, we argue that "free trade is not free." These costs have been borne overwhelmingly by the United States, the only nation that has had both the motivation and capacity to maintain a global navy and other military assets. These vast assets have effectively subsidized global "order."

We further argue policy makers are motivated primarily by the desire to serve national, not global, interests. Until fairly recently, the national interests of the United States were broadly consistent with the expansion and maintenance of global economic order, since, during the Cold War, the primary motivation was to incentivize allies to counter the threat of the Soviet Union. Thus, the increase in global trade and the prosperity that it engendered were byproducts of this more pressing national interest.

This peculiar alignment of national interests and globally beneficial policies is now waning. We contend the cost-benefit calculus, from a US policy perspective, has been fundamentally altered due to two broad factors. First, *transaction costs* associated with protecting international waterways and serving as the world's police—including, importantly, the growing fiscal constraints of the federal government—have increased substantially from their Cold War levels. Second, the *benefits* of participating in global trade *for the United States* have likely fallen as random events and the disruptions caused by recent geopolitical conflicts have increased. As a result of these changing factors, the United States is unlikely to continue its extensive support for globalization. Greater economic integration among the complementary economies of NAFTA nations means the United States will be less dependent on the rest of the world than it was in the past.

More recent policies support our position that the US pullback from globalization is likely a long-term one. Since at least the start of the Trump administration, the United States has shifted from a strong commitment to "the Washington consensus" to an "American first" style of industrial policy. Many observers initially viewed Trump's policy shifts, especially toward China, as a bizarre aberration that would be quickly corrected when more steady hands regained power. These observers were wrong. The Biden administration has actually doubled down on this policy shift, not least by offering huge subsidies for both American and foreign companies to relocate their production facilities to the United States (Muro 2023).

This policy retreat, in the case of the United States, is therefore not caused by flawed analysis or misguided populist pressures. The United States will largely abandon the "grand" vision of globalization because it no longer has the motivation—or the capacity—to pay the transaction costs that have subsidized global trade for so long.

We should, in conclusion, be clear that we are in no way endorsing this new American industrial policy, which is increasingly oriented toward subsidizing domestic industries. These policies come with their own array of problems, largely documented in the trade literature over many decades. We merely want to point out that the underlying rationale for this major policy adjustment is not simply a misunderstanding of the benefits of trade or misfit populists. Furthermore, any moves to counter the deglobalization trend must presumably start with the correct diagnosis of the underlying problem.

Acknowledgements We would like to thank James Breen, Vincent Carret, Stephen Jones-Young, and Sheilagh Riordan for their helpful comments. Jakee is grateful for the research support of the Wilkes Honors College at Florida Atlantic University.

References

Agrawal R (2023) The White House's case for industrial policy. Foreign Policy, Mar 2. https://foreignpolicy.com/2023/03/02/live-industrial-policy-katherine-tai-trade-economy-chips-inflation/. Accessed Mar 2024

Anderson K (2016) Contributions of the GATT/WTO to global economic welfare: empirical evidence. J Econ Surv 30(1):56–92

Bernhofen D, El-Sahli Z, Kneller R (2016) Estimating the effects of the container revolution on world trade. J Int Econ 98:36–50

Brands H (2024) The US' waning naval dominance and China's surge should worry you. American Enterprise Institute Op-Ed, Mar 21. https://www.aei.org/op-eds/the-us-waning-naval-dominance-and-chinas-surge-should-worry-you/. Accessed Mar 2024

Buchanan J (1984 [1979]) Politics without romance: a sketch of positive public choice theory and its normative implications. In: Buchanan J, Tollison R (eds) The theory of public choice-II. University of Michigan Press

Buchanan J, Wagner R (1977) Democracy in deficit: the political legacy of Lord Keynes. Academic Press, New York

Coase R (1960) The problem of social cost. J Law Econ 3(1):1–44

Congressional Budget Office (CBO) (2024) The long-term budget outlook: 2024–2054. https://www.cbo.gov/system/files/2024-03/59711-Long-Term-Outlook-2024.pdf. Accessed Mar 2024

Copeland D (2022) When trade leads to war: China, Russia, and the limits of interdependence. Foreign Affairs, Aug 23. https://www.foreignaffairs.com/china/when-trade-leads-war-china-russia. Accessed Mar 2024

Cowen T (1985) The Marshall plan: myths and realities. In: Bandow D (ed) U.S. aid to the developing world: a free market agenda. Heritage Foundation, Washington, DC

Cramer M (2022) A year after Suez blockage, another evergreen ship is mired in the Chesapeake. The New York Times, Mar 15. https://www.nytimes.com/2022/03/15/business/ever-forward-stuck-chesapeake-bay.html. Accessed Mar 2024

Dahl MH (2024) The Panama canal is running dry. Foreign Policy, Jan 15. https://foreignpolicy.com/2024/01/15/panama-suez-canal-global-shipping-crisis-climate-change-drought/. Accessed Mar 2024

Dappe MH, Jooste C, Suárez-Alemán A (2017) How does port efficiency affect maritime transport costs and trade? World Bank Policy Research Working Paper 8204. https://documents1.worldbank.org/curated/en/388141506343576100/pdf/WPS8204.pdf. Accessed Mar 2024

Goldstein J, Rivers D, Tomz M (2007) Institutions in international relations: understanding the effects of the GATT and the WTO on world trade. Int Organ 61(1):37–67

Goodwin M, Eatwell R (2018) National populism: the revolt against liberal democracy. Pelican Books, London

Haidt J (2012) The righteous mind: why good people are divided by politics and religion. Penguin Books, London

Hanson G (2024) Washington's new trade consensus and what it gets wrong. Foreign Aff 103(1):164–172

Hookway J (2024) Who are the houthis? what to know as red sea attacks continue. Wall Street Journal, Jan 18. https://www.wsj.com/world/middle-east/houthis-yemen-rebels-us-strike-explained-75697f9c. Accessed Mar 2024

Hume D (1739 [1896]) A treatise of human nature. Clarendon Press, Oxford. http://files.libertyfund.org/files/342/0213_Bk.pdf. Accessed Jan 2024

Ikenberry J (2011) Liberal Leviathan: the origins, crisis, and transformation of the American world order. Princeton University Press, Princeton

Infantino L (2020) Adam Smith and the problem of unintended consequences. J Public Financ Public Choice 35(2):219–236

Institute for Policy Studies (2022) U.S. still spends more on military than next nine countries combined. National Priorities Project. https://ips-dc.org/u-s-still-spends-more-on-military-than-next-nine-countries-combined/. Accessed Mar 2024

International Monetary Fund (IMF) (2023) European Union datasets. World Economic Outlook. https://www.imf.org/external/datamapper/profile/EU. Accessed Mar 2024

Jakee K (2022) Modern political economy I: a brief history. In series pathways to research. EBSCO Information Services

Jakee K, Spong H (2003) The normative bias in entrepreneurial theory. Div Labour Trans Costs 3(2):81–105

Jakee K, Turner S (2002) The welfare state as a fiscal commons: problems of incentives versus problems of cognition. Public Financ Rev 30(6):481–508

Jakee K, Turner S (2023) Contingent compliance: a reconsidered calculus of consent. Paper presented at Mercatus markets and society conference, 34 pp.

Kagan R (2012) The world America made. Vintage Books, New York

Kagan R (2018) The jungle grows back: American and our imperiled world. Alfred A. Knopf, New York

Kilfoyle M (2023) Ukraine: what's the global economic impact of Russia's invasion? Economics Observatory, Oct 24. https://www.economicsobservatory.com/ukraine-whats-the-global-economic-impact-of-russias-invasion. Accessed Mar 2024

Mearsheimer J (2018) The great delusion: liberal dreams and international relations. Yale University Press, New Haven

Muro M (2023) Biden's big bet on place-based industrial policy. Commentary, Mar 6. Brookings Institution, Washington, DC. https://www.brookings.edu/articles/bidens-big-bet-on-place-based-industrial-policy/. Accessed Mar 2024

North D (1990) Institutions, institutional change, and economic performance. Cambridge University Press, Cambridge

Peterson Foundation (2023) The United States spends more on defense than the next 10 countries combined, Apr 23. https://www.pgpf.org/blog/2023/04/the-united-states-spends-more-on-defense-than-the-next-10-countries-combined. Accessed Mar 2024

Posen A (2022) The end of globalization? what Russia's war in Ukraine means for the world economy. Foreign Affairs, Mar 17, pp 1–11

Posen A (2023) America's zero-sum economics doesn't add up. Foreign Policy, Mar 24. https://foreignpolicy.com/2023/03/24/economy-trade-united-states-china-industry-manufacturing-supply-chains-biden/. Accessed Mar 2024

Prasad E (2023) The world will regret its retreat from globalization. Foreign Policy, Mar 24, pp 1–11

Rajan R (2023) The gospel of deglobalization: what's the cost of a fractured world economy? Foreign Aff 102(1):155–162

Rasmussen DC (2017) The infidel and the professor: David Hume, Adam Smith, and the friendship that shaped modern thought. Princeton University Press, Princeton

Smith A (2007 [1776]) An inquiry into the nature and causes of the wealth of nations. MetaLibri, New York. https://www.ibiblio.org/ml/libri/s/SmithA_WealthNations_p.pdf. Accessed 3 Sep 2021

Stockholm International Peace Research Institute (SIPRI) (2022) World military expenditure passes $2 trillion for first time. SIPRI for the Media. https://www.sipri.org/media/press-release/2022/world-military-expenditure-passes-2-trillion-first-time. Accessed Mar 2024

Stratfor (2011) The geopolitics of the United States, part 1: the inevitable empire. https://www.mvd.usace.army.mil/Portals/52/docs/STRATFOR%20article.pdf. Accessed Mar 2024

Subramanian A, Freeman J (2020) How deglobalization is hurting the world's emerging economies. World Economic Forum. https://www.weforum.org/agenda/2020/09/convergence-threatened-by-deglobalization-covid19/. Accessed Mar 2024

Tullock G (1981) The rhetoric and reality of redistribution. South Econ J 47(4):895–907

United Nations Conference on Trade and Development (UNCTAD) (2017) Review of maritime transport 2017. United Nations, New York. https://unctad.org/system/files/official-document/rmt2017_en.pdf. Accessed Mar 2024

US Navy (2017) US ship force levels: 1886-present. Naval History and Heritage Command. https://www.history.navy.mil/research/histories/ship-histories/us-ship-force-levels.html. Accessed Mar 2024

Wallerstein E (2024) A $1 trillion conundrum: the US Government's Mounting Debt Bill. The Wall Street Journal, Feb 16. https://www.wsj.com/finance/the-u-s-government-will-soon-spend-more-on-interest-payments-than-defense-ee6fbeec. Accessed Mar 2024

Williamson OE (1975) Markets and hierarchies. Free Press, New York

Wintour P (2024) German living standards plummeted after Russia invaded Ukraine, say economists. The Guardian, Mar 18. https://www.theguardian.com/world/2024/mar/18/german-living-standards-plummeted-after-russia-invaded-ukraine-say-economists. Accessed Mar 2024

World Bank (2022) Correcting course: poverty and shared prosperity 2022. The World Bank, Washington, DC. https://openknowledge.worldbank.org/server/api/core/bitstreams/b96b361a-a806-5567-8e8a-b14392e11fa0/content. Accessed Mar 2024

Export Subsidies

Veronique de Rugy

One of the biggest fallacies about trade is that the ultimate value of trade for a country is found in that country's exports, with imports being valuable only insofar as they better enable the country to export. But in reality, the opposite is true: Imports are the end and exports are the means. If we could acquire imports without exporting anything, that would be the best of all worlds for us. Unfortunately, foreigners won't work for us for free. They want things in return for what they produce for us, and so we must export.

As a result of this confusion over the role of imports and exports, politicians spend taxpayer money and use up a great deal of resources trying to promote exports through a variety of policies and strategies aimed at enhancing the competitiveness of domestic industries on the global stage. These measures are supposedly designed to support domestic businesses in expanding their market reach beyond national borders, thereby contributing to economic growth and job creation. Some common ways politicians promote exports include currency policies or export subsidies.

V. de Rugy (✉)
George Gibbs Chair of Political Economy, Mercatus Center at George Mason University, Arlington, VA, USA
e-mail: vderugy@mercatus.gmu.edu

Export Subsidies: Prohibited Versus Authorized

Export subsidies are one of the few trade measures prohibited by World Trade Organization rules. The prohibited export subsidies include:

> The grant by governments (or special institutions controlled by and/or acting under the authority of governments) of export credits at rates below those which they actually have to pay for the funds so employed (or would have to pay if they borrowed on international capital markets in order to obtain funds of the same maturity and other credit terms and denominated in the same currency as the export credit), or the payment by them of all or part of the costs incurred by exporters or financial institutions in obtaining credits, in so far as they are used to secure a material advantage in the field of export credit terms.[1]

They are called "prohibited subsidies," as WTO documents explain that "members "shall" not use them."[2] Why this special treatment? Because members see export subsidies as particularly distortive. Export subsidies make the subsidized products cheaper on the international market than they are in the domestic market, making competition unfair and potentially imposing on industries in importing countries harms unrelated to economic efficiency.

The Agreement on Subsidies and Countervailing Measures (SCM Agreement) under the WTO explicitly bans subsidies that are contingent upon export performance, as these are seen to directly distort trade flows. US law has the same treatment of export subsidies. Here's how the Department of Commerce puts it: "They ... are viewed as particularly harmful under the Subsidies Agreement and US law."[3]

The WTO allows certain types of export subsidies to be paid, but only under specific conditions. The SCM Agreement provides some leeway for developing and least-developed countries, recognizing their need for economic development and diversification of their export base. These countries are allowed to use subsidies to reduce the costs of marketing exports or cover indirect costs of exporting products for a limited period. The WTO also permits subsidies aimed at promoting environmental conservation, research, and development, provided these meet certain criteria and that the amount

---

[1] World Trade Organization, "Agreement on Subsidies and Countervailing Measures," part I, art. 1.1, http://www.wto.org/english/docs_e/legal_e/24-scm_01_e.htm.

[2] https://www.wto.org/english/docs_e/legal_e/24-scm_03_e.htm#annI and https://www.trade.gov/trade-guide-wto-subsidies#:~:text=A%20subsidy%20granted%20by%20a,of%20domestic%20over%20imported%20goods.

[3] https://www.trade.gov/trade-guide-wto-subsidies.

of the subsidies are not directly linked to export performance. The Agreement on Agriculture under the WTO has its own set of rules regarding export subsidies. While the Nairobi Ministerial Decision of 2015 aimed for a commitment to eliminate agricultural export subsidies, there are exceptions and provisions for developing countries to support their agricultural sectors under specific conditions.

The distinction between prohibited and allowed export subsidies is based on several considerations. The primary goal is to ensure fair competition in the global market. Prohibiting export subsidies that distort trade flows helps maintain a level playing field for all countries. Second, recognizing the economic challenges faced by developing and least-developed countries, the WTO allows certain subsidies to support their growth and integration into the global economy. Finally, subsidies that promote environmental conservation and research are seen as serving global interests and are therefore treated differently from those that merely aim to boost exports.

The WTO's approach to export subsidies allegedly reflects a balance between promoting free and fair trade and recognizing the diverse needs and challenges of its member countries. By prohibiting subsidies that distort trade while allowing those that support development, environmental, and research goals, the WTO aims to foster an equitable global trading system.

Unfortunately, the export subsidies that are allowed do none of this.

Is There an Academic Case for Export Subsidies?

In the introduction to *Empirical Studies of Strategic Trade Policy*, the Nobel-laureate economist Paul Krugman wrote "The revolution that swept through the theory of international trade in the first half of the 1980s-the rise of the so-called new trade theory'-left many of the insights of traditional trade theory intact.... Yet the new trade theory also suggests some new reasons why government intervention in international trade might prove beneficial."[4] It is in that context that export subsidies were explored in a series of academic papers under the rubric of strategic trade policy.

The term strategic trade policy was coined in a 1985 paper by James Brander and Barbara Spencer making the foundational case for export subsidies.[5] They argue that export subsidies have the potential to benefit a country at the expense of its international rivals, although only under very specific conditions. It is not a general result. And even when these subsidies work,

---

[4] Krugman (1994).
[5] Brander and Spencer (1985).

they are never costless since they raise the cost of imports and shrinks total world output and consumption. In addition, some value is lost when the government shifts market share from unsubsidized goods to subsidized ones. This mechanism operates the same, irrespective of whether the opposing government employs subsidies.[6]

It is not an exaggeration to say that Brander-Spencer analysis gave a new lease on life to advocates of aggressive trade policies. But it was also quickly followed by a lot of pushbacks. A few years after the Brander and Spencer paper, Avinash Dixit and Gene Grossman broadened the scope of the export-subsidy model to consider a scenario where multiple industries engage in "oligopolistic" trade.[7] They find that when industries vie for limited resources, such as specialized labor, the economy is harmed more than in the Brander-Spencer model relative to the free-trade stance. In a landscape populated by numerous industries, the overall economic health improves in the absence of widespread export subsidies.

Next, Ignatus Horstmann and James Markusen demonstrated that the advantages of strategic trade policy could be eroded by new firms entering the market and the consequent overcapacity.[8] In their 1988 study titled "Contradictory Results from Competing Assumptions," Markusen and Anthony Venables examined how oversimplified assumptions are driving any positive outcome associated with export subsidies.[9] A significant finding of their research was that export subsidies are most effective in markets dominated by a few large players.

What the literature reveals is that the outcomes of export-subsidy theories are inherently and very sensitively tied to the assumptions within each model. These assumptions often include an all-knowing government focused solely on maximizing resident income, domestically owned subsidized firms, and static technology and industrial structures. In practice, of course, governments are neither omniscient nor unfailingly devoted to promoting public welfare.

Real-world governments operate with imperfect information and typically juggle conflicting objectives. The presumption that governments can accurately predict trade outcomes and set optimal policies is challenged by

---

[6] The main difference with the traditional trade model, Krugman explains, "we imagine two firms, from each of two countries, competing for some export market. Domestic consumers in this sector are ignored or assumed away, 3 Introduction so that the approach is inherently biased toward a view of trade as competition rather than mutual gain. The firms compete by choosing the level of some strategic variable: perhaps output, perhaps capacity, perhaps R&D".

[7] Dixit and Grossman (1986).

[8] Horstmann and Markusen (1986).

[9] Markusen and Venables (1988).

real-world complexities. Moreover, the influence of lobbying on trade policy has been well-established and suggests a deviation from theoretical ideals, aiming more at profit maximization of the lobby firms rather than enhancing the national income.[10]

Another common assumption of this literature involves domestic ownership of subsidized firms. In their analysis, Brander and Spencer state that they "are assuming an economy with identical consumers who receive the same income based on identical endowments and an equal share of the profits of the imperfectly competitive domestic firm. This is the usual assumption one makes so as to abstract from the problem that the national distribution of income affects demand and welfare." Essentially, this means the researchers presuppose that every citizen equally owns the exporting firm, thereby equally benefiting from any subsidies it receives.

This assumption also overlooks the global nature of finance, ensuring that subsidies often produce benefits for foreign investors. Furthermore, the static nature of the model prevents it from accounting for the dynamic nature of policy and industrial change—meaning that real-world subsidies dispensed in accordance with the model's recommendations might in fact stifle competition and innovation by artificially supporting established monopolies.

As Krugman summarized:

> What this academic critique showed was not that the strategic trade policy concept was wrong, but that it was not necessarily right. Or to put it more accurately, the case for strategic trade policies was not like the traditional case for free trade, which (in the old trade theory) could be made a priori without consideration of the specific details of industries. Strategic trade policies could be recommended, if at all, only on the basis of detailed quantitative knowledge of the relevant industries. So what the new trade theory gave rise to was not a prescription for policy, but a program of research.[11]

Several decades after this research program started, however, attempts to confirm strategic trade theory with empirical data have largely failed to demonstrate the effectiveness of the strategy, including the beneficial use of export subsidies, at surpassing the benefits of a policy of unilateral free trade. In a paper called "Export-Import Bank: What the Scholarship Says," economist Salim Furth summarized the Krugman-edited volume laying out the empirical evidence in the following way:

---

[10] Gawande and Bandyopadhyay (2000).
[11] Krugman (1994).

Gernot Klepper found that Europe's subsidies for Airbus hurt European consumers. Kala Krishna, Kathleen Hogan, and Phillip Swagel conclude that it is not possible to know what the optimal trade policy is for any given industry, and prove that optimal trade policy depends heavily on industry structure. Anthony Venables simulated nine British industries and found net losses, sometimes "extremely large," in six of them. In the other three cases, he cautions that the "magnitude of the gains remains extremely modest." Andrew Dick found that global market share for different firms moved in the opposite direction as Krugman's prediction in a paper in which Krugman proposed using protectionism to promote exports. A decade later, Kyle Stiegert and Shinn-Shyr Wang looked back at the effort to connect strategic trade theory to real-world industries and found very little of practical value.[12]

Export Subsidies in the Real World

The failure to show that in the real-world strategic trade policy has the potential to benefit a country didn't stop governments around the world from using export subsidies. The USA, for instance, employs various forms of support that can be considered as export subsidies, although direct export subsidies are generally restricted under World Trade Organization (WTO) rules. Here are some of the main forms of export support that have been used in the USA:

1. Export financing and insurance: The Export-Import Bank of the USA (ExIm Bank) is a key agency that provides American exporters with financial assistance. This includes direct loans, loan guarantees, and insurance to help foreign purchasers buy US goods and services when private sector lenders are unable or unwilling to provide financing.
2. Agricultural subsidies: The US Department of Agriculture (USDA) administers various programs that support American agricultural producers, some of which have implications for exports. Programs under the farm bill, such as the Market Access Program (MAP) and the Foreign Market Development Program (FMDP), are designed to enable US agricultural producers to enter and expand in international markets by sharing the costs of overseas marketing and promotional activities.

---

[12] Salim Furth. The Export-Import Bank: What the Scholarship Says. The Heritage Foundation. https://www.heritage.org/trade/report/the-export-import-bank-what-the-scholarship-says#_ftnref11.

3. Tax incentives: Certain tax provisions can act as indirect subsidies for exporters. For example, the Foreign-Derived Intangible Income (FDII) deduction, introduced by the Tax Cuts and Jobs Act of 2017, offers a lower tax rate on certain income earned from serving foreign markets, encouraging companies to develop and keep their intellectual property in the USA.
4. Small business support: The Small Business Administration (SBA) offers programs to assist small businesses in exporting. These include financing options like the Export Working Capital Program, which provides working capital to support sales to international customers, and the International Trade Loan Program, which offers long-term financing for businesses expanding because of export sales or adversely affected by imports.
5. State-level programs: Various states have their own programs to support exporters, including grants, loans, and assistance in finding foreign buyers. These programs are often designed to complement federal initiatives and provide more localized support.

Defenders of these programs not only ignore the lack of strong evidence that strategic use of subsidies works in practice as it does in theory, but they also devise new arguments allegedly justifying export subsidies.

Countervailing Trading Partners' Export Subsidies

In recent years, a prevalent excuse for export subsidies is that these are an effective tool for countervailing China's export subsidies. It has certainly been the case with the ExIm Bank in the last eight years. But the argument that export subsidies are necessary to "level the playing field" has been around for a long time. Level playing fields is one of the outcomes the American Export Credit Agency (called the Export-Import Bank of America and referred to as ExIm Bank in this paper) describes itself as pursuing. Its website reads "We also help to level the playing field for US exporters by matching the financing that other governments provide to their exporters." The same argument is used for export subsidies paid to support agricultural products.

The level-the-playing-field argument is also used to justify keeping subsidies in place indefinitely. According to this line of argument, removing export subsidies is the equivalent of unilateral disarmament. Doing so, it is argued, would penalize domestic exporters when they compete globally against firms that are subsidized by their government. It is argued that without any equivalent reduction of foreign export subsidies, reducing subsidies paid to domestic exporters will deprive them of market share, which in turn will cause them to decrease production and shed employment.

Although in an ideal world no governments would be subsidizing their domestic firms and no companies would have to compete against subsidized firms, a domestic government's policy should be to promote the general welfare and allow the national economy to perform at its best as opposed to promoting the welfare of particular industries and firms. We do not operate in an ideal world. A look at the ExIm Bank, for instance, reveals that most of the benefits are captured by a few large exporters and are concentrated in a few sectors like air transportation, oil and gas, and manufacturing. This creates an unlevel playing field between subsidized exporters and all other domestic firms (whether they are exporters or not). Like other subsidies, export-subsidy programs are a heavier burden for domestic taxpayers in the granting nation than for foreign competitors.

Furthermore, there is a lingering claim that China is subsidizing its products more than Europe and the USA, which in turn justifies more export subsidies. But data compiled by the Centre for Economic Policy Research (CEPR) of 18,137 corporate subsidies awarded by China, the EU, and the USA since November 2008 reveal that this is not the case. The USA, along with the EU, accounts for 12,629 entries in the inventory, challenging the notion that extensive subsidization is unique to China. The findings suggest that subsidies are also prevalent in market-based economies like the USA and have significant implications for global trade.

The link between government-backed export and export performance is weak. Take the US ExIm Bank, for instance. There is no connection between how a county ranks as an exporter and its rank as a credit subsidizer. This makes sense since export subsidies affect a relatively low share of exports. The Exim Bank 2023 Competitive Report looks at 29 countries subsidizing their exports through ECAs.[13] Looking at the share of the total exports backed by ECA financing for each country reveals that no country has more than five percent of its exports backed by government support, and for almost all countries on this list, the share of exports backed by ECA financing is below two percent. That includes China.

The country with the largest dollar amount of exports backed by an ECA is Italy ($14.8 billion). Yet, only 2.3% of the country's exports are backed by ECA financing. In most other countries, over 98% of exports happen without government backing. These data suggest that ECA financing is irrelevant to

---

[13] Export Import Bank. Competitiveness Report: https://img.exim.gov/s3fs-public/reports/competitiveness_reports/EXIM_2023_CompetitivenessReport_Final_Print.pdf.

the overall health of the export market and does not move the needle on growth or jobs.

At the heart of the problem is that the typical ECA acts as though the chief determinant of how well its economy can compete globally is how many subsidies it is dispensing relative to how many subsidies are dispensed by foreign ECAs. The Competitiveness Report includes sentences like these: "Increase amount of ExIm financing relative to foreign ECAs," and "Increase amount of ExIm MLT financing in particular industries that have historically sought ExIm support, but where ExIm has fallen behind in terms of ECA activity relative to the significant market presence of US companies in such industries." The number of subsidies, not economic growth of the country, is the target in that framework.

The obsession with what other ECAs are doing signals that the bureaucrats staffing these agencies believe that economic growth and jobs come down to hand-to-hand combat between government banks. This notion is obviously nonsensical. Again, take the case of Italy, which ExIm's Competitiveness Report highlights as a hyperactive ECA, one that is presumably an example to follow. But why? The Italian ECA's hyperactivity appears to have had little impact on the country's economic growth or employment.

Finally, we must recall the very narrow conditions identified by Brander and Spencer (1985) under which a country could benefit from using export subsidies. Furth reminds us that the narrow case for export subsidies in Brander and Spencer's framework would break down if the market exhibits even one of the following eight conditions: "(1) There are more than two significant global exporters in every market; (2) corporate ownership is public and international; (3) most large exporters are multinational and have global supply chains, so their production is not exclusively in the USA; (4) there are many US industries that export globally and on a large scale; (5) the US market is a significant portion of the global market; (6) world markets are complex and not easily understood by government; (7) lobbying efforts are influential in setting trade policy; (8) large exporters mostly operate in high-tech, high-innovation sectors, then a country granting export subsidies will be hurt by its own export subsidies."[14]

---

[14] Salim Furth. The Export-Import Bank: What the Scholarship Says. The Heritage Foundation. https://www.heritage.org/trade/report/the-export-import-bank-what-the-scholarship-says#_ftnref11.

Countervailing Capital Market Failures

Central to the argument in support of export credit agencies' subsidies is the presumption that capital markets are imperfect. Specifically, the presumption is that high risks scare private financiers away from funding high-value projects. This argument is especially popular for justifying subsidies to help so-called infant industries. But the logic of this argument is inherently flawed because private investors are not likely to leave value on the table. And so private investors will not be scared away by high risks when the payoff from success is sufficiently high. If a project's risk-adjusted rate of return is positive—a condition necessary to justify funding—private investors have every incentive to fund that project.

Not all high-risk projects should find financing. Projects with negative risk-adjusted rates of return should be unpursued. Prohibitively high risks serve as a signal that investment funds can be more effectively spent elsewhere. There is simply no credible reason to believe that government officials—spending other people's money—will have a better track record at accurately determining different projects' risk-adjusted rates of return than do private investors spending their own money. As the 1981 Congressional Budget Office (CBO) report on the ExIm Bank notes,

> The mere absence of a loan offer from the private market at terms desired by the borrower does not prove that capital markets are imperfect. Many borrowers are too risky or too small to finance their credit needs in bond markets and must instead go to banks; some borrowers are so risky that even banks will not lend them the amounts they desire.[15]

The inability of high-risk projects with slim prospects for repayment to secure financing reflects a deliberate mechanism within capital markets, signaling the excessive risk associated with these ventures compared to other available opportunities. This aspect of capital markets is a feature, not a bug. Proponents of these subsidies nevertheless insist that "financing gaps" that arise from imperfect capital markets must be filled out of the public purse. But unless and until subsidy proponents offer a credible account of how government officials will get information about project risks that is more reliable than the information obtained by participants in private capital markets, there is no viable justification of export subsidies.

---

[15] The Benefits and Costs of the Export-Import Bank Loan Subsidy Program (Washington, DC: Congressional Budget Office, March 1981), p. viii, https://www.cbo.gov/sites/default/files/cbofiles/ftpdocs/113xx/doc11311/1981_03_export.pdf.

Trade economists examining the operations of America's ExIm Bank point out that, without addressing a genuine market failure, such interventions merely shift income from taxpayers and unsubsidized firms to domestic exporters or residents of the borrowing nation. In essence, the true "financing gap" is the disparity between the earnings that exporters could achieve without intervention and those they manage to secure with government-endorsed advantages. It is not the proper role of the government to offer discount financing to firms with political connections.

Let us, however, imagine for the moment that true market imperfections do exist. One such imperfection, for instance, could be asymmetry of information. Underlying the ExIm Bank's intervention is the built-in assumption that it has special insight or information that the about which transactions are creditworthy and which ones aren't that private lenders either don't have or have no incentives to get access to. Having looked at the additionality criteria used by the Bank to decide how to extend a loan or not, I can testify that the agency doesn't have such information. Even in such a case, the first-best solution is to correct the imperfections directly. For instance, it is unclear why the Bank couldn't share its information with reluctant lenders as opposed to simply extending a subsidy. As Arvind Panagariya notes, "Only if such solutions are not available, a case for temporary protection can be made on the usual 'second-best' grounds."[16]

Another such imperfection might be unavailable credit. That's one of the arguments used by the Bank when it insists that it serves as a lender of last resort. One can imagine that credit would be unusually tight during a financial crisis when global markets tend to freeze, and global trade tends to drop. However, trade economists have found that the main reason for the drop in financing is the lack of demand rather than the lack of loanable funds.[17]

Nevertheless, in reality, the vast majority of export subsidies are extended during good times when the economy is growing, and capital is unquestionably plentiful. In the case of the ExIm Bank, the agency's top foreign beneficiaries are in relatively high-income countries that have no difficulty attracting private capital or investments on their own. Data available on the OECD website show that a relatively small share of the export credits provided by OECD countries go to low-income countries. In 2019, the level of financing by ECAs in high-income countries was more than double

---

[16] Panagariya (2000).
[17] Mora and Powers. See also, Eaton et al. (2010).

the amount in low-income countries. In earlier years, the ratios were much higher: 22-to-1 in 2018, 5-to-1 in 2017, and 24-to-1 in 2016.[18]

As these data show, the American ExIm Bank and other OECD's ECAs are competing in markets where commercial lenders are capable of, and are indeed, doing brisk business. The ECAs' relatively low default rates suggest that it is extending support to creditworthy countries and projects. This puts a dent in the idea that export subsidies are necessary to countervail capital-market failure.

If export subsidies aren't correcting a market imperfection, the subsidies are shifting resources away from other and better uses. In the case of ExIm, for instance, a below-market rate loan or guarantee extended to the agency's beneficiaries is pulling capital away from other uses leaving non-subsidized projects to face higher interest rates on their loans.

Finally, it is worth pointing out that the actual operation of ECAs—including, of course those in Europe and the USA—is to perpetuate oligopoly power. The main beneficiary of ExIm subsidies is Boeing. Meanwhile, one of the largest beneficiaries of its EU counterpart is Airbus. The subsidies add to the existing barriers to entry for Airbus and Boeing unsubsidized competitors.

Export Subsidies to Achieve Diversification

Export diversification falls into the category of what Bhagwati and Srinivasan call the "non-economic" objectives.[19] Here, the case for export subsidies is made as a way to achieve goals such as the "promotion of small businesses" or "minority business exporting."

There is no evidence that export subsidies are the most cost-effective way to achieve a certain level of export diversification. But diversification arguments are used often when it comes to justifying export subsidies granted through ECAs. The ExIm Bank, for instance, is supposed to extend at least 20% of its activities to small businesses. Also, advocates for the Bank argue that without the support, small and medium businesses would be having a hard time accessing credit to export.

It's unlikely. ExIm only backs around 2% of exports, as mentioned earlier. Small businesses account for less than 20% of the American ECA's activities. According to the Small Business Administration, small business exports

---

[18] OECD: Export Credit Statistics, 3. Arrangement Official export credits—Destination countries by income levels (billion USD). And Veronique de Rugy and Justin Leventhal: ExIm Favors High Income Countries.

[19] Bhagwati and Srinivasan (1969).

account for roughly 35% of US exports.[20] In other words, virtually all exports by small businesses take place without any government support.

As a reminder, the abstract theoretical justification for export subsidies exists only for monopolies or near-monopolies. Since small businesses almost always operate in highly competitive markets, there isn't even a theoretical case for export subsidies paid to small businesses.

It is worth keeping in mind that Columbia University economist Arvind Panagariya also makes a powerful case in his paper "Evaluating the Case for Export Subsidies" against another non-economic objective: Export Expansion.

The East Asian Experience

As suggested by Panagariya, "the evaluation of the possible role of export subsidies will be incomplete without a brief discussion of the East Asian experience." He is correct as one very common argument made in favor of export subsidies is that growth in China, Japan, South Korea, and other Asian countries that are rich today was enhanced by export policies these countries pursued in the past. A 1993 World Bank report describes the East Asian miracle, when the economies in the region grew faster than in all other regions of the world and managed to sustain that growth over a long period.[21] Most the high growth was concentrated in Japan, the four Asian Tigers (Hong Kong, South Korea, Singapore, and Taiwan), China, and the Southeast Asian economies (Indonesia, Malaysia, and Thailand). It is true that Asian countries have grown very fast. It is also correct that some of them have, or have had, export subsidies in place.

The questions, however, one must ask are whether the export-subsidy policies pursued by the countries play a crucial role in stimulating exports and growth in the countries in the region, and, if they did, should other countries copy them?

Panagariya writes:

> The answer to the first question is controversial. To begin with, the NBER project headed by Bhagwati and Krueger found that once all incentives and disincentives to exports and imports are taken into account, the domestic relative price of tradables closely tracks the world relative price [Bhagwati (1988)].

---

[20] Small Business Administration. What do we know about small businesses that export? Office of Advocacy. Issue Brief n. 19. March 5, 2024. https://advocacy.sba.gov/wp-content/uploads/2024/03/Issue-Brief-No.-19-Small-Business-Exports.pdf.
[21] World Bank (1993).

As such, even though export subsidies were actually present, they did not tilt the relative prices in favor of exportables in aggregate. From the available econometric evidence, the only East Asian country for which subsidies have been shown to have a statistically significant effect on export performance is the Republic of Korea (Westphal and Kim 1982).[22]

The World Bank analysis effectively accepted Bhagwati and Krueger's result but dug deeper into the specific issue of the role played by export subsidies in the East Asian miracle. The report acknowledges three export push policies pursued by these countries. But as Panagariya notes,

> Though the East Asian Miracle study employs the term "export push" uniformly across these approaches, it is fair to say that the first approach is no different than free trade. The trade regime in Hong Kong and Singapore cannot be described as having tilted the balance in favor of exports either on the average or in specific industries. On balance, the third approach is also closer to a movement towards a free-trade regime rather than having an outright bias in favor of exports even in selected industries. Free-trade regime for inputs used in exports simply moves towards removing the bias against exports rather than creating a bias in favor of them. Though the institutional support policies have a more direct bias in favor of exports, they do no more than partially offset the import protection that has existed in the Southeast Asian economies. Thus, only in the case of the second approach, pursued principally by South Korea and Taiwan, China, some of the policies can be characterized as positively "export push" policies.[23]

With that in mind, does the evidence point to the existence of a causal relationship between pro-export interventions and economic growth? While the report notes that "in most of these economies, in one form or another, the government intervened—systematically and through multiple channels," the authors also conclude that "it is very difficult to establish statistical links between growth and a specific intervention and even more difficult to establish causality."

According to the World Bank report, "private domestic investment and rapidly growing human capital were the principal engines of growth. ... In this sense there is little that is "miraculous" about the [high-performing Asian economies'] superior record of growth; it is largely due to superior accumulation of physical and human capital."[24]

---

[22] Panagariya (2000).
[23] Panagariya (2000).
[24] World Bank.

Even if we were to assume that export subsidies played any role in the Asian countries' growth, it begs the question of whether other countries should emulate them. The answer is no. After observing the use of export subsidies for many years in the USA, the evidence shows that the correction of one distortion by the introduction of another distortion is clearly inferior to removing the original distortion. What's more, the introduction of the alleged corrective subsidy eliminates the pressure to remove the original distortion, and the two distortions are likely to become permanent due to rent-seeking behavior.

Countervailing Existing Tariff Distortions

There is a theoretical case that can be made to justify export subsidies as a means of neutralizing the negative effects of tariffs on imports. As Panagariya notes, "if all imports are subject to tariffs at a uniform rate and cannot be removed, via the Lerner Symmetry theorem, they can be fully neutralized by export subsidies to all products at the same, uniform rate." In practice, however, this isn't what happens. The first-best policy is the removal of the tariffs, insofar as the payment of export subsidies will incite foreign governments to retaliate either with higher tariffs or export subsidies of their own. Further, the desired welfare-improving effect of greater exports will not come to pass.

A Better Way Than Export Subsidies

The case for ending all export subsidies is strong. However, it's losing in the court of political opinion. These days a common case for export subsidies goes something like this: "We are in a global race against China. China is massively subsidizing their exports, dumping them on the global market, and creating unfair trade. We must be more like China in order to fight China."

It isn't true though. The solution is not to impose more consumer punishing tariffs that will add to the overall global market distortions. It is not to subsidize domestic industry either. These policies are a net negative to the economy of any country whose government imposes them.[25] And neither of them will produce results that are superior to a free-trade regime.

---

[25] Bryan Riley. Foreign Export Subsidies: Kill Them Don't Copy Them. https://www.heritage.org/trade/report/foreign-export-credit-subsidies-kill-them-dont-copy-them#_ftnref25.

However, since politicians are rarely satisfied with the idea of doing nothing, they should consider the following alternatives to subsidies.

When China acceded to the WTO in December 2001, they agreed to eliminate all noncompliant subsidies. In a 2018 article, Bryan Riley notes that "This section includes the WTO's limit on export credit subsidies. The USA should take full advantage of existing WTO rules to challenge export subsidies used by China and other foreign governments."[26]

Cato Institute's Scott Lincicome agrees. He recently wrote:

> All 164 WTO members, including the United States and China, have agreed to abide by the SCM Agreement's rules, which are intended to encourage international trade by both preventing the proliferation of trade-distorting subsidies and providing reasonable dispute-settlement mechanisms for adjudicating subsidy-related disputes. The SCM Agreement 1) defines what is and isn't a "subsidy"; 2) prohibits the most trade-distorting subsidies (those tied to exports or the recipients' use of local content over imports); 3) lets a WTO member challenge other subsidies (i.e., ones that harm the member's domestic companies at home or in overseas markets) at the WTO or via a "countervailing duty" (CVD) investigation; and 4) sets forth procedures for CVD cases.[27]

If he had to choose, he would prefer using global anti-subsidy rules' alternative process—a WTO dispute—since it "is a much better approach than unilateral CVDs. Most importantly, WTO cases are adjudicated by respected independent arbiters approved by all WTO members." Over at International Law and Economic Blog, Simon Lester also argues that using the WTO's adverse effects complaints is a better route to take than the domestic CVD route.[28] Still both CVDs investigations and WTO beat using export-subsidy policies.

In sum, the evidence is clear that doing nothing against countries who use export subsidies is the least distortive economic approach. But the USA and other countries are facing a resurgence of calls for protectionism not seen in decades. In the interest of fencing off some of our worst instincts, the least costly response is for all countries to scale back their subsidies and either recommit to the WTO's agreement on subsidy rules or design a new set of anti-subsidy rules. Else, we risk spiraling into costly subsidy wars, costly trade wars, and a declining standard of living.

---

[26] Au (2013).
[27] Lincicome (2024).
[28] Lester (2024).

References

Au TH (2013) Reconciling WTO general exceptions with China's accession protocol. Tsinghua China Law Rev 5(2). http://www.tsinghuachinalawreview.org/articles/PDF/TCLR_0502_AU.pdf

Bhagwati J, Srinivasan TN (1969) Optimal intervention to achieve non-economic objectives. Rev Econ Stud 36(1):27–38

Brander JA, Spencer BJ (1985) Export subsidies and international market share rivalry. J Int Econ 18(1–2):83–100

Congressional Budget Office (1981) The benefits and costs of the export-import bank loan subsidy program. https://www.cbo.gov/sites/default/files/cbofiles/ftpdocs/113xx/doc11311/1981_03_export.pdf

De Rugy V (2015). The export-import bank: winners and losers of government-granted privilege. Mercatus Center. https://www.mercatus.org/publications/export-import-bank/export-import-bank-winners-and-losers-government-granted-privilege

De Rugy V and Leventhal J. Ex-Im favors high income countries

Dixit AK, Grossman GM (1986) Targeted export promotion with several oligopolistic industries. J Int Econ 21(3–4):233–249

Eaton J, Kortum S, Neiman B, Romalis J (2010) Trade and the global recession. National Bank of Belgium Working Paper no. 196. http://papers.ssrn.com/sol3/papers.cfm?abstract_id=1692582

Export-Import Bank of the United States (2023) Report to the U.S. congress on global export credit competition. https://img.exim.gov/s3fs-public/reports/competitiveness_reports/EXIM_2023_CompetitivenessReport_Final_Print.pdf

Furth S. The Export-Import Bank: what the scholarship says. The Heritage Foundation. https://www.heritage.org/trade/report/the-export-import-bank-what-the-scholarship-says. Accessed 15 May 2024

Gawande K, Bandyopadhyay U (2000) Is protection for sale? Evidence on the Grossman-Helpman theory of endogenous protection. Rev Econ Stat 82(1):139–152

Horstmann IJ, Markusen JR (1986) Up the average cost curve: inefficient entry and the new protectionism. J Int Econ 20(3–4):225–249

International Trade Administration. Trade guide: WTO subsidies agreement. https://www.trade.gov/trade-guide-wto-subsidies. Accessed 15 May 2024

Krugman P (1994) Introduction. In: Krugman P, Smith A (eds) Empirical studies of strategic trade policy. University of Chicago Press, pp 1–10. https://www.nber.org/system/files/chapters/c8673/c8673.pdf

Lester S (2024) WTO adverse effects complaints vs. domestic CVD cases. Int Econ Law Policy Blog. https://ielp.worldtradelaw.net/2024/02/wto-adverse-effects-complaints-vs-domestic-cvd-cases.html

Lincicome S (2024) What should America do about Chinese overcapacity? the answer may surprise you. The Dispatch. https://www.cato.org/commentary/what-should-america-do-about-chinese-overcapacity

Markusen JR, Venables AJ (1988) Trade policy with increasing returns and imperfect competition: Contradictory results from competing assumptions. J Int Econ 24(3–4):299–316

Organization for Economic Co-operation and Development. Arrangement official export credits—destination countries by income levels (billion USD). Export Credit Stat 3.

Panagariya A (2000) Evaluating the case for export subsidies. Policy Research Working Paper 2276. World Bank. https://documents1.worldbank.org/curated/en/836621468750545367/pdf/multi-page.pdf

Riley B. Foreign export credit subsidies: Kill them, don't copy them. The Heritage Foundation. https://www.heritage.org/trade/report/foreign-export-credit-subsidies-kill-them-dont-copy-them. Accessed 15 May 2024

Small Business Administration, Office of Advocacy (2024) What do we know about small businesses that export? Issue Brief no. 19. https://advocacy.sba.gov/wp-content/uploads/2024/03/Issue-Brief-No.-19-Small-Business-Exports.pdf

World Bank (1993) The East Asian miracle: economic growth and public policy. Oxford University Press, New York

World Trade Organization. Agreement on subsidies and countervailing measures. Part I, Article 1.1. http://www.wto.org/english/docs_e/legal_e/24-scm_01_e.htm. Accessed 15 May 2024

Germany's Costly Hidden Export Subsidies

Gunther Schnabl

Germany's Costly Export Subsidization

Germany is a successful exporting country. Brands such as Volkswagen, Bayer, and Haribo are known worldwide. After World War II, "*Made in Western Germany*" became a quality seal. At the end of the 1950s, West Germany overtook the UK as the leading export nation in Europe. Between 2003 and 2008, Germany's exports even surpassed the much larger USA as shown in Fig. 1. Germany was the "*Export World Champion.*" Then, China passed by. According to the World Bank, today, exports represent around 50 percent of GDP of Germany. In France, it is only 34%, in Italy 37%.

Over time the driving force of German exports has changed, however. After World War II, for a long time, the German mark was under appreciation pressure. This constituted a persistent pressure on the German industry to increase efficiency and to develop highly sophisticated products, which were resistant to exchange rate-induced price increases in foreign markets (Schnabl 2023). With the introduction of the euro, the circumstances changed. The euro not only eliminated the exchange rate and appreciation risk for the German export industry with respect to exports to the member states of the

---

A previous, policy-oriented version of the paper was published in Schnabl (2024).

G. Schnabl (✉)
Institute for Economic Policy, Leipzig University, Leipzig, Germany
e-mail: schnabl@wifa.uni-leipzig.de

Flossbach von Storch Research Institute, Cologne, Germany

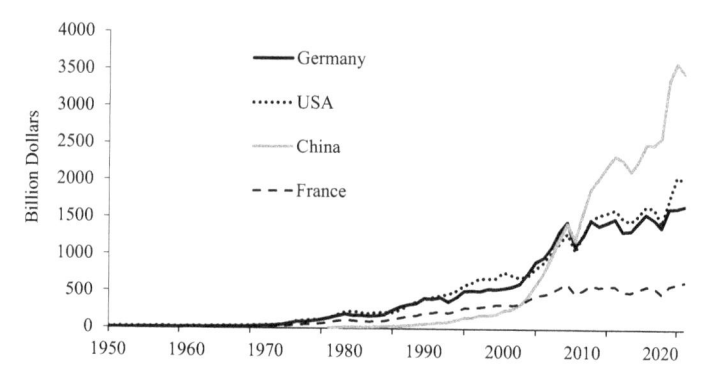

Fig. 1 Exports of large export nations. *Source* International Monetary Fund. 2023 Approximation

European Monetary Union. As the European Central Bank became increasingly inclined to set interest rates low and to allow for a deprecation of the euro, the German export industry also became addicted to hidden subsidies.

An export subsidy is generally defined as a government policy to encourage exports of goods through direct payments, low-cost loans, tax relief for exporters, or government-financed international advertising (see Brander and Spencer 1985; Melitz and Messerlin 1987; Collie 1991). As will be shown, in the case of Germany since the turn of the millennium, the export subsidies not only took the form of persistent low interest rate policies and corporate bond purchases of the European Central Bank. Also, the euro rescue policies may have been motivated from a German perspective by the goal to sustain Germany's exports, with the transmission taking the detour via public international credit provision (Müller and Schnabl 2019; Murai 2024).

Capital Outflows Drive Export Surpluses

Germany had a positive current account in most years after World War II, which was usually attributed to the high competitiveness of its industry. But there were also times when a negative current account balance persisted, for example in the 1990s. While West Germany still had been recording trade and current account surpluses in most of the 1980s, the current account of Germany suddenly turned negative in the early 1990s after the reunification as shown in Fig. 2. The high investments in East Germany and the catch-up demand of East Germans in consumption had caused a sharp rise in imports.

Figure 2 also shows that for Germany—as for all other countries—the current account is a mirror image of the financial account, which represents

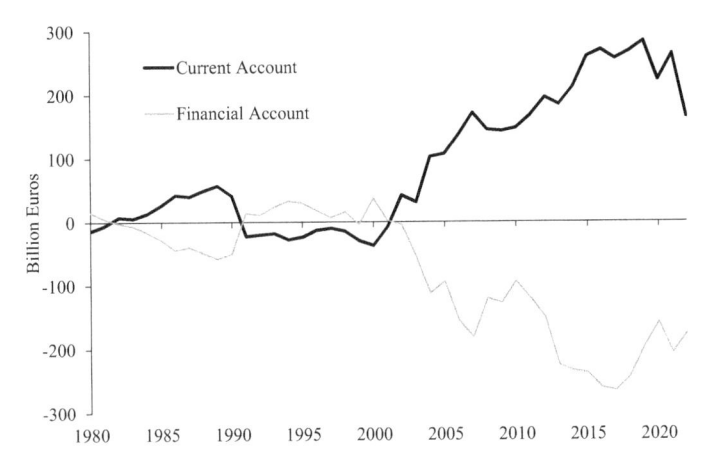

Fig. 2 Current and financial account of Germany. *Source* Oxford Economics. Until 1990 West Germany, from 1991 unified Germany. 2023 Forecast

net capital inflows (positive sign) or net capital outflows (negative sign).[1] If, as in Germany since the turn of the millennium, the financial account is negative, more capital flows out than capital flows in over a year. There is a long discussion as to whether the flows of goods and services drive capital flows or vice versa (see for instance Böhm von Bawerk 1914; Obstfeld 2012).

Yet, in a world of liberalized capital markets, in which since the 1970s more and more capital has been flowing around the globe, capital flows had a major impact on the flow of goods and services as confirmed by Murai (2024) for Germany. Thus, before the European financial and debt crisis, Greece could not have imported as many goods, if they had not received large amounts of loans from abroad (Abad et al. 2013). For Germany, this implies that in these times, the impressive export surpluses can not only be attributed to the excellent quality of the German goods but also to accelerating capital outflows since the turn of the millennium.

The financial account in the wider sense, which measures how much private and public capital flows across borders within a year, has an impact on a country's so-called net foreign assets. The net foreign assets correspond to the difference between the assets held by Germans abroad and the assets held by foreigners in Germany. Figure 3 shows that Germany, China, and Japan have accumulated large wealth abroad thanks to persistent current account surpluses. In Germany, this process starts since the turn of the millennium. There are two reasons for the rising current account surpluses, which are linked to the macroeconomic policy mix (Murai and Schnabl 2021).

---

[1] See also the absorption approach to the current account (Alexander 1952).

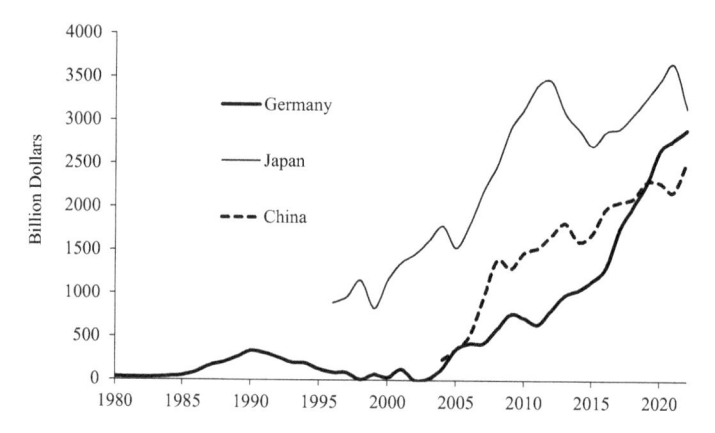

Fig. 3 Net foreign assets of Germany, Japan, and China. *Source* International Monetary Fund

First, in response to the bursting of the dot-com bubble in March 2000, the European Central Bank cut interest rates significantly, from 4.75 in April 2000 to 2.0% in June 2003. Falling interest rates favor capital exports. The euro area interest rate remained low until December 2005 before gradually rising again. Second, during this time, the German government—in contrast to other euro area countries—made efforts to keep public finances under control, as the national debt had risen sharply as a result of the reunification. Due to the high costs of the reunification, Germany had not only reached the debt limit of the European Monetary Union equivalent to 60% of GDP. The German corporations had also lost significantly in international competitiveness due to rising wages and social security contributions as reflected in the current account deficits of the 1990s (Sinn 2003).

The former Chancellor Gerhard Schröder reacted boldly with the so-called Agenda 2010 from 2003, which referred to the European Union's Lisbon Strategy. The European Union's objective was to become the "*most competitive and dynamic knowledge-based economy in the world.*" The reforms aimed at creating more room for private initiative, reducing unemployment, limiting public debt, and preparing the social security system for demographic change. The government relaxed employment protection, which lowered the company's payroll costs. It reduced unemployment benefits and created pressure to enter the labor markets, with a large low-wage sector being created (Eichhorst and Marx 2011).

The government reduced the benefits of statutory health insurance and made the rise in pensions dependent on demographics. Early retirement incentives were eliminated to increase the employment of aged people. As the reforms reduced the expected statutory pension benefits, state support for private pension provision was provided. When in the year 2005 Angela Merkel took over the Chancellorship, she explicitly thanked her predecessor for the courageous reforms (Deutscher Bundestag 2005).

The reforms affected the financial account as they increased aggregate savings. Households saved more because the government promoted private retirement provision. At the end of 2007, there were more than 10 million so-called Riester contracts for private pension provision.[2] The state was holding back on spending, particularly in terms of personnel costs and investment. In 2007, a public sector surplus was reached. Companies saved because the reforms created a large low-wage sector that kept down the wage level. Figure 4 shows the sharp rise in overall savings since 2003.

While savings correspond to the supply on the domestic capital market, investments represent the demand for capital. If capital would not be allowed flow across borders, the capital supply and demand would align over the interest rate. In Germany, domestic investment remained sluggish as the dot-com bubble had burst in March 2000, with the reforms further depressing economic sentiment. As shown in Fig. 4, investments did not keep up with the steep rise in savings. The demand for credit was crippling, with savings piling up at German banks.

The upshot is that German banks started looking for lending opportunities abroad. They found two particularly attractive regions. First, a small economic miracle was developing in the south of the euro area, after interest rates had sharply declined in the course of euro accession. (Previously, given a

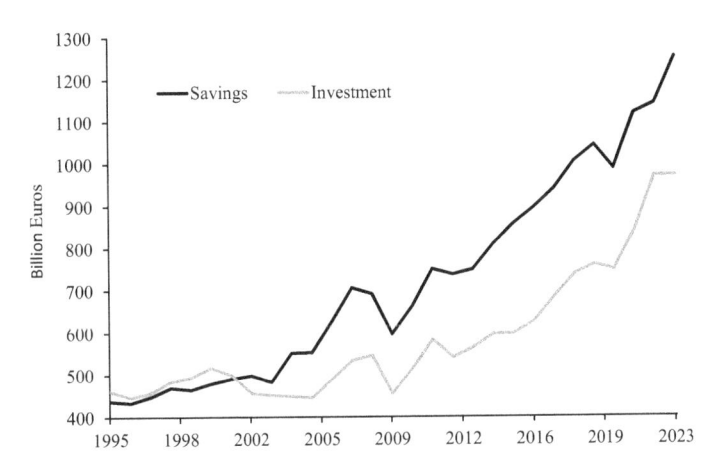

Fig. 4 Savings and investment in Germany. *Source* International Monetary Fund

---

[2] Named after Walter Riester, who created the concept.

high degree of macroeconomic instability, interest rates had been high.) The economy also boomed in the Baltic countries and Iceland. Second, the Fed's interest rate cuts in response to the bursting of the dot-com bubble had triggered a boom in the US real estate market, which was boosting bank lending there. German banks participated in both lending booms.

Even though foreign loans are more risky than domestic ones, the German banks' foreign lending increased sharply (Sepp et al. 2024). If, as in the case of the Asian Financial Crisis, the currency of a debtor country is devalued, and lending is denominated in the currency of the creditor country, the debt and interest burdens of the debtor country rise sharply in domestic currency, which increases the risk of default (McKinnon and Schnabl 2004). With the euro, exchange rate risks within the euro area were eliminated, which made lending to other euro area countries more attractive. The Baltic countries had not yet introduced the euro but had credibly pegged their exchange rates to the euro. Despite the exchange rate risks, investments in the USA were attractive to German banks. Public and private banks channeled German savings into the US mortgage market. American banks handed out large-scale loans to low-income people, later referred to as "*ninjas*, ("people with "*no income, no job, and no assets*"), with property prices going sharply up.

Investment banks bundled these real estate loans into securities, so-called asset-backed securities, with rating agencies awarding them the highest AAA rating. Many German banks, in particular publicly owned banks such as Sachsen LB, WestLB, HSH Nordbank, and BayernLB, purchased these securities through subsidiaries in Ireland, with possible risks not being reflected in their balance sheets. While the volume of outstanding loans from German banks abroad in 1999 was just over 700 billion euros, they rose to over 2,400 billion euros until the outbreak of the global financial crisis in 2008, as shown in Fig. 5.

In the southern euro area countries, the USA, and other countries, the additional loans allowed companies and households to import more German goods. German savings may have also taken the detour via other countries, such as France or the Netherlands. The credit booms abroad brought about import booms, which came along with fast-rising current account deficits (Unger 2017), which particularly benefited the large German export-oriented industrial companies. At the same time, in Germany, domestic consumption stagnated because real wages barely rose. Even more, in 2006, the new German government further curtailed consumption by raising value-added tax from 16 to 19%—the "biggest tax increase since 1949."

German exports rose from $471 billion in 2001 to $1450 billion in 2008, as Fig. 1 shows. The German automotive industry experienced an

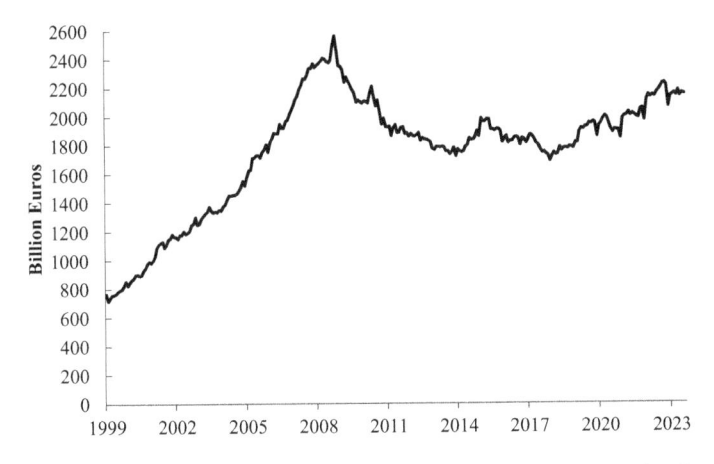

Fig. 5 Outstanding loans from German banks abroad. *Source* Deutsche Bundesbank

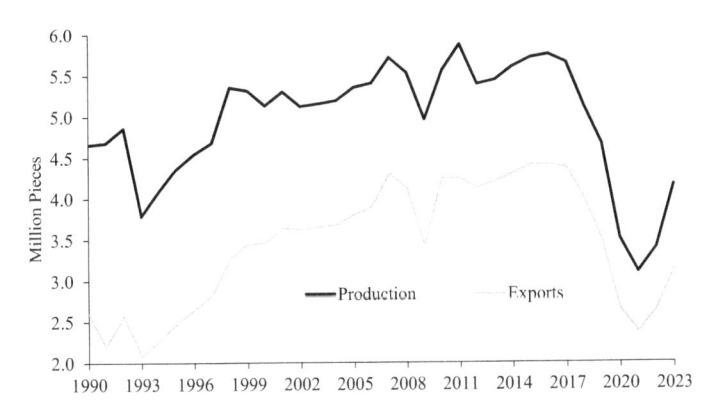

Fig. 6 Production and exports of the German automotive industry. *Source* VDA. 2023 Forecast

outstanding boom. It exported 4.30 million vehicles in 2008, up from 3.64 million vehicles in 2001 (see Fig. 6). Stock prices rose. However, with the outbreak of the global financial crisis, exports and production fell sharply in 2008 and 2009. A lucrative business model threatened to be lost.

How the ECB and the German Government Secured Exports

As German foreign loans had played a major role for the export boom, the crisis threatened to lead into a major export crisis. Public banks such as WestLB and Sachsen LB were bankrupt and could no longer lend abroad. To reduce the balance sheet risks exposed to the foreign credit, many other banks withdrew their foreign loans. Thus, when exports and production collapsed in 2008, particularly of the German car industry, the German government not only stabilized domestic demand by creating a "car-scrap bonus".[3] It also stabilized car exports by stabilizing the southern euro area countries.

In the USA, the Fed had mitigated the crisis by cutting interest rates quickly. As early as December 2008, the Fed began unprecedented purchases of government bonds and other assets via *quantitative easing*. At the same time, the US government decided on major economic stimulus programs and supporting measures for the financial sector. In Asia, the Bank of Japan greatly expanded its purchases of government bonds. In China, the government launched a huge stimulus package to fight the global crisis. Thus, German exports to the USA and East Asia were stabilized.

But most German exports went to the European Union. Between 2001 and 2008, the proportion of exported goods going to the partner countries of the European Union had risen from 50 to 84 percent of total exports. As households and governments in southern Europe had lived beyond their means during this period, a sharp decline in imports and thus in German exports could be expected with an economic downturn in these regions. Even a possible collapse of the euro came on the agenda. Strong devaluations of the currencies of the southern euro area countries would have made imports from Germany much more expensive.

The European Central Bank's interest rate cuts stabilized the banking sector across the euro area and prevented the crisis from expanding further. The extensive support provided for the euro crisis countries by the European Union, the European Central Bank, and the International Monetary Fund not only rescued the euro but also constituted a rescue program for the German export industry. In 2010, German exports were already growing again (see Fig. 6 for automobiles). Yet, as the crisis continued to simmer, the bargaining power of the German trade unions remained weak, helping to keep the wage costs of German companies low.

The so-called Target2 balances within the Eurosystem played a crucial role for the cohesion of the euro (Sinn 2012). The Eurosystem consists of the European Central Bank and the national central banks of the euro area, which implement the monetary policy decisions for the ECB governing council. The European Central Bank had originally set up the payment system Target2 (originally Target) to speed up cross-border financial transactions between

---

[3] ...Owners of old cars received a subsidy from the government, if they decided to scrap their car and buy a new one.

banks. With the outbreak of the financial crisis, a second function unexpectedly emerged: A kind of credit mechanism. The Deutsche Bundesbank built up large Target2 claims against the European Central Bank, while southern crisis countries such as Italy and Spain accumulated large liabilities versus the European Central Bank.

The Target2 claims of the Deutsche Bundesbank rose to around 1,200 billion euros by the end of 2022, as shown by Fig. 7. Sinn (2012) argued that the Deutsche Bundesbank was providing large amounts of credit to the southern euro area countries through the Target2 system. The recipient countries such as Italy and Spain were initially able to refinance their current account deficits thanks to growing Target2 liabilities to the European Central Bank. Later, austerity programs of the EU aiming to curtail public debt, restrained imports, and thereby helped to cure the current account deficits.

Yet, when investors withdrew their deposits from Italian banks and brought them (inter alia) to Germany, some Italian banks would probably be in disarray, if they had not received loans from Banca d'Italia as compensation. Banca d'Italia refinanced itself through the Target2 system with the European Central Bank, which in turn received deposits from the Deutsche Bundesbank. Sinn (2012) criticized that lending to the southern central banks was automatic and did not require any explicit approval by the Deutsche Bundesbank. There was no clear ceiling for these loans and the European Central Bank did not reward any interest payments for the Target2 claims of the Deutsche Bundesbank at the time.

Hellwig (2018a), a former member of the European Systemic Risk Board, which is based at the European Central Bank, contradicted. The Target2

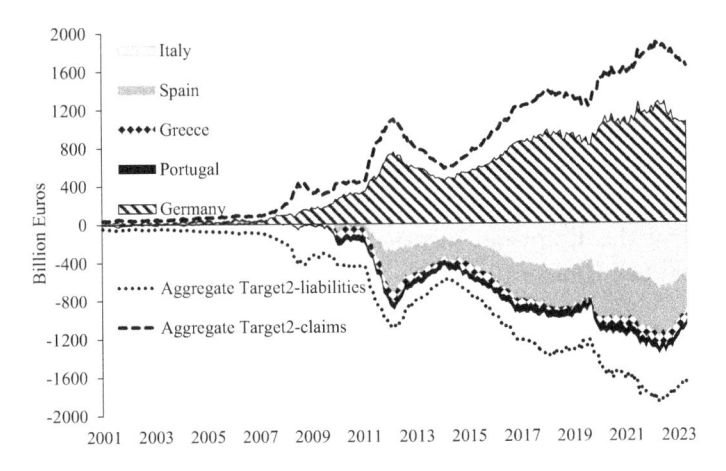

Fig. 7 Target2 balances in the Eurosystem. *Source* European Central Bank

claims of the Deutsche Bundesbank were no loans; possible losses were negligible because the claims were not rendering interest. Isabel Schnabel, today a member of the Executive Board of the European Central Bank, argued in a hearing in the German parliament that the discussion about the Target2 balances was characterized by misunderstandings and misrepresentations, which led to an overestimation of the risks from the Target2 balances in the German public (Deutscher Bundestag 2019).[4]

While the conflict has not been resolved to this day, the Deutsche Bundesbank's statistics indicate the increasing Target2 claims as an international investment, i.e., as a capital export. The statistics of the International Monetary Fund account for the Target2 claims of the Deutsche Bundesbank as part of the German foreign assets. As the Target2 claims stabilized the banks and the economy in the recipient countries as well as the euro, they also stabilized the demand for German export goods.

Even more, the public Kreditanstalt für Wiederaufbau (KfW), which has been responsible for export and project financing since 1950, helped to cover the risks of export corporations. In 2008, it outsourced this business area to IPEX-Bank as a wholly owned subsidiary. The Bank for International Project and Export Finance (IPEX) provides medium- and long-term targeted financing to support the export industry, the development of economic and social infrastructure as well as environmental and climate protection projects in other countries. The KfW Group continuously expanded its export financing, so that it has risen to more than 71 billion euros by 2022.

The upshot is that the German government and the European Central Bank have played a crucial role in German capital exports. Initially, it was private capital outflows that were driven by uncoordinated monetary and fiscal policy decisions. Since the outbreak of the European financial and debt crisis, the European governments and the European Central Bank have created a comprehensive network of national and European rescue measures that have not only saved the euro, but also promoted German exports. While many people see the German export surpluses as an expression of the high competitiveness of the German economy, at the latest since 2008, they were supported by the European Central Bank, the German government, and other European institutions.

---

[4] "In our opinion, no comprehensive reforms of the target system are necessary, as this system does not pose any significant risks to the German taxpayer." Schnabel said (Deutscher Bundestag 2019).

Stupid German Money?

The southern European countries repeatedly complained that Germany subsidizes its exports by low wages (Bonatti and Fracasso 2013). The European Commission saw the continued high export surplus of Germany as a risk to the European economy (The Spiegel Online 2013). Chancellor Angela Merkel replied, however, that it makes no sense to artificially reduce Germany's competitiveness. It would be absurd to cut production and to make cuts to the quality of German products. (Der Spiegel Online 2013).

In 2017, US President Donald Trump, on a visit to Brussels, said: "The *Germans are bad, very bad*". "*See the millions of cars they sell in the US. Terrible. We will stop this.*" (Müller 2017). The then-German Finance Minister Wolfgang Schäuble responded that those, who were counting on economic growth, needed to also rely on free trade and not on protectionism. Chancellor Angela Merkel explained to students of a High School in Berlin that the German export surplus was driven by the depreciation of the euro and the low price of oil. Both factors were not within the sphere of influence of the German government, which could not order that goods which the Germans wanted to buy would be produced in other EU countries (Reuters Online 2017).

Thus, whether or not current account surpluses are beneficial for a country depends on the point of view. Current account surpluses can be considered as savings of a country for the future because capital is invested abroad. In the 1980s, Germany has invested capital abroad, which could be repatriated in the wake of the reunification to finance the necessary investments. Yet, the sudden withdrawal of German capital from abroad triggered several crises at the time, including the UK (Masson 1994). Under normal circumstances, credit renders interest and will eventually be repaid. Today's capital exports finance more imports from abroad tomorrow. On the other hand, a foreign borrower benefits from investing the funds, which allows repayment in the future.

Currently, the US economy grows faster than the German economy, which is throttled by the governments' green transformation plans. The innovative companies for artificial intelligence are concentrated in the USA. The US financial market is highly developed and robust. Why not invest there for the future? With German capital inflows promoting growth in the USA, the USA is benefiting from German savings. If Germany's funds are well-invested in the USA, the USA will be able to repay its debts without any problems in the future, which would be beneficial for the aging German society.

The problem is, however, that on average, German investment abroad does not yield high returns. A study by the Kiel Institute for the World Economy (2019) suggests that the return on German foreign assets is significantly lower than that of other countries. Between 2009 and 2017, the average annual income was more than five percentage points lower than that of US foreign investments. Other European countries, such as Italy, France, and the Netherlands, have performed significantly better, with German capital exports being dubbed a "*billion dollar grave.*" In particular, the investment of German banks in the US subprime market turned out to be a disaster.

Financial assets abroad are not necessarily repaid. They are more risky than domestic financial assets because information about the reliability of foreign borrowers is limited. In the case of crises, it is more difficult to assert claims across borders than in the case of domestic claims. Many of the assets that Germans have acquired abroad in the last twentyfive years have lost their value. The term "*stupid German money*" was originally coined by the US film industry, after tax-subsidized media funds in Germany had attracted savings into unlucrative US film productions. Since investors were able to deduct losses in the film industry from taxable income, films "with a flop guarantee" were tempting for German doctors and pharmacists (Welt am Sonntag 2007).

Huge investments by German state-owned banks in the US mortgage market suddenly turned out to be worthless in the global financial crisis. In July 2008, the German finance minister had to urge a consortium of German banks to take over the risks of the private German Industrial Bank (IKB) amounting to 3.5 billion euros in July 2008. That the state-owned KfW took over a share of 2.5 billion euros indicates that the public sector was strongly involved in the failed investments abroad. The losses of German state-owned banks in course of the US mortgage market crisis were estimated to be more than 70 billion euros (Hellwig 2018b).

German industrial companies also lost substantial amounts with takeovers of foreign competitors. The "*marriage of horror,*" as *the Süddeutsche Zeitung* has described the takeover of Chrysler by the German car producer Daimler, is said to have cost nearly 40 billion euros (Süddeutsche Zeitung Online 2010). BMW's acquisition of the English car manufacturer Rover for 2 billion marks in 1994 ended six years later with the sale of MG Rover for ten British pounds to a financial investor. The losses are estimated to have totaled up to 10 billion euros. The costly acquisition of Monsanto by the German chemical giant Bayer in 2018 created immense legal risks in the USA, strongly pulling down the share price up to the present.

The total loss in value of German investments abroad is difficult to quantify but is likely to be considerable. At the end of 2022, Germany's officially

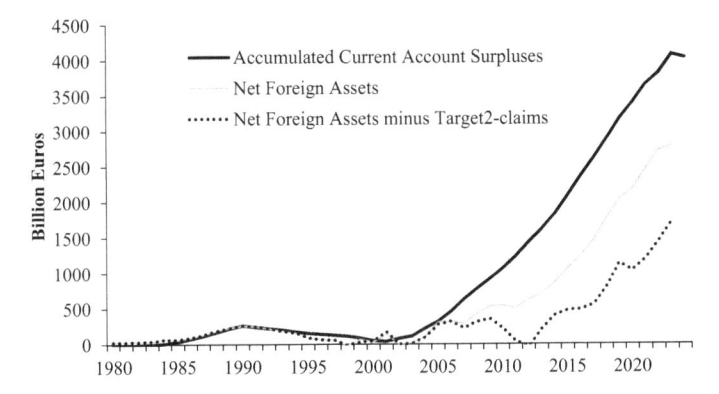

Fig. 8 Estimates of Germany's net foreign assets. *Source* German Bundesbank and own calculations

declared net foreign assets stood at 2,720 billion euros (Fig. 8). Net foreign assets correspond to the difference in German assets abroad minus foreign assets in Germany. If all current account surpluses and deficits in Germany since 2000 are added up as a proxy for net foreign assets without losses, the figure is around 3,850 billion euros (Fig. 8). This would imply a loss of around 1,130 billion euros, i.e., around 13,000 euros per inhabitant.

If the Target2 claims of the Deutsche Bundesbank, which at the end of 2023 still amounted to around 1000 billion euros, are additionally deducted, the net foreign assets at the end of 2023 would be only 1,696 billion euros. The loss would be equivalent to 2,420 billion euros, i.e., around 28,600 euros per capita. Albeit the total size of the losses will remain unknown, it should be certain that much of the austerity in consumption, which allowed German companies to export and maintain industrial jobs, will not bring more consumption to the German consumers in the future.

Welfare and Distribution Effects of Lost Capital Exports

In view of the high losses on German foreign investments, however, it is doubtful that—given the underlying hidden subsidies—current account surpluses are beneficial for German citizens. Moreover, it seems that the Germans give away their export goods to abroad for free. But why did the German government repeatedly defend the German export surpluses so vigorously despite international criticism? Wouldn't it have been better to increase wages in Germany that would have increased household consumption, thereby reducing the risky international assets? Wage levels could have risen more strongly, constituting a countermeasure against growing political discontent.

One answer could be that policy makers did not know it better, believing in the high competitiveness of the German export industry. Alternatively, some players have benefited from the export surpluses. Since the turn of the millennium, the German export industry—above all the car industry—had a pleasant tailwind due to the capital export boom. The consumers abroad were subsidized. On the other hand, the Germans did not consume the capital that went abroad, which is likely to have been at the expense of small companies in the service sector, whose business depends on the purchasing power of the domestic population.

Since the year 2010, the number of restaurants, bars, and small retail stores has continued to decline. In the smaller cities, the shop windows are becoming increasingly empty. Whereas the centers of large cities are still very lively, this is much less the case in smaller cities and villages. This indicates not only a significant loss of wealth but also that the success of the large export corporations is particularly at the expense of the small-scale service sector. Goods that are given abroad for free increase the output per capita. But consumption abroad does not benefit the domestic consumer.

The illusion of a rich country can be maintained by referring to the successful export industry, but wealth that has been given abroad does not come to the attention of the people. From this point of view, the large export surpluses were and still are a major redistribution in favor of the large export companies, their suppliers, their managers, and their employees at the cost of the rest of the German population.

Meanwhile, as the ECB has increased interest rates and therefore painfully increased the financing cost of German corporations, the demands for subsidies have become louder. The Kiel Institute for the World Economy has shown that the German government has dramatically expanded the volume of subsidies, often justified by environment or climate protection (Laaser et al. 2023). Subsidies have increased from 38 billion euros in the year 2000 to 98 billion euros in 2022 and are estimated to increase to 208 billion euros in 2023 as shown in Fig. 9. Including the financial aid from the federal states and tax concessions the estimation even goes up to 362 billion euros for the year 2023.

Although all kind of subsidies are included in this estimation and not all of them are going directly to the corporations, it is likely that the large export-oriented corporations are most successful in bargaining for public

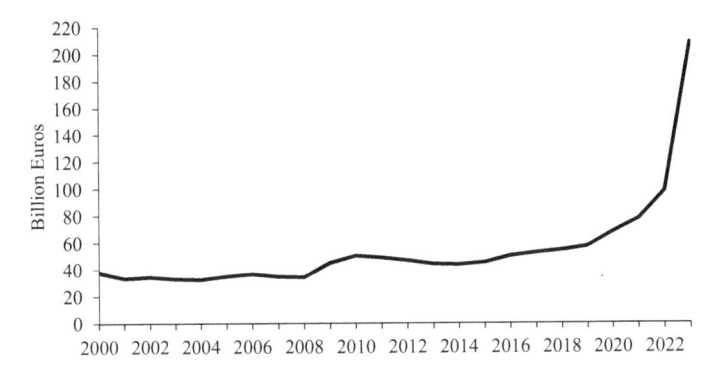

Fig. 9 Subsidies in Germany. *Source* Kiel Institute for the World Economy. 2023 projection

support, particularly by stressing their crucial role in greening the German economy and achieving the ambitious climate goals of Germany and the European Union. Meanwhile, the flourishing subsidies are becoming a threat to the common market of the European Union, i.e., the free movement of goods, services, capital, and labor. To prevent distortions to free competition within the common market subsidies are forbidden and exceptions have to be authorized by the European Commission.

The European Commission, however, has increasingly become inclined to make exemptions, particularly for German and French companies. Germany has exerted pressure to soften the restrictions on state aid in the European Union, with representatives of smaller countries such as the Czech Republic and the Netherlands raising complaints (Packroff and Noyan 2023). The executive vice-president of the European Commission, Margrethe Vestager, has proposed a "Temporary Crisis and Transition Framework" for state aid, which facilitates subsidies for renewable energy technologies and tax breaks for companies in strategic sectors that are at risk of diverting investments to third countries outside Europe (Allenbach-Ammann 2023). This may be a way for the large German export-oriented corporations to maintain their international competitiveness despite rising energy and wage costs. Yet, this new model of export promotion is far from the originally high competitiveness of the German industry.

References

Abad J, Löffler A, Schnabl G (2013) Fiscal Divergence and TARGET2 Imbalances in the EMU. Intereconomics 48(1):51–58

Alexander S (1952) Effects of a Devaluation on a Trade Balance. IMF Staff Pap 2(2):263–278

Allenbach-Ammann J (2023) EU Commission's Vestager proposes change to state aid rules. *Euractiv* 13.1.2023. https://www.euractiv.com/section/economy-jobs/news/eu-commissions-vestager-proposes-change-to-state-aid-rules/

Böhm von Bawerk E (1914) Unsere passive Handelsbilanz, In: Weiss, Franz (ed): *Gesammelte Schriften von Eugen von Böhm-Bawerk.* Leipzig: Hölder-Pichler-Tempsky

Bonatti L, Fracasso A (2013) The German model and the European Crisis. J Common Market Stud 51(6):1023–1039

Brandner J, Spencer B (1985) Export subsidies and international market share rivalry. J Int Econ 18:83–100

Bundestag D (2005) Stenografischer Bericht, 4. Sitzung, Plenarprotokoll 16/4, 30. November 2005, 78, https://dserver.bundestag.de/btp/16/16004.pdf

Bundestag D (2019) Experten wollen Target2-System beibehalten, https://www.bundestag.de/dokumente/textarchiv/2019/kw23-pa-finanzen-644412

Collie D (1991) Export subsidies and countervailing tariffs. J Int Econ 31:309–324

Der Spiegel Online (2013) Merkel verteidigt Handelsüberschüsse, 21.11.2013, https://www.spiegel.de/wirtschaft/soziales/merkel-verteidigt-handelsuebersch uesse-a-934944.html

Die Welt am Sonntag Online (2007) Stupid German Money für Hollywood, 2.8.2007, https://www.welt.de/wams_print/article776804/Stupid-German-Money-fuer-Hollywood.html

Eichhorst W, Marx P (2011) Reforming German labour market institutions: a dual path to flexibility. J Eur Soc Policy 21(1):73–87

Hellwig M (2018a) Target2-Falle oder Empörungsfalle? Perspekt Wirtsch 19:345–382

Hellwig M (2018b) Germany and the Financial Crisis 2007–2017, https://www.riksbank.se/globalassets/media/konferenser/2018/germany-and-financial-crises-2007-2017.pdf

Kiel Institute for the World Economy (2019). Deutschland verdient weniger mit Auslandsanlagen als andere Länder, 4.7.2019, https://www.ifw-kiel.de/de/publikationen/aktuelles/deutschland-verdient-weniger-mit-auslandsanlagen-als-andere-laender/

Laaser CF, Rosenschon A, Schrader K (2023) Kieler Subventionsbericht 2023: Subventionen des Bundes in Zeiten von Ukrainekrieg und Energiekrise, Kiel

Masson P (1994) The credibility of the United Kingdom's commitment to the ERM: intentions versus actions. IMF Working Paper WP/94/147

McKinnon R, Schnabl G (2004) The East Asian dollar standard, fear of floating, and original sin. Rev Dev Econ 8(3):331–360

Melitz J, Messerlin P (1987) Export credit subsidies. Econ Policy 2(4):149–167

Müller S, Schnabl G (2019) The brexit as a forerunner: monetary policy, economic order and divergence forces in the European Union. Econ Voice 16:1

Müller P (2017) Trump in brussels: The Germans are bad, Very bad, 26.5.2017. https://www.spiegel.de/international/world/trump-in-brussels-the-germans-are-bad-very-bad-a-1149330.html

Murai T (2024) The relationship between the German current account and financial account: evidence from Toda-Yamamoto causality approach. Econ Voice 21:1

Murai T, Schnabl G (2021) Macroeconomic policy making and current account imbalances in the euro area. Credit Capital Markets 54(3):347–373

Obstfeld M (2012) Does the current account still matter? Am Econ Rev 102(3):1–23

Reuters Online (2017) Merkel weist Kritik an deutschem Exportüberschuss zurück. https://www.reuters.com/article/idUSKBN18I16H/

Packroff J, Noyan O (2023) Germany under fire for push to revamp EU-subsidy rules, *Euractiv* 16.1.2023. https://www.euractiv.com/section/politics/news/germany-under-fire-for-push-to-revamp-eu-subsidy-rules-2/

Schnabl G (2023) Seventy-five years west German currency reform: crisis as catalyst for the erosion of the market order. Kyklos 77(1):77–96

Schnabl G (2024) Deutschlands fette Jahre sind vorbei. Finanzbuchverlag, München

Sepp T, Israel KF, Treitz B, Hartl T (2024) Monetary policy and bank-type resilience in Germany from 1999 to 2022. Universität Leipzig, Wirtschaftswissenschaftliche Fakultät, Working Paper 181

Sinn H-W (2003) Ist Deutschland noch zu retten. Econ Verlag, Berlin

Sinn H-W (2012) Die Target2-Falle—Gefahren für unser Geld und unsere Kinder. Hanser Verlag, München

Süddeutsche Zeitung Online (2010) Hochzeit des Grauens, 17.5.2010, https://www.sueddeutsche.de/wirtschaft/daimler-und-chrysler-hochzeit-des-grauens-1.464777

The Spiegel Online (2013) Complaints about German Exports Unfounded, 5.11.2013

Unger R (2017) Asymmetric credit growth and current account imbalances in the Euro Area. J Int Money Financ 73:435–451

Trading Away Freedom: How Non-trade Elements Came to Dominate Trade Agreements

Iain Murray

The American writer Jonah Goldberg regularly suggests that free trade agreements should consist of one sentence on one piece of paper: "There shall be free trade between [the countries.]" Henceforth I shall call this Platonic Ideal of the free trade agreement a "Goldberg agreement." Yet we all know that Goldberg Agreements are a fantasy.

The very need for any sort of agreement on trade suggests why. Each country has its own domestic barriers to trade and the trade agreement exists precisely to try to remove or lower the presence of these barriers. A Goldberg Agreement would imply the sweeping away of every such barrier, from tariffs through product safety standards to warranty requirements and beyond. It would allow the importation and sale of snake oil. (By which I mean fraudulent medication, not the actual product, which is available at Amazon. There truly are markets in everything.)

Indeed, a Goldberg Agreement actually reveals that the case for free trade is essentially a unilateral one. If lowering domestic trade barriers is a good thing, why not do it in the absence of an agreement with other parties? No agreement is needed. A genuine free trade policy recognizes that governments do not trade with each other, individuals and businesses do, so let them. There is no role for governments, or an agreement between them.

Once governments insert themselves into these peaceful economic transactions, however, the very idea of negotiation introduces mercantilist concepts

I. Murray (✉)
Competitive Enterprise Institute, Washington, DC, USA
e-mail: Iain.Murray@cei.org

into those negotiations. So, the best a free trader can hope for is something approaching a Goldberg Agreement, with mutual lowering of trade barriers such that economic transactions between citizens of the two nations are unimpeded by anything but the most basic considerations. Such an agreement might not be a sentence long, but it might only be a few pages.

While such complete deregulation via trade agreement may be a dream to satisfy the desires of the most ardent anarcho-capitalist, it is unlikely to happen in the modern world. Although tariff barriers can be overcome relatively easily via a process of give and take, non-tariff barriers and technical barriers to trade have proven stickier.

This is at least partly because domestic barriers are precisely that—domestic. They have, at least in aggregate, been the product of a considerable amount of deliberation and political maneuvering that in many cases represents a compromise between various interest groups within the nation. A trade agreement that asks politicians and officials essentially to reopen those debates has to offer a considerable amount in compensation.

And for the most part, during the era when trade was governed by the General Agreement on Tariffs and Trade, trade agreements did so. The reduction primarily in tariff barriers offered a great deal in exchange. Politicians in many countries also recognized that their internal domestic rules represented a drag on domestic economic growth and so pursued domestic liberalization alongside trade liberalization. The result was a huge boost to many economies around the world, from China to New Zealand and from India to Mexico.

In other places, trade agreements advanced along the lines of what Ikenson, Lester, and Hannan call "mercantilist reciprocity," whereby one country agrees to expose its domestic sectors to greater competition only in exchange for reciprocal greater access to the other country's markets for their merchants' exports. The approach therefore blended the mercantilist idea that imports were costs with the Ricardian principle of comparative advantage, as the reciprocity was not direct, but allowed specialization to occur.

As Ikenson et al. summarize, these "managed trade" deals "simultaneously liberalize, divert, and stymie trade and investment flows." While liberalizing trade in some areas, they erect or reinforce protectionist barriers for some industry sectors. Politicians announcing trade deals routinely celebrate their "wins" for the export industry alongside the protections for domestic sectors, with the gains from imports rarely being mentioned.

The Changing Nature of US Trade Agreements

What this chapter will attempt to demonstrate is that as the gains from reduced tariffs have mostly been achieved thanks to the results of GATT the characteristics of trade deals have changed.[1] They have become gradually more about the stronger party in the trade deal, normally the US or European Union, exporting their domestic protections in certain areas to the weaker party, imposing restrictions on that party's abilities to liberalize and specialize. These protections largely cluster around two areas—labor regulation and environmental regulation—that will be discussed in detail below.

Another underappreciated aspect of this change has been the move away, particularly in the U.S., from larger multilateral trade deals toward bilateral deals that allow for greater leverage by the larger party on the smaller. After the North American Free Trade Agreement (NAFTA) in 1994 and the creation of the World Trade Organization (WTO) in 1995, the U.S. proceeded to negotiate a series of much smaller bilateral deals:

- Jordan–United States Free Trade Agreement—Signed in 2000.
- Chile–United States Free Trade Agreement—Signed in 2003.
- Singapore–United States Free Trade Agreement—Also signed in 2003.
- Australia–United States Free Trade Agreement—The first of four agreements signed in 2004.
- Morocco–United States Free Trade Agreement—Signed in 2004.
- Bahrain–United States Free Trade Agreement—Signed in 2004.
- Oman–United States Free Trade Agreement—Signed in 2006.
- Peru–United States Trade Promotion Agreement—Signed in 2007.
- Colombia–United States Trade Promotion Agreement—Signed in 2006 but did not go into effect until 2012.
- Korea–United States Free Trade Agreement (KORUS)—Signed in 2007 and put into effect in 2012 (the United States' largest free trade agreement since NAFTA.)
- Panama–United States Trade Promotion Agreement—Signed in 2007 and enacted in 2012.

The only multilateral agreement signed during this period was the Dominican Republic–Central America Free Trade Agreement (CAFTA-DR)—signed in 2004 with Costa Rica, El Salvador, Guatemala, Honduras,

---

[1] Daniel J, Ikenson, Simon Lester, Daniel Hannan, "The Ideal U.S.-U.K. Free Trade Agreement: A Free Trader's Perspective," Cato Institute, Sept. 18, 2018. https://www.cato.org/white-paper/ideal-us-uk-free-trade-agreement-free-traders-perspective.

Nicaragua, and later joined by the Dominican Republic in 2005. Nevertheless, the combined size of the economies on the other side of the agreement from the U.S. was still quite small. However, toward the end of this period of bilateral agreements there were serious plans for multilateral agreements, most notably the Trans-Pacific Partnership (TPP) and the US-EU Transatlantic Trade and Investment Partnership (T-TIP.)

A proliferation of bilateral agreements necessarily increases bureaucracy. Consider, for example, the form of Goldberg Agreement with a few pages mentioned earlier. Some of those few pages will describe "Rules of Origin" so that the two parties can be sure that the benefits of trade accrue only to the two nations and not to other nations whose citizens insert themselves into the process. Bureaucracies and their guidance policing these rules of origin will grow. In doing so, these bilateral agreements introduce discrimination among products in a manner contrary to the original principle of the GATT, which was non-discriminatory.[2] Even multilateral regional agreements do this, although in a less harmful way than bilaterals.

The domestic bipartisan opposition to the US-negotiated Trans-Pacific Partnership (TPP) demonstrated in the 2016 election may have represented the final demise of multilateral agreements from the U.S. Both presidential candidates decried the deal as not gaining enough for US domestic interests, and the Biden administration has shown no appetite for re-entering the deal that was negotiated by the administration in which Joe Biden was vice president. This was the same time that T-TIP negotiations stalled, as the incoming President Donald Trump expressed a strong desire for bilateral agreements over multilateral agreements, saying one week into his presidency:

> We've also withdrawn from the Trans-Pacific Partnership, paving the way for new one-on-one trade deals that protect and defend the American worker. And believe me, we're going to have a lot of trade deals. But they'll be one-on-one. There won't be a whole big mash pot.[3]

The subsequent renegotiation of the North American Free Trade Agreement by the Trump administration into the United States-Mexico-Canada Agreement (USMCA) was also an act of political power on behalf of the United States—the other parties had little choice but to go along with it. As we shall see, while achieving some welcome liberalizations and introducing a

---

[2] General Agreement on Tariffs and Trade (1947)—Article XIII: Non-discriminatory Administration of Quantitative Restrictions https://www.wto.org/english/docs_e/legal_e/gatt47_01_e.htm#articleXIII.

[3] Administration of Donald J. Trump, Remarks at the "Congress of Tomorrow" Republican Member Retreat in Philadelphia, Pennsylvania, January 26, 2017, https://www.govinfo.gov/content/pkg/DCPD-201700514/html/DCPD-201700514.htm.

new element on regulatory coherence that could prove especially beneficial, the renegotiated agreement also included much stronger labor and environmental provisions as well as increased protectionism—and therefore less free trade—particularly in the automotive sector than its predecessor agreement for all the parties involved.

Another thing to note in this brief history of US trade agreements is the gradual disappearance of the word "free" from the titles of the agreements. Apart from Korea-US, trade agreements since 2006 have been styled "trade promotion agreements" rather than "free trade agreements," representing a recognition of a change in approach from promoting free trade to promoting managed trade. The Obama-era negotiations of multilateral agreements emphasized the word "partnership" over trade.

One final thing to consider before we move on to more detailed analysis is that the only new trade agreements negotiated by the US during the Trump administration (the US-Japan Trade Agreement, and the "Economic and Trade Agreement Between the Government of the United States of America and the Government of the People's Republic of China," commonly known as the "Phase One Trade Agreement," signed in 2019 and 2020 respectively) were expressly designed not to need Senate approval. As "executive agreements," they derive their authority from existing delegated powers and therefore do not rise to the level of treaties, which would require approval. This is an important distinction given the role afforded treaties in the US Constitution. It further underlines the idea that these agreements are primarily administrative and regulatory in nature.

What Happened with NAFTA—Environmental Side-Agreement

When NAFTA was being negotiated in the early 1990s, early objections were raised to the progress of negotiations by a variety of special interests, including labor and environmental organizations and lobby groups. Political opposition was led by prominent figures across the political spectrum—old right conservative Pat Buchanan, third party presidential candidate and populist Ross Perot, and leftist environmental and consumer advocate Raph Nader.

The overlapping objectives of these interest groups led to novel alliances, such as US labor organizations allying with international environmental pressure groups. Charges of "social dumping" were leveled by both groups. First President George H. W. Bush and then President Bill Clinton agreed to open side negotiations on these issues. These translated into side-agreements that were pursued parallel to NAFTA that achieved many of the special interests' objectives. As a study by the Federal Reserve Bank of Dallas put it at the time:

> [W]hile NAFTA opens trade, NAFTA related agreements open broader opportunities for protectionists to reduce trade through appeals against environmental and workplace enforcement in areas with little direct effect on the international exchange of goods and services.[4]

These groups had successfully linked their issues to trade directly for the first time, with an official infrastructure created to support them. Future agreements would have to take account of them. For example, the NAFTA environmental side-agreement contained the following provisions:

- A new Commission for Environmental Cooperation, which would consist of the top environmental official from each member nation, a Joint Advisory Committee, and a secretariat to support them;
- Treaty obligations on each signatory to "ensure that its laws provide for high levels of environmental protection and shall strive to continue to improve those laws";
- Dispute settlement processes to be followed should a party fail to enforce its environmental laws and obligations under the treaty;
- Monitoring arrangements on the environmental effects of trade between the parties; and
- Immediate workplans aimed at eliminating certain chemicals and pesticides within the treaty area.

For the first time, therefore, the U.S. allowed for the internationalization of environmental policy, and it did so largely by exporting its own attitude toward environmental law to Mexico (Canada already having similar environmental laws). This set a precedent for harmonization of environmental law in future treaties and agreements.

It should be noted that this agreement implicitly recognized that Mexico's existing environmental law represented an unfair trading practice. In addition to its work on chemicals and pesticides, the Commission early on set about introducing cooperative regulations on matters such as pollution, emissions, habitat protection, and energy efficiency. Even as early as 1995, the Commission was beginning work on assessing the effects of climate change.

---

[4] William C. Gruben and John C. Welch, "Is NAFTA Economic Integration?" Economic Review (Federal.
Reserve Bank of Dallas) Second Quarter, 1994. https://www.dallasfed.org/~/media/documents/research/er/1994/er9402c.pdf.

As James M. Sheehan of the Competitive Enterprise Institute inventoried in 1995, early work from the Commission was already resulting in significant changes to Mexico's environmental laws. Sheehan summarized:

Upward Harmonization of Regulations is Progressing in Several Areas:

- *Mexico's laws are being patterned after U.S. laws in the areas of transportation, forestry, fisheries, soil, and water standards.*
- *In advance of NAFTA harmonization meetings, Mexico's transport ministry published 125 pages of regulations classifying hundreds of important industrial materials as officially "hazardous" under the United Nations guidelines. Other rules were issued covering vehicle emission standards, engine manufacturing requirements, and fuel standards in preparation for the NAFTA harmonization of weights and transport regulations.*
- *NAFTA officials drafted harmonized rules through a Land Transportation Standards Subcommittee. Reports were translated from Spanish to English to French and back again, and the NAFTA-crats [sic] settled on the official definition of a "NAFTA truck."*
- *Raising its standards to U.S. levels, Mexico enacted an "Emergency Response Guidebook," which classifies transported materials according to "U.N. Recommendations on the Transport of Dangerous Goods." Mexican environmental authorities declare that "We are going to work closely with the [U.S.] EPA to standardize what we mean by waste."*[5]

While many of these reforms may have been desirable and in pursuit of other treaty obligations, we should not lose sight of the fact that, for example, reforms to forestry regulations were prioritized in the name of a trade agreement.

In doing so, the NAFTA agreement lost sight of one of the most important considerations in international trade—the principle of comparative advantage. It is entirely possible (indeed likely given current debates over the requirements of the National Environmental Policy Act) that US environmental law over-protects the environment in comparison with other considerations. If that is the case, then exported US standards may be even more out of proportion to Mexico's needs. To put it another way, lower standards of environmental protection might form some of the comparative advantage Mexico has over the U.S., allowing it to produce certain goods more affordably.

---

[5] James M. Sheehan, "Two Years after NAFTA: A Free Market Critique and Assessment," Competitive Enterprise Institute," December 1, 1995. https://cei.org/studies/two-years-after-nafta-a-free-market-critique-and-assessment/

By exporting its environmental law to "level the playing field" the US nullified this comparative advantage. The principle, to briefly reiterate, holds that both parties gain from comparative advantage. Even if Portugal is better at producing cloth than England, it still makes sense for it to import cloth from England if its comparative advantage is in producing wine. Both England and Portugal gain from the trade.

Thus, the U.S. not only hurt Mexico. By insisting on it raising its environmental law to the same standards as the U.S., it also hurt itself. In many ways the principle of comparative advantage is simply an application of the concept of opportunity cost. The environmental provisions of NAFTA were actually an imposition of opportunity costs on the American economy.

Moreover, the effects of these changes on Mexico's environmental performance suggest that they interfered with the country's progress along the environmental Kuznets Curve. The concept of the curve, which posits that countries first increase the amount of environmental damage they produce as their economies grow then start to reduce it, was actually developed during the NAFTA debate.[6] Research by Lipford and Yandle suggests that while Mexico was within range of the turning point of the Kuznets Curve when NAFTA was signed, it has failed to generate enough income growth since NAFTA to actually pass it.[7] They conclude:

> Simply put, while NAFTA's institutional framework alone may have reduced pollution below levels that would have otherwise prevailed, the treaty has not resulted in the rapid economic growth necessary for Mexico to reach and surpass turning points for pollutants other than those that most directly affect human health and welfare (water and sanitation). Mexico will have to wait for further income growth before progress begins on other pollutants and Mexico begins its race to the top.

It is therefore possible that NAFTA's environmental provisions caused it to fail both as a trade agreement, by causing Mexico's economy to fail to grow as much as would have been desirable from a trade treaty, and as an environmental agreement, by failing to incentivize the economic growth necessary for environmental improvement, despite the imposition of significant changes in environmental law.

---

[6] Gene M. Grossman and Alan B. Krueger, Environmental Impact of a North American Free Trade.
Agreement, Working Paper 3914, Cambridge, MA: National Bureau of Economic Research (1991).

[7] Jody M. Lipford and Bruce Yandle, "NAFTA, Environmental Kuznets Curves, and Mexico's progress,".
Global Economy Journal 10(4):4–4, January 2011. https://www.mercatus.org/research/working-papers/nafta-environmental-kuznets-curves-and-mexicos-progress.

Nevertheless, the NAFTA side-agreement on the environment was an important and influential precedent (as was the side-agreement on labor, as we shall see later). It proved so important that it influenced the main US law governing future trade agreements, the Trade Promotion Authority Act, when it was re-authorized in 2002.

The US Constitution vests power over trade with other nations in the US Congress, not in the president. However, to allow for the president and the US trade representative to conduct trade negotiations, the Congress regularly grants the president trade promotion authority (TPA) to both negotiate and then "fast track" trade agreements so that they are voted up or down quickly and are not bogged down in Congressional back-and-forth (the latter consideration is why TPA became known as "fast track").

As part of the grant of TPA, the Congress sets out its objectives and constraints for presidential negotiations. During the TPA debates running up to the 2002 re-authorization labor and environmental interests demanded that labor and environmental matters be included in every trade agreement, thereby elevating NAFTA's side-agreements to full articles of any trade treaty.

The intent was to ensure that any trade agreement imposed labor and environmental standards more demanding than those of existing, separate multilateral labor and environmental treaties. As John Audley of the Carnegie Endowment for International Peace, one of the chief players in the 2002 reauthorization put it, "The Trade Act of 2002 reflects an important shift in U.S. trade policy. The argument over whether or not environment belongs in trade negotiations is now over; environmental policy is here to stay as an element of trade negotiations."[8]

All future trade agreements negotiated by the U.S. therefore contained some form of labor and environmental provisions. Other countries followed suit. Trade agreements would therefore routinely include some form of mercantilist protectionism in the form of these provisions.

---

[8] John Audley, Trade, Equity, and Development, "Environment's New Role in U.S. Trade Policy," Carnegie Endowment for International Peace, September 2002 https://carnegieendowment.org/2002/09/24/environment-s-new-role-in-u.s.-trade-policy-pub-9039.

Exporting Environmental Politics and Bureaucracy

After NAFTA's precedent for the export of US environmental law and regulations, it was only natural that future agreements would provide for the export of US environmental politics. The CAFTA-DR trade agreement mentioned above provides a helpful case study for how this happened.

The environmental provisions in CAFTA include the creation of and Environmental Cooperation Commission that establishes a work program for environmental "programs, projects, and activities."[9] These programs have largely been funded by the U.S. under the guise of trade promotion.

For instance, in the first few years of the agreement, the George W. Bush administration spent nearly $40 million (2008 dollars) "to support trade-related environmental initiatives."[10] These initiatives included:

- Strengthening institutions for more effective implementation and enforcement of environmental laws;
- Promoting biodiversity and conservation;
- Promoting market-based conservation; and
- Promoting private-sector environmental performance.

The U.S. continues to spend large amounts of taxpayer money on CAFTA-DR partners' environmental regimes. The Environmental Protection Agency is currently sponsoring programs on air quality management, public participation in the environmental impact assessment process, solid waste management, and marine litter, all under the authority of trade promotion.[11]

As with the example of NAFTA's environmental agreement and Mexico, serious questions arise as to whether these initiatives promote trade. They would seem to reduce the CAFTA-DR countries' comparative advantage and hinder the development of economic infrastructure. Environmental impact assessments, for instance, have a well-known tendency to become bloated, and their compilation, especially with significant public participation, often delays much-needed projects. This hindrance of needed infrastructure might in turn cause environmental Kuznets Curve issues, suggesting that all the

---

[9] Chapter 17.9 of the CAFTA-DR Agreement https://www.caftadr-environment.org/wp-content/uploads/2015/04/Chapter_17_CAFTA_-_DR.pdf.
[10] Fact Sheet: CAFTA-DR Environment Projects, Office of the Spokesman, US Department of State, January 30 2008. https://2001-2009.state.gov/r/pa/prs/ps/2008/jan/99875.htm.
[11] US EPA, Capacity-Building Programs Under the Dominican Republic-Central America-United States Free Trade Agreement (CAFTA-DR). https://www.epa.gov/international-cooperation/capacity-building-programs-under-dominican-republic-central-america. Accessed May 3, 2024.

bureaucracy for which the U.S. is paying might harm the environment in the long run.

An example of the bureaucracy exported is the CAFTA-DR Secretariat for Environmental Matters, to which under the treaty any citizen or organization can submit a complaint that a party is not enforcing its environmental responsibilities.[12] Dealing with a complaint is a bureaucratic process. The secretariat receives the complaint, determines if more information is needed, then decides whether the complaint has met the requirements for further action. If it decides it has, it requests a response from the party. The party may form a technical committee to investigate the matter and following the report of the committee submit a response to the secretariat. Further back-and-forth may continue. If necessary, an arbitration panel is formed.

Many of the submissions to the Secretariat have come from environmental groups, suggesting that US environmental politics is being exported to the CAFTA-DR parties. This is backed up by the capacity building projects being undertaken by US agencies with US funding. For instance, the US Agency for International Development funded the US-based pressure group Social Accountability International which worked with the US-based Rainforest Alliance to "build producers' capacity for sustainable compliance with labor and environmental standards through incentive structures, social management systems, and social dialogue" in Costa Rica and the Dominican Republic.[13] There are many such examples.

Thus, trade has been used as the basis for a massive expansion of US environmental law and politics into countries across the world, funded largely by the US taxpayer. Most citizens of the U.S. and its trading partners are unaware that this is being done under the auspices of agreements that are supposed to be primarily about trade. Thus, while the ideal Goldberg Agreement would force countries to reduce regulation, trade agreements in the real world are being used to impose regulation, with little democratic input.

Indeed, Mauel Ayau of Universidad Francisco Marroquin in Guatemala warned in a Wall Street Journal article in 2003, "CAFTA will involve many legal requirements to satisfy labor and environmental interests in the U.S. This effort…will damage Central America's ability to compete. Moreover, when these restrictions are incorporated into an international treaty they will be more difficult to correct than sovereign decisions would be."[14]

---

[12] Secretariat for Environmental Matters website—Legal Basis http://www.saa-sem.org/en/legal-basis/. Accessed May 3, 2024.
[13] Environment and Labor Excellence for CAFTA-DR, Social Accountability International. https://sa-intl.org/programs/usaid-program-ele/. Accessed May 3, 2024.
[14] Manuel F. Ayau, "An Unfree Trade Agreement for Central America," Wall Street Journal, August 8, 2003.

The US funding US-based pressure groups to engage in partners' domestic politics under the aegis of "trade-related" activity simply makes this problem more acute for its partners. If this problem is to be solved, it will have to be solved in the U.S. So a question must be asked: What should US trade negotiators negotiate about?

Paul Krugman's Answer

That is exactly what Nobel Prize-winning economist Paul Krugman asked in 1997.[15] In reviewing a two-volume book titled "Fair Trade and Harmonization: Prerequisites for Free Trade?" edited by Jagdish Bhagwati and Robert E. Hudec, Krugman asked whether the academic arguments that regulatory harmonization was necessary for trade held water.

Krugman makes the point that has been made several times already in this overview. Gains from trade result fundamentally from differences in relative prices across countries, irrespective of whether those differences arise from technology, resources, policies, or any other source. Therefore, far from undermining the case for trade, differing policies in different countries enhance the potential gains from trade insofar as those policies result in differing prices. Moreover, harmonization of policies prevents individual countries from setting policies appropriate to their own preferences and income levels.

The issue, as Krugman says, is not that the case for free trade is unsound or ambiguous, but that "policy-oriented economists must deal with a world that does not understand or accept that case." In the imagination of much of the public and much of the political class, mercantilist theory is dominant. Exports are good and imports are bad. It is an excellent example of what the late economist David Henderson called "Do-It-Yourself Economics"— folk lore misunderstandings of economics that dominate political debates.[16] Special interests, moreover, will always engage in special pleading.

Sometimes those pleadings take the form of "second-best" arguments, such as the idea that failing to agree environmental standards will result in a "race to the bottom" as countries slash environmental regulation in the name of lowering costs. However, there is little empirical evidence for such a thing

---

[15] Krugman, Paul. "What Should Trade Negotiators Negotiate About?" Journal of Economic Literature 35, no. 1 (1997): 113–20. http://www.jstor.org/stable/2729695.
[16] David Henderson, "The Power of Do-it-Yourself Economics," Reith Lecture, BBC Radio 4, November 6, 1985. https://www.bbc.co.uk/programmes/p00h1g2t. Accessed May 3, 2024.

happening, and Krugman notes that some countries might engage in a "race to the top," with ever-increasing environmental stringency.

Yet the arguments continue to be made. Savvy proponents of special interest pleading recognize that this is the political reality, and sometimes even admit it. Krugman provides an illuminating example:

> When the United States recently imposed utterly indefensible restrictions on Mexican tomato exports, an Administration official remarked off the record that Florida has a lot of electoral votes while Mexico has none. The economically correct rebuttal to this sort of thing is to point out that the other 49 states contain a lot of pizza lovers; the politically effective answer is to subject U.S. Mexican trade to a set of rules and arbitration procedures in which the Mexicans do too have a vote.

Thus the Goldberg Agreement recedes ever more into the background. The "politically effective answer" is always to try to regulate the problem away, if only to placate otherwise frenzied special interests.

Krugman points to one way out. The international legal structure is that of Westphalian states (referring to the Seventeenth Century Treaty of Westphalia) where each country is sovereign to itself. Experts in international law tend to agree that retaining this structure is for the best, so international harmonization should be the exception rather than the rule. This would suggest that smaller countries would do well to resist the lure of bilateral or regional trade agreements. However, for many of them the lure of access to the huge markets of America or the European Union is likely to prove too appealing not to swallow. While mercantilist arguments prevail within those larger countries/blocs, the problem is not going to go away.

The Growth of Environmental and Labor Clauses in US Trade Agreements

It is worth looking at each of the US trade agreements mentioned above in some detail to appreciate the outsized role labor and environmental issues have come to play in trade agreements. Agreements before NAFTA, whether in the U.S. or abroad, tended not to touch on them much, if at all. The US-Israel agreement of 1985 ran to just 14 pages and had no environmental or labor clauses. The ANZCERTA agreement between Australia and New Zealand, from 1983, has no environmental clauses and just two relating to labor protection.

That all changed with NAFTA's side-agreements. The environmental agreement had 7 clauses in 40 pages, most of which were dedicated to enforcement procedures. The labor agreement featured 7 clauses in 34 pages, establishing objectives related to workers' rights and quality of life, provided for public awareness of labor law, and called for fair processes to resolve labor disputes (which had been the object of US labor law since the New Deal).

The Jordan-US deal in 2000/1 was only 19 pages long and dedicated only two of those pages to labor and environmental issues.[17] However, both focused on "race to the bottom" arguments and the labor section committed the agreement's joint committee to regular reviews of how to "improve labor standards," outlining those standards in terms that reflected the practice of American labor law.

By the time of the raft of trade deals that were signed in 2004, the office of the US Trade Representative (USTR) had established advisory committees on labor and environmental issues, which were to henceforth give recommendations about the draft agreements. The tabulation in the appendix outlines the attitudes of both committees as well as the resulting labor and environmental clauses, together with their main provisions, in all US agreements from 2004 to 2015, spanning the George W Bush and Barack Obama administrations.

As can be seen, the labor environmental committee routinely opposed the deals as not going far enough while the environmental committee routinely approved the deals as significant expansions of environmental regulation.

Labor disagreements focused on the lack of what the committee saw as appropriate expansions of workers' rights in the partner countries and on the supposed effects on jobs domestically. Nevertheless, virtually all these agreements include clauses on dispute resolution, introduce labor cooperation institutions such as a Labor Council, and ensure recognition of fundamental labor rights such as the right to bargain collectively. These provisions were strengthened after a 2007 fast track agreement between Congress and the administration. Moreover, workers with job losses attributable to trade became eligible for "trade adjustment assistance" as early as 1974, with expansions to the program after NAFTA and on several occasions since.[18]

Nevertheless, the US-style labor provisions proved extremely influential. As University of Miami law professor Kathleen Claussen summarized:

---

[17] Agreement Between the United States of America And The Hashemite Kingdom of Jordan on the Establishment of A Free Trade Area, October 24 2000. https://ustr.gov/sites/default/files/Jordan%20FTA.pdf.

[18] Congressional Research Service, Trade Adjustment Assistance for Workers and the TAA Reauthorization Act of 2015, CRS Report R44153. https://crsreports.congress.gov/product/pdf/R/R44153. Accessed May 6, 2024.

At the end of 2005, only 21 trade agreements notified to the WTO had labor provisions. As of 2016, 77 out of 267 FTAs included labor provisions. The language used in these agreements largely tracks the language used by the United States in its FTA labor chapters. Given the outsized role of the U.S. Congress in determining that language..., as other countries have adopted the U.S. trade agreement language on labor, the U.S. Congress has become, de facto, a primary drafter of the only transnationally enforceable labor law provisions in the world.[19]

By contrast to the labor committee, the environmental advisory committee regularly approved draft trade deals on two grounds. First, the deals were seen as significantly expanding environmental law and accountability in the partner countries. Secondly, the committee often recognized the principle of the environmental Kuznets Curve, that growing wealth would lead to environmental improvement. The growing enthusiasm of the environmental movement for trade deals with major ecological elements can be seen as reflected in the growing scope of the agreed upon language. The creation of environmental councils mentioned above in the CAFTA-DR deal would be reflected in most deals afterward and the number of pages and clauses dedicated to environmental issues grew over time (Korea-US may have been an exception, which seems to have been attributable to a higher level of existing environmental protection in Korea than in other partner countries at the time of the deal.)[20]

TPP and USMCA: The draft agreement for the Trans-Pacific Partnership was built on these two trends. The labor provisions were substantively like the usual but included references to labor standards beyond those demanded by the International Labor Organization[21] as well as an enhanced dispute resolution procedure that may have gone some way toward meeting the outstanding criticisms of labor interests and the labor advisory committee.[22] The environmental elements also included enhanced dispute resolution that went beyond previous commitments and established a new standard for environmental trade agreements.

It is therefore worth remembering what happened to TPP. When Congressional approval was within sight, major labor and environmental interests

---

[19] Claussen, Kathleen, Reimagining Trade-Plus Compliance: The Labor Story (August 1, 2018). 23 J. Int'l Econ. L 25 (2020), Available at SSRN: https://ssrn.com/abstract=3258639.
[20] Final Environmental Review: United States—Korea Free Trade Agreement, Office of the U.S. Trade Representative, September 2011.
[21] Such as minimum wages, working hours, and occupational health and safety rules.
[22] Kolben, Kevin, A New Model for Trade and Labor? The Trans-Pacific Partnership's Labor Chapter and Beyond (2017). New York University Journal of International Law and Politics (JILP), Vol. 49, No. 4, 2017, Available at SSRN: https://ssrn.com/abstract=3084379.

lined up to *oppose* the deal.[23] Both labor and environmental opponents agreed on one thing—that the deal gave too much weight to corporate interests. This was because the draft, like all its predecessors, included an Investor-State Dispute Settlement procedure, allowing corporations to challenge over-stringent regulations that acted as a restraint on trade.

The Sierra Club told the Washington Post that the deal as drafted would "empower big polluters to challenge climate and environmental safeguards in private trade courts." AFL-CIO's then-President Richard Trumka echoed this, saying, "Rushing through a bad deal will not bring economic stability to working families, nor will it bring confidence that our priorities count as much as those of global corporations."

Moreover, opposition to the deal quickly became bipartisan. Both presidential candidates in 2016 opposed the deal. Hillary Clinton announced her opposition days after her own President unveiled it, saying, "I don't believe it's going to meet the high bar I have set."[24] Later on the campaign trail she said, "I will stop any trade deal that kills jobs or holds down wages, including the Trans-Pacific Partnership. I oppose it now, I'll oppose it after the election and I'll oppose it as president."

Donald Trump's initial opposition focused on the absence of currency manipulation provisions, but he soon transitioned to similar arguments to Clinton, alleging that she would sign the deal and "we will lose millions of jobs and our economic independence for good."[25] Trump, of course, eventually withdrew the U.S. from the TPP after becoming president.

It had become apparent that the problem with the Trans-Pacific Partnership was that it would do too much to encourage trade, which was now identified as destroying rather than creating jobs and harming rather than improving environmental protection. To garner support, any future trade deal would have to promote those considerations at the expense of trade-expanding provisions like an ISDS or would have to bypass somehow the Congressional approval process.

Thus, the next major trade deal that America negotiated was the first to restrict trade against the existing agreement when USMCA replaced NAFTA

---

[23] Catherine Ho, "Industry, Labor and Environmental Groups Gear Up to Oppose TPP Trade Deal," Washington Post, Oct. 6, 2015, https://www.washingtonpost.com/news/powerpost/wp/2015/10/06/industry-labor-and-environmental-groups-gear-up-to-oppose-tpp-trade-deal/

[24] "Hillary Clinton says she does not support Trans-Pacific Partnership," PBS.org, October 7, 2015. https://www.pbs.org/newshour/politics/hillary-clinton-says-she-does-not-support-trans-pacific-partnership Accessed May 6, 2024.

[25] Full transcript: Donald Trump NYC speech on stakes of the election, Politico.com, June 22 2016. https://www.politico.com/story/2016/06/transcript-trump-speech-on-the-stakes-of-the-election-224654#ixzz4CLWcQtqa Accessed May 6, 2024.

in 2020. In large part, the agreement was based on segments of the TPP draft. But although the deal kept in place most of the zero tariff arrangements of NAFTA and expanded trade in some areas, such as Canada's notoriously protectionists dairy sector, there were significant trade-restricting and problematic non-trade elements:

- The labor provisions essentially dictated to Mexico what its labor policy should be. It is notable that the main issue highlighted on the USMCA's US webpage at time of writing is "Through the Rapid Response Mechanism (RRM), we were able to address a workers' rights issue at a General Motors factory in Silao, Mexico, by reaching a fast course of action."[26]
- It imposed several new non-tariff barriers, including export quotas, sourcing requirements, and provisions on monetary policy.
- Introduced further non-trade elements such as provisions on intellectual property and pharmaceutical regulations.

Owing to the massive disruptions to international trade thanks to the COVID pandemic it has not proved possible yet to assess the economic impact of USMCA replacing NAFTA, especially given other trade-related issues (such as the Trump/Biden trade war with China) and huge increases in domestic spending (such as the CHIPS Act and Inflation Reduction Act) that favored near-shoring and shorter supply chains.

One thing the USMCA did not do was introduce climate-related elements into the environmental provisions. The agreement is up for review in 2026 and there will be significant pressure in all three parties for them to be incorporated. Whether this will happen will depend on the results of the 2024 presidential election, but given other developments in trade agreements around the world we can expect it be likely that the U.S. will start entwining trade with climate at some point.

EU-Japan: Environmental Strategic Partnership: In 2018, the European Union and Japan signed a "strategic partnership agreement" (SPA) with Japan, which preceded an economic partnership agreement signed in 2019. The SPA commits the two parties to work together on challenges such as energy security, climate change, and aging populations. Trade is now simply a part of this overarching partnership, and so trade agreements between the parties must reflect this.

While the EU-Japan agreement is undoubtedly an advance in trade-specific terms, creating the world's largest trade agreement and significantly reducing

---

[26] Office of the USTR, USMCA web page https://ustr.gov/usmca Accessed May 6, 2024.

tariff and many non-tariff barriers, it needs to be set alongside such things as the EU-Japan Green Alliance that commits both countries to ambitious environmental goals which, for instance, promote "more sustainable, circular practices in production and consumption" and "increased regulatory cooperation and business exchange to drive global uptake of low-carbon technologies." These policies will create new non-tariff barriers.

With respect to the impact on trade, the parties recognize "the need to keep in mind the interaction of these measures and policies with their shared commitment to *fair and open* international trade and with the risk of carbon leakage in the global economy" (emphasis added.) The ideal of *free* trade is not mentioned, while "the risk of carbon leakage" refers to the possibility that industries might locate in places with less stringent emissions standards. In other words, the agreement is concerned that developing nations might seek to exercise comparative advantage.

We can expect further EU-negotiated deals to progress along similar lines—an overarching SPA with trade reduced to just one element in the development of the partnership, and probably not the most important one. As far as the EU is concerned, the free trade agreement model is a thing of the past. This would suggest that a potential US-EU deal would no longer be a "trade and investment" partnership but something much more ambitious, which makes it far less likely to happen.

The Limited Potential for a Game-Changing Treaty

The EU, however, is now missing a previously important member. The United Kingdom withdrew from the European Union in January 2020. The current administration has shown little interest in conducting a trade treaty with Brexit Britain. However, it is plausible that a future administration might show more interest, and if so the labor and environmental elements might either go in a different direction to that of USMCA and/or the EU approach or reinforce them.

The shape of a future agreement will depend on which parties are in power at the same time, and the possible shapes of the agreement are summarized in the table below. We have known since Brexit that the UK conservative government and US democratic administrations have shown little mutual interest in a trade deal, so the prospect for any deal between these parties is low. Should a future democratic administration open talks with a future conservative government, it is likely, given party commitments on both sides, that environmental aspects will form a major part of any deal. The main source of conflict is likely to lie in the labor arena, where the conservatives will probably seek to defend the Thatcher-era labor reforms against an attempt by labor interests in the U.S. to impose something like USMCA's Rapid Response Mechanism.

UK Government/US Administration	Republican	Democrat
Conservative	High likelihood Weak labor provisions Conflict over/moderate environmental provisions	Low likelihood Conflict over labor provisions Strong environmental provisions
Labor	Low likelihood Conflict over labor provisions Conflict over environmental provisions	Moderate likelihood Strong labor provisions Strong environmental provisions

The likelihood of an agreement between a US Republican administration and a UK Labor government is also low. There will be conflict over the labor and environmental elements, despite the possibility that a labor government might see a US trade deal as an essential element of a post-Brexit strategy.

A UK Labor/US Democratic agreement is more likely than a UK Conservative/US Democratic agreement as both sides share common interests, although US domestic considerations might still prevent enthusiastic negotiations. If a deal is agreed, it will likely contain strong labor and environmental provisions as the two sides attempt to cement policy in these areas against future changes in leadership. The deal might however founder on simple trade issues—Democrats who represent agricultural states will demand access to British markets, which British agricultural interests will resist strongly, spreading stories about "chlorinated chicken," for example. It is therefore possible that a Democrat-Labor deal will be even more about these non-trade elements, leaving expanded market access for trade out in many areas.

However, a UK Conservative/US Republican deal offers perhaps the only chance for a radically different approach, reinstating the primacy of trade in an international agreement. Neither side will be enthusiastic for strong labor provisions, and while the UK Conservatives are markedly more "green" than US Republicans, they are unlikely to risk the deal by insisting on, say, strong climate provisions. Instead, it is likely that the environmental provisions will center around endangered species and fisheries protection and the like.

This suggests that the main feature of a US-UK deal in those circumstances will likely be some agreement on regulatory coherence, building on the provisions on those lines in USMCA. Such provisions could result in a trade agreement based around mutual recognition of regulatory competence, rather than around regulatory harmonization.

If an agreement between the US and UK along those lines also contained an accession agreement, then it could form the basis of a new global trade alliance, one that takes a different approach to the EU partnership model. It could thereby allow for competition among trade frameworks.

Conclusion

American and indeed global trade agreements are no longer primarily about free trade. The word "free" has disappeared from their titles and "trade" is following suit. The willingness of American Presidents of both parties to use tariffs to protect domestic interests suggests that mercantilist thinking has come to dominate American approaches to trade once again. Moreover, the insistence of other special interests that their issues must be given great weight in international agreements, together with continued political acquiescence to that insistence, means that the benefits of trade, particularly for smaller parties, will be reduced as agreements work to wipe away comparative advantage.

The only way for this cycle to be broken is if a groundbreaking trade agreement that uses a different approach is signed between two relatively internationally important parties. The best prospect for that lies in an agreement between the United States and United Kingdom. However, even in that case, it will require political stars to align. While the possibility of a trade-focused model for international agreement is not yet dead, the prospect of Goldberg Agreements, or any similarly simple deal, is remoter than ever.

Acknowledgements The author would like to thank Daniel Hannan, Ryan Young, Jeremy Lott, Narupat Rattanakit, and above all Mitchell Thornton for their thoughts and contributions to this chapter.

Appendix: Labor and Environmental Aspects of US Trade Deals 2004–2015.

Chile–US Trade Deal—2004.

- The Labor Advisory Committee advised that the FTA did not meet congressional standards under TPA and was a step back from the Jordan FTA. The committee complained about how trade deficits had increased since NAFTA.
- The Environmental Advisory Committee advised that the deal reached all relevant standards regarding environmental protections and struck a balance in utilizing both nations' resources to solve issues.
- The Labor section is 8 pages with 8 clauses:
    - It includes an "anti-race to the bottom" provision discouraging deregulation to attract investment
    - It includes a conflict resolution section that requires promoting awareness regarding labor laws
    - It requires establishing a Labor Affairs Council and creating a panel of labor experts to resolve disputes
    - It includes an annex encouraging better dispute resolution mechanisms.
- The Environmental section is 11 pages with 14 clauses:
    - It recognizes each nation's right to establish its own environmental laws
    - It establishes an Environmental Affairs Council to discuss solving environmental issues. It encourages public participation
    - It includes required and recommended steps to improve both nations' environments, including the U.S. helping reduce pollution from Chilean mines
    - It provides a dispute resolution mechanism including developing an environmental panel

US–Singapore Trade Deal—2004.

- The Labor Committee did not explicitly endorse or oppose the deal but recommended a framework for improving then-current labor issues in Singapore
- The Environmental Committee supported the trade deal, acknowledging no significant changes in environmental impacts
- The Labor section is 5 pages with 7 clauses:
    - It includes an "anti-race to the bottom" provision

- It raises public awareness of labor laws. It establishes a Labor Cooperation Mechanism (an additional 2 pages and 4 clauses)
- It provides for labor consultations.

• The Environment section is 5 pages with 10 clauses:

- It includes an "anti-race to the bottom" provision
- It establishes the principle of public participation
- It encourages environmental cooperation between parties
- It includes a section on corporate environmental stewardship.

Australia–US Trade Deal—2004.

• The Labor Committee opposed the trade deal, citing anti-union laws in Australia and a lack of protection for workers' jobs in the United States
• The Environmental Committee supported the trade deal, seeing trade as an opportunity to increase economic prosperity in both nations, opening more opportunities to protect the environment
• The Labor section is 5 pages with 7 clauses:

- It provides a framework for dispute resolution
- It encourages increasing public awareness regarding labor laws
- It increases international cooperation

• The Environment section is 4 pages with 9 clauses:

- Both nations must enforce their own environmental laws
- It provides for public awareness of environmental laws and public participation
- It encourages voluntary mechanisms to better the environment
- It provides a framework for dispute resolution.

Morocco–US Trade Deal—2006.

• The Labor Committee opposed the trade deal, citing exclusion of support for international workers' rights
• The Environmental Committee supported the deal, although it would have preferred more public participation sections like in previous deals. However, it believed the deal improved environmental regulations over NAFTA.
• The Labor section is 8 pages with 6 clauses:

- It has an anti-race to the bottom section
- It provides a framework for resolving disputes
- It encourages cooperation between the parties.

- The Environmental section is 7 pages with 8 clauses:
  - It has an anti-race to the bottom section
  - It encourages cooperation on environmental issues
  - It includes a section on dispute resolution
  - It incentivizes private actors to improve the environment. It encourages public participation.

Bahrain–US Trade Deal—2006.

- The Labor Advisory Committee argued that the trade deal did not address workers' rights and was a step backward since the Jordan FTA, including allegations about outsourcing jobs and decreasing American prosperity
- The Trade and Environmental Committee agreed that the FTA met environmental standards but argued the agreement could be improved by including some new provisions.
- The Labor section is 6 pages with 7 clauses:
  - It includes text attempting to prevent a regulatory "race to the bottom"
  - It includes a section discouraging child labor
  - It has specific enforcement procedures for international companies violating labor laws
  - It has a 2-page annex requiring international labor standards cooperation between parties
- The Environmental section is 5 pages with 10 clauses:
  - It includes wording discouraging a "race to the bottom" through deregulation
  - It requires a fair system to resolve violations of environmental laws
  - It encourages governments to enact voluntary environmental support mechanisms
  - It encourages public participation. It allows individuals to request consultations to resolve environmental disputes.

CAFTA-DR 2006

- The Labor Advisory Committee opposed the deal, arguing it would cost American jobs
- The Environmental Advisory Committee supported the deal as meeting congressional standards. It added that trade should be encouraged as increased economic prosperity leads to a better environment.

- The Labor section is 10 pages with 7 clauses:
    - It discourages a regulatory "race to the bottom"
    - It specifies that no country can enforce its labor laws extraterritorially
    - It provides a mechanism for settling labor disputes
    - It has provisions for public understanding of labor laws
    - It forms a Labor Council
    - It creates a panel on labor regulations.
- The Environmental Section is 13 pages with 12 clauses:
    - It discourages a "race to the bottom"
    - It allows access to a dispute resolution system and enforcement of judgments
    - It encourages incentivizing private companies to improve the environment
    - It allows opportunities for public participation
    - It creates a panel to settle disputes.

Oman–US Trade Deal—2009.

- The Labor Committee opposed the deal, arguing it would not protect "fundamental human rights of workers"
- The Environmental Committee supported the deal, although it would have preferred larger sections related to public participation. It considered it an improvement over NAFTA.
- The Labor section is 6 pages with 6 clauses:
    - It has an anti-race to the bottom section
    - It increases public awareness
    - It provides a framework to resolve disputes
    - It increases cooperation between countries to resolve disputes.
- The Environmental section is 7 pages with 9 clauses:
    - It has an anti-race to the bottom section
    - It provides a framework to resolve disputes
    - It encourages voluntary mechanisms to enhance environmental performance
    - It encourages cooperation to improve the environment.

Peru–US Trade Deal 2009.

- The Labor Committee opposed the deal, citing a lack of enforceable labor standards or other workers' rights issues

- The Environmental Committee supported the deal overall, arguing it did not have an extensive enough public participation framework but was more rigorous than NAFTA.
- The Labor section is 10 pages with 12 clauses:
  - It supports fundamental labor rights
  - It requires actively enforcing labor laws
  - It provides a framework to settle disputes
  - It increases labor cooperation between nations.
- The Environmental section is 22 pages with 14 clauses:
  - It requires nations to enforce their environmental laws
  - It provides a procedural framework for resolving disputes
  - It encourages incentivizing private companies to improve the environment
  - It creates an Environmental Affairs Council
  - It increases opportunities for public participation
  - It provides a framework for enforcement and record-keeping
  - It encourages environmental cooperation
  - It encourages biological diversity
  - It has an annex including combating illegal logging/wildlife trade and creating a subcommittee on this issue.

Colombia–US Trade Deal—2012.

- The Labor Advisory Committee opposed the trade deal on the grounds that it lacked enforcement mechanisms to prevent a "race to the bottom"
- The Environmental Committee supported the trade deal as an improvement over NAFTA in enforcement and public participation.
- The Labor section is 10 pages with 8 clauses:
  - It requires adopting "fundamental labor rights" related to unionization and non-discrimination
  - It includes provisions regarding dispute resolution procedures
  - It establishes a Labor Affairs Council
  - It encourages public participation.
- The Environmental section is 14 pages with 14 clauses:
  - It recognizes national sovereignty while promoting multilateral environmental agreements
  - It allows interested persons to request investigations into alleged environmental law violations

- It recommends incentivizing private companies to improve the environment
- It establishes an Environmental Affairs Council
- It requires opportunities for public environmental law education and participation
- It provides for enforcement when parties fail to enforce environmental laws
- It promotes public participation to conserve environmental diversity
- It creates a panel to handle environmental disputes
- It requires following CITES and other environmental treaties

Korea–US Trade Deal—2012.

- The Labor Committee opposed the Korean FTA, asserting that it was actually the worst FTA since NAFTA and could have a negative impact on jobs and wages.
- The Environmental Committee supported the trade deal, although it expressed concerns over the language related to expropriation. It expressed support for trade because increased wealth helps the environment.
- The Labor section is 7 pages with 4 clauses:
  - It includes support for collective bargaining
  - It discourages a "race to the bottom" in labor standards
  - It includes an enforcement mechanism for resolving disputes
  - It creates a Labor Council.
- The Environmental section is 9 pages with 10 clauses:
  - It has an anti-race to the bottom section
  - It includes an enforcement section for resolving disputes and creates an Environmental Affairs Council, while also encouraging public participation
  - It encourages incentivizing private industries to improve environmental performance
  - It requires parties to follow international environmental agreements, such as on endangered species and environmental protection.

References

Agreement Between the United States of America And The Hashemite Kingdom of Jordan on the Establishment of A Free Trade Area, October 24 2000. https://ustr.gov/sites/default/files/Jordan%20FTA.pdf

Audley, John. "Environment's New Role in U.S. Trade Policy." Trade, Equity, and Development, Carnegie Endowment for International Peace, September 2002. https://carnegieendowment.org/2002/09/24/environment-s-new-role-in-u.s.-trade-policy-pub-9039.

Ayau, Manuel F., "An Unfree Trade Agreement for Central America," Wall Street Journal, August 8, 2003

Chapter 17.9 of the CAFTA-DR Agreement, https://www.caftadr-environment.org/wp-content/uploads/2015/04/Chapter_17_CAFTA_-_DR.pdf

Congressional Research Service (2024) Trade adjustment assistance for workers and the TAA reauthorization Act of 2015. CRS Report R44153. https://crsreports.congress.gov/product/pdf/R/R44153. Accessed May 6

Environment and Labor Excellence for CAFTA-DR (2024) Social Accountability International. https://sa-intl.org/programs/usaid-program-ele/. Accessed May 3

US EPA (2024) Capacity-building programs under the Dominican Republic-Central America-United States free trade agreement (CAFTA-DR). https://www.epa.gov/international-cooperation/capacity-building-programs-under-dominican-republic-central-america. Accessed May 3

Claussen, Kathleen. "Reimagining Trade-Plus Compliance: The Labor Story." SSRN, 1 Aug. 2018. https://ssrn.com/abstract=3258639.

Full transcript: Donald Trump NYC speech on stakes of the election (2016) Politico.com, June 22 2016. https://www.politico.com/story/2016/06/transcript-trump-speech-on-the-stakes-of-the-election-224654#ixzz4CLWcQtqa. Accessed May 6, 2024

General Agreement on Tariffs and Trade (1947) Article XIII: Non-discriminatory administration of quantitative restrictions. https://www.wto.org/english/docs_e/legal_e/gatt47_01_e.htm#articleXIII

Gruben WC, Welch JC (1994) Is NAFTA Economic Integration? Economic review, Federal Reserve Bank of Dallas, Second Quarter. https://www.dallasfed.org/~/media/documents/research/er/1994/er9402c.pdf

Henderson D (1985) The power of do-it-yourself economics. Reith Lecture, BBC Radio 4, 6 Nov. https://www.bbc.co.uk/programmes/p00h1g2t

Hillary Clinton says she does not support Trans-Pacific Partnership (2015) PBS.org, October 7, https://www.pbs.org/newshour/politics/hillary-clinton-says-she-does-not-support-trans-pacific-partnership Accessed May 6, 2024

Ho C (2015) Industry, labor and environmental groups gear up to oppose TPP trade deal, Washington Post, Oct. 6, https://www.washingtonpost.com/news/powerpost/wp/2015/10/06/industry-labor-and-environmental-groups-gear-up-to-oppose-tpp-trade-deal/

Ikenson DJ et al (2018) The ideal U.S.-U.K. Free trade agreement: a free trader's perspective. Cato Institute, 18 Sept. https://www.cato.org/white-paper/ideal-us-uk-free-trade-agreement-free-traders-perspective

Kolben K (2017) A new model for trade and labor? The trans-pacific partnership's labor chapter and beyond. SSRN, 2017. New York University Journal of International Law and Politics (JILP), Vol. 49, No. 4, Available at SSRN: https://ssrn.com/abstract=3084379

Krugman P (1997) What should trade negotiators negotiate about? J Econ Lit 35(1):113–120

Lipford JM, Yandle B (2011) NAFTA, Environmental Kuznets curves, and Mexico's progress. Global Econ J 10(4):4–4

Secretariat for Environmental Matters website—Legal Basis http://www.saa-sem.org/en/legal-basis/. Accessed May 3, 2024

Sheehan JM (1995) Two years after NAFTA: a free market critique and assessment, Competitive Enterprise Institute, December 1, https://cei.org/studies/two-years-after-nafta-a-free-market-critique-and-assessment/

Trump DJ (2017) Administration of Trump DJ, Remarks at the Congress of Tomorrow Republican Member Retreat in Philadelphia, Pennsylvania, 26 Jan

U.S. Department of State (2008) Office of the Spokesman. Fact Sheet: CAFTA-DR Environment Projects. 30 Jan

U.S. Office of the Trade Representative (2011) Final Environmental Review: United States—Korea Free Trade Agreement. Sept

United States—Mexico—Canada Agreement website

Trade Adjustment Textbook Chapter

Scott S. Lincicome

Introduction

The recent rise in global populism has been accompanied by protectionist policies intended to help a working class citizenry victimized by free trade and the widespread "deindustrialization" that it inflicted on the developed world. Populist politicians like US presidents Donald Trump and Joe Biden further claim that these wrongs can be reversed, and that middle class living standards can be improved by tariffs, subsidies, localization mandates, and other measures that restrict imports.

China is modern protectionists' most common target, and, in the United States at least, criticism of free trade and support for protectionism (against imports from China *or* other countries) usually cites the "China Shock"—a 12-year surge of Chinese imports into the United States beginning in 2000 and a series of economic papers documenting their effects on the US workforce and US economy. The papers, led by economists David H. Autor, David Dorn, and Gordon H. Hanson, concluded that the increase in imports from China accounted for some of the decline in US manufacturing employment from the late 1990s to 2011. Their papers have been joined by others producing similar employment results, such as one by economists Justin Pierce and Peter Schott focused on the US granting of "permanent normal trade relations" (PNTR) to China as part of the nation's accession to the World Trade Organization (WTO). The collection of studies has supported

S. S. Lincicome (✉)
Cato Institute, Washington, DC, USA

still other economics research employing various methodologies and data—and often finding statistically significant harms to American workers and their communities. Combined, these papers form the academic backbone of arguments against free trade and globalization, of the current political narrative surrounding past US-China trade policy, and of concrete protectionist actions targeting Chinese and other imports today.

This chapter will not seek to refute the populists' general claims about free trade and globalization, nor will it assess the economic and political efficacy of their protectionist policies—other chapters have done so masterfully. Instead, it will address other fundamental errors in the populist/protectionist approach to trade policy. First, it misunderstands that the China Shock does not justify new protectionism today. Second, it erroneously contends that trade is uniquely costly when compared with other types of market-based disruption, such as automation. Third, it ignores the important economic benefits that accompany this "creative destruction," thanks in large part to individuals' and companies' adjustment thereto; and, finally, it overlooks all the government policies that thwart adjustment to disruption, whether due to trade or any other market phenomenon.

Ignoring the China Shock's *Benefits*

The China Shock is commonly characterized as not merely supporting but *advocating* US government restrictions on Chinese imports due to the China Shock's damage to the US economy writ large and *especially* to American manufacturing employment. None of this, however, is accurate.

First, the academic papers assess only job losses incurred by *specific local labor markets* due to the China Shock and thus have little to say about the overall effect of Chinese imports on the US labor market and economy. Although the Autor, Dorn, and Hanson (ADH) papers cite a top-end figure of 2.4 million lost jobs (around 1 million in manufacturing) between 1999 and 2011, their central estimates were around half those amounts and came amid an economy-wide *gain* of approximately 2.2 million jobs.[1] Even the top-end number of 1 million lost manufacturing jobs, meanwhile, accounted for less than 20% of the total manufacturing job losses over the same time frame—and a fraction of the *tens of millions* of job separations that occur in the United States each year.[2] Thus, even the ADH papers confirm that

---

[1] Federal Reserve Bank of St. Louis (2024).
[2] Bureau of Labor Statistics (2024).

dislocations caused by Chinese imports were at best a plausible contributor to—not the main driver of—US workforce trends during the 2000s.

Just as importantly, ADH does not examine whether imports from China boosted jobs in the nation overall. Several other economists have explored this issue in depth, finding mostly positive results. Nicholas Bloom and colleagues, for example, concur with Autor, Dorn, and Hanson that the China Shock caused manufacturing job losses, especially for those without college degrees, *but* they add that the losses were offset by gains in service jobs in other regions.[3] Several other studies have similarly found that a decline in US manufacturing jobs during the China Shock period was accompanied by increases in American service-sector jobs.[4] The results from Zhi Wang and colleagues were even more positive: they found that, after accounting for the effects of Chinese imports throughout the supply chain, specific jobs were indeed lost, but overall employment and wages increased, *even in regions that experienced large manufacturing employment declines* (contra Autor, Dorn, and Hanson).[5]

The original China Shock papers also did not examine the consumer and aggregate economic effects of trade with China for the United States. Other economists have filled this gap too, again with mostly positive results. Xavier Jaravel and Erick Sager, for example, found that for each percentage point increase in Chinese imports, consumer prices fell by nearly 2 percentage points, with savings from both imports and domestically produced goods (thanks to heightened competition).[6] They estimate that, overall, American consumers saved an estimated $411,000 for every US manufacturing job lost from Chinese import competition. Notably, middle- and low-income households enjoyed a disproportionate amount of these benefits, as the most affected products were those often sold at big-box retailers, such as Target and Walmart.[7] Other studies have found Chinese imports to have provided similar reductions in consumer prices as well as significant benefits for American manufacturers that consume imported inputs.[8]

Autor, Dorn, and Hanson have recently acknowledged these consumer benefits, which their earlier work had excluded. In particular, their 2021 reassessment of the China Shock found that once Chinese imports' consumer benefits were considered (using Jaravel and Sager's estimates), only 6.3%

---

[3] Bloom et al. (2019).
[4] Caliendo and Parro (2023).
[5] Wang et al. (2018).
[6] Jaravel and Sager (2020).
[7] Broda and Romalis (2008).
[8] Lincicome (2020).

of the US population—or 82 of the 722 US localities (commuting zones) examined—experienced net losses from that same import competition.[9] This represents a far smaller share of China Shock "losers" than that found in the authors' original estimates, though they still view the losses as significant.

The China Shock's overall impact on US living standards (referred to here as "welfare") has also been found to have been positive—in line with previous research on trade liberalization. Caliendo and Parro, in particular, find that between 1995 and 2011 the United States experienced an aggregate welfare gain of 3.4% due to trade with China. Other research also found gains in overall welfare, with sizable majorities of Americans (though of course not all) benefiting from this bilateral trade. Summarizing this research, Caliendo and Parro state that "[a]ggregate gains from trade are widely agreed upon by trade economists, and the increased trade integration between the United States and China over the past 20 years has allowed researchers to confirm this view." And Autor, Dorn, and Hanson agree in their 2021 paper.

Ignoring Adjustment to the China Shock *and* Other Market Disruptions

Even more importantly, American protectionists fail to grasp that the China Shock's major and novel contribution to the economics literature related not to the trade effects but to what happened after the disruption—affected American workers' inability to adjust to the shock. In particular, ADH found that displaced manufacturing workers did not, as economists expected, quickly move to other regions or industries but instead became unemployed or exited the labor force. This effect was more pronounced for workers without a college education and for low-earning workers. In their 2021 paper, ADH assert that the negative effects of the China Shock persisted through 2019.[10] Thus, the ADH paper states plainly that the problem in US labor markets is not the impact of Chinese imports but rather that "adjustment in local labor markets is remarkably slow, with wages and labor force participation rates remaining depressed and unemployment rates remaining elevated for at least a full decade after the China trade shock commences."

This lack of adjustment is important but says little about the value of trade with China or any other nation because the issue applies to *any* type of labor market disruption, not just ones resulting from import competition. When

---

[9] Autor et al. (2021).
[10] Autor et al. (2021).

releasing a previous study of US-China trade, David Autor in 2012 stated, "I'm not anti-trade, but it is important to realize that there are reasons why people worry about this issue." He elaborated: "We do not have a good set of policies at present for helping workers adjust to trade or, for that matter, to any kind of technological change." His co-author Gordon Hanson told the *New York Times* in 2016: "The problem is not trade liberalization.... The problem is that labor market adjustment is too slow."[11] In fact, ADH themselves find "ultimate and sizable net gains" from trade, and as the *New York Times* reported in 2016, "Mr. Autor, like most economists, is still persuaded of the long-established benefits that global trade confers on the economy as a whole."[12]

Thus, Autor, Dorn, and Hanson emphasize that policies addressing the problems identified in their papers should focus on helping workers adjust to trade or other disruptions, *not* stopping the disruptions from occurring (e.g., with tariffs or other forms of protectionism). As Hanson writes in a 2021 article, "The China trade shock hurt many US workers and their communities. But so, too, have automation, the Great Recession, and the COVID-19 pandemic. And because the scarring effects of job losses are the same whether imports, robots, or a virus is responsible, responses to the damage should not depend on the identity of the culprit."[13]

Corroborating the economists' emphasis on adjustment is the fact that many places in the United States affected by import competition have adjusted and thrived since the 1980s—often with the help of trade and foreign investment. That the longer-term effects of Chinese imports vary dramatically from place to place—even in states or regions that faced similarly intense trade competition[14]—undermines the notion that the China Shock was a *national trade* problem (necessitating national protectionism) as opposed to a *more localized adjustment* problem (necessitating local and adjustment-related solutions).

In fact, many cities and towns in America that were once known for low-skill manufacturing and faced intense import competition in the 1990s and 2000s have since adapted and thrived. As previously noted, several studies show that most US regions ended up better off following the China Shock, though some areas—particularly those with low human capital—struggled.

A 2018 Brookings Institution report, moreover, finds that 115 of the 185 US counties identified as having a disproportionate share of manufacturing

---

[11] Barro (2016).
[12] Schwartz and Bui (2016).
[13] Hanson (2021).
[14] Caliendo et al. (2015).

jobs in 1970 had "transitioned successfully" from manufacturing by 2016, and that of the remaining 70 "older industrial cities," 40 exhibited "strong" or "emerging" economic performance between 2000 and 2016.[15] The "strong" localities, achieving high marks for growth, prosperity, and inclusion, include not only well-known success stories such as Pittsburgh and cities close to Boston and Manhattan but also smaller places such as Beaumont, Texas; Waterloo, Iowa; and Bethlehem, Pennsylvania. Overall, only 30, or about 16%, of those "struggling 1970s mill towns" we read so much about were still struggling a decade ago.

Anecdotal evidence reiterates these findings: towns that once depended on low-skill manufacturing, such as Greenville, South Carolina; Tuscaloosa, Alabama; Hickory, North Carolina; Warsaw, Indiana; and Danville, Virginia, are now home to growing companies and local economies that succeeded by adapting to the market, including through international trade and investment.[16] One can drive down U.S. Interstate 85 from Charlotte, North Carolina, to Montgomery, Alabama, and see all the multinational factories firsthand[17]—a region the Federal Reserve Bank of New York emphasized in its 2019 examination of the recent surge in US manufacturing jobs.[18]

By contrast, Youngstown, Ohio—often called the poster child of deindustrialization—has been unable to adjust in the face of new competition, namely an influx of more efficient foreign *and domestic* steel in the 1970s and 1980s. The abrupt 1977 closure of Youngstown Steel and the loss of 50,000 steelworker jobs (known as "Black Monday") unsurprisingly crippled the regional economy. Despite repeated political promises to return steel production to Youngstown, a manufacturing revival never occurred. Today, the city continues to struggle economically and, as a result, has lost more than half of its population in the last 40 years.[19]

The contrast between American bustling towns like Greenville and struggling ones like Youngstown—both hit by trade shocks that ended decades ago—indicates that the problem those shocks revealed was not import competition but the latter communities' inability to adjust to seismic economic changes, just as the China Shock authors themselves concede.

---

[15] Berube and Murray (2018).
[16] Byrnes (2016), Torres and Saraiva (2018), Allen (2017), Cunningham (2016), Paquette (2017), Sasso (2019) and Fallows (2019).
[17] Warren (2018).
[18] Abel and Deitz (2019).
[19] Stanford (2014).

Ignoring that Disruption is Good, and Trade Isn't Uniquely Disruptive

Economists understand that international trade is disruptive. It creates competition, which can be challenging for incumbent companies that lose sales or reduce prices because of new market entrants offering better, cheaper, or simply different alternatives. That can, in turn, mean layoffs or bankruptcies that are obviously difficult for the people and communities involved. On the other hand, this same disruption has many benefits. Consumers get lower prices, higher quality, or more variety, and the money they save buying imports can be used elsewhere in the economy, thus supporting other businesses and workers. Trade also gives domestic companies new customers and investors from abroad, and the United States is one of the world's top exporting nations and recipients of foreign direct investment, much of it concentrated in manufacturing. Foreign competition, meanwhile, pressures domestic firms to boost efficiency or invent new products, and if they fail to do so, the resources (labor, raw materials, capital, etc.) once dedicated to their operations can be deployed elsewhere in the national economy in more productive and viable businesses. Overall, "winners" far outnumber "losers," living standards rise, and the economy is better off on net—a result repeatedly found in the economics literature on trade, including on the China Shock.

That said, economists also understand that the effects of international trade are economically no different from those of other beneficial market activities. Competition is difficult for incumbents whether it comes from a person across the street or in another state or from an alternative product or new technology. That pressure can, in turn, generate layoffs or bankruptcies, none of which are easy. But in these cases, too, economists know that the disruptions' benefits far outweigh their costs, and that the risk of facing new competition—of being disrupted—is the "price" we all must pay to live in a dynamic, modern, and prosperous economy. Just as we wouldn't want to live in a world of horse-drawn carriages, abacuses, and phlebotomy, we wouldn't want to live in a world without trade—over short *or* long distances.

Indeed, economists often try to explain this reality by noting that trade is just another form of technology, like cars or robots or computers. In the "Iowa Car Crop," for example, Professor Steven E. Landsburg explains:

> There are two technologies for producing automobiles in America. One is to manufacture them in Detroit, and the other is to grow them in Iowa. Everybody knows about the first technology; let me tell you about the second. First you plant seeds, which are the raw material from which automobiles are constructed. You wait a few months until wheat appears. Then you harvest the

wheat, load it onto ships, and sail the ships eastward into the Pacific Ocean. After a few months, the ships reappear with Toyotas on them.[20]

Or we can consider a more recent and concrete example: fast food ordering kiosks, which have recently proliferated due to the high cost of labor (and recently increased minimum wages) in many US cities. In California, the voice inside the kiosk is a "bot" (artificial intelligence), while in New York it's an actual person living in the Philippines.[21] We can argue about which approach is better for business or which is more humanitarian, but their local economic effects—on American workers, employers, competitors, consumers, the economy, and so on—are identical. And those effects are mostly good.

Indeed, studies have repeatedly found it difficult to distinguish the employment effects of trade from those of technology. After documenting the evolution of American manufacturers in their China Shock paper, for example, Fort, Pierce, and Schott acknowledge that the "data provide support for both trade- and technology-based explanations of the overall decline of [manufacturing] employment over this period, while also highlighting the difficulties of estimating an overall contribution for each mechanism."[22] In fact, some papers have—contra the protectionist narrative—found that technology is *more* disruptive and "costly" for local workers than is trade. For example, a 2019 International Monetary Fund cross-country analysis of trade and technology shocks found that while both can have adverse regional employment effects (raising unemployment and lowering labor force participation), only *automation* has long-lasting harms and that regions hit by trade shocks actually ended up *better off* a couple years later.

Very few economists believe that protectionism is the correct policy response to trade-related disruptions for the same reason they oppose blocking new technologies or blocking interstate commerce. They advise that policymakers should instead focus on helping individuals and communities prepare for and adjust to disruptions, whether they come from trade or anything else. This approach not only preserves the disruptions' net benefits, but also can generate spillover gains. That 2019 IMF paper, for example, found that national policies encouraging more flexible labor markets can improve both adjustment in regional labor markets and their resilience to shocks, and that countries with less stringent product market regulation,

---

[20] Perry (2015).
[21] Kavilanz (2024) and Chen (2024).
[22] Fort et al. (2018).

lower administrative costs for starting a business, and *greater trade openness* had lower regional inequality.[23] Yale's James Bessen has found that the United States' relatively flexible labor market that allowed American workers displaced by computers to find new jobs in different occupations or industries.[24] Research from economist Niklas Engbom shows that more fluid labor markets with higher job-to-job mobility tend to have higher wage growth, higher lifetime earnings, more skills accumulation, and higher national productivity.[25] And recent research from economists Kyle Handley, Fariha Kamal, and Wei Ouyang finds that, while only 6% of US firms in manufacturing and services are "goods traders," these firms account for *half* of economy-wide employment today and supported 60% of all new net jobs created after 2008, primarily through the establishment of new businesses.[26]

Of course, these points do not prove that free trade is seamless, or that economists have always accurately predicted regional labor market responses to large-scale trade disruptions. But they *do* show why policy should focus on helping workers adjust to disruption, rather than trying to prevent the disruption from ever happening in the first place.

Ignoring Policy that Often Thwarts Necessary and Beneficial Adjustment

Unfortunately, just as technology, globalization, recessions, and the pandemic were increasingly disrupting our world and workplaces, governments across the United States were enacting policies that hinder American workers' ability to adjust and prosper in a modern, globalized economy. This includes:

Labor regulation: Numerous US government policies regulate private-sector work agreements, often predicated on the assumption of unequal bargaining power between employers and employees. Such regulations, instead of fostering mutually beneficial agreements, frequently impose constraints on both workers and firms, diluting workers' freedom to contract their labor and employers' flexibility to manage. Examples include anti-discrimination laws safeguarding individuals based on sex, gender, race, age, religion, or national origin, alongside minimum wage laws, overtime pay regulations, scheduling

---

[23] International Monetary Fund (IMF) (2019).
[24] Bessen (2016).
[25] Engbom (2022). See also Karahan et al. (2017).
[26] Handley et al. (2021).

laws, restrictions on independent contracting, and mandates for employer-provided benefits like family leave and medical coverage. While such laws are presumed to benefit workers, economic evidence suggests they can limit job availability and mobility and alter workers' compensation unfavorably. At best, these laws help some workers enjoy more security or higher pay, but they do so at the expense of others. For example, the bulk of research on increasing minimum wage levels finds that they raise hourly pay for most affected workers but that they lower overall employment levels or hours worked, thus reducing job prospects for young and unskilled workers.[27]

Occupational licensing: Since the 1950s, the share of US jobs requiring a license has soared from 5 to 22% in 2021, creating barriers that disproportionately affect young workers starting their careers, people with low incomes, interstate movers, people switching occupations, veterans, and individuals with criminal records.[28] These regulations, varying across states, mandate specific educational, training, and testing prerequisites for numerous professions, ranging from doctors and lawyers to barbers and massage therapists. The recent surge in occupational licensing restrictions poses a significant impediment to work and mobility in the United States, contrasting with its otherwise relatively flexible labor markets. One researcher estimates that occupational licensing can result in up to 2.85 million fewer jobs nationally, with an annual consumer cost of $203 billion.[29]

Home business regulation: Fueled in part by the pandemic-induced shift toward remote work, an increasing number of individuals are recognizing the benefits of running businesses from the comfort of their homes. However, state and local regulation restricts—often severely—the ability of individuals to operate a business from their residence. Local governments impose zoning rules that restrict or even prohibit home businesses. These outdated rules, rooted in twentieth-century practices, were designed to separate residential, commercial, and industrial zones to mitigate potential negative externalities such as noise and congestion,[30] but studies show that the regulations are based on tradition rather than actual analyses of externalities.[31] Many states also impose industry-specific barriers on home businesses, such as cottage food producers, daycares, hair stylists, and music producers.[32] Collectively,

---

[27] Neumark and Shirley (2022).
[28] U.S. Bureau of Labor Statistics (2022). The 1950s figure is from Kleiner and Vorotnikov (2018).
[29] Kleiner (2015).
[30] Lemar (2019).
[31] Gonzalez and Gray (2020) and Gray and Gonzalez (2020).
[32] McDonald (2022).

barriers to home businesses make it harder for American workers to make a living, whether by choice or necessity.

Criminal justice policy: Criminal justice policies in the United States present significant barriers to employment for millions of Americans. With over 30% of adults having been arrested and nearly 8% holding a felony record, employment opportunities for this population are hindered by their record rather than their capacity or willingness to work.[33] In fact, studies repeatedly show that a criminal record—not the underlying crime—is a significant reason for unemployment, and that the United States' increasing felony-history share since the 1980s translated to about 1.7 million Americans not working because of their record.[34] Government policy exacerbates these challenges. Many states restrict the ability of people with criminal records to become licensed professionals in certain industries. These restrictions are generally limited to charges related to the occupation being pursued, but five states even permit licensing boards to deny an application based on any felony conviction, even if it is unrelated to the license at hand.[35] Criminal records can also be a barrier to self-employment. For example, applicants to the Small Business Administration (SBA)'s largest loan programs must disclose all criminal records and histories, including any expunged records. Federal law, meanwhile, reduces federal transportation funding to states that do not suspend driver's licenses of individuals convicted of drug offenses. Many states also deny driver's licenses to individuals with minor arrest records or unpaid court debts, thus harming their employment prospects.[36] Finally, broader issues such as overcriminalization (e.g., for drugs or gambling), coercive plea bargaining, and juvenile detention burden many individuals with an undeserved criminal history.

Transportation policy: US transportation-related policies contribute to an inefficient and costly system, costing workers time and money while limiting their geographic mobility. Travel within the U.S. is often fraught with gridlocked streets, unreliable mass transit, and subpar rail and air transport that compare poorly to their counterparts overseas. Commutes have lengthened over the years, with American workers spending more time traveling than their European counterparts.[37] The financial toll is significant, with congestion alone costing drivers an average of $1348 per year. Numerous

---

[33] Umez and Pirius (2018) and Shannon et al. (2017).
[34] Bushway et al. (2022), Larson et al. (2022) and Lincicome (2021).
[35] Sibilla (2022).
[36] DeHaven and de Rugy (2011).
[37] U.S. Census Bureau (2021) and Eurostat (2020).

policies contribute to these problems. Passenger vehicle prices are inflated by thousands of dollars, thanks to US tariffs on imported vehicles and parts (particularly the 25% tax on imported light trucks); federal Corporate Average Fuel Economy (CAFE) standards; and state laws restricting direct-to-consumer sales by manufacturers, adding hundreds or thousands of dollars to vehicle prices.[38] Gasoline prices are increased by not only state taxes but federal regulations like the Jones Act, which mandates the use of US-flagged vessels for domestic shipping, and the renewable fuel standard, which requires biofuels be blended into gasoline. Local zoning laws discourage density, thus extending commutes and increasing road wear. Buy America requirements and the Davis-Bacon Act, which requires union labor, increase the cost of building public transportation infrastructure. State and federal localization rules (e.g., Buy America) also increase the cost and decrease the quality and availability of mass transit. And air cabotage laws prohibit foreign airlines from operating domestic routes and thus subject American air travelers to higher prices and fewer routes, further reducing mobility.

Remote work policy: Despite remote work's continued popularity among both employers and employees, government policy has failed to adapt to this new reality, thus restricting workers' job and physical mobility. Several US states apply onerous "convenience of the employer" laws, which can lead to double taxation of remote workers living in one jurisdiction for a company headquartered in another. State laws also impose tax withholding and filing obligations for remote workers that have spent as little as one day working and residing in the state. Federal tax treatment of remote work-related issues, such as fringe benefits, deductions, and home offices, remain unclear, further discouraging the practice. And occupational licensing rules often prevent remote workers from practicing across state lines (e.g., in telemedicine). Collectively, these rules can constitute a significant barrier to American workers finding new employment without moving to a new state or locality.

Employee benefits and health care: Current federal and state policies subsidize employers' provision of health, childcare, and other benefits to their employees and limit workers' ability to use these services upon quitting or being fired. Most importantly, the federal tax exclusion for employer-sponsored insurance creates implicit penalties for workers that might prefer to take cash instead and buy health insurance and care independent from their companies. Because employer-provided insurance is not fully portable, the tax

---

[38] Bourne (2018).

exclusion fosters "job lock" (a situation where workers forgo better employment opportunities for fear of losing insurance coverage) and "entrepreneurship lock" (discouraging workers from going out on their own for the same reason). Indeed, a majority of studies surveyed by AARP [formerly called the American Association of Retired Persons] in 2015 found that health insurance-related job lock reduced workers' propensity to change jobs, to start businesses, and to retire or work part-time.[39] Bae and Meckel (2022) found, moreover, that the Affordable Care Act's mandate that private insurance plans extend coverage to adult dependents under the age of 26 had the unintended consequence of increasing job lock among numerous parents who would have otherwise left their employers.[40] Other types of benefits subsidized by the federal government and tied to workers' employers, rather than to workers, raise similar concerns regarding worker choices, wasteful spending, and job lock. This includes various flexible spending accounts for qualified medical, dental, or dependent care expenses or pensions that employers control or manage for retirement savings.

Welfare policy: Government efforts to combat poverty have consisted of substantial financial investment, with the US government alone allocating over $1.1 trillion to more than 100 anti-poverty programs in 2021. However, many programs are designed in ways that discourage recipients' economic and geographic mobility. Most notably, the majority of welfare benefits today are provided not in cash but rather as in-kind benefits: direct cash assistance programs, including refundable tax credits, made up just 22% of federal assistance in 2020. Virtually all of these programs are limited to government-sanctioned purchases and locations, thus pushing recipients into narrowly concentrated neighborhoods clustered around subsidized housing—neighborhoods have been shown to inhibit residents' upward income mobility.[41] Other welfare programs discourage work altogether. The most troubling of these is the current Social Security Disability Insurance (SSDI) system, which, because of its generous benefits, lax eligibility criteria, and lack of rigorous enforcement, has become, according to one expert, "a permanent dole for a rising number of adults with limited earning potential who clearly are physically able to work."[42]

Childcare policy: Expensive childcare in the United States can deny parents the types of childcare they prefer or that is better suited to their work needs. It

---

[39] Baker (2015).
[40] Bae and Meckel (2022). See also Shi (2020).
[41] Chetty and Hendren (2017) and Whatley (2021).
[42] Winship (2015).

can also create a barrier to better job matching, human capital accumulation, and physical mobility that could deliver higher wages or better opportunities, along with a more vibrant and productive economy overall. Consider, for example, that in 2022 full-time center-based care for an infant in Washington, DC, cost an average of $24,400 per year, while in Mississippi, it cost $5800.[43] For a working family looking to move from the latter location to the former, the childcare cost differential could be prohibitively high. For a family already in Washington, high childcare costs could force one parent to stay home instead of work.

That childcare is expensive is not—contrary to what many critics say—a "market failure" in need of government intervention. Stringent state staff-to-child ratio requirements substantially increase prices with little beneficial effect on observed childcare quality. Educational qualifications and training requirements for licensed caregivers have similarly large price effects on childcare prices. Federal subsidies tied to these state regulations further entrench them (and their economic harms). Furthermore, many state and local governments consider home daycares a "problem use" and have therefore used zoning restrictions to ban them, thus reducing the availability of childcare in the affected neighborhoods and further increasing prices. Finally, the supply of potential childcare workers, au pairs, and babysitters is further reduced through lengthy foreign labor certification processes, low visa caps, and limited visa availability for nannies living outside the home of care.

Housing policy: US housing policy discourages adjustment and dynamism in two ways. First, sky-high rents and home prices in thriving local economies (e.g., New York City or Silicon Valley) prevent workers from moving there for better employment opportunities. In the past, Ganong and Shoag (2015) found that less-skilled workers could not afford the higher housing costs in heavily regulated cities that have strong economic opportunities, and so these workers became stuck in lower-cost areas that had lesser job prospects.[44] Davis and Haltiwanger (2024) have further found that housing prices, economic dynamism, and employment are highly intertwined, so much so that the 2008–2010 housing crisis accounted for about three-quarters of the decline in young firm employment.[45] Yet numerous government policies increase construction costs and home prices. For example, tariffs have

---

[43] Childcare Aware of America (2022) (Arlington, VA: Childcare Aware of America).
[44] Ganong and Shoag (2015).
[45] Davis and Haltiwanger (2024).

increased the cost of a wide variety of construction materials and other essential home goods.[46] Federal tax deductions for property and mortgage interest also increase home prices by making houses more valuable and increasing people's willingness to pay, thereby making it harder for first-time homebuyers to afford down payments.[47] Federal tax law also requires developers to write off the construction costs for new apartments over decades, thus increasing the cost of development.[48] Federal policies also restrict the availability of land for housing, notably in states with high levels of in-migration and federal land ownership. Finally, federal rules governing manufactured housing allow local governments to regulate these homes more restrictively than pricier "stick-built" homes.[49]

Second, federal subsidies for home ownership—tax deductions for mortgage interest, direct homebuyer subsidies, and federal government involvement in housing finance (mortgage insurers, mortgage security guarantees, and government-sponsored enterprises)—can inhibit geographic mobility, especially for people with significant mortgage debt or living in struggling localities. Analyzing data from the Netherlands, Bernstein and Struyven (2022) suggested that, in fact, having a mortgage can be a serious impediment to geographic mobility when a loan exceeds a home's value (known as "negative equity," which often occurs during economic downturns).[50]

Personal savings. Various laws also discourage personal savings, which can provide crucial for workers experiencing or at risk of disemployment. A larger financial cushion, for example, can give workers more freedom to pursue new job opportunities, to start their own businesses, or to move when local economic problems arise. Unfortunately, personal savings are disadvantaged at the federal level compared to spending, with the exception of narrow government-specified savings goals (e.g., health care or retirement).[51] Laws and regulations governing benefits give workers less control over their compensation—shifting part of it into mandated or encouraged benefits that, if provided as cash, might otherwise be directed to savings. Overgenerous unemployment insurance (UI), meanwhile, can delay unemployed

---

[46] Lincicome (2021).
[47] Joint Economic Committee Republicans (2020).
[48] Lincicome (2020).
[49] Schmitz (2020) and "Manufactured Housing and Standards—Frequently Asked Questions," U.S. Department of Housing and Urban Development, Office of Manufactured Housing Programs.
[50] Bernstein and Struyven (2022).
[51] Bourne and Edwards (2017).

Americans' return to the workforce[52] or discourage workers' geographic mobility.[53]

Individually, these impediments to worker adjustment may be surmountable. Collectively, however, they can present impossible hurdles to workers moving on with their lives after economic disruption occurs—whether caused by trade or technology or anything else. Protectionists, however, rarely consider them at all.

Conclusion

The populist narrative that free trade has uniquely and irreparably harmed the working class and their communities is almost entirely wrong. In reality, the vast majority of workers in the United States have benefited from open markets, have adjusted to trade-related disruptions, and are better off today than they were decades ago. This does not mean, however, that trade or any other type of beneficial disruption is not without its downsides, at least in the short term. That is particularly the case for workers and places that, unlike their peers, did not quickly adjust—finding new jobs, vocations, or communities—in response to an economic shock. Those situations are real and worthy of policymakers attention, but the solutions lie not in stopping the shocks from occurring—stagnation that would make us all worse off—but in reforming all the policies that prevent those affected from moving on with their lives. Doing that would boost not only those workers, but also broader labor dynamism, productivity, and economic growth. It also would avoid the common trap of simply throwing more money at an existing program or creating yet another new program to address the challenges caused by previous ones—creating higher costs, strained budgets, and more distortions in the process.

Bibliography

Abel JR, Deitz R (2019) Where are manufacturing jobs coming back? Liberty street economics (blog). Federal Reserve Bank of New York

---

[52] For negative employment effects, see Schmieder and Wachter (2016).
[53] See, for instance, Nunn et al. (2018) (finding that the Extended Benefits program, which ties weekly benefits to state unemployment rates instead of workers, "is associated with diminished worker mobility" across state lines) and Fernandez-Navia (2021).

Allen K (2017) Shrinking cities: population decline in the World's Rust-Belt Areas. Financial Times

Autor D, Dorn D, Hanson G (2021) On the persistence of the China shock. Brookings Institution Press 2021(2):381–476

Bae H, Meckel K (2022) Dependent Coverage and parental 'job lock': evidence from the affordable care act. National Bureau of Economic Research Working Paper No. 30200

Baker D (2015) Job lock and employer-provided health insurance: evidence from the literature. AARP

Barro J (2016) So what would it mean to 'Beat China' on trade? New York Times

Bernstein A, Struyven D (2022) Housing lock: Dutch evidence on the impact of negative home equity on household mobility. Am Econ J Econ Pol 14(3):1–32

Berube A, Murray C (2018) Renewing America's economic promise through older industrial cities. Brookings Institution

Bessen J (2016) How computer automation affects occupations: technology, jobs, and skills. Boston University School of Law and Economics Working Paper No. 15-49

Bloom N et al (2019) The impact of Chinese Trade on U.S. employment: the good, the bad, and the apocryphal. Working paper, Stanford University

Bourne R (2018) Government and the cost of living: income-based vs. cost-based approaches to alleviating poverty. Cato Institute Policy Analysis No. 847:12-14

Bourne R, Edwards C (2017) Tax reform and savings: lessons from Canada and the United Kingdom. Cato Institute Tax and Budget Bulletin, No. 77

Broda C, Romalis J (2008) Inequality and prices: does China benefit the poor in America? Working paper, European Trade Study Group

Bureau of Labor Statistics (2022) Labor force statistics from the current population survey: data on certifications and licenses

Bureau of Labor Statistics (2024) Job openings, hires, and separations levels, seasonally adjusted. https://www.bls.gov/charts/job-openings-and-labor-turnover/opening-hire-seps-level.htm. Accessed 5 April 2024

Bushway S et al (2022) Barred from employment: more than half of unemployed men in their 30s had a criminal history of arrest. Sci Adv 8(7)

Byrnes N (2016) Learning to prosper in a factory town. MIT Technol Rev

Caliendo L, Dvorkin MA, Parro F (2015) Trade and labor market dynamics: general equilibrium analysis of the China Trade Shock. Federal Reserve Bank of St. Louis Working Paper No. 2015–009H. Revised February 21, 2019

Caliendo L, Parro F (2023) Lessons from US-China trade relations. Annu Rev Econ 15:513–547

Census Bureau (2021) Census bureau estimates show average one-way travel time to work rises to all-time high

Chen S (2024) The fried chicken is in New York. The cashier is in the Philippines. New York Times

Chetty R, Hendren N (2017) The impacts of neighborhoods on intergenerational mobility I: Childhood exposure effects. National Bureau of Economic Research Working Paper No. 23001

Childcare Aware of America (2022) Appendices of demanding change: repairing our child care system

Cunningham E (2016) No, Wall Street Journal, Chinese imports didn't kill my hometown. The Federalist

Davis SJ, Haltiwanger J (2024) Dynamism diminished: the role of housing markets and credit conditions. Am Econ J Macroecon 16(2):29–61

DeHaven T, De Rugy V (2011) Terminating the small business administration. Downsizing the Federal Government (blog), Cato Institute

Engbom N (2022) Labor market fluidity and human capital accumulation. National Bureau of Economic Research Working Paper No. 29698

Eurostat (2020) Majority commuted less than 30 minutes in 2019

Fallows J (2019) Lessons from Danville. The Atlantic

Federal Reserve Bank of St. Louis (2024) All employees, total nonfarm (PAYEMS). https://fred.stlouisfed.org/series/PAYEMS#0. Accessed 5 April 2024

Fernandez-Navia T (2021) Unemployment insurance and geographical mobility: evidence from a quasi-natural experiment. SSRN

Fort TC, Pierce JR, Schott PK (2018) New perspectives on the decline of US manufacturing employment. National Bureau of Economic Research Working Paper No. 24490

Ganong P, Shoag D (2015). Why has regional income convergence in the U.S. declined? Harvard University, John F. Kennedy School of Government

Gonzalez O, Gray N (2020) Zoning for opportunity: a survey of home-based-business regulations. Center for Growth and Opportunity at Utah State University Policy Paper No. 2020.006

Gray N, Gonzalez O (2020) Home-based businesses are coming. As COVID-19 accelerates remote working, are cities prepared? City J

Handley K, Kamal F, Ouyang W (2021) The rise of exporters and importers in US job growth: insights from newly released data. VoxEU, Centre for Economic Policy Research

Hanson GH (2021) Can trade work for workers? The right way to redress harms and redistribute gains. Foreign Affairs

International Monetary Fund (IMF) (2019) Chapter 2: Closer together or further apart? Subnational regional disparities and adjustment in advanced economies. World Economic Outlook: Global Manufacturing Downturn, Rising Trade Barrier. IMF, Washington, pp 65–92

Jaravel X, Sager E (2020) What are the price effects of trade? Evidence from the U.S. and implications for quantitative trade models. FEDS Working Paper No. 2019-68

Joint Economic Committee Republicans (2020) Priced out: why federal tax deductions miss the mark on family affordability

Karahan F et al (2017) Do job-to-job transitions drive wage fluctuations over the business cycle? Am Econ Rev 107(5):353–357

Kavilanz P (2024) California just hiked minimum wage for fast food workers. Some restaurants are replacing them with Kiosks. CNN

Kleiner MM (2015) Reforming occupational licensing policies. Hamilton Project Discussion Paper No. 2015-01, p 6

Kleiner MM, Vorotnikov ES (2018) At what cost? State and National Estimates of the Economic Costs of Occupational Licensing. Institute for Justice

Larson R et al (2022) Felon History and Change in US Employment Rates. Social Science Research 103(102649)

Lemar AS (2019) The role of states in liberalizing land use regulations. North Carolina Law Rev 97(2):293–354

Lincicome S (2020) Testing the "China Shock": was normalizing trade with China a mistake? Cato Institute Policy Analysis No. 895

Lincicome S (2020) Why (some of) the rents are too damn high. The Dispatch

Lincicome S (2021) How U.S. Trade Policy helped construction materials costs go through the roof. Cato at Liberty (blog)

Lincicome S (2021) Not ready for prime time. The Dispatch

McDonald J (2022) Entrepreneur from home. Institute for Justice

Neumark D, Shirley P (2022) Myth or measurement: what does the new minimum wage research say about minimum wages and job loss in the United States? National Bureau of Economic Research Working Paper No. 28388

Nunn R, Kawano L, Klemens B (2018) Unemployment insurance and worker mobility. Tax Policy Center

Paquette D (2017) In this part of the Midwest, the problem isn't China. It's too many jobs. Washington Post

Perry MJ (2015) Economics at its best—the story of the 'Iowa Car Crop'. American Enterprise Institute

Sasso M (2019) Lost jobs of North Carolina are gone for good. Few seem to mind. Bloomberg

Schmieder JF, Von Wachter T (2016). The effects of unemployment insurance benefits: new evidence and interpretation. National Bureau of Economic Research Working Paper No. 22564

Schmitz JA (2020) Solving the housing crisis will require fighting monopolies in construction. Federal Reserve Bank of Minneapolis

Schwartz ND, Bui Q (2016). Where jobs are squeezed by Chinese Trade, voters seek extremes. New York Times

Shannon SKS et al (2017) The growth, scope, and spatial distribution of people with felony records in the United States, 1948–2010. Demography 54(5):1795–1818

Shi M (2020) Job lock, retirement, and dependent health insurance: evidence from the affordable care act. Columbia University

Sibilla N (2022) Barred from working. Institute for Justice (website)

Stanford E (2014) How youngstown, Ohio, became a poster child for post-industrial America. CNBC

Torres C, Saraiva C (2018) The new startup south. Bloomberg Businessweek

Umez C, Pirius R (2018) Improving access to licensed occupations for individuals with criminal records. National Council for State Legislatures

United States Department of Housing (nd) Manufactured Housing and standards—frequently asked questions. U.S. Department of Housing and Urban Development, Office of Manufactured Housing Programs

Wang Z et al (2018). Trading with China on local labor markets: a supply chain perspective. National Bureau of Economic Research Working Paper No. 24886

Warren M (2018) What Trump doesn't understand about South Carolina and BMW. Weekly Standard

Whatley V (2021) The importance of neighborhoods and intergenerational economic inequality in the United States. Washington Center for Equitable Growth

Winship S (2015) How to fix disability insurance. National Affairs

Challenges in Export Growth and Financial Compliance for Latin America

Jorge Jraissati

Introduction

Economic development has long been intertwined with the ability of a country to expand its export base, both in volume and in the sophistication of the goods produced. Increasing exports is pivotal for economic growth, as it enables countries to leverage their comparative advantages, integrate into global markets, and benefit from technology transfers and economies of scale.

The theoretical underpinnings of export-led growth can be traced to the economic principles of comparative advantage and structural transformation. Comparative advantage posits that countries benefit from specializing in goods they can produce efficiently, while structural transformation involves shifting resources from low-productivity to high-productivity sectors (Rodrik 2006). This dual approach has been instrumental in the rapid economic growth observed in most developed economies, where deliberate policy interventions have fostered export diversification and industrial upgrading.

More recently, the economic literature has emphasized the importance of a country's "export sophistication," which measures the income level associated with a country's export basket. In essence, countries exporting more

---

I am grateful to Valery Jraissati and Eduardo Royo for the research assistance and commitment to this area of work.

J. Jraissati (✉)
President, Economic Inclusion Group, Brussels, Belgium
e-mail: jorge@econinclusion.org

© The Author(s), under exclusive license to Springer Nature Switzerland AG 2025
M. Rangeley and D. Hannan (eds.), *Free Trade in the Twenty-First Century*, https://doi.org/10.1007/978-3-031-67656-7_29

complex goods tend to grow faster. The production and export of these goods often require the development of advanced skills, technologies, and infrastructures. Having a "more sophisticated" export portfolio allows countries to capture bigger profit margins while also benefiting from positive externalities in other sectors (Hausmann et al. 2006). For instance, India, Taiwan, and Japan have achieved remarkable growth rates by diversifying their exports into more sophisticated products, moving up the global value chain.

The role of export sophistication is further elaborated through the concept of "cost discovery," where entrepreneurial ventures into new products generate knowledge spillovers that benefit the broader economy. These spillovers are particularly critical in developing countries where initial production costs are uncertain and high, as successful ventures reveal profitable opportunities for other firms (Hausmann et al. 2006). The ability to produce and export more sophisticated goods, often associated with higher productivity, results in faster economic growth.

Similarly, empirical data reveals that countries with a large and well-diversified manufacturing sector are better positioned for sustained economic growth. Manufacturing drives productivity through technological advancements and the accumulation of production know-how by a firm, usually referred to as the process of "learning by doing." It also creates backward and forward linkages that stimulate other sectors of the economy (Rodrik 2006). The experience of East Asian economies highlights the effectiveness of targeted preferential policies and export promotion strategies in fostering economic development.

In contrast, regions that have failed to diversify their exports or that remain dependent on primary commodities often experience slower growth and greater economic volatility. Latin America exemplifies this issue, where reliance on primary commodities has contributed to economic instability and slower growth rates. Moreover, there is vast evidence of the negative relationship between resource abundance and democratic stability, including the non-discriminatory provision of public goods, which are essential for economic development.

From this evidence, diversifying into manufacturing and high-value-added exports is therefore a crucial step to achieve sustained economic development. In the context of Latin America, the region's struggle with the middle-income trap underscores the importance of increasing export sophistication. Overcoming this challenge requires deliberate policies to enhance productive capabilities, foster technological innovation, and support industrial diversification. These policies help create the conditions necessary for moving up the value chain and breaking into markets for more technologically advanced products and services.

To unlock this export-led development path, policymakers must find solutions to the various growth constraints in their economies. These constraints include domestic institutional challenges such as extractive policy arrangements, lack of rule of law, contractual security, property rights, and monetary stability, among others. Additionally, there are domestic structural issues, such as the absence of substantial comparative advantages or an inward-looking productive composition. Common growth constraints also involve international factors, such as rising geopolitical tensions that could undermine trade flows, supply chains, and territorial security. Changes in the global economic environment, like declining demand for certain goods and services or the downturn of a major trading partner, also pose challenges. Finally, shifts in the global regulatory environment, including policies governing the energy sector, global banking, and tax controls, present additional obstacles.

When analyzing these factors, there is not much literature on the relationship between export-growth development and the state of today's global financial regulatory architecture. The purpose of this paper is, therefore, to analyze this issue. When doing so, it becomes clear that emerging markets are facing a historically challenging global regulatory financial environment, characterized by escalating costs and unintended consequences. This trend is led by the ever-increasing complexity of a series of regulations known as Anti-Money Laundering and Counter-Terrorism Financing laws (AML/CFT). Collectively, these regulations impose demanding compliance costs in the form of extensive monitoring, reporting, and due diligence procedures, among others. They also produce negative economic effects, including market concentration, barriers to innovation, supply chain disruptions, and financial exclusion. These challenges are particularly present in emerging markets like Latin America, whose institutions, industries, and communities are considered riskier by the Financial Action Task Force (FATF) as well as other global financial intelligence units (FIUs).

By examining this critical international challenge for the Latin American export sector and economy as a whole, this chapter aims to equip policymakers with the knowledge needed to formulate more effective development strategies for their respective countries, thereby fostering improved development outcomes for their populations. The chapter is structured as follows: Section "Latin America's Trade Outlook" provides a brief analysis of Latin America's trade outlooks. Section "The Rise of AML/CFT Laws and Their Impact on Compliance Costs in Emerging Markets" elaborates on the complexity and economic effects of AML/CFT laws. Section "Policy Recommendation" offers a policy recommendation to address this issue.

Latin America's Trade Outlook

The 33 countries forming the Community of Latin American and Caribbean States (CELAC) collectively represent the European Union's fifth-largest trading partner and the United States' third-largest. This underscores the region's critical role in global trade dynamics, despite its inherent structural and economic complexities (EPRS 2023).

From the early twentieth century to the present, Latin America's international trade dynamics have undergone significant transformations, influenced by global economic trends, regional policies, and domestic economic strategies. The region's trade policies have oscillated from protectionist approaches to more open practices and vice versa. This has resulted in suboptimal economic results in the region, as economic growth is negatively correlated with policy uncertainty and instability.

During the early twentieth century, many Latin American countries adopted protectionist trade policies aimed at fostering domestic industries. These policies, characterized by high tariffs, import quotas, and subsidies, were underpinned by the import substitution industrialization (ISI) strategy. ISI sought to reduce dependency on foreign goods by encouraging local production of industrial products and developing nascent industries.

This approach often led to inefficiencies, as local industries were shielded from international competition and innovation. By the mid-twentieth century, the limitations of ISI became apparent. The economic crises of the 1980s caused in part by ISI strategies, marked by high debt levels and inflation, prompted many Latin American countries to adopt structural adjustment programs advocated by the International Monetary Fund (IMF) and the World Bank. These programs emphasized trade liberalization, deregulation, and privatization. They became the core of the so-called "Washington Consensus" paradigm in Latin America.

As a result, governments across the region reduced trade barriers, eliminated quotas, and lowered tariffs by sector and margin. These reforms also included significant privatization of state-owned enterprises in sectors such as telecommunications, electricity, and banking, leading to increased efficiency and attracting substantial foreign investment. Financial liberalization was another critical component, with countries dismantling capital controls to attract foreign portfolio investment, though this also exposed economies to greater financial volatility.

The 1990s also saw the emergence of regional trade agreements aimed at enhancing economic cooperation and integration. Notable agreements include the North American Free Trade Agreement (NAFTA) between the United States, Canada, and Mexico, and the Southern Common Market (MERCOSUR) between Argentina, Brazil, Paraguay, and Uruguay. These agreements facilitated tariff reductions, increased trade flows, and attracted foreign direct investment (FDI) to the region.

However, the Washington Consensus delivered mixed results in the region, partially because of problems related to not only policy implementation, pace, and sequencing but also political stability, which includes public support for such a drastic reform agenda. As a result, in the 2000s, Latin America saw the rise of the so-called "Socialism of the XXI Century," which included the governments of Chavez in Venezuela, Morales in Bolivia, and Kirchner in Argentina. These governments intensified trade relationships beyond traditional partners in North America and Europe to engage more with Asia, particularly China. China's demand for raw materials and commodities has driven significant export growth for countries like Brazil, Chile, and Peru. Chinese FDI in Latin America is growing, focusing on minerals, petroleum, and food production. This shift has increased Latin America's political connections with China and its dependency on commodity exports, making the region vulnerable to global price fluctuations.

Despite these changes, trade and investment between the United States and Latin America grew significantly from 2000 to 2012. Since then, the composition of US trade with the region has evolved, influenced by various factors, including policy shifts, the rise of China, and changes within global value chains (GVCs). The United States has comprehensive reciprocal trade agreements with most major Latin American economies, covering over three-quarters of total US trade with the region. Notable agreements such as NAFTA, CAFTA-DR, and bilateral FTAs with Chile, Peru, Panama, and Colombia have boosted US-LAC trade and investment. Despite not having an FTA with the US, Brazil remains the second-largest US trade partner in the region.

Currently, Latin American countries are undertaking several policy initiatives to enhance their trade performance and economic stability. The Mercosur-EU trade agreement, which aims to eliminate tariffs on 90% of goods traded between the two blocs, is expected to boost trade by providing preferential access to both markets and encouraging foreign direct investment (FDI) (European Commission 2021). The Pacific Alliance, comprising Chile,

Colombia, Mexico, and Peru, continues to work on deepening economic integration and expanding trade partnerships beyond the region. Efforts also include negotiating free trade agreements with countries in the Asia-Pacific region.

Brazil has implemented policies to enhance the competitiveness of its manufactured goods, including tax incentives and support for research and development (R&D) in high-tech industries. The country's National Plan for Logistics and Transport (PNLT) aims to improve infrastructure by reducing logistics costs and facilitating trade. Mexico has focused on strengthening its automotive and aerospace sectors, which are significant contributors to its export economy. The National Development Plan includes initiatives to enhance productivity and innovation in these industries.

Overall, Latin America's trade outlook remains uncertain. The region faces significant challenges, but also immense opportunities. A clear example of this is seen in LAC's energy sector. Not only does Latin America have extensive oil and gas reserves, its large share of lithium and copper supplies guarantees it will continue leading this sector as the world transitions away from fossil fuel. To capitalize on these opportunities, however, Latin America has to change. Despite the efforts mentioned above, the region remains more economically closed than most regions. The Mercosur area bears witness to this, as can be seen from the high common external tariff of between 10 and 12%, while the average international tariff is around 5.5% (Briceño 2022). In economies like Brazil and Argentina, trade represents less than 30% of GDP. In comparison, the global average is 45%, and many emerging market competitors have much higher trade-to-GDP ratios (O'Neil 2022). Moreover, less than 20% of trade in Latin America occurs within the region, compared to much higher rates in other parts of the world. This lack of regional integration limits the benefits of globalization. Plus the lack of integration into global value chains has left Latin America at a disadvantage.

The Rise of AML/CFT Laws and Their Impact on Compliance Costs in Emerging Markets

Over the past few decades, the financial sector has experienced a notable rise in compliance expenses, particularly related to Anti-Money Laundering and Counter-Terrorism Financing (AML/CFT) regulations. These regulations refer to the laws, regulations, and procedures designed to prevent criminals from disguising illegally obtained funds as legitimate income, as well as the measures to detect, deter, and disrupt the financial support networks of terrorist organizations. They have become increasingly rigorous, necessitating substantial investments in compliance infrastructure and processes.

These regulations are led by the Financial Action Task Force (FATF), an intergovernmental organization established in 1989 by G7 countries to combat money laundering. The organization sets international standards and promotes legal, regulatory, and operational measures to combat money laundering, terrorist financing, and other related threats to the integrity of the international financial system. The FATF's Recommendations, first issued in 1990, have become the cornerstone of global AML/CFT efforts. Compliance with these standards involves severe customer due diligence (CDD), transaction monitoring, and the filing of suspicious activity reports (SARs).

The increasing implementation of AML/CFT laws has significantly raised compliance costs for businesses, especially in emerging markets. These regulations, aimed at curbing illicit financial activities, need extensive monitoring, reporting, and due diligence procedures that often require substantial financial and human resources. On a global scale, financial institutions incur compliance costs exceeding $200 billion, representing more than 12% of global research and development (R&D) spending.

In Latin America, the regulatory environment poses specific challenges due to a combination of factors such as varying levels of regulatory maturity, economic constraints, and high levels of informality in the financial sector. Financial institutions in Latin America often struggle with the dual burdens of complying with international AML/CFT standards while navigating local regulatory landscapes that may lack consistency and clarity. These institutions face higher relative costs of compliance due to less developed regulatory frameworks and technological infrastructure.

The direct costs of AML/CFT compliance include investments in technology, human resources, and training. Financial institutions are compelled to deploy sophisticated software solutions capable of detecting suspicious transactions and maintaining compliance with evolving regulatory requirements. Additionally, there is significant expenditure on hiring and training compliance professionals who are well-versed in regulatory standards and capable of managing complex compliance systems. In the context of Latin America, these costs are exacerbated by the need to adapt international best practices to local realities, which can be resource-intensive and challenging.

Beyond the direct financial burden, AML/CFT compliance imposes significant indirect costs. These include the opportunity costs associated with the allocation of resources toward compliance activities instead of revenue-generating functions. Moreover, compliance requirements can lead to reduced operational flexibility and increased friction in customer onboarding processes, potentially impacting customer satisfaction and retention. In Latin America, where financial inclusion remains a critical goal, these compliance requirements can hinder the ability of financial institutions to expand their customer base, particularly among underserved populations.

AML/CFT regulations can sometimes lead to unintended consequences such as de-risking. To avoid the possibility of non-compliance, financial institutions may engage in terminating or restricting relationships with clients or correspondent banks deemed high-risk. This can lead to reduced access to financial services, particularly in vulnerable regions, industries, or communities perceived as high-risk. In Latin America, this has been a significant issue, with many businesses losing access to essential banking services (Gutiérrez and Carbo 2018). Similarly, AML/CFT regulations also require stringent monitoring and verification of transactions, causing significant delays in processing international transactions. These delays can disrupt supply chains and cash flow, which are critical for maintaining smooth business operations.

Similarly, higher risks and compliance costs have resulted in the decline of correspondent banks, which provide local accounts and payment services for international banks. This arrangement allows international banks to incur cross-border payments, which represent about 20% of the total transactions in the payments industry. However, as these banks are deemed more susceptible to money laundering than direct originator bank-to-beneficiary payments, financial institutions have to apply "significant AML and KYC processes to ensure they are not inadvertently offering services for illicit activity" (Nice Actimize 2022: 1).

This has resulted in lower profitability and increased risk of owning and operating correspondent banks, which has resulted in a 22% drop in correspondent banks from 2011 to 2019, according to data gathered by the Bank for International Settlements (2020). The BIS also reports that Latin America has been among the regions more affected by decline with a 34% drop in its correspondent banking sector. Overall, this phenomenon is leading to financial exclusion as well as a higher concentration of transactions in fewer banks, despite the growth in the volume of cross-border payments.

From an industrial policy perspective, the high cost of compliance can influence market dynamics by disproportionately affecting smaller financial institutions and businesses, which may struggle to meet regulatory demands compared to their larger counterparts. This disparity can lead to reduced competition and increased market concentration and pricing power of established firms, stifling innovation, and reducing consumer choice as well as the efficiency of markets. In Latin America, where small and medium-sized enterprises (SMEs) play a crucial role in economic development, the impact of these costs can be particularly detrimental.

Moreover, the complex regulatory environment can stifle innovation, particularly in the financial technology (fintech) sector. Startups and tech companies may find it challenging to navigate intricate compliance landscapes, slowing the development and adoption of new technologies. Regulatory hurdles can limit fintech growth, affecting the broader financial sector's ability to leverage technological advancements for improved efficiency and security (IMF 2023; KPMG 2023). In Latin America, where fintech is seen as a critical driver of financial inclusion and innovation, these regulatory challenges can significantly impede progress.

Empirical evidence supports the assertion that AML/CFT compliance costs are a significant concern for businesses in emerging markets. For example, a study by the World Bank highlights that banks in Sub-Saharan Africa face some of the highest compliance costs globally, which can account for up to 10% of their operating expenses (World Bank 2016). In Latin America, similar challenges exist, with financial institutions facing significant compliance burdens that affect their profitability and ability to provide affordable financial services, potentially exacerbating financial exclusion in the region.

Global penalties for breaching AML regulations have risen sharply, from $4.27 billion in 2018 to $10.4 billion by 2020, highlighting the increasing regulatory pressure on the private sector to combat ML proactively (True Cost of Compliance, 2023). Compliance costs for financial institutions reached a staggering $274 billion in 2022 (Pol 2018). Yet, despite these immense expenditures on compliance, the overall impact of AML/CFT policies is minimal, according to numerous studies. As Elucidate (2023) reports, "more than 99% of money laundering proceeds remain in the hands of criminal gangs" despite the increasing global expenditure on enforcing AML/CFT laws.

Policy Recommendations

In conclusion, the path to sustained economic growth for Latin American countries lies in their ability to diversify and sophisticate their export base. Theoretical and empirical evidence consistently underscores the significance of export sophistication—shifting toward the production and export of more complex goods—as a catalyst for higher economic growth. Countries that have successfully navigated this transition, such as those in East Asia, demonstrate the efficacy of targeted sectorial policies aimed at fostering export diversification and industrial upgrading (Hausmann et al. 2006).

However, the contemporary global financial regulatory environment presents unique challenges to this export-led development trajectory. Stringent AML/CFT regulations impose disproportionately high compliance costs on emerging markets, which have to reallocate factors of production from revenue-generating to compliance-focused activities. It also stifles innovation, especially in the fintech sector, which is a critical driver of financial inclusion in the region. It creates market concentration by overwhelmingly affecting small and medium-sized enterprises. Lastly, it creates financial exclusion by incentivizing a "zero-risk" policy among financial institutions, which then terminates or restricts relationships with clients or correspondent banks deemed high-risk. Overall, these regulatory burdens exacerbate the already significant challenges these countries face in achieving export-led growth.

As a result, there needs to be a concerted and prioritized effort among Latin American governments to align international regulatory frameworks with the developmental needs of emerging markets. Policymakers in Latin America have to engage with the Financial Action Task Force (FATF) to advocate for proportionate AML/CFT compliance measures that consider the specific contexts of developing economies, thereby reducing the compliance burden and fostering a more conducive environment for exports and business in general.

This means advocating for simplified compliance requirements for Latin American firms, financial institutions, and citizens, instead of the universal enforcement of highly complex global standards. Since most individuals and firms operate within fairly standard and small business models, the simplifications of rules would not compromise the integrity of the financial system. Yet, it would result in increased financial inclusion and economic activity. This would reverse the current one-size-fits-all nature of current AML/CFT regulations, characterized by its "no-risk" bias, which is proven prejudicial for emerging markets and vulnerable communities.

This argument is supported by various experts within and beyond the financial sector. For instance, according to the General Manager of the Bank for International Settlements, Agustín Carstens, applying the proportionality approach would result in "very large" potential benefits in terms of expanding financial inclusion globally, while only marginally increasing ML risks (Bank for International Settlements 2022: 2). For this reason, Carstens argues for this approach in both entity-based and activity-based AML/CFT regulations, including the alleviation of know-your-customer (KYC) requirements for basic financial services. He then invites standard-setting bodies (SSBs) to incorporate "financial inclusion considerations into their work and accept the principle that good regulation should also minimize any unintended adverse impact on other social policy goals" (Bank for International Settlements 2022: 1).

Carstens' position, of enhancing the provision of basic payment accounts for firms and individuals deemed "high-risk" due to current AML/CFT procedures, goes in line with my own policy recommendation to the Parliamentary Assembly of the Council of Europe (PACE) on the subject of "Addressing the Financial Exclusion of Latin American Immigrants," where I advocate for financial reforms that guarantee a "right to banking" for immigrants, with a special emphasis on analyzing existing AML/CFT laws (Jraissati 2024). As a result of my policy recommendation, over twenty members of PACE pushed forward a resolution proposal with the same title, with hopes to start addressing this issue in the 46 member states of the Council of Europe (Bartulica 2024). Similar work should be initiated in other international institutions.

As part of these government-led efforts to reform the predominant AML/CFT approach, involving commonly underrepresented sectors of civil society is crucial. This includes businesspeople representing small and medium-sized enterprises, rising entrepreneurs representing the interests of young people and tech innovators, non-profit leaders, as well as immigrants and refugee seekers. This would address the institutional and sectorial bias present in the deliberations and recommendations proposed by FATF as well as other regulatory agencies dealing with international finance. Ultimately, FATF and domestic FIUs have to include financial inclusion as part of their primary mandate—not only to address the unintended consequences of AML/CFT regulations but also to recognize that greater financial inclusion would contribute to the effectiveness of combating money laundering.

Acknowledgements I would like to thank Economic Inclusion Group Research Fellows Alberto Arape and Raul Carrasco Contero for their research assistance.

References

Bank for International Settlements (2020) New correspondent banking data—the decline continues at a slower pace. https://www.bis.org/cpmi/paysysinfo/corr_bank_data/corr_bank_data_commentary_2008.htm

Bank for International Settlements (2022) Speech by Agustín Carstens, general manager of the BIS. https://www.bis.org/speeches/sp221107.pdf

Bartulica (2024) Addressing the financial exclusion of Latin American immigrants. https://pace.coe.int/en/files/33363

Briceño RJ (2022) La flexibilización del Mercosur. En 30 años del Mercosur. Trayectoria, flexibilización e interregionalismo, coord. Caetano, Gerando y Hernández N., Diego, pp 114–115. Montevideo: Universidad de la República

Commission E (2021) The EU-Mercosur trade agreement: overview. European Commission, Brussels

Elucidate (2023) 5 reasons why the global anti-money laundering system is failing financial institutions. https://www.elucidate.co/blog/5-reasons-why-the-global-anti-money-laundering-system-is-failing-financial-institutions

European Parliamentary Research Service (EPRS) (2023) EU trade with Latin America and the Caribbean: overview and figures. European Parliament, Brussels

Gutiérrez E, Carbo J (2018) Financial inclusion in Latin America and the Caribbean. World Bank Working Paper.

Hausmann R, Hwang J, Rodrik D (2006) What you export matters. J Econ Growth 12(1):1–25

International Monetary Fund (IMF) (2023) Anti-money laundering and combating the financing of terrorism. https://www.imf.org

Jraissati J (2024) Proposal for a resolution in the Parliamentary Assembly of the Council of Europe (PACE) to address the financial exclusion of Latin American immigrants. https://drive.google.com/file/d/1Eiwe9dADz_JpPvRIe2rWg7BLiuaQqaEI/view?usp=sharing

KPMG (2023) Fraud and financial crime: 2023 regulatory challenges. https://home.kpmg

LexisNexis Risk Solutions (2023) True cost of compliance 2023 report. https://risk.lexisnexis.co.uk/insights-resources/white-paper/true-costs-of-compliance#form

NICE Actimize (2022) Correspondent banking: mitigate risk, not de-risk. https://www.niceactimize.com/Lists/InsightsArticles/aml_insights_article_correspondent_banking_mitigate_risk_not_de_risk.pdf

O'Neil S (2022) Why latin America lost globalization and how it can win now, council on foreign relations. Available at: https://www.cfr.org/article/why-latin-america-lost-globalization-and-how-it-can-win-now

Pol A (2018) Anti-money laundering and its impact on financial inclusion: a critique of the current regulatory framework. J Financ Crime 25(4). Available at: https://www.tandfonline.com/doi/full/10.1080/25741292.2020.1725366

Rodrik D (2006) Industrial development: stylized facts and policies. In: Industrial development for the 21st century. United Nations Department of Economic and Social Affairs, New York

World Bank (2016) The cost of compliance in the financial sector: evidence from Sub-Saharan Africa. World Bank, Washington, DC

Free Trade and Free Markets

How Free Trade Helps Businesses Thrive

Daniel Lacalle

It is surprising to witness a growing negative press regarding free trade. There is a global advancement of old and failed ideas like autarky and protectionism, which collide with the undeniable benefits that free trade has generated for society.

A recent paper by the IMF (Growing Threats to Global Trade, Goldberg and Reed 2023a, b) reminds us that "the era of 'hyper globalization' that took shape from the 1990s onward was associated with great economic achievement. Extreme poverty as defined by the World Bank was dramatically reduced and expected to be eliminated in all but a small number of institutionally fragile countries, partly thanks to dramatic growth in East Asian countries. Standards of living, as measured by income per capita, increased across the world." "While numerous factors contributed to this rise in living standards, openness and other market-oriented policies played an essential role. Trade with (at the time) low-wage countries influenced goods prices and wages in advanced economies, benefiting consumers in these countries and workers in exporting economies. Inflation remained surprisingly low, despite quantitative easing and increasing debt in the U.S. Finally, the Western world enjoyed a historically rare, extended period of peace that fostered prosperity. The tight global interconnectedness achieved by the end of the twentieth

---

Daniel Lacalle: PhD Economist and author of Freedom and Equality (Post Hill Press).

D. Lacalle (✉)
Chief Economist, Tressis SV, Madrid, Spain

century was arguably a major contributing factor by giving everyone an incentive to behave."

Despite these positive results from free trade, protectionist measures and limits to free trade have soared, particularly in the past decade, due to a misinformed view of globalization as the culprit of weakening living standards for workers in developed economies, something that has more to do with increases in direct and indirect taxes and destruction of the purchasing power of the currencies due to inflationary policies. Interventionist politicians are eager to impose any form of control, even if it is harmful to the economy.

As I commented in 2018 (Tariffs are the Worst Way to Combat Protectionism), "protectionism only protects the government. It does not defend obsolete industries, does not create jobs, and certainly does not support growth. It only protects the government that imposes it." In essence, barriers to trade are only a desperate attempt from the side of government that prefers control to progress, presenting themselves as saviors of the negative side effects of something that they have caused with interventionist policies, shifting causation toward a foreign external enemy: trade and competition.

As Henry George said, "What protectionism teaches us is to do to ourselves in times of peace what enemies seek to do to us in times of war."

According to the World Bank (Protectionism Is Failing to Achieve Its Goals and Threatens the Future of Critical Industries, 2023), "Since 1990, global trade has increased incomes by 24% worldwide and by 50 percent for the poorest 40% of the population. This growth has lifted more than one billion people out of poverty. Trade has also played a pivotal role in shaping the global economy and promoting positive socioeconomic outcomes. Today, however, protectionist measures are on the rise. And trade tensions and geopolitical challenges are raising concerns about the trajectory of globalization. As a result, deglobalization—the process of reducing global economic interdependence—has been at the forefront of current policy discussions."

Politicians all over developed economies demand free trade and open markets while imposing barriers in their home territories. The political elite and its crony sectors like rising exports but dislike competition.

Interventionist practices are allowed because political powers use bilateral treaties to grant unnecessary advantages to semi-state-owned conglomerates or decide to look the other way at other countries' barriers to trade. If the World Trade Organization (WTO) imposed real and severe fines on anti-competitive practices and did so effectively and quickly, this would not happen. But the mirage of growth and thinking that if you look elsewhere, countries will stop imposing anti-trade practices that have clouded society's perception of economic reality.

If we believe that we can impose barriers to trade and, at the same time, expect to export more goods and services, we are simply dreaming.

The rise of China as an economic powerhouse, the eurozone stagnation, COVID, and the war in Ukraine have made politicians dust off the worst economic ideas in history: autarky and protectionism.

As I explained in The Stupidity of Autarky (March 2022), autarky is based on the belief that if our nation produced everything we needed, we would all be better off because we would not depend on others. The idea comes from a deep lack of understanding of economics. There is no such thing as autarky. There is no such thing as covering all the needs of a population based on the limits of a politically defined border. It makes no sense. If I told you that I want to make my city self-sufficient, you would laugh about it, understanding that it is impossible and that the reason my city thrives is because of the interaction and commerce with other cities. However, when a group of politicians define a nation's border, we are immediately led to believe that those limits contain every resource that citizens may need and that everything else is irrelevant.

The other fallacy about autarky is that anyone can understand that limiting the economy to the confinement of a random limit of land is an extremely poor way to develop, grow, and prosper. It is almost laughable to read from politicians in the eurozone how they want to achieve full independence and limit imports while at the same time bragging about its enormous trade surplus. It is funny to see how the most autistic politicians want to increase exports at the same time.

We also forget that our progress also comes from the development of the nations we trade with. Our security of supply and our improvement are only a function of everyone else's growth.

How can autarky and protectionism be sold to citizens? By selling the false idea of a zero-sum game in the economy. If someone is selling oil to us, they win, and we lose. If someone is selling solar panels to us, they win, and we lose. We would win if we sold everything to ourselves. However, it is simply false. Politicians who sell a zero-sum game in the economy know it is false, but they also know that protectionism and autistic aspirations give them power and make citizens more dependent on political power.

It is precisely through the development of other nations and making the best use of trade that we can grow faster and have access to more goods and services at better prices.

Productivity, technology, trade, and cooperation are essential factors for prosperity. Autarky and protectionism are essential drivers of stagnation and poverty.

The recent inflation and supply shortage problem does not come because of the evils of globalization and the mistakes of free trade, but because of the trend of interventionism and protectionist measures that have plagued the world in the past years. There is only one way in which countries can overcome the impact of a war in a country that sells a significant percentage of the world's cereals, oil, and gas: with more trade and better diversification of sources of supply, not with autarky and protectionism.

If recent crises can tell us anything, it is that we need more cooperation and trade with even more countries to avoid hunger, shortages, and lack of access to essential goods.

The solution to the challenge presented by the polarization of the world is to develop even more trade and cooperation agreements with the world. Thankfully, technology and human action are dissolving what once seemed like impenetrable borders.

Autarky leads to a collapse in productivity and much worse real wages.

Protectionism is rising and it is using new disguises, like "green policies." According to Le Monde, taxing carbon emissions means reshaping the landscape of world trade. In 2021, University of Zurich professor Mathilde Le Moigne published a study titled "Buy Green, Not Local: How International Trade Can Help Save Our Planet." She wrote that, if a uniform tax on carbon emissions was implemented across the globe, "it would favor the countries of the global North (Germany, Japan, Finland, and the United States), which are major producers in the world and relatively less carbon intensive. Conversely, it would affect the countries of the South, such as Cambodia, Peru, and the BRICS countries (Brazil, Russia, India, China, and South Africa), whose global emission share is higher than their production share." (How the rise of green protectionism penalizes poor countries, Boissou 2022)

The external enemy is a very convenient escape goat for governments and the easiest one to use these days is climate. Citizens would immediately be against a border tax on imports from emerging economies because they understand they would suffer higher prices while hurting poor countries. However, announcing it in the name of climate change goals makes it much easier to sell. Politicians will announce large subsidies—that you pay—to mitigate the impact on jobs of the weaker economies while charging yet another tax that limits free trade. If they really wanted to tackle climate change, they would facilitate the development of technology and support competition to make emerging markets richer so they could invest in green policies. However, the ultimate goal is control and serfdom, so they use taxation, which enlarges the size of government in the economy while making domestic consumers poorer as they must finance the subsidies and the higher cost of goods and services.

There are no reasons for deglobalization and politically imposed "reshoring" if we understand how the economy works. The insanity of thinking of the economy in artificial border terms. With free trade, everyone wins. The only way in which populists may try to convince us of the benefits of deglobalization and reshoring is by resorting to envy, fear, and greed. No one who believes in cooperation and collaboration can ever agree on these different forms of interventionism.

Envy of those that are more competitive, thinking they take our jobs when reality has proven that employment thrives thanks to global cooperation and trade.

Fear of an inexistent enemy. Thinking that a nation that sells to us wants to harm us, which makes no sense,

Greed is when politicians make citizens believe, especially in developed economies, that they will enjoy the benefits of global trade sharing without benefiting our trading partners.

Competitiveness is not achieved by eliminating our trading partners, but through technology, added value, and innovation.

In its core, protectionism adopts the Marxist view of value. For Marx, the value of a commodity is determined by socially necessary labor time, or the amount of time "required to produce an article under the normal conditions of production and with the average degree of skill and intensity." It is such an outdated and incorrect view that it should have been abandoned many decades ago, but there is still a significant group of interventionist policymakers that fall under the trap of believing that value is determined by cost addition and, as such, if someone else is selling below the calculation made in our country, then it should be taxed, limited, or prohibited.

It is important to remind the reader that the evils of free trade are sold to us by people who benefit from imposing barriers. Interventionism and trade barriers empower politicians, who then present themselves as the solution to supply shortages by reaching bilateral agreements.

We must not forget that there is no single defender of protectionism and trade barriers who believes that exports are bad. They just want free trade one way. Theirs. However, making emerging economies poorer does not make us richer. Trade barriers, like tariffs, always backfire. Our trading partners become poorer when we limit their exports to our nation and, in turn, have increasing difficulties purchasing our goods. There is no such thing as deglobalization and rising exports. And there is no such thing as deglobalization and declining exports with rising domestic prosperity.

Deglobalization is inflationary, as the prices of goods and services soar in real and nominal terms, not just from the higher costs but due to the destruction of the purchasing power of the currency the protectionist nation issues—inflation—and makes poverty rise, inside and outside our borders, adding fuel to the fire of global conflicts. By invoking our greed and desire to shelter our nation from the world, we achieve the opposite.

Deglobalization and protectionism are like communism. Everyone knows they have failed but there is always someone trying to sell us the idea that it will work if they implement it.

No one can deny the atrocious results of autarky and interventionism in European nations in the past, yet a few politicians think this time will be different.

It is no coincidence that economic stagnation, massive public debt, poor productivity growth, and weakening real wage growth across the world have coincided with a period of rising protectionism. Yet, despite the evidence of its poor results, the answer from the populist interventionists is that we need even more intervention.

Interventionism always fails, and when citizens complain about their eroding quality of life, politicians resort to the three most common excuses:

It was not enough.

We need more.

Repeat.

No one would defend protectionism if they understood what it really is: a subsidy to obsolete sectors paid for by consumers and workers alike.

Why Do Small and Large Businesses and Workers Benefit from Free Trade?

The global benefits of free trade are evident. However, those benefits escape the average citizen and particularly small businesses.

One of the most important benefits of a free trade world is the development of a sophisticated and efficient financial market that facilitates transactions, credit, and insurance inside and outside the borders of a nation.

Small businesses today have unprecedented access to credit and insurance instruments at affordable costs that would not exist if we did not have a thriving global free trade environment.

Today, even a small shop can trade globally and hire a container with goods insurance at the click of a button and the affordable rates they enjoy cannot exist if there was no mutualization and large developed financial institutions that can syndicate risk and offer the best options for citizens, be it in a small shop or a medium-sized manufacturer.

Small businesses may not understand that the competitive financing and ample liquidity they enjoy in a competitive financial services industry would never exist if there was no free trade and large shippers and companies all over the world originated the merchandise moves that cement the pillars of the financial industry.

A startup company can access customers all over the world and offer their goods and services thanks to a global network of financial institutions, investment banks, insurance brokers, and other service providers that were created, thanks to the development of world trade. Furthermore, it is not just a global financial system that offers competitive rates. Imagine for a second the type of financing costs a small business would suffer if there was no free and open trade. In fact, most small businesses would have no access to liquidity and financial support.

We should not underestimate the benefits of free trade in the access to world class legal support and counseling. Today, small businesses have the possibility of using the services of legal firms that have built a wide range of capabilities and specialized services due to the development of free trade globally. Small and medium enterprises today enjoy more protection and can extract the most out of their competitive advantages thanks to the globalization of services that offer legal and investor security.

A fundamental tool for small businesses to conduct their activities is mediation in conflict. This tool, which is more affordable, faster, and more efficient than litigation or arbitration, is essential for small and medium enterprises that want to continue growing without large liabilities from judicial processes. Mediation would not exist without the benefits of free trade and a global financial and legal framework that creates these competitive services, thanks to the existence of large transactions between multinationals.

And how do small and medium enterprises become multinationals? Tapping into a pool of global investors that can take positions and finance the growth of services and manufacturing businesses all over the world. Without a global free trade system no one can think there would be access to the global network of investors for capital raising as well as origination and financing of credit for investment projects.

Autarky and protectionism also mean strangled liquidity and expensive, if any, access to credit.

The access to a global financial system is not just a competitive advantage for small and medium businesses. It means cheaper rates, support in challenging times through advanced insurance mechanisms, security in payment, and resolution of conflicts.

These benefits are also evident for citizens. The entire credit system of the world is built on two main pillars, the global transaction and financing of governments through the acquisition of sovereign bonds as well as the origination of financing for global trade.

An average household may not know it, but one of the reasons why they can access a personal loan or a mortgage at competitive rates with many institutions offering financial support is because the government itself can sell its bonds to investors and central banks all over the world, and these institutions accept sovereign debt as a reserve, a low-risk investment and collateral.

Protectionism and autarky significantly reduce the access to credit and legal support for households and businesses.

We must remember that when a government imposes barriers to trade it is literally telling the world it does not want their business, and the nation cannot expect that the world will react by purchasing their sovereign bonds and providing them with credit. The reader may think that a nation may not need the rest of the world if it has its own banks, but the previously mentioned problem happens equally. What do you think is the reserve for those banks? The sovereign bond. If those bonds are rejected by the rest of the world because the government closes its borders to trade, the immediate consequence is the inability of local banks to provide affordable or any credit to businesses and families.

Families and small businesses suffer more in a protectionist nation because the reserve issued by the government, its sovereign debt, is rejected globally. When this happens, the government can only issue debt in foreign currency, and by closing trade and imposing protectionist measures, it also destroys the purchasing power of its currency.

If a family or business thinks that free trade does not affect them, they should look at the disastrous situation that closing borders to trade has generated in countries like Argentina or North Korea.

Rejecting free trade has a double negative financial impact. It creates a massive slump in exports, as the world rejects products from countries that impose barriers on others, while it generates a significant deterioration of the purchasing power of the currency as the government's credit diminishes.

The reader may think this applies to small nations, but not to giants like the United States or China. However, that perception is misguided. China and the United States may be enormous markets with significant resources, but they cannot close their borders to trade. China, as a global competitive manufacturer, needs free trade to provide its goods and services to the world. If it closes its trade, the currency loses value, and this means weaker purchasing capacity of real wages. The United States needs free trade, open and independent institutions as well as a thriving financial sector to finance its fiscal deficit and continue to enjoy the benefits of having a global reserve currency. This is the same for the euro area. Protectionism hurts any economy, regardless of its size, and the damages manifest in a deteriorating currency and weaker standards of living.

Defenders of protectionism argue that it is unfair to have open economies and free trade when other nations play with different rules, lower salaries, and less taxes. This is a myopic view. These nations were, at one point, the lowest cost, salary, and tax nation and if anyone had imposed trade barriers on them, they would have justifiably seen it as unfair. The United States was the low-cost producer for the developed Great Britain or France. The way to compete is through added value, innovation, and technology, not a race for the lowest cost. This is the only way in which nations like China have developed and now do not compete only on price and volume, but technology and innovation. The best way to combat the protectionist temptations of interventionist governments is with more free trade, not less.

Businesses also benefit from free trade because they learn, adapt, and become more competitive. Innovation is an unstoppable force. Protectionism only serves as a tool to make companies lazy and avoid being more efficient and innovative. It is not a surprise to see that nations that implement massive subsidies and enormous barriers to trade, using regulation as a protectionist tool, lose the technology battle and end up having higher unemployment and weaker productivity companies than open economies.

The reader may believe that innovation can also exist if a nation limits free trade if it has a large enough population. It is a grave mistake. Innovation benefits from the access to diverse cultures and markets. In fact, reality has shown that even in nations like China innovation thrives when companies sell their products globally. This process of understanding global needs and trends and providing goods and services that address the demand from all consumers is precisely what allows added value to increase, margins to improve, productivity growth, and with it, higher real wages for all workers.

What reduces the real wages of workers in developed nations is not free trade, but the constant debasement of the currency coming from a monetary policy that disguises the rising government debt and passes the imbalances to citizens through inflation—both of assets and consumer prices. Reagan was right when he said "Inflation—that's the price we pay for those government benefits everybody thought were free." Individual prices may rise due to an exogenous factor like a war or a supply disruption, but that does not make inflation rise, consolidate, and continue rising annually, which is the rise in aggregate prices. The only thing that makes aggregate prices rise at the same time and continue increasing through time is when governments issue more currency—debt—than what the private economy demands. Inflation is the destruction of the purchasing power of the currency. Governments increase inflation passing their fiscal imbalances to the consumer via inflation and taxes, free trade limits that inflationary process.

Maybe the reader believes that inflation is still high, but what they are not considering is that the level of current consumer prices would be even higher without free trade and technology.

Inflation, the hidden tax on the poor, is what is hurting the middle class destroying the purchasing power of real wages and deposit savings while artificially increasing asset prices.

Artificial money creation is never neutral. It disproportionately benefits the first recipient of money, the government that issues it, and massively hurts the last recipients, real wages, and deposit savings. Artificial money creation is a transfer of wealth from workers to governments.

This is what is hurting the middle class, artificial money printing created by bloating the government size in the economy through public debt, not free trade.

Government interventionism does not redistribute from the rich to the poor, but from the middle class to government.

Free trade makes families and businesses increasingly economically independent, richer, and more productive. It is the only way in which a small business can become a large one. Without free trade, credit, liquidity, affordability, and innovation disappear.

Trading globally makes business managers better understand the needs of their customers, inside and outside their headquarters' borders. It also helps businesses anticipate important trends and prepare themselves for changes in customer demands. A company that competes with international peers is also one that can prepare itself in a better way for the challenges and opportunities coming from global trends, including demographics and technological changes.

Eliminating free trade is destroying freedom and the negatives outweigh any positive that populists try to sell us. Limiting trade is limiting innovation, lowering quality of life for all.

Limiting free trade is like cutting the flow of blood to one limb thinking it will benefit from the accumulated blood and its own tissue. It rots and dies.

Furthermore, unless amputated, it will kill the body. Free trade is the blood flow of the world. Putting barriers to trade is the same as putting barriers to the flow of oxygen to the body.

Bibliography

Bouissou J (2022) How the rise of green protectionism penalizes poor countries. https://www.lemonde.fr/en/economy/article/2023/06/22/how-the-rise-of-green-protectionism-penalizes-poor-countries_6034961_19.html

Caselli F, Koren M, Lisicky M, Tenreyro S (2020) Diversification through trade. Quart J Econ 135(1):449–502

Goldberg PK, Reed T (2023a). "Is the Global Economy Deglobalizing? And if So, Why? And What Is Next?" Brookings Papers on Economic Activity (March).

Goldberg PK, Reed T (2023b) Growing threats to global trade. International Monetary Fund (IMF, June 2023). https://www.imf.org/en/Publications/fandd/issues/2023/06/growing-threats-to-global-trade-goldberg-reed

Lacalle D (2018) Tariffs: the worst way to combat protectionism. https://app.hedgeye.com/insights/66095-tariffs-the-worst-way-to-combat-protectionism

Lacalle D (2022) And now for a really bad response to political calamity: autarky (Mises, 2022). https://mises.org/mises-wire/and-now-really-bad-response-political-calamity-autarky

Martin TL (1989) Protection or free trade: an analysis of the ideas of henry George on international commerce and wages. Am J Econ Sociol 48(4):489–501 (JSTOR). http://www.jstor.org/stable/3487565. Accessed 15 Apr 2024

Marx K "Capital" (1867) https://www.d.umn.edu/cla/faculty/jhamlin/4111/MarxReadings/1867%20Capital%20I%20--%20Ch_%20I.htm#:~:text=The%20labour%2Dtime%20socially%20necessary,intensity%20prevalent%20at%20the%20time

World Bank (2023) Protectionism is failing to achieve its goals and threatens the future of critical industries. https://www.worldbank.org/en/news/feature/2023/08/29/protectionism-is-failing-to-achieve-its-goals-and-threatens-the-future-of-critical-industries

Colombia's Uber Wars: Anarchy, Legalism, and the Politics of Regulatory Capture

Daniel Raisbeck

On the corner of 76th street and 11th *carrera*, you will find a stately, Tudor house that, now firmly within Bogotá's urban sprawl, once overlooked the city's leafy outskirts. Inside there once stood Colombia's foremost private library, with over 27,000 volumes centered around the Greco-Roman classics and the Western canon's great books.[1] Within these confines, the house's learned owner lambasted the modern, bourgeois world. His weapon: a collection of aphorisms that, though never meant for publication, have earned him posthumous comparisons to Friedrich Nietzsche.[2] But Nicolás Gómez Dávila was no nihilist, let alone a Marxist. He relished the term "reactionary" without any intention to thwart history's relentless tide.

Gómez Dávila was a Catholic thinker whom German writer Martin Mosebach described as an "emigrant from the present," a hermit who lived and wrote "in a place of exile," a cold, rainy city "at the edge of the inhabited world."[3] Not that Gómez Dávila resented such descriptions of his native Santafé de Bogotá. As he himself wrote, he had resolved "the basic problem of all former colonies" with "maximum simplicity;" in the face of "intellectual

---

[1] Goenaga Olivares, 97.
[2] See, for instance, Fuentes (2010).
[3] Mosebach, 5–6.

D. Raisbeck (✉)
Washington, D.C., USA
e-mail: draisbeck@cato.org

servitude, a paltry tradition, and enforced, shameful imitation," he decided: "Catholicism is my country."[4]

Gómez Dávila's aphorisms, "discovered" by German and Italian scholars before they were much recognized in Colombia itself, constitute short notes to an "implicit" text. In one of his longer "notes," he reflects upon Spanish colonial history with remarkable insight.

The *conquistadors*, Gómez Dávila writes, were ambitious adventurers who, covetous of wealth and power, unleashed anarchy across their New World domains, lands that they "began to deliver into chaos."[5] Hernán Cortés provides a good example. The conqueror of the Aztec Empire did not have official permission to launch an expedition into Mexico. Rather, he disobeyed his superior, Diego Velásquez, and left from Cuba to Yucatán in an act of mutiny. Only his magnificent success won him legitimacy and honor.

But, Gómez Dávila remarks, the Spanish Crown soon moved to rein in such rogue figures. It imposed upon their incipient American states a "severe and rigid administration," which Spain itself had inherited, via the House of Aragon, from the Kingdom of Naples.[6] Already in the twelfth and thirteenth centuries, the Norman kingdom of Sicily, precursor to the Neapolitan state, had weakened the nobility and centralized power in the monarch's hands.[7] Four hundred years later, Spanish kings had no intention to leave their American colonies outside of their distinctly inflexible system of political control.

Cortés learned this the hard way; his rule of "New Spain" as Captain General was soon checked by the newly created Audiencia. An ocean away from the seat of royal power, the swashbuckling Cortés nonetheless fell under the close supervision of royally appointed officials.

From its *sui generis* founding, Gómez Dávila found, "Spanish America inherits the two factors of its history." The first is anarchy, the *conquistadors*' legacy, which drags countries in the region "from revolution to revolution, and turns every Spanish American individual into a permanent antagonist to the state." The second factor is the state itself, which accounts for "a perennial legalism, an inability to act in the economic sphere without the state's assistance, and an easy tolerance of dictatorships."[8] The uneasy merger between anarchy and legalism unleashed tensions that, across the region, are still felt to this day. In Bogotá, you encounter them soon after you fly into the city.

---

[4] Gómez Dávila (2001).
[5] Idem (1953, 195).
[6] Ibidem.
[7] See Abulafia, 202 ff.
[8] Gómez Dávila (1953, 195).

* * *

In a rare display of commercial nous, the Colombian authorities named the Bogotá airport El Dorado, a reference to a mythical city of gold that *conquistadors* sought—in vain—to find on this high Andean plateau inhabited by the Muisca people. Conversely, El Dorado, "the gilded one," referred to the local chieftain at Guatavita, a circular lake in the nearby highlands. Early Spanish sources mention a coronation ritual that involved smothering the freshly anointed ruler's naked body with powdered gold before rowing him out to the middle of the lake on a raft, whence he would proceed to bathe in the water, sacred as it was to the Muisca mother goddess.[9]

As you step off your flight in El Dorado, you are unlikely to spot gilded royalty. But you will notice a Colombian twist to the standard amenities of international aerodromes: duty free shop shelves loaded with bottles of the state-produced *aguardiente* schnapps ("fire water"), currency exchange kiosks eager to sell you heavily devalued pesos, and local fast-food chains that will introduce you—via, for instance, *arepas*—to the maize-based, homegrown culinary tradition that provided hungry *conquistadors* with some respite when they first came across a Muisca village. But one thing you won't find at El Dorado are the signs—prevalent at any major US airport—leading you to a ride-sharing waiting lot.

Colombian regulation is ambivalent about arriving passengers' ability to catch a ride at the airport via Uber or any other similar web application.[10] Instead, passengers without pre-arranged transportation are expected to use either the bus system[11] or the officially sanctioned taxi service. All taxis that operate legally belong to a single company, Taxi Imperial, whose contract with the conglomerate that runs El Dorado grants it a virtual monopoly over the airport's incoming traffic.[12] With 35.5 million passengers arriving in 2022,[13] Taxi Imperial's owners have truly struck gold at El Dorado.

* * *

---

[9] See Quintero Guzmán.

[10] According to Uber's website, it does provide a service *from* El Dorado Airport. However, this is not clearly permitted for the reasons explained below. And as late as 2023, a YouTube video explained how to order an Uber ride from El Dorado, emphasizing that it should be done clandestinely and from the second floor, an area not used regularly for passenger pick-up. In April, 2019, police officers fired several shots at an Uber driver, who was wounded, in an incident during a late-night raid at the second floor of the airport. See RCN Radio (2019).

[11] Hernández Torres.

[12] Aeropuerto El Dorado. "Taxi Imperial es la empresa autorizada para transportar a los viajeros de la terminal aérea".

[13] Gimenez Mazó.

If given a choice, would incoming passengers use Uber to reach their destination?[14] Foreigners who already use the service in their home countries almost certainly would, but the same applies to locals. In fact, Uber's user growth in Bogotá was extraordinary once it arrived in 2013.[15] Operating originally as a "luxury service" with the sole use of special white vehicles—it soon included—through a service called "UberX"—drivers of private cars that met minimum requirements.[16] The company thus created a much-publicized luxury niche, which it soon democratized. With its double-pronged approach, Uber quickly filled a void in a captured market in which customers desperately sought security, convenience, and transparency.

Uber succeeded in Bogotá by unleashing a flight to safety. Living in the city, you are lucky if you merely know someone who has—and have not yourself been—the victim of the unique mugging method known as the "millionaire's ride."[17] In its standard form, a pair of armed criminals—clearly in cahoots with the driver—trap a taxi's passenger by forcing their way through each of the car's rear doors. At gunpoint or under the threat of a knife's blade, the victim is then driven for several hours to a series of ATM machines, forced to hand over as much cash as possible, and finally left—alive, if fortunate—in a remote part of the city, usually without a mobile telephone, a watch, or any other valuable. By 2014, the millionaire's ride had become so commonplace that insurance companies offered policies to protect their clients from the adverse financial effects of this unique brand of "micro-kidnapping."[18]

By minimizing passengers' risk of experiencing the millionaire's ride or similar heists, any company that provided a safe alternative to Bogotá's yellow taxis would have been an instant success. In Uber's case, they verified the identity of the drivers on the app and ensured that they held no criminal records. They also georeferenced the trajectory of each ride and, with their rating system, created positive incentives for drivers to provide a good service. Unsurprisingly, Uber's ability to offer the high likelihood of a safe ride to their passengers proved popular.

But users were also looking for a reliable, non-arbitrary way to reach their homes or places of work. Taxi drivers, on the other hand, often reject passengers on the street if they deem their destination to be inconvenient.[19] Uber, again, solved this problem by connecting passengers with a driver willing to

---

[14] "Uber" will be used as a term that encompasses ride-sharing applications in general.
[15] La República.
[16] Acevedo.
[17] See Newsweek.
[18] See Revista Semana (2012 (2)).
[19] See Publimetro.

take them to a specific destination for a pre-determined fee. The system also ensured that the driver picked passengers up at their precise location.

The fee itself, to which users agree before ordering the ride, was another advantage. Passengers of taxis were tired of inconsistent and unreliable meters, whose inaccuracies often seem to skew to the upside.[20] Besides, Uber, unlike taxis, would accept payments with debit and credit cards and not strictly with cash. Although some users, journalists, and social media activists criticized Uber's surge pricing—when pent up demand and limited supply significantly increases rates for passengers—this missed an essential point: users are always free not to use the service. Besides, Uber's drawbacks simply lent entry opportunities to competitors, and several companies did indeed join the fray by offering very similar services.

If Uber and similar apps rapidly acquired tens of thousands of passengers while, at the same time, providing a flexible source of income for thousands of drivers who also joined the service, surely lawmakers and regulators would have sought to adapt the existing rules to accommodate the new technology. This took place in the United States, where the federal system allows individual states to take the lead in experimenting with new policies, with others free to emulate any instance of success. In 2014, Colorado was the first to address certain insurance issues and allow Uber and its competitor, Lyft, to operate legally.[21] The rest of the country eventually followed. In highly centralized Colombia, on the other hand, events unfolded differently.

* * *

Colombian politicians are loath to upset the taxi lobby, and not without good reason. In 2001, Bogotá's mayor was Antanas Mockus, an academic of Lithuanian descent. He had come to national prominence as the president of Colombia's state-run National University, where he silenced hundreds of his unruly students at an event by taking the stage, dropping his trousers, and revealing his bare behind to the audience.[22] The stunt made Mockus a celebrity and set him on the path to victory in the 1994 mayoral election. During his second term, Mockus decided that the previous mayor's restrictions on private vehicles—which were only allowed to circulate at certain times according to their license plate number—should also apply to previously exempt taxis. The ensuing reaction brought the city to a standstill.

---

[20] See RCN Radio (2023).
[21] Vuong.
[22] Caballero.

On August 2, 2001, taxi drivers mobilized en masse and blocked at least 40 of Bogotá's busiest streets, avenues, and thoroughfares. The result, one daily newspaper reported, was one of "the most chaotic days in the city's recent history."[23] While traffic chaos is routine in Bogotá, this particular traffic jam became legendary; the road system was so clogged that children had to sleep inside their school buses or classrooms. The next day, public transport remained paralyzed and thousands of people failed to show up at work.[24] The taxi drivers eventually relented before Mockus's heavy-handed measures. Nonetheless, they had proven that they were a force to be reckoned with.

It was also a highly concentrated force, wielded in truth by only two men. Uldarico Peña and José Eduardo Hernández met in 1978 while driving taxis to and from El Dorado Airport, where they detected a business opportunity. They used the three cars they owned to create Radio Taxi Aeropuerto, Colombia's first taxi company to allow its users to order a service on the telephone[25] (ironically in light of later events, Peña and Hernández started out as tech entrepreneurs.) By 1987, 200 taxis were under their banner and 20 operators worked full time to answer customers' calls at the emblematic 2111111 number, which the company obtained from the public telephone monopoly. During the following decades, the partners expanded their business by creating numerous companies; among them was Taxi Imperial,[26] the extant airport monopoly. By the 2010s, they controlled around 35,000 taxis[27]—well over half of the city's total fleet—either by owning them directly or charging their owners to join their network.

Peña and Hernández built a business with extremely high barriers to entry; a wide moat in Warren Buffett's terminology.[28] But this was due to government favoritism, not to customer satisfaction. In 1992, the city of Bogotá, in one of its many attempts to reduce congestion by decree, capped the number of official taxi permits at 30,000, with the owners of scrapped taxis free to sell their permits in the market.[29] Nonetheless by 2010, there were over 49,000 taxis circulating in the city, with many of the 19,000 additional vehicles operating illegally. Others obtained their permits through fraud.[30] In 2019, the

---

[23] Cortés Fierro.
[24] Ibidem.
[25] La Silla Vacía.
[26] Revista Semana (2012 (1)).
[27] La Silla Vacía.
[28] See Corfina.
[29] D. Rodríguez.
[30] Ibidem.

Bogotá Secretary of Transport revealed that 48,473 taxis were authorized to operate in the city.[31]

As the city's population grew, the cap on taxi permits, which is still in place, made the costs of each permit skyrocket. Originally purchased from the city for around COP $500,000, permits sold at one point for COP $150 million, around three or nearly four times the cost of a new taxi.[32] The secular bull market in taxi permits, however, could last only while passengers remained without alternatives to yellow taxis. This was also the reason why taxi drivers could get away with providing a subpar and even dangerous service. Soon enough, however, the market's barriers to entry would cave in.

It was one thing, in fact, for the taxi lobby to fight authoritarian and, frankly, counterproductive traffic regulations in the early 2000s; the license plate-based restriction, still in place and known as *pico y placa* (peak and plate), has incentivized the purchase of second vehicles, thus helping to increase the total number of cars and, thereby, congestion.[33] But the threat to the taxi industry in the mid-2010s was of a different nature altogether. Suddenly, the dominant players were rapidly losing market share to a technology platform that makes use of people's excess capacity—namely, private cars that otherwise would remain mostly idle—and connects drivers—who are supply-side users of the platform—with other users who demand a travel service. All of which is done in an ad hoc manner and through a transparent method for the parts to set prices and either make or receive payments.[34]

The existing regulations did not even contemplate the degree to which this "ride-sharing" technology upended traditional public transport. As such, Uber operated in a legal vacuum. Its methods, however, made the taxi permit system obsolete, and the price of permits fell accordingly; by 2022, a permit sold for COP $80 million.[35] This time, it was the taxi guild's leaders themselves who demanded authoritarian and counterproductive traffic regulations from the government.

In early 2014, taxi industry pressure groups protested and urged officials to shut down Uber's services due to its perceived unfair competition practices.[36] Already in May of that year, the police—allegedly tipped off and encouraged

---

[31] Secretaría de Movilidad.
[32] Revista Semana (2020a, b).
[33] As in other Latin American cities. See Rivas, Suárez-Alemán, and Serebrisky, 9.
[34] See Bergh, Funcke, and Wernberg.
[35] Ibidem.
[36] El Tiempo (2014).

by taxi drivers themselves—set up checkpoints where passengers who were caught using Uber were forced to exit their vehicles.[37]

On June 17th, 2014, the minister of transportation declared that Uber operated illegally in Colombia,[38] only for her vice-minister to claim some weeks later that the government was contemplating measures to allow the company to function as a special service.[39] The latter statement infuriated the taxi lobby. A taxi union leader, Hugo Ospina, threatened the Bogotá and national governments with a 2001-style blockade of the capital unless Uber was forced to leave the country.[40] To a certain extent, his rage was justified. The start of the Uber polemics coincided with the most closely fought presidential election in decades. As tensions rose and the mudslinging intensified, politicians of the highest rank went to the taxi lobby as Greeks bearing gifts.

*　*　*

In early June, 2014, sitting President Juan Manuel Santos was struggling to win reelection.

On May 25th, he had lost the first round of voting by a small yet, for him, alarming three-point margin. In 2010, he had breezed to victory against Antanas Mockus, the former, mooning mayor of Bogotá, whom Santos thumped in a run-off by 42 points. On that occasion, however, he had run on the right and with the backing of incumbent Alvaro Uribe, a two-term president whose law-and-order agenda proved immensely popular, and whom Santos had served as minister of defense. In 2014, however, Santos was in the middle of negotiations to amnesty the Revolutionary Armed Forces of Colombia, a Marxist guerrilla group that had come to dominate the country's cocaine trade.[41] This had caused a rupture between Uribe and Santos, who was now running to the left of Uribe and against his new candidate, former finance minister Oscar Iván Zuluaga. Some polls suggested Zuluaga was likely to win; others put Santos slightly ahead. A thin margin, it seemed, would decide the election.

Less than two weeks before voters returned to the polls, the Santos campaign flaunted the public support of Bogotá's taxi drivers. On June 5th, the candidate himself ordered a taxi by telephone from his campaign headquarters, where he and his family boarded a fleet of yellow taxis that drove them to the city's main soccer stadium. There, Santos spoke to over 1000 taxi

---

[37] Ibidem.
[38] Arango.
[39] El País.
[40] El Espectador (2014).
[41] See The Economist.

drivers about his government's plans to offer them social security coverage and housing subsidies. But he also assured them that he would cancel "the applications that foment illegality" and piracy, including any "special services."[42] Santos, a University of Kansas graduate, had once been known for his "neoliberal" economic agenda.[43] And here he was, assuring the local taxi guild that, if reelected, he would move against the multinationals that pestered them.

Santos ended up winning the election against Zuluaga handily, by over seven percentage points. Regardless, as tensions rose over the Uber issue, Santos resorted to a preferred technique of a certain school of modern political leadership: he washed his hands and delegated the problem to his vice-president, Germán Vargas Lleras, who was entrusted with the task of fixing the Uber matter once and for all via decree.[44] Vargas, a career politician and, like Santos, the scion of a political dynasty, had his own eyes on the presidency. He knew that the upcoming election for mayor of Bogotá in October of 2015 would be a prelude to the 2018 presidential campaign, in which he was already the favorite. His own party was in a strong position to play kingmaker. As such, he was in no rush to stir the Uber controversy any further.

Vargas deliberately lingered as the campaign for mayor, in which I took part as an independent candidate, unfolded.[45] This prolonged the legal *lacuna* in which Uber had operated for nearly two years. In no mood for patience, some members of the taxi guild decided to take the law into their own hands.

One instance involved a late-night car chase in early September, the aftermath of which appeared in a video posted on social media. A group of taxi drivers had pursued an "Uber car" in northern Bogotá and forced it to come to a full stop. In the video, they harass the driver and try to compel the passenger, a woman in her early 20s, to exit the vehicle. They accuse her of using a "pirate" service. In tears, she pleads for them not to use violence. One of them replies: "if we have to end piracy with violence, so be it." Astoundingly, a police officer witnesses the entire exchange. The passenger repeatedly asks him to intervene to no effect. Meanwhile, the taxi drivers order the policeman to call a transit cop who can fine the Uber driver. It is they—and not the city authorities—who are calling the shots.[46]

---

[42] Caracol Radio (2014).
[43] Hernández-Mora.
[44] El Universal.
[45] El Espectador (2015).
[46] See La FM (2015 (1)).

In debates and interviews throughout the campaign for mayor, the main candidates—as backed by major parties—either sidestepped the Uber question or openly supported the taxi guild. Left-winger Clara López, a former designated mayor, claimed that, by using Uber, "high earners were looking for a service that is absolutely illegal." Social democrat Rafael Pardo, Santos's former labor minister, insisted that Uber engaged in unfair competition. He gained the backing of hundreds of taxi drivers.[47] The eventual winner, former mayor Enrique Peñalosa, an urban planner who ran for Vice President Vargas's party, courted and received Peña's public support.[48] Only my campaign, which ran on a shoe-string budget, supported the new applications' right to operate in the city and proposed ending the taxi quota system.[49]

* * *

On November 23rd, once the electoral dust had settled, Vargas and Santos himself held an event at the presidential palace to reveal the details of their decree to regulate "luxury taxis." Henceforward, the document proclaimed, only black cars registered under a taxi company would be allowed to provide a "luxury service." Thus, the drivers of white cars who used Uber were left out in the cold. Also, any digital platform used to make a payment for transportation would have to belong to a taxi company or a third party.[50] Peña, who was at the palace for the government's press conference, commented that his company had its own payment platform ready.[51] Finally, the decree forbade private vehicles from providing transportation services. Within six months, any company that did provide such services would have to register as a taxi company. A satirical website, referring to Peña as the de facto minister of transportation, perhaps put it best: the only thing missing from the government's decree was Peña's company logo.[52]

Taxi guild representatives told the media that they were satisfied with the decree's contents,[53] but not everyone on the anti-Uber side of the argument was quite as sanguine. Senator Jorge Enrique Robledo, a maoist and lifelong campaigner against multinational corporations, raged since "Uber's *gringo*"—company representative Michael Shoemaker, "a promoter of illegality and

---

[47] Caracol Radio (2015).
[48] La FM (2015 (2)).
[49] Moreno.
[50] El Tiempo (2015a, b (1)).
[51] El Tiempo (2015a, b (2)).
[52] Actualidad Panamericana.
[53] El Tiempo (2015 (2)).

corruption" in Robledo's view—had also been invited to the presidential palace for the press conference. The decree, Robledo maintained, was a mere smokescreen meant for taxi owners and drivers to fall asleep at Uber's feet.[54]

Beyond his neo-Luddite dogma and anti-Americanism—perhaps the only type of xenophobia the Colombian media tolerates—the senator did have a point. By focusing on "luxury taxis," an ultimately small segment of the market, the government's decree ignored the real issue at stake, which was the immense growth of UberX in the far larger sector of standard ride-sharing. The legal vacuum remained unfilled. And, as Shoemaker said to a reporter at the palace, Uber was supporting a legislative project to regulate ride-sharing apps, which a sitting senator—a member of Vargas's party—was set to introduce the next day.[55] Despite the fanfare and all the legalistic ink spilled on the decree, the Santos government had merely tossed the Uber problem over to Congress.

* * *

In its ensuing stages, the Uber saga is worthy of the picaresque, this despite the absence of a memorable hero. Congress, it turned out, was about as willing as the government to legalize ride-sharing, so that the Uber-backed bill failed without even being debated in the chamber.[56] In March of 2016, the Superintendence of Ports and Transport fined Uber for offering illegal transportation services.[57] Uber responded that, as a technology company, it was following constitutional norms.[58]

However, when the government faced pressure to ban Uber's application from the internet in 2017, the Ministry of Technology responded that this was impossible due to the country's official commitment to web neutrality. As far as the technology minister was concerned, Uber operated legitimately unless the law expressly forbade it, which it did not.[59] To crown the Santos cabinet's conflicting views on Uber, the head of Colombia's tax authority admitted that the company did pay a hefty amount of taxes to the state. But, he added with Delphic clarity, this did not imply that Uber operated legally in the country.[60]

---

[54] Robledo.
[55] El Tiempo (2015 (2)).
[56] Publimetro (2016).
[57] El Tiempo (2016).
[58] Ibidem.
[59] Peña Castañeda o (2017).
[60] Blu Radio.

Meanwhile, the black luxury taxis—those supposed to replace Uber's white car service within six months of the November, 2015 decree—never came in the market. As late as June, 2017, Bogotá's Secretary of Transportation was promising that black taxis would be released "by the end of the year," assuring also that only two companies met the requirements to operate them.[61] To no one's surprise, they both belonged to Peña and Hernández.

In the meantime, ride-sharing continued to grow at a hectic pace. By mid-2017, there were more drivers linked to UberX (53,000) than there were taxis with an official permit.[62] For passengers, however, using the service involved—as it still does—mastering underhand methods to evade the authorities' attention. Drivers usually request that you sit in the front seat even if you are the sole customer. If you are heading to the airport, where the police can be on the lookout for roving Ubers, they sometimes drop you off in the parking lot. As you first step into the car, drivers often provide you with a pre-arranged story to parrot to the police in case you run into a checkpoint. In order to give credence to a fictional, previous acquaintance, you could play the role of, say, spouse to the driver's distant cousin, or it might be his distant cousin's stepbrother's business partner whatever works to conceal the incriminating fact that you are an Uber customer on your way to the dentist.

* * *

On August 7, 2018, Santos finished his second term in office with the Uber question still in limbo. The new president, Iván Duque, who was Alvaro Uribe's new protégé, was supposed to introduce a pro-business, entrepreneurship-friendly agenda. Not that this made any difference in the Uber conundrum. Duque's transportation minister, Angela Orozco, proved inflexible in her stance that Uber was illegal.[63] As late as 2014, however, she had defended the app on Twitter, likening its proposed ban with restricting the internet for the sake of the fax machine business.[64]

In August of 2019, the Superintendence of Industry and Commerce (SIC)—whose head is appointed by the president—imposed a fine on Uber worth USD $629,000 for not allowing its officials to access the company's databases as part of an investigation.[65] The company, however, continued to operate, in part because the Ministry of Technology stuck to its line

---

[61] Noticiero del Transporte.
[62] Revista Semana (2017).
[63] Revista Semana (2020a, b).
[64] Forbes Colombia (2020 (1)).
[65] Trucco.

that Uber could function under web neutrality rules.[66] The shillyshallying continued until December of 2019, when an SIC judge ruled that Uber did indeed engage in unfair competition practices against a taxi company that had sued the platform.[67] For the first time, Uber was ordered to cease all of its operations in Colombia.[68]

The ruling against Uber came in the wake of a series of union-led strikes against Duque's government, in the midst of which Uribe publicly opposed a new initiative in Congress to legalize all ride-sharing platforms. His party's priority, he stated, was to support taxi drivers.[69] Although Uribe's party denied that it had negotiated with the taxi guild to sacrifice Uber, union leader Ospina confirmed that he had met Uribe in the context of the strike, which taxi drivers did not join, to discuss the problem.[70] After the judge's ruling against Uber, Duque publicly supported taxi drivers, assuring that his government was promoting fair competition without attacking technology.[71] By January of 2020, the taxi guild appeared to have gotten its way once again, as Uber launched a P.R. campaign to bid farewell to Colombia.[72] Still, the company, which stated that 88,000 drivers used their platform in the country, announced it would challenge the judge's ruling.[73]

In late February, 2020, as the COVID-19 virus spread through Western Europe, Uber announced that it would renew its operations in Colombia under "vehicle rental contracts." According to their terms, drivers would agree to use Uber's services while acknowledging that "Uber is a technology service provider that does not offer transportation services, does not function as a carrier, and does not operate as an agent for passenger transportation."[74] The news went largely unnoticed; within days, the Colombian authorities began to impose some of the world's most Draconian lockdowns, with citizens barred from traveling from one municipality to the next, and Bogotá residents only allowed to leave their house on certain days according to their national identification (*cédula*) number.[75] Perversely, the *pico y placa* traffic restriction had morphed into *pico y cédula*, a euphemism for general house arrest.

---

[66] Revista Semana (2019a, b (1)).
[67] Reuters.
[68] Feiner.
[69] Meléndez.
[70] Semana (2019 (2)).
[71] Ruiz.
[72] Long.
[73] Associated Press.
[74] Arbeláez.
[75] Alcaldía de Bogotá. See also Raisbeck.

Amid the lockdown, another news item was mostly overlooked: in June, a Bogotá tribunal overturned the SIC's ruling against Uber, albeit for procedural reasons. The plaintiffs, the tribunal ruled, had filed their lawsuit over two years after they had become aware of Uber's unfair competition practices, thus overstepping the allowed time period.[76] Uber, it appeared, was back in business. But its underlying legal status still remained unresolved.

In October of 2022, the new government of hard leftist Gustavo Petro, whom Ospina supported during his 2022 campaign,[77] announced that it considered Uber and like platforms illegal.[78] On January 30, 2023, the media reported that the Superintendence of Transportation, a regulator attached to the transportation ministry, was about to order internet providers to block Uber and other "unregulated" technology platforms, with fines of COP $10 million for riders caught using their services.[79] The next day, however, the Petro government softened its stance, announcing that it would seek "dialogue" with representatives from the ride-sharing apps.[80]

Faced with a taxi drivers' strike on February 22nd, the government issued a statement to assert that only transportation companies and registered vehicles were allowed to provide legal services to passengers. Any change to the law, the statement added, had to pass through Congress.[81] Yet the legislative branch had not moved to regulate Uber when, in October, the Supreme Court ruled that the use of technology could not be deemed an unfair competition practice in the transport sector.[82]

The Supreme Court ruling was interpreted as a clear mandate for Uber to operate legally in Colombia. Nonetheless, on April 16, a taxi drivers' protest against Uber drivers led to what the media deemed a "pitched battle" between both groups in the vicinity of the airport.[83] In May, as the taxi guild threatened new strikes against Petro's government, the SIC launched a new investigation against Uber and its competitors, accusing them formally of carrying out unfair competition practices and providing illegal services through non-authorized vehicles.[84]

In mid-2024, over a decade has passed since Uber first began to operate in Colombia; five years have already gone by since the company's IPO, and

---

[76] Forbes Colombia (2020 (2)).
[77] Semana (2022).
[78] Acosta.
[79] Caparroso.
[80] El Colombiano.
[81] Caracol Radio (2022)
[82] Pinto Duitama.
[83] J. Rodríguez.
[84] La Silla Vacía (2024).

six since the death of Bogotá taxi mogul Uldarico Peña. *Tempus fugit* indeed. And yet the Uber war, with all its farcical elements, rages on.

* * *

During Colombia's Uber saga, the political class has proven to be as skilled at muddling and shirking off responsibility as it is beholden, regardless of professed ideology, to the same set of professional blackguards. But this is mere spectacle. The struggle's defining factors sit at two extremes.

On the one hand, there is the impractical obsession with the letter of the law, which is itself oblivious of citizens' needs and their daily choices in the market. Hence, a slew of official decrees, rulings, and pronouncements—made upon arcane technicalities—turn out to be impossible to uphold, not least due to the authorities' tendency to contradict themselves. On the other hand, the law's patent hollowness ushers in the law of the jungle, as the threatened beneficiaries of an unpopular monopoly, granted and sustained by bureaucratic fiat, use street violence to uphold a privilege that the state can sanction, but cannot enforce.

As absurd as this present, digital-era dilemma may seem, its causes, I think, lay far in the past. They stem from the anarchy-legalism paradox that harks back to Spanish America's conquest.

Bibliography

Abulafia D (1988) Frederick II: a medieval emperor, London
Acevedo J (2016) Uber y los taxis. La Silla Vacía, 29 June 2016. https://www.lasillavacia.com/red-de-expertos/red-cachaca/uber-y-los-taxis/
Acosta J (2022) Para el gobierno, las plataformas de transporte son ilegales, 6 Oct 2022. https://www.portafolio.co/economia/gobierno/para-el-gobierno-las-plataformas-de-transporte-son-ilegales-572237
Actualidad Panamericana (2015) Decreto de Uber salió con membrete de Taxis Libres, 23 Nov 2015. https://actualidadpanamericana.com/decreto-de-uber-salio-con-membrete-de-taxis-libres/#google_vignette
Aeropuerto El Dorado (2024) Servicio de transporte autorizado. https://www.uber.com/global/en/r/airports/bog/. Consulted on 30 May 2024
Alcaldía de Bogotá (2020) Así funcionará el pico y cédula en Bogotá desde el 16 de junio de 2020, 14 June 2020. https://bogota.gov.co/mi-ciudad/salud/asi-sera-el-pico-y-cedula-en-bogota-desde-el-16-de-junio-de-2020
Arango T (2014) Mintransporte señaló que Uber no está autorizado para funcionar en el país. La República, 16 June 2014. https://www.larepublica.co/empresas/mintransporte-senalo-que-uber-no-esta-autorizado-para-funcionar-en-el-pais-2134781

Associated Press (2020) Lawsuit forces Uber to stop operating in Colombia, 10 Jan 2020. https://apnews.com/general-news-a7a7950eca33b1107bc708c0f688ecd1

Bergh A, Funcke A, Wernberg J (2017) Timbro sharing economy index. https://timbro.se/ekonomi/timbro-sharing-economy-index/attachment/tsei-version-17_web/

Blu Radio (2018) Cobro de IVA a Uber no implica que su servicio sea legal: DIAN, 7 June 2018. https://www.bluradio.com/economia/cobro-de-iva-a-uber-no-implica-que-su-servicio-sea-legal-dian

Caballero MC (2004) Mayor Mockus of Bogotá and his spectacularly applied theory. Harvard Gazette, 11 Mar 2004. https://news.harvard.edu/gazette/story/2004/03/academic-turns-city-into-a-social-experiment/

Caparroso J (2023) Gobierno Petro buscaría el bloqueo de plataformas de movilidad como Uber, Cabify e Indriver, 30 Jan 2023. https://forbes.co/2023/01/30/actualidad/gobierno-petro-buscaria-el-bloqueo-de-plataformas-de-movilidad-como-uber-didi-cabify-e-indriver

Caracol Radio (2014) Más de mil taxistas se unen a la campaña de Santos, 5 June 2014. https://caracol.com.co/radio/2014/06/04/nacional/1401917460_258846.html

Caracol Radio (2015) Próximo alcalde de Bogotá no cambiará el pico y placa. October 2, 2015. https://caracol.com.co/programa/2015/10/02/hora_20/1443821515_908436.html

Conozca el decreto que reglamenta el servicio de taxis de lujo, 23 Nov 2015. https://www.eltiempo.com/archivo/documento/CMS-16439095

Consejos para identificar un taxímetro adulterado: evite cobros excesivos, 11 July 2023. https://www.rcnradio.com/tecnologia/consejos-para-identificar-un-taximetro-adulterado-evite-cobros-excesivos

Corfina M (2014) Explaining economic moats to an 8-year-old. Morningstar, 21 Feb 2014. https://sg.morningstar.com/sg/news/121611/explaining-economic-moats-to-an-8-year-old.aspx

Cortés Fierro E (2001) Bogotá, sitiada por buses y taxis. El Tiempo, 3 Aug 2001. https://www.eltiempo.com/archivo/documento/MAM-454328

¿Cuánto vale un cupo de taxi en Bogotá? 10 Feb 2020. https://www.semana.com/amp/cuanto-vale-un-cupo-de-taxi-en-bogota/281403/

Decreto de taxis de lujo pone reglas a servicios como Uber, 23 Nov 2015. https://www.eltiempo.com/archivo/documento/CMS-16439271

Decreto para reglamentar Uber será emitido en noviembre. Vargas Lleras, 22 Sept 2015. https://www.elespectador.com/politica/decreto-para-reglamentar-uber-sera-emitido-en-noviembre-vargas-lleras-article-588059/

El Colombiano (2023) Gobierno no radicará proyecto que prohíbe apps de transporte hasta que no haya consenso, 31 Jan 2023. https://www.elcolombiano.com/colombia/multar-por-montar-en-uber-o-cabify-llevan-a-reunion-de-condcutores-de-aplicaciones-con-gobierno-BC20223741

El Espectador (2014) Taxistas anuncian paro si Gobierno regula servicio de Uber, 16 July 2014. https://www.elespectador.com/bogota/taxistas-anuncian-paro-si-gobierno-regula-servicio-de-uber-article-504667/#google_vignette

El Espectador (2015) Decreto para reglamentar Uber será emitido en noviembre. Vargas Lleras. September 22, 2015. https://www.elespectador.com/politica/decreto-para-reglamentar-uber-sera-emitido-en-noviembre-vargas-lleras-article-588059/

El País (2014) Afinan decreto para reglamentar taxis en aeropuertos y servicio de Uber, 15 July 2014. https://www.elpais.com.co/colombia/afinan-decreto-para-reglamentar-taxis-en-aeropuertos-y-servicio-de-uber.html

El Tiempo (2014) Uber, la aplicación que desató la ira de los taxistas, 5 May 2014. https://www.eltiempo.com/archivo/documento/CMS-13939898

El Tiempo (2015a) Conozca el decreto que reglamenta el servicio de taxis de lujo. November 23, 2015. https://www.eltiempo.com/archivo/documento/CMS 16439095

El Tiempo (2015b) Decreto de taxis de lujo pone reglas a servicios como Uber. November 23, 2015. https://www.eltiempo.com/archivo/documento/CMS-16439271

El Tiempo (2016) Supertransporte sanciona a Uber con 451 millones de pesos. March 7, 2016. https://www.eltiempo.com/archivo/documento/CMS-16530000

El Universal (2015) Santos delega al vicepresidente Vargas Lleras el tema de Uber, 16 Sept 2015. https://www.eluniversal.com.co/colombia/2015/09/16/santos-delega-al-vicepresidente-german-vargas-el-tema-de-uber/

Feiner L (2020) Uber to end service in Colombia after regulatory crackdown. CNBC, 10 Jan 2020. https://www.cnbc.com/2020/01/10/uber-to-end-service-in-colombia-after-regulatory-crackdown.html

Forbes Colombia (2020) Así defendía Uber la ministra hace unos años, 15 Jan 2020. https://forbes.co/2020/01/15/actualidad/asi-defendia-la-ministra-de-transporte-a-uber-hace-unos-anos

Fuentes R (2010) Nicolás Gómez Dávila: un Nietzsche colombiano. Centro Virtual Cervantes, July 2010. https://cvc.cervantes.es/el_rinconete/anteriores/julio_10/28072010_02.htm

Gimenez Mazó E (2023) El Dorado desplazó a Guarulhos como el segundo aeropuerto con más pasajeros de Latinoamérica. Aviación Online, 2 July 2023. https://www.aviacionline.com/2023/02/el-dorado-desplazo-a-guarulhos-como-el-segundo-aeropuerto-con-mas-pasajeros-de-latinoamerica/

Goenaga Olivares FE (2017) La biblioteca de Nicolás Gómez Dávila, el cronotopo de una novela infinita. Boletín cultural y bibliográfico LI(92):96–115

Gómez Dávila N (1953) Escolios a un texto implícito: Selección: Bogotá, 2001. Notas: Bogotá

Gómez Dávila N (2001) Escolios a un texto implícito: Selección, Bogotá

Hernández Mora S (2010) 'El gabinete de lujo' de Juan Manuel Santos. El Mundo, 2 Aug 2010. https://www.elmundo.es/america/2010/08/02/colombia/1280784817.html

Hernández Torres TA (2023) Aeropuerto El Dorado: ¿Cuáles son las rutas de SITP que lo pueden llevar?" El Tiempo, 19 Oct 2023. https://www.eltiempo.com/bogota/aeropuerto-el-dorado-cuales-son-las-rutas-de-sitp-que-lo-pueden-llevar-817911

Hugo Ospina dice que hubo reunion con Uribe para hablar de Uber, 23 Dec 2019. https://www.semana.com/vicky-en-semana---hugo-ospina-dice-que-hubo-reunion-con-uribe-para-hablar-de-uber/646291/

Hugo Ospina, líder taxista, confirmó que votará por Gustavo Petro: 'No le temo', 16 June 2022. https://www.semana.com/confidenciales/articulo/video-hugo-ospina-lider-taxista-confirmo-que-votara-por-gustavo-petro-no-le-temo/202207/

La FM (2015) Nathalie Prieto, la pasajera de Uber que terminó acorralada por taxistas, 7 Sept 2015. https://www.lafm.com.co/bogota/nathalie-prieto-la-pasajera-de-uber-que-termino-acorralada-por-taxistas

La República (2022) Así fue el desembarco de Uber en Colombia, 12 July 2022. https://www.larepublica.co/empresas/asi-fue-el-desembarco-de-uber-en-colombia-entre-protestas-y-amenazas-de-salidas-3401699

La Silla Vacía (2021) Uldarico Peña (QEPD), 12 Feb 2021. https://www.lasillavacia.com/quien-es-quien/uldarico-pena-qepd/

La Silla Vacía (2024) SIC investiga a Uber, Didi y Cabify por 'infringir la libre competencia. May 14, 2024. https://www.lasillavacia.com/en-vivo/sic-investiga-a-uber-didi-y-cabify-por-infringir-la-libre-competencia/

Long G (2020) Uber says goodbye Colombia after competition ruling. Financial Times, 1 Feb 2020. https://www.ft.com/content/9e32cc1a-4549-11ea-aeb3-955839e06441

Meléndez J (2019) Uribe dice que su partido no apoyará legalización de Uber. El Tiempo, 21 Nov 2019. https://www.eltiempo.com/politica/congreso/alvaro-uribe-dice-que-su-partido-no-apoyara-legalizacion-de-uber-435906

Moreno H (2015) 'Soy el único candidato que apoya 100 % a Uber,' Daniel Raisbeck. Publimetro, 12 July 2015. https://www.publimetro.co/co/bogota/2015/07/13/unico-candidato-que-apoya-100-uber-daniel-raisbeck.html

Mosebach M (2005) Nicolás Gómez Dávila: Ensiedler am Rand der bewohnten Erde. Sinn und Form (1):5–9

Newsweek (2013) The danger of the millionaire ride. Newsweek, 26 June 2013. https://www.newsweek.com/2013/06/26/danger-millionaire-ride-237630.html

No nos hemos reunido con Uber porque son ilegales, 14 Jan 2020. https://www.semana.com/pais/articulo/ministra-de-transporte-habla-sobre-caso-uber-en-colombia/280763/

Notas (1953) Bogotá

Noticiero del Transporte (2017) Taxis de lujo comenzarán a operar a finales del 2017, 8 June 2017. https://noticierodeltransportemeta.jimdofree.com/2017/06/08/taxis-de-lujo-comenzarán-a-operar-a-finales-de-2017/

Nuevo seguro contra fleteo y paseo millonario, 9 Feb 2012. https://www.semana.com/nuevo-seguro-contra-fleteo-paseo-millonario/44339/

'Odian a los taxistas pero todo el mundo quiere jugar a ser uno': Hugo Ospina, 22 May 2017. https://www.semana.com/pais/articulo/hugo-ospina-habla-sobre-taxis-y-legalizacion-de-uber-colombia/245644/

Paro de taxistas se levanta tras acuerdo de 17 puntos con el Gobierno, 22 Feb 2023. https://caracol.com.co/2023/02/22/paro-de-taxistas-se-levanta-tras-acuerdo-de-17-puntos-con-el-gobierno/

Peña Castañeda CA (2017) Bloquear 'apps' viola el principio de neutralidad de la red. El Tiempo, 23 Marzo 2017. https://www.eltiempo.com/tecnosfera/novedades-tecnologia/mintic-dice-que-bloquear-uber-viola-el-derecho-de-neutralidad-de-internet-70690

Pinto Duitama K (2023) Uber podrá seguir funcionando en Colombia gracias a sentencia de la Corte Suprema, 11 Oct 2023. https://www.larepublica.co/empresas/uber-podra-seguir-funcionando-en-colombia-gracias-a-sentencia-de-la-corte-suprema-3726636#:~:text=La%20Corte%20Suprema%20de%20Justicia,desleal%20y%20solicitaban%20que%20fuera

Próximo alcalde de Bogotá no cambiará el pico y placa, 2 Oct 2015. https://caracol.com.co/programa/2015/10/02/hora_20/1443821515_908436.html

Publimetro (2016) Se cae en el Congreso proyecto para legalizar Uber, 8 June 2016. https://www.publimetro.co/co/colombia/2016/06/09/se-cae-congreso-proyecto-legalizar-uber.html

Quintero Guzmán JP (2023) El Dorado offerings in lake Guatavita: a Muisca ritual archaeological site. Cambridge University Press, Aug 2023. https://www.cambridge.org/core/journals/latin-american-antiquity/article/el-dorado-offerings-in-lake-guatavita-a-muisca-ritual-archaeological-site/CCCA4FF23E90BA66FD0A1353C353434F

Raisbeck D (2020) Topos, ovejas y lobos. El Nuevo Siglo, 4 Aug 2020. https://www.elnuevosiglo.com.co/columnistas/topos-ovejas-y-lobos

RCN Radio (2019) Policías disparan contra un conductor de Uber en el Aeropuerto El Dorado, 30 Apr 2019. https://www.noticiasrcn.com/colombia/policias-disparan-contra-un-conductor-de-uber-en-el-aeropuerto-el-dorado-339194

RCN Radio (2023) Consejos para identificar un taxímetro adulterado: evite cobros excesivos. July 11, 2023. https://www.rcnradio.com/tecnologia/consejospara-identificar-un-taximetro-adulterado-evite-cobros-excesivos

Reuters (2019) Colombia orders Uber to cease ride-hailing, cites competition rules violation, 20 Dec 2019. https://www.reuters.com/article/us-colombia-uber/colombia-orders-uber-to-cease-ride-hailing-cites-competition-rules-violation-idUSKBN1YP00R/

Revista Semana (2012) Monopolio de taxis: imperialismo Amarillo, 26 Oct 2012. https://www.semana.com/monopolio-taxis-imperialismo-amarillo/266991-3/

Revista Semana (2017) Odian a los taxistas pero todo el mundo quiere jugar a ser uno: Hugo Ospina. May 22, 2017. https://www.semana.com/pais/articulo/hugo-ospina-habla-sobre-taxis-y-legalizacion-de-uber-colombia/245644/

Revista Semana (2019a) Sigue limbo jurídico en las plataformas tecnológicas. July 13, 2019. https://www.semana.com/economia/articulo/sigue-limbo-juridico-enlas-plataformas-tecnologicas/623310/

Revista Semana (2019b) Hugo Ospina dice que hubo reunion con Uribe para hablar de Uber. December 23, 2019. https://www.semana.com/vicky-en-semana---hugo-ospina-dice-que-hubo-reunion-con-uribe-para-hablar-de-uber/646291/

Revista Semana (2020a) No nos hemos reunido con Uber porque son ilegales. January 14, 2020. https://www.semana.com/pais/articulo/ministra-de-transporte habla-sobre-caso-uber-en-colombia/280763/

Revista Semana (2020b) ¿Cuánto vale un cupo de taxi en Bogotá? February 10, 2020. https://www.semana.com/amp/cuanto-vale-un-cupo-de-taxi-enbogota/281403/

Revista Semana (2022) Hugo Ospina, líder taxista, confirmó que votará por Gustavo Petro: 'No le temo. June 16, 2022. https://www.semana.com/confidenciales/articulo/video-hugo-ospina-lider-taxista-confirmo-que-votara-por-gustavo-petro-no-letemo/202207/

Rivas ME, Suárez-Alemán A, Serebrisky T (2019) Políticas de transporte urbano en América Latina y el Caribe: Dónde estamos, cómo llegamos aquí y hacia dónde vamos. Banco Interamericano del Desarrollo, Washington

Robledo JE (2015) Los trinos de Robledo sobre Uber y el decreto para taxis de lujo. Jorgerobledo.com, 24 Nov 2015. https://www.jorgerobledo.com/los-trinos-de-robledo-sobre-uber-y-el-decreto-para-taxis-de-lujo/

Rodríguez D (2010) El problema de los taxis piratas. El Espectador, 10 Sept 2010. https://www.elespectador.com/bogota/el-problema-de-los-taxis-piratas-article-223781/

Rodríguez JD (2024) Así fue la 'batalla campal' de taxistas y conductores de aplicaciones en El Dorado, tras protestas. Infobae, 17 Apr 2024. https://www.infobae.com/colombia/2024/04/17/reportan-batalla-campal-de-taxistas-y-conductores-de-aplicaciones-en-el-dorado-tras-protestas/

Ruiz C (2020) Presidente Duque respalda a taxistas y dice que no está atacando la tecnología, 13 Jan 2020. https://canal1.com.co/noticias/nacional/presidente-duque-respalda-a-taxistas-y-dice-que-el-gobierno-no-esta-atacando-la-tecnologia/

Secretaría de Movilidad, Alcaldía Mayor de Bogotá D.C. (2019) La administración distrital, comprometida con la mejora del servicio de taxi en Bogotá, 9 June 2019. https://www.movilidadbogota.gov.co/web/Noticia/la_administraci%C3%B3n_distrital_comprometida_con_la_mejora_del_servicio_de_taxi_en_bogot%C3%A1

SIC investiga a Uber, Didi y Cabify por 'infringir la libre competencia', 14 May 2024. https://www.lasillavacia.com/en-vivo/sic-investiga-a-uber-didi-y-cabify-por-infringir-la-libre-competencia/

Sigue limbo jurídico en las plataformas tecnológicas, 13 July 2019. https://www.semana.com/economia/articulo/sigue-limbo-juridico-en-las-plataformas-tecnologicas/623310/

Supertransporte sanciona a Uber con 451 millones de pesos, 7 Mar 2016. https://www.eltiempo.com/archivo/documento/CMS-16530000

Taxista se vuelve famoso por su 'hasta allá no voy', 2 Mar 2018. https://www.publimetro.co/co/bogota/2018/03/02/taxista-se-vuelve-famoso-en-eredes.html

The Economist (2000) The gringos land in Colombia, 31 Aug 2000. https://www.economist.com/the-americas/2000/08/31/the-gringos-land-in-colombia

Tribunal revoca decisión de la SIC que ordenó a Uber salir de Colombia, 19 June 2020. https://forbes.co/2020/06/19/actualidad/tribunal-revoca-decision-de-la-sic-que-ordeno-a-uber-salir-de-colombia

Trucco F (2019) Multan a Uber en Colombia con 629.000 dólares. CNN en Español, 13 Aug 2019. https://cnnespanol.cnn.com/2019/08/13/alerta-multan-a-uber-en-colombia-con-629-mil-dolares/

Uber (2024) El Dorado International Airport. https://www.uber.com/global/en/r/airports/bog/. Consulted on 30 May 2024

Uldarico Peña dice que no está comprando votos para Enrique Peñalosa, 21 Oct 2015. https://www.lafm.com.co/bogota/uldarico-pena-dice-que-no-esta-comprando-votos-para-enrique-penalosa

Vuong A (2014) Colorado first to authorize Lyft and Uber's ridesharing services. The Denver Post, 5 June 2014. https://www.denverpost.com/2014/06/05/colorado-first-to-authorize-lyft-and-ubers-ridesharing-services/

Globalization, Long May It Reign

Deirdre Nansen McCloskey

It Merely Makes an Economic Neighborhood

The word "globalization" delights some, and terrifies others. But it's merely the gradual emergence on our little globe of a single economy.

It's a natural and beneficial result of humans doing what humans have done since the beginning, making their families better off—working hard, inventing new stuff, keeping alert, looking around, and making little deals. The result of all this human liberty of choice has been globalization. At various scales of time it's been happening from the caves to the modern world, or from 1350 to 1800, or from 1776 to 2024.

Your neighborhood is a "single economy." Most people in Manhattan don't own cars, and so the economic neighborhood in effect is smallish. A grocery store at the corner of Broadway and West 143rd Street can't get away with charging $10 for a loaf of bread when another store two blocks away is charging $2. Within ten blocks or so the prices of the same brand of bread and the wages of the same quality dentist and the interest charged on a bank loan for the same credit rating will be pretty much the same.

On Long Island everyone has a car, or two, or three, and the approximate sameness of prices extends for miles. And the overlap of neighborhoods means that anything that can move or can be offered easily to people who do move—bread, cars, dentists, bank loans—but not so much for houses, pretty

D. N. McCloskey (✉)
Chicago, USA
e-mail: deirdre.nansen.mccloskey@gmail.com

much immoveable by nature, and not so much across restricted borders, pretty much immovable by law—is pretty much the same from the redwood forest to the Gulf Stream waters. And the overlap of the overlaps, if not restricted by legal interventions by the state in the prices permitted, means that even globally, from the Amazon forest to the North Sea waters, the prices of wheat and iron and AK 47s are pretty much the same.

The rough sameness of prices is not caused by a sweet state official enforcing a just price, or by an evil monopolist imposing an unjust price. It's caused by moderately alert customers making the sameness happen, by exercising their liberty to shift from this to that purveyor of cars or dentistry or bread. No one will pay $10 for a loaf when she knows that a couple of blocks away she can pay $2. And the $2 grocery store will make sure she is alert to the difference. In Miami, which has a large population or retied people on fixed incomes, the prices of milk and toilet paper differ from store to store very little, within extraordinarily tight limits, a cent or two. The old people spend their days in comparison shopping and sharply buying. Fool me once, shame on you; fool me twice, shame on me. If you thrill to economic jargon, you can call this obvious piece of common sense "arbitrage." (And then you can watch people edging away from you at the party tonight.)

Globalization puts everyone whose government permits it into a global neighborhood, in which the price of a Samsung TV at a Best Buy in Washington is pretty much the same as in Beijing or New Delhi. Big price differences in the same neighborhood would mean that you could do better easily. For example, you as a low-price buyer could re-sell to a high-price buyer. Or you as the low-price seller could advertise. Or you as a high-price buyer could get smarter and look around for a better deal. The deals are voluntary, and therefore must benefit both buyer and seller, a little or a lot. If permitted widely in a society, GDP per head goes up, a little or a lot. It happens by arbitrage, globalization, common sense, the natural result of people liberated to better themselves while bettering others.

If the price of TVs is higher in Beijing, then suppliers will send TVs there, instead of Washington. Ordinary prudence recommends "Buy low, sell high," until the arbitrage of suppliers and demanders makes the price difference come down to a level at which no more deals are profitable. Economists call the result of such a mutual exhaustion of deals and the uniform prices that signal its achievement "Pareto efficiency." (Go ahead. Using that if economic jargon at the party will kill conversation.)

Arbitrage applies also, though often at a slower pace, to the labor, capital, materials, and especially to the technical know-how that goes into the Samsung TV. Again, it's all about liberty. China opened economically after

1978, permitting exports and imports, and permitting people to move to new jobs, and permitting people to start new businesses. In the largest migration in human history, hundreds of millions of Chinese from the interior moved one-by-one to the coast to work in the new factories at higher wages than at home. And the Communist Party let wages and prices be set by business-suppliers and citizen-demanders instead of by the state. Arbitrage ruled, and China waxed pretty prosperous.

Contrary to what you might have heard, however, there's no "Chinese model" to be seen as an intriguing if authoritarian alternative to Western economic liberalism. The Communist Party of China would like you to believe there is. Nope. After 1978 the Party merely started to permit an economic liberalism of the sort partially implemented in the West in the nineteenth century—though of course the Party did not permit anything like a corresponding liberalism in politics. The "Chinese model" is merely "the capitalist road."

The economic result of liberty in the economy? China's income per head in 1978 was then about the same as South Sudan's. It's now 25 times higher, about the same as Brazil's, which is in turn about the global average. The figure is still only a third of the U.S. income per head. But it's on the way to parity in one or two generations, if Premier Xi Jinping does not succeed in reverting to economic anti-liberalism, with central planning and controls on prices. India likewise after 1991 opened to global prices, and as a result, if Premier Modi in India like Xi in China does not leave liberalism behind, can expect parity with Europe and the U.S. in two or three long generations. Latin America and Africa cannot be far behind. Globalization, which is to say the force of arbitrage exercised by liberated people in the economy, spreads prosperity.

New Transport Does It, Blocking by States Undoes It

Globalization has gone forward, and occasionally backward, from two sources.

The big source for going forward has been innovation in transport, and the resulting fall in the price of moving goods and people. It came again from individual choice, not by state action. The voyageurs in New France adopted the birchbark canoe from the First Nations, driving down the price differential on furs between the supply in the interior of Canada and the demand in Montreal. The shipping container invented in North Carolina in

1955 drove down the price differential of soybeans between the supply in Iowa and the demand in Shanghai.

An original monopoly in the neighborhood—such as the country store in town in 1800 or the sole purchaser of wheat in the local county in 1850 or Peabody Coal in a company town in 1900—could search out high prices for its selling or buying. But the steady fall in transport costs as people, especially in the last two centuries of a frenetic innovation suddenly permitted by liberalism, permitted new entrants to break the monopolies. Enterprise monopoly has steadily declined, because of the coming of better roads, longer canals, the railway, the telegraph, riverboats, ocean steamships, bicycles, streetcars, subways, downtown department stores, mail-order companies, telephones, autos, longer hours of business, airplanes, superhighways, strip malls, containerization, the internet, and Amazon.com. Prices converged. Prosperity spread, because at the same prices faced by all, there were no more reallocations for additional arbitrage o make both sides of a deal better off. Buying low and selling high had done its good job. Economic activity was doing as well for people as it could. The economist's "efficiency" was achieved. (Use that jargon, too. You'll lose all your friends. We economists have.)

The other significant source of globalization has been the reversal, intended or not, of state-supported monopolies *against* the trade in goods or the flows of financial capital or the migration of the poor. Globalization, that is, came from allowing more arbitrage, by dropping instead of raising the taxes on imports on foreign goods—the jargon for the taxes is "tariffs"—and dropping the restrictions on where you can invest, and dropping the legal rules keeping retail prices up, and dropping the laws against selling on Sundays, and especially by dropping the numerous state-supported monopolies such as telephones and taxis and citizenship itself. Drop, drop, drop, and you get more arbitrage and more globalization and more income. We all end up trading in the same global neighborhood. We get richer, because we all get the best deals available. The right people specialize in making TVs and the right people specialize in buying them. (Yes, there's jargon for that, too. The result is called "following comparative advantage to achieve global efficiency." Seriously, though, please, spare your friends.)

Globalization has occasionally gone backwards, because of fresh, brilliant, coerced schemes for state laws to block the arbitrage of prices of goods and people and ideas, globally or locally. "Trading blocs" such as the Comecon in Eastern Europe until the fall of Russian-imposed communism blocked trade with the West, and also administered by bureaucrats the trading within the bloc in a way that prevented complete arbitrage between, say, Poland and Romania. Block, block, block, and globalization stops or reverses. And you get poorer when you could so easily be richer. The Comecon did. Its fall after 1989 made Eastern Europe much richer.

Exactly where melons, say, are grown and where they are eaten matters only if globalization has *not* happened. If everyone under globalization pays pretty much the same price, from where they are best grown, and they will go to where they are most eagerly eaten. It's all for betterment in a pretty good globalized world. No drama, no corrupt "protection" for Paul at the expense of Peter. But Japan, once protected its small group of melon growers. They were incompetent compared with its Toyota employees, speaking relative to US melon on growers compared with Detroit auto makers, and therefore Japan was violating its comparative advantage in autos as against melons. Japan imposed heavy tariffs on importation of melons from the Philippines or the U.S. Melons costing $1.40 to consumers in Manila or Los Angeles cost $20 in Tokyo, wrapped in lovely tissue paper and elegantly boxed as wedding gifts. Japanese GDP per head was a little lower than it could have been with thorough globalization.

If people are allowed to buy and sell where they want, geography gradually stops mattering much. We come to live in one big economic neighborhood. Marketed income is higher, because the trades that constitute it are accomplished as efficiently as can be. During the 1950s an American could buy only from three and a half Detroit auto manufacturers. Then the tariffs and quotas on foreign cars, imposed when the US makers of policy were still hostile to free trade, were eliminated, slowly, with much anger in Detroit about the evils of Volkswagens and Toyotas. Now American consumers of cars have the choice of twenty companies competing with each other, in hundreds of models. Look at the frenetic car-company advertisements on TV. Or look at simply the number of competitors, existing ones and now even Chinese.

To consume much, when you come right down to it, we *must* trade. Homework in cooking and child care is a true and significant part of a properly defined national product. But as the centuries marched down to the present we've more and more traded away our own work in farm and factory and office to get the benefit of the work of others. A hunter-gatherer band, true, gets most of its consumption inside the band. Yet Aboriginal Australians traded gemstones and boomerangs over hundreds of miles, and prices converged. A medieval village was not averse to trading butter for blacksmithing inside. But the self-sufficiency of a European medieval village is exaggerated in imagination. It imported iron from other neighborhoods, and sold its grain into the little urban markets.

Anciently, a massive trade in grain from Egypt supported bread and circuses in the city of Rome. As commerce revived in medieval Europe (much earlier than was once believed) wheat prices between the European lowest level, Poland as a supplier, and the highest, Venice as a consumer, converged. The same was true inside China and inside vast swathes of the rest of the world. In central Mexico from 1000 BCE down to the Conquest the locals in the Valley of Mexico mined obsidian, an extremely sharp volcanic glass used for knives. As it was shipped north on the backs of men from the neighborhood of present-day Mexico City it of course became more and more expensive and was sliced finer and finer. In what is now New Mexico archeological sites show it sliced very fine indeed. The Spaniards with their horses caused the price differential to fall. The transport cost had put a big wedge between prices, and innovation caused the wedge to become smaller. It was arbitrage, and rising income from the more efficient trade in obsidian.

As late as 1900, a third of Americans still lived on farms. At about the same time only 15% of global population lived in substantial cities. Now it's about 60% globally. But in 1900 even urban households even in the relatively rich U.S. were little factories of "autarchy." (It means g in Greek "self-rule," in this economic context meaning not trading at all, self-sufficiency. That's another piece of wonderful economic jargon. You're welcome.) A mother would typically spend 40 hours in a week on food-preparation alone, and would make most of the clothing for herself or the children, and would store in glass jars the vegetables from her garden for consumption in winter, and, before innovation in antibiotics made purchased medical doctoring a good idea, would work as the sole doctor/nurse for most diseases. "Man works from sun to sun," the proverb went, "Woman's work is never done."

A hermit could refuse to take advantage of globalization, and achieve self-sufficiency in his own little hut. It sounds lovely and brave. Grow your own wheat. Make your own accordion. But it's been calculated that nowadays a hamburger made *wholly* self-sufficiently would cost about $83. Perhaps it would be better to work a little in a market and then take the earnings to spend at the neighborhood McDonalds. When Thoreau went to be self-sufficient for two years 1845–47 on the banks of Walden Pond in Concord, Massachusetts, he still bought nails in town for his hut, and iron hoes for his crops, and books to read. Every Sunday he went into town for dinner. Towns and trade are mighty tempting, with their low prices in production achieved by specialization and their low prices in marketing achieved by arbitrage.

Self-sufficiency, true, charms people. But it also serves the self-interest of monopolies sitting inside the sufficient place. Medieval market towns run by monopolizing guildsmen arranged to keep the mere indwellers from buying anywhere else. During the early modern period the same policy at the level of the entire nation was called "mercantilism." The accumulation of gold in the nation, a "positive balance of payments" (more jargon: no extra charge), was achieved by making exports large and making imports small. Getting gold was seen as just the ticket. Wait a minute. It's like saying that it's good for you as a little nation to work to earn money but bad for you to spend the money on groceries. Keep money piled up in the back yard, like Scrooge McDuck.

Modern mercantilism has the same illogical logic. Both the Trump and the Biden Administrations in the U.S. after 2016 tried to raise exports of airplanes and reduce imports of steel. Negotiation over "trade agreements" have the same rhetorical structure. "I'll let your exports into the U.S. only if you let U.S. exports into your country." Exports are good, the rhetoric in the negotiation says, imports are bad. Working is good, eating is bad.

Such talk is of course lunacy, though still the basis of public policy worldwide, as it was anciently. You have, after all, a balance of payments deficit with your grocer. The grocer accumulates the money. Has the deficit kept you up at night worrying? Not likely. Yet the stop–go policy of the British state during the 1950s and 19060s was based on just such mercantilist lunacy, and crippled real growth. Words matter. Words like "self-sufficiency" and "protection" and "balance of payments deficit" lead us far astray, and make us poor. Better get the economic rhetoric right, and achieve prosperity, by speaking of "arbitrage," "efficiency," and "globalization."

Globalization Flowed and Ebbed, 1848–1948

The First Globalization came to its height in the 1890s. An economics-driven ideology in the U.K. had inspired in the mid-nineteenth century a brief flurry of "free trade," that is, allowing international trade to happen free of let or hindrance. Buy what and where you will. The state will not obstruct you. Reject mercantilist rhetoric.

Free trade was part of a wider liberalization. It began in theorizing by A. R. J. Turgot and Adam Smith and Thomas Paine and Mary Wollstonecraft in the late eighteenth century, to be applied massively in the nineteenth century by governments now increasingly "of, by, and for the people." Liberalism rejected for the first time a rule "of, by, and for the masters." It ended slavery and serfdom, broke down city guilds, and inspired free international trade in goods, people, and investments. A country like Sweden was in 1800 clotted with blocked opportunity for arbitrage, and its people were among the poorest in Europe. In the mid-nineteenth century it began to liberalize, and began its long rise, by the 1930s, to a position among the richest.

The First Globalization, then, was notably British. Britain after the 1840s essentially let anyone trade with it free of state-imposed restrictions, and became the central market of the world. With few exceptions the result by the 1890s globally was startlingly free trade in wheat and wine, free migration of people to the New World or the Colonies, and unhindered liberty to invest in Argentinian and Indian railways.

Notice that the liberalization of the First Globalization was in goods, yes, but also in migrants and in investments. A deep economic point is that any one of the three liberalizations is a substitute for the other two. You can trade internationally with Juan Valdez in far Colombia, by buying his product and letting it be shipped to you, in this case the coffee that he grows. Or Juan can move to your town, and trade domestically with you, as a worker in a local restaurant, say. Except for Juan's location, the results in the prices of goods, workers, capital tend to be similar whether he stays in Colombia and is permitted to trade goods with you or comes to your town and is permitted to trade labor with you. Prices and wages and interest rates tend to converge internationally whether people trade internationally in goods or migrate internationally in person or invest their capital abroad. Capital flowing into new factories and extended railways abroad is, again, a substitute for goods imports and human migration. To get around a US tariff, for example, a foreign company opens a factory in Tennessee. Eventually, the economist predicts, and the history of globalization shows, all the world will have the same prices and wages and interest rates and so forth, and much greater prosperity. For example, if present barriers to migration were removed now, it has been plausibly calculated, GDP per head in the globe would increase 50%.

Until the 1960s, the German and American and most other governments never did sign on to free trade with anything like the nineteenth-century British enthusiasm. Germans long protected farmers from Ukrainian and American wheat and the Americans protected steelmakers from German and British steel. Yet so large did Britain, as the first industrial nation, weigh in the world's economy that such corrupt and foolish machinations mattered little to the making of a global neighborhood.

Down to the coming of the income tax in 1913, the U.S. Federal government depended on revenues from tariffs on foreign trade. The word "tariffs" sounded scientific, and obscured that they were simply taxes on imports. Yet a tariff was a tax that unlike a tax on domestic beer or incomes could be claimed to be imposed on the dammed foreigners. The economic claim was silly, because prices of wheat and steel and the rest were by the nineteenth century largely determined in global markets, over which even an increasingly bulky US economy had little influence. A tariff on steel merely raised the price of, say, rails in the U.S., to the world price *plus* the tariff. It's still true. A tariff on steel imports means that Americans themselves pay for cutting off their noses to spite their faces. They lose the low price of foreign goods, on the false premise that doing so makes Americans in general better off. It is why countries should adopt free trade even if other countries don't. Keep your own nose, and the lower price of steel, even if others adopt the mercantilist fashion of cutting off theirs.

But especially in the nineteenth century such corruptions and foolishness didn't matter much to prosperity in the U.S., and not much more in the German Empire, so large were both internally. Wide trade from Chicago to Boston in meat made domestic markets into one big neighborhood. The pressure of domestically arbitraged prices bore great fruit. By article I, section 9, clause 5 of the U.S. Constitution the individual American states were forbidden from the outset to impose tariffs on each other. Such tariffs still happen between modern Indian states, and happened among European nations before the formation of the European Union. In 1960 trucks crossing from Switzerland to Italy lined up for miles to pay tariffs, and on passenger trains everyone's passport was checked when crossing from the Netherlands to Belgium. Bettering deals were evidently available. But they weren't taken up. Result? Lower income.

A widespread retreat from globalization happened worldwide during and after the First World War, a Great De-Globalization. New walls were erected at national borders on the arbitrage of goods, migrants, and capital. Until well after the Second World War the economic world had reverted to economic autarchy, nation-by-nation. The disastrous interlude of retreat from the First Globalization began during the 1920s and especially the 1930s. Hard cases make bad law, and hard recessions make bad economic and political policy. The Great Depression of the 1930s, presaged in Britain by a slump in the 1920s, radically undermined earlier liberalism, in both the economy and the politics. In the Great De-Globalization even the British abandoned free trade. Fascist and communist parties flourished worldwide. The three major political ideas dreamed by intellectuals during the past couple of centuries have been, in sequence, liberalism after 1776, nationalism after 1789, and socialism after 1848. The liberation and consequent Great Enrichment of the globe has come from the first one. But if you think you like the other two, maybe you'll like Germany's "national socialism," 1933–1945, or its recent rebirth in white nationalism. I hope not.

Then We Recovered Our Economic Senses

But then our present, Second Globalization happened, and the Second Political Liberalization. Thank God.

Yet understand that blocking and blocking and blocking arbitrage in order to benefit this or that special interest never completely stops, even now, well into the Second Globalization, even with approximately liberal politics. For example, new schemes have been implemented recently making the Uber taxi service illegal in Germany and imposing a tax on cheap Chinese solar panels imported into the U.S. They are always justified as "protecting" Hans the taxi driver in Hamburg or Harriet the stockholder of Hanwha Q CELLS in Dalton, Georgia. Never mind the rest of us. A journalist covering home improvement for the business magazine *Forbes* ("capitalist tool") writes that the tariffs imposed by the Trump administration on imported solar panels "result in financial benefit for solar customers."[1] You bet. Hamburg customers, you see, get financial benefit from paying higher prices for blocked rides. Uh huh. A most ingenious paradox. Homeowners in the U.S. benefit from paying higher wages to their lawn services from blocked immigration form Central America. Oh, sure. And British people benefited from the £50 block imposed in 1966 on the number of pounds sterling allowed to be taken on holidays abroad. Go to Calais, dears, buy a nice if not too expensive French dinner, stay one night in a French hotel, and next afternoon board the ferry back to Dover. Financial benefit. Ha, ha.

The Second Globalization commenced only after fascism had been defeated in the Second World War and communism was being resisted in the Cold War. The various economic nationalisms started to recede. A crux was the so-called Kennedy Round 1964–67 of tariff reductions under the new General Agreement on Tariffs and Trade, known to its friends as GATT. Its surviving son is the World Trade Organization, the WTO, administered in Geneva. The United States, once addicted to tariffs, began after the Second World War to take adult responsibility as the dominant economy in the world. Suddenly—through something of a political and rhetorical accident—it became enthusiastically free trading. In 1962 Congress passed the Trade Expansion Act which authorized the government to negotiate tariff cuts of up to 50%. Wow.

If the neo-mercantilism of the 1930s, or for that matter the long-running opposition on the left of politics to "neo-liberalism," as the left calls it, and

---

[1] Shelby Simon, "Everything You Need To Know About American Solar Panel Manufacturers." *Forns Home* Oct 20, 2022. Reprinted in Wikipedia https://www.forbes.com/home-improvement/solar/american-solar-panel-manufacturers/. Retrieved June 1, 2023.

now also on the right in the "new economic nationalism," was a good, idea the Kennedy Round and the GATT/WTO and the Second Globalization would have been a global disaster. It would have impoverished the poor of the world. One can buy bumper stickers declaring, "Milton Friedman, Father of Global Poverty." But in 1960, 4 out of the 5 billion people on the globe lived at an appalling $2 a day in 2024 prices, cooking over cow-dung fires, hauling water two miles for drinking, dying young, illiterate. It was how almost all humans had lived from the beginning. By now 1 billion of the present 8 billion people still live in such misery. But the other 7 billion have leapt forward, many to the "super-abundance" that the economists Marian Tupy and Gale Pooley have recently chronicled. It happened in the face of gloomy predictions that rising population would starve us all, that our best days were behind us. Real income per head on the globe has risen during the Second Globalization from a little over $2 a head per day to about $50 a day.

The World Bank reckons that it will keep rising at about 2% per year into the indefinite future, if we don't kill it with bloody war or policy panic, of just the sort that causes the Great De-Globalization, 1918–1945. Two percent doesn't sound like much. But at such rates the average person on the planet, more globalized and urbanized and educated and cured over the next century, will come to earn in real, inflation-adjusted terms three or four times more than a present-day Swiss or American person. Again: wow.

The Doubts Don't Make a Lot of Sense

But wait. Surely the anxieties about globalization have *some* economic and historical justification. Surely, it's not all rosy.

One reason people say so is that pessimistic histories and predictions are popular. You are more cool—if that is what you worry about being—to predict disaster even though it doesn't happen, and to paint the future in dark colors though they are false, than to adopt the optimistic bet on the century to come and the optimistic history of the two centuries past.

From 1776 to the present, though, the optimistic bet and history has been much the wiser one. One important instance, contrary to what you hear about the rich getting richer and the poor poorer, is that globalization has radically reduced inequality of incomes. For one thing, the enrichment of the globe brought a great many of the wretched of the earth to a pretty good standard of comfort, the $50 a day. In 1901 the American economist John Bates Clark predicted that "the typical laborer will increase his wages [in real terms, allowing for inflation] from one dollar a day to two, from two to four and from four to eight. Such gains will mean infinitely more to him than any possible increase of capital can mean to the rich.... This very change will bring with it a continual approach to equality of genuine comfort."[2] His prediction was spot on.

And in any case, envy of the rich is not a sound basis for social policy, being insatiable. You can envy almost anyone, as Shakespeare put it, "wishing me like to one more rich in hope, / Featured like him, like him with friends possessed, / Desiring this man's art and that man's scope." The football star or rock musician or entrepreneur might inspire envy, but after all they achieved their wealth by making you better off. You pay to get their services, voluntarily, and you gain. If you don't think so, please give me your season tickets to the Washington Nationals. (Well, maybe it's not such a good example, painful as it is to watch them.) Better: give me your access to Walmart or Amazon.com. Oh, wait, I already have it. Liberty of trade.

Furthermore, the force of arbitrage works to erode pools of great wealth. The Nobel economist William Nordhaus has calculated that the gain from all the innovations in the U.S. since the Second World War went overwhelmingly to us, the customers, American and foreign, when competitors to General Motors, General Electric, and General Foods rushed in. Once upon a time we faced the terrible "monopolies" of Kodak, Nokia, IBM, Toys R Us, Tower Records, and Blockbuster. They are all now one with Nineveh and Tyre. Eighty-five percent of the *Fortune* 500 firms in 1955 are no longer. That's good, not bad. New ideas replace the old ones, and then new investment replaces the old, and new jobs replace the old, which is to our benefit.

The result is that during the Second Globalization contrary again to what you may have heard on TV, the inequality of income worldwide has dramatically fallen. As China and India have enriched, their large share of global population have risen from utter misery. Other successes such as Botswana and Ireland have added to the result that individuals on the globe are much more equal than ever. Want to see enormous inequality? Go back to 1800, and compare the Duchess of Norfolk with the average English peasant.

Another worry, especially from the left, is that globalization seems a terrible "minotaur," as the one-time Finance Minister of Greece, Yannis Varoufakis calls it, a beast eating Athenian maidens. Yanis' case—that there is something sinister about investors moving investments around the globe in response to opportunities for arbitrage in returns on capital—would have at least a surface

---

[2] Clark (1901).

plausibility if it had not corresponded to the largest enrichment of the poor in human history.

Another is that the very enrichment from globalization is destroying the planet environmentally. But the invention of the automobile ended horrible pollution in cities from horse poop. Imposition of rules against soft-coal burning, and the replacement in heating by electricity, stopped life-shortening smog. And so forth. Want to save the environment? First get rich by globalization and then watch the many millions of new engineers and entrepreneurs do it.

Fearful myths proliferate. For example, the decline in the U.S., and every other rich country, in the share of the labor force making things such as cars and drill presses inspires fears of "deindustrialization." It didn't happen. What the fearful folks mean is that the share of manufacturing *employment* has fallen. Bu the share of its *output* has not. That's good, not bad. American and British and French manufacturing is getting more productive per person. Rising productivity is the only way that real income per head can rise. If we don't have a bigger pie, the slices to everyone can't get larger.

Yet left and right and middle cry, "Bring back manufacturing to the U.S., and establish self-sufficiency in the making of physical things." The local version of the cry is "Keep money in the neighborhood." "Buy American." "Buy local." But if these are such fine ideas, why not bring manufacturing back to your own house alone? Mk everything yourself. It's crazy. The crazy notion comes from the conviction that genuine output is a material good, an apple or an auto or an airplane, not "mere" services such as banking and insurance. It's part of the prejudice against the middleman dating back to Aristotle and Confucius. It's not sensible, as St. Thomas Aquinas among others noted. We need middleman to do the necessary middle job of arbitrage, buying low and selling high to our benefit in efficiency.

The master myth haunting the fearful folk is that trade is war, or at best zero sum. They believe that what the U.S. gains other countries have to lose. British writers in the 1890s declared imports from Germany an "invasion." Such a way of talking about peaceful trade was not a small cause of actual shooting war in 1914. According to the war metaphor an immigrant, too, "invades," a Juan Valdez giving you a good, cheap meal in Iowa City. It echoes the mercantilist and Calvinist feeling that production is good, a win, yet consumption is bad, a loss. But we produce in order to consume, not consume in order to produce. You would want your labor to be less, your consumption to be more, yes? Of course.

In the seventeenth century the English raised similar fears against the commercial Dutch, erecting protectionist policies against them and fighting three Anglo-Dutch wars. Nowadays similar "invasion" by enriching East Asian nations arouses fears that would not now be applied to trade with the same Dutch, or the British. In the 1980s the Japanese were feared by the fearful folk, and now the Chinese are. Hmm. East Asians both. Is a little racism involved? Of course it is. China today might well be a military threat to the liberal order. Taiwan is a liberal country. But giving Americans TV sets in exchange for a little soybeans and a few airplanes is not war.

Yet even if you can persuade the fearful that imports are not warfare and that globalization raises the goods and services available to us all, many folk fear *cultural* "invasions." Globalization is widely viewed as making world culture drearily uniform, "McDonaldization." But globalization has opened a cultural trade, as for instance in the explosion of world cuisine, using tastes and techniques from abroad. Keeping out foreign food, music, ideas, science clearly makes no sense. The old Soviet Union tried to keep out American jazz and blue jeans, because they were from "capitalist" America and especially because they both carried a message of liberal spontaneity. The Soviet masters favored authoritarian, top-down music, like a symphony under a conductor or a ballet under a choreographer, and favored conventional pants from centrally planned factories, too. They hated improvisation. Plan, plan, plan, and impose the plan coercively.

Local arts are commonly encouraged, not suppressed, by what the economist Tyler Cowen praises as "commercial culture." Soapstone sculptures and woven cloth by First Nations in Canada and Guatemala end up in fashionable shops on Michigan Avenue, and the makers back in the village prosper. The fear of cultural globalization causing cultural uniformity is overblown. South Asians learned the game of cricket from the British Raj. But now they play it their own way, the "great *tamasha.*" As the anthropolinguists tell us, goods and procedures are reshaped by other cultures for their own purposes.

Quit being fearful about globalization.

And It's Ethical

The ethical case for globalization is not simply that it enriches us all, though it does. It's also that permitting arbitrage is an implication of allowing you to buy and sell with anyone you wish. It's elementary liberty. And liberty is liberty is liberty. The liberty to trade is a piece with the liberty to speak and read and vote and live and love.

The left and the right, and often enough the center, disagree. They want to stop you from buying a joint of marihuana or buying a Toyota or buying a book with gay characters, even in the Land of the Free. The economic historian J. R. T. Hughes pointed out long ago that Americans have two contradictory positions, "Don't tread on me" and "Don't do *that*." That "*that*" consists of things like dressing as you want or loving whom you want or buying where you want. Globalization is part of liberty.

Such individual liberties are… well… individual. Not collective. A collective "general will" justifies "Don't do *that*." The only even approximately just notion of a general will is the economist's GDP per head. Leaving people alone to work and trade, in line with the notion new in the eighteenth century of "Don't tread on me," led in fact to a Great Enrichment, that rise from $2 to $50 and beyond. Globalization by arbitrage was innovation's necessary environment, without which it wouldn't have happened.

But there's a crucial caveat. The Great Enrichment 1776 to the present corrected for inflation was on the order of a 3000% rise of income per head. But compared with such an astonishing order of magnitude, greater efficiency by itself accounts only for modest increases. Improvements in the English constitution in 1689, or the free migrations of the First Globalization, or the dropping of tariffs in the Kennedy Round, were all to the good, to be sure. But their good was nothing like 3000%. They resulted in economic enrichments on the order or, say, 10%, or, even 100%. Jolly good. But not 3000%, even if you add up all of the merely efficiency-yielding arbitrages. Doing the same old routines a little better is of course a good idea, and liberal arbitrage makes it happen in both production and consumption. Get the marginal opportunity cost lined up with the marginal utility (that one will kill every party you've been at). Fine and dandy. But the really big developments, as the economist Israel Kirzner puts it, come from "the incentive… to try to get something for nothing, if only one can see what it is that can be done."[3] Creativity is permitted to more and more humans. Massive invention therefore occurs. Innovation with arbitrage in markets makes it happen. The outcome has been the modern world, the bulk of the Great Enrichment, 3000% and more.

That is, wholly new ideas, such as the steam engine and AC electricity and the modern corporation and careers for married women eventually permitted by the new liberalism of the eighteenth-century theorists like Adam Smith and Mary Wollstonecraft, are mainly what made us rich. Yet these, too, depended upon globalization. If governmental protectionism in goods

---

[3] Kirzner (1973, p. 84) and Diamond (2019).

or migrants was such a good idea, why not exclusively a Russian science in Russia or Australian music in Austria or US technology in the U.S.? Confining, say, the sonata form in classical music to Italy by strict law would be in fact advantageous only to a few Italian musicians, and disadvantageous to everyone else. Ideas flow, too. But they follow material trade. National systems of patents and copyrights attempt to obstruct the flow of ideas. Fortunately, they usually fail, even in the short run, and always have since 1776 in the long run. The notion of "intellectual property" raises incomes for lawyers and reduces the incomes of everyone else. Let's stop saying it and implanting it.

"Material" globalization, as it might be called, puts pressure on the more consequential globalization of ideas to take place. India protected its breakfast cereal industry by preventing Kellogg from entering India. Indian cold breakfast cereal was awful, until after the liberalization from 1991 the tariff was dropped. When auto tariffs into the U.S. were dropped the US auto makers were here forced to achieve Toyota standards of excellence. They learned new ideas, such as having one ley for ignition, entry, and the trunk. Wow.

Globalization, in short, has been the great teacher, in the first instance in doing a good old at old jobs and in the long run in creating massively new ideas for doing new jobs. Efficiency and innovation, both.

Long, long may it reign.

References

Clark JB (1901) The society of the future. In: Gail K (ed) The independent 53 (July 18): 1649–1651, reprint. Democracy and the gospel of wealth. Problems in american civilization. Boston, Heath, 1949 (pp 77–80)

Diamond AM (2019) Openness to creative destruction: sustaining innovative dynamism. Oxford University Press, New York

Kirzner IM (1973) Competition and entrepreneurship. University of Chicago Press, Chicago

Social Market Economy, Ordoliberalism and Neoliberalism. An Introduction

Annette Godart-van der Kroon

Social Market Economy. Definition and its Working

Until the years 1870, the (old) Liberalism with its theory of Laissez-faire prevailed, but then the attitude changed, under the influence of the theories of the Historical School and Marxism (Meijer 1988, 2), especially in Germany where Bismarck wanted to prevent social unrest with several (social) regulations.

In the beginning of the twentieth century and certainly after WWII, Classical Liberals rejected the idea of laissez-faire and wanted to pursue a political policy to create a social market economy that could flourish (Meijer 1988, p. 17). They wanted to break through the rigidity of views à tort et travers of the Liberals in the nineteenth century, like Bastiat, Spencer, the Manchester School etc. (Meijer 1988, 8).

The term of social market economy was first used by A. Müller-Armack in 1946 (Müller-Armack 1947, 480–484).

Müller-Armacks theories and ideas did not differ much from those of Röpke and Rüstow. He agreed with their sociological ideas, but he wanted

---

Speech pronounced at the 36th Heilbronn Symposium "The origins and changes of the social market economy".

A. Godart-van der Kroon (✉)
Ludwig Von Mises Institute Europe IVZW, Brussels, Belgium
e-mail: annette.godart@vonmisesinstitute-europe.org

to elaborate the concept of redistribution of income with the instruments necessary for that (Meijer 1988, 20).

Let us first consider the meaning of the word social and then the theory of Müller-Armack.

Hayek analysed the word "social", which is connected with an enormous amount of nouns: "social awareness, social conscience, social responsibility, social activities, social welfare, social politics, social justice, social insurance, social rights, social control, social legislation, social democracy. I would like to know what aims of a democracy can be said to be not social and why. The word "social" presupposes the existence of known and common aims behind the activities of a community, **but does not define them**" (von Hayek 1967, 242).

Hayek calls it a "word which always confuses and never clarifies the issue". He wonders why in the last decades the words "moral" or simply "good" have been replaced by "social" (von Hayek 1967, 239). To be social is not the same as being "good" or "righteous". According to him the truly social is in this sense of its very nature, anonymous and non-rational (von Hayek 1967, 141, with reference to von Wieser 1919, 115). Then there remains little or nothing in life which is not 'social' in one sense or another, and the word becomes meaningless" (von Hayek 1967, 242). The word "social" is used also in the context of inflation:

As die Zeit wrote: "However, the ECB is not intended to generate new growth. Their primary task is to limit price increases. Incidentally, this is also a social task" (Die Zeit 9-6-2022, 22).

"Society thus assumes a dual personality; it is firstly a thinking entity with aspirations of its own that are different from those of the individuals of whom it is composed. Secondly by identifying it with them, it becomes the personification of the views held by certain individuals who claim to be endowed with a more profound insight of moral values" (von Hayek 1967, 243).

To conclude, Hayek notes that "what we have experienced under the banner of the social concept has been a metamorphosis from service *to* society to a demand *for* an absolute control of society, from a demand for the subordination of the State to the free forces of society to a demand for the subordination of society to the State" (von Hayek 1967, 246).

The market economy can be divided in

- A free economy, a planned economy and a mixed economy.
- A planned economy which means that only the state is entitled to provide goods and services, possesses all the means of production, which eliminates the market mechanism (balance between supply and demand). A

planned economy is a so-called top-down economy, meaning, that at the highest level of an imaginary pyramid, the economy is determined by a few people, and propagated downwards to the lowest level (the consumer). In a planned economy, the consumer can only control the supply by persuading politicians to do so. That is why we talk about a supply-oriented economy. There is also the problem of the calculation of prices, which according to von Mises and von Hayek cannot exist in a planned economy (von Mises 1920; von Hayek 1935, 111 etc.).

- A free market economy is an extreme form (basic form) of economic order in which the allocation problem is solved through the free play of supply and demand (the price and market mechanism). The U.S. economy (U.S.) has most of the characteristics of this economic order.
- In a mixed economy, the producers and consumers decide on production, investment and consumption within limits set by the government. It is a mixture between the centrally managed economy and the free exchange economy.

In all three market forms it concerns the calculation of prices; of supply and demand. Where can the social element come in? The social safety net for those who need it, is usually provided for by the state but also by private institutions. Think of the pension funds in the Netherlands. Or should the prices be regulated by the government? Then we can speak of a planned economy.

According to van Empel (1984, 5) the proper functioning of the market also requires a certain mobility of the factors of production and a certain flexibility in business operations.

The market economy can be defined in several different ways:

Entrepreneurship is important. Kirzner and Schumpeter wrote about that aspect: the private property of the means of production, the stock exchange and competition. Hayek did distinguish between planning for competition and planning against competition. The second group has measures that prohibit the working of the price formulation (Meijer 1988, 17).

It can also be defined as the social system of the division of labour under private ownership of the means of production. And as a means of reconciliation of different knowledge and different aims-in short catallaxy (von Hayek 1973–1979, II, 110).

The Influence of Müller-Armack

In 1953 the Aktionsgemeinschaft Soziale Marktwirtschaft (ASM) was founded in Heidelberg. In fact the influence of the ideas of the social market order was especially accepted in Germany under the influence of Müller-Armack, who was a politician and worked at the Federal Ministry for Economic Affairs of the BDR until 1965 (Meijer 1988, 38). For his economic policy credo, Müller-Armack had invented the formula of the "social market economy" in 1947, which, after Ludwig Erhard adopted it as a label for his economic policy from 1950, became the trademark of the Federal Republic and its "economic miracle":

The famous quote was: "Sinn der Sozialen Marktwirtschaft ist es, das Prinzip der Freiheit auf dem Markt mit dem des sozialen Ausgleichs zu verbinden". Also with regard to the "core" of their cooperation, the social market economy, Erhard and Müller-Armack were demonstrably not necessarily one heart and one soul.

Ludwig Erhard found this statement at least incomplete. For him, freedom on the market and social balance were only acceptable if this was combined with the "moral responsibility of the individual towards the whole" (Schirmer 2017). According to Erhard, redistribution can only ever take place at the expense of third parties. Without moral limitations—moral responsibility in Ludwig Erhard's case—redistribution becomes an end in itself. While for Müller-Armack the social market economy is an instrument for fulfilling social goals, Erhard sees it as an instrument for the development of a liberal economic and social order.

Müller-Armack thus interprets the further developments of this "economic style" from the end of the 19th to the 30s of the twentieth century, the formation of interdependencies between the economy and the state, through which entrepreneurial freedom of action is more and more restricted, as the result of politics (Haselbach 1989, 722).

According to its diagnosis of the Great Depression of 1932, the modern intervention state is a self-contradiction. On the one hand, entrepreneurship as the basis of social dynamics is increasingly restricted by interventionism, on the other hand, that entrepreneurial dynamic remains the economic basis of all state power—this is the thesis of the contradiction of the tax and intervention states, which is also known from the recent discussion of the welfare state.

Müller-Armack connects to Max Weber's thesis of Protestantism, which, like Weber, justifies the emergence of capitalism in Calvinist religiosity. However Weber was by no means concerned with making religious sentiment the sole cause of the formation of economic structures, but this is exactly Müller-Armack's thesis: for him, religious orientation is realised in a historical "overall sense" or "principle of form", according to which history divides into epochs (Haselbach 1989, 722).

Edith Eucken-Erdsiek also discussed in her review of Müller-Armacks book, the fact that for him the connection of religion and economy was very important (Eucken-Erdsiek 1961, 347). In this point he connects to the theory of Weber, but he expands it. He emphasises the fact that the Calvinists were excluded from the posts of civil servant and therefore were pushed into free professions. Edith Eucken-Erdsiek stresses the fact that the Prussian state relies on a Calvinist upper class, and a state-loyal Lutheran population. The Lutherans got used to entrust their entire existence to the state and to expect that the State would take the usual decisive decisions for them (Eucken-Erdsiek 1961, 346). In short: the Calvinists were mostly free entrepreneurs and Lutherans served the state. That might be applicable for Germany, but for example in the Netherlands this metaphor does not apply: there the Calvinists were the upper class and more or less ruled the country and there were no Lutherans, only Dutch reformed protestants.

In this context, Meijer's opinion on Müller-Armack was as follows: he wanted to reconcile several groups, Catholicism, Protestantism, Socialism and Liberalism. According to Müller-Armack it is important that not one of those four groups would prevail. These groups should—while preserving their ideas—move to a common point of view on society. The emphasis of the social aspects the first three groups adhere, should be answered by a policy that combines the market economy and social policy. The situation between socialists and liberals was one of a rapprochement. This was due to the common experience with the centrally planned economies in their economic and social aspects (Meijer 1988, 275).

In fact the aim was to show that the market economy is more social than the planned economy, but it had to show also the possibilities that the market economy offers. Mostly it is the other way round and then the planned economy is described as the more social one. Experiences in the former Soviet Union and its satellites have shown that the planned economy was not social at all.

Although Hayek published articles in the Ordo Jahrbuch, he was not pro-social market economy. He said: "not only many of my friends in Germany deem it appropriate and desirable to qualify the term "free market economy" by calling it a "social market economy", but even the constitution of the Federal German Republic instead of adhering to the clear conception of a "Rechtsstaat", used the new and ambitious phrase "a social Rechtsstaat."

The Connection of Social Market Economy with Neoliberalism and the Role of Röpke and Rüstow

The meaning and the role of Neoliberalism:

Neoliberalism was preceded by several initiatives before WW II, but was only developed after the war; Like Centre International des Etudes pour la Rénovation du Liberalisme. The report of the meeting was published only in 1961. Or le Colloque Lippmann, where there were hardly any representatives of the Anglo-Saxon world (Meijer 1988, 32–33). Only after WW II the Mont Pelerin Society was founded by Hayek in 1947, and it exists until this very day.

Gerrit Meijer gives six elements for Neoliberalism:

1. The stability of the monetary value
2. Open markets. That means a free entry to the market.
3. Private property, also of the means of production
4. Freedom of contract, but not to affect the basic principle
5. Full liability for economic transactions
6. Constancy of politics (Meijer 1988, 18).

In connection with the last element, one can add: the regulations and laws should be clearly formulated so that the citizen knows in advance what they can expect.

After WWII Neoliberalism exerted a great influence on politics. The issue was not to seek acceptance of ideas, but more the solution of problems. They had a hearable voice, first in West-Germany, Austria, Italy and Switzerland. Later in France (after 1958) and in the UK (after 1979).

Eucken calls the expression of neoliberalism as tendentious. He does not see it as laissez-faire, but as a system in which the government is strongly concerned with economic life (Eucken 1960, 374–375).

In their sharp critique of capitalism, the neoliberals go a long way with the socialists and Marxists (Meijer 1988, 3).

As Röpke put it: "Im engeren Bereiche der Wirtschaft bedeutet ein solches Programm Bejahung der Marktwirtschaft, unter gleichzeitiger Ablehnung eines entarteten Liberalismus" (Röpke 1946, 18–19, 45–46).[1]

---

[1] In the narrower spheres of the economy, such a program means affirming the market economy, while at the same time rejecting a degenerate liberalism.

At the same time the Neoliberals distanced themselves from direct intervening in economic life and centralisation of the economy.

Meijer wanted also to discuss the coherence (or the connection) of neoliberalism with the underlying idea of the social market economy (Meijer 1988, 7). According to him this connection is so strong, that the social market economy can be considered as a variant of neoliberalism put into practice (Meijer 1988, 19), although the tendency is to call a centralised economy social and the market economy not social. That is in fact wrong. According to Röpke and Rüstow a policy should be shaped that aims at creating a social structure in which the market economy can thrive. This has been greatly neglected by the liberals of the last century. To this end, the fight against proletarianisation, the promotion of agriculture and crafts and the decentralisation and distribution of industry are necessary (Meijer 1988, 17). Müller-Armack wanted to take a step further. He spoke of redistribution of income. To combine the principle of freedom on the market with social balance. Müller-Armack regarded the social market economy as a "third way" between liberalism and the centrally organised economy. His goal was "Prosperity for all" and his motto "As much freedom as possible, as much state coercion as necessary!".

Nawroth called the social market economy a variant of neoliberalism (Nawroth, 1962).

Hayek made a distinction between false and real individualism. He criticised the laissez-faire. He criticised cartel and trust formation As a matter of fact, Hayek was in the beginning against monopolisation. Later he was less severe concerning cartels and monopolisation.

Another point was the impossibility of economic calculation in a centrally organised economy. That was stressed by von Mises. In an article on "Economic Calculation in a Socialist Community," which appeared in spring of 1920, he demonstrated that the possibility of rational calculation in our present economic system was based on the fact that prices expressed in money provided the essential condition which made such reckoning possible. The essential point on which Professor von Mises went far beyond anything done by his predecessors was the detailed demonstration that an economic use of the available resources was only possible if this pricing was applied not only to the final product but also to all the intermediate products and factors of production and that no other process was conceivable which would in the same way take account of all the relevant facts as did the pricing process of the competitive market (von Hayek 1935).

Schiller argued: "Wettbewerb wenn möglich, Planung so weit wie nötig" (Schiller 1957, 227). This formulation has been used later by Frans Timmermans, the EU commissioner, in a different context.

Nawroth declares that "The principle of market conformity is not identical with the principle of social conformity" (Nawroth 1962, 152).

The Meaning and the Role of Ordoliberalism

Ordoliberalism was started after WW II with the publication of the "ORDO—Jahrbuch für die Ordnung von Wirtschaft und Gesellschaft", a yearbook starting from 1948 on. In fact it started already after WW I, because the influence of Socialism and Communism increased. The economic problems like unemployment and unstable valuta seemed to show the need of a government intervention. After WWII there was a slight revival of liberal ideas, because the public opinion had seen the results of dictatorial and totalitarian regimes. The abandonment of the gold standard and the return of protectionism seemed to herald the definitive end of the free world economy. The attempts to restore and improve the principles of liberal politics failed. The attempts to prolong prosperity and ensure full employment through credit and money expansion, eventually created a global inflationary movement to which employment adapted so much that inflation could not be stopped without creating extensive unemployment (von Hayek 1978, 130–131).

Ordoliberalism is a direction of a revisionist liberalism, wrongly called neoliberal, better called social liberal, which adheres to the liberal principle of private ownership of the means of production but strives after a market economy order that seeks to prevent a use of private property directed against the general interest by disempowering monopolistic market positions (Ordo 1955). The supreme moral principle is the pure principle of performance based on compensatory justice.

The term Ordoliberalism was coined to identify a particular neoliberal direction based on the yearbook ORDO. In the ORDO Yearbook, the concept of the social market economy was theoretically developed.

Ordoliberalism has clearly refuted the widespread conviction as if historical liberalism had finally exhausted the possibility of a liberal order of society, state and economy.

Equality, Value and Merit

These values together with social justice are also connected with the social market economy. They are analysed by Hayek and his view is that Equality, Value and Merit is not compatible with freedom.

Hayek distinguishes between value and merit and these terms he deduces to justitia distributiva and justitia commutativa. These notions were already used by Aristoteles and later by Thomas of Aquino. In fact Hayek describes more the Justitia distributiva, or distributive justice, later called social justice than the Justitia commutativa. That term is more difficult to define. It could mean to equate it with reward for merit, which Hayek says is pursued by liberalism (see also von Hayek 1960, 440–444). The difference lies in the fact that in one case one rewards a performance with a service in return (remuneration according to merit) and pays the appropriate price (justitia commutativa) or that one distributes favours or rewards from above (Justitia distributiva). In fact it is the same difference between merit and value. J. S. Mill has as first aligned the term social justice with distributive justice (Mill {1861} 1917, 57–58; von Hayek 1973–1979 II, 63). In this context the notion of social justice leads directly to a fully developed socialism. As he put it: "In the terminology current since Aristotle we can express the difference by saying that a free economy can always achieve only commutative justice, while socialism -and in a great measure the popular ideal of social justice-demands distributive justice. Commutative justice means here a reward according to the value which a person's services actually have to those of his fellows to whom he renders them, and which finds expression in the price of the latter are willing to pay. This value has, as we must concede, no necessary connection with moral merit. It will be the same, irrespective of whether a given performance was in the case of one man the result of great effort and painful sacrifice while it is rendered by another with playful ease and perhaps even for his own enjoyment, or whether he was able to meet at the right moment as a result of prudent foresight or by sheer chance. Commutative justice takes no account of personal or subjective circumstances of needs or good intentions, but solely of how the results of a man's activities are valued by those who make use of them" (von Hayek 1967, 257–258). The results of such remuneration according to the value of the product must appear as highly unjust from the point of view of distributive justice. Examples are: Zuckerberg produced Facebook, Bezos produced Amazon and Elon Musk created even more and it looks like they did achieve their success without much effort.

Nurses and doctors should be rewarded highly according to Justitia commutativa because they are so needed, but especially nurses are not well rewarded. Houses are needed as well and the prices are going up, because of the current financial policy using low interest rates, investors invest in houses.

It seems most unfair that someone speculating at the bourse can win a fortune in a few hours or an inventor who has been anticipated by another by a few days remains unremunerated. That seems most unfair.

But in such a society there is freedom of choice concerning the choice of profession, of production and of the services to be rendered. This in contrast to countries where Justitia distributiva rules. So, free choice of occupation and of production are irreconcilable with distributive justice.

The opposite is a society, that aims at social justice, and where people are rewarded according to their own ideas of merit instead of objective standards. It is the kind of justice which may and perhaps must prevail within a military or bureaucratic organisation.

It is the justice of a command society or command-economy and irreconcilable with the freedom of each to decide what he wants to do and with freedom of opinion. Distributive justice therefore demands not only personal unfreedom but the enforcement of an indisputable hierarchy of values in other words a strictly totalitarian regime (von Hayek 1967, 258).

When the opinion of the community decides what different people shall receive, the same authority must also decide what they shall do. This conflict between the ideal of freedom and the desire to "correct" the distribution of incomes so as to make it more "just" is usually not clearly recognised. But those who pursue distributive justice will in practice find themselves obstructed at every move by the rule of law. They must, from the very nature of their aim, favour discriminatory and discretionary action. The ultimate result of their efforts will necessarily be not a modification of the existing order but its complete abandonment and its replacement by the command economy" (von Hayek 1960, 231–232).

Keynes

When Keynes wrote his big opus "The General Theory of Employment, Interest, and Money (1935–36)" the term of social market economy did not exist yet.

However, he published the article: "*THE END OF LAISSEZ-FAIRE*" in 1926, where he describes the decline of the use of Laissez-Faire, but he does not mention that the liberals themselves wanted to get rid of this expression already before WW II.

Keynes had won the battle between him and Hayek and his policy prevailed during decades. The reason: his political theory was easier for politicians. Based on his theory, they could make debts to answer the desires of the population and the whole concept could better be "sold" to the people.

The people would not accept falling prices or loans, but they would accept the falling prices via inflation.

The socialist policy however turned out to be disastrous in the seventies everywhere in Europe, but especially in the UK: in 1978/79 there were strikes all the time. Garbage was not collected and even the undertakers went on strike: dead people were not buried. It was a total mess. Hence the election in 1979 of Margaret Thatcher, as prime minister.

Conclusion and the Future

What can be concluded? What is or was the influence of Neoliberalism in the society of today? What became of the idea of a social Market economy?

Whatever the arguments are: examples show that the working of a market where the state is not interfering is the most profitable: the economy in China grew the fastest in the eighties, when Deng Xiaoping started to throw overboard the theories of Mao. Since the beginning of the eighties, the Chinese economy has always grown the fastest on average where the state withdrew most consistently from the market. The private sector provided for 70% of all innovations in China and created for 90% new jobs (Die Zeit 15-6-2022, 10).

Hayek is praised and jeered at. He has brought and enlightened ideas that outlived him. For example his price theory was revolutionary. Today it is mainstream. Prices are like a language that everyone speaks. They solve social coordination problems. For example in the sharp rise in gas prices lies the information that one should perhaps not consider the supply in the coming months as secure. Hayek was firmly convinced that prices should not be falsified (Die Presse 19-3-2022, 16–17). When the side effects of the Keynesian economic policy became apparent in the late 60s—like very high inflation rates and the unemployment rates did not decrease—liberal forces gained in Momentum and Hayek experienced a renaissance a little later as an economist. In fact, Keynes had won the battle between him and Hayek and his policy prevailed during decades. The socialist policy however turned out to be disastrous especially in the seventies in the UK:

Nowadays the situation is totally different. Instead of the blind trust Neoliberals had in the working of the market, the predominance of the state takes this role. Neoliberalism is not predominant anymore and more: according to the public opinion it is the cause of all the misery. State aid is now quite normal in questions like minimal wages, clearing (state) debts, industrial policy, minimum wages, taxonomy, climate protection and Supply Chain Act: the state is on the right track according to many people. Now, it is normal that a government gives rules/directions how a house should be built or heated etc. Clemens Fuest, an influential German economist, speaks of a creeping, spreading neodirigisme. According to Fuest not an exaggerated belief in the market is the problem today, but an exaggerated state credibility (Die Zeit 17-2-2022, 21).

The EU Commission wants to assess when companies make a sustainable social contribution to society. Fuest continues "The idea of sorting the whole economy, which is diverse and constantly changing into a political process according to which to be decided who is good and who is bad, is absurd" (Die Zeit 17-2-2022, 21).

There will always be two groups with opposite views on the matter: on the one hand the pro-market economists who say, that spending this big amount of money will slow down recovery (why search for a job, if doing nothing is rewarded) and on the other hand the state economists who draw the opposite conclusion: Because helicopter money brings too little, the state must bypass the citizen: and invest in trains, power lines, iPads for children, social housing etc. Larry Summers on the other hand wants to go back to a politics "that stops inflation" (Die Zeit dd 27-5-2021, 22).

Some remarks on poverty

Poverty has always been a topic that occupies the mind.
 Now two different results were published.
 The first one shows an optimistic result[2]:
 The amount of the "working poor" has been halved. Now there are 630 million employees who work in poverty, but 25 years ago (in 1994), the amount of those working poor was the double. Those numbers have been published in the edition of 2020 of "*World Employment and Social Outlook*".
 The IAO (The International Labor Organization) indicates that there are two categories of working poor:
 The first group (234 million = 7.1% of the working world population) that earns less than 1.90 dollar per day and who lives in extreme poverty and

---

[2] De Standaard 21-1-2020 p. 25.

the second group (402 million = 12.2% of the total employees population) who has to survive on a salary of 3.20 dollar and does not live in a better situation.

However what counts, is that the amount of the working poor has dramatically been reduced in the last decades, although nowadays these numbers are going up again.

The second result is not optimistic: according to a research, the gap between rich and poor is increasing:

The amount of billionaires is at the moment 2.153 and they possess more money than the 4.6 billion (or 60% of the world population) together.[3]

The question arises: should we bother that much about the second result or count the results of the first outcome? After all, the most important result is that the working poor will be lifted out of their misery and be able to lead a dignified life. Redistribution of income/capital requires constant re-adjustments. Commutative justice requires perhaps re-adjustments but not constantly. There is an example for this in the past: the ten guilder that was provided by Minister Lieftinck after WW II in the Netherlands: everybody received 10 guilder, but that brought no equality: the result was inequality again. After all, people react differently: they either spend, save or invest money.[4]

Also subsidies will not help: they simply do not come there, where they should land.

Of course, redistribution of income can reinforce the idea of justice, but will it help to improve the life of those 4.6 billion (or 60% of the world population)?

I doubt that. If it were so easy to distribute money fairly in society through laws, then this would have happened long ago (Die Zeit 6–7-2023, 6).

List of Literature

De Standaard 21-1-2020, p 23

---

[3] De Standaard 21-1-2020, p. 23.
[4] Shortly after the Second World War, on 26 September 1945, all Dutch people received ten guilders during the great purge of money that Lieftinck set up. In the week in which all old banknotes and coins had to be returned—and then exchanged for new money—one had to live on this ten guilders. This was preceded by the invalidation of the 100 guilder notes on 6 July 1945 and on 26 September 1945 all Dutch paper money became invalid in one fell swoop. At the same time, all bank balances were frozen. In the following months, access to a credit was only granted after it had been proved that the money had been lawfully obtained.

Die Presse (2022, 19 Mar) Was wir heute von Hayek lernen können, Vienna, pp 16–17
Die Zeit 17-2-2022 Der neue Superstar, p 21
Die Zeit 27-5-2021 Wem helfen Joe Bidens Geldgeschenke wirklich? p 22
Die Zeit 15-6-2022 Die Weltmachtblase, p 10
Eucken W (1960) Grundsätze der Wirtschaftspolitik. ORDO, Hamburg
Eucken-Erdsiek E (1961) Der Hebel der Zivilisation. Zu Müller-Armacks Werk "Religion und Wirtschaft". ORDO, pp 339–349
Haselbach D (1989) Philosophische anthropologie und "Soziale Marktwirtschaft": Alfred Müller-Armack. SSOAR Social Science Open Access Repository
Keynes JM (1935–36) The general theory of employment, interest, and money
Meijer G (1988) Neoliberalisme. van Gorcum Assen/Maastricht
Mill J-St. ((1861) 1971) Utilitarianism, liberty and representative government, New York
Müller-Armack A (1947) Soziale Marktwirtschaft. Wirtschaftsspiegel, Jg 2, pp 480–484 reference by Meijer G (1988), p 28
Nawroth EE (1962) Die sozial-und wirtschaftphilosophie des Neoliberalismus, F.H. Kerle Verlag
ORDO (1955) Jahrbuch für die Ornung von Wirtschaft und Gesellschaft, Band VII
Röpke W (1946) Civitas Humana, Erlenbach-Zürich
Schiller K (1957) Sozialismus und Wettbewerb. Frankfurt am Main, quoted by Meijer 1988, p 288
Schirmer A (2017, 13 Oct) Die Erfindung der Sozialen Marktwirtschaft. Newsletter Ludwig-Erhard-Stiftung e.V.
van Empel F (1984) Eerherstel van het marktmechanisme, Leiden
von Hayek FA (1935) Collectivist economic planning, London, p 111 etc.
von Hayek FA (1948) Individualism and economic order. University of Chicago Press
von Hayek FA (1960) The constitution of liberty. Routledge, London
von Hayek FA (1967) Studies in philosophy, politics and economics. Routledge & Kegan
von Hayek FA (1973–1979) Law, legislation and liberty. Routledge & Kegan Paul, London
von Hayek FA (1978) New studies in philosophy, politics, economics and the history of ideas, Chicago
Von Mises L ((1920) 2012) Economic calculation in the socialist commonwealth. Mises Institute
von Wieser F (1919) Österreichs Ende, quoted by Hayek FA

Revealing the Benefits of Trade to University Students

Anthony J. Evans and Wioletta Nawrot

Free trade will be the link to bind
Each nation to the other;
'Twill harmonize the rights of man
With every fellow brother.
Origin unknown (cited by Evans (2020, p. 327))

Teaching Trade Theory in the Classroom

One of the largest joys of being an economics instructor is the ability to introduce students to profound insights that affects their view of the world. And perhaps the greatest of these is the concept of free trade. This chapter shares the methods and key findings of a well-known classroom activity—called 'The Bag Game'—which reveals the gains from trade in a simple yet powerful format.

There are various ways to teach economics, and trade theory is particularly adept at being made engaging. One option is to assign allegorical

A. J. Evans (✉)
Economics, ESCP Business School, London, UK
e-mail: aevans@escp.eu

W. Nawrot
Economics (Teaching), ESCP Business School, London, UK
e-mail: wnawrot@escp.eu

readings, which draw explicit parallels between theory and practice. Good examples include 'The Stranger' (which can be found in Ingram 1970, and Evans 2020); the 'Iowa car crop' (see Landsburg 1993); or the conversation between a corporate executive and the ghost of David Ricardo, as presented by Roberts (1994). Another option is group based activities. Becker (2000) and Bergstrom and Miller (2000) provide good examples of resources that advise instructors on how to use class room games, and Jacobson and Luedtke (2023) introduce articles with instructions for activities that vary from serving simple economic applications to targeting complex interdisciplinary learning objectives. Cruickshank and Telfer (1980) present a strong case for the utilisation of games and simulations, and the doyen of the field is Holt (1999). For a recent symposium see Jacobson and Luedtke (2023). In terms of evidence, Emerson and English (2006) find that students that receive experiential learning obtain higher learning outcomes than those who do not, and several other studies confirm the positive impact of classroom experiments on teaching objectives (see Durham et al. 2007; Emerson and English 2016).

The Bag Game has been used for decades, and although the precise origins appear unclear, there are several available resources (in particular see Houston and Hoyt 2001; Strow and Strow 2004; Smith 2019).[1] While our purpose when conducting this activity is to educate students as part of their formal education, we also recognise the impact these ideas have on them as citizens, and trade theory is particularly notable for demonstrating the gap in perspectives between professional economists and the general public. While economists are often criticised for being unable to find common agreement with each other, Fuller and Geide-Stevenson (2003) find that, 'consensus is particularly strong for propositions of free international trade and capital flows'. According to Whaples (2006), 88% of members of the American Economic Association (AEA) agreed with the statement 'the U.S. should

---

[1] There is a good description from the "Starting Point" website, which is written by Tisha Emerson and cites James Henderson at Baylor University as performing the activity. See https://serc.carleton.edu/econ/experiments/examples/36305.html. There is also a good video overview provided by The Foundation for Teaching Economics, available here: https://youtu.be/j__9arjgwK0?si=OtuC4iqBUCNVgoBV. In our opinion, the best collection of freely available resources to understand and perform The Bag Game is Scott Walla's version, presented by the Federal Reserve Bank of St Louis. See here: https://www.stlouisfed.org/education/is-trade-a-zero-sum-game. It is part of a range of educational resources that are extremely useful for economics instructors of all levels. The origins of our awareness of the Bag Game was when one of the authors attended a Market-Based Management® workshop hosted by the Charles G. Koch Charitable Foundation. There is also a strong oral tradition of the Bag Game, as most economics instructors will be familiar with it regardless of whether they have actually deployed it in a classroom setting.

eliminate remaining tariffs and other barriers to trade',[2] and N. Gregory Mankiw has confidently declared that:

> few propositions command as much consensus among professional economists as that open world trade increases economic growth and raises living standards. (Mankiw 2006).

And yet these sorts of ideas are much less popular among the general public. Sapienza and Zingales (2013) found that while almost all surveyed economists agreed with the claim that 'NAFTA increased welfare', less than half of the general public did.[3] It is a sad indictment of the public outreach of economic communicators that the general public remain so hostile to something that professionals consider so beneficial.

This chapter reveals how practical experience can aid students to fully understand the core economic concepts that underpin trade theory, and in doing so help to close the gap between economists and the public. Our purpose is to share our experience as educators and reveal the important learning outcomes of this activity. The chapter will proceed as follows. Section 2 will explain how the bag game operates, and provides complete instructions to enable readers to not only understand the activity but also perform it for themselves. Section 3 will then summarise the key learning outcomes of the game and discuss the implications for our wider understanding of the benefits of free trade.

How We Played the Game

We introduced The Bag Game to first-year Bachelor of Management (BIM) students studying at the London campus of ESCP Business School. Founded in 1819, ESCP is the oldest business school in the world and has accreditation

---

[2] The AEA is the main professional body for academic economists, with over 20,000 members. It published the most prestigious journal in the discipline (the *American Economic Review*) and co-hosts the most important conference (the *Allied Social Science Associations*) each January.

[3] The North Atlantic Free Trade Agreement (NAFTA) came into effect in 1994 and created a free trade area between Canada, Mexico and the United States. It constitutes one of the largest free trade zones on the planet and has prompted significant attention and debate. The topic of free trade was not the biggest difference between expert economists and the average American, however. Statements that drew even larger discrepancies included '"Buy American' has a positive impact on manufacturing employment" as well as those relating to healthcare sustainability and carbon taxes. We find it notable that for most disciplines if there is a discrepancy between academic experts and the general public there would be no controversy in recognising that the former are expected to be correct. And yet when it comes to economics the anti-market bias is so prevalent it will not always settle things! (see Caplan 2002).

from Equis, AACSB and EFMD. It is a French grand ecole and has its own campus in five European cities and the BIM students study in three different countries over three years. The activity being shared in this chapter took place in 2017 when the authors participated in a collaborative course called 'Introduction to Business'. This was an early year of the BIM programme and the aim was to expose students to the core ideas of the respective disciplines of an array of faculty members. For those studying in London the authors were asked to deliver a short seminar that would be fun, engaging, and carry a powerful message about economics. The Bag Game was an obvious choice.

A simple overview of the Bag Game is that students each receive a paper bag containing a gift. They are asked to consider how highly they rate that gift before being given the opportunity to trade with a classmate. As the game progresses students are permitted to trade with an increasing number of other students, monitoring their satisfaction levels at the end of each trading period. The instructors collect and publish the results to establish how much wealth (as measured through self-assessed satisfaction) is created through trade.

There are different ways of running the game, especially when it comes to the choice of items students receive from the instructor, the satisfaction measurement system, and the number of rounds of trade. Some version may use sweets or chocolate (e.g. Strow and Strow 2004) however we used a variety of small items purchased from Flying Tiger. Items ranged from random chemist supplies (such as bandage tape) as well as school supplies and little toys. The bags normally contain one item each, but there is also the possibility to have a set of items, such as a handful of different kinds of sweets. However, having more than one item in a bag may unnecessarily complicate the game, with some risk of confusion over the instructions and the interpretation of the results. We therefore opted for a simple set up for our experiment. We adopted the 0–5 rating scheme to measure the satisfaction students derive from owning these items. Finally, a key consideration for the game is the number of students taking part and the time allowed for it. We worked with 5 groups of 24–28 students each, summing up to 130 students in total in 5 × 1.5-h learning sessions. This allowed us to analyse the results for each individual group and to compare the results between these groups. Our set up allowed for a total of 3 rounds for each group.

Briefing

Usually, the session starts with a short discussion allowing students to reflect on the reasons why people trade. It is useful to record their responses on a whiteboard as 'student hypotheses' to be 'tested' during this classroom experiment and to allow a reflection on these hypotheses at the end of the experiment.

The bags are randomly distributed among students and students are instructed not to open them until further notice. Students are informed that what they will find in the bag is a gift and their 'private property' and that they will be allowed to take it home with them at the end of the session. This is a very important factor of this activity as student behaviour changes considerably, with an inverse effect on the results, if students are not persuaded that the items in the bags are theirs.

Round 1

Instructors invite students to look in their bag, without removing the item or showing it to anyone else. They are asked to rate their satisfaction on a simple 5-point scale which gets recorded on an individual student record sheet and also as a frequency distribution within an Excel file being shown on a large screen.

We find that helping students to interpret the scoring system in an easy-to-understand way, such as using face mimics or by a precise description of what each of the ratings from 0 to the maximum number of points means, helps in having comparable rating data. We opted for a visual, body language description of the meaning of these ratings. Our students were given a record sheet, and the summary results were recorded on the screen. We find that asking students to show with their fingers the level of their satisfaction derived from owning the allocated item is a nice icebreaker at the beginning of the simulation and stimulates students' engagement. We pooled students by having all the 5s raise their hands and recorded the number of them on the screen. We followed with all 4s, then all 3s, and down to the lowest satisfaction rating of 0. As a result, we built a table with all the ratings from 0 to 5 in one column and the corresponding number of students choosing these ratings, which became our starting point for this activity.

Round 2

Students are then asked to remove the items from their bags and show them to others. At this moment there is a flexibility as to what will happen next. Either the instructor decides to allow students to consider trading with only one student (their immediate neighbour) or allows the trade to take place in small subgroups.[4] In the second-round students are again reminded of their 'property right' to the item in their bag, and are reassured that they can do with it what they wish.

In our setting students were allowed to trade with the closest few neighbours, and we found it practical to give them some examples of what they could choose to do with their items—they could eat it (if the item was edible), divide it up (if an item was divisible), fully or partially trade it, or they also could decide not to trade it at all. The only condition was that they were allowed to interact with the closest few neighbours only, but they were also allowed to trade as many times as they wanted.

It was an interesting experience to observe them interacting with students sitting next to them and to notice the first signs of excitement when they could achieve a beneficial trade. We also saw a note of disappointment if they could not make any exchange, due to their item being met with a lack of interest from other students. What also attracted our attention is the emotional response students had when they compared their benefit from trade with the benefit other students derived—their happiness was reinforced if they perceived their trade to be more beneficial than the trade of other students, and disappointment was more pronounced in the opposite case.

At the end of round 2 students were again asked to rate their satisfaction with the new 'private property' in their current possession, and to record it on their individual sheet. We recorded their results on the screen alongside those from round 1. Even if the level of satisfaction increased after the trade was allowed, we did not intend to attract too much attention to this yet.

Round 3

The instructors can decide on the number of rounds they wish to allow, depending on the particular needs they want to address. We found that having 3 rounds in total works effectively and the results are clear. In our third and final round students were allowed to trade with everyone in class. We encouraged students to mingle and interact far away from their seats, and noticed that even the shy students became fully engaged. The classroom layout obviously plays a role in facilitating the unrestricted movement of students (which assists a discussion about the physical architecture of a

---

[4] Some instructors might add a letter-code to each of the bags indicating a subgroup (A, B, C, D, etc.) and permit students to trade with their same group. We find that an instruction that students are only allowed to trade with the closest neighbours is sufficient, which can be enforced by discouraging students from leaving their chair.

Total satisfaction

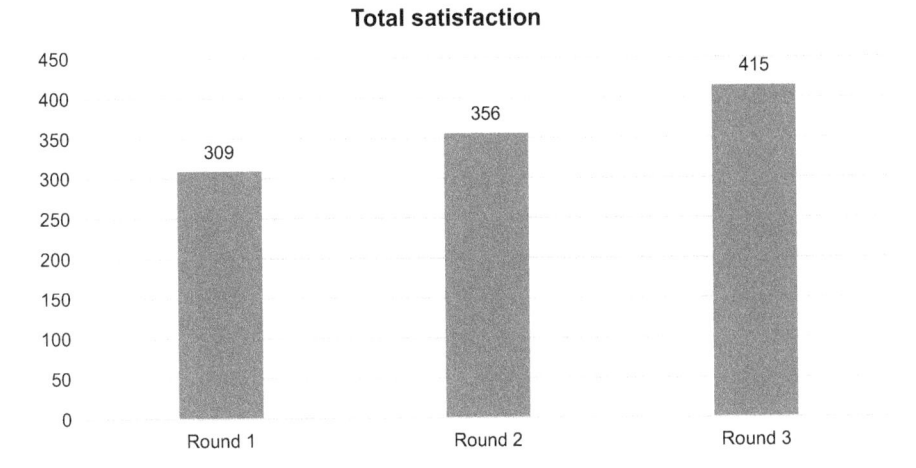

[Bar chart showing Round 1: 309, Round 2: 356, Round 3: 415]

Fig. 1 Total satisfaction

marketplace), and the activity therefore works better in large, flat classrooms rather than amphitheatres with fixed desks.

After the round had ended we again asked students to record their satisfaction level, and the collective results were displayed on the screen. When the time to debrief comes, having the results of the student satisfaction in all the rounds displayed one next to the other provides a useful comparison. It is expected that the overall satisfaction from round to the round increases even if not all the students are necessarily happy with their trading activity, but it is not immediately clear to the students why this happens. A discussion about the benefits of trade facilitates the understanding of it later on.

As Fig. 1 shows, total satisfaction increased over the course of the game, from 309 units of satisfaction in round 1, to 415 at the end. This reveals a 15% increase in satisfaction in round 2, and a 34% in satisfaction in round 3.

We can also report the average satisfaction, shown in Fig. 2, which rose from 2.38 to 3.29. This constitutes an 38% increase in wealth based on the parameters of the exercise.

Debrief

The game reveals that voluntary trade is mutually beneficial and leads to an increase in wealth. We define wealth as the value we place on the assets that we own, and for the purposes of this activity it is measured by using the 5

Average satisfaction

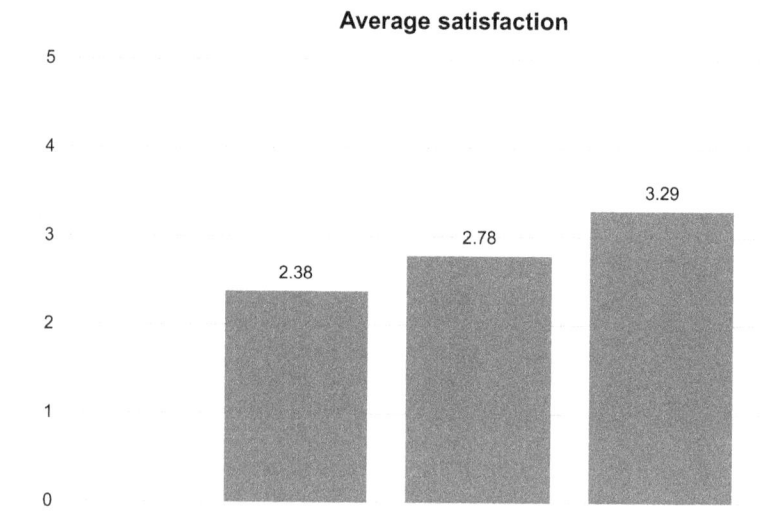

2.38   2.78   3.29

Fig. 2 Average satisfaction

point scale.[5] We found it particularly interesting to reflect on what happened during the course of the game. Figure 3 shows the number of students that assigned each of the 5 ratings in rounds 1, 2 and 3. We can clearly see that the lower ratings (0, 1 and 2) declined and the higher ratings (3, 4 and 5) increased. The mirrored progression is a sweet visualisation of the power of the activity.

Our classroom discussion covered some of the typical debrief questions that are used for this game.[6] These include:

- Did anyone choose not to trade, and if not why not?
- Who benefits the most from trade? Is it the people who have worst endowments or those who make the most trades?
- Would you engage in trade if it made you worse off?
- Did both sides of the transaction benefit from each trade?
- Is trade therefore a zero-sum game or a positive-sum game?
- In the real world what is the equivalent of moving from round 1, to round 2, to round 3?
- Are there any other real-world considerations that we should discuss?

---

[5] These "values" can also be considered utility. Throughout the main text we use the term "satisfaction" to keep it relatable.
[6] These are taken from the Federal Reserve Bank of St Louis version, see https://www.stlouisfed.org/education/is-trade-a-zero-sum-game.

Student ratings in each round

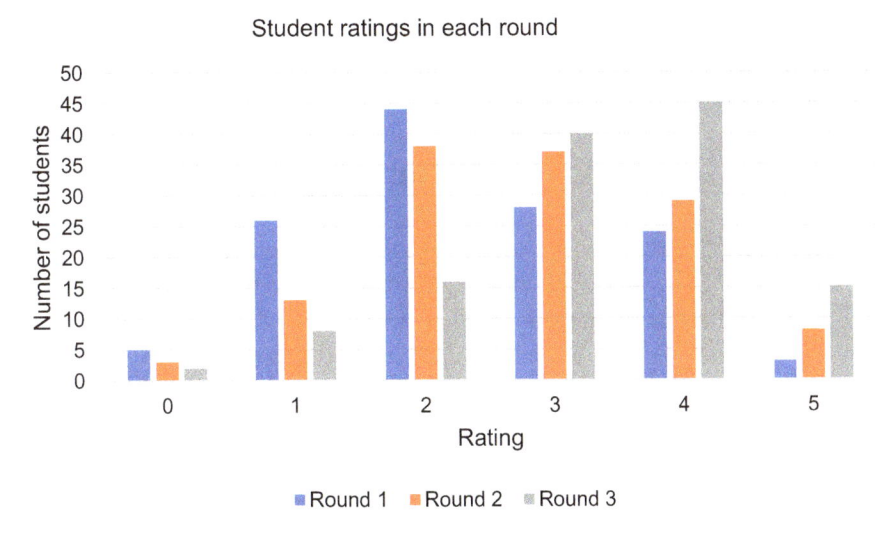

Fig. 3 Student ratings in each round

During the debrief we also tried to highlight the targeted learning objectives. These included the fact that there are no costless trades, and therefore to gain from a transaction (i.e. to 'benefit') you must give something up (this constitutes an 'opportunity cost'). We discussed the assumption that people are rational, and therefore only voluntarily engage in trades where the 'benefit' exceeds the 'opportunity cost' which realises the 'gains from trade'. We can then clearly demonstrate that trade creates wealth. Trade allows goods to be directed to those who value them most, so even if the number or the quality of items doesn't change, the 'economic wellbeing' of parties improves as items move to the people who value them more. The recognition that trade is a technology that increases wealth without requiring any increase in the quality or quantity of goods available is a remarkable lesson to learn! And our classroom experiment clearly demonstrated it—when we progressed to the last round and participants had more opportunities to trade, even more wealth was created than in the second round. Instructors can also introduce the concept of trade interventions such as tariffs, and it tends to be unambiguously recognised that any restrictions on trading opportunities would have reduced overall scores. We can also consider how unfair and arbitrary it would be to restrict trading partners to the same nationality, or their geographical origins. If we think of round 2 as going to regional trade, then round 3 is full globalisation.

At this point we needed to guide student understanding that the creation of wealth doesn't guarantee that everyone would be wealthier, but instead the overall level of wealth increases. We used the example of students who didn't trade because nobody wanted what they had in their bags to illustrate this very important learning point.

Our Reflections and Key Findings

In our summary of the session, we mentioned the importance of institutions (i.e. the rules of the game) in order for wealth creation to take place. We reminded students that what they received in their bags was their own 'private property' and that they were aware of this before they engaged in this activity. Also, we reminded them that no one was forced to make a trade.

The learning benefits of the activity chosen for our classroom experiment were clear, but also the overall student experience was clearly affected. We noted that students were more engaged in this classroom activity than when we present the same content in the form of a theoretical lecture. Everyone wanted to engage in trade, and they tried hard to find partners even if they were unlucky and started off with the least desirable items. Students visibly enjoyed this activity, and reacted with enthusiasm when they made a beneficial exchange. It was a direct observation of our natural proclivity to truck, barter, and exchange (to quote Adam Smith), and we saw that it drew people together.

Indeed, a nice example of how trade links prompt human connections is the fact that many Australian cattlemen supported South Korea during the 2002 FIFA world cup. As Sudha Shenoy has explained, this was because South Korea was such a large importer of Australian beef (see Shenoy 2003). Our classroom resembled an extended market order, where each step away from our original locality constituted an increase in opportunity for beneficial trade and greater manifestation of wealth creation. One of the most powerful insights in economics is that free trade is a positive sum game, and that wealth creation is limited by the extent of the market. There was nothing in the Bag Game that isn't in a standard economics textbook, but the practical experience of witnessing how wealth increases in step with the diversity of trading partners is a stunning revelation. We hope that student carry this insight into their professional careers and also their lives as well informed global citizens.

As mentioned, we conducted the Bag Game as part of a first-year undergraduate course called 'Introduction to Business'. One of the authors also contributes to a collaborative course called 'Business Frontier Technologies', which forms part of the ESCP Master in Digital Transformation. Students arrive expecting a survey of state-of-the-art tools that are finding their way into exciting new business models. Indeed, they receive plenty of those examples throughout the course, but that should not distract from core economic principles. We consider the situation facing a company that makes sanitary wear products. The question posed is as follows:

> If we think of "frontier technology" as cutting-edge innovation, then what types of products or services might be launch next year?

We typically brainstorm things like thinner pads, or perhaps specially contoured versions that are conducive to different types of sporting activity. This example comes from Rosling (2019, pp. 149–150) who points out that in the countries we are likely imagining—those with an income at the highest level of the global distribution, which is level 4—there are around 300 million menstruating women. And yet if we look lower down the distribution, at levels 2 and 3, there are over 2 billion menstruating women. Their demands are much simpler. They just want low cost and reliable products. And not only is the market much bigger, it's also growing much faster. Indeed, by 2040 the number of people in level 3 is expected to double. There are of course valid reasons why Western manufacturers may struggle to break into these markets. There are greater logistical challenges, and exposure to more political risks. But Rosling (2019) argues that the business leaders he spoke to did not provide such excuses. They were simply ignorant of the opportunity. The upshot here is that instead of treating frontier technology as cutting-edge innovation, we might also recognise that trade is a technology, and that the 'frontier' is emerging markets. This gives us a radically different approach to product innovation. As the Bag Game teaches us, we do not need any new resources to create wealth. We can make dramatic improvements in living standards simply by expanding the scope of the market place as broadly as possible. Treating trade as a technology, and expanding the geographical frontiers as far as possible, is the path to prosperity.

Of all the areas where economists find consensus, free trade is one of the most notable. And yet surveys suggest that the general public don't fully appreciate the benefits of mutually advantageous exchange. We believe the solution to this division is economic education, and that classroom games are perfect way to achieve this. Free trade works in the classroom and works in practice.

Acknowledgements We appreciate the help from all of the BIM students who participated in the original study. Any errors are our own.

References

Becker WE (2000) Teaching economics in the 21st century. J Econ Perspect 14(1):109–119

Bergstrom T, Miller J (2000) Experiments with economic principles: Microeconomics. McGraw-Hill

Caplan B (2002) Systematically biased beliefs about economics: robust evidence of judgemental anomalies from the survey of Americans and economists on the economy. Econ J 112(479):433–458

Cruickshank DR, Telfer R (1980) Classroom games and simulations. Theory Pract 19(1):75–80

Durham Y, Mckinnon T, Schulman C (2007) Classroom experiments: not just fun and games. Econ Inq 45(1):162–178

Emerson TLN, English LK (2006) Classroom experiments teaching specific topics or promoting economic way of thinking. J Econ Educ 47(4):288–299

Emerson TLN, English LK (2016) Classroom experiments—is more more. Am Econ Rev Pap Proc 106(5):363–367

Evans AJ (2020) Economics: a complete guide for business. London Publishing Partnership

Fuller D, Geide-Stevenson D (2003) Consensus among economists: Revisited. J Econ Educ 34(4):369–387

Holt CA (1999) Teaching economics with classroom experiments: a symposium. South Econ J 65(3):603–610

Houston RG, Hoyt GM (2001) International trade and money: a simple classroom demonstration. Classroom Expernomics 10

Ingram J (1970) International economic problems. Wiley

Jacobson S, Luedtke AO (2023) Games in the classroom: a symposium. J Econ Educ 54(2):126–127

Landsburg S (1993) The armchair economist. The Free Press

Mankiw NG (2006) Outsourcing redux. Greg Mankiw's blog, 7 May. http://gregmankiw.blogspot.com/2006/05/outsourcing-redux.html

Roberts R (1994) The choice: a fable of free trade and protectionism. Pearson

Rosling H (2019 [2018]). Factfulness. Sceptre

Sapienza P, Zingales L (2013) Economic experts vs. average Americans. Chicago Booth research paper, pp 13–11

Shenoy S (2003) The global perspective. Mises Daily Articles, 8 Dec

Smith C (2019) Is trade a zero-sum game? The answer lies in chocolate. Open Vault Blog, Federal Reserve Bank of St. Louis, 30th Jan. https://www.stlouisfed.org/open-vault/2019/january/trade-zero-sum-game-chocolate

Strow BK, Strow CW (2004) Illustrating trade in the classroom: how free trade can create wealth and decrease hunger, literally. J Econ Finan Educ 3(2):41–46

Whaples R (2006) Do economists agree on anything? Yes!" The Economists' Voice. 3(9):6

Free Trade Myths and Realities

Wayne Winegarden and Rowena Itchon

Creative Destruction is the essential fact about capitalism
—Joseph A. Schumpeter.[1]

The expansion of global trade over the past three decades has improved people's lives in rich and poor nations alike and has helped lift a billion people out of poverty.[2] Despite this impressive record, public support for international trade is showing signs of faltering.[3]

While troubling, wavering support for global free trade periodically occurs. International trade, like all positive contributions to economic growth, is a creatively destructive process that improves our lives by disrupting the old

---

[1] Schumpeter JA Capitalism, Socialism and Democracy, 1950 (3rd edition), Harper & Row.
[2] "Trade Has Been a Powerful Driver of Economic Development and Poverty Reduction" The World Bank, February 12, 2023, https://www.worldbank.org/en/topic/trade/brief/trade-has-been-a-powerful-driver-of-economic-development-and-poverty-reduction.
[3] Goldberg PK and Reed T "Growing Threats to Global Trade" International Monetary Fund, June 2023, https://www.imf.org/en/Publications/fandd/issues/2023/06/growing-threats-to-global-trade-goldberg-reed, Johnson L "What Europe Thinks…About Trade" Internationale Politik Quarterly, January 4, 2023, https://ip-quarterly.com/en/what-europe-thinks-about-trade, and Younis M "Sharply Fewer in U.S. View Foreign Trade as Opportunity" Gallup, March 31, 2021, https://news.gallup.com/poll/342419/sharply-fewer-view-foreign-trade-opportunity.aspx.

W. Winegarden · R. Itchon (✉)
Pacific Research Institute, Pasadena, CA, USA
e-mail: ritchon@pacificresearch.org

way of doing things. While necessary to generate broad-based prosperity, these disruptions are not without a cost.

The growth in internet retailers, for instance, has brought a wider array of more affordable goods and services directly to people's doorsteps around the world. Between 2007 and 2017, it also created nearly a half million new jobs in fulfillment centers and e-commerce companies in the U.S. alone that paid nearly a third more than brick-and-mortar retail jobs on average.[4] While the job gains in the new economy also caused job losses and business closings for brick-and-mortar retailers, on net, e-commerce has vastly improved our quality of life and overall prosperity.

These net benefits result whether that trade occurs within a country or when those exchanges are conducted across national borders. While few people in the U.S. would doubt that Nebraskans benefit when they purchase high-tech services from a firm in Seattle, Washington rather than Omaha, Nebraska, too many forget or ignore the mutual benefits from trade when these transactions occur between people living in different countries. They consequently raise all sorts of concerns should Nebraskans purchase those same services from a technology firm located across an imaginary line in Vancouver, Canada.

But the transactions are the same economically and, in this case, even geographically given how close Seattle and Vancouver are. Empowering people and businesses to choose the firm that provides the most compelling goods or services, regardless of its location, improves the outcome for buyers, sellers, and the broader economy. Failing to recognize that international free trade creates the same large benefits as domestic free trade jeopardizes opportunities to improve people's quality of life. Simply put, promoting expanded free trade is an essential part of a pro-growth policy environment that will help reinvigorate global growth.

This inability to account for the full economic benefits from expanded free trade leads to many fallacies. Commonly expressed fallacies include trade deficits are always harmful, tariffs can be helpful (particularly if a country is running a trade deficit), international trade only benefits the rich while harming lower-income workers, and exports can raise consumer prices in the exporting country.

When policymakers accept these fallacies as correct, they thwart efforts to expand free trade to the detriment of prosperity in their own country as well as their potential trading partners.

---

[4] Mandel M "How Ecommerce Creates Jobs and Reduces Income Inequality" Progressive Policy Institute, September 2017, https://www.progressivepolicy.org/wp-content/uploads/2017/09/PPI_ECommerceInequality-final.pdf.

Why Trade?

Before debunking these myths, it is helpful to briefly summarize the benefits from expanding international free trade. These benefits were clearly described more than 250 years ago by Adam Smith and David Ricardo and are just as applicable today as they were in the late eighteenth/early nineteenth century.[5]

Greater international trade allows people to produce those goods and services that they can provide more efficiently and purchase the ones they produce less efficiently. Since people can now focus on what they do best, international trade increases our total productive capacity. Greater productive capacity enables both countries to produce more total goods and services and improves overall prosperity.

By leveraging the benefits of specialization, international trade increases the ability of producers to discover new innovations and implement more efficient production processes. These innovations and efficiency gains build upon one another creating a beneficial cycle that incentivizes continual technological advancements. Sometimes these innovations are evolutionary improvements in mundane business processes, such as improved logistics, that may not elicit great excitement but meaningfully improve businesses' ability to provide better products to people at lower costs. Other times the opportunities are revolutionary changes that create whole new products and industries, for instance applying exciting cutting-edge technologies such as fracking to expand productive capacities or the development of artificial intelligence whose potential benefits are still uncertain as of this writing. More innovations and greater efficiencies generate even higher incomes and more prosperity.

International trade is often couched in terms of goods and services, but open economies also foster exchanges of ideas and knowledge. These exchanges of knowledge, whether intentional or unintentional, accelerate learning and foster an even more productive environment that creates more and better innovations that further enhance prosperity.

Then there are the intangible benefits that more intense competition creates. Competition encourages companies to work harder, innovate, and lower prices all to the benefit of consumers. The companies that fail to do these tasks risk losing their customers and ultimately risk their survival. In the same way that sports rivalries encourage athletes to train harder and reach performance benchmarks that were thought to be out of reach, competitive

---

[5] Smith A The Wealth of Nations, 2018 (1776), CreateSpace Independent Publishing Platform; Ricardo D On the Principles of Political Economy and Taxation, 2004 (1817), Liberty Fund.

markets encourage companies to continually find new and better ways to serve their customers.

These benefits are not merely theoretical. Empirical studies find that expanding international trade provides widespread benefits to the average family. The accelerated economic growth that countries joining the EU experience exemplify these gains. Prior to EU membership, trade between a non-EU country and an EU country is subject to all sorts of obstructions. Membership removes these barriers, expands international trade, and accelerates economic growth. A 2014 study found that "the 1980s and 2004 enlargements" increased per capita GDP of the nations' joining the EU by around 12%.[6] Not only are people wealthier, but EU membership also provides residents access to a wider range of cheaper products, particularly necessities such as food and clothing.[7]

In the U.S., the expansion of international free trade from the end of World War II through 2007 increased incomes by "$1 trillion, or $9,000 per household".[8] Trade was also linked to net job creation in the U.S. and more affordable goods and services.[9]

These results are not atypical, they are the norm. International trade is not a zero-sum transaction, these exchanges create win-win opportunities that expand the economic pie and improve the well-being of both trading partners.

Generating prosperity requires a dynamic society that embraces change. International trade is an important source of dynamism that promotes innovation, introduces new ideas, and encourages better ways of doing things. It is noteworthy that, while often overused, legitimate geopolitical considerations do exist, as well as important questions of property right protections. These important issues do not take away from the economic case for free trade nor lend any credibility to the myths debunked below.

---

[6] Coricelli F, Moretti L, Campos N "Ho much do countries benefit from membership in the European Union?" CEPR, April 9, 2014, https://cepr.org/voxeu/columns/how-much-do-countries-benefit-membership-european-union.

[7] "1 The WTO can...cut living costs and raise living standards" World Trade Organization, https://www.wto.org/english/thewto_e/whatis_e/10thi_e/10thi01_e.htm.

[8] "Trade Delivers Growth, Jobs, Prosperity and Security at Home" United States Trade Representative, February 2008, https://ustr.gov/archive/assets/Document_Library/Fact_Sheets/2008/asset_upload_file804_15077.pdf.

[9] "Trade Delivers Growth, Jobs, Prosperity and Security at Home" United States Trade Representative, February 2008, https://ustr.gov/archive/assets/Document_Library/Fact_Sheets/2008/asset_upload_file804_15077.pdf; and "The Economic Benefits of U.S. Trade" Executive Office of the President of the United States, May 2015, https://obamawhitehouse.archives.gov/sites/default/files/docs/cea_trade_report_final_non-embargoed_v2.pdf.

Accounting Fallacies and Trade Deficit Confusion

Given all these benefits, a natural question arises: Why does the accusation that free trade imposes net costs on domestic economies persist? The short answer is the opponents ignore the much larger benefits from international trade and emphasize the destructive side of the growth process. The long answer requires an understanding of national economic accounting.

Like corporate or personal accounting, national accounting (e.g., measuring GDP) is a double-entry system. For every buyer there is a seller, for every expenditure there is an offsetting revenue, and for every asset there is an offsetting liability or equity. When it comes to international transactions, offsetting transactions are typically incurred by different entities and occur on different dates. This transactional separation can obscure the benefits from expanding free trade. However, properly accounting for all the related transactions reveals the net benefits from international trade and the flaws in most criticisms.

Take the argument that trade deficits are always harmful. This myth arises because the national accounting definitions lend themselves to a simplistic error. When calculating the size of a country's GDP (the widely accepted measure of an economy's size), imports are subtracted from the other major components of the economy (e.g., consumption, investment, government expenditures, and exports). If only focusing on this transaction, it seems to logically follow that imports are detrimental to growth. After all, if the size of an economy increases when exports are higher, but declines when imports are higher, then it seems to follow that the more a country imports the smaller its economy will be. But this logic is the epitome of incomplete thinking that ignores economic fundamentals.

To see how a complete accounting of the transaction reveals that imports do not detract from growth, consider a simple economy where there is initially no international trade—consumers can only purchase goods that are produced domestically (say in the U.S.). From this initial state where there are no imports, if one consumer now decides to spend $100 on a good produced by a company in another country (say the U.K.), then an incomplete accounting of the transaction would conclude that this transaction lowers overall GDP. After all, $100 of spending was switched from the domestic consumption category that increases U.S. GDP to the import category that subtracts from GDP.

The conclusion is wrong. As demonstrated above, typically consumers choose the import over a domestically produced good because it is either better, cheaper, or both. Focusing on the cost savings scenario for simplicity (a similar argument would hold for purchases of higher quality products), this means that the consumer's purchasing power increases when they choose an import. Therefore, total consumption of domestic and imported goods increases.

The accounting of the domestic benefits from purchasing the import is still incomplete, however, because only the initial transaction has been considered. The ultimate uses of the money that the U.K. company has received has not yet been recorded.

Citizens in the U.K. do not transact in U.S. dollars. By holding the U.S. dollar, the U.K. company is expressing an interest in conducting a transaction in the U.S. One possibility is that the U.K. company wants to directly purchase goods or services from a U.S. company or invest that money into a U.S. based asset. When the U.K. company executes its desired transaction then either consumption increases in the U.S. (if the U.K. company directly purchases a good or service), investment increases (if it invests these resources into a private asset), or government expenditures increase (if it purchases a government bond). Regardless of its choice, the offsetting transaction offsets the supposed reduction in GDP when the U.S. consumer purchased a product from the U.K. company.

The other possibility is that the U.K. company has no desire to conduct another transaction in the U.S. In this case, the company needs to convert its dollars into pounds so it can transact in the U.K. Whoever is willing to give up pounds to acquire the company's dollars does so because there is some other entity that wants to purchase either goods, services, or assets in the U.S. market. In other words, the willingness to accept a U.S. dollar implies that there is a demand for a future U.S. transaction. That transaction could be a purchase of a different good or service or an investment in a U.S. asset.

These two facts—(1) voluntarily choosing imports improve consumers well-being and often purchasing power, and (2) all imports are counterbalanced by either an export of a different good or service, or a capital investment in the domestic economy—demonstrates that trade deficits do not reduce domestic growth, they expand it.

A country running a trade deficit is, by definition, not offsetting all imports with an equal value of exports. This means that countries running trade deficits must be simultaneously running capital surpluses. The use of the terms deficit or surplus is confusing because a large trade deficit sounds terrible while a large capital surplus sounds wonderful. Yet, these are two different ways to measure the exact same economic phenomenon. They are accounting identities that, by definition, must be the exact inverse of one another.

Without government interference, a U.S. trade deficit means that Americans are purchasing more goods and services from abroad because they prefer the quality and cost combinations offered by these products. Reciprocally, the U.S. has a capital surplus because people from other countries, on net, invest more in the U.S. because they prefer the diversity, return, and risk benefits available in the U.S. markets. These investors benefit from greater investment choices and the U.S. economy benefits from an increased capital stock that funds the construction of new buildings, new entrepreneurial ventures, or the large U.S. budget deficit. In short, these investments improve overall standard of living in both the U.S. and abroad. It is a win-win outcome.

Whether a country is running a trade deficit / capital surplus, or a trade surplus / capital deficit, depends on its relative investment climate. A country running a trade deficit over an entire year, decade, or several decades, must also be a place where people, businesses, and institutions from outside of the country want to invest their money (e.g., purchase domestic assets). The investors from outside of the country obtain the resources to invest in the domestic country by selling more goods and services into the country than they purchase from it—there must be a surplus of currency from trade to raise the requisite resources to purchase the desired assets.

On net, there are some countries, like the U.S., where domestic residents buy more goods and services from other countries than people in all other nations purchase from the U.S. Simultaneously, people in all other nations "purchase" more investments from the U.S. than people from the U.S. "purchase" from these countries. There are other countries, such as Japan, where the opposite economic trends apply. The existence of a trade deficit/capital surplus or trade surplus/capital deficit does not portend any particular outcome. To understand the economic implications, more information is needed.

As a final observation, if trade deficits are antithetical to economic growth, then why over the last half-century have trade deficits in the U.S. shrunk during recessions but increase during economic expansions? The clear answer is that trade deficits do not harm growth.

U.S. trade deficit as a percentage of GDP 1970 Q1 through 2023 Q4. *Source* U.S. Bureau of Economic Analysis

The Tariff Temptation

Tariffs are often justified as a means for protecting domestic industries, countering or punishing unfair trade practices, and a useful tool for reducing a country's trade deficit. The previous section demonstrates the folly of the last justification—trade deficits are not detrimental growth; therefore, their existence does not require corrective action nor justify the imposition of tariffs. But what about the first two justifications?

There is a long and sad history of countries using tariffs to protect domestic companies and the outcomes have never been pretty. Latin America's experience using tariffs and other trade barriers in a vain attempt to foster economic development in the 1950s exemplifies the large costs.

During this period, many Latin American nations followed the advice of anti-trade economists to implement what was called an import substitution trade strategy. The basic theory was to use tariffs and quotas (regulations that set strict restrictions on the quantity of products that can be imported into the country) to protect the nation's developing industries. These policies were supposed to create breathing room for the domestic companies and provide the time to acquire the scale and skills necessary to compete in the global marketplace.

The greater domestic sales were then expected to generate more domestic income, which would then create a positive growth cycle. The result would be faster economic development that fostered broad-based wealth in the country. Once this growth process was well established, and the companies gained greater competencies and efficiencies, the country could then reduce tariffs as the domestic industries would no longer require protection. Things did not work out this way.

Import substitution failed as the expected efficiency gains and accelerated economic growth never occurred. Perhaps the best way to visualize these failings is to compare the economic fortunes of these Latin American nations that used tariffs and trade barriers to protect their domestic industries to the East Asian nations of South Korea, Taiwan, Singapore, and Hong Kong who contemporaneously imposed low trade barriers and embraced international trade as an economic development strategy. Today, incomes in Latin America severely lag the average incomes in these countries, which are among the highest in the world even though, as the International Monetary Fund notes, "in the early 1960s, Latin America's per capita income was more than double that of East Asia."[10]

This transformation in fortunes demonstrates the folly of imposing tariffs to protect domestic industries. Rather than creating protection, tariffs impose large taxes on the economy that deter growth and disincentivize innovation. Imposing tariffs on foreign goods raises the price of these goods when they are sold in the domestic economy and are anti-growth tax increases paid by consumers.

The lessons apply to rich and poor nations alike. More recently, the U.S. has imposed tariffs on steel, tires, and other products and faced similar consequences. Take the recently implemented steel tariffs in the U.S. as an example. A 2020 study by the U.S. Bureau of Labor Statistics studied the impact from the 2002 steel tariffs on domestic steel prices.[11] Their review of the data showed that steel prices significantly increased following the implementation of the tariffs. While beneficial for the steel producers in the U.S., consumers and most other industries were harmed. Since steel using industries had to pay more for their steel, consumers of products such as cars, appliances, and utensils also faced higher prices and were made worse off. Just as bad, there

---

[10] "Missed Opportunities: The Economic History of Latin America" International Monetary Fund, October 5, 2017, https://www.imf.org/en/News/Articles/2017/10/05/NA100517-Missed-Opportunities-The-Economic-History-of-Latin-America.

[11] Hergt B "The effects of tariff rates on the U.S. economy: what the Producer Price Index tells us" Bureau of Labor Statistics, Prices & Spending, October 2020 Vol. 9 No. 13, https://www.bls.gov/opub/btn/volume-9/the-effects-of-tarifff-rates-on-the-u-s-economy-what-the-producer-price-index-tells-us.htm.

are now fewer dollars available for people from other nations to invest in the U.S. economy. With less investment, there will be fewer productive resources available to raise wages and power future growth.

The steel example raises another problem created by tariffs, around one-half of global trade is "intermediate goods" or inputs into the production process.[12] Trade in intermediate goods allow companies in industrialized countries to improve their supply chain efficiencies and offer consumers higher quality products for less. The improved efficiencies and increased purchasing power expands economic activity in the industrialized nation while the ability to become a supplier to major global companies expands activity in the developing nation—a win-win outcome.

Imposing tariffs on the sales of intermediate goods reverse these gains. Since the tariffs raise costs for domestic producers, tariffs on goods that are inputs into the domestic production process are akin to direct taxes on the operations of domestic companies. While the companies in the developing nations will likely share in the burden, the higher cost structure will harm the domestic economy by either reducing domestic companies' profitability or raising costs for consumers. Either way, tariffs on intermediate goods impose net costs on both nations.

If tariffs cannot be justified based on the argument that they protect domestic industries, what about the justification that tariffs are an effective negotiation tool to address unfair trade practices? Some advocates of tariffs may even recognize that imposing tariffs will create economic harm, but claim that tariffs are valuable tools, nonetheless. They will argue that the threat of imposing these harms on both countries is an encouragement for trading partners to address other issues, such as the very real problem of intellectual property protections.

History teaches that tariffs are not effective negotiation tools. When one country imposes tariffs, other countries respond by implementing even more destructive tariffs. The costs are borne by the average person across the globe in terms of less opportunity and greater poverty.

Italy's termination of its trade agreement with France in the late 1880s led to successive retaliatory tariffs that damaged both countries' economies and exacerbated tensions leading up to World War I.[13]

---

[12] "Global Trade Outlook and Statistics" World Trade Organization, Update: October 2023, https://www.wto.org/english/res_e/booksp_e/gtos_updt_oct23_e.pdf.

[13] Palen WM "Here are Three Examples of Why Trade Wars are Damaging" Austrian Center, March 7, 2018, https://austriancenter.com/three-examples-trade-wars-damaging/; Magness PW "The Problem of the Tariff in American Economic History, 1787 – 1934" Cato Institute, September 26, 2023, https://www.cato.org/publications/problem-tariff-american-economic-history-1787-1934.

The Smoot–Hawley tariffs that the U.S. imposed in 1930 led to retaliatory tariffs from countries across the globe and exacerbated the damages from the Great Depression. The "volume of world trade (measured in 1934 dollars) declined from almost $3 billion in January 1929 to just $992 million in January 1933."[14] As U.S. agricultural exports were particularly hard hit, the tariffs exacerbated the insolvency crisis on farm mortgages and worsened the financial crisis.[15]

In a more recent example, the steel tariffs President Trump imposed in 2018, and the trade war that followed, cost the U.S. economy more than a quarter of a million jobs, cut nearly one percent from GDP growth, lowered corporate profits, and reduced U.S. wage growth.[16]

These large and inevitable costs tariffs impose on the countries that impose them undermine their utility as a negotiation tool.

Free Trade Benefits the Rich at the Expense of Lower-Income Workers

Other critics assert that free trade harms lower-income families. This criticism is typically connected to industrialized nations trading with developing nations with much lower wages. Trade with low wage countries allegedly drives down incomes in wealthier countries and increases unemployment. Lower-income workers allegedly bear these costs to a greater extent than upper-income workers. Interrelated, leveraging their cost advantages, the low-wage countries ultimately filch industries from the high-income countries, which enables their development by de-industrializing the rich nations—particularly, the manufacturing sector.

Undoubtedly, businesses in industrialized countries that are in a tradable sector and whose production process relies on low-cost labor—industries such as clothing, furniture, and sporting equipment—will be harmed by trade. This is the destructive part of economic advancement.

Just as obvious, businesses in the industrialized countries that rely on higher-skilled labor and higher technology processes typically benefit from trade. Expanding international trade opportunities increases revenues

---

[14] Magness PW "The Problem of the Tariff in American Economic History, 1787–1934" Cato Institute, September 26, 2023, https://www.cato.org/publications/problem-tariff-american-economic-history-1787-1934.

[15] Ibid.

[16] Hass R and Denmark A "More pain than gain: How the US-China trade war hurt America" Brookings Institution, August 7, 2020, https://www.brookings.edu/articles/more-pain-than-gain-how-the-us-china-trade-war-hurt-america/.

for these industries and creates more high paying jobs in the domestic economy. Additionally, many businesses source resources from lower-cost global suppliers. For instance, next generation automobile manufacturers may source their steel production from suppliers in lower-cost countries. The less expensive steel helps to create a more efficient production process and enables the expansion of high value industries. Historically, the job gains from this process have exceeded the job losses.

However, the criticism is not about net job gains but the distribution of these gains and losses. This distribution appears to support the critics assertions but the beneficial market process that free trade jumpstarts go beyond these direct impacts.

Imports from developing nations increase the purchasing power of households and families across the economy of the industrialized nation. This improvement in affordability is particularly valuable for low-income households, many of whom work in non-tradable services sectors that are not subject to job losses. In fact, accounting for the dynamic benefits that the greater purchasing power from imports enables, jobs and salaries in these non-tradable sectors expand and are often of direct benefit to lower-income households.

Supporting this impact, an analysis from the Federal Reserve Bank of Cleveland found, "that lower income households, though possibly more exposed to the labor market costs, benefit more than do higher-income households from the reduction in prices that trade induces. This is because low-income and low-wealth households use a larger fraction of their expenditures on tradable goods and services. …Overall, this suggests that the gains from trade are more equally distributed than previously thought."[17]

There are also additional benefits generated due to the increased growth in highly skilled and high technology industries. The expansion of these industries and the increased job opportunities created will accelerate overall economic growth. This economic growth will increase employment opportunities and incomes for people who directly support these activities and indirectly benefit from the increased prosperity. These widely recognized dynamic benefits from expanded economic activity increase opportunities for higher-income and lower-income workers alike.

Risks of job loss for many low-wage workers goes beyond international trade as well. Many of the jobs at-risk to international trade are already vulnerable to economic dislocations, such as technological innovations, or

---

[17] Carroll D and Hur S "The Winners and Losers from Trade" Federal Reserve Bank of Cleveland: Economic Commentary, Number 2019-15, September 30, 2019.

offer little hope of substantial income gains. The best way to create opportunities for these workers and moderate the costs from the creatively destructive growth process, regardless of the source, is to implement a more efficient social safety net. There are many reasons why people may need to retrain or reinvent their career, and economic dislocations are an important one. Regardless of the source, the social safety net should focus on minimizing the duration of these dislocations and help transition people toward more promising career paths.

On net, international trade creates job opportunities for low-income and high-income workers alike. The broad-based gains in productivity, jobs, and income are an essential part of improving people's quality of life and generating broad-based prosperity.

Exports Raise Domestic Prices

A troubling myth has arisen with respect to exports of liquefied natural gas from the U.S. that is worthy of dispelling due to the economic and environmental importance of natural gas. According to this myth, the U.S. should abstain from exporting natural gas (technically liquefied natural gas, LNG) because doing so will raise domestic prices. Allegedly, greater LNG exports will expand the demand for natural gas causing supply shortages in the exporting country (in this case the U.S.). Consequently, prices in the exporting country will increase.

This theory is simply inconsistent with the empirical data, see the below figure.

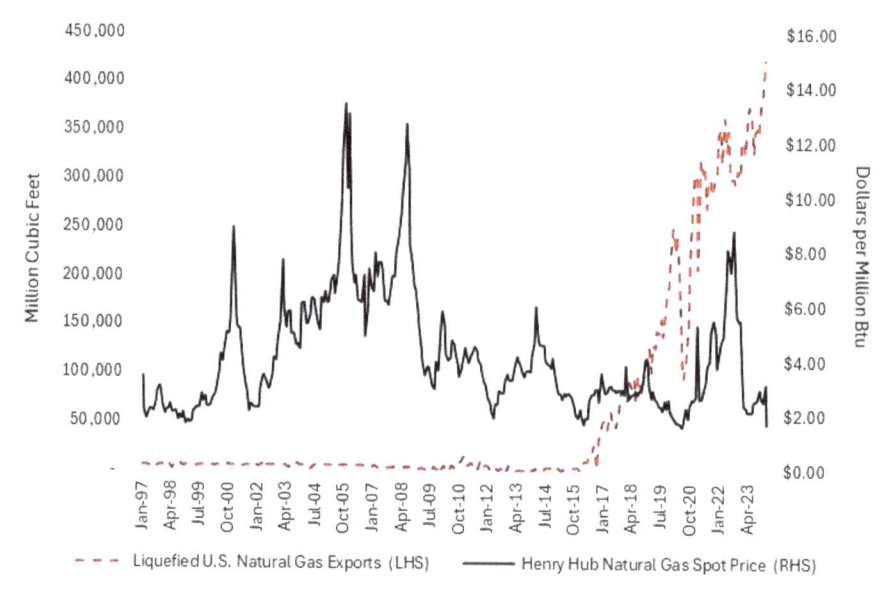

Henry hub natural gas spot price compared to U.S. liquefied natural gas exports January 1997 through February 2024. *Source* U.S. Energy Information Administration

The figure presents the spot prices for natural gas beginning in January 1997 through February 2024. The long time series provides perspective on the long-term price trends for natural gas, which can be volatile. Over this entire period, the average spot price for natural gas was $4.18 per million Btu but was as high as $13.42 per million Btu in October 2005.

U.S. LNG exports show a very different pattern. For most of the time series, the U.S. exported virtually no natural gas. This changed in 2017. While not without volatility, the total volume of LNG exports grew substantially since then and averaged around 356,951 million cubic feet, which is about 70 times larger than the average volume of exports in 1997.

If exports raised prices, then there should be a positive correlation between the rising LNG exports since 2017 and spot prices—spot prices should be consistently rising about the $4.18 per million Btu price. No such correlation exists. In fact, while U.S. exports of natural gas were virtually nonexistent prior to 2017, spot prices were more volatile and averaged $4.48 per million Btu. Once exports expanded, and they expanded a lot, spot prices for natural gas were less volatile and averaged $3.35—25% lower!

Simply put, a review of the price and export data debunks this myth. If anything, greater exports of natural gas have caused prices to decline in the U.S. not increase.

The fatal flaw of this myth is its quintessentially static logic. Clearly, if demand increases for a finite resource, then prices will increase. But resources are rarely finite. In the case of natural gas, exports expanded the market, which then encouraged greater production, more exploration, and the search for improved efficiencies. These dynamic responses enabled the U.S. (the exporting country) to provide valuable resources to trading partners while also improving the availability and pricing in the domestic economy.

These positive incentives, and the dynamism it inspires, are not unique to the natural gas market. They exemplify the pro-growth benefits international trade creates. Often those benefits are not clear from a static view of the economy, but economies are never static. Assuming they are static is a flaw that leads to many inaccurate assertions about international trade.

Conclusion

Expanding international trade is an integral part of a pro-growth policy environment that fosters broad-based and sustainable economic growth. Trade myths such as trade deficits are necessarily bad, tariffs can promote economic prosperity, and international trade harms low-income workers are so costly because the actual benefits are so great.

In practice, expanding international trade provides countries with many potential economic opportunities. When countries embrace international trade, companies can focus on producing those goods and services where they have a production advantage, consumers can purchase more desirable goods and services at more competitive prices, and investors can seek out investment opportunities that offer the most compelling risk-reward attributes. It is a quintessential win-win-win that promotes broad-based economic prosperity and incentivizes innovation.

Despite these benefits, it is too easy to accept the myths to be true because all drivers of economic growth, including international trade, are creatively destructive processes. All too often, the smaller adverse consequences are readily apparent while the larger beneficial impacts are less noticed. The unfortunate result is unwarranted opposition to expanding international trade. Yet, a comprehensive accounting of the costs and benefits from trade clearly demonstrates that countries create barriers to trade at their own peril.

References

Carroll D, Hur S (2019) The winners and losers from trade. Federal Reserve Bank of Cleveland: economic commentary, Number 2019-15, Sept 30

Coricelli F, Moretti L, Campos N (2014) Ho much do countries benefit from membership in the European Union? CEPR, Apr 9

Executive Office of the President of the United States (2015) The economic benefits of U.S. trade.

Goldberg PK, Reed T (2023) Growing threats to global trade. International Monetary Fund

Hass R, Denmark A (2020) More pain than gain: how the US-China trade war hurt America. Brookings Institution

Hergt B (2020) The effects of tariff rates on the U.S. economy: what the producer price index tells us. Bur Labor Stat Prices Spend 9(13)

Johnson L (2023) What Europe thinks…about trade. Internationale Politik Quarterly, Jan 4

Magness PW (2023) The problem of the tariff in American economic history, 1787–1934. Cato Institute, Sept 26

Mandel M (2017) How ecommerce creates jobs and reduces income inequality. Progressive Policy Institute

Missed opportunities: the economic history of Latin America. International Monetary Fund, Oct 5, 2017

Palen WM (2018) Here are three examples of why trade wars are damaging. Austrian Center, Mar 7

Ricardo D On the Principles of Political Economy and Taxation, 2004 (1817), Liberty Fund

Schumpeter JA (1950) Capitalism, socialism and democracy, 3rd edn. Harper & Row

Smith A (2018 [1776]) The wealth of nations. CreateSpace Independent Publishing Platform

United States Trade Representative (2008) Trade delivers growth, jobs, prosperity and security at home

World Bank (2023) Trade has been a powerful driver of economic development and poverty reduction, Feb 12

World Trade Organization (2023) Global trade outlook and statistics

World Trade Organization, The WTO can…cut living costs and raise living standards

Younis M (2021) Sharply Fewer in U.S. view foreign trade as opportunity. Gallup, Mar 31

Free Trade Versus Interventionism

Jörg Guido Hülsmann and Karl-Friedrich Israel

Introduction

Ever since the days of Adam Smith, economists have championed free trade quite unanimously. They have demonstrated that trade policies—designed to encourage exports and to discourage imports—are likely to make all nations poorer rather than richer (Smith 2007 [1776]; Ricardo 2001 [1821], 1951 [1822]; Say 2011 [1803]). The economic argument in favour of free trade does not rely on the real or imagined perfections of a free-market economy. Rather, it highlights the adverse effects of government interventions (Mises 2011 [1929]). Repressive trade policies in the form of tariffs, quotas, and product regulation curtail the international division of labour and thereby stymie labour productivity at home and abroad (Mises 1998 [1949], pp. 741–749; Röpke 1942). Whatever the imperfections of a free-market economy are, they are likely to be reinforced by protectionism.

But this line of argument can be generalised. It does not only concern *repressive*, but also *permissive* policies (Hülsmann 2024, pp. 268–275). In our present contribution, we shall focus on the latter. Permissive trade policies most notably come in the form of export subsidies and of expansionary monetary policy designed to boost exports. In what follows, we shall study

---

J. G. Hülsmann (✉)
Université d'Angers, Angers, France
e-mail: guido.hulsmann@univ-angers.fr

K.-F. Israel
Université Catholique de L'Ouest, Angers, France

how such policies affect aggregate output, the international division of labour, the volume of foreign trade in real terms and in money terms, as well as the relative importance of foreign trade in comparison to the domestic economy. As we shall see, permissive trade policies are not quite as harmful as their repressive cousins, but they tend to be sterile in respect to the division of labour and harmful in regard to aggregate output.

We shall start off by considering foreign trade in a hypothetical world without government interventions and a constant world money stock (I). This will serve as a foil to contrast the impact of export subsidies (II) and the impact of expansionary monetary policies (III). Throughout, we shall neglect the role of financial flows and of foreign direct investments.

I Trade Without Government Interventions

In a first step, suppose that the world economy is operating within a framework of private-property rights, yet without any government interventions that deliberately violate existing property rights. Suppose furthermore that all agents of the world economy use the same type of money and that the overall money stock is fixed.

In such a world, the division of labour (DOL) and the corresponding real trade volumes would be both a cause and a consequence of economic growth. Trade volumes largely depend on the level of aggregate output, while the division of labour between the residents of any given area (home) with the rest of the world (ROW) also depends on the *relative* size of the home economy as compared to the ROW economy. Let us walk through a few scenarios to explain these connections.

The Pricing Process in a Growing Economy

Suppose that aggregate output increases once and for all times in the home economy, while the ROW is at first stagnating at its previous output level. The ensuing adjustment process would be driven by market prices and increasing specialisation. Let us first look only at the pricing process. In the economic literature, it is known as the specie-flow mechanism (see Lechner 1988, pp. 371ff).

The increased output at home would entail a tendency for all money prices at home to drop (price-deflationary growth). Indeed, economic growth means that a greater quantity or variety of real goods is supplied to the market. If the overall money stock stays put, as we have assumed, then the unavoidable consequence is that money prices at home would tend to fall. This concerns both product prices and the prices of factors of production (labour services, raw materials, intermediate goods and fixed-capital goods).

It follows that goods produced at home would be relatively cheaper than similar goods produced abroad. They become more price-competitive. It becomes more attractive to buy at home and less attractive to buy from the ROW. Exports from home to the ROW would increase *in real terms*. If the foreign demand for these goods is price-elastic, then the volume of exports from home *in money terms* would also increase. If it is inelastic, it would diminish. But as long as the price-level difference prevails, there will also be exports of *other goods* than those that have been exported before the output increase. It is therefore likely that exports from the home economy increase not only in real terms, but also in money terms. The money stock is therefore likely to increase in the home economy and to diminish in the ROW.

This is why the initial competitive advantage of the home economy is bound to be temporary. For how would the money units flowing in from abroad be used? Some would be hoarded because the demand for cash would increase as a consequence of growing wealth. Some would be spent on goods produced at home, thereby increasing their prices. Some would also be spent on real goods produced abroad, most notably on goods which cannot be produced at home. The bottom line is that *not all* of the additional money units coming in from abroad would return to the ROW. The volume of imports into the home economy, in money terms, would lag behind the volume of exports from home. The nominal cash balances held at home would *permanently* increase, while the nominal cash balances held abroad would permanently diminish. As a consequence, the money price level abroad would eventually tend to shrink as well, and this would re-establish a competitive equilibrium between home and the ROW.

As long as the home economy grows faster than the ROW, this process would reiterate. Prices at home would drop, money-term exports from home would be higher than money-term imports into the home economy, cash balances would build up at home and shrink abroad, so that prices abroad diminish, until a new equilibrium be reached.

In each new final equilibrium, exports and imports would eventually be equal in money terms. The trade balance and the balance of payments would be equilibrated. However, there are also four significant changes as compared to the situation before the output increase in the home country. One, the division of labour (DOL) focuses more strongly on the home economy, both at home and in the ROW. Two, the volume of foreign trade *in real terms* is now greater than before. Three, the volume of foreign trade *in money terms* is also likely to increase. Four, foreign trade is less important relative to the home economy and more important relative to the economy of the ROW.

Indeed, if output surges in the home economy while it stays put in the ROW, then the division of labour (DOL) would focus more strongly on the home economy. Home residents would allocate a greater share of their time and material resources to serve the needs of other home residents. In the short run, this occurs most notably because of the price advantages that the growing home economy enjoys over the ROW. Home residents would purchase more products manufactured at home, because home prices drop relative to prices in the ROW. But we have seen that these price advantages are only temporary. The true reason why the DOL would focus more strongly on the home economy is that the productivity of the latter has increased relative to the ROW. The real revenues and the money revenues of the home residents have increased relative to the corresponding revenues of residents in the ROW. And this means that home residents will be able to not only purchase more goods and services than before, but *relatively* more goods and services than will be purchased by the ROW. And they will also purchase relatively more goods *from* other home residents (rather than from the ROW) simply because these others now produce a greater share of world output.

The worldwide DOL would therefore be geared more strongly to the home country. The home residents would allocate a greater share of their time and material resources to serve the needs of their compatriots. And the ROW, too, would allocate a greater share of their time and material resources to serve the needs of the residents of the home country. If the different growth rates persist for a prolonged time, then the home country would eventually grow into the role of a metropolitan area, whereas the ROW would turn into the home's periphery or economic hinterland.

Since the agents of the home economy are increasingly trading amongst themselves, one may think that, in the new equilibrium, the *money volume* of foreign trade is likely to diminish, even though the real volume will increase, as compared to the initial situation. But we also need to keep in mind that money revenues and nominal cash balances in the home country have permanently increased. Therefore, even though, for the reasons we have discussed, the spending on imports is likely to decline in the home country relative to domestic spending, the absolute level may very well increase. For example, the residents of the home country may initially have had an aggregate revenue of 100 units of money, out of which 20 were spent on imports. When the economy grows relatively to the ROW, its aggregate revenue may increase to 200, out of which 30 are spent on imports. In the initial situation, foreign trade was relatively more important for the home country, but in absolute terms it spent less on imports because its overall revenue was smaller. By contrast, in the ROW, foreign trade will become more important, not only in real terms, but also in money terms and relative to the domestic economy.

Analogous consequences would follow, *mutatis mutandis*, if the ROW grows while the home economy initially stagnates. Then imports from the ROW to the home economy would increase, with corresponding money outflows, and not all this money would flow back. The home price-level would therefore eventually diminish, and a new equilibrium be reached. The DOL would be reoriented, and a relatively greater share of time and material resources be allocated to serve the needs of the ROW. The real volume of foreign trade would increase, as would its money volume, while foreign trade would become more important relative to the home economy and less important relative to the ROW. The latter may eventually turn into an economic centre of the world economy, while the home turns into a hinterland.

If *all* areas of the world economy are growing at approximately the same rate, then the world price level would drop, yet without any major regional disparities. In this case, foreign trade could not be reshaped under the mere impact of the price-level changes that we have discussed so far. But it will be reshaped under the impact of another repercussion of economic growth, namely, diversification. Let us look at this in a bit more detail.

Specialisation in a Growing Economy

Economic growth comes with product differentiation. A growing economy does not need ever more haircuts and bread. Sooner or later, it needs *better* haircuts, better bread, and *new* products serving needs that were hitherto not provided for. This movement, too, is typically prompted by the price-deflationary impact of economic growth. In order to avoid or mitigate the reduction of their monetary revenues, producers at home and in the ROW will seek to side-step price competition and cater to niche markets. In many cases, this is only possible through geographical extensions of the customer base.

The trade volume in both money and real terms then tends to increase beyond what it would have been under the mere impact of price-level changes. If only the home economy grows while the ROW initially stagnates, then the DOL would still be reoriented to the benefit of the home economy. The spending on imports relative to domestic spending is likely to decline in the home country and to increase in the ROW, but the relative decline would be mitigated at home, and the relative increase reinforced in the ROW, by virtue of product differentiation and specialisation.

If *all* areas of the world economy are growing at approximately the same rate, trade patterns would not be driven by any price-*level* differentials, but by the intensification of the DOL and corresponding changes in individual prices (i.e. in the price *structure*). Specialisation and product diversification would increase. Each producer would more and more cater to customers all over the world, rather than only at home (see Mises 1916). In all countries, foreign trade would then increase relative to purely domestic trade. It would increase in real terms and in money terms.

II Trade Driven by Export Subsidies

Let us now abandon our previous assumption that the world economy is operating without any government interventions that deliberately violate existing property rights. Suppose that governments exist and that they intervene into the economy with permissive trade policies. But they do not meddle with the money stock. We still suppose that the latter is fixed and that the same money is used all over the world.

Permissive policies pursue the deliberate objective of facilitating exports from home (imports into the ROW). They come in various forms and shapes. They can be volume-based (e.g. the government pays to exporters X pounds per vehicle of type Z sold to customers abroad) or value-based (e.g. the government pays a subsidy of X percent on the price paid by customers abroad). Often, they also come in the form of government-funded export insurance, or in the form of industrial policies designed to create "national champions" that are especially competitive on a worldwide scale. (By contrast, tax rebates and tariff drawbacks are *not* subsidies, see Adam Smith 2007 [1776], p. 388.)

Winners and Losers

Export subsidies enable more foreign trade in the subsidised products. Their primary beneficiaries are the subsidised exporters, as well as their suppliers and employees. They all receive additional revenue out of the public purse. Their customers abroad benefit, too, since they usually do not have to pay the full price of the services that they receive from the exporter.

Notice however that the foreign customers do *not always* gain from the export subsidy. This is because the *intended* beneficiaries are not always the real beneficiaries. In the political process, an export subsidy is *presented and justified* as a subsidy to attract foreign customers. But it may very well turn out to be a *cross-subsidy on internal sales*, in which case it would mainly benefit costumers at home. If a car manufacturer receives from his government 10 million pounds for cars he sells abroad, he may use a part or all this money, not to reduce his prices abroad, but at home. Of course, in his official accounting he would impute the subsidy to exports only. His sales abroad would show a profit, while the sales at home would show a loss. But this might not be his internal accounting.

Again, such a cross-subsidisation *may be* the unintended effect of an export subsidy. But it may also be implemented for the deliberate (though hidden) purpose of benefitting the export business at home, rather than abroad.

Export subsidies also create losers. The subsidies must be financed by the rest of the home economy in the form of taxes or in the form of an inflation of the money stock. In the present section we still suppose that no extension of the money stock takes place. In that case, all subsidies must be funded out of taxes, and taxes reduce the business revenues and household revenues of the taxpayers. They therefore also reduce the revenues of *their* suppliers and employees. The squeezed profit margins can lead to insolvencies and unemployment. While more resources (capital, labour, raw materials) will be re-allocated into the subsidised industry, less resources will be used elsewhere.

If the subsidy is fully funded by taxation, the amount of the subsidy is exactly equal to the amount that has been levied on the taxpayers. The overall net effect on aggregate revenues and aggregate production is therefore likely to be zero. To be true, this is not how things usually *appear* to be. The reason is that the subsidies are typically concentrated on a few beneficiaries, while the corresponding taxes are typically paid in small increments by a great number of taxpayers. The benefits are therefore highly visible, while the costs are widely dispersed and often seem to be outright negligible for each individual taxpayer (see Salin 2020 [1985], p. 174).

An export subsidy is quite frequently justified as a beggar-thy-neighbour policy: not nice, but does the job. The home country seems to gain at the expense of hapless foreigners who are lured into buying more of the subsidised products. But the beggar-thy-neighbour idea falls short of its promise. It is true that the subsidised businesses gain an advantage at the expense of their foreign competitors. But this microeconomic advantage cannot be generalised. Recall that we are still supposing that the worldwide money stock does not change. In that case, each additional pound that the ROW customer pays on the subsidised product is a pound that is not spent elsewhere. As a consequence, the prices of *other* goods in the ROW will eventually drop, and these goods will therefore become more price-competitive. If Britain subsidises cheddar cheese on the French market, then Frenchmen will likely purchase (marginally) more British cheddar. But all the money spent on cheddar is not spent elsewhere in the French economy. The prices of other goods will therefore (marginally) drop and become (marginally) more competitive, not only within France, but also internationally. In other words, a policy of export subsidies, while benefitting any *one* line of business in the short run, nurtures competitors to *other* British businesses in the longer run.

A Zero-Sum Game

It would be wrong to infer that export subsidies are zero-sum games. In fact, they are negative-sum games. The recipients of the subsidies may benefit, but the home country as a whole is likely to lose. Two important considerations lead to this conclusion.

The first one has been spelled out by Adam Smith in 1776, by Murray Rothbard in 1970, and by hosts of other economists in the past and in the present. Subsidies bring about an allocation of resources that businessmen would not have chosen in the absence of government coercion. Without the subsidy, the exporter would have to sell his products in a foreign market at a price "which does not replace to him his capital, together with the ordinary profit" (Smith 2007, p. 390). In that case he might not export his goods and services at all, or sell less of them, because such exports would entail a loss. Thanks to the subsidy, capital, raw materials, and labour are now used in a way that is less productive than existing alternative uses which, under normal circumstances, would have been chosen instead. Lines of production which *really are less profitable* than others are *becoming profitable* from the microeconomic point of view of the subsidised beneficiary, at the expense of the rest of the economy. It is arguably rational for individual entrepreneurs to seize this artificially created profit opportunity, but it is pointless from a macroeconomic point of view. Economists call this a rationality trap.

The second reason is that some of the available resources are not redirected into other lines of business, but diverted into bureaucracy and political rent seeking. Additional bureaucracy is needed to execute the subsidy programme. Political rent seeking is needed because the subsidy is a one-off advantage. In order to turn it into a perennial benefit for the recipient, it must be renewed again and again. That is, it must be defended in the political process through constant lobbying and bribery. The growth of political rent seeking causes regime uncertainty und undermines long-term investments and real economic growth (Higgs 1997, 2012).

This is why subsidies tend to be deadweight losses for the home economy. Subsidies of all forms, according to Rothbard (2009 [1970], p. 1255) "coercively penalize the *efficient* for the benefit of the *inefficient*." He points out:

> This is most clearly seen in the case of government transfer subsidies paid from tax or inflation funds—an obvious taking from Peter to give to Paul. Let the subsidy method become general, then, and everyone will rush to gain control of the government. Production will be more and more neglected, as people divert their energies to the political struggles, to the scramble for loot. It is obvious that production and general living standards are lowered in two ways: (1) by the diversion of energy from production to politics, and (2) by the fact that the government inevitably burdens the producers with the incubus of an inefficient, privileged group. The inefficient achieve a legal claim to ride herd on the efficient. *This is all the more true since those who succeed in any occupation will inevitably tend to be those who are best at it.* (p. 1256)

Export Subsidies and Foreign Trade

We now turn to the impact of exports subsidies on foreign trade. The real exports *of the subsidised businesses* will increase. Their exports in money terms may or may not increase, depending on the price-elasticity of the demand for the subsidised goods. Let us assume for the sake of argument that foreign demand is relatively elastic, so that the overall selling proceeds (exports in money terms) increase for the subsidised businesses.

Even then, it is not certain at all that the *overall exports* of the home country will in the long run increase in either real or money terms. Indeed, as we have seen, the increased spending of the ROW on the subsidised goods willy-nilly goes hand in hand with diminished spending on other goods. The prices of ROW goods will therefore eventually drop relative to the prices of goods from the home country. The non-subsidised exporters from the home country will therefore have a harder time marketing their products to the ROW. It is therefore very well possible that the export subsidies have no impact on the *overall* export volume (money terms and real terms), and it is even possible that the overall volume diminishes.

Let us assume for the sake of argument that the export subsidies increase the overall volume of exports from home. More money is then flowing into the home economy thanks to the permissive trade policy. But this does not represent any overall advantage to the home economy as compared to the ROW. It simply means that the international division of labour has been restructured in an inefficient way. Foreign trade swells to the detriment of the domestic economies at home and abroad, but there is no aggregate benefit.

Indeed, whenever export subsidies increase the overall volume of exports from home in money terms, this is likely to bring about an increase in imports as well. The reason is that there would be no reason to *hoard* the additional money units. After all, aggregate wealth has not increased and may even tend to diminish, for the reasons discussed above. All or next to all money units coming into the home country would therefore be exchanged for non-monetary goods. As a consequence, the home price-level would tend to increase. In the ROW, it would be the other way around. Money is leaving the ROW area, and the ROW price level is therefore likely to fall. The overall result is that products from the ROW would become increasingly competitive in comparison to home products. Exports from the ROW (imports into the home country) will therefore tend to increase.

To sum up, it is by no means certain that export subsidies have any positive impact on the overall volume of foreign trade. Sectoral subsidies of the sort that we have discussed so far have no systematic impact on overall trade volumes at all. *Even if* the overall export volume were to increase, it would likely entail an increase of overall imports as well. Superficially, such an inflation of foreign trade would resemble the case of the growth-driven expansion of foreign trade that we discussed in section I. But notice the difference. Economic growth brings about a systematic, permanent, and productive increase of foreign trade, whereas export subsidies entail this result only accidentally, temporarily, and parasitically. Growth-driven foreign trade is an organic extension, or spill-over, of the division of labour into the international realm, whereas any subsidy-driven growth of foreign trade is doomed to be a destructive redistribution of income and wealth. It is a waste of time and money from the overall point of view.

III Trade Driven by the Printing Press

Until now we have reasoned from the hypothetical premise that all agents of the world economy use the same type of money and that the overall money stock is fixed. Let us now drop this hypothesis and assume that governments do intervene in the production and use of money.

Assume furthermore that, as a consequence of these interventions, there are national currencies the stock of which may be expanded without any technical or legal constraints (Hoppe 1990). It does not matter for the purposes of our argument whether these national currencies are produced by privileged private agents or provided by government-sponsored central banks. Neither does it matter whether these national currencies come in the form of money substitutes (inside money) or in the form of base money (outside money). It only matters that the government exercise control over the production and allocation of new money units. As a shorthand, we will use the metaphor of the central bank controlling the printing press to refer to this situation.

A government may use the printing press to pursue a permissive trade policy. It is able to increase the money stock at virtually zero marginal costs. It can therefore artificially reduce the value of its own currency on the foreign exchange markets. Assume, for example, that the current exchange rate between the home money and the ROW money is $H1.20$–$R1$. The home central bank, which controls the home printing press, could decide to buy ROW money at $H1.80$ and keep these money units in its forex cash balance. This would correspond to a 50% devaluation of the home money against ROW money. All forex market participants would immediately buy at the new rate. No seller of ROW money would be willing to sell below $H1.80$, because he could always obtain this price at the home central bank. And no buyer of ROW money would therefore find anybody willing to sell below this threshold.

This means that goods from the home economy are now cheaper for buyers abroad. ROW customers would rush to the forex markets, exchange their money for the home money, and then purchase goods and services from the home economy. Exports from the home economy would therefore increase in money terms and real terms. Most importantly, exports from *all* branches of the home economy would increase, not only exports from specific firms or branches, as in the case of export subsidies. All exporting businesses are likely to have higher revenues. All exporting businesses are therefore likely to have higher profits. They may all hire additional people, pay higher wage rates, and make additional investments.

But this stimulus is bound to be of temporary value only, just as in the case of subsidies. Indeed, as we have seen, the new units of home money, which had been created through a central-bank intervention on the forex markets, quickly find their way into the domestic home economy. At first, they are paid to the exporters. But the latter will then use them to remunerate their employees and suppliers. And then these other people will spend them, too, and so on and on. One round of spending therefore leads to the next. The new money units trickle through the economy, thereby increasing revenues and prices. The different individual prices will not increase in the same proportion and at the same time (Cantillon effects), but they definitely tend to increase (Mises 1998 [1949], pp. 413ff; Hülsmann 2014; Dorobat

2015). While more money units have been created out of thin air thanks to the powers of the central bank, these powers are insufficient to create more goods out of thin air that can be exchanged for money. The home money supply is therefore bound to become relatively more abundant as compared to the supply of non-monetary goods, and the consequence is an increase of the price level.

This price-level increase will quickly become problematic for all the business that primarily serve the domestic market. Their top-line revenue has not increased, or increased only insignificantly, but now their costs are rising because the exporters spend their selling proceeds and thereby bid up factor prices. This means that the forex intervention may turn into a zero-sum game of sectoral gains and losses. The exporters gain, but their advantage comes at the expense of corresponding losses amongst the firms that primarily serve the domestic market.

The same problem will eventually befall the exporters themselves. Suppose the initial forex intervention occurred only once. Today the home central bank buys ROW money at $H1.80$, but tomorrow it abstains from any further intervention. This would give a one-time advantage to the lucky few who buy the home money today. It also would provide a one-time advantage to the exporters and increase their top lines. As from tomorrow, however, the bonanza would disappear and the exporters would revert to normal business. For it to have any significant impact, the forex intervention must therefore be repeated, again and again, as in the case of export subsidies. Eventually, the central bank must purchase ROW money at higher prices than $H1.80$ because factor prices will have caught up to that level. The permanent expansion of the home money stock to buy ROW money at a price of $H1.80$ sooner or later pushes up the price level at home so much that $H1.80$ is now the going market rate and no longer requires any further intervention. In order to procure advantages to the export firms, the exchange rate then has to be propped up to $H1.90$ or $H2.00$.

The benefits of forex interventions for the exporters and their customers, suppliers, and employees are therefore only temporary. This implies that such policies are likely to entail significant log-rolling and other forms of rent-seeking by the beneficiaries, along with corresponding deadweight losses for the economy as a whole.

But there are other losses as well. We have already pointed out that the benefits of the exporters come at the expense of businesses that primarily serve the home economy. Moreover, consider that a rising exchange rate of ROW money means a dropping exchange rate of the home money. It means that all ROW goods and services become more costly to home residents. It means that the division of labour between home customers and their suppliers from the ROW is hampered. For the same reason that exports receive a short-run boost, imports are likely to be curtailed.

Furthermore, we need to ponder the significance of the above assumption that the home central banks purchases ROW money at artificially high prices to keep it in its forex cash balance. This seems to be a very unrealistic assumption. Present-day central banks, to the extent that they seek to bid down the exchange rate of the home money (think of China and Japan), do not keep ROW money in cash, but purchase ROW financial assets. However, in an era of extremely low interest rates by historical standards, this policy comes close to hoarding cash. Moreover, and most importantly, from an overall point of view it is just as problematic as cash hoarding, and possibly even more so. For what the policy means *in real terms* is that the central bank subsidises ROW customers of the home exporters and then uses the selling proceeds to subsidise ROW debtors. Where is the benefit for the home economy? It creates products for customers abroad and in exchange obtains only promises of future payments. Clearly, such a policy carries the definite risk of turning the home economy into a slave serving foreign masters. At any rate, it means that the division of *labour* is curtailed. True cooperation is replaced by unilateral production in exchange for promises.

Speaking of ROW financial assets brings us to what is probably the most momentous disadvantage of unilateral forex interventions, namely, that they tend to dissuade potential investors from all over the world. Investors from the home country will be reluctant to invest at home if they must expect the exchange rate to deteriorate for extended periods of time. For the same reason, investors from the ROW would rather stay in their countries than expose themselves to a capital loss.

In short, a policy of foreseeable forex interventions with the purpose of reducing the exchange rate of the home money are bound to have catastrophic consequences for capital flows, *unless they are compensated by other factors*, such as savings and genuine entrepreneurship. China and Japan are casebook examples. In both countries, central banks have been able to pursue forex interventions of the sort that we have discussed, yet without suffering capital outflows, because the policy-induced devaluations of the yuan and yen on the forex markets have been more than compensated by the vigorous growth of the real economy.

But this does not alter the impact of the policy *as such*. Without the intervention, the exchange rates of the yen and of the yuan would have been substantially higher, with corresponding gains for Japan and China as a whole, in terms of the volume of foreign trade, of the integration into the international division of labour, and of capital flows. Their ill-advised monetary policies have entailed a *relative impoverishment* of these countries. They have become poorer as compared to the wealth that they could have attained in the absence of these policies. Thanks to compensating factors, this relative impoverishment has not turned into an absolute one.

To sum up, when the printing press is used to pursue a permissive trade policy, it is unlikely to have any beneficial impact at all from an aggregate point of view. In the short run it is likely to create as many immediate winners as immediate losers. In the medium run, it jeopardises the international division of labour and encourages political rent-seeking. In the long run, it is bound to discourage capital investments unless the ill-faded policy is neutralised or overcompensated by the exploits of the private sector.

Conclusion

International trade volumes can be artificially inflated, at the expense of domestic trade and the domestic economy, through central-bank monetary policy and other forms of interventionism. Such policies have a negative *aggregate* impact on the economy by encouraging capital exports and by increasing bureaucratic red tape, cronyism, and regime uncertainty (Table 1). They are often perceived to be beneficial for the economy as a whole because they go hand in hand with concentrated and visible gains for the few winners and hidden losses for the many losers. Genuine free trade requires that such permissive policies be abrogated. Free trade should not be conceived in opposition to *protectionism*, but to *interventionism*. The proper policy objective of free traders should be to get the government out of the picture as far as possible.

Table 1 Overview

	Same growth at home and in ROW	Growth at home Stagnation in ROW	Export subsidy	Inflationist exchange rate policies
Trade volume (real)	Increase	Increase	Unsystematic	Short-run increase of exports Short-run implosion of imports. Long-run decrease of exports and imports
Trade volume (money)	Increase	Increase	Unsystematic	Increase in terms of the home money. Decrease in terms of ROW money
Relative importance of foreign trade	Increase	Decrease at home Increase in ROW	Unsystematic	Increase at home. Decrease in ROW
International division of labour	Increase	Increase (more strongly oriented towards the home economy)	Decrease	Decrease

References

Dorobat CE (2015) Cantilllon effects in international trade: the consequences of fiat money for trade, Finance, and the International Distribution of Wealth. Doctoral dissertation, Université d'Angers.

Higgs R (1997) Regime uncertainty: why the great depression lasted so long and why prosperity resumed after the war. Independent Rev 1(4):561–590

Higgs R (2012) Regime uncertainty: some clarifications. Mises Daily Articles. https://mises.org/library/regime-uncertainty-some-clarifications

Hoppe H-H (1990) Banking, nation states, and international politics: a sociological reconstruction of the present economic order. Rev Austr Econ 4:55–87

Hülsmann JG (2014) Fiat money and the distribution of incomes and wealth Howden D and Salerno JT (eds), The fed at one hundred—a critical view on the federal reserve system (Berlin: Springer-Verlag), pp 127–138

Hülsmann JG (2024) Abundance, generosity, and the state. Auburn: Mises Institute

Lechner HH (1988) Währungspolitik. de Gruyter, Berlin

Mises LV (1916) Vom Ziel der Handelspolitik. Archiv für Sozialwissenschaft und Sozialpolitik 42(2)

Mises LV (1998 [1949]) Human action: a treatise on economics. The scholar's edition. Auburn: Ludwig von Mises Institute

Mises LV (2011 [1929]) A critique of interventionism. Auburn: Ludwig von Mises Institute

Ricardo D (2001) On the principles of political economy and taxation. Batoche Books, Kitchener

Ricardo D (1951 [1822]) On the protection of agriculture. In: The works and correspondence of David Ricardo, Vol IV, edited by Sraffa P, London: Cambridge University Press

Röpke W (1942) International Economic Disintegration. William Hodge, London

Rothbard MN (2009) Man, economy, and state: a treatise on economic principles—with power and market: government and the economy. Auburn: Ludwig von Mises Institute

Salin P (2020 [1985]) Fiscal Tyranny (Cheltenham, UK: Edward Elgard)

Say J-B (2011) [1803]): *Traité d'économie politique, ou simple exposition de la manière dont se forment les richesses.* Institut Coppet, Paris

Smith A (2007 [1776]) An inquiry into the nature and the causes of the wealth of nations. MetaLibri

Globalization: Free Trade Versus Managed Trade

Richard M. Ebeling

> International economic relations can be carried out in three different ways: exclusively by private individuals and corporations; exclusively by governments; or by private persons and corporations on the one side and by governments and government institutions on the other side.
>
> Moritz J. Bonn (1945, 123)

In 1831, Sir Henry Parnell (1776–1842), a long-time Chairman of the Financial Committee of the House of Commons, published *On Financial Reform*, in which he made the case for freedom of trade at a time when trade protectionism was mostly the order of the day in Great Britain, especially in agriculture:

> If once men were allowed to take their own way, they would very soon, to the great advantage of society, undeceive the world of the error of restricting trade, and show that the passage of merchandise from one state to another ought to be as free air and water. Every country should be as a general and common fair for the sale of goods, and the individual or nation which makes the best commodity should find the greatest advantage.
> Happily, the time, if not yet arrived, is rapidly approaching, when the desire to reduce the principles of trade to a system of legislative superintendence will be placed in the rank of other gone-by illusions. The removal of obstacles is

---

R. M. Ebeling (✉)
The Citadel: Military College of South Carolina, Charleston, SC, USA
e-mail: rebeling@citadel.edu

all that is required of the legislature for the success of trade. It asks nothing from Government but equal protection to all subjects, the discouragement of monopoly, and a fixed standard of money. All that is wanted is to let loose from commercial restriction, protection, and monopoly, the means the country has within itself by force of individual exertion of protecting and promoting its interests, to secure its future career in all kinds of public prosperity (Parnell 1831, 292-293).

Sixteen years later in June 1846, Parnell's hope came to fulfillment with the unilateral abolition of the Corn Laws that had secured the British landed aristocracy a profitable protection from foreign competition in farming, especially in wheat production. The British prime minister at this time, Sir Robert Peel (1788–1850), had been placed in that office by the Tory Party to assure the continuance of agricultural protectionism against the supporters of free trade. But with the worst crop failures in living memory in 1845–1846, and with growing hardship and threatened starvation among the low-income members of British society, Peel came around to the free trade position of Richard Cobden (1804–1865) and John Bright (1811–1889). With the support of the free trade advocates and a sufficient number of Tory members in the House of Commons and the House of Lords, the importation of less expensive foreign wheat and other food products unilaterally became the law of the land on 26 June 1846.

Furious with Robert Peel's defection, the Tory landowners forced his removal as prime minister. In his last speech before stepping down from his position, Peel declared:

If other countries choose to buy in the dearest market, such an option on their part constitutes no reason why we should not be permitted to buy in the cheapest. I trust the Government. Will not resume the policy which they and we have felt most inconvenient, namely the haggling with foreign countries about reciprocal concessions, instead of taking the independent course we believe conducive to our own interests. Let us trust to the influence of public opinion in other countries – let us trust that our example, with the proof of practical benefit we derive from it, will at no remote period ensure the adoption of the principles on which we have acted, rather than defer indefinitely by delay equivalent concessions from other countries (Quoted in Hobson 1919, 41).

British Unilateral Free Trade and the Beginnings of Globalization

Great Britain, thus, became the symbol of a policy of freedom of trade, regardless and indeed in spite of any restrictive and protectionist policies maintained or introduced by other countries. Of course, not every tariff was actually reduced to zero or as a modest revenue tariff. But certainly, after Britain's commercial treaty with France in 1860, for all intents and purposes Great Britain practiced what it preached. And soon, a growing number of other European countries followed the British and French examples and lowered their trade barriers.

The idea and ideal of unilateral free trade became the basis of British thinking in the face of any and all proposals for restricting imports in the name of retaliation against the protectionist policies of other countries or waiting for reciprocity before any modification on remaining duties on imported goods. Toward the end of the nineteenth century its logic was emphasized by Henry Dunning Macleod (1821–1902). Trade retaliations and reciprocations merely harmed the citizens of one's own country far more than it imposed any supposed damage on a protectionist trading partner. "If the present hostile tariffs destroy an incalculable amount of commercial intercourse, a resort to reciprocity and retaliation would destroy it infinitely more. If foreign nations smite us on one check by their hostile tariffs, if we followed the advice of the reciprocitarians, and retaliated, we should simply smite ourselves very hard on the cheek. The true way to fight hostile tariffs is by free imports" (Macleod 1896, 82 & 84).[1]

---

[1] Also, Sir Louis Mallet, "If as is alleged, protection is only sought for the sake of reciprocity, it is impossible to understand why a one-sided Free Trade should not be better than no Free Trade at all. The mutual relaxation of restrictions is a mutual advantage; the mutual creation of restrictions is a mutual injury. If one tariff is bad, two must be worse. It matters nothing whether the barrier be raised in one country or the other, the effect is precisely the same" (Mallet, 1891, 124). And Charles P. Villiers: "Sir Robert Peel set forth exhaustively the facts and reasons which justified the Free Trade policy for which he was responsible, and boldly maintained that the principle of Protection to domestic industry–meaning thereby duties on imports imposed for that purpose and not for revenue– was a vicious principle, and that the best way to compete with hostile tariffs was to encourage free imports" (Villiers, 1896, 224-225). In addition, Henry Fawcett: "England, it is argued, is suffering because with regard to the abolition of protective duties there has not been sufficient reciprocity between her and other countries. It is in fact argued that free trade is excellent when all countries adopt it, but that a country pursues a too generous course, and one involving too much self-sacrifice, if she abolishes protective duties whilst her neighbors retain them. It is no doubt perfectly true that England would be benefited if other countries adopted free trade. We therefore have every inducement to do all in our power to make them take such a course. It is also equally true that other countries have shared the advantages which England has derived from free trade; but if we re-imposed protective duties because other countries are sufficiently unwise to retain then, the only result would be that we should inflict an injury upon ourselves in order to avenge the unwise financial policy imposed by other countries. England would be largely benefited by the active stimulus which

As a consequence of these movements toward more universal freedom of trade, the age of globalization truly emerged and encompassed a growing part of the planet. By the end of the nineteenth century, in fact, economists could hail the amazing social, cultural, and economic integration that had and was occurring through the internationalizing of commerce, trade, and investment (Delaisi 1925, 86–134). For instance, the Irish economist, Charles Bastable (1855–1945), explained:

> One of the most striking features of modern times is the growth of international relations of ever-increasing complexity and influence. Facilities for communication have brought the closer and more constant intercourse between different countries of the world, leading to many unexpected results. This more intimate connection is reflected in all the different sides of social activity. International law, that two hundred years ago was almost wholly confined to the discussion of war and its effects, no contains a goodly series of chapters treating in detail of the conduct of nations during peace. It draws the bulk of materials from the large and rapidly-growing body of treaties that regulate such matters, and form so many fresh links between the states that sign them. Literature, Science and Art have all been similarly affected; their followers are engaged in keenly watching the progress of their favorite pursuits in other countries and are becoming daily more and more sensitive to any new tendency or movement in the remotest nation.
> "But, as might be expected, it is in the sphere of material relations that the increase in international solidarity has been most decisively marked and can best be followed and appreciated. The barriers that in former ages impeded the free passage of men and of goods from country to country have been—it cannot unfortunately be said removed, but very much diminished; and more particularly during the last fifty years the extraordinary development and improvement of transport agencies both by land and sea have gone far toward obliterating the retarding effects of legislative restraints or national prejudices. So little attention is ordinarily paid to the great permanent forces that govern the changes of societies, in comparison with the interest excited by the uncertain action of minor disturbing causes, that it is eminently desirable to emphasize as strongly as possible the continuous increase of international dealings. In spite of temporary checks and drawbacks, the broad fact stands beyond dispute, that the transfer of human beings from country to country

---

would be given to her iron trade if America would remove protective duties upon manufactured iron. But we would be acting with ignorant perversity if we refused to buy the wheat from America which we so urgently require, because America refuses to purchase as much English iron as we are willing to sell her. It is therefore evident that with regard to free trade there is reciprocity, but in a sense directly opposed to those who desire that protective duties should be re-imposed because other countries will not abolish them. The advantages associated with free trade are reciprocal, because even if only one country adopts such a policy, the benefits resulting are diffused over every country with which commerce is carried out" (Fawcett 1874, 389-390).

which is known as 'migration,' as also similar movement of goods described as 'commerce' is not merely expanding, but if periods sufficiently lengthy for fair comparison are taken, expanding at an accelerated rate (Bastable 1899, 1-2).

The world was, increasingly, a single market, especially due to the global nature of the British Empire, which served as one, vast free trade zone. All were more or less welcome to trade, invest, and reside regardless of any individual's nationality or politics. Following the end of the Napoleonic Wars in 1815, Great Britain and many other European counties did away with the formalities of passports and visas, with the right of freedom to move an increasingly accepted principle in the middle decades of the nineteenth century. It is worth recalling that Karl Marx moved to London in 1849 and lived there for the rest of his life, without any visa requirement, or residency or work permits. (Torpey 2000, 57–92).

The Three Freedoms of the Nineteenth-Century Globalization

It is true that protectionism was making a return in the 1880s, most especially in Imperial Germany, with Bismarck's reintroduction of an extensive political paternalism in the form of the institutions of the modern interventionist-welfare state and tariffs meant to more directly influence German industrial and agricultural development (Dawson 1904). But, nonetheless, it is not an exaggeration to say that in comparison to the world before the nineteenth century and much that occurred in the twentieth century, the middle and late decades of the 1800s stand out as an epoch of what the German economist, Gustav Stolper (1888–1947) called the era of the three freedoms: free movement of men, money, and goods:

> The economic and social system of Europe was predicated on a few axiomatic principles. These principles were considered as safe and unshakeable by that age as the average American citizen even today considers his civil liberties embodied in the Bill of Rights. They were free movement for men, for goods, and for money.
> Everyone could leave his country when he wanted and travel or migrate wherever he pleased without a passport. The only European country that demanded passports (not even visas!) was Russia, looked askance for her backwardness with an almost contemptuous smile. Who wanted to travel to Russia anyway?

The trend of migration was westward—within Europe from the thinly populated agricultural east to the rapidly industrializing center and west, and above all from Europe to the wide-open Americas.

There were still customs barriers on the European continent, it is true. But the vast British Empire was free-trade territory open to all in free competition, and several other European countries, such as the Netherlands, Belgium, Scandinavia, came close to free trade. For a time, the Great Powers on the European continent seemed to veer in the same direction. In the sixties of the nineteenth century the conviction was general that international free trade was the future. The subsequent decades did not quite fulfill that promise. In the late seventies reactionary trends set in. But looking back at the methods and the degree of protectionism built up at that time we are seized with a nostalgic envy. Whether a bit higher or a bit lower, tariffs really never checked the free flow of goods. All they effected was some minor price changes, presumably mirroring some vested interest.

And the most natural of all this was the freedom of movement of money. Year in, year out, billions were invested by the great industrial European Powers in foreign countries, European and non-European. These billions were regarded as safe investments with attractive yields, desirable for creditors as well as to debtors, with no doubts about the eventual return of both interest and principal. Most of the money flowed into the United States and Canada, a great deal into South America, billions into Russia, hundreds of millions into the Balkan countries, and minor amounts into India and the Far East. The interest paid on these foreign investments became an integral past of the national income of the industrial Powers, protected not only by their political and military might but – more strongly – by the general unquestioned acceptance of the fundamental capitalist principles: sanctity of treaties, abidance by internal law, and restraint on governments from interference in business (Stolper 1942, 7-8)[2]

---

[2] Also, Oskar Morgenstern: "Before 1914, there was freedom of travel without passports, freedom of migration, and freedom from exchange control and other monetary restrictions. Citizenship was freely granted to immigrants. Short-term or long-term capital could move unsupervised in any direction and these movements took any form. Direct foreign investments were common and welcome; securities of other countries were freely traded on most stock markets. Transfer of profits was unhampered, and foreign investments were not confiscated after they had begun to show a yield. Monetary standards in most countries were firmly established in gold. It is also noteworthy that international financial and commercial transactions before 1914 were among individuals (and corporations) and rarely among countries dealing as a whole. National boundaries were thus of small importance, as was the fact that most countries had different currencies. There were colonial wars, but they did not leave deep scars. There were also other wars such as the Spanish-American, the Russo-Japanese, and the Balkan war, but they were localized and occurred at the periphery of economic centers" (Morgenstern 1959, 17, 19, 21).

Globalization Before 1914 Versus After the World Wars

This period before the First World War stands out for two reasons relating to the issue of globalization. First it was in stark comparison to the world that followed in 1920s and 1930s. The interwar years saw the rise of political and economic nationalism, along with the emergence of totalitarian regimes that overturned what remained of the prewar era of those three freedoms after the four years of World War One. In their place, was a strongly anti-globalization movement, as many governments imposed high tariff walls as part of their implementation of systems of domestic control, command, and planning, none of which was in anyway compatible with open and free international trade if national interventionist and planning goals and targets were to be pursued (Mises 1943, 145; 1944, 3).

The Swedish economist, Gustav Cassel (1866–1945), penned a monograph for the League of Nations with the title, *Recent Monopolistic Tendencies in Industry and Trade: Being an Analysis of the Nature and Causes of the Poverty of Nations* (Cassel 1927), highlighting the opposite direction the world economy was moving compared to the nineteenth century. A variety of governments especially in the totalitarian regimes of Soviet Russia, fascist Italy, and National Socialist (Nazi) Germany pursued autarkic economic policies, determined to reduce their dependencies on the international system of division of labor in pursuit of political and military goals (Gregory 1931; Tippetts 1933; Angell 1936; Rappard 1936; 1937; 1938; Fisher 1939; Bresciani-Turroni 1940).

The second reason the globalizing trends before the First World War stand out is that it differed in essential ways from the attempt to restore an international environment conducive to a return to a global economic order of human cooperation after the Second World War. The distinguishing characteristic of nineteenth-century Europe and North America and the globalization that was fostered is that, however inconsistently and imperfectly it might have been practiced, the hundred-year period between 1815 and 1914 can rightly be said to have been the product of the classical liberal spirit.

The guiding principle that directed much of public policy in most of the countries of the "civilized world" was the *depoliticizing* of social life. With the triumph of free trade over mercantilism and protectionism in the early and middle decades of the nineteenth century, with the elimination of many of the domestic regulations, monopoly privileges and restraints on private enterprise, the State was dramatically removed from the affairs of everyday life (Ebeling 1995). In its place arose civil society, the blossoming of the "private sector," an extension of the network of "intermediary institutions" of voluntary association and market relationships. As Nassau Senior (1790–1864) expressed it:

> The advocate of freedom dwells on the benefit of making full use of our own peculiar advantages of situation, wealth, and skill, and availing ourselves to the utmost of those possessed by our neighbors.... The principle of free trade is non-interference; it is to suffer every man to employ his industry in the manner which he thinks most advantageous, without pretense on the part of the legislature to control or direct his operation (Senior 1828, 1 & 68).

The Liberal Ideal of Globalization Through Private Enterprise

In especially the second half of the nineteenth century, governments did form international associations and reached various agreements with each other. But for the most part (and separate from various changing political and military alliances), their associations and agreements were designed to facilitate the smooth functioning of private intercourse between citizens and subjects. They included international river commissions, railway and transportation agreements, telegraph and postal unions, health rules and guidelines, procedures for uniform weights and measures, and respect for patents and copyrights. The thinking behind these arrangements was to establish general "rules of the game" to assist in the further globalization of private commercial and cultural exchange.

Within these rules of the game, individuals were to be left free and at liberty to direct their own lives and determine how best they thought the use of their own labor and private property; individuals freely and voluntarily associated and exchanged goods and services, along with investment capital and resource uses. The forms, the directions, and the effects of globalized trade and investment were matters of individual and private enterprise decision-making, guided by market prices in determining the coordination of internationally connected and interdependent supplies and demands. It would be an exaggeration to say that governmental "affairs of state" never intruded itself into the private sector, but they were far more the exception than the rule. Especially in the case of Great Britain, as one noted economic historian of the period explained:

Like those who carried on industry and trade for their own profit, those who had capital to invest, and those whose business it was to deal in investments claimed the right to carry on their activities without government hinderance and control. Their affairs, they argued, were best run, judged by their own interest and national interest, without government interference. To this laissez-faire argument official opinion subscribed… Thus, the government attempted no formal regulation of capital investment, except to prevent fraud and to prevent activities judged socially unwholesome… Save in exceptional instances where some British interest, usually political, seemed to be threatened, there was little wish for formal official interference (Feis 1930, 83-84).

Thus, globalization before the First World War was based on and the result of the (classical) liberal ideas and ideals of individual freedom, private property, free enterprise at home and free trade abroad, with impartial rule of law under de facto or de jure constitutionally limited government. It was basically presumed that Adam Smith was right when he argued that both personal freedom and mutual economic betterment will be most likely attained when the determination and the direction of resources, labor services, and capital of every society is guided by each person's self-interested pursuit of improvement (as he defined it) without political hinderance or support in any direction. By doing so, as Smith said, "The sovereign is completely discharged form a duty… of which no human wisdom or knowledge could ever be sufficient; the duty of superintending the industry of private people, and of directing it towards employments most suitable in the interest of society" (Smith 1776, 651).

The fundamental premise was that the purpose of production was consumption, that the role of supplies was to meet and satisfy consumer demands in the least cost and most efficient ways, so as to maximize the economic wellbeing of as many people in society as possible. It was best to leave it to the knowledge and judgments of the individuals in the various corners of the division of labor see to it that the scarce means of production were employed in such ways that a system of absolute and comparative advantage assured the most effective achievement of people's ends through the employment of means. Not only did this not require the guiding or influencing hand of governments, but as Adam Smith also said, the assigning of any such authority to those in political power, "could be safely trusted, not only to no single person, but to no council or senate whatever, and which would nowhere be so dangerous as in the hands of a man who had the folly and presumption enough to fancy himself fit to exercise it" (Smith 1776, 423).

Trade Liberalization Through Managed Trade

The policies of the 1920s and 1930s had turned such arguments and reasoning on its head. The state, in both totalitarian and democratic countries, returned to the pre-free trade ideas of the mercantilists that government knew better than all the individuals about how the economic and social affairs of society should be organized and directed. The post-World War II era seemed to be a restoration of a free global international economic order only because in the context of the economic nationalism, protectionism, and autarkic policies advocated and implemented in the interwar and war years, the liberalizing tendencies introduced in the years after 1945 seemed so "liberating" in comparison. As Gottfried Haberler said in the late 1970s, the postwar decades were "a period of unprecedented growth and prosperity. Compared with the interwar period, the entire postwar period. Must be judged a great success. World trade grew by leaps and bounds" (Haberler 1979, 354–355; 1976).

During the Second World War, the Allied countries, led by the United States, decided that a continuation of policies of autarky and economic nationalism would be a disaster. International trade and commerce, global access to raw materials and the opportunity for foreign investments were essential elements if a new world order was to be constructed. But the new world order that arose out of the ashes of World War II was not like the world order before 1914. Instead, the new globalization was based upon and managed in the context of a set of international governmental organizations. The new system would revolve around three intergovernmental institutions: the World Bank for long-term loans for economic reconstruction; the International Monetary Fund (IMF) for long-terms monetary stability through shorter-term loans; and the General Agreement on Tariffs and Trade, out of which has grown the World Trade Organization (WTO), to coordinate trading rules and procedures among the member countries. (Osterfeld 1994, 186).

Why and how did this new globalization structure come into existence? While proclaiming the belief in free trade and globalized commerce, the world in the postwar period increasingly became enveloped in a spider's web of welfare statist programs that required governments to secure redistributive shares of income and market shares for selected and privileged sectors of their respective economies. Given the institutional responsibilities that modern governments took upon themselves in the name of the "social good," the "national interest," and the "general welfare," the state's use of domestic policy tools to serve special interests feeding at the trough of the government became inevitable.

Those institutions established after 1945 have reflected this ideological, political, and economic trend. Whether it be the IMF, or the World Bank, or the WTO, the purpose has been for governments to oversee, manage and direct the patterns of international trade and investment. The IMF and the World Bank have expanded and extended their activities to more greatly influence the distribution of loanable funds to both governments and private investors, especially in what used to be called Third World, i.e., lesser developed, countries. They have also taken upon themselves the responsibility of tying such loans and credits to guidelines for economic policy reform in the recipient nations. During their existence, the IMF and World Bank have followed the various interventionist and collectivist fads and fashions that have dominated public policy, whether in developed countries or in the lesser developed nations: financial support for nationalized industries or government privileged "private" enterprises; below-market interest rate loans for loss-making sectors of the economy; billion-dollar credit lines for governments in lesser developed countries; planning schemes to foster politically determined "balanced growth"; fiscal policies pushing tax increases rather than absolute and consistent cuts in government spending and regulations (Tumlir 1985; Bhagwati 1988; Lindsey 2002, 264–266; Easterly 2006; Lal 2006, 62–90).

The Swings Between Liberal and Illiberal Managed Trade

As we saw, in the first several decades of international trade relations after the Second World War, global trade and commerce was noticeably liberalized, with tariff barriers and import restrictions being significantly lowered. Yet this was not the result of an ideology and policy of free trade, per se, but rather of the particular pattern of politically managed trade agreed upon by the international trading partners. It remained in effect only for as long as the member governments desired to regulate global markets in the direction of freer trade.

However, beginning in the 1970s and 1980s, the world came to be dominated by a different set of ideas about when international trade can be considered "fair" or "just" (Bovard 1991). The central problem with an idea like "fair trade" is that it is an empty and ambiguous a term as "social justice," being able to mean almost anything that the user of the concept wishes it to.

(Ferrer 1904, 1–3; Hayek 1976). As Jaghish Bhagwati pointed out, under the heading of "fair trade" nearly anything that one country does in terms of its domestic and trading policies can be rationalized by another government as involving "unfair" trade practices that negatively affect or threaten its domestic industries' market circumstances, and to which the affected nation has to respond. "If everything becomes a question of fair trade," Bhagwati said, "then 'managed trade' will be the outcome, with bureaucrats allocating trade according to what domestic lobbying pressures and foreign political muscle dictate" (Bhagwati 1991, 22).

The 1990s saw a partial return to the idea of trade liberalization with the demise of the Soviet Union and the collapse of the socialist central planning ideal. Socialism-in-practice had brought too much of a social and economic disaster in all the countries burdened with the task of living the Marxian ideal (Ebeling 2020). So, in China after the death of Chairman Mao in 1976 and then in the Eastern European nations and many of the Third World countries with the end of Soviet socialism, market-oriented institutional reforms introduced more of an economic liberal agenda around the globe. New open markets and expanding international trade and globalization saw world-wide rising standards of living through trade, investment, and a major increase and intensification of the division of labor. Supply-chains of interdependency offered even many of the poorest corners of the globe ways to find their niche to bring about improvements in the conditions of more and more of mankind (Legrain 2004; Wolf 2004).

From Illiberal Managed Trade to a New Global Central Planning

But with the global financial crisis of 2008–2009 and the breaks in the global supply-chains due to the national lockdowns and shutdowns during the Coronavirus crisis of 2020–2021, new calls were heard for national economic security against similar disruptions of essential resource availabilities and production capabilities. This has been exacerbated by the growing political tensions and war fears resulting from Russia's military aggression in Ukraine and China's drive for political, economic, and military ascendancy in East Asia and beyond. Concerns over economic and political conflicts serve as revived reasons and rationales for national or regional protectionism against imports and justifications for artificial subsidies and supports for domestic suppliers to provide import substitutions. But, inescapably all of this is at a great cost in less competition from international rivals, inefficient and wasteful misallocations of scarce resources to produce at home what could be more easily and cost-effectively bought from abroad. Standards of living are imperiled, with many in those societies seeing threatened with higher costs and reduced qualities of what is bought. Even if in absolute terms standards of living continue to rise, it is still the fact that any such improves are less than would was possible if freedom of trade was followed by one, some, or all. Humanity is less well off than it could have been.

The most recent danger to global trade and exchange is the reemergence of the central planning mindset under the name of "stakeholder capitalism," which is meant to fight climate change and impose a new social order of supposed equity and inclusion. A model for this has been formulated by the World Economic Forum. The intention is to impose a series of controls and commands on every corporation and business enterprise in the world, first through seemingly "voluntary" association, but finally, as proposed, on the basis of political dictate via national and international governmental authorities. Prices, wages, work conditions, methods of production and types of output, along with employment quota systems based on racial, ethnic and gender group classifications and identifications would steer and direct the global economy. (WEF 2019, 2020).

Such a political-economic agenda and the governmental policy implementations to bring it about, if sufficiently or fully pursued could result in a global central planning—regardless of any name officially given to it. It might easily be called Global Fascism—government command and control over private enterprises having little or no real and autonomous discretion over their own decision-making. If this seems extreme, already the European Union political and bureaucratic structures impose an increasingly tight spider's web of rules, regulations, and restrictions over virtually every form of manufacturing and farming among the member states. In the United States, both major political parties advocate "industrial policies" to design the future of the American economy based on the ideological goals and special interest desires that interact in legislative processes that result in the tapestry of interventions and redistributions that redirect the outcomes of the market from what they would have been if government politics did not interfere with resource uses, production decisions, and relative income shares.

The respective national and domestic regulatory, planning and income-share goals necessarily come into conflict with each other in the arena of international trade, commerce, and investment. The wheeling and dealing of how these polices will be compromised or end up in irreconcilable opposition with each other on the international stage determines the configuration of the global economy. Everything becomes "affairs of state" that threaten tensions and economic warfare. Any attempt to coordinate national politics at the international level through a global agenda such as the one proposed by the World Economic Forum would only exacerbate the conflicts due to arguments and dogmas over who gets what share based on a world-wide system of "diversity, equity and inclusion," plus who will bear the economics costs of "saving the planet," and by how much in terms of restrained or reduced standards of living. (Ebeling 2023).

Conclusion: Liberal Globalism Versus a Planned World Economy

This is not what was meant by a global economy in the minds of its earlier proponents in the nineteenth century. To the classical liberals of that time, a central purpose for freeing trade from the heavy hand of governments was precisely to take politics out of the marketplace, by making all such interactions private matters of peaceful mutual agreement and association; that competition was not to be affairs of political power and military aggrandizement. Global competition in all its forms and facets was meant to be the means and methods for peaceful rivalries in discovering, implementing, and offering more, better, and less expensive goods and services and life opportunities to as many of the broad mass of humanity as was possible. The world was to benefit from everyone's knowledge, abilities, and talents by precisely leaving individuals at liberty to apply themselves as they thought best through the globalized division of labor of peaceful and productive human association.

These are the two opposing visions and possibilities for globalization in the remainder of the twenty-first century: free trade or managed trade. Only the classical liberal idea and ideal of free trade is consistent with liberty, peace, and prosperity. Managed trade only offers constant conflicts as governments and "politics" attempt to bend market outcomes, domestically and internationally, to power-grabbing visions of planning and regulating ideologues and to special interest groups desirous of using political power for themselves at the expense of the rest of humankind (Ebeling 2016, 2019, 2021

References

Angell N (1936) This have and have-not business: political fantasy and economic fact. Hamish Hamilton, London
Bastable CF (1899) The commerce of nations. Methuen, London

Bhagwati J (1988) Protectionism. The MIT Press, Cambridge, MA
Bhagwati J (1991) The world trading system at risk. Princeton University Press, Princeton, NJ
Bonn MJ (1945) International economic relations between governments: a source of world peace or friction?" Proceedings of the academy of political science, pp 122–135
Bovard J (1991) The fair trade fraud. St. Martin's Press, New York
Bresciani-Turroni C (1940) Living space versus an international system, Revue Al Qanoun Wal Iqtisad (Cairo, Egypt), pp 36–68
Cassel G (1927) Recent monopolistic tendencies in industry and trade: being Ana analysis of the nature and causes of the poverty of nations. League of Nations, Geneva
Dawson WH (1904) Protection in Germany: a history of German fiscal policy in the nineteenth century. P. S. King, London
Delaisi F (1925) Political myths and economic realities. Noel Douglas, London
Easterly W (2006) The white man's burden: why the west's efforts to aid the rest have done so much ill and so little good. Penguin Press, New York
Ebeling RM (2023) The Failure of Central Planning and Its Revival as Stakeholder Capitalism. In: Sielska A (ed) Transition Economics in Central and Eastern Europe: Austrian Perspectives. Routledge, London, pp 7–23
Ebeling RM (1995) World peace, international order, and classical liberalism, Int J World Peace, pp 47–54
Ebeling RM (2016) Austrian economics and public policy. Fairfax, VA: Future of Freedom Foundation
Ebeling RM (2019) For a new liberalism. Great Barrington, MA: American Institute for Economic Research
Ebeling RM (2021) Socialism-in-practice was a nightmare, not utopia: Ludwig von Mises's critique of central planning and the fall of the soviet union, Review of Austrian Economics, pp 431–448
Fawcett H (1874) Manual of political economy. MacMillan, London
Feis H ([1930] 1974) Europe, the World's Banker, 1870–1914. Clifton, NJ: Augustus M. Kelley
Ferrer TH (1904) Free trade versus fair trade. Cobden Club, London
Fisher AGB (1939) Economic self-sufficiency. Oxford University Press, Oxford
Gregory TE (1931) Economic nationalism, Int Affairs, pp 289–306
Haberler G ([1976] 1985) The world economy, Money, and the great depression, 1919–1939, reprinted in, Anthony Y. C. Koo, ed., Selected Essays of Gottfried Haberler. Cambridge, MA. The MIT Press, pp 363–403
Haberler G ([1979] 1993) The liberal international economic order in historical perspective, Reprinted in, Anthony Y. C. Koo, ed., The Liberal Economic Order, Vol. 1: Essays on International Economics by Gottfried Haberler. Brookfield, VT: Edward Elgar, pp 349–370
Hayek FA (1976) Law, legislation, and liberty, Vol 2: The Mirage of Social Justice. Chicago: University of Chicago Press

Hobson JA ([1919] 1968) Richard Cobden: The International Man. London: Ernest Benn

Lal D (2006) Reviving the invisible hand: the case for classical liberalism in the twenty-first century. Princeton University Press, Princeton, NJ

Legrain P (2004) Open world: The Truth about Globalization. Chicago: Ivan R. Dee

Lindsey B (2002) Against the dead hand: the uncertain struggle for global capitalism. John Wiley & Sons, New York

Macleod HD (1896) The history of economics. Bliss, Sands, London

Mallet SL (1891) Free exchange: papers on political and economical subjects. Kegan Paul, Trench, Trubner, London

Mises LV ([1943] 1990) Autarky and its consequences, in Richard M, Ebeling (ed), Money, method, and the market process: essays by Ludwig von Mises. Norwell, MA: Kluwer Academic Publishers, pp 137-154

Mises LV (1944) Omnipotent government: the rise of the total state and total war. Yale University Press, New Haven, CT

Morgenstern O (1959) International financial transactions and the business cycle. Princeton University Press, Princeton, NJ

Osterfeld D (1994) The world bank and the IMF: misbegotten sisters, in Peter J, Beottke (ed), The collapse of development planning. New York: New York University Press, pp 185–209

Parnell H (1831) On financial reform. John Murray, London

Rappard WE (1936) The common menace of economic and military armaments: being the Richard Cobden lecture for 1936. Cobden-Sanderson, London

Rappard WE (1937) Economic Nationalism. Authority and the individual: Harvard tercentenary conference of the arts and sciences. Harvard University Press, Cambridge, MA, pp 74–112

Rappard WE (1938) Postwar efforts for freer trade. Geneva Research Centre, Geneva

Senior NW ([1828] 1966) Three lectures on the transmission of the precious metals from country to country and the mercantile theory of wealth, in Selected writings on economics by Nassau W, Senior. New York: Augustus M. Kelly

Smith A ([1776] 1937) An inquiry into the nature and causes of the wealth of nations, Edwin Cannan edition. New York: Modern Liberty

Stolper G (1942) This age of fable: the political and economic world we live in. Reynal & Hitchcock, New York

Tippetts CS (1933) Autarchy: national self-sufficiency. University of Chicago Press, Chicago

Torpey J (2000) The invention of the passport: surveillance, citizenship, and the state. Cambridge University Press, New York

Tumlir J (1985) Protectionism: trade policy in democratic societies. American Enterprise Institute for Public Policy Research, Washington, D.C.

Villiers CP (1896) Reply to the Cobden club's corn law repeal jubilee address, in Richard Coben and the jubilee of free trade. T. Fisher Unwin, London

Wolf M (2004) Why globalization works: the case for the global market economy. New Haven, CT: Yale University Press

World Economic Forum (2019) Davos Manifesto 2020: The universal purpose of a company in the fourth industrial revolution. Davos, Switzerland

World Economic Forum (2020) Measuring stakeholder capitalism: toward common metrics and consistent report of sustainable value creation. Davis, Switzerland